THE KITCHEN ECOSYSTEM

THE
KITCHEN
ECOSYSTEM

EUGENIA BONE

Photographs by Ben Fink

Integrating
Recipes
to Create
Delicious
Meals

CLARKSON POTTER/PUBLISHERS
NEW YORK

All rights reserved.
Published in the United States
by Clarkson Potter/Publishers,
an imprint of the Crown
Publishing Group, a division
of Random House LLC, a
Penguin Random House
Company, New York.
www.crownpublishing.com
www.clarksonpotter.com

CLARKSON POTTER is
a trademark and POTTER
with colophon is a registered
trademark of Random House
LLC.

Library of Congress
Cataloging-in-Publication Data
has been applied for.

ISBN 978-0-385-34512-5
Ebook ISBN 978-0-385-34513-2

Printed in China

Book and cover design by
Rae Ann Spitzenberger
Cover photographs by Ben Fink

10 9 8 7 6 5 4 3 2 1

First Edition

To Carson and Mo

CONTENTS

INTRODUCTION. I

HOW TO USE THIS BOOK. 5

   About Substitutions 5

The Recipes

APPLES 7

APRICOTS 16

ARTICHOKES. 24

ASPARAGUS 31

BEEF 41

BEETS WITH GREENS 49

CABBAGE 56

CARROTS
WITH GREENS. 65

CHERRIES 72

CHICKEN 82

CORN 92

CRANBERRIES . . . . IOI

CUCUMBERS IO9

CURRANTS II7

DUCK. I24

FENNEL I33

FIGS I4I

GINGER I47

GRAPES I56

LEMONS I65

LOBSTER. I76

MUSHROOMS

   Cultivated Mushrooms I83

   Wild Mushrooms I92

MUSSELS 2OI

PAGE 44

PAGE 271

STRAWBERRIES 319

TOMATOES 326

TROUT.............................. 337

WATERMELONS 346

ZUCCHINI.......................... 351

CONDIMENTS, NECESSITIES,
AND LUXURIES.................. 359

Preserving and Recipe Techniques

ABOUT PRESERVATION

Water Bath Canning 373

Pressure Canning..................... 376

Freezing.............................. 381

Curing 383

Smoking 384

Drying 384

Preserving in Oil 387

Preserving with Alcohol.............. 388

A Final Word on Canning............ 389

How to Sterilize 389

Altitude Adjustments................. 389

RECIPE TECHNIQUES

Preparing Stocks 390

Preparing Pasta in Stocks 392

Preparing Juices 393

Preparing Granitas 393

Preparing Fruit Syrups 394

Preparing Ice Cream by Hand 394

Preparing Pastry by Hand............ 395

Preparing Crepes..................... 395

ONIONS 208

ORANGES 214

PEACHES 222

PEAS 228

PEPPERS: SWEET,
CHERRY, AND HOT............... 237

PLUMS.............................. 253

PORK................................. 260

RADISHES WITH
GREENS 270

RASPBERRIES..................... 276

RHUBARB.......................... 285

SALTWATER FISH

Salmon.............................. 293

Tuna 300

White-Fleshed Fish 306

SHRIMP 313

ACKNOWLEDGMENTS 397

INDEX 398

INTRODUCTION

There are three steps to preparing really delicious food: (1) make dishes with as many seasonal ingredients as possible, using some, while the ingredients are fresh, in dishes to eat that night, and preserving the rest to use in the off-season; (2) replace the commercial products in the pantry with homemade ones; and (3) prepare base recipes from the parts you usually throw away, like bones and peels, and use them to bump up the flavor of other dishes. That's it.

But honestly? It took me twenty-five years to get there.

I suppose it started with preserving. I used to put up large batches of jams and jellies and pickles from recipes I read in preserving classics like *Putting Food By*. But I found it totally discouraging to spend a long, sweaty day prepping fruit and processing a dozen jars of jam only to have the whole batch end up loose or overly sweet or just *nasty*. And then, when the preserves did work out well, I was stuck with way more strawberry jam than anyone over the age of five could possibly consume.

So I started doing small-batch canning. I'd do just a few jars of any given product, about what I thought I'd use over the course of a year. This was a good solution because I found if I screwed it up, it wasn't such a tremendous loss of time and treasure. What's more, I discovered that by putting up only a couple of jars I could not only do a preservation recipe from whatever I was cooking for dinner that night, but I could also do it at the same time I was hanging around cooking in the kitchen anyway. If I was making a fresh tomato and watermelon salad, for example, I'd buy an extra pound or two of tomatoes and put up a pint jar. All it took was another burner on the stove.

It wasn't long before I became interested in putting up all sorts of foods. Because the stakes are low in small-batch preserving, I felt at liberty to preserve a wider and wider array of products. I would think of the ingredients I used in a dish—say, beef, carrots, thyme, and pearl onions—and I would pressure can a couple of pints of this combo so I could make a beef pot pie by just opening the jar and adding a puff pastry crust. If fresh ginger was cheap and crisp in a Chinatown market, I'd buy enough to cook with a fish for dinner, ferment some for ginger soda, and make a cup of ginger syrup to hold in the fridge for a week or so. With the syrup, I'd flavor panna cotta and poached pears. If I found a load of wild mushrooms I might cook them with osso buco for dinner, then dry the remainder, to add to soups and sauces another day.

As I became a more experienced home cook and preserver, I recognized the potential of the scraps left over from preparing fresh or preserved foods. I hated to throw away the bones and peels of foods because I knew they had flavor in them. It seemed a waste to get rid of the, well, waste. So I started to turn scraps into stocks and marinades, granitas, zests, and juices; by-products that made my recipes taste much better.

Whether it was drawn from fresh or preserved foods, my cooking really improved as a result of my collection of homemade supplemental ingredients. Eventually it became habitual. After I've cooked a chicken I dump the bones into a stockpot instead of the garbage and make a small amount of stock. I might make stracciatella with the stock for dinner, or can it for another day. I save the boiled disks of ginger left over from making syrup, candy them, and make ginger-studded chocolate bark. I'll zest all my oranges before juicing them and make up a batch of orange bitters or a bottle of orange baking extract. I don't do all this right away: I don't cook constantly. But I get to most things in the fridge eventually. Many times my daughter has pulled a bag of parsley stems out of the fridge and asked, "Are you really saving this, Ma? *Really?*"

So I discovered that most of my favorite ingredients could be used in three ways: I could eat some fresh, preserve some, and turn the stuff I would normally toss into useful ingredients. My kitchen was becoming an ecosystem, and I was creating, in essence, a kind of perpetual pantry. Preserved foods and products made from preparing one dish could boost the flavor in the next dish, which in turn generated even more preserved foods, and so on.

I actually became rather infatuated with how many dishes I could spin off an ingredient. I even drew cladograms, which are like family trees, to help me visualize just how many recipes could be squeezed out of a couple of pounds of something. For example, from a few pounds of asparagus I'll make roasted asparagus with garlic or an asparagus and Parmesan cheese frittata. Then I'll pickle a pint to use in a salad of cauliflower with pickled asparagus and chopped herbs, and freeze a half-pint of asparagus pesto to use as a sauce for ravioli or broiled fish.

But once I started using the scraps and peels and bones and shells—the waste stream of foods—I upgraded to Preserving 2.0. When you prepare asparagus to preserve (or cook), you usually discard the lower half of the spear because it is hard and stringy. But it's also full of flavor. Asparagus ends can be boiled in water, then pressed through a food mill to make an aromatic asparagus stock. This stock can be pressure canned or frozen or used right away. I use that stock to make even more recipes, like asparagus-flavored risotto (which can be garnished with shrimp or another vegetable) or spaghettini cooked in the asparagus stock and topped with grated ricotta salata or homemade ricotta.

I found flavor in the scraps of many foods: The bones and shells from fish, poultry, and meat make stocks and sauces, as do the pods and leaves and stems of mushrooms and vegetables and herbs; fat can be rendered and strained and reused; leftover marinades and pickling liquid from putting up pickles can be repurposed after the pickles are all eaten; the watery juice produced while prepping fruits for processing can be preserved separately, to make granitas and cocktails and sodas; and the peels of some fruits can be used to make pectin and zests.

Along the way I started to replace the commercial condiments I regularly use with homemade condiments, because I found that whenever I used homemade mayo instead of commercial mayo in a recipe, the dish tasted better. Open your refrigerator door: Almost everything in there can be made pretty easily. It used to be that when I was out at the market shopping for, say, beef to roast, and knew I needed horseradish, I could never remember if I had any. So I'd buy a jar and then when I got home I'd realize I had one open in the fridge and another in the pantry from the last time I made this same mistake. But once I started to make my own horseradish, I never forgot I had it. I think when you preserve a food it becomes a little more meaningful.

Cooking is not a full-time job for most of us. If a recipe is convoluted or really labor-intensive, it's very hard for me to fold it into my lifestyle. However, if I can preserve or glean useable flavoring agents from the foods I have to prepare for dinner anyway, then I'll do it. Often that means making nanobatches: I don't turn up my nose at making just a pint of stock. Why not? It's handy. And over time, my pantry and freezer and fridge have become loaded with lovely preserved foods and useful by-products that lend flavor and convenience to the daily job of making dinner.

I have what amounts to a kitchen ecosystem: a set of interconnected recipes and foods that defines my palate, which is mostly Mediterranean, primarily Italian. It also reflects my politics, because I believe in supporting regional, organic food producers. By eating regionally I am keep my dollars local and what's more, by preserving I keep my

COBS SAVED FOR STOCK

dollars local year-round. And the small chores of maintaining an array of support ingredients like stock actually save me time and money when it comes to putting dinner together. Usually all I have to do is buy the main fresh ingredient, like a chicken or a bunch of beets, and I can rustle up a couple of meals.

Shopping is key to cooking. If you use fresh, ripe locally grown vegetables and fruits, animals that have been raised with care, and wild products, your cooking will taste better. But beyond this commonsense approach, binging on seasonal foods is the healthiest and most natural way to eat. When my daughter was little she'd eat avocados for a month, then switch to a month of eating hot dogs, and so on. I worried she wasn't getting proper nutrition. But when I consulted her pediatrician he said that if I looked at what

THE BAR CABINET, WITH HOME-CANNED CRANBERRY JUICE, LIMONCELLO, APRICOT SHRUB, AND ORANGE BITTERS.

she ate over the course of a year, I would see she was actually getting a pretty well-rounded diet. This was a revelation to me, and it reinforces the wisdom of seasonal eating. The only way you can get a range of foods in a *daily* diet is if you eat some foods out of season, and those foods must, of course, be picked early and processed to accommodate the stress of shipping. Since out-of-season foods are less nutritious than seasonal foods, I think the whole idea of a daily food pyramid is bogus. So I have embraced the idea of a well-rounded *annual* diet, and jag on seasonal foods while they are at their nutritional peak. And just to keep it interesting and tasty, I augment my local and seasonal diet with preserved foods, put up when they were best sourced and at their freshest.

In the last five years or so, lots of people have gotten interested in preserving foods. I love it: It feels like a revolution. But I think the next step is to value and use the waste streams of our foods. Most of us make stock from the Thanksgiving turkey carcass, but to cook better every day we need to have on hand a single pint of stock from the hard shiitake mushroom stems, or a single pint of chicken stock from the bony back of a roasted chicken. We need to catch juices, render fats, reserve waters vegetables were boiled in, save herb stems and cheese rinds and citrus zests, and use them to enhance our cooking. This is how my Italian grandmother cooked. It is thrifty, and it produces robust taste. Very flavorful food is not a matter of one exceptional recipe— although there are many of those. It is a matter of thinking of your kitchen as a system.

HOW TO USE THIS BOOK

The ingredients in this book were selected in large part because they are foods that produce edible waste streams. I don't have a string bean or blueberry section, for example, because you eat the whole thing. But some foods are included because I use what's left over from cooking or preserving them, like the brine from pickling onions or zucchini. So this collection is really more idiosyncratic than prescriptive. In fact, I hope it will provide as much inspiration to do your own thing as it does actual recipes to follow. Because ultimately, the recipes you use are a reflection of your kitchen ecosystem: what makes sense for you and your region, your lifestyle, and your palate.

This book, this kitchen ecosystem, is riddled with cross-references. They point to recipes for homemade versions of ingredients, like chicken stock or vanilla extract, and instructions like altitude adjustments, and substitutions that explain how you can do the same recipe with a different ingredient. I would have loved to publish every recipe as a unique document, but I haven't for two reasons. First, it would make reading the book rather redundant to see water bath processing instructions over and over again, and secondly, it would have made for such a huge book you'd probably end up using it as a doorstop, rather than, well, *using* it. So cross-referencing was a trade-off. Don't let it drive you crazy. I mean, I use home-canned tomatoes, but you don't have to. However, if you find yourself attracted to recipes that call for them, maybe this fall you should give canning them a whirl.

I have a pretty well equipped kitchen, and there are tools that I highly recommend, like a food processor, for big jobs like breaking up horseradish or shrimp shells, an immersion blender for fast in-pot purees, and a food mill for separating out the skins and seeds from fruits and vegetables. A candy thermometer is helpful if you are going to make jams and jellies without pectin, and stuff like yogurt and ricotta. And definitely you need tools for some preserving projects, like a pressure canner (which is described in "Pressure Canning," page 376), but these conveniences aren't what make my food taste good. While I got my palate and many recipes from my father, who is a very fine cook, I actually learned how to cook on a hot plate and a toaster oven. After a few years, I added a Cuisinart food processor, a birthday gift from my parents. I cooked using that setup in a grungy dark loft in lower Manhattan from 1981 to 1988, when I married into a kitchen with a window. So while the gizmos of cooking are very useful, I can tell you from experience that good cooking is not the result of stuff. It's the result of practice.

About Substitutions

Many primary ingredients can be substituted for one another in recipes. And I love all kinds of substitutions. It's the first step in recipe development and once you get a feel for it, great fun. Here's a guideline to substitutions for the recipes in this book:

Baked goods: All the cakes can be muffins, just bake them for 5 to 10 minutes less. All the muffins can be cakes, but to be on the safe side, cook muffin recipes in tube cake pans. Cakes take 5 to 10 minutes longer to bake. The ultimate test is when you can smell a baked product; that usually means it's done.

Citrus: Oranges, grapefruit, and lemons are interchangeable in the marmalade recipe, and any combination of the three will work. Likewise, the zests are interchangeable in recipes but keep in mind, lemon has the strongest flavor, grapefruit the most subtle.

Dairy products: You can substitute crème fraîche for sour cream, or use it as a substitute for a whipped cream topping. Plain yogurt and sour cream can be substituted for one another in recipes that don't call for baking.

Herbs: You can substitute any tender herb (parsley, tarragon, cilantro, basil, chervil) with another, in both fresh and preserved recipes. It will change the flavor of the recipe, but you may love the result.

Fresh berries: All the berries and cherries are interchangeable in the dessert recipes.

Dried fruits: Any of the dried fruits used in sweet recipes can be substituted with other dried fruits.

Fruit jams: You can make a crostata or shortbread, or stuff a crepe, ricotta ball, scones, or fried ravioli with any jam (but not a jelly—it liquefies).

Fruit juices and syrups: Any fruit juice or fruit syrup can make a granita or a soda, and you can combine juices. Why not? I often do when I don't have enough of one flavor.

Fruit preserves: You can make the skillet tart recipes or the rice pudding with any fresh fruit or fruit preserve (not a jam or jelly). Just strain off the excess syrup and save it for a granita.

Fruit purees: You can make dessert soufflés, coffee cake, yeast buns, or panna cotta with any fruit puree, including fresh.

Fish and shellfish: You can substitute any white-fleshed saltwater fish for another. The main thing to keep in mind is the cut of fish, as the cut affects timing: Fillets are more delicate and take less time to cook than steaks. Shrimp and scallops are interchangeable in recipes.

Greens: Broccoli rabe, beet greens, radish greens, and feral greens, separately or in combination, are interchangeable.

Mushrooms: All the mushroom species are interchangeable, with two exceptions: porcini for making dried porcini powder; and candy caps. As candy caps are the only sweet mushroom in this book, you really can't substitute them.

Pasta: You can substitute rigatoni or shells for penne, spaghettini for linguine fini, and spaghetti for linguine.

Pestos: You can use the pea, asparagus, nettle, and ramps pestos interchangeably. You can make pestos thinned with oil with any tender herb and you can use any type of nut.

Stock: Any stock can be used to cook pasta or make risotto as long as it isn't too thick (and if it is, add water to make it about the consistency of skim milk). Just remember the corn stock is sweet. You can make any of the soup recipes with any stock except for the seafood stocks, which are best in seafood recipes.

APPLES

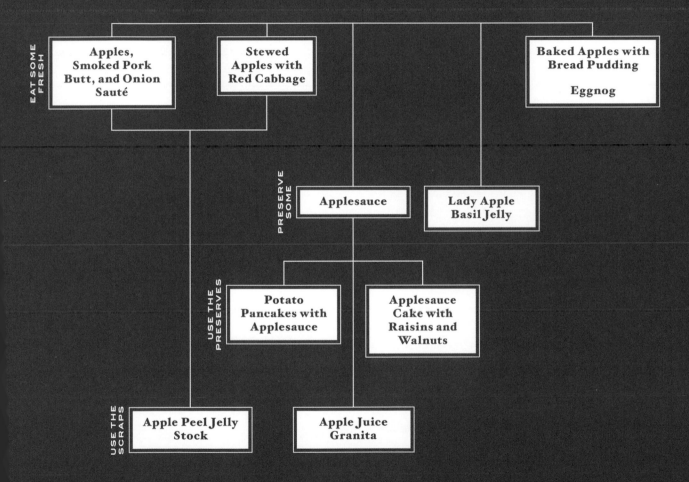

EAT SOME FRESH

Apples, Smoked Pork Butt, and Onion Sauté

Stewed Apples with Red Cabbage

Baked Apples with Bread Pudding

Eggnog

PRESERVE SOME

Applesauce

Lady Apple Basil Jelly

USE THE PRESERVES

Potato Pancakes with Applesauce

Applesauce Cake with Raisins and Walnuts

USE THE SCRAPS

Apple Peel Jelly Stock

Apple Juice Granita

Apples, Smoked Pork Butt, and Onion Sauté

This is excellent served on a TV tray with a dark beer on Super Bowl Sunday. Cortland, Granny Smith, and Rome Beauties are all good apples to use as their flesh maintains its integrity well under heat.

SERVES 4

> 2 to 4 tablespoons unsalted butter
>
> 1½ pounds smoked pork butt, cut into 8 slices (½ inch thick)
>
> 2 large onions, cut horizontally into 8 slices (½ inch thick)
>
> 2 baking apples, cored and cut horizontally into 8 rings (½ inch thick)
>
> ½ cup apple cider
>
> Salt and freshly ground black pepper
>
> A few sprigs of fresh thyme (optional)

In a large skillet, melt 2 tablespoons butter over medium-low heat. Add the pork and cook until golden on both sides, 3 to 5 minutes. Remove the pork to a platter and cover loosely with foil to keep warm. Cook the pork (and the onions and apples) in batches depending on the size of your skillet. You will need to add additional butter to grease the bottom of the skillet between batches.

Add the onion slices to the pan. Cook for 3 to 4 minutes, or until just golden. It's okay if they blacken a bit on the edges. Remove the onions and add them to the platter with the pork.

Add 2 more tablespoons of butter if the pan seems dry. Once the butter is melted, add the apples and cook until they pick up some golden color, 2 to 3 minutes. Add the apples to the platter with the pork and onions.

Pour the apple cider into the pan and scrape up the browned bits as the cider boils. Cook until reduced by half. Return the pork butt, onions, and apples to the pan, and season with salt and pepper to taste. Cook for 2 to 3 minutes longer to meld the flavors.

Serve promptly, garnished with thyme, if you'd like.

Stewed Apples with Red Cabbage

My friend Bart Byuck taught me this recipe. It is a traditional dish from his hometown of Ghent in Belgium. When I made it for him he closed his eyes, chewing in a kind of nostalgic reverie. Use Jonathans, Granny Smiths, or Galas in this recipe, or you can use applesauce. This dish is usually served with a plain pork sausage cooked on the grill. **Save the apple peels for Apple Peel Jelly Stock (page 14).** SERVES 4

> 2 tablespoons unsalted butter
>
> 4 cups finely sliced red cabbage (1 small head)
>
> 2 cups chopped peeled apples or 1 pint applesauce (for homemade, page 10)
>
> 1 bay leaf
>
> ¼ teaspoon ground cloves
>
> Salt and freshly ground black pepper

In a large pot, melt the butter over medium heat. Add the cabbage, cover, and cook until the cabbage is wilted, 3 to 4 minutes. Add the apples, bay leaf, cloves, and salt and pepper to taste. Cover and cook until the apples are hot and tender, 3 to 4 minutes longer.

Baked Apples
with Bread Pudding

I am not a huge fan of sweet baked apples, but I kept making them half hoping something would change. Then something did. I made a bread pudding and put a couple of smashed baked Cortland and Jonathan apples on top, then put the whole thing in the oven. You can also chop peeled apples and add them to the custard when you add the bread, which makes the bread pudding perhaps a bit less primitive looking. Sometimes I substitute the chopped apples and brandy with pitted sweet cherries and hazelnut liqueur. I like to serve this pudding for breakfast or as a dessert with Eggnog (recipe follows). **SERVES 8**

APPLES

4 small or 2 large baking apples (about 1 pound)

4 teaspoons light brown sugar

2 tablespoons raisins (for homemade, page 161)

1 tablespoon grated orange zest

2 tablespoons unsalted butter, cut up

1 cup apple cider

BREAD PUDDING

1 cup heavy cream

1 large egg plus 2 large egg yolks, beaten together

⅓ cup granulated sugar

2 tablespoons brandy

3 cups cubed bread (I like firm white sandwich bread, brioche, or challah best)

1 tablespoon unsalted butter (for the pan)

Preheat the oven to 350°F.

For the apples: Slice off the stem end of the apples and scoop out the core and seeds, making a cavity inside the apple large enough to hold 2 tablespoons. I use a melon baller for this. Slice the blossom ends off the apples so they'll stand upright.

Dividing evenly, stuff the apple cavities with the brown sugar, raisins, and orange zest. Top each apple with butter.

Place the apples in a baking pan where they fit snuggly (I use a loaf pan) and pour in the cider. Bake for 30 minutes, or until the apples are soft. Remove them and set aside. Leave the oven on.

Meanwhile, for the bread pudding: In a large bowl, whisk together the cream, eggs, granulated sugar, and brandy. Add the bread and let it soak while you butter an 8-inch baking dish.

Pour the bread and custard into the baking dish. With a metal spatula, gently smash the baked apples until they are flattened. Place the apples on top of the pudding.

Place the baking dish in a roasting pan that is larger and deeper. Pour in enough very hot water to come halfway up the sides of the baking dish.

Place the pudding in the oven and bake for 45 minutes, or until the bread is golden and the custard set. Do not overcook bread pudding or it will get tough.

EGGNOG

I drizzle eggnog over the bread pudding with baked apples. I also sometimes serve the eggnog in a shot glass alongside, for diners to either pour on the bread pudding or drink. **MAKES 1½ CUPS**

1 cup whole milk

½ cup sugar

3 large egg yolks, beaten

¼ cup bourbon

¼ cup heavy cream

Pinch of grated nutmeg

In a medium pot, combine the milk and sugar and heat over medium-low heat until the sugar dissolves. Add the egg yolks, whisking all the while. Cook until the mixture coats the back of a spoon, about 5 minutes. Allow the mixture to cool. Stir in the bourbon, heavy cream, and nutmeg. Chill.

Applesauce

The best applesauce is made from sweet apples like Cortland or Jonathan (or better yet, a combination of sweet apples), not tart apples like Granny Smiths, which need more sugar. A hand-cranked food mill is the best tool for making applesauce (and tomato sauce and many other things). You can also use a food processor or potato masher, but you should peel and core the apples before cooking them if you do. **Save the peels and cores for Apple Peel Jelly Stock (page 14).** MAKES 3 TO 4 PINTS

> 3 pounds sweet apples (about 9 medium)
>
> 2 to 4 cups cider, unsweetened apple juice, or water, or a combination
>
> Sugar
>
> Flavorings (optional): Calvados, grated orange zest, ground cinnamon, or grated nutmeg

Quarter the apples and core. (Also peel them if you are using a food processor.) Pour the cider into the bottom of a big pot. There needs to be enough liquid to come up at least 2 inches in the pot. Add the apples, cover, and place over medium-low heat. Cook until the apples are soft, about 15 minutes.

Allow the apples to cool, then scoop them out with a slotted spoon and press them through a food mill.

There will be excess juice in the bottom of the pan after cooking the apples. Pour it into a sterilized jar and refrigerate it. Drink it straight or use it to make Apple Juice Granita (page 15).

Pour the applesauce into a medium pot and bring to a boil. Add sugar to taste, and stir to dissolve the sugar, then turn off the heat. If you'd like, you can flavor your applesauce at this point. Spike it with Calvados, orange zest, cinnamon, or nutmeg . . . none of which will affect the processing instructions.

Have ready 4 clean pint jars and bands, and new lids that have been simmered in hot water to soften the rubberized flange. You can also do half-pints, or a combination of pints and half-pints. Spoon the applesauce into the jars leaving ½ inch of headroom. Wipe the rims, place on the lids, and screw on the bands fingertip tight.

Process the jars in a water bath (see page 375) for 15 minutes. Eight half-pints are processed for the same amount of time, and 2 quarts are processed for 20 minutes. Be sure to make altitude adjustments when preserving (see page 389). The fruit at the top of the jar may darken over time. It's okay.

Lady Apple Basil Jelly

Delicate, with an herby fragrance, this jelly firms up well because apple skins are full of pectin. It has a beautiful pale color, too. You can flavor it with fresh thyme or mint instead of the basil if you'd like, or forgo the herbs altogether. MAKES 2 HALF-PINTS

2 pounds lady apples, halved, with blossom
ends and stems removed

1½ cups sugar

2 tablespoons fresh lemon juice

About 6 large basil leaves

Place the apples in a large pot with enough water to just cover (about 4 cups). Boil the apples gently over medium-high heat, covered, until the fruit is soft, about 30 minutes. The apples will look like they have exploded. Don't mash the apples. Take the pot off the heat, uncover, and allow the apples to cool in the cooking liquid.

Arrange a jelly bag or a sieve lined with two layers of cheesecloth over a deep pot. Wet the bag or cheesecloth so it doesn't absorb any of the juice. Ladle the apples and their cooking liquid into the jelly bag and let the juice drip through into the pot. (It's okay to squeeze the jelly bag to speed things up, because although this is a murky juice, it becomes clear when you boil the juice with the sugar.) Measure the juice. You should have about 2 cups. If you have more or less that's okay. Just adjust the sugar accordingly. You can prepare the juice ahead of time and refrigerate. It holds well for 2 to 3 days.

Place the juice, sugar, and lemon juice in a heavy-bottomed 6- to 8-quart pot. Bring to a boil over medium-low heat, allowing the sugar to gently dissolve. Increase the heat and boil the juice hard for about 15 minutes, then add the basil leaves and boil hard for a few minutes more. Watch the bubbles: When the jelly bubbles seem to increase their volume, and take on color, the jelly is usually ready. Check the temperature with a candy thermometer. It will jell at 220°F at sea level, or 8°F over boiling temperature wherever you are. (To calculate the boiling temperature at your altitude, see page 389). Or you can test the jelly by letting a spoonful cool in the fridge for a couple of minutes. If the jelly drips off the spoon in dribbles, it's not ready. If it shears off the spoon in a single drop, it is.

Have ready 2 sterilized half-pint jars and bands, and new lids that have been simmered in hot water to soften the rubberized flange. (See "How to Sterilize," page 389.) Remove the basil leaves and spoon the jelly into the jars leaving ¼ inch of headroom. Wipe the rims, place on the lids, and screw on the bands fingertip tight.

Process the jars in a water bath (see page 375) for 5 minutes. Process a 1 pint jar for the same amount of time. Be sure to make altitude adjustments when preserving (see page 389).

LADY APPLE BASIL JELLY

POTATO
PANCAKES WITH
APPLESAUCE

Potato Pancakes
with Applesauce

Around Hanukkah every year my friend Diane throws a potato pancake party. Hers are the best I've ever had. They are rich and light, crispy and potato-y, and blessedly easy to make. My small contribution to the party is homemade applesauce. The trick to these pancakes is to fry them in small batches. Diane knocks herself out to make a hundred of them for a party, but I think 16 pancakes for 4 people are perfect. They make a great side dish, too, and are wonderful with a piece of broiled fish on top. You can refrigerate the pancakes for a few days after frying them, or freeze them for up to 2 months. The baking step will crisp them up beautifully. SERVES 4/MAKES 14 TO 16 PANCAKES

4 large baking potatoes (about 4 pounds)

3 tablespoons all-purpose flour

½ teaspoon baking powder

Dash of ground cinnamon

Salt and freshly ground black pepper

¼ cup minced onion

2 large eggs, beaten

Neutral oil, such as safflower, for frying

1 cup applesauce (for homemade, page 10)

1 cup sour cream (optional)

Preheat the oven to 350°F.

Peel the potatoes and place them in a bowl of cold water.

In a small bowl, combine the flour, baking powder, cinnamon, and pepper to taste. Set aside.

Pat the potatoes dry and grate them on the large holes of a grater. Long grated shreds are best. You will get about 1 heaping cup of grated potato per baking potato. Place the grated potatoes in a large bowl, add the onions, and toss well. Add the flour mixture and toss well, breaking up the clumps. This may take a bit of time as the dry ingredients must be well distributed. Add the eggs and combine well.

In a large nonstick skillet, heat about 1 inch of oil over high heat. Test the heat by inserting a little piece of potato in the oil. If it bubbles violently, the oil is ready.

Using a slotted spoon, scoop up a spoonful of the potato mixture, allowing excess liquid to drain off. Drop the spoonful of potatoes into the oil. Add more spoonfuls of potatoes. I usually fit 8 to 10 pancakes in a large skillet. Fry until just golden, about 2 minutes on each side. Do not flip the pancakes over until they are golden on the underside, otherwise they will fall apart and may get greasy. They will not be cooked through. It's okay, because they finish cooking in the oven. Drain on brown paper bags or paper towels. Continue until all of the potato mixture is used. As you get toward the bottom of the bowl, the potatoes will be wetter. They will take a bit of pressing to remove the extra liquid, and will take a bit longer to cook. If you're using a large skillet you probably won't need to add more oil, but if you do add oil, then wait until the oil has come up to a high heat before adding more pancakes.

Arrange the pancakes on a baking sheet and bake for about 10 minutes on each side. They will turn a rich golden brown. They may need to be blotted on a paper towel before serving. Season with salt to taste.

Serve with applesauce and sour cream, if you like.

Applesauce Cake with Raisins and Walnuts

You can substitute the raisins with currants, dried cranberries, dried cherries, or bits of dried apricots, and the walnuts with pecans if you'd like, but keep to the quantities in the recipe or the cake could be heavy. This light and spicy cake is great on its own and I serve it simply with whipped cream; but a confectioners' sugar glaze is good, and a cream cheese or fudge frosting is luscious. You can make a dozen cupcakes with this recipe, too. They will take about 10 minutes less time in the oven. **MAKES ONE 9-INCH TUBE CAKE (10-CUP CAPACITY)**

> 8 tablespoons (1 stick) unsalted butter, at room temperature
>
> 1 cup sugar
>
> 1 cup applesauce (for homemade, page 10)
>
> 1½ cups all-purpose flour
>
> ¾ teaspoon baking soda
>
> ½ teaspoon ground cinnamon
>
> ½ teaspoon grated nutmeg
>
> ½ cup golden raisins (for homemade, page 161)
>
> ½ cup chopped walnuts
>
> ¾ teaspoon vanilla extract (for homemade, page 361)

Preheat the oven to 325°F. Butter a 9-inch tube pan.

In a large bowl, beat the butter and sugar together until light and fluffy. Beat in the applesauce until well combined. The batter will look curdled. It's okay.

In a second large bowl, sift together the flour, baking soda, cinnamon, and nutmeg.

Measure out 2 tablespoons of the flour mixture and transfer to a small bowl. Add the raisins and walnuts and toss them in the flour.

Add the flour mixture to the butter mixture and combine well, but do not beat beyond combining or the crumb of the cake will be tougher. Stir in the vanilla and the flour-coated fruit and nut mixture.

Pour the batter into the prepared tube pan. Tap the pan on the counter to distribute the batter evenly. Bake for about 45 minutes, until you can smell the cake and a cake tester comes out clean. Let the cake cool in the pan for a few minutes, then turn the cake out onto a rack to cool completely.

Apple Peel Jelly Stock

Jelly stock is a thick, pectin-rich juice that can be added to help low-pectin jams and jellies jell. How much jelly stock to use in canning is a bit of an art form, but in general, add 1 cup jelly stock to every 2 cups of fruit juice or 2 pounds of mashed fruit. Then use a recipe for jelly or jam using liquid pectin and that particular fruit to determine sugar and acid (usually lemon juice) quantities and canning instructions. Jelly stock can be frozen for up to a year. For small-batch canning, it is useful to freeze the jelly stock in ½-cup quantities. **MAKES 1 CUP**

> 2 pounds apple peelings, seeds, and cores (green apple peels have the highest pectin)
>
> 4 cups water

Place the apples and water in a deep, heavy-bottomed pot and bring to a boil over high heat. Reduce the heat to medium, cover, and cook until the peels and cores are mushy, about 20 minutes.

Arrange a jelly bag or a sieve lined with two layers of cheesecloth over a deep pot. Wet the bag or cheesecloth so it doesn't absorb any of the juice. Ladle the apples and their water into the jelly bag and let the juice drip through into the pot. This can take a few hours. You should have about 2 cups of juice.

Pour the juice into a heavy-bottomed pot and boil over medium-high heat until the juice is reduced by half, about 20 minutes.

Jelly stock holds in the fridge for a few days, or you can freeze it. (See "How to Freeze Foods," page 382.)

Apple Juice Granita

The apple juice left over from cooking apples for applesauce is a treasure. It is very intense and sweet. Feel free to experiment with warm spices like cinnamon and nutmeg. A shot of Calvados (apple brandy) in this granita is pretty tasty, too. You can also make this granita with commercial unsweetened apple juice or apple cider. SERVES 4

- 3 cups apple juice
- ½ cup sugar
- ¼ cup orange juice (optional)
- 1 tablespoon fresh lemon juice

Prepare according to the technique for making granitas on page 393.

APPLE JUICE GRANITA (GREAT WITH GINGER COOKIES, PAGE 148)

APRICOTS

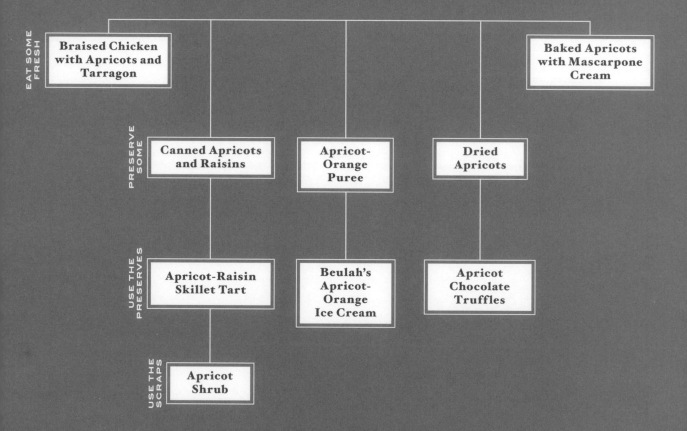

EAT SOME FRESH

Braised Chicken with Apricots and Tarragon

Baked Apricots with Mascarpone Cream

PRESERVE SOME

Canned Apricots and Raisins

Apricot-Orange Puree

Dried Apricots

USE THE PRESERVES

Apricot-Raisin Skillet Tart

Beulah's Apricot-Orange Ice Cream

Apricot Chocolate Truffles

USE THE SCRAPS

Apricot Shrub

Braised Chicken with Apricots and Tarragon

I make this recipe with chicken thighs that I collect over the course of a few whole chicken purchases, but a mixture of parts will do. The bright taste of the apricots is especially nice with tarragon, though you can play with other herbs as well, like parsley or cilantro. It's a lovely summer dish. SERVES 4

- 8 bone-in, skin-on chicken thighs
- ¼ cup chopped guanciale (pork jowl), pancetta, or bacon
- 2 tablespoons minced garlic
- 10 whole cloves
- 2 tablespoons minced fresh tarragon
- ⅔ cup dry white wine
- 1 heaping cup pitted fresh apricots, halved if small and quartered if large (about 4 large apricots or ½ pound)
- Freshly ground black pepper
- Chicken stock (optional; for homemade, page 89)

Place the chicken skin-side down in a large cast-iron skillet or nonstick skillet. Sprinkle the guanciale, garlic, the cloves, and 1 tablespoon of the tarragon on top of the chicken. Pour the wine around the meat.

Cover the skillet and place it over medium-low heat. Cook until the chicken is nicely browned, about 25 minutes, then flip the meat over, allowing the other ingredients to spread throughout the pan. Add the apricots and remaining 1 tablespoon tarragon and cook for 5 to 10 minutes longer to finish browning the chicken. You may not need to salt this dish but a few grinds of black pepper are very good. If the dish seems a bit dry at any point, add a little water or chicken stock to the skillet.

Remove the cloves before serving. Serve warm or at room temperature.

Baked Apricots with Mascarpone Cream

This is a simple dessert that really showcases the wonderful sweet and tart flavor of fresh apricots. I like to garnish the apricots with a sprinkle of crushed amaretti cookies (which seem to last in my cabinet for years), but crushed biscotti or graham crackers work well, too. SERVES 4

- 4 large fresh apricots, halved and pitted
- 2 tablespoons unsalted butter, cut into little bits
- 4 tablespoons sugar
- 8 ounces mascarpone cheese, at room temperature
- ½ cup heavy cream
- ½ cup crushed amaretti cookies

Preheat the oven to 400°F.

Lay the apricots in a baking dish or skillet cut side up in a single, snug layer. (I like to use an 8-inch cast-iron skillet.) Sprinkle the butter over the apricots, then sprinkle with 2 tablespoons of the sugar.

Bake the apricots for about 5 minutes, or until tender but not browned. Remove from the oven and let cool to room temperature.

Meanwhile, in a small bowl, combine the mascarpone cheese and remaining 2 table-spoons sugar. In a separate bowl, with an electric mixer, beat the heavy cream to soft peaks. Fold the whipped cream into the mascarpone cheese.

To serve, spoon the mascarpone cream into the cavities of the apricots and sprinkle with crushed amaretti.

BAKED
APRICOTS WITH
MASCARPONE
CREAM

Canned Apricots and Raisins

It's best not to can very ripe apricots or you'll end up with mushy fruit. Apricots continue to ripen after being picked, so keep that in mind when planning to can. I always put up a few pints of these apricots in order to make Apricot-Raisin Skillet Tart (page 20), my go-to, last-minute dessert. You can leave out the raisins if you'd like. **You will have excess syrup; save it for Apricot Shrub (page 23).** MAKES 3 PINTS

- 3 cups water
- 1 cup sugar
- 2½ pounds fresh apricots (about 20), halved and pitted
- 3 tablespoons golden raisins (for homemade, page 161)

Have ready 3 clean pint jars and bands, and new lids that have been simmered in hot water to soften the rubberized flange.

In a large, heavy-bottomed pot, combine the water and sugar and bring to a boil over medium heat, stirring to dissolve the sugar. Add the apricots. As soon as the syrup comes to a boil again, stir in the raisins, and take the pot off the heat.

Remove the apricots and raisins with a slotted spoon and drop them into the pint jars. Pack the apricots loosely. Pour the syrup over the apricots leaving ½ inch headroom. Wipe the rims, place on the lids, and screw on the bands fingertip tight.

Process the jars in a water bath (see page 375) for 20 minutes. Be sure to make altitude adjustments when preserving (see page 389). The apricots may float. It's okay. There may be some discoloring of the fruit at the top of the jar over time. That's okay, too.

Apricot-Orange Puree

Some years the apricots I get are very meaty, other years more juicy. This is a reality of orchard-fresh fruit, and it means that you have to adjust recipes a bit. If the apricots are very juicy you'll want to cook them a bit longer in order to thicken this puree, which should be about as thick as porridge. (You can make this puree chunky, too—it will not affect the processing.) This is a great sauce to spoon onto Orange Olive Oil Pound Cake (page 215), to pour onto pancakes, or flavor Beulah's Apricot-Orange Ice Cream (page 21). MAKES 4 HALF-PINTS

- 2 pounds fresh apricots (about 16), halved and pitted
- 1½ cups sugar
- ¼ cup fresh lemon juice
- ¼ cup orange juice

In a blender or food processor, combine the apricots, sugar, lemon juice, and orange juice and puree. Pour the apricot puree into a large heavy-bottomed pot and bring to a boil over medium-low heat. Boil gently, uncovered, until the mixture thickens to the consistency of porridge, about 20 minutes.

Have ready 4 sterilized half-pint jars and bands, and new lids that have been simmered in hot water to soften the rubberized flange. Pour the puree into the jars leaving ¼ inch of headroom. Wipe the rims, place on the lids, and screw on the bands fingertip tight.

Process the jars in a water bath (see page 375) for 5 minutes. Be sure to make altitude adjustments when preserving (see page 389). There may be some discoloring of the fruit at the top of the jar over time. It's okay.

Dried Apricots

Dried apricots should be leathery but pliable. If the weather is humid, it will take longer for the apricots to dry. Commercial apricots are usually treated with the preservative sulfur dioxide, which ensures a very soft, bright orange product. Without sulfur, dried apricots are a bit tougher and darker in color, even with an ascorbic acid soak. I use dried apricots in Apricot Chocolate Truffles (page 22); or as a substitute for raisins in Applesauce Cake (page 14) and Granola with Raisins (page 162); or to replace the cherries in Dried Cherry Chunkies (page 80).

MAKES ½ POUND

- 4 cups water
- 2 tablespoons plus 2 teaspoons ascorbic acid (to mitigate discoloration)
- 3 pounds fresh apricots (about 30), halved and pitted

In a large bowl, combine the water and ascorbic acid. Mix to dissolve the acid and add the apricots. Allow them to soak for 10 minutes.

Drain the apricots and place them cut side up in the trays of a food dehydrator (or see page 385 for instructions on oven-drying). Do not pack them tightly. It is better to give the apricots a bit of space. Set your dryer to 135°F. The apricots should take about 12 hours. See "How to Dry" (page 385) for information on "conditioning" the dried apricots.

Apricot-Raisin Skillet Tart

This is the fastest, easiest tart that I make. You can use any of your canned fruit in it, like Canned Cherries (page 00). **Save the drained syrup to make Apricot Shrub (page 23).** SERVES 4

APRICOT-RAISIN SKILLET TART

APRICOT-RAISIN SKILLET TART

1 tablespoon unsalted butter, for buttering
   the pan

1 pint Canned Apricots and Raisins (page 19)

¼ cup sugar

¼ cup slivered blanched almonds (optional)

1 sheet frozen puff pastry, thawed in the
   refrigerator

Crème fraîche (for homemade, page 362) or
   whipped cream, for serving

Preheat the oven to 350°F.

Butter an 8-inch nonstick ovenproof skillet. (Unless you have an awesomely seasoned cast-iron skillet, using anything other than nonstick will disappoint.) Drain the apricots and pour them into the skillet. Add the sugar. If you'd like, add the slivered almonds. They add texture.

Cut out a round of puff pastry the size of the pan and place it on top of the apricots. Punch holes all over the pastry with the tines of a fork (to let the steam out).

Bake for 10 to 15 minutes, or until the pastry is puffed up and golden. Remove the skillet and let cool a bit. Remember the handle of the skillet is very hot and stays hot (I've gotten some horrid burns from making this dish). The pastry will deflate some. It's okay.

Flip the tart over onto a serving plate. Serve with crème fraîche or whipped cream.

Beulah's Apricot-Orange Ice Cream

Years ago I learned how to make Apricot-Orange Puree (page 19) from Beulah Fletcher of Paonia, Colorado, when she was 98 years old. She mentioned that she makes ice cream with the puree. I'd always wanted to follow up on the recipe, and also pay my respects to her, but time slipped by and a few years passed. When I finally did call, her son answered and said she had died two days earlier. I can think of a hundred things that weren't as important, things that I did instead of calling her. Such is the nature of regret. I eventually made the ice cream, but for me, the recipe is Beulah's. **SERVES 4**

1 cup whole milk

¼ cup sugar

1 cup heavy cream

1 half-pint Apricot-Orange Puree (page 19)

In a small heavy-bottomed saucepan, heat the milk over a medium-low heat. Add the sugar and cook a few minutes, stirring to dissolve the sugar.

Transfer the milk mixture to a stainless steel container. Stir in the heavy cream and apricot puree, mixing well. Chill in the refrigerator for a few hours.

Transfer the chilled mixture to an ice cream maker and freeze according to the manufacturer's directions (or make by hand; see page 394). The ice cream holds for about 1 month.

Apricot Chocolate Truffles

These truffles are utterly delicious and totally easy to make, though they do take time. I roll my truffles rather small, the size of gumballs. You can roll them as large as you like, but they become more difficult to cover smoothly with chocolate the larger they are. Chocolate chips work as well as chocolate that comes in a block, but use the best chocolate you can find. Substitute Dried Sweet Cherries (page 77) for the apricots and kirsch for the Cointreau if you'd like.

MAKES ABOUT 45 TRUFFLES

> 6 ounces (about 1 cup) dried apricots (for homemade, page 20), minced
>
> ½ cup orange juice
>
> Heaping ¼ cup sugar
>
> ½ cup heavy cream
>
> 4 tablespoons (½ stick) unsalted butter, cut up
>
> 1½ tablespoons light corn syrup
>
> 2 pounds bittersweet chocolate, cut into small bits or shaved
>
> 2 tablespoons Cointreau or other orange liqueur

In a small heavy-bottomed pot, combine the apricots, orange juice, and sugar. Bring to a boil over medium heat and cook until the sugar dissolves and the fruit absorbs the liquid, about 5 minutes. Remove from the heat.

In a medium heavy-bottomed pot, combine the cream, butter, and corn syrup and heat over medium-low heat until the butter melts and the cream starts to boil. Remove from the heat.

In a double boiler or bowl set over a pan of hot water, combine one-third of the chocolate and the Cointreau and stir to melt.

Add the chocolate mixture to the cream mixture. Stir to combine, then add the apricot mixture. Pour the chocolate apricot mixture into two 9-inch cake pans and place in the freezer for a few hours until hard. (If you put all of the chocolate mixture into one 9-inch pan it will take much longer to harden.)

Line a baking sheet with wax paper or parchment paper. Remove one pan of chocolate from the freezer (leave the other in the freezer while you work on the first). The chocolate should be very hard. Scoop out marble-size portions of the chocolate mixture (I use a melon baller, but you can use a spoon) or cut out pieces with a knife. Roll the pieces of chocolate mixture between your palms to make balls. (This is a messy business. I have to wash my hands frequently. But be sure to dry them well as rolling with wet palms makes the mess worse.) The balls won't be perfectly round. That's life. As you work, place the truffles on the lined baking sheet. Continue with the second cake pan. Place the baking sheet in the refrigerator and chill for a couple of hours.

Line a second baking sheet with wax paper or parchment paper.

In a double boiler or bowl set over a pan of hot water, melt the remaining chocolate (I actually prefer a bowl here because the rounded bottom of the bowl makes it easier when it comes time to roll the truffles in the chocolate). Stir until smooth.

When the chocolate is melted, dip the balls in the chocolate: Dipping the balls in chocolate is not as easy as it sounds. I've used chopsticks, tongs, two forks, but at the end of the day, what works for me is a butter knife or other flat utensil for rolling the truffle in the chocolate, and a fork for lifting it out. The main trick is completely covering the truffle in melted chocolate. Trying to cover a truffle with scant chocolate resources is a drag, like trying to stay warm under a blanket that is too small for your bed.

As you work, place the truffles on the baking sheet to cool. Then place all the truffles back in the fridge to chill. Once the shells are hard you can pack the truffles in candy boxes. They hold in the fridge for about 2 weeks.

Apricot Shrub

A shrub is a vinegar-based drink. My friend Willy mixes all kinds of shrubs with prosecco. Shrubs are easy to make, either using leftover syrup from canning fruit or fresh syrup (see Note). More of a method than a recipe, the following is how you make a shrub with syrup left over from canning fruit. This example happens to be from Canned Apricots and Raisins, but the same method can be applied to the syrup left over from canning any fruit. To serve, pour a tablespoon or less of the shrub in a champagne glass and top with cold prosecco. **MAKES 1 HALF-PINT**

½ cup apricot-flavored syrup (see Canned Apricots and Raisins, page 19)

½ cup white wine vinegar or cider vinegar

When you are done canning the apricots, there should be ½ cup or so of apricot-flavored syrup left in the bottom of the pot. Combine this apricot syrup with an equal amount of vinegar.

The shrub is quite tart at first, but over time it will mellow. If you want to use the shrub right away, boil the syrup/vinegar mixture for 5 minutes. This reduces some of the acidity and makes for a mellower product.

Bottle and refrigerate or, for shelf-stable shrub, water bath process it. (There is no USDA recommendation for canning apricot shrub, however I did a pH test on this shrub and it fell well within safe limits [3.5]. Therefore the canning time here is based on the USDA recommendation for apple juice, which has about the same pH.)

Have ready 1 sterilized half-pint jar for every cup of shrub, along with a sterilized band and a new lid that has been simmered in hot water to soften the rubberized flange. Pour the shrub into the jar, leaving ¼ inch of headroom. Wipe the rim, place on the lid, and screw on the band fingertip tight.

Process the jar in a water bath (see page 375) for 5 minutes. Be sure to make altitude adjustments when preserving (see page 389).

Note: If you don't have any fruit syrup around and still want to make a shrub, combine equal weights of berries or coarsely chopped stone fruit (skin-on) and sugar in a large bowl. Place the bowl on your kitchen counter, cover with plastic wrap, and leave to macerate for 2 days. The sugar will dissolve and become watery, and the fruit may start to look shriveled and dehydrated. That's all good.

Strain the fruit and sugar mixture through a jelly bag or a few layers of cheesecloth. It is okay to squeeze the bag of fruit in order to get as much juice out as you can. Measure the syrup. For ½ pound berries and ½ pound sugar I usually get about 1 cup of syrup.

ARTICHOKES

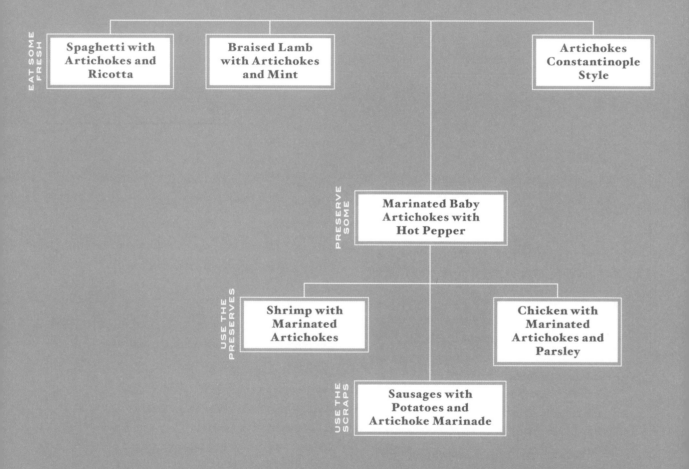

EAT SOME FRESH

Spaghetti with Artichokes and Ricotta

Braised Lamb with Artichokes and Mint

Artichokes Constantinople Style

PRESERVE SOME

Marinated Baby Artichokes with Hot Pepper

USE THE PRESERVES

Shrimp with Marinated Artichokes

Chicken with Marinated Artichokes and Parsley

USE THE SCRAPS

Sausages with Potatoes and Artichoke Marinade

How to Trim an Artichoke

To trim a large artichoke for cooking, first rinse and brush off the film on the surface of the leaves. This biofilm, which is naturally produced by the artichoke, can lend a bitter flavor. Cut off the top inch of the artichoke with a serrated knife, and only about ½ inch off the stem: The artichoke stem is a continuation of the heart and tastes good, so don't remove it unless you need the artichoke to sit upright for serving. Long stems should be peeled with a vegetable peeler down to the pale green flesh. The artichoke and stem can be cooked together, or the stem chopped and cooked separately. Snip off the thorns on the tip of the leaves. Rub the cut ends of the artichoke with a half lemon if you want to prevent browning. You can also place the artichokes in a bowl of water and lemon juice, or water and a pinch of ascorbic acid to prevent browning. To trim a baby artichoke, remove the tough outer leaves, reducing the volume of the vegetable by half, until the artichoke has the shape of a teardrop or candle flame and is pale green to yellow and soft to the touch. With a paring knife, cut around the base, removing all of the rough surfaces. Halve the artichoke lengthwise and pluck out any thistly interior leaves.

Spaghetti with Artichokes and Ricotta

This dish balances the tartness of artichokes cooked in wine with the sweet cream of ricotta. Homemade ricotta is best (see page 367). You'll need 4 cups of milk, and the ricotta can be prepared while the artichokes are cooking. I often make the artichokes in this recipe as a side dish. SERVES 4

  2 pounds baby artichokes (about 10), trimmed (see above)

  ¼ cup dry white wine

  ¼ cup olive oil

  ¼ cup water or chicken stock (for homemade, page 89)

  1 tablespoon sliced garlic

  1 tablespoon fresh lemon juice

  1 tablespoon fresh thyme leaves (optional)

  1 bay leaf

  Salt and freshly ground black pepper

  12 ounces spaghetti

  8 ounces (1 cup) ricotta cheese (for homemade, page 367)

  2 tablespoons chopped flat-leaf parsley

  Extra virgin olive oil, for serving

Arrange the artichokes in a pot that will hold them snugly in a single layer. Add the wine, oil, water, garlic, lemon juice, thyme (if using), bay leaf, and salt to taste. The braising liquid should come about halfway up the sides of the artichokes. A little more is okay. Bring to a boil, then reduce the heat to low. Cover and gently braise the artichokes until very tender, about 30 minutes. You may need to rotate the artichokes, or turn them over for even cooking. The artichokes will be softened and their color bleached out some. Remove the bay leaf.

Bring a large pot of salted water to a boil and add the pasta. Cook until al dente and drain.

Toss the pasta in a serving bowl with the artichokes and residual juices. Add the ricotta and toss gently to combine.

Garnish with black pepper and the parsley. If the pasta seems a bit dry, then add a drizzle of extra virgin olive oil.

BABY
ARTICHOKES

Braised Lamb with Artichokes and Mint

This is typical of the kind of dish I grew up eating on a school night. The vegetable and protein are cooked together in one pot. The original recipe was published in 1971 in Italian Family Cooking *by Edward Giobbi, my father.* **SERVES 4**

- 2 tablespoons olive oil
- 1½ pounds boneless lamb leg, cut into 1-inch cubes
- Salt and freshly ground black pepper
- 1 large onion, thinly sliced (about 2 cups)
- 2 garlic cloves, peeled
- 8 baby artichokes, trimmed (see page 25)
- 2 bay leaves
- One 4-inch sprig of fresh rosemary
- 3 tablespoons unsalted butter
- 1 cup dry white wine
- 2 tablespoons chopped fresh mint

Preheat the oven to 400°F.

In a large Dutch oven, heat the oil over high heat. Add the lamb and salt and pepper to taste and cook until the lamb is browned, 5 to 10 minutes. Add the onion and garlic and cook for about 5 minutes, or until the onions are translucent.

Add the artichokes, reduce the heat to medium, cover, and cook for 5 minutes, then add the bay leaves, rosemary, and butter. Cover and cook until the butter is melted, a few minutes. Add the wine and mint, reduce the heat to medium low, cover, and gently cook for about 5 minutes until it loses its winey taste. Add a little water, about ½ cup, if the pot looks dry.

Place the pot in the oven and bake for 15 minutes, or until the artichokes are tender.

ARTICHOKES CONSTANTINOPLE STYLE

Artichokes Constantinople Style

My Greek friend Stathis showed me this delicious olive oil braise, which is even better the next day. You can make this with frozen artichoke hearts if you'd like, but it is really great with small spring artichokes. **SERVES 4**

- 4 small Yukon Gold potatoes, peeled and halved
- 2 cups sliced carrots (2-inch-long planks)
- 20 pearl onions, peeled
- 1 cup olive oil
- 1 cup water
- 4 baby artichokes, trimmed (see page 25)
- 2 tablespoons fresh lemon juice
- ¼ cup chopped fresh dill
- 2 tablespoons chopped fresh fennel leaves (optional)
- Salt and freshly ground black pepper

Cut a round of parchment paper to fit inside a medium sauté pan. Cut a hole in the center of the parchment round about the size of a quarter.

Place the potatoes, carrots, and onions in the pan. Add the oil and heat over medium heat until the oil is just barely boiling. Cook the vegetables in the hot oil until they begin to soften, about 10 minutes.

Add the water, artichokes, lemon juice, dill, fennel (if using), and salt and pepper to taste. Place the parchment over the vegetables and gently boil until they are very tender, 20 to 25 minutes.

MARINATED BABY ARTICHOKES
WITH HOT PEPPER

Marinated Baby Artichokes with Hot Pepper

There is no USDA data for water bath canning artichokes. I developed this recipe, which has a pH of 3.5, well within the safety limits for water bath canning. The processing time is based on the recommended time for marinated peppers, which contain similar quantities of olive oil—an important consideration when water bath processing foods. Rather than discard the outer leaves, boil them for about 10 minutes. Chill and serve with mayonnaise (page 365); or serve hot, with melted butter for dipping. **The marinade left over after you've finished the jar of artichokes is delicious and can be used to flavor other dishes, like Sausages with Potatoes and Artichoke Marinade (page 30).**

MAKES 2 PINTS

> 24 baby artichokes (about 6 pounds), trimmed (see page 25)
>
> ½ cup fresh lemon juice
>
> 1 cup white wine vinegar (5% acidity)
>
> ½ cup olive oil
>
> 2 garlic cloves, sliced
>
> 1 teaspoon pickling salt
>
> ½ teaspoon hot pepper flakes

In a large nonreactive pot, combine the lemon juice, vinegar, oil, garlic, pickling salt, and pepper flakes. Bring to a boil. Add the artichokes, cover, and boil for 10 minutes.

Have ready 2 clean pint jars and bands, and new lids that have been simmered in hot water to soften the rubberized flange. Remove the artichokes from the marinade with a slotted spoon and pack them into the jars, filling the jars about three-fourths full. Resist the temptation to overpack or you will compromise the seal. Cover the artichokes

SHRIMP WITH MARINATED ARTICHOKES

with the marinade, distributing the garlic and hot pepper evenly and leaving ½ inch of headroom. (Refrigerate any leftover marinade: It holds for months.) Wipe the rims, place on the lids, and screw on the bands fingertip tight.

Process the jars in a water bath (see page 375) for 25 minutes. You can process 4 half-pints for the same amount of time. Be sure to make altitude adjustments when preserving (see page 389). The artichokes will be ready to eat in 2 weeks.

Shrimp with Marinated Artichokes

This is an adaptation of a dish from Marche, where my father's family is from. It makes a lovely first course, and we often have it as part of the antipasto plate at La Vigilia, a traditional Italian fish dinner served on Christmas Eve. **Save the marinade drained off the artichokes for Sausages with Potatoes and Artichoke Marinade (page 30). Save the shrimp shells for Shrimp Shell Sauce (page 317). SERVES 4 AS AN APPETIZER**

1 pound large shrimp, peeled and deveined

1 cup marinated artichokes (for homemade, opposite), drained

3 tablespoons minced flat-leaf parsley

Salt and freshly ground black pepper

Bring a medium pot of salted water to a boil over medium-high heat. Add the shrimp and cook until pink, about 4 minutes. Drain and rinse in cold water. Slice the shrimp on an angle.

Coarsely chop the marinated artichokes (they are also nice sliced).

In a serving bowl, combine the shrimp, artichokes, parsley, and salt and pepper to taste. Toss gently and serve at room temperature.

Chicken with Marinated Artichokes and Parsley

*You can make this dish with thighs as well as breasts, or use a combination of the two. Be sure to drain the fat off the chicken after cooking, because the artichokes are oily from the marinade. **Save the marinade drained off the artichokes for Sausages with Potatoes and Artichoke Marinade (right). Save the rendered chicken fat in a jar in the fridge for sautéing vegetables or roasting potatoes—it adds a lovely flavor.** SERVES 4*

- 2 cups marinated artichokes (for homemade, page 28), drained
- 1 tablespoon olive oil
- 2 whole bone-in chicken breasts, split and then halved (for a total of 8 pieces)
- 1 cup chicken stock (for homemade, page 89)
- 2 tablespoons minced flat-leaf parsley

Preheat the oven to 250°F.

Spread the artichokes on a baking sheet and bake for about 20 minutes, to dry them out a bit.

Meanwhile, in a large skillet, heat the oil over medium heat. Add the chicken pieces and cook until browned all over, about 20 minutes. Remove the chicken and pour off the fat.

Return the chicken to the pan and add the chicken stock and artichokes. Cover and cook over medium heat until the artichokes start to fall apart and the chicken is well done, about 10 minutes. Garnish with the parsley.

Sausages with Potatoes and Artichoke Marinade

The marinade at the bottom of a jar of marinated artichokes, whether homemade or store-bought, is a great flavoring agent. It turns a simple dish of sausages and potatoes into something special. SERVES 4

- 1½ pounds Italian pork sausage (andouille is good in this dish, too)
- 1 cup marinade drained from a jar of marinated artichokes (for homemade, page 28)
- 1 pound small potatoes, such as fingerlings or baby Yukon Golds
- Salt and freshly ground black pepper
- 2 tablespoons chopped flat-leaf parsley

Heat a large skillet over medium heat and add the sausages. Cook until browned all over, about 10 minutes. Add the marinade, cover, and cook for 15 minutes.

Meanwhile, bring a large pot of water to a boil. Add the potatoes, cover, and cook until the potatoes are fork-tender, about 15 minutes. Drain and keep warm in the pot.

Uncover the sausages and let the marinade reduce at a boil, about 5 minutes longer.

Slice the potatoes and place in a serving bowl with a spoonful of the hot marinade from the sausages. Slice the sausages and add them and the remaining marinade to the bowl with the potatoes. Season with salt and pepper to taste. Garnish with the parsley.

ASPARAGUS

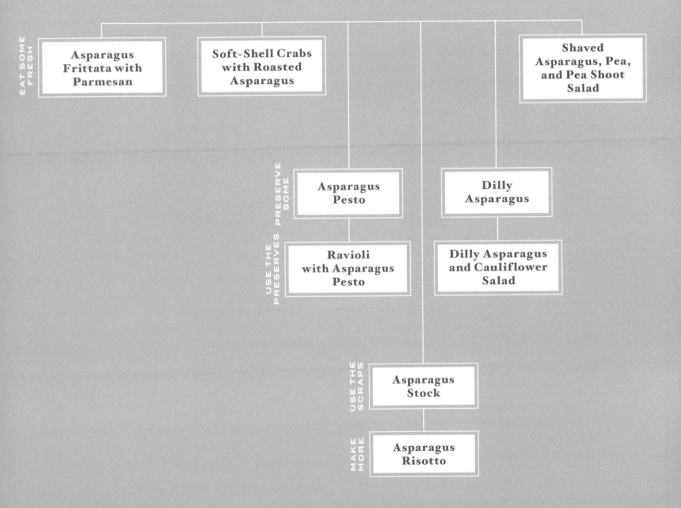

EAT SOME FRESH

Asparagus Frittata with Parmesan

Soft-Shell Crabs with Roasted Asparagus

Shaved Asparagus, Pea, and Pea Shoot Salad

PRESERVE SOME

Asparagus Pesto

Dilly Asparagus

USE THE PRESERVES

Ravioli with Asparagus Pesto

Dilly Asparagus and Cauliflower Salad

USE THE SCRAPS

Asparagus Stock

MAKE MORE

Asparagus Risotto

How to Trim Asparagus

You can use all of the asparagus spear. If the stem ends are tough, peel only the lower half of the asparagus and cut off just the dry part at the bottom. Otherwise no need to peel asparagus. You can also snap off the tough ends: Hold the end of a spear and gently bend; it will break at the point where the tender part of the asparagus ends. Save the tougher ends of the spears and/or any asparagus peelings (they have plenty of flavor) to make Asparagus Stock (page 37).

Asparagus Frittata with Parmesan

I serve this simple frittata at room temperature. It is delicious with a few dashes of Hot Vinegar Sauce (page 365) and perfect for buffets and picnics and take-along lunches. You can add sliced onions, chopped leeks, or fresh morels to the asparagus sauté if you'd like. **Save the asparagus ends or peels for Asparagus Stock (page 37).** SERVES 4

> 12 to 16 medium to thick spears asparagus (about 1½ pounds), trimmed (see above)
>
> 2 tablespoons olive oil
>
> 4 garlic cloves, minced
>
> Salt and freshly ground black pepper
>
> 8 large eggs
>
> ¼ cup grated Parmesan cheese
>
> 2 tablespoons vegetable oil

Cut the asparagus crosswise into ½-inch pieces.

Preheat the broiler and place an oven rack in the center of the oven.

In a 9-inch well-seasoned cast-iron skillet or nonstick ovenproof skillet, heat the olive oil over medium heat. Add the garlic and cook

until it becomes aromatic, about 2 minutes. Do not brown. Add the asparagus and salt and pepper to taste, and cook for 5 minutes. Add a few tablespoons of water to keep the garlic from scorching and to create a bit of steam. Cover the skillet and continue cooking until the asparagus are fork-tender, a few minutes longer. Remove from the heat.

In a medium bowl, beat the eggs until blended. Add the asparagus, Parmesan, and salt and pepper to taste.

Wipe out the skillet that you cooked the asparagus in. Heat the vegetable oil in the skillet over medium heat until hot. Pour the egg and asparagus mixture into the hot skillet. The edges will cook and separate quickly. Reduce the heat to medium-low and cook, uncovered and without stirring, for 3 to 5 minutes, until the eggs are set on the bottom (you will smell the eggs cooking).

Place the skillet under the broiler and broil for about 8 minutes, or until the frittata is golden brown and puffy.

Allow the frittata to rest for a few minutes—it will deflate some—then flip it over onto a board and allow it to come to room temperature. Slice into wedges to serve.

Soft-Shell Crabs with Roasted Asparagus

I make this dish in the late spring, when the asparagus and the soft-shell crabs are both in season. The roasted asparagus buds get rather crunchy, and the garlic browns, lending a nutty flavor. Be sure that you do not use pencil-thin asparagus for this.

(Sometimes I hurry up the cooking by placing the asparagus under the broiler instead of roasting them in the oven, but you've got to keep an eye on them: They burn easily, and only a bit of burn is good.) This makes a great entrée with rice, or a wonderful open-face sandwich on bruschetta with a spoonful of aioli (minced garlic added to homemade mayonnaise, page 365). **Save the asparagus ends or peels for Asparagus Stock (page 37).** SERVES 4

- **12 to 16 medium to thick spears asparagus (about 1½ pounds), trimmed (opposite)**
- **3 garlic cloves, minced**
- **6 tablespoons olive oil**
- **Salt and freshly ground black pepper**
- **8 soft-shell crabs, cleaned (see Note)**
- **¾ cup white wine**
- **2 tablespoons unsalted butter**
- **2 tablespoons chopped flat-leaf parsley**

Preheat the oven to 400°F.

Place the asparagus on a baking sheet in a single layer. Sprinkle the garlic and 3 table-spoons of the oil over the asparagus. Season with salt and pepper to taste. Roast the asparagus for about 10 minutes, or until the asparagus are fork-tender (thicker asparagus take a bit longer).

Meanwhile, season the crabs with salt and pepper. In a large nonstick skillet, heat the remaining oil over medium-high heat. Add the crabs and cook a few minutes per side, until they are opaque. Add the wine and cook until the wine reduces by half and the crab is pink, about 5 minutes. Add the butter and swirl it around. Remove from the heat.

Arrange the asparagus on a platter and add the crabs. Garnish with the parsley.

Note: When buying soft-shell crabs, look for live ones that have very thin shells. Leathery shells will cook up tough. Ask your fishmonger to kill and clean them, or you can do it yourself. To kill a crab, cut off the face with kitchen scissors. Leave the "mustard" (that yellowish stuff under the top shell). It has flavor. Lift the sides of the shell and snip the gills (those gray fibrous things). Turn the crab over and snip off the belly flap.

Shaved Asparagus, Pea, and Pea Shoot Salad

I have served this surprisingly rich salad as a second course after a pasta dish, or on top of a piece of broiled fish. **Save the pea pods to make Pea Pod Stock (page 236), a flavorful soup base.** *When choosing pea shoots, look for small pale leaves with plenty of thin, curling tendrils. Avoid large stemmy pea shoots, which are tougher. But if you do find them in the market with very long stems you can cut the stems off and throw them in Pea Pod Stock.* **Save the asparagus ends or peels for Asparagus Stock (page 37).** SERVES 4

- **1½ cups shelled fresh peas (about 1 pound in the shell)**
- **12 thick spears asparagus, trimmed (opposite)**
- **1 large garlic clove, smashed and peeled**
- **½ teaspoon mustard powder**
- **1 teaspoon fresh lemon juice**
- **1 whole anchovy (see Note), chopped**
- **2 tablespoons olive oil**
- **¼ pound pea shoots**
- **Salt and freshly ground black pepper**
- **1 tablespoon grated Parmesan cheese**

SHAVED
ASPARAGUS,
PEA, AND PEA
SHOOT SALAD

In a pot of boiling water, cook the peas until tender, about 10 minutes. Drain.

Using a very sharp knife (or a mandoline if you have one), cut the asparagus into very thin slivers on an angle. Raw asparagus must be very thinly sliced to be edible.

Rub the garlic clove around the inside of a wooden bowl. Add the mustard powder and lemon juice. Mix until the mustard powder dissolves. Add the anchovy and combine well. Add the oil, mixing all the while. Add the peas, asparagus, and pea shoots and toss in the dressing. Season with salt and pepper to taste and toss with the Parmesan cheese.

Note: I prefer whole anchovies cured in salt, which you can find in Italian markets. Soak them for 10 minutes to remove the salt, then rinse and fillet them. You don't have to get all the bones, just the spine.

Asparagus Pesto

This puree is great to have on hand. It makes an excellent sauce for broiled fish or for pasta like Ravioli with Asparagus Pesto (page 38). With added cream and seasoning, it's also perfect as a warm soup. It is not thick, but loose and light. Save the asparagus cooking water and ends or peels for Asparagus Stock (page 37). MAKES 1 PINT

> 1 pound asparagus, trimmed (see page 32)
> 2 garlic cloves, sliced
> 2 tablespoons olive oil
> 4 teaspoons fresh lemon juice
> Salt

Cut the asparagus in large pieces and place them in a large pot. Add just enough water to barely cover and bring to a boil over high heat. Reduce the heat to medium, cover, and boil the asparagus gently until they are fork-tender, about 10 minutes for slender asparagus, longer for thick ones. Reserving the cooking water, drain the asparagus.

Place the asparagus in a food processor along with ¼ cup of the reserved cooking water and the garlic. Add the oil, lemon juice, and salt to taste and pulse to combine. If necessary, add a bit more cooking water to get a smooth pesto.

The asparagus pesto holds in the freezer for 8 to 12 months. See "How to Freeze Foods," page 382.

Dilly Asparagus

I pickle a few jars of asparagus every year and then use the asparagus in a variety of dishes. Asparagus are low in acidity, but since these asparagus are pickled, they are safe to water bath process. Larger than a half-pint but smaller than a pint, the tall and widely available 12-ounce jar is perfect for asparagus (though in order to fit the asparagus into a jar you will need to cut the ends, sometimes a lot). You can also pickle chopped asparagus and pack them into half-pint or pint jars. Chopped pickled asparagus are a great substitute for capers: Among other dishes, they are good in the French bistro classic, skate wing with browned butter and capers, or in chicken piccata, or in Lamb Tonnato (page 303). Whole pickled asparagus are great in a Bloody Mary. Save the cut ends of asparagus for Asparagus Stock (page 37). MAKES THREE 12-OUNCE JARS

2½ pounds asparagus (see Note)

1 cup plus 2 tablespoons white wine vinegar
(5% acidity)

1 cup plus 2 tablespoons water

¼ cup pickling salt

2 garlic cloves, slivered

1 teaspoon dill seeds

¼ teaspoon hot pepper flakes

9 leafy sprigs fresh dill

Cut the ends off the asparagus so they fit very snugly standing upright in a 12-ounce jar. The tips must not poke above the screw threads of the jar, so you will have to cut them quite short. I end up cutting at least 3 inches off the bottoms.

Place about 2 inches of water in a shallow pan wide enough to hold the asparagus in a single layer. Bring to a boil over medium-high heat. Lay the asparagus that fit into the jar in the pan and allow the water to return to a boil. As soon as the water comes back to a boil, remove the asparagus and run them under very cold water or dunk them in ice water to stop the cooking. Drain well. This sets the green color.

In a saucepan, combine the vinegar, water, pickling salt, garlic, dill seeds, and pepper flakes and bring to a boil over medium heat. Stir to dissolve the salt. Do not boil past the point where the salt has dissolved. Acetic acid evaporates more quickly than water and you could upset the water to vinegar ratio if you boil for too long.

Have ready 3 clean 12-ounce jars and bands, and new lids that have been simmered in hot water to soften the rubberized flange. Pack the asparagus into them. You really have to wedge the asparagus in, or once you add the vinegar

solution, they will bob above the rim. Cut the sprigs of dill to fit the jar and stuff 3 in each jar.

Add the vinegar solution, enough to cover the tops of the asparagus leaving ½ inch of headroom. Distribute the spices throughout the jars. Wipe the rims, place on the lids, and screw on the bands fingertip tight.

Process the jars in a water bath (see page 375) for 10 minutes. (You can process pint jars for the same amount of time as 12-ounce jars.) Be sure to make altitude adjustments when preserving (page 389). Don't leave the jars in the water to cool or the asparagus will overcook and come out pale and withered. As is, they do wash out and shrink, so the asparagus may bob. It's okay. They will be ready to eat in 4 weeks.

Note: Jersey Giants, the purple-topped asparagus, are delicious and meaty but they will stain the vinegar solution. It's okay.

Dilly Asparagus and Cauliflower Salad

This lovely sharp salad is great served with barbecue, brisket, and homemade pastrami (page 61). **SERVES 4**

1 small head cauliflower, broken into florets
(about 4 cups)

1½ cups chopped Dilly Asparagus (page 35)

⅓ cup extra virgin olive oil

Salt and freshly ground black pepper

3 tablespoons pine nuts

3 tablespoons finely chopped flat-leaf parsley

Bring a large pot of salted water to a boil over high heat and add the cauliflower. Boil until the cauliflower is fork-tender, about 5 minutes. Drain and transfer to a serving bowl.

DILLY ASPARAGUS AND CAULIFLOWER SALAD

Add the Dilly Asparagus, oil, and salt and pepper to taste. Toss gently.

Heat a small skillet over high heat. Add the pine nuts and toast for a minute or two, shaking the skillet often. Garnish the salad with the toasted pine nuts and the parsley.

Asparagus Stock

I make asparagus stock with the trimmed off ends of asparagus spears. You can hold the stock in the fridge, but it tends to ferment quickly; so it is best to freeze or pressure can it. While there is no USDA data for asparagus stock, I have based my pressure canning time on the recommendation for whole raw asparagus tightly packed into a pint jar. This is the same timing as the Ball Complete Book of Home Preserving *uses for pints of vegetable stock.* **MAKES 2 PINTS**

1 pound asparagus trimmings, cut into 2-inch pieces

Place the asparagus in a deep pot and cover with about 1 inch of water. Bring to a boil over medium heat, cover, and gently boil until the asparagus are very, very soft, about 45 minutes or longer. Add more water to be sure the asparagus stems stayed covered if necessary. Let cool in the water.

Because you are using the woody, stringy stem ends of the asparagus, you need to grind the asparagus in a food processor with a little of the cooking water. (You may not be able to grind up the woodiest parts. It's okay.) Then pass the ground asparagus plus the rest of the cooking water through a food mill. You will get about 1 quart of stock, mostly green water with about one-third the volume in pulp. For refrigeration and freezing, see the technique for making stocks (page 390).

To make shelf-stable stock, pressure can the jars. Have ready 2 clean pint jars and bands, and new lids that have been simmered in hot water to soften the rubberized flange. Pour the stock into the jars leaving 1 inch of headroom. Wipe the rims, place on the lids, and screw on the bands fingertip tight.

Process the jars in a pressure canner at 10/11 psi for 30 minutes. (See "How to Pressure Can," page 379.) Be sure to make altitude adjustments when preserving (see page 389). You may notice some separation of the pulp and water in the jar. It's okay.

Ravioli with Asparagus Pesto

Making the ravioli takes time, but it is worth the trouble because it is so sweet and satisfying. However, if you have a good pasta shop in your neighborhood, try this sauce with their ricotta-stuffed ravioli. The sauce is also fantastic on fettuccine tossed with a little ricotta. You can make this dish with Pea Pesto (page 233), too. This is my grandmother's ravioli recipe. It doubles perfectly. SERVES 4

PASTA
1½ cups all-purpose flour

A pinch of salt

2 large eggs

Olive oil, for oiling the dough

RAVIOLI WITH ASPARAGUS PESTO

RICOTTA FILLING
1¼ cups ricotta cheese (for homemade, page 367)

¼ cup grated Parmesan cheese

1 large egg, lightly beaten

Freshly ground black pepper

SAUCE
1 heaping cup Asparagus Pesto (page 35)

3 tablespoons unsalted butter

Salt

Freshly ground black pepper and grated Parmesan, for serving

For the pasta: Combine the flour and salt on a board or countertop. Make a mound with a well. Crack the eggs into the well. Using a fork, gradually combine the flour with the eggs. When half of the flour is incorporated, switch to using your hands. Combine the flour and eggs thoroughly, then knead for about 15 minutes or less, until the pasta is smooth and pliable. Rub a few drops of olive oil all over the dough, cover it in plastic, and leave it at room temperature for about 1 hour.

For the ricotta filling: In a bowl, mash together the ricotta, Parmesan, egg, and pepper to taste with a fork.

Cut the pasta in half. Press each half through the rolls of a pasta machine, in ever decreasing thicknesses, until the pasta has passed through the narrowest thickness. (If you roll out by hand, just keep at it: You want the pasta to be as thin as you can get it, about ⅒ inch.) Lay one sheet of the pasta out on a floured board. Place teaspoon-size dollops of the ricotta mixture on the pasta spaced about 4 inches apart. Place the second sheet of pasta on top. Press the dough down between the stuffing

and cut the dough around the stuffing, leaving about a 1-inch margin. You can cut the ravioli into squares, or use a cookie cutter to make disks. Have ready a small cup of water. Wet the tines of a fork and press firmly all around the edges of the ravioli to seal. (If you have small children they will love this job. I did.)

Bring a large pot of salted water to a boil. Place the ravioli on a baking sheet and then carefully slip the ravioli in the water. When a ravioli floats, it is done. It will also look whiter and soft. Do not overcook. Remove with a slotted spoon and place on a platter.

For the sauce: In a large sauté pan or skillet, heat the asparagus pesto and butter over medium-low heat. Season with salt to taste.

Gently toss the cooked ravioli in the sauce. Garnish with pepper and Parmesan. Serve hot.

Asparagus Risotto

Styles of cooking risotto vary, but once it is done it should be eaten right away, otherwise the risotto begins to thicken and dry out. I like to serve it soft enough so that if you rock the bowl the risotto undulates. I've made this risotto in the middle of winter with canned asparagus stock and frozen asparagus tips, garnished with chopped Canned Shrimp (page 316) and a knob of butter at the end of cooking. The trick to making risotto is knowing when to stop cooking it, so taste the rice for doneness as you go. **SERVES 4**

ASPARAGUS RISOTTO

> 4 tablespoons (½ stick) unsalted butter
>
> 1 cup minced onion (1 medium)
>
> 1 cup carnaroli, vialone nano, or Arborio rice
>
> ½ cup dry white wine
>
> 2 pints Asparagus Stock (page 37)
>
> Salt and freshly ground black pepper
>
> 1 heaping cup chopped asparagus tips
>
> 1 tablespoon minced garlic
>
> 1 small whole dried hot pepper or a pinch of hot pepper flakes
>
> A few sprigs of flat-leaf parsley
>
> 6 tablespoons grated Parmesan cheese
>
> Extra virgin olive oil, for serving (optional)

In a wide, shallow heavy-bottomed pot, heat 2 tablespoons of the butter over medium heat. (A wide shallow pot will cook risotto faster and more evenly than a deep small one unless you stir it all the time.) Add the onion and cook until the onion is translucent, about 5 minutes. Add the rice and stir until it is well coated with butter. The rice will become slightly translucent and the grains will individuate. This is good. Add the white wine (it will boil up rapidly for a moment then settle down). Reduce the heat to medium-low and cook until the wine is absorbed, a few minutes.

Add 1 cup of asparagus stock and stir. Cook until the rice absorbs almost all the stock, about 5 minutes. The rice may stick, so stir often (though you don't have to stir it constantly). Add another cup of asparagus stock, stirring frequently as it becomes absorbed, and so on until you have used all the stock. Season with salt to taste. Test the rice for doneness by sampling a grain. It should be yielding but firm to the bite, and the texture of the overall dish should be as soft as porridge.

Meanwhile, in a small skillet, heat the remaining 2 tablespoons butter over medium heat. Add the asparagus tips, garlic, and the hot pepper. Sauté the asparagus until they are fork-tender, 6 to 8 minutes. Remove the hot pepper if cooked whole. Season with salt to taste.

Stir the sautéed asparagus and the Parmesan into the risotto. Check the seasoning and add a lot of good black pepper. Serve the risotto in shallow bowls garnished with parsley. You can also drizzle a little extra virgin olive oil over the dish, if you'd like.

BEEF

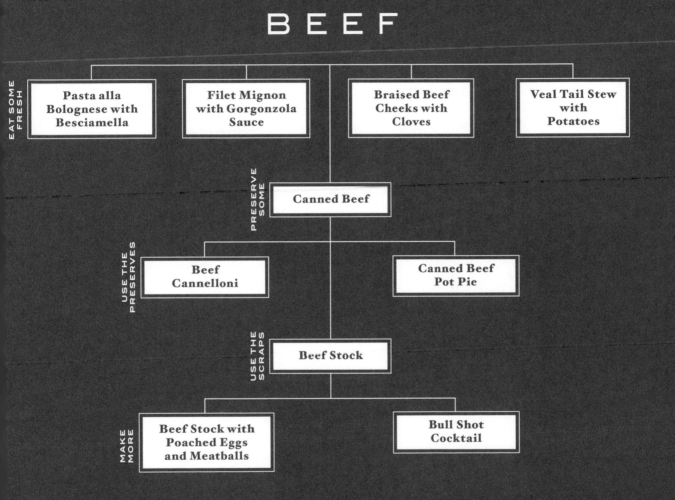

EAT SOME FRESH

Pasta alla Bolognese with Besciamella

Filet Mignon with Gorgonzola Sauce

Braised Beef Cheeks with Cloves

Veal Tail Stew with Potatoes

PRESERVE SOME

Canned Beef

USE THE PRESERVES

Beef Cannelloni

Canned Beef Pot Pie

USE THE SCRAPS

Beef Stock

MAKE MORE

Beef Stock with Poached Eggs and Meatballs

Bull Shot Cocktail

How to Tell Your Beef Is Done

I usually use the thumb test for estimating doneness when cooking beef in the oven or over a flame: Open your palm and press on the fleshy thumb muscle. That is raw, and when you press the meat, raw beef will have the same amount of give. Bring your thumb and pinky together and press on the fleshy thumb muscle. That is well done, or about 160°F. Bring your thumb and ring finger together and press on the fleshy thumb muscle. That is medium, or about 140°F. Bring your thumb and middle finger together and press on the fleshy thumb muscle. That is medium-rare, or about 130°F. Bring your thumb and index finger together and press on the fleshy thumb muscle. That is rare, or about 120°F.

Pasta alla Bolognese with Besciamella

*To make an authentic tasting Bolognese sauce, use grass-fed beef if you can. It is more like Italian beef, which is lean and subsequently a bit tough. A light béchamel sauce (*besciamella *in Italian) makes a very rich pasta alla Bolognese. Layers of Bolognese sauce and besciamella make the most delicious lasagna, too.* **SERVES 6**

BOLOGNESE

1 tablespoon rendered pork or duck fat (for homemade, page 126)

1 cup chopped onion

2 teaspoons chopped garlic

1 pound ground grass-fed beef

⅓ cup white wine

1 teaspoon dried oregano

1 bay leaf

2 tablespoons tomato paste (for homemade, page 331)

4 cups beef stock (for homemade, page 47), warmed

Salt and freshly ground black pepper

1 pound tagliatelle

BESCIAMELLA

1 cup whole milk

1 tablespoon unsalted butter

1 tablespoon all-purpose flour

¼ teaspoon grated nutmeg

¼ cup grated Parmesan cheese

2 tablespoons finely chopped flat-leaf parsley

For the Bolognese: In a large skillet, heat the fat over medium-low heat. Add the onion and garlic and cook until the onions are translucent, about 5 minutes. Add the beef and cook, breaking it up with a wooden spoon, until it is browned, about 10 minutes. Add the wine, oregano, and bay leaf and continue cooking until the wine cooks out, about 10 minutes. Stir in the tomato paste and 2 cups of beef stock. Stir well and simmer the sauce for about 15 minutes until the sauce begins to dry out. Add another cup of beef stock and cook the sauce until it begins to dry out, about 15 minutes longer. Add the final cup of stock and cook the sauce for another 10 minutes or so, until the meat in the sauce is so broken down it is like a thick meaty gravy. Season with salt and pepper to taste. Set aside.

Bring a large pot of salted water to a boil and add the pasta. Cook until al dente, and drain.

Meanwhile, for the besciamella: In a small saucepan, warm the milk over medium heat. In a separate small saucepan heat the butter over medium heat. As soon as the butter melts, add the flour, whisking until well blended. Add the warmed milk to the butter mixture in a slow drizzle, whisking all the while. Add salt to taste and the nutmeg. Reduce the heat to low and gently cook until there is no raw flour taste left to the sauce, about 10 minutes.

Toss the pasta with the Bolognese sauce and the besciamella. Garnish with the Parmesan and parsley.

Filet Mignon with Gorgonzola Sauce

Filet with Gorgonzola dolce and wilted radicchio is one of my favorites. I usually prepare about ⅓ pound filet per person because it is so rich. **Since you only need a few radicchio leaves to make this recipe, save the rest to broil (page 84).** SERVES 4

> 1⅓ pounds filet mignon, at room temperature
> Salt and freshly ground black pepper
> 1 tablespoon neutral oil, such as safflower
> 4 radicchio leaves
> 6 ounces Gorgonzola dolce cheese
> ¼ cup white wine (optional)

Cut the filet into 3 pieces and tie each filet around the waist horizontally with kitchen twine. This holds the meat together. Season the meat on both sides with salt and pepper.

Heat a medium skillet over high heat. Add the oil and as soon as the oil wrinkles, swirl it around the pan to coat. Add the filets. For medium rare, sear for about 4 minutes on one side, then turn them over. Place a radicchio leaf on each filet, then cover the filets with a lid that fits inside the skillet to weigh down the filets and sear on the second side for another 4 minutes, then remove from the pan, and cover with foil. Let the filets rest about 10 minutes.

Meanwhile, in a small saucepan, melt the Gorgonzola over medium heat. Watch the cheese to make sure it doesn't boil. If the cheese seems dry, add the white wine 2 tablespoons at a time to thin it out. The sauce should be like light cream.

To serve the filets, place a puddle of Gorgonzola sauce on each plate. Place the radicchio leaf on top of the sauce, and the filet on the radicchio leaf. Oh boy.

Braised Beef Cheeks with Cloves

The first time I asked our local meat co-op in Colorado if I could buy beef cheeks, there was a long pause. "Well, we could sell you the whole head," said the lady on the phone doubtfully. I may be a DIY enthusiast, but that was more than I was willing to take on. Eventually the butchers cut off the cheeks for me and I have been buying them ever since. Beef cheeks are inexpensive and outrageously sweet when cooked to the point of utter surrender. They are wonderful with a loaf of bread and a watercress salad. SERVES 4

> 1½ pounds beef cheek meat
> 1 teaspoon ground cloves
> Salt and freshly ground black pepper
> 2 tablespoons olive oil
> 2 cups sliced onions
> 4 cups beef stock (for homemade, page 47)
> ½ cup red wine

If the cheeks have fatty gristle on them, trim it away. Season the meat with the cloves and salt and pepper to taste.

In a heavy-bottomed pot or Dutch oven, heat the oil over medium-high heat. Add the meat and brown all over, about 5 minutes. Add the onions and cook until translucent, about 5 minutes. Add the stock and red wine. Reduce the heat to very low, cover, and cook until the meat is falling apart, about 3 hours. (You can also make this in a slow cooker or in a 300°F oven.)

Veal Tail Stew with Potatoes

Veal tails contain a lot of gelatin. Not only is the gelatin very good for you, it is super sweet, a natural sauce thickener, and adds a soft, velvety quality to the stew. You can make this recipe with oxtails as well.

SERVES 4

2 pounds veal tails

Salt and freshly ground black pepper

All-purpose flour, for dredging

6 tablespoons olive oil

2 tablespoons fresh rosemary leaves or 2 teaspoons dried

1 medium onion, finely chopped (about 1 cup)

1 red bell pepper, sliced (optional)

4 garlic cloves, finely chopped

2 tablespoons finely chopped flat-leaf parsley

¾ cup dry white wine

1 tablespoon dried basil

2 cups chicken stock (for homemade, page 89), warmed

8 small potatoes, such as Yukon Gold, peeled

Season the veal tails with salt and pepper and lightly dredge them in flour.

In a Dutch oven (or heavy-bottomed pan wide enough to hold the veal tails without overlapping), heat the oil over medium heat. Add the veal tails and rosemary and cook until the veal tails are lightly browned all over, about 10 minutes. Remove the veal tails and cover them with foil so they stay warm.

Add the onion, bell pepper (if using), garlic, and parsley to the pan. Cook until the onions are translucent, about 5 minutes. Add the veal tails and any accumulated juices, the wine, and basil. Cook until the wine cooks out, about 5 minutes. Add the chicken stock, cover, reduce the heat to low, and cook for about 1 hour, until the veal tails are tender.

Add the potatoes. Adjust the seasoning and continue cooking until the potatoes are tender, about 20 minutes. The veal tails will be very tender at this point.

Canned Beef

This is fast food, my way: the jars, filled with raw meat, vegetables, and herbs, are pressure canned and remain shelf stable for a year. So, for a year, I can pop open a jar, top it with thawed puff pastry from the freezer, and make a Canned Beef Pot Pie (opposite) in as much time as it takes to heat one from the store. I can also make a quick beef stew, or warm the beef with cooked beans and garnish with chopped raw onion to make a cowboy bowl, or grind the meat to make lovely Beef Cannelloni (page 46).

MAKES 3 PINTS

2⅓ pounds boneless beef, such as stew meat or shank meat

¾ cup sliced carrots (about ½ inch thick— chunks are okay but thin slices will get mushy)

½ cup fresh shelled peas (optional)

9 to 12 pearl onions, peeled

15 or so black peppercorns

6 sprigs of fresh thyme

6 sprigs of flat-leaf parsley

3 small bay leaves

¾ teaspoon salt

CANNED BEEF

CANNED BEEF POT PIE

Have ready 3 clean pint jars and bands, and new lids that have been simmered in hot water to soften the rubberized flange.

Chop the meat into 2-inch chunks. Dividing evenly, pack the meat, carrots, peas (if using), and onions into the 3 jars. Distribute the peppercorns, thyme, parsley, bay leaves, and salt equally among the jars. Do not add any liquid. Wipe the rims, place on the lids, and screw on the bands fingertip tight.

Process the jars in a pressure canner at 10/11 psi for 1 hour 15 minutes. (See "How to Pressure Can," page 379.) Be sure to make altitude adjustments when preserving (see page 389). The meat will shrink and will be mostly covered with brown meat stock.

Canned Beef Pot Pie

With canned beef on hand, dinner doesn't get any quicker than this. If you want to go really country, you can cut the puff pastry to fit the top of the canning jar, place on a baking sheet, and proceed with cooking. The jar is ovensafe. For a fancier presentation, prepare the pot pie in individual ramekins. **SERVES 3**

> **3 pints Canned Beef (opposite)**
>
> **Salt and freshly ground black pepper**
>
> **3 medium sized potatoes, boiled and sliced (optional)**
>
> **1 sheet frozen puff pastry, thawed in the refrigerator**
>
> **1 small egg beaten with 1 tablespoon water**

Preheat the oven to 350°F.

Drain the canned beef. Pour the meat and vegetables into a 9-inch pie plate. Season with salt and pepper. Add the potatoes if you are using them. Cut the puff pastry to fit the top of the pie plate. Lay the puff pastry on top and make a few slits with a knife so steam can escape during baking. Brush the egg wash over the pastry. Bake for 15 minutes, or until the pastry is browned and puffy and the meat is bubbling.

Beef Cannelloni

This easy but labor-intensive recipe is one step easier if you have your own canned beef. You can use dried cannelloni pasta in this recipe—I recommend the no-boil type if you can find them—but using homemade crepes makes for a very tender and extra-delicious dish. If you do use cannelloni tubes, increase the oven temperature to 400°F and cook for 30 minutes.

SERVES 4

CREPES
¾ cup all-purpose flour

1 teaspoon baking powder

½ teaspoon salt

2 large eggs, beaten

⅔ cup whole milk

⅓ cup water

2 tablespoons unsalted butter, for greasing the pan and cooking the crepes

SAUCE
¼ cup olive oil

1 medium onion, chopped (about 1 cup)

3 garlic cloves, chopped

2 cups fresh or canned chopped tomatoes (for home-canned, page 328)

1 tablespoon chopped flat-leaf parsley

Salt

2 tablespoons unsalted butter

⅓ cup heavy cream

BEEF STUFFING
2 pints Canned Beef (page 44), stock poured off and herbs removed

1 tablespoon chopped flat-leaf parsley

1 tablespoon grated Parmesan cheese

¼ teaspoon grated nutmeg

Salt

1 cup grated Parmesan cheese, for topping

Freshly ground black pepper, for serving

For the crepe batter: In a medium bowl, combine the flour, baking powder, and salt. In a small bowl, combine the eggs, milk, and water. Add the wet ingredients to the dry ingredients and whisk together. Don't worry about the lumps. Place the bowl in the refrigerator for about 30 minutes.

For the sauce: In a saucepan, heat the oil over medium heat. Add the onion and garlic and cook until the onion is translucent, about 5 minutes. Add the tomatoes, parsley, and salt to taste. Simmer, uncovered, until the tomatoes have broken up, 15 to 20 minutes. Puree the sauce with an immersion blender or in a food processor or blender, and return to the pan. Do not put back on the heat. Add 1 tablespoon of butter and stir to melt, then add the cream and stir well.

Preheat the oven to 350°F. Butter a 9 × 13-inch baking pan with 1 tablespoon butter.

Prepare the crepes (see page 395). You should get about 12 crepes.

For the beef stuffing: In a food processor, combine the canned beef (and vegetables), parsley, Parmesan, nutmeg, and salt to taste and pulse to grind.

To assemble, place 2 tablespoons of beef stuffing in the center of each crepe and roll it up. Place the rolled crepe seam-side down in the buttered baking pan. Continue this process until all the crepes and beef stuffing are used.

Pour the sauce over the crepes, and sprinkle with the 1 cup Parmesan. Bake for 20 minutes, or until the cheese is melted and the cannelloni are heated through. Garnish with a few grinds of black pepper.

Serve promptly.

Beef Stock

You can purchase beef soup bones; they're cheap. But I always make stock with the bones left over from a standing rib roast or a T-bone steak. **MAKES 2 QUARTS**

> 3 pounds beef bones
> 1 large onion, peeled, with 5 cloves stuck in it
> 2 celery ribs
> 3 carrots, cut in half
> ½ cup flat-leaf parsley (stems are okay)
> 20 black peppercorns
> Salt
> 4 quarts water

In a large soup pot, combine the bones, onion, celery, carrots, parsley, peppercorns, salt to taste, and water and bring to a boil over high heat. Reduce the heat to medium, cover, and gently boil for 2 hours. Skim off the scum periodically while it is boiling. Uncover and cook the stock until reduced by half, about 30 minutes longer. Adjust the seasoning and strain the liquid. Defat the stock with a gravy separator, or chill the broth in the refrigerator for a couple of hours. The fat will rise to the top and harden. Remove the fat.

Transfer the broth to quart jars and refrigerate or freeze (see the technique for making stocks, page 390).

To make shelf-stable stock, pressure can the jars. Have ready 4 clean pint jars or 2 quart jars and bands, and new lids that have been simmered in hot water to soften the rubberized flange. Pour the stock into the jars leaving 1 inch of headroom. Wipe the rims, place on the lids, and screw on the bands fingertip tight.

Process the jars in a pressure canner at 10/11 psi for 20 minutes for pints, 25 minutes for quarts. (See "How to Pressure Can," page 379.) Be sure to make altitude adjustments when preserving (see page 389).

Beef Stock with Poached Eggs and Meatballs

Poached eggs in beef stock are nothing new, but adding meatballs is pretty novel. I credit the talented photographer and chef Jonathan Gayman for coming up with this fabulous combination. The meatball recipe makes twice the amount you need for this dish, but it just seems crazy not to make enough meatballs to have for later (see Note), maybe with spaghetti and marinara sauce (page 332)? **SERVES 4**

> MEATBALLS
> ½ cup breadcrumbs (for homemade, page 362)
> ¼ cup whole milk
> ⅓ pound ground beef
> ⅓ pound ground pork
> ⅓ pound ground veal
> ½ cup minced onion
> 1 large egg, beaten

¼ cup grated Parmesan cheese

3 tablespoons water

1 tablespoon chopped fresh thyme leaves

Salt and freshly ground black pepper

2 tablespoons olive oil

¼ cup white wine

BROTH AND EGGS

4 cups beef stock (for homemade, page 47)

1 teaspoon distilled white vinegar

4 large eggs

Salt and freshly ground black pepper

2 tablespoons chopped flat-leaf parsley

For the meatballs: In a small bowl, combine the breadcrumbs and milk. In a large bowl, combine the beef, pork, veal, onion, egg, Parmesan, water, thyme, and salt and pepper and mix well. Add the breadcrumbs and milk. Combine well. I use my hands. The mixture will be on the wet side. This is good. The softer the meat mixture, the more tender the meatballs. Roll the meat into balls the size of golf balls. You should get about 24.

In a large nonstick skillet, heat the oil over medium heat. Add the meatballs and brown them, turning often, about 10 minutes. Add the white wine, cover, and cook an additional 5 minutes. Remove the cover and let the wine cook out, a few minutes more. Set aside half of the meatballs to use in another dish (see Note).

For the broth: Heat the beef stock in a sauce pan. Have ready 4 shallow soup bowls. Place 3 meatballs in each bowl. Bring a deep pot of water to a high simmer over medium heat. Add the vinegar. Crack an egg into a ramekin, then slide the egg into the water to avoid breaking the yolk. Poach 2 eggs at a time, until the whites are opaque, then carefully lift them out with a slotted spoon. Place an egg in each bowl, then poach the remaining eggs.

Cover with the stock. Season with salt and pepper and garnish with parsley. Serve promptly.

Note: Refrigerate the cooked meatballs to use in the next day or two, or freeze them: Let the meatballs come to room temperature, place on a baking sheet, and chill in the fridge. Then transfer them to the freezer. Once frozen, pack into a freezer bag and freeze.

Bull Shot Cocktail

A Bull Shot is a variation on a Bloody Mary, only it is made with beef stock instead of tomato juice. While usually made with vodka, I like it better with bourbon. **SERVES 1**

½ cup beef stock (for homemade, page 47), warmed

½ teaspoon lemon juice

Dash of Worcestershire sauce (for homemade, page 369)

Dash of Tabasco sauce or hot sauce (for homemade, page 365)

Salt and freshly ground black pepper

2 ounces vodka or bourbon

In a small saucepan, combine the stock, lemon juice, Worcestershire sauce, Tabasco, and salt and black pepper to taste and heat to a simmer. Pour the hot stock into a heatproof cup. Stir in the vodka or bourbon.

BEETS
WITH GREENS

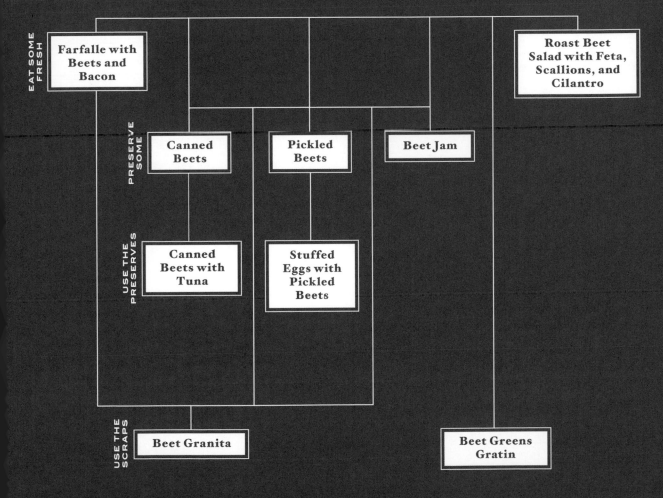

EAT SOME FRESH

Farfalle with Beets and Bacon

Roast Beet Salad with Feta, Scallions, and Cilantro

PRESERVE SOME

Canned Beets

Pickled Beets

Beet Jam

USE THE PRESERVES

Canned Beets with Tuna

Stuffed Eggs with Pickled Beets

USE THE SCRAPS

Beet Granita

Beet Greens Gratin

Farfalle with Beets and Bacon

It may be a very, well, pink *dish to look at, but pasta with beets is absolutely yummy. This is a version of a recipe my dad and I developed years ago for my first book,* At Mesa's Edge. ***Save the greens for Beet Greens Gratin (page 55) or as a substitute for radish greens in Skillet-Cooked Radish Greens (page 275).*** SERVES 4

> 8 slices bacon (for homemade, page 263)
>
> 1 pound beets (about 2 the size of an apple), greens removed
>
> 1 cup minced onion (about 1 medium)
>
> 1 tablespoon minced garlic
>
> 1 cup chicken stock (for homemade, page 89)
>
> ¼ cup minced flat-leaf parsley
>
> Salt and freshly ground black pepper
>
> ¾ pound farfalle pasta
>
> ½ cup ricotta cheese (for homemade, page 367) or crumbled ricotta salata

In a large skillet, cook the bacon over medium-high heat until the fat is rendered and the bacon is golden, 5 to 10 minutes. Remove the bacon and drain on paper towels or brown paper bags and reserve 3 tablespoons of the bacon grease in the skillet. When the bacon is cool enough to handle, crumble.

Wash and peel the beets. Grate the beets on the large holes of a box grater or on the julienne blade of a mandoline.

Heat the bacon grease in the skillet. Add the beets and cook over a medium heat until the beets are soft, about 10 minutes. Add the onion and garlic and cook for 5 minutes more, until the onions are translucent. Add the chicken stock, parsley, and salt and pepper to taste. Cook for 5 minutes to meld the flavors. You can set the sauce aside for a couple of hours at this point, or refrigerate it. The beets will absorb a great deal of the stock, so have a little more stock on hand to soften things up when it comes time to finish the recipe.

Bring a large pot of salted water to a boil. Add the pasta and cook until al dente and drain. Add the pasta to the beet sauce. The pasta will turn a deep pink. Toss well and make sure all the pasta is stained by the beet sauce. Adjust the seasoning. Serve the pasta garnished with the ricotta and bacon bits.

Roast Beet Salad with Feta, Scallions, and Cilantro

This is a rich, really delicious, make-ahead luncheon salad, a nice use of garden-fresh beets. Sometimes I substitute the feta with ricotta salata. ***Save the greens for Beet Greens Gratin (page 55) or as a substitute for radish greens in Skillet-Cooked Radish Greens (page 275).*** SERVES 4

> 4 medium beets (about 1½ pounds), greens removed
>
> 4 slices bacon
>
> ¼ cup vinaigrette (for homemade, page 368)
>
> ¼ cup crumbled feta cheese
>
> ¼ cup chopped scallions
>
> 2 tablespoons chopped cilantro
>
> Salt and freshly ground black pepper

ROAST BEET SALAD WITH FETA, SCALLIONS,
AND CILANTRO

Preheat the oven to 400°F.

Wash the beets but don't peel them. Wrap
them individually in foil, place on a rack in
the center of the oven, and bake the beets for
45 minutes to 1 hour, until fork-tender. Allow
the beets to come to room temperature.

Meanwhile, cook the bacon in a skillet until
browned and crisp. (Or place the bacon on
a rimmed baking sheet and bake in the oven
along with the beets for 10 to 15 minutes.)
Drain the bacon on paper towels or brown
paper bags, then crumble.

When the beets are cool enough to handle,
peel, cut in half and cut into bite-size slices.
Toss the beets in a bowl with the vinaigrette.

Arrange the sliced beets on a serving platter.
Garnish with the feta, scallions, bacon, and
cilantro. Season with salt and pepper to taste,
but be careful: Both the feta and bacon may
already be quite salty.

Pickled Beets

This recipe is adapted from the Ball Complete
Book of Home Preserving. *I added the spices,
which you can vary if you'd like; try cloves,
cinnamon, peppercorns. I use these pickles in a variety
of dishes, but one of my favorites is Stuffed Eggs
with Pickled Beets (page 54).* **Save the greens for
Beet Greens Gratin (page 55) or as a substitute for
radish greens in Skillet-Cooked Radish Greens
(page 275). Reserve the cooking liquid from
boiling the beets to make Beet Granita (page 55).**
MAKES 3 HALF-PINTS

> 1 pound medium beets, greens removed
>
> 1 cup white wine vinegar (5% acidity)
>
> 1 cup sugar
>
> 1 teaspoon caraway seeds
>
> 1 teaspoon coriander seeds
>
> 1 teaspoon pickling salt

Bring a large pot of water to a boil over high
heat. Wash the beets. Add the beets to the
boiling water and cook until fork-tender, 15 to
20 minutes. Drain. When cool enough to
handle, peel and slice the beets.

Have ready 3 clean half-pint jars and bands, and
new lids that have been simmered in hot water
to soften the rubberized flange. Pack the beets
tightly in the jars.

In a small saucepan, combine the vinegar, sugar,
caraway seeds, coriander seeds, and pickling
salt and bring to a boil over high heat, stirring
until the sugar and salt are dissolved. Pour
the hot liquid over the beets, making sure
the seeds are distributed evenly among the
jars, leaving ½ inch of headroom. Wipe the
rims, place on the lids and screw on the bands
fingertip tight.

Process the jars in a water bath (see page 375) for 30 minutes. Be sure to make altitude adjustments when preserving (see page 389). The beet slices may float. It's okay.

Beet Jam

*This is a wonderful savory/sweet jam that I serve with cheese. The jam is loose—kind of like sauerkraut—and delicious. Note this jam calls for pressure canning. There is no USDA data for beet jam, so I process it for the same amount of time as canned beets. Indeed, I put up canned beets and beet jam at the same time, in the same pressure canning session. **Save the greens for Beet Greens Gratin (page 55) or as a substitute for radish greens in Skillet-Cooked Radish Greens (page 275). Reserve the cooking liquid from boiling the beets to make Beet Granita (page 55).** MAKES 2 HALF-PINTS*

> ¾ pound medium beets, greens removed
> ¼ cup water
> 1 teaspoon grated lemon zest
> 1 tablespoon fresh lemon juice
> ¾ cup sugar
> Pinch of salt

Bring a large pot of water to a boil over high heat. Wash the beets. Add the beets to the boiling water and cook until fork-tender, 15 to 20 minutes. Drain. When cool enough to handle, peel and shred the beets on the large holes of a box grater.

Transfer the beets to a medium saucepan and add the water, lemon zest, and juice. Stir to combine. Add the sugar and salt. Bring to a boil over medium-high heat, then reduce the heat to medium and cook for 5 minutes to dissolve the sugar.

Have ready 2 clean half-pint jars and bands, and new lids that have been simmered in hot water to soften the rubberized flange. Pour the jam into the jars leaving 1 inch of headroom. Wipe the rims, place on the lids, and screw on the bands fingertip tight.

Process the jars in a pressure canner at 10/11 psi for 30 minutes. Process 1 pint for the same amount of time. (See "How to Pressure Can," page 379.) Be sure to make altitude adjustments when preserving (see page 389).

Canned Beets

*I like to have canned beets on hand to make composed salads in the off-season. The fresh beet dishes in this book can all be made with canned beets. You need about ¾ of a pound of beets per pint of canned. **Save the greens for Beet Greens Gratin (page 55) or as a substitute for radish greens in Skillet-Cooked Radish Greens (page 275). Reserve the cooking liquid from boiling the beets to make Beet Granita (page 55).** MAKES 2 PINTS*

> 1½ pounds beets, greens removed

Bring a large pot of water to a boil over high heat. Wash the beets. Add the beets to the boiling water and cook until fork-tender, 15 to 20 minutes. Drain.

Have ready 2 clean pint jars and bands, and new lids that have been simmered in hot water to soften the rubberized flange.

As soon as the beets are cool enough to handle, peel, slice, and pack them into the jars. Cover the beets with hot water leaving 1 inch of headroom. Wipe the rims, place on the lids, and screw on the bands fingertip tight.

CANNED BEETS
WITH TUNA

Process the jars in a pressure canner at 10/11 psi for 30 minutes for pints, 35 minutes for 1 quart. (See "How to Pressure Can," page 379.) Be sure to make altitude adjustments when preserving (see page 389).

Canned Beets with Tuna

To prepare this delicious, elegant dish, just open the jars. I like to serve this as part of an antipasto platter, with other fish-based salads like Shrimp with Marinated Artichokes (page 29). **SERVES 4 AS AN APPETIZER**

- 1 pint (2 cups) cooked beets (for homemade, page 52)
- 1 half-pint canned tuna (for homemade, page 301)
- 2 tablespoons extra virgin olive oil
- Squeeze of fresh lemon juice
- Salt and freshly ground black pepper
- 2 tablespoons minced flat-leaf parsley

Drain the beets and pour them into a serving bowl. Drain the tuna and flake the meat over the beets. Drizzle the oil over all, and squeeze on some lemon juice. Add salt and pepper to taste and garnish with the parsley.

Stuffed Eggs with Pickled Beets

When I was a child, my Southern grandmother always had a tray of stuffed eggs in the "ice box," protected by a sheet of plastic wrap. It seemed so extravagant to me that this treat was available whenever someone was hungry, but actually it was typical of her era's gracious style. Adding pickled beets to this humble dish just makes them better. I prefer stuffed eggs that have never been chilled, but they do hold up perfectly well in the fridge for a day or two. To ensure the yolks of your boiled eggs are centered, flip them over the night before boiling. **MAKES 6 STUFFED EGGS**

- 3 large eggs (see Note)
- 2 tablespoons crème fraîche (for homemade, page 362) or sour cream
- 1 tablespoon mayonnaise (for homemade, page 365)
- Salt and freshly ground black pepper
- 3 tablespoons finely chopped Pickled Beets (page 51)

Place the eggs in a deep pot and cover with water. Cover and bring the water to a boil over medium heat. Turn off the heat and let the eggs rest in the hot water for 12 minutes. Remove the eggs and let them come down to room temp.

Peel the eggs and halve them from pole to pole. Gently remove the yolks and place in a small bowl. Add the crème fraîche, mayonnaise, and salt to taste and mix until smooth.

Spoon the yolks back into the boiled egg whites. You can pipe the yolks in if you'd like, but I think that makes the eggs look a little cruise-shippy.

Garnish with the chopped pickled beets and pepper.

Note: Use older eggs to hard-boil: They shell more easily. You can tell an egg is hard-boiled by spinning it on your counter. If it spins fast and easily, it is ready.

Beet Greens Gratin

Whenever I go to the farmers' market and hear shoppers tell the farmers to cut off the beet greens, I swoop in. "Can I have those?" I ask, and they always comply with a nod of recognition. Beet greens are one of the sweetest greens I know. I never buy beets without them. **Even the water you use to boil the greens is flavorful. I'll store a quart jar of it in my fridge for a few days and use it the next time I make a vegetable dish or soup and need water.** *This dish is a great side for a grilled steak.* SERVES 4

Unsalted butter for greasing the baking dish

½ pound beet greens (weight of a typical bunch), washed

⅓ cup heavy cream

½ cup grated Gruyère cheese (or other melting cheese, like cheddar, or a combination)

Salt and freshly ground black pepper

¼ cup breadcrumbs (for homemade, page 362)

BEET GREENS GRATIN

Preheat the oven to 400°F. Butter a 7 × 10 × 2-inch baking dish (I use a shallow oval dish).

Bring a large pot of salted water to a boil. Add the beet greens and cook until the water returns to a boil. Drain the greens. Allow the greens to cool, then chop into bite-size pieces.

In a large bowl, combine the greens, cream, and Gruyère. Season with salt and pepper to taste.

Spread the greens mixture in the baking dish. Sprinkle the breadcrumbs on top.

Bake for 10 minutes, until golden brown and bubbling.

Beet Granita

I've tried drinking beet water warm (too health-foodie) and making cocktails with it (altogether too weird), but using it to make a granita is divine. Sometimes I make this with less sugar to serve between rich courses. For dessert, I serve it with whipped cream. SERVES 4

2 cups beet water

¾ cup sugar or to taste

2 tablespoons fresh lemon juice or to taste

In a medium saucepan, combine the beet water and sugar. Heat over medium heat, stirring to dissolve the sugar. When the sugar has dissolved take it off the heat. Chill the beet and sugar water in the fridge. Add the lemon juice and pour the beet mixture into a pan that conducts cold well.

Prepare according to the technique for making granitas on page 393.

CABBAGE

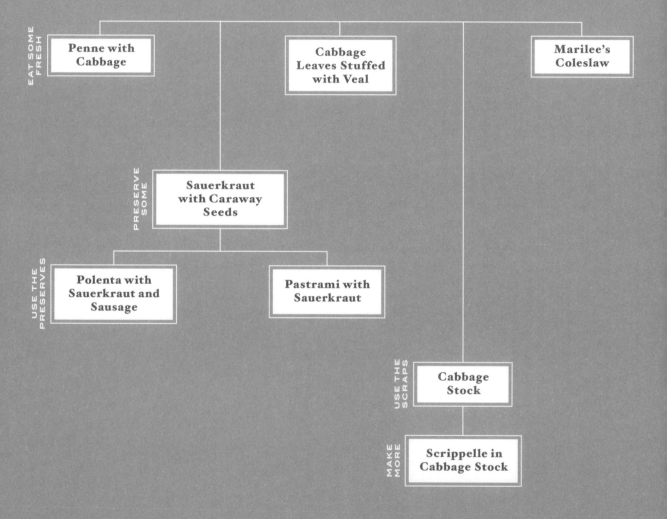

EAT SOME FRESH

Penne with Cabbage

Cabbage Leaves Stuffed with Veal

Marilee's Coleslaw

PRESERVE SOME

Sauerkraut with Caraway Seeds

USE THE PRESERVES

Polenta with Sauerkraut and Sausage

Pastrami with Sauerkraut

USE THE SCRAPS

Cabbage Stock

MAKE MORE

Scrippelle in Cabbage Stock

Cabbage Leaves Stuffed with Veal

My dad taught me this dish and it is a winner. You won't need all of the cabbage, only about half, but you will need the large outer leaves. You can make this dish with fish by substituting the veal with 1 pound of chopped sole or flounder, omitting the raisins, garlic, and marjoram, and instead smearing the inside of the cabbage leaf with basil pesto. Note it cooks for 1 hour, less if you prepare it with fish. **Save the rest of the cabbage to make Sauerkraut (page 60) or Marilee's Coleslaw (page 58).** SERVES 4

- 1 large head white or green cabbage, about 3 pounds
- 1 pound ground veal
- ½ cup breadcrumbs (for homemade, page 362)
- 2 to 3 tablespoons golden raisins (for homemade, page 161)
- 1 tablespoon minced garlic
- 1 large egg, beaten, or 2 egg whites
- 1 teaspoon dried marjoram or oregano
- Salt and freshly ground black pepper
- 2 tablespoons olive oil
- ½ cup minced onion
- 2 cups canned crushed tomatoes (for homemade, page 328) or canned whole tomatoes in water, drained and crushed
- 2 cups chicken stock (for homemade, page 89), warmed
- ¼ cup chopped flat-leaf parsley, for garnish

Preheat the oven to 450°F.

Remove 12 leaves whole from the cabbage. To do this, I make a cut at the base of each leaf and then gently pull the leaf off the head. If the cabbage is very tight and you find the leaves tearing, boil the cabbage for about 5 minutes, then the leaves will come off easily. Cut the tough stem end off the leaves.

CABBAGE LEAVES STUFFED WITH VEAL

Bring a large pot of water to a boil over high heat. Add the cabbage leaves and blanch for 1 minute (unless you preboiled the cabbage, as described above). Remove and allow the cabbage leaves to come down to room temperature.

In a large bowl, combine the veal, breadcrumbs, raisins, garlic, egg, marjoram, and salt and pepper to taste. I use my hands to combine. At first the meat will be wet and sticky, but as you incorporate the ingredients it will become dryer. Make 12 meatballs the size of golf balls, then flatten them each into an oval.

Have ready a 9 × 13-inch baking pan, or two 9 × 4-inch loaf pans. Place a cabbage leaf cup side up on your counter and lay a veal oval inside. Gently roll up the cabbage leaf, tucking in the sides as you roll. Place the cabbage leaf seam side down in the pan(s). For best results, the cabbage rolls should fit snugly.

In a medium saucepan, heat the oil over medium heat. As soon as it wrinkles, add the onion and cook until translucent, about 5 minutes. Add the tomatoes and bring to a gentle boil. Add the chicken stock and cook 10 minutes until the flavors meld and the sauce is slightly thickened. Season with salt and pepper to taste.

Pour the sauce over the stuffed cabbage leaves. Cover the pan(s) with foil and bake for 1 hour, until the veal is cooked through, the cabbage leaves are very tender, and the sauce has thickened significantly.

To serve, place 4 stuffed cabbage leaves on a plate and spoon some tomato sauce over them. Garnish with the chopped parsley.

Penne with Cabbage

This is a lovely pasta dish, a perfect last-minute dinner, but it's also nice enough for company, served before a game entrée. Without the pasta, the cabbage/ onion mixture makes a wonderful vegetable accompaniment for duck or brisket. **SERVES 4**

- ¼ cup olive oil
- 1 large onion, thinly sliced (about 1¼ cups)
- 1½ pounds crimped leaf cabbage (like Savoy), shredded (about 6 cups)
- 1 cup chicken stock (for homemade, page 89)
- Salt and freshly ground black pepper
- ¾ pound penne pasta
- 6 tablespoons grated Parmesan or pecorino cheese
- Extra virgin olive oil, for serving

In a large skillet, heat the olive oil over medium heat. Add the onion, cover, and cook until translucent, about 5 minutes. Add the cabbage, stock, and salt to taste. Cover and cook over medium-low heat, stirring often, until the cabbage is tender, about 15 minutes.

Meanwhile, bring a large pot of salted water to a boil and add the pasta. Cook until al dente and drain.

Toss the cabbage and pasta together in a serving bowl. Check the seasoning. Toss with grated cheese and serve each portion with a drizzle of extra virgin olive oil and a few cranks of freshly ground black pepper.

Marilee's Coleslaw

This is the best, freshest coleslaw I've ever had. My friend Marilee lives on Four Directions Farm in Colorado. She is a marvelous home cook, and this is her grandmother's recipe. My friend Ben Fink (he took the photos for this book) adds raw peanuts to this dish. You can cut the cabbage with a sharp knife (Marilee does), but I find a mandoline does the job better than I can do by hand. Because this slaw is so light and crisp, it is a wonderful garnish on foods like stewed meat. **SERVES 4**

- 1 pound white or green cabbage
- 2 to 3 tablespoons white wine vinegar
- 2 tablespoons extra virgin olive oil (optional)
- 1 to 2 tablespoons sugar, to taste
- Salt and freshly ground black pepper

Shred the cabbage and toss in a large bowl with the vinegar, oil (if using), sugar, and salt and pepper taste. Serve within 20 minutes. Don't dress this slaw too far in advance of eating it. If you do, the salt will have time to draw out water from the cabbage and the slaw will get soggy.

MARILEE'S
COLESLAW

Sauerkraut with Caraway Seeds

Caraway seeds transform ordinary sauerkraut into extraordinary sauerkraut. I use white or green cabbage (crinkled leaf cabbage, like Savoy, is too soft). Very fresh cabbage is best, as it will produce the most water during the brining period. If you start with an old soft cabbage, then your end product will be mushy. Crisp into the brining pot means crisp out of the brining pot.

*Sauerkraut is a dry-salt pickle: The salt pulls liquid out of the cabbage, which creates a brine. The brine protects the cabbage from air while it ferments. Fermenting turns the sugars in the cabbage into acids, which inhibit the growth of spoilers. The sauerkraut is acidic enough to safely process in a water bath for long-term shelf life. **Save the leftover tough outer leaves and cores of the cabbage to make a terrific Cabbage Stock (page 62).** MAKES 4 PINTS*

> 1½ pounds white or green cabbage, core and tough outer leaves removed, shredded (about 6 cups)
>
> 3 tablespoons pickling salt
>
> 4 teaspoons caraway seeds
>
> 1 quart water

In a 1-gallon ceramic crock or deep nonreactive bowl, combine the cabbage, 1½ tablespoons of the pickling salt, and caraway seeds. Press the cabbage down with your hands to compact it in the crock.

In a separate bowl, combine the water and remaining 1½ tablespoons pickling salt and pour into a 1-quart zipseal plastic food storage bag. Place the bag filled with brine on top of the cabbage. This will weight down the cabbage and keep the vegetable submerged in the brine. You put the brine in the bag so that if the bag leaks, it only releases brine.

Place the crock in a cool place and allow it to rest for 2 weeks. Check after 24 hours to see if there's enough brine to cover. Very fresh cabbage will produce enough brine naturally. Older cabbage will need additional brine to cover, so if after 24 hours your cabbage has not produced enough brine, make up a batch: 1 quart of water with 1½ tablespoons of pickling salt dissolved in it. Pour in enough brine until the cabbage is covered.

Take a look at the sauerkraut every once in a while. You will notice it will bubble and froth a bit. That is good. It will also smell quite strong after a couple of days and then become increasingly mellow. When the 2 weeks are up, you will notice the fermentation is over—no more bubbling or frothing.

Have ready 4 clean pint jars and bands, and new lids that have been simmered in hot water to soften the rubberized flange.

Transfer the kraut and brining liquid to a large pot and bring to a boil over medium-high heat. Stir frequently so that it doesn't scorch. Pack the hot sauerkraut tightly into the jars. Cover with the hot brine, leaving ½ inch of headroom. Loosen any air bubbles in the jar with a butter knife. Wipe the rims, place on the lids, and screw on the bands fingertip tight.

Process the jars in a water bath (see page 375) for 10 minutes for pints, 15 minutes for 2 quarts. Be sure to make altitude adjustments when preserving (see page 389).

Note: If you do not can the sauerkraut you can keep it in a jar in your fridge for a couple of weeks. The live probiotic bacteria in the kraut is very good for you.

Polenta with Sauerkraut and Sausage

I'd made focaccia with sauerkraut and sausage and that was pretty good, but this dish, which comes from Verona, is so much better. Got hungry teenagers to feed? This is your dish. **SERVES 4**

- 8 links Italian sweet sausage
- 2 cups water
- 1 teaspoon salt
- ½ cup fine or coarse cornmeal
- 2 tablespoons unsalted butter
- 1 pint sauerkraut (for homemade, opposite), drained
- Extra virgin olive oil, for drizzling
- Salt and freshly ground black pepper
- ⅓ cup grated pecorino cheese

Preheat the broiler.

Heat a large skillet over medium-high heat and add the sausage. Brown it slowly all over, about 20 minutes. If you are using very thick sausage, you can add ½ cup water after the sausage has browned. Cover and let the water steam the sausage to finish cooking. Remove and slice lengthwise or in rounds.

In a medium saucepan, bring the 2 cups water and salt to a boil over high heat. Add the cornmeal in a thin stream, whisking all the while. Reduce the heat to low and cook, covered, for 5 minutes or until the water is absorbed and the cornmeal has lost its raw taste. Add the butter and stir into the polenta.

Pour the polenta into the bottom of an 8 × 12 × 2-inch metal baking pan. Add the sausage slices and distribute the sauerkraut on top of the sausage. Drizzle some olive oil over the top, add pepper to taste, and sprinkle the pecorino over all.

POLENTA WITH SAUERKRAUT AND SAUSAGE

Place the pan 5 to 6 inches below the broiler and broil for 10 minutes, or until the sauerkraut dries out a little and even gets a bit crispy. Watch it carefully, though, as it can burn.

Pastrami with Sauerkraut

Pastrami with sauerkraut, especially your own homemade kraut, is unbelievably satisfying. I was pleasantly surprised to discover how easy pastrami is to make, and how inexpensive! The flavor of this pastrami is terrific, but since I don't use pink salt, the color is brown, not red. There are 3 steps to making pastrami and it takes 3 days. But it's worth it. I use my Cameron stovetop smoker, but you can rig a smoker, too. See page 384 for instructions. **MAKES 8 AWESOME SANDWICHES**

3 quarts water

¾ cup kosher salt

1 whole garlic bulb, cloves separated, smashed, and peeled

2 tablespoons granulated sugar

1 tablespoon black peppercorns

1 tablespoon juniper berries

1 tablespoon coriander seeds

1 bay leaf

2 pounds brisket (don't trim the fat)

RUB

3 tablespoons coriander seeds

2 tablespoons black peppercorns

1 tablespoon yellow mustard seeds

2 tablespoons light brown sugar

2 tablespoons wood chips: hardwood (such as oak) or fruitwood (such as cherry)

16 slices rye bread

1 pint sauerkraut (for homemade, page 60), drained

Mustard to taste (for homemade, page 366)

For the brine: In a large pot, combine the water, salt, garlic, granulated sugar, peppercorns, juniper berries, coriander seeds, and bay leaf and heat over medium heat until the salt and sugar have dissolved. Remove from the heat and allow the brine to cool.

Place the brisket in a bowl and cover with the brine. Refrigerate for 48 hours. Remove the brisket and place in a bowl covered with fresh water for 24 hours. Drain.

For the rub: In a spice grinder or with a mortar and pestle, combine the coriander seeds, peppercorns, and mustard seeds and grind. Transfer to a small bowl and stir in the brown sugar.

Dry the brisket and rub it with the spice rub.

Prepare your stovetop smoker (see "How to Smoke Indoors," page 384) with the wood chips. Place the brisket on the rack. Close the smoker and place over medium heat. Smoke the brisket for 1 hour 30 minutes. You will smell the brisket as it cooks.

Turn off the heat and allow the smoker to come down to room temperature. Remove the brisket. Store in the refrigerator wrapped in foil.

To serve, pastrami should be steamed to heat it up. I use my pasta pot with its fitted colander if I am steaming the whole brisket. (For smaller amounts, I use a standard basket steamer over a small pot of boiling water, with a lid.) Add 3 inches of water to the pasta pot. Place the brisket in the steamer basket. Cover and steam the brisket over a high heat for about 15 minutes to heat it through.

Slice the brisket and make sandwiches on rye bread with sauerkraut and mustard.

Cabbage Stock

I was surprised that cabbage stock is so good. It has a deep, rich flavor. You can refrigerate, freeze, or pressure can this stock. It is wonderful to have on hand as a base for soups and stews, or to serve as is.
MAKES 1 QUART

2 tablespoons olive oil

½ cup chopped guanciale or thick-cut plain or smoked bacon

½ pound onions, coarsely chopped

1 pound cabbage leaves and cores

2 quarts water

Salt

In a large soup pot, heat the oil over medium heat. Add the guanciale and cook until the fat is rendered, about 5 minutes. (It may seem counterintuitive to heat the pork in oil but the pork will render faster in oil because fat attracts fat.) Be careful the pork doesn't burn.

Add the onions and cook until the onion is translucent, about 5 minutes. Add the cabbage and water, increase the heat to medium-high, cover, and bring to a boil. Then reduce the heat to medium-low, uncover, and gently boil the stock for 1 hour. The stock should reduce by about 50 percent. If it doesn't, that's okay. The intensity of the stock is up to you. Strain and season with salt to taste.

Transfer the broth to quart jars and refrigerate or freeze (see the technique for making stocks, page 390).

For longer storage, pressure can (see Note). Have ready 1 clean quart jar or 2 clean pint jars and bands, and new lids that have been simmered in hot water to soften the rubberized flange. Pour the stock into the jar(s) leaving 1 inch of headroom. Wipe the rims, place on the lids, and screw on the bands fingertip tight. Process the jar(s) in a pressure canner at 10/11 psi for 30 minutes for pints, 35 minutes for 1 quart (see "How to Pressure Can," page 379). Be sure to make altitude adjustments when preserving (see page 389).

Note: There is no USDA canning data for pressure canning vegetable stock. The *Ball Complete Book of Home Preserving,* a reliable source, calls for 30 minutes. The USDA does have data for pressure canning meat stock (beef, pork, lamb): it's for 20 minutes. When in this situation (vegetable stock with pork) I opt for the longer processing time.

Scrippelle in Cabbage Stock

Scrippelle are thin omelets flavored with Parmesan cheese and parsley. Usually served in a fine chicken broth, I think they are terrific in cabbage stock.

SERVES 4

> 1 quart Cabbage Stock (opposite)
> 2 tablespoons unsalted butter
> 8 large eggs, beaten
> ½ cup grated Parmesan cheese
> ¼ cup minced flat-leaf parsley
> Salt and freshly ground black pepper

In a large pot, heat the stock over low heat.

Have ready a few sheets of wax or parchment paper. Heat a small nonstick skillet over medium heat and add about ¾ teaspoon of the

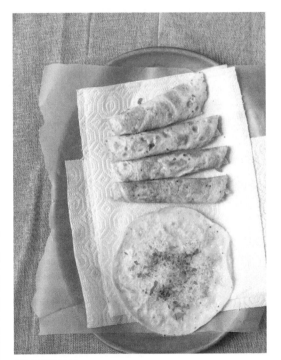

SCRIPPELLE

butter. Pour ¼ cup or so of beaten egg into the pan and swirl it around to cover the bottom of the pan. Allow the scrippella to cook for a few minutes, until the edges look dry. You do not need to flip it over. Slide the scrippella off the pan and onto a sheet of wax or parchment paper. Sprinkle the scrippella with 1 tablespoon of the Parmesan, a pinch of parsley, and salt and pepper to taste. Roll the scrippella up. Continue making more scrippelle, adding more butter as you go.

To serve, place two scrippelle in the bottom of each of 4 shallow soup bowls. Pour the hot stock over them. Add a bit more parsley and black pepper, if you'd like.

SCRIPPELLE IN CABBAGE STOCK

CARROTS
WITH GREENS

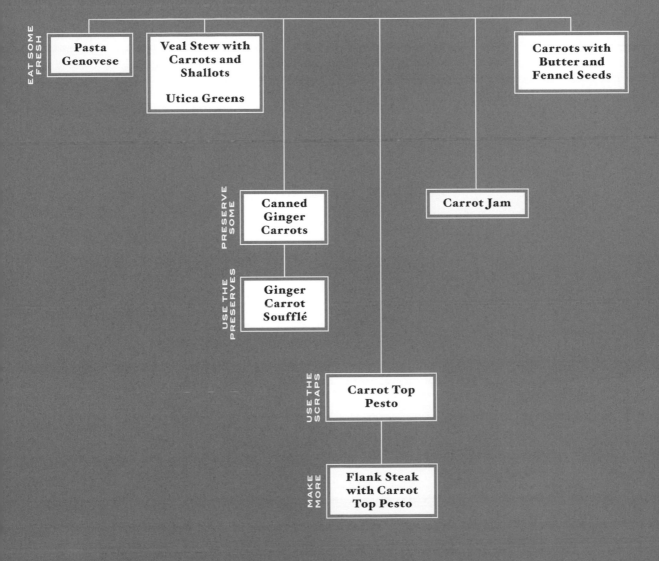

EAT SOME FRESH

Pasta Genovese

Veal Stew with Carrots and Shallots

Utica Greens

Carrots with Butter and Fennel Seeds

PRESERVE SOME

Canned Ginger Carrots

Carrot Jam

USE THE PRESERVES

Ginger Carrot Soufflé

USE THE SCRAPS

Carrot Top Pesto

MAKE MORE

Flank Steak with Carrot Top Pesto

Pasta Genovese

This hearty dish from Naples, not Genoa, is sweetened by the carrots and onions. My friend Natalie Smith, who owns Global Table in New York City where most of the tableware in this book's photos came from, gave me this easy and satisfying winter recipe. You can serve the pasta with vegetables as a first course, and the meat as a second course. **Save the carrot greens for Carrot Top Pesto (page 70).**
SERVES 4

- 1 pound skirt steak, pounded ¼ inch thick
- Salt and freshly ground black pepper
- ⅓ cup golden raisins (for homemade, page 161; optional)
- ¼ cup pine nuts
- 3 garlic cloves
- 2 tablespoons coarsely chopped flat-leaf parsley
- 3 tablespoons olive oil
- ⅓ cup chopped pancetta or bacon
- ½ cup dry white wine
- 3 cups minced carrots
- 2 cups minced onions
- 1 cup minced celery
- ½ cup water
- ¾ pound large-cut pasta, such as paccheri or rigatoni
- ⅓ cup grated pecorino cheese

Season the skirt steak with salt and pepper and cut it into 4 pieces.

In a mini food processor, grind the raisins (if using), pine nuts, garlic, parsley, and 1 tablespoon of the oil to a coarse mash. (You can also do this by hand: very finely chop together everything but the oil, then mix in the oil.) Place ¼ of this mixture onto a piece of steak. Roll the steak up and tie with kitchen twine. Do the same with the remaining mixture and steak pieces.

In a large Dutch oven or heavy-bottomed pot, heat the remaining 2 tablespoons oil over medium-high heat. Add the pancetta and cook until the fat has rendered, about 5 minutes. Add the steak rolls and brown all over, about 5 minutes. Add the wine and cook until the wine has reduced by half, about 5 minutes. Add the carrots, onions, and celery. Cover, reduce the heat to medium-low, and cook for 1 hour. Add the water and cook until the meat is very tender and the vegetables saucy, about 30 minutes longer. If the rolled steaks still need more time to get tender, it's okay. Just add a bit more water and continue cooking until the meat cuts with a fork. Check the seasoning.

Bring a large pot of salted water to a boil and add the pasta. Cook until al dente and drain.

Remove the beef rolls from the vegetable sauce, cut off the strings, and set aside. The rolls will hold together, though the meat will tear a bit where the strings held them. Pour the cooked pasta into the pot with the vegetables and stir to combine. (Sometimes I grind up the vegetables with an immersion blender or a regular blender to make a smoother sauce, before adding the pasta. Other times I leave it chunky. You can also push the vegetables through a food mill. Add a little water to loosen.)

Serve the pasta with the vegetable sauce, garnished with the pecorino and a few grinds of black pepper, and the beef rolls as a second course.

Veal Stew with Carrots and Shallots

The carrots make this cozy dish sweet, a version of which my dad made often when I was growing up. I like to serve this stew with polenta or grits, combined with a handful of grated Romano cheese and lots of salt and black pepper, or Utica Greens (recipe follows). **Save the carrot greens for Carrot Top Pesto (page 70).** SERVES 4

3 tablespoons olive oil

1½ pounds veal breast, fat trimmed, cut into serving-size pieces

¼ cup all-purpose flour

Salt and freshly ground black pepper

½ cup chopped shallots

½ cup dry Marsala wine or white wine

1 cup chicken stock (for homemade, page 89)

8 large carrots, sliced into rounds (about 4 cups)

2 tablespoons unsalted butter

2 tablespoons finely chopped flat-leaf parsley

In a Dutch oven, heat 2 tablespoons of the oil over high heat. Dredge the meat in the flour. Season it with salt and pepper. Drop the floured meat into the hot oil and brown all over, about 5 minutes. Transfer the meat to a plate and cover with foil to keep warm.

Add the remaining 1 tablespoon oil and the shallots to the Dutch oven. Reduce the heat to medium and cook until the shallots are translucent, a few minutes, then add the Marsala. Stir, scraping up the browned bits on the bottom of the pan while the wine cooks. Allow the wine to boil gently for a few minutes to reduce by half. It will be like a thin syrup. Add the veal and accumulated juices. Add the stock, cover, and cook until the veal is very tender, about 1 hour. You may have to add about ½ cup water at some point to keep everything moist.

Meanwhile, bring a large pot of water to a boil over high heat and add the carrots. Boil until they are fork-tender, 5 to 10 minutes. Drain. In a medium saucepan, melt the butter over medium heat and add the carrots. Mix well to coat the carrots with butter.

Add the carrots and butter to the stew and cook an additional 5 minutes. Check the seasoning before serving. Garnish with the chopped parsley.

UTICA GREENS

I tasted a version of this dish in Syracuse, New York, which has a large Italian population. I've made it many different ways since. It is wonderful as is, but great with cooked orecchiette mixed in, or eggs poached on top. SERVES 4

3 tablespoons olive oil

½ cup chopped prosciutto

1 cup chopped onion

1 tablespoon minced garlic or skordalia (for homemade, page 368)

1 tablespoon chopped cherry pepper (optional)

2 large bunches escarole, washed and chopped in big pieces

¼ cup grated Parmesan cheese

⅓ cup breadcrumbs (for homemade, page 362), toasted

Salt and freshly ground black pepper

In a deep pot (I use my pasta pot), heat the oil over medium heat. Add the prosciutto and cook until the prosciutto turns pink, a few minutes. Add the onion, garlic (or skordalia), and cherry pepper (if using) and cook until the onion is translucent, about 5 minutes. Add the escarole. Cover and cook until the escarole is wilted, about 5 minutes. Stir the escarole up a bit. Add the Parmesan and breadcrumbs and stir. Add salt and pepper to taste (sometimes the prosciutto and cheese makes the dish salty enough).

Carrots with Butter and Fennel Seeds

Carrots and fennel seeds are a lovely combination. If you'd like to sweeten your carrots, you can add a tablespoon or two of brown sugar when you add the butter. **Save the carrot greens for Carrot Top Pesto (page 70).** SERVES 4

1 pound carrots, cut into batons (like little sticks)

2 cups water

2 tablespoons unsalted butter

2 teaspoons fennel seeds

Salt and freshly ground black pepper

Place the carrots in a large pot and add the water. Bring to a boil over medium heat, cover, and cook for 7 minutes. Uncover and let the carrots continue to boil. Add the butter, fennel seeds, and salt and pepper to taste. Cook until the liquid has almost completely evaporated, another 3 minutes or so.

Serve promptly.

CARROTS WITH BUTTER AND FENNEL SEEDS

Canned Ginger Carrots

This is an instant side dish. One pint serves two. I usually buy 2 big bunches of carrots to make this recipe. **Save the carrot greens for Carrot Top Pesto (page 70).** MAKES 2 PINTS

    1½ pounds sliced carrots, about ¼ inch thick
    2 tablespoons grated fresh ginger or
        2 teaspoons ground ginger
    1 teaspoon salt

Place the carrots in a large pot and cover with water. Bring to a boil and cook for 5 minutes.

Have ready 2 clean pint jars and bands, and new lids that have been simmered in hot water to soften the rubberized flange.

Using a slotted spoon, remove the carrots from the water and pack into the jars. It is okay to press them down. Divide the ginger and salt between the jars. Cover the carrots with the water they were boiled in, leaving 1 inch of headroom. Wipe the rims, place on the lids, and screw on the bands fingertip tight.

Process the jars in a pressure canner at 10/11 psi for 25 minutes for pints, 30 minutes for 1 quart. (See "How to Pressure Can," page 379.) Be sure to make altitude adjustments when preserving (see page 389).

Carrot Jam

This recipe is adapted from Putting Food By. *I've altered the flavorings to make the jam less spicy. Carrot jam is wonderful with cheeses and great on a mozzarella sandwich. I macerate the carrots overnight in the fridge to help shorten the cooking time, though you don't have to.* **Save the carrot greens for Carrot Top Pesto (page 70).** MAKES 2 HALF-PINTS

    1 pound carrots, coarsely grated
        (about 2½ cups)
    1½ cups sugar
    2 teaspoons grated lemon zest
    ¼ cup fresh lemon juice
    ½ teaspoon salt
    One 3-inch cinnamon stick
    8 whole cloves
    ½ cup water
    Pinch of grated nutmeg

In a Dutch oven or heavy-bottomed pan, stir together the carrots, sugar, lemon zest, lemon juice, and salt. Tie up the whole spices in a piece of cheesecloth and add to the carrots. (You can put the spices in loose, but you will need to fish them out before canning, so if you do, count those cloves!) Cover and let rest in the fridge to macerate overnight.

The next day, add the water and nutmeg to the carrot mixture. Bring to a boil over medium heat and boil the jam, stirring often to prevent scorching, until the syrup has mostly evaporated and is thickened and orange, and the carrots are glossy, 20 to 30 minutes. If you boil the carrots too long they will become gluey. It's not the end of the world. Go ahead and process them, but loosen them up a bit with some warm water before serving.

Have ready 2 clean half-pint jars and bands, and new lids that have been simmered in hot water to soften the rubberized flange. Remove the spices, then pour the carrot mixture into the jars leaving ¼ inch of headroom. Wipe the rims, place on the lids, and screw on the bands fingertip tight.

Process the jars in a water bath (see page 375) for 10 minutes. Be sure to make altitude adjustments when preserving (see page 389).

Ginger Carrot Soufflé

I have made this savory soufflé from canned carrots, fresh carrots (½ pound cooked until tender), or from carrots left over from making chicken stock. The soufflés are sumptuous yet easy to make. I use my immersion blender to puree the carrots right in the jar. I just open the jar, drain, and insert the blender. But you can mash by hand with a potato masher or a fork. **SERVES 6**

- 3 tablespoons unsalted butter
- 3 tablespoons all-purpose flour
- Pinch of ground ginger
- 1 cup whole milk
- 3 large eggs, separated
- 1 pint Canned Ginger Carrots (page 69), drained and mashed to a puree
- ½ cup grated Gruyère cheese
- 1 tablespoon chopped flat-leaf parsley

Preheat the oven to 400°F. Use 1 tablespoon of the butter to grease six 1-cup ramekins or one 6-cup soufflé dish.

In a double boiler, heat the remaining 2 tablespoons butter over medium-high heat. When the butter is melted, whisk in the flour. Cook the roux for a few minutes, whisking all the while. Add the ginger. Add ½ cup of the milk and whisk to blend. In a minute or so the sauce will thicken. Add the remaining ½ cup milk and whisk to blend. Cook the sauce, whisking often, for 3 to 4 minutes, until the sauce is thick and smooth, like runny yogurt. Take the sauce off the heat and stir in the egg yolks, combining well. Add the carrot puree and combine well. Mix in the Gruyère and parsley. (You can let this mixture sit for up to 1 hour before completing the soufflé.)

In a bowl, with an electric mixer or whisk, beat the egg whites until they form soft peaks. Add a spoonful or two of egg whites to the carrot mixture to lighten it, then carefully fold in the remaining egg whites so as not to deflate the mixture.

Pour the carrot mixture into the ramekins, filling each about three-fourths full, or the soufflé dish. Bake for 30 minutes for the ramekins or 35 minutes for the large soufflé, until golden brown and puffy.

The soufflés are quite hot, so wait a few minutes before serving.

Carrot Top Pesto

Delicious and refreshing—I've never bought carrots without the greens since I discovered how to make this (you have to blanch the greens first or the pesto is too grassy). Be sure you separate the greens as soon as you get them home as they pull moisture out of the carrots. **Save the carrot stems for stock (see techniques for stocks, page 390).** **MAKES ABOUT ½ CUP**

- Greens from 1 medium bunch of carrots
- 3 tablespoons olive oil
- 1 tablespoon pine nuts
- 2 garlic cloves
- Squirt of fresh lemon juice
- Salt

Pull the feathery leaves off the stems. You should have about 2 loosely packed cups of leaves. Bring a small pot of water to a boil and drop in the carrot leaves. Cook for 1 or 2 minutes to blanch, then drain. The greens will reduce to about ½ cup.

Transfer the greens to a food processor or blender and add the oil, pine nuts, garlic cloves, lemon juice, and salt to taste. Blend to a puree.

Refrigerate the pesto, preserve it in oil (see "How to Preserve in Oil," page 387), or freeze it (see "How to Freeze Foods," page 382).

Flank Steak with Carrot Top Pesto

This is a simple, fabulous dinner: I just have to buy steak, carrots with the greens, and some fresh thyme. The other stuff I usually have on hand. I like to marinate the steak in the morning or the night before, but if you only get in 1 hour of marinating, that's fine, too. You can substitute skirt steak for the flank steak if you'd like. This is great accompanied by Carrots with Butter and Fennel Seeds (page 68). **SERVES 4**

  1½ pounds flank steak
  3 tablespoons olive oil
  Small bunch of fresh thyme
  4 garlic cloves, smashed and peeled
  Juice from ½ lemon (about 2 tablespoons)
  Salt and freshly ground black pepper
  2 tablespoons safflower oil
  Carrot Top Pesto (opposite)

Pound the steak with a mallet to tenderize.

Place the steak, olive oil, thyme, garlic, lemon juice, and salt and pepper to taste in a sturdy plastic food storage bag and refrigerate for at least 1 hour and up to overnight.

About 1 hour before you are ready to start cooking, take the bag out of the fridge and let the meat come to room temperature.

FLANK STEAK WITH CARROT TOP PESTO

In a grill pan or heavy skillet, heat the safflower oil over high heat. Remove the steak from the bag. Don't worry if there is garlic or thyme stuck to it. Place in the pan and cook for about 10 minutes, searing both sides, for medium-rare.

Remove the meat and let it rest for 5 minutes. Slice the meat against the grain and on an angle, and serve with the carrot pesto. You can serve this dish at room temperature or warm, both are good.

CHERRIES

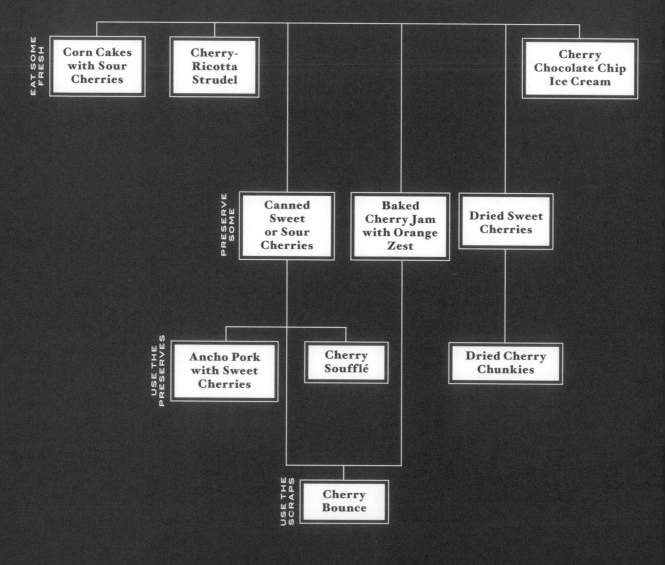

EAT SOME FRESH

Corn Cakes with Sour Cherries

Cherry-Ricotta Strudel

Cherry Chocolate Chip Ice Cream

PRESERVE SOME

Canned Sweet or Sour Cherries

Baked Cherry Jam with Orange Zest

Dried Sweet Cherries

USE THE PRESERVES

Ancho Pork with Sweet Cherries

Cherry Soufflé

Dried Cherry Chunkies

USE THE SCRAPS

Cherry Bounce

Pitting Cherries

Pitting Cherries

Cherry pitters, whether you use handheld olive pitters or the kind that punches the pit out, work great with sweet cherries, but forget about sour cherries. They are too small and too soft and get crushed. The best technique is to pinch out the seeds by hand, like a zit. It's slow going but by the second pound you'll be a pro. Sour cherries produce tons of juice, so pit them over a bowl to capture the liquid. If the cherries you buy are very firm and hard to pit, freeze them first, then defrost and pit them. When it comes to canning, there is some controversy over whether to leave the pits in or not—but really it's a matter of aesthetics. A cherry preserved with the pit in will be plumper. Pitted cherries use less volume in the jar, so keep that in mind when canning.

Corn Cakes with Sour Cherries

Corn cakes take a few more minutes to cook than regular all-flour pancakes. You can substitute the sour cherries with blueberries if you'd like. **MAKES 12 CAKES**

> 1 cup all-purpose flour
>
> 6 tablespoons cornmeal
>
> ¼ cup sugar
>
> 2 teaspoons baking powder
>
> Pinch of salt
>
> 1 cup whole milk
>
> ¼ cup vegetable oil, like canola
>
> 2 large eggs, beaten
>
> 1 teaspoon almond extract
>
> 2 tablespoons unsalted butter
>
> 1 cup pitted sour cherries
>
> Butter and maple syrup, for serving

In a bowl, combine the flour, cornmeal, sugar, baking powder, and salt. In a second bowl, whisk together the milk, oil, eggs, and almond extract. Add the wet ingredients to the dry ingredients and combine well.

In a large nonstick skillet or griddle, heat 1 tablespoon of the butter over medium to medium-high heat. When the butter is sizzling, pour ¼ cup batter per pancake into the skillet. Drop cherries onto the corn cake. Cook about 2 minutes until golden brown, then flip over with a spatula. Repeat for the remaining butter and batter.

Serve with butter and maple syrup. Yum.

Cherry-Ricotta Strudel

Using frozen phyllo dough is a lot quicker than making strudel dough, and I always have it on hand. You can also make this delightful strudel with blueberries; a combination of blueberries and cherries is good too. If you use blueberries, mash them with a fork. If you use sour cherries, increase the sugar by 2 tablespoons. **SERVES 4**

> ¾ cup ricotta cheese (for homemade, page 367)
>
> ½ cup plus 2 tablespoons sugar
>
> ½ teaspoon vanilla extract (for homemade, page 361)
>
> ¼ cup heavy cream
>
> 1 cup pitted and chopped sweet or sour cherries (or a combination)
>
> Grated zest of ½ lemon
>
> 8 sheets phyllo dough
>
> 4 tablespoons (½ stick) unsalted butter, melted

In a medium bowl, combine the ricotta, ¼ cup of the sugar, and the vanilla. In a bowl, with an electric mixer, whip the cream until soft peaks form. Add a spoonful of the whipped cream to the ricotta to lighten it. Then fold in the remaining cream. Place the ricotta cream in the refrigerator for about 30 minutes to chill.

Preheat the oven to 350°F.

In a medium bowl, combine the cherries, lemon zest, and ¼ cup of the sugar.

Line a baking sheet with wax paper or parchment paper. Lay a sheet of phyllo on the baking sheet. Brush the dough with some melted butter. Lay another sheet of phyllo dough on top, and brush on some more butter. Continue until all the phyllo has been used.

Smear the ricotta cream over the lower third of one long side of the phyllo dough. Spoon the cherries on top. Gently roll the filled portion of the strudel over the unfilled portion of the phyllo dough. As you come close to the end

of the dough, tuck the sides of the dough in, and continue rolling. Set the strudel seam side down. Brush the remaining butter over the top of the strudel and sprinkle the remaining 2 tablespoons sugar on top.

Bake the strudel for 25 minutes, or until golden. Let cool before serving.

Cherry Chocolate Chip Ice Cream

For one whole summer, every day after I picked up my children from swimming at the town pool, we stopped at the hardware store in Hotchkiss, Colorado, to buy Ben & Jerry's Cherry Garcia ice cream pops. They are adults now, and I make this ice cream for them as a kind of sentimental offering. Keep in mind that sweet cherries don't continue to ripen (or sweeten) once picked, so taste before buying. MAKES 1½ PINTS

> 1 cup heavy cream
>
> 1 cup whole milk
>
> 2 large eggs, beaten
>
> ⅓ cup sugar
>
> 1 teaspoon vanilla extract (for homemade, page 361)
>
> ½ cup chopped sweet cherries
>
> ¼ cup chopped bittersweet chocolate
>
> 4 heaping tablespoons blanched slivered almonds

In a heavy-bottomed medium saucepan, combine the cream and milk. Heat over medium-high heat until the milk is very hot but not boiling, a few minutes.

In a medium bowl, combine the eggs and sugar and whisk until they are well blended. Whisk in a few tablespoons of the hot milk to warm

CHERRY CHOCOLATE CHIP ICE CREAM

Cherries

Some of the most delicious cherries in the world are grown in southwest Colorado, and the little town of Paonia is ground zero for the big lusty Bing, the impossibly delicate Rainier, and the Montmorency, a sour cherry of perfect mouth-puckering juiciness.

Just about every Fourth of July for the last ten years or so I have attended the Cherry Days festival in Paonia, an orderly little town of brightly painted western-style buildings surrounded by orchards, some of them among the oldest on the Western Slope of the Rockies. It's a diverse place, with room for dozens of tiny churches, dreadlocked hippies, conservative farm folk, sophisticated oenophiles, and strange meeting-of-like-minders like the Ladies Anarchist Sewing Circle. It seems like practically everyone in town either listens to or hosts a show on the groovy local radio station, KVNF, which plays everything from punk to polka.

Paonia (the name derives from *Paeonia*, the genus of the peony—the plant traveled to Colorado in 1881 with the town founder) rests at 5,600 feet and there is something special about high-altitude orchards. The fairly consistent weather during the season—hot days and cool nights—and ample ground (not rain) water are perfect for growing succulent fruit. Cherries don't ripen after harvest the way pears or peaches do. As a result, when the harvest is in, it's *in*! And it is this bounty that led to the establishment of Paonia's Cherry Days festival in 1947.

The festival is held in Town Park, with its ancient cottonwoods and stone-lined ditches running with cold snowmelt. Families picnic under the shady trees; the old folks lie on their sides eating cherries, their gnarled hands holding a collection of pits, watching young parents chase after their toddlers. There are corn dog stands and pony rides, and a greasy, creaky Ferris wheel.

The cherry part of the Cherry Days festival consists of the crowning of Cherry Days royalty, the cherry cobbler and ice cream social, and the Cherry Days rockabilly dance. And we always buy chocolate-covered cherries from a couple of high school girls in cowboy hats and cut-off jeans sitting on a cooler ignoring the bandy-legged boys that hover near, their eyes bright with expectation and mischief.

up the eggs, then transfer the egg mixture to the pan with the milk in it. Heat, whisking all the while, until the mixture thickens, about 5 minutes. You can tell the mixture has thickened enough if the custard coats the back of a spoon. Stir in the vanilla. Pour the custard into a stainless steel bowl or other cold conductive container and chill in the refrigerator until very cold.

Transfer the chilled custard to an ice cream maker. Add the cherries, chocolate bits, and almonds. Freeze according to the manufacturer's directions (or make by hand; see page 394). The ice cream holds for about a month.

Canned Sweet or Sour Cherries

*You can pit cherries for canning. If you do, the cherries will take less space, and so you will not be able to fill the fourth pint jar in this recipe. If that is the case, process 1 half-pint jar (or up to 7 half-pints). They process for the same amount of time, and can be processed in the same batch as pints. **If you pit the cherries, do so over a bowl (especially the sour cherries, which are very juicy) and retain the juice for Cherry Bounce (page 80).*** MAKES 4 PINTS

> 3 pounds sweet or sour cherries, stemmed, and pricked twice with a pin, so they don't burst during processing
>
> 3 cups sugar (regardless of whether you are canning sweet or sour cherries)
>
> 2 to 3 cups water (2 cups for sour cherries, 3 cups for sweet)

In a large heavy-bottomed pot, combine the cherries, sugar, and water and heat over medium heat until the sugar dissolves and begins to boil. The cherries will look glossy.

Have ready 4 clean pint jars and bands, and new lids that have been simmered in hot water to soften the rubberized flange. Using a slotted spoon, fill the jars with the cherries—it's okay to press them down gently. Cover the cherries with the syrup, leaving ½ inch of headroom. Wipe the rims, place on the lids, and screw on the bands fingertip tight.

Process the jars in a water bath (see page 375) for 15 minutes for pints, or 20 minutes for 2 quarts. Be sure to make altitude adjustments when preserving (see page 389).

Baked Cherry Jam with Orange Zest

*This jam is slow cooked in the oven, which results in a cooked fruit taste. The method, which I learned from the chef Jacques Pépin, works well with apricots and peaches too. I used the USDA timing for "cherry topping," a dense product similar to this one. **If your cherries are especially juicy, you will have excess syrup. Save it! The syrup can be used in Cherry Bounce (page 80).*** MAKES 3 HALF-PINTS

> 1 pound sweet cherries, pitted
>
> 1 cup sugar
>
> 2 tablespoons grated orange zest

Preheat the oven to 200°F. Line a rimmed baking sheet with foil or a silicone baking mat.

Place the cherries on the prepared baking sheet and sprinkle with the sugar. Bake for up to 2 hours, until the cherries are dark and wrinkly and release their juice. But watch carefully to make sure the juice doesn't burn. Transfer the cherries to a bowl with a spatula and mash them with the orange zest. You will have leftover syrup in the baking sheet. Do not discard.

BAKED CHERRIES

Have ready 3 clean half-pint jars and bands, and new lids that have been simmered in hot water to soften the rubberized flange. Spoon the cherries into the jars and cover with the syrup from the baking sheet, leaving ½ inch of headroom. Wipe the rims, place on the lids, and screw on the bands fingertip tight.

Process the jars in a water bath (see page 375) for 15 minutes. Be sure to make altitude adjustments when preserving (see page 389). The fruit at the top of the jar may darken over time. It's okay.

Dried Sweet Cherries

Dried cherries should be leathery but pliable like raisins. I use these in Dried Cherry Chunkies (page 80) and in place of raisins in Granola with Raisins (page 162). **MAKES ABOUT ½ CUP**

1 pound sweet cherries, pitted
2 cups water
4 teaspoons ascorbic acid

Bring a large pot of water to a boil over high heat. Drop in the cherries and blanch for 30 seconds. Drain. This cracks the skin, which will allow the cherries to dry more effectively.

Place the water and ascorbic acid in a large bowl and add the cherries. Soak 10 minutes.

Drain the cherries and place, pit opening up, in the trays of a food dehydrator (or see page 385 for instructions on oven-drying). Do not pack them tightly. It is better to give the cherries a bit of space. Set your dryer to 135°F. The cherries should take about 24 hours, or until they are raisin-like. See "How to Dry" (page 385) for information on "conditioning" the dried cherries.

Ancho Pork with Sweet Cherries

We eat this dish in small bowls with warmed tortillas on the side, a squeeze of lime juice, and a bit of cilantro to garnish. It's also nice served with a plain or cheese omelet. If you are using canned cherries with the pits in, just squeeze them out before using; it's easy since the flesh is soft from processing. I often make a large batch of this ancho chile sauce (you can easily double or quadruple the recipe) and keep it in 1-cup containers in the fridge or freezer. It is great to have on hand whenever there are pork leftovers. **Save the cherry syrup drained from the jar for Cherry Bounce (page 80).** SERVES 4

ANCHO SAUCE

1 ancho chile

1 medium onion, coarsely chopped

½ cup coarsely chopped cilantro

½ cup chicken stock (for homemade, page 89), warmed

1 large garlic clove, coarsely chopped

Salt

PORK RIBS

2 tablespoons olive oil

Salt

2 pounds boneless country-style pork ribs, cut into 2-inch pieces

1 cup chicken stock (for homemade, page 89)

1 pint Canned Sweet Cherries (page 76), drained and pitted

For the ancho sauce: In a small bowl, cover the ancho chile in hot water and soak until softened, about 1 hour. Keep the chile submerged to ensure that it softens. I hold it down with a small pot lid. Drain the ancho and remove the stem and seeds.

In a blender, combine the chile, onion, cilantro, chicken stock, and garlic and blend to a fine puree. Add salt to taste. (If you are making a large batch of the sauce to freeze, puree in batches to avoid spillage, and don't add the salt until you use it.)

Pour the ancho sauce into a saucepan and bring to a low boil over medium heat. Allow the sauce to cook for about 10 minutes to meld the flavors. Watch for spatter if the sauce boils too high.

For the pork ribs: In a large heavy-bottomed pot, heat the oil over medium-high heat. Salt the ribs and add them to the oil. Brown the ribs until they release easily from the bottom of the pot, about 20 minutes.

Reheat the chili ancho sauce over medium heat. Add the ancho sauce and chicken stock to the pork. Reduce the heat to medium-low, cover, and cook until the meat is tender, about 1 hour.

Uncover and cook until the sauce is reduced by about half, about 30 minutes. If the sauce separates, with mahogany-colored oil around the periphery, don't worry. It's okay (actually, it's delicious). Just stir it back in. Break up the meat with a fork and adjust the seasoning. Add the cherries and heat through, a few minutes.

Cherry Soufflé

I make this incredibly light dessert with my canned cherries, but you can use fresh, too. A dessert to be inhaled rather than eaten, the soufflé will start to collapse as soon as it comes out of the oven because there is no flour or egg yolks to give it structure, but it is heavenly. To prepare a soufflé at altitude, you will have to use a béchamel-based recipe (see Variation).
If using canned cherries, save the syrup for Cherry Bounce (page 80). Save the egg yolks (but not for long, as they dry out quickly): you can use them to make dough for a sweet or savory tart crust (page 157). SERVES 4

- 1 tablespoon unsalted butter
- 8 tablespoons sugar
- 2 pints unpitted Canned Sweet or Sour Cherries (page 76), drained, or 1 pint pitted fresh cherries (see Note)
- ½ teaspoon almond extract
- 3 large egg whites
- Pinch of cream of tartar
- 2 tablespoons ground blanched almonds

Position a rack in the center of the oven and preheat to 425°F. Use the butter to grease four 1-cup ramekins or one 4-cup ramekin. Sprinkle 2 tablespoons of the sugar into one ramekin, swirl it around, and tilt the sugar into the next ramekin, and so on until the ramekins are all lined with sugar.

If using canned unpitted cherries, pit them. Place the cherries in a food processor or blender and puree.

Transfer the puree to a medium saucepan and add 4 tablespoons of the sugar. Heat over medium-low heat, stirring often, until the sugar dissolves. Take the puree off the heat. Allow to cool to room temperature. Stir in the almond extract. (This stage can be done ahead.)

In a large bowl, with a whisk or electric mixer, beat the egg whites until foamy. As the whites pick up volume, add the remaining 2 tablespoons sugar and the cream of tartar. Beat until the whites hold soft peaks.

Pour the puree into a large bowl and add a scoop of the whites to lighten up the fruit mixture. Then add the remaining whites, carefully folding them in.

Spoon the batter into the ramekins and sprinkle with ground almonds. Place the ramekins on a baking sheet and bake for 15 minutes, or until they are golden brown and high. A larger soufflé will take a few minutes longer to cook.

Serve the ramekins on plates: They will be hot!

Note: If using fresh cherries, first cook them in 1 cup water until they look exploded. Drain and proceed with the recipe.

VARIATION

High-Altitude Soufflé: At altitude, soufflés need the structure of a béchamel base. Here's how: Heat 2 tablespoons butter in a double boiler over medium-high heat. When the butter is melted, whisk in 3 tablespoons all-purpose flour. Cook for a few minutes, whisking all the while. Whisk in ½ cup whole milk to blend and cook for a minute or so to thicken the sauce. Whisk in another ½ cup milk to blend. Cook the sauce, whisking often, until the sauce is thick and smooth, like runny yogurt, 3 to 4 minutes. Take the sauce off the heat and stir in 3 egg yolks. Combine well and add the cherry puree. Pick up the main recipe where you beat the egg whites and continue with the rest of the recipe as directed.

Dried Cherry Chunkies

I make these chunkies for hiking trips, ski trips, and mushroom foraging. You can use any combination of dried fruit and nuts. Got dried apricots? Chop them up and throw them in. Walnuts? Pistachios? Dried cranberries? Candied grapefruit peel? They are all good. Sometimes I even add cinnamon red hots for Valentine's Day. **MAKES ABOUT 12 CANDIES**

- 1 pound bittersweet chocolate, chopped
- 6 tablespoons dried cherries (page 77)
- 6 tablespoons chopped blanched almonds
- 1 teaspoon orange extract (for homemade, page 361)

In a double boiler, melt the chocolate over medium heat. Stir until smooth. Pour the chocolate into a bowl and add the cherries, almonds, and orange extract.

Lightly oil a 9 × 5-inch loaf pan. Pour in the chocolate mixture. Refrigerate the chocolate for about 6 hours. Turn the chocolate out onto a large piece of wax paper.

Heat a large knife by pouring boiling water over it and drying it off. Gently slice the chocolate into 2-inch squares. Wrap in wax paper and store in the refrigerator.

The chocolate will be fine for up to 1 month. If the chocolate is exposed to varying temperatures, a bloom will appear. It does not affect the taste of the chocolate.

VARIATION: Instead of pouring the chocolate mixture into a pan to create chunkies, you can make elegant individual chocolates. Drop about 1 tablespoon melted chocolate onto a piece of wax paper fitted into a baking sheet. Drop a combination of nuts and dried fruits on top. Chill.

DRIED CHERRY CHUNKIES

Cherry Bounce

This is a traditional American cordial with both Southern and New England roots. There are about a million recipes for it, but this recipe is a basic one. I make this cordial with leftover cherry syrup from making Baked Cherry Jam with Orange Zest (page 76). If you don't have leftover cherry syrup, make a fresh syrup with cherry juice; see the technique for fruit syrups on page 394. **MAKES 1½ CUPS**

- ¾ cup cherry syrup
- ¼ cup rum
- ¼ brandy
- ¼ cup water

Combine and chill.

Holds forever in the fridge.

CHICKEN

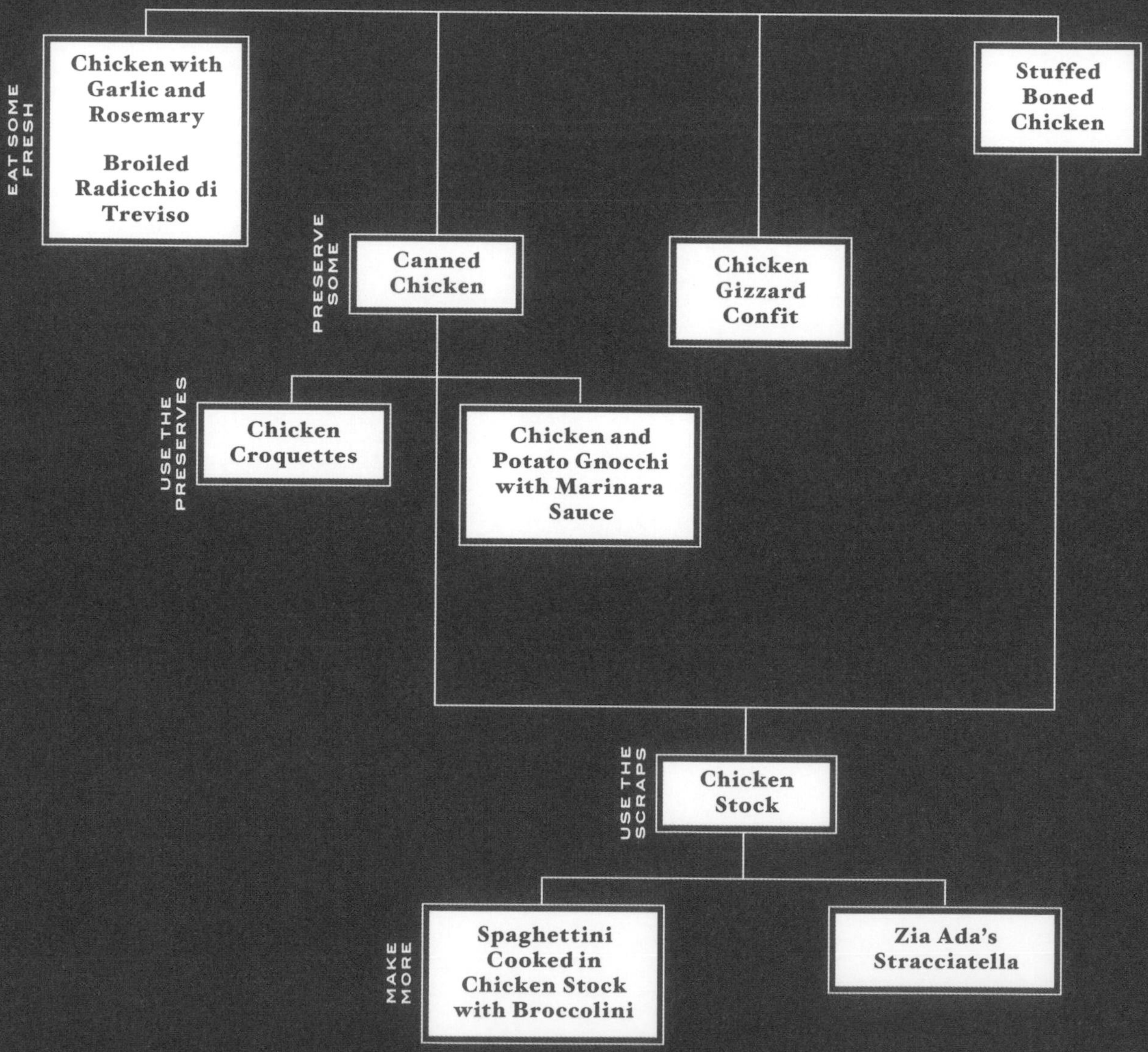

EAT SOME FRESH

Chicken with Garlic and Rosemary

Broiled Radicchio di Treviso

Stuffed Boned Chicken

PRESERVE SOME

Canned Chicken

Chicken Gizzard Confit

USE THE PRESERVES

Chicken Croquettes

Chicken and Potato Gnocchi with Marinara Sauce

USE THE SCRAPS

Chicken Stock

MAKE MORE

Spaghettini Cooked in Chicken Stock with Broccolini

Zia Ada's Stracciatella

Chicken Preparation

The most economical way to buy chicken is to purchase a whole bird and cut it into parts. If I want to cook just thighs, I'll buy two chickens, cut them into pieces, make a huge stock, and freeze or can the breast meat and legs for another day. Otherwise, one 4-pound chicken will feed four, with raw bones left over to produce about 2 pints of stock.

Here's how to cut a chicken into parts: Place the chicken on its back. Dislocate a wing by snapping it away from the body. Cut through the joint with a sharp knife. Repeat for the other wing. Grab a thigh and cut the skin where the thigh attaches to the body. Dislocate the joint by snapping the thigh away from the body and cut through the joint, capturing as much of the thigh meat that encroaches on the back as possible. Dislocate the joint between the thigh and the leg and cut through the joint. Repeat for the other thigh and leg. With a paring knife, cut out the wishbone. Flip the chicken over and cut through the rib bones to remove the sternum. Chop the breasts into four pieces.

How to Truss a Chicken

Take a piece of kitchen twine about 2 feet long. Place the chicken on its back, cavity away from you. Place the center of the twine under the tail. Bring the two ends of the twine up and cross over the legs, then loop the twine under the ankles of the chicken and pull tight. Pull the two ends of the twine toward you, over the wing drumettes. Flip the bird over and cross the strings. Catch the neck and tie it down with a knot. Fold the wing tips back. Flip the chicken back over and tuck the breast tip down to close the cavity.

CHICKEN WITH GARLIC AND ROSEMARY WITH OLIVES

Chicken with Garlic and Rosemary

I grew up with this chicken dish. On Sundays my Zia Ada, who lived and died in Centobuchi, Italy, would cook this and rabbit similarly but separately, then mix the rabbit and chicken together. You can add 24 to 30 pitted green olives or a dollop of Green Olive and Orange Tapenade (page 217) when you add the second half of the garlic to the pan. Zia served this dish at room temperature with Broiled Radicchio (recipe follows). **SERVES 4**

> One 4-pound chicken
>
> Salt and freshly ground black pepper
>
> 2 tablespoons olive oil
>
> 2 tablespoons chopped garlic
>
> ½ cup dry white wine
>
> 3 tablespoons fresh rosemary leaves

Cut the chicken into 14 pieces (you can ask your butcher to do this): Chop the breast, on the bone, into 6 pieces. Chop each thigh into 2 pieces. Remove the wings tips but reserve the drumettes. Chop off the bony end of the drumstick.

Season the chicken with salt and pepper to taste. In one large seasoned cast-iron or stainless steel skillet (you won't have as good a result if you use nonstick) or 2 medium skillets, heat the oil over medium heat. Add the chicken, skin side down, in a single layer. Be sure the chicken pieces do not overlap. Cook over medium heat until browned, about 10 minutes; as the skin browns it will loosen from the pan. Turn over the pieces.

Add 1 tablespoon of the garlic. Continue cooking, pouring off the fat as it accumulates, until the chicken is browned all over, about 10 minutes more.

Add the wine and 2 tablespoons of the rosemary. Cover, reduce the heat to medium-low, and cook until the wine has mostly cooked out, about 5 minutes. Uncover, add the remaining garlic, and cook for 10 minutes longer to meld the flavors. Check the seasoning and garnish with the remaining 1 tablespoon rosemary.

BROILED RADICCHIO DI TREVISO

My relatives in Italy never use balsamic vinegar in a salad—it's too sweet and thick. They use balsamic vinegar to garnish roasted and broiled vegetables, like radicchio, and fruit such as figs. You can also roast the radicchio: Cook in a 500°F oven for 5 to 10 minutes. **SERVES 4**

> 2 heads radicchio (Chiogga or Treviso will do)
>
> 3 tablespoons olive oil
>
> 2 tablespoons balsamic vinegar
>
> Salt and freshly ground black pepper

Preheat the broiler.

Cut the radicchio into wedges. Do not cut off the stem end as this holds the leaves together. Lay the slices on a nonstick baking sheet. Sprinkle the radicchio with 1 tablespoon of the oil.

Broil until browned—the tips of the leaves will be blackened—a few minutes (more if you are using an electric oven). Turn the slices over and continue cooking until the second side is browned.

Transfer the radicchio to a platter. Dress the radicchio with the remaining 2 tablespoons oil, a drizzle of balsamic vinegar, and salt and pepper to taste.

Stuffed Boned Chicken

I often make this dish for dinner parties because it can be made ahead of time and served at room temperature, and it is swanky looking. Besides, everybody likes chicken. You can stuff the chicken with anything you like: sautéed greens like chard or spinach, sweet peppers, breadcrumbs, sausage meat. I used to debone chicken myself. I saw Jacques Pépin do it in a cooking class once and it was like the bones just wanted to come out of that chicken. It literally took him 52 seconds. When I do it, the bird looks massacred, though if I am doing more than one, the second one looks okay. But now I just ask my butcher Pino to do it. Plus, they give me the bones for soup. **SERVES 4**

> 2 tablespoons unsalted butter
>
> 4 cups minced mushrooms
>
> 2 cups minced onions
>
> Salt and freshly ground black pepper
>
> One 4-pound chicken, boned
>
> ½ cup white wine
>
> ¼ cup olive oil

Preheat the oven to 350°F.

In a large skillet, heat 1 tablespoon of the butter over high heat. Add half the mushrooms and half the onions. (It is best to prepare the mushrooms in two batches, because if the skillet is full of mushrooms, they will steam and be too wet.) Cook until the mushrooms give up their liquid, and the liquid evaporates, about 10 minutes. Dump in a bowl and repeat with the remaining butter, mushrooms, and onions. Combine both batches of mushrooms and season with salt and pepper to taste.

STUFFED BONED CHICKEN

Spread the chicken on its back. Spread the mushroom mixture ½ inch thick on the chicken. Close the breast meat around the stuffing. I like to secure the meat with poultry pins. Truss the chicken as you would a beef roast.

Place the chicken on a rack over a roasting pan. Pour the wine in the bottom of the pan (if you use a large pan you might need to add more wine, or wine and water—you need enough to cover the bottom of the pan) and drizzle the oil over the chicken. Season the chicken with salt and pepper. Bake the chicken for 1 hour, or until the skin is golden brown and the juices run clear.

Allow the chicken to rest for about 10 minutes before carving. This chicken is served in slices.

Canned Chicken

When I took my master canner class in Colorado I sat next to a woman who ran a ranch pretty far away from civilization, and she canned like crazy. One day she brought in her canned chicken for me to see. She cans on the bone, with vegetables and herbs. It was a revelation to me: Here was a beautiful, delicious looking canned product with a huge use potential. It is like having leftover chicken and stock on hand all the time. Canning poultry is easy and safe if you use a pressure canner. Cheap, too: I like to can turkey after Thanksgiving, when the meat is on sale. If you pressure can bone-in poultry, you will need more jars and the processing time goes down to 1 hour 5 minutes. MAKES 4 PINTS

- 4 strips of lemon zest
- 16 black peppercorns
- 2 teaspoons salt
- 16 sprigs of fresh thyme
- 16 sprigs of flat-leaf parsley
- 4 small bay leaves
- 3 pounds boneless chicken or turkey meat, cut into pieces

Have ready 4 clean pint jars and bands, and new lids that have been simmered in hot water to soften the rubberized flange.

Place in each jar a strip of lemon zest, 4 peppercorns, ½ teaspoon salt, 4 sprigs thyme, 4 sprigs parsley, and 1 bay leaf. Pack the chicken or turkey meat into the jars leaving 1¼ inches of headroom. Do not add any liquid. Wipe the rims, place on the lids, and screw on the bands fingertip tight.

Process the jars in a pressure canner at 10/11 psi for 1 hour 15 minutes. (See "How to Pressure Can," page 379.) Be sure to make altitude adjustments when preserving (see page 389).

Chicken Gizzard Confit

It can be hard to find gizzards—much less organic ones—so I save mine from when I make roast chicken. This recipe is adapted from one that the winemaker Yvon Gross prepares at the Leroux Creek Vineyards in Hotchkiss, Colorado. According to Yvon, the gizzards can be stored in the duck fat for 3 months in the fridge. I think you can count on a month, as long as they stay buried in the fat in the fridge.

SERVES 4 AS AN HORS D'OEUVRE

- 1 pound chicken gizzards (about 12 big gizzards), with silver skin, fat, and grit duct removed
- 1 tablespoon salt
- 4 sprigs of fresh thyme or 1 teaspoon dried leaves
- 2 small bay leaves
- One 3-inch sprig of fresh rosemary
- 4 cups rendered duck fat (for homemade, page 126)
- 1 small onion, stuck with 3 cloves
- 12 to 24 bite-size chunks of fresh apricot or peach

Place the gizzards, salt, thyme, bay leaves, and rosemary in a sturdy zipseal food storage bag and shake well to distribute the salt and herbs. Refrigerate for 6 hours.

Preheat the oven to 250°F.

Wash the gizzards very well. (Yvon says to rinse them 5 times. The French. Sheesh.)

In a deep heavy-bottomed, flameproof casserole with a fitted top, melt the duck fat over medium heat. Tuck the gizzards into the fat to cover. It is very important the gizzards be completely covered in fat, otherwise the bits of gizzard poking above the fat will dry out and be tough. Add the onion. Cover, place in the oven, and cook for about 4 hours, until the gizzards are meltingly tender when probed with a fork. (You can make the recipe ahead to this point. Bring the pot with the gizzards to room temperature, then refrigerate.)

Wipe the fat off the gizzards (this doesn't need to be a thorough job). Heat a skillet over medium-high heat. Sear the gizzards in the skillet, a couple of minutes.

Spear the gizzards on toothpicks with a piece of fresh apricot or peach. (If the gizzards are very large, cut them in half.)

Chicken and Potato Gnocchi with Marinara Sauce

These gnocchi are very tender, light, and delicate. I use my canned chicken to make them, but you can use leftover boiled chicken, too. In this recipe I dress the gnocchi with marinara sauce (page 332), but I also serve them with melted butter mixed with minced fresh sage, salt, and black pepper; or I serve them in chicken stock. See the variations that follow.

SERVES 4

- 2 cups Canned Chicken (opposite), chopped
- 2 cups mashed potatoes (unseasoned), cooled
- 2 large eggs plus 1 large egg yolk
- 1 scant tablespoon grated lemon zest
- ½ teaspoon grated nutmeg
- Salt and freshly ground black pepper
- All-purpose flour, for dredging
- 2 quarts chicken stock (for homemade, page 89) or salted water
- 2 cups marinara sauce (for homemade, page 332)
- ½ cup grated Parmesan cheese, for serving

In a food processor, combine the chicken, mashed potatoes, whole eggs and yolk, lemon zest, nutmeg, and salt and pepper to taste and pulse to combine the ingredients very well. You can also mash the ingredients together in a bowl using a fork. Place the chicken and potato mixture in a bowl in the refrigerator and let rest, covered, for at least 2 hours and up to overnight.

Pour about 1 cup of flour into a shallow bowl. Shape the chicken mixture into 1-inch dumplings, roll them in the flour, and place on a plate. The gnocchi are very soft, so you can't handle them long or they just fall apart. Try to roll them quickly, and with a light touch. You should have around 24 gnocchi. Put them in the refrigerator while you heat the stock.

In a large pot, bring the stock or water to a boil over medium heat. Reduce the heat to maintain the liquid at a hot simmer. Carefully drop the gnocchi into the simmering liquid. At first they will drop to the bottom of the pot, then they will rise. When they rise to the top of the water, scoop them out with a slotted spoon. The gnocchi will look very soft and pale. Place on a serving plate. Some will break. That's life.

Meanwhile, warm the marinara sauce in a medium pot over medium heat.

Gently toss the gnocchi in the marinara sauce. Serve with the Parmesan.

VARIATIONS

Gnocchi with Sage Butter: Form and cook the gnocchi as directed above. In a small saucepan, melt 1 stick of butter, 2 tablespoons of chopped fresh sage, and salt and pepper to taste. Gently toss the gnocchi with the sage butter. Garnish with grated Parmesan as in the main recipe.

Gnocchi in Broth: Form the gnocchi as directed. Cook the gnocchi in chicken stock, not water. Strain the stock in which you boiled the gnocchi, as it will have bits of gnocchi in it, and then rewarm. Add 1 tablespoon lemon juice and continue cooking for a few more minutes. To serve, place 8 or so gnocchi in a bowl and cover with the stock. Serve the soup garnished with the grated Parmesan cheese. A little minced parsley is nice, too.

Chicken Croquettes

I make this dish with home-canned chicken or turkey or when I have leftover boiled or roasted chicken or turkey. I use panko rather than homemade breadcrumbs because it's crunchier, and serve the croquettes with lemon wedges and a nice green salad. When they were little, my kids liked them with homemade Tomato Ketchup (page 330). **SERVES 4**

> 2 tablespoons unsalted butter
>
> 1 cup minced onion
>
> 1 cup plus 1 heaping tablespoon all-purpose flour
>
> ¾ cup chicken stock (for homemade, opposite)
>
> 4 cups chopped Canned Chicken (page 86)
>
> 1 large egg yolk, beaten
>
> A few dashes of Worcestershire sauce (for homemade, page 369)
>
> Salt and freshly ground black pepper
>
> Hot sauce (optional; for homemade, page 365)
>
> 2 large eggs, beaten
>
> 2 cups panko breadcrumbs
>
> Neutral oil, such as safflower, for frying
>
> Lemon wedges, for garnish

In a large nonstick skillet, heat the butter over medium heat. Add the onion and cook until translucent, about 5 minutes. Add 1 heaping tablespoon of the flour and stir to coat the onion. Add the chicken stock, stirring. The sauce will thicken up quickly. Add the chopped chicken and stir well. The chicken will begin to disintegrate and become rather mushy. (This is good. If it doesn't, don't worry; your croquettes will still taste good. It just means you chopped it too large, or the chicken was a bit dry or tough to start with.)

Take the chicken off the heat and stir in the egg yolk to combine. Return to the heat for a few minutes. Add the Worcestershire sauce and season with salt and pepper to taste. (A little hot vinegar sauce is good, too.) Dump the chicken mixture into a bowl and pack it down. Cover with plastic wrap and refrigerate for at least 6 hours and up to 2 days.

Have ready 3 shallow bowls. Place the 1 cup of flour in one, the beaten whole eggs in another, and the panko in a third.

Remove the chicken mixture from the fridge. Scoop out the mixture by the ¼ cup and form into an oblong shape. Roll in the flour, then the egg, then in the panko and place on a plate. Continue to make all the croquettes. You will end up making 12 to 16 croquettes. This is a messy job. Frequent hand washings are in order. You can refrigerate the croquettes for up to 24 hours at this point.

To fry the croquettes, put ½ inch of oil into a large nonstick saucepan and heat over medium heat. Throw a bit of breadcrumb into the oil and if it sizzles and pops the oil is hot enough. Add the croquettes—I usually do about 6 at a time—and fry until golden brown all over, just a couple of minutes. Drain on brown paper bags or paper towels. Be sure to let the oil come back up to heat before frying the next batch. (The fried croquettes will hold in the fridge for a couple of days. Just rewarm them in a 350°F oven for about 5 minutes.)

Serve hot with lemon wedges for squeezing.

Chicken Stock

*How often have you opened a quart carton of chicken stock, only to use half and then let the rest go bad in your fridge? Making a small amount of stock—even as little as a pint—from the carcass of a roast chicken is not only easy, it is convenient, and tastes better than the commercial stuff to boot. If you've got other tender herbs (dill, cilantro, thyme, tarragon) throw them in. If you've got some bones from a steak dinner, throw them in. Got a turnip, shallots, garlic? Throw them in. **When you strain the stock, save the carrots to make Ginger Carrot Soufflé (page 70).** MAKES ABOUT 4 PINTS*

CHICKEN STOCK INGREDIENTS

    1 roast chicken carcass, plus the roasting
        drippings, or the neck, back, and wing tips of
        a raw chicken

    2 carrots, halved

    1 celery stalk, halved

    1 onion, halved

    1 small bunch flat-leaf parsley (just the stems
        are okay)

    A few whole cloves

    1 bay leaf

    1 piece of Parmesan cheese rind (if you have it)

    2 teaspoons salt

    2 quarts water

In a soup pot, combine the chicken, carrots, onion, parsley, cloves, bay leaf, Parmesan rind (if using), salt, and water. Partially cover and bring to a boil over high heat, then reduce the heat and boil gently for at least 2 hours, but the longer the better.

Strain. You should have about 4 pints. If you cooked it longer, you may have less. Transfer the stock to jars and refrigerate or freeze (see the technique for making stocks, page 390).

For shelf stable stock, pressure can it. Have ready 4 clean pint jars and bands, and new lids that have been simmered in hot water to soften the rubberized flange. Pour the stock into the jars leaving 1 inch of headroom. Wipe the rims, place on the lids, and screw on the bands fingertip tight.

Process the jars in a pressure canner at 10/11 psi for 20 minutes for pints, 25 minutes for 2 quarts. (See "How to Pressure Can," page 379.) Be sure to make altitude adjustments when preserving (see page 389).

SPAGHETTINI
COOKED IN
CHICKEN STOCK
WITH BROCCOLINI
AND RICOTTA

Spaghettini Cooked in Chicken Stock with Broccolini

I've made this dish as a quick supper and as an elegant dinner party first course. It goes both ways, which is key to its charm and longevity in my cooking repertoire. The sauce is created when the starch from the pasta mixes with the chicken stock. One bunch of broccoli rabe can be substituted for the broccolini, but be sure you peel the tough stems. In the summer I garnish this dish with minced cilantro, parsley, or basil, garlic, and fresh tomatoes. This recipe is my winter version. (The sautéed broccolini is delicious as a side vegetable, or tossed with roast chicken pieces. I also combine cooked broccolini with grilled sausages and cooked white beans.) SERVES 4

> 2 bunches broccolini (about 1½ pounds)
>
> 4 to 6 tablespoons olive oil
>
> 2 tablespoons minced garlic
>
> Salt and hot pepper flakes
>
> ¾ pound spaghettini
>
> 1½ quarts chicken stock (for homemade, page 89)
>
> ½ cup ricotta cheese (for homemade, page 367) or ricotta salata

Bring a large pot of water to a boil and drop in the broccolini. As soon as the water comes back to a boil, drain the broccolini.

In a large skillet, heat 4 tablespoons of the oil over medium heat. Add the garlic and cook for a minute to soften. Do not brown. Add the pepper flakes to taste and the broccolini. Cook over medium-low heat until the broccolini is tender, about 15 minutes. You may need to add a bit more oil. Adding a little water is okay, too, if the pan seems dry. Snip the broccolini into little pieces. Add salt to taste.

Cook the pasta according to the technique for cooking pasta in stock on page 392.

Pour the pasta into a serving plate and garnish with the broccolini and the crumbled ricotta.

Zia Ada's Stracciatella

My Aunt Ada would always serve us stracciatella when we first arrived in Centobuchi from New York. She believed air travel upset the stomach, and so made this delicate soup to comfort us on our first night in Italy. SERVES 4

> 6 cups chicken stock (for homemade, page 89)
>
> 4 large eggs
>
> 3 tablespoons grated Parmesan cheese
>
> 1 tablespoon grated lemon zest
>
> Salt and freshly ground black pepper
>
> Juice of ½ lemon
>
> 2 tablespoons minced flat-leaf parsley, for garnish

In a large soup pot, heat the stock over medium-low heat. In a bowl, beat together the eggs, Parmesan, lemon zest, and salt and pepper to taste. Whisking all the while, add the egg mixture to the hot stock. Do not let the stock come to a boil. A high simmer is good. Add the lemon juice and garnish with the parsley. Serve with additional Parmesan, if you'd like.

CORN

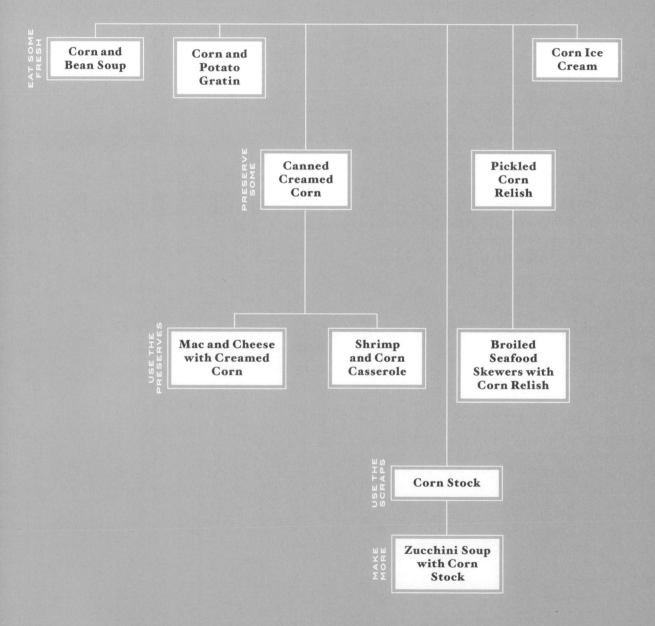

EAT SOME FRESH

Corn and Bean Soup

Corn and Potato Gratin

Corn Ice Cream

PRESERVE SOME

Canned Creamed Corn

Pickled Corn Relish

USE THE PRESERVES

Mac and Cheese with Creamed Corn

Shrimp and Corn Casserole

Broiled Seafood Skewers with Corn Relish

USE THE SCRAPS

Corn Stock

MAKE MORE

Zucchini Soup with Corn Stock

How to Dry Corn Husks

When you husk your corn, remove the husk in as large pieces as possible. Wash the husks and remove all corn silk. Dry them and lay the husks out on a sunny counter or in a box in a sunny protected spot and air-dry for a couple of days until the green color is washed out and the husks are as dry as paper. Store the husks in plastic bags in a cool dry place for up to a year. To use (to make tamales, for example), soak the husks in warm water for about 30 minutes, drain, and blot dry.

Corn and Potato Gratin

*This is our go-to side dish for grilled summer steaks. The recipe is simple, so have fun with garnishes. I usually top this gratin with crumbled fried bacon, sometimes cracklings left over from making Home-Rendered Lard (page 268), or chopped fresh tender herbs. You can also make this dish with Canned Creamed Corn (page 96). Simply substitute 1 cup of creamed corn for the fresh corn in the recipe. **Save the corncobs for Corn Stock (page 99).** SERVES 4*

>   1 tablespoon unsalted butter, for the baking dish
>   1 pound baking potatoes
>   2 large ears corn, husked
>   ½ cup heavy cream
>   ½ cup grated mild cheddar or Gruyère cheese, or a combination
>   1 tablespoon minced garlic
>   ¼ teaspoon grated nutmeg
>   Salt and freshly ground black pepper
>   ½ cup breadcrumbs (for homemade, page 362)

Preheat the oven to 350°F. Butter an 11 × 6 × 2-inch baking dish. (I use an oval gratin dish.)

Peel and slice the potatoes crosswise. Cut the kernels off the cobs.

In a large bowl, combine the potato, corn, cream, cheese, garlic, nutmeg, and salt and pepper to taste. Pour the ingredients into the baking dish and sprinkle the breadcrumbs on top. Bake for 35 minutes, or until the breadcrumbs are golden brown and the cream is bubbling.

Corn and Bean Soup

This is a very sweet, delicious summer soup. Sometimes I add about 4 peeled shrimp per person at the same time as the corn, which makes it even lovelier. SERVES 4

>   4 tablespoons olive oil
>   1 cup chopped onion
>   1 tablespoon chopped garlic
>   1½ cups chopped tomatoes
>   6 cups water, Corn Stock (page 99), chicken stock (for homemade, page 89), or a combination
>   2 cups dried cannellini beans, soaked overnight with a big pinch of salt, then drained
>   3 large ears corn, husked, kernels cut off (about 2 cups), corncobs reserved
>   2 teaspoons salt
>   1 cup chopped pancetta
>   ¼ cup grated Parmesan cheese
>   Freshly ground black pepper

In a large soup pot heat 2 tablespoons of the oil over medium heat. Add the onion and garlic and cook gently until the onions are translucent, about 5 minutes. Add the tomatoes and cook gently until the tomatoes have melted, about 10 minutes.

Add the water or stock and the beans, increase the heat, and bring to a boil. Then reduce the heat to medium-low and gently boil for 1 hour.

CORN AND
BEAN SOUP

Add the corn kernels, corncobs, and salt and cook until the corn is tender, 5 to 10 minutes longer. Turn off the heat and let come down to room temperature.

When you are ready to serve, discard the corncobs. In a small skillet, heat the remaining 2 tablespoons oil over medium heat. Add the pancetta and cook until the fat is rendered and the pancetta bits are golden.

Garnish the soup with the hot pancetta and rendered fat, the Parmesan, and black pepper to taste.

Note: Save Parmesan rinds in the freezer. If you add one to bean soups and other stews it will lend the dish a rich cheesy flavor.

USE THE COBS TO MAKE STOCK

Corn Ice Cream

Usually I am not so interested in savory foods used in sweet concoctions, but corn is different. It is naturally sugary, although once picked, the sugars convert to starch rapidly, so use very fresh corn. The real trick is to get the ice cream smooth. Grainy corn ice cream is slightly repulsive, so be sure you really blend those kernels to a smooth puree and pass them through a sieve. **MAKES 1 PINT**

 2 large ears corn, husked
 1 cup whole milk
 1 cup heavy cream
 ⅓ cup plus ¼ cup sugar
 2 large eggs

Over a large bowl, cut the kernels from the cobs, then scrape the cobs with the edge of a spoon to push all the milk out of the cob. Break the cobs in two.

In a medium saucepan, combine the corn kernels, corncobs, milk, cream, and ⅓ cup of the sugar. Bring to a boil over medium heat and then turn the heat off. Leave the cobs and cream mixture in the pot, covered, until cool. Remove the cobs (be sure to scrape all the cream and corn juices off the cob back into the pot) and discard.

Puree the corn and cream with an immersion blender or a regular blender. To ensure a very smooth ice cream, pass the corn mixture through a fine-mesh sieve into a bowl, pushing it through with a rubber spatula.

In a medium bowl, beat the eggs with the remaining ¼ cup sugar until frothy. Combine with the corn mixture and pour into a double boiler. Bring the water in the lower chamber to a boil over medium heat. Cook, stirring often, until the mixture is slightly thickened, about

CORN ICE CREAM

10 minutes. Dip a metal spoon into the mixture and if it coats the back of the spoon, it is ready. Pass the mixture through a fine-mesh sieve into a metal bowl (something that will conduct cold well). Chill in the refrigerator a few hours.

Transfer the chilled mixture to an ice cream maker and freeze according to the manufacturer's directions (or make by hand; see page 394). The ice cream holds for about 1 month.

Canned Creamed Corn

Creamed corn is a dense combination of milky corn juice and corn kernels. After cutting off the kernels, run the edge of a spoon or butter knife along the cob, pushing out the sweet milk. This is known as creaming or milking the cob. Creamed corn is so sweet and versatile, you will never buy frozen corn again. Corn is a low-acid food, so you have to pressure can it

to store it safely on the shelf. It takes about 3 medium ears of corn to fill a pint jar. **MAKES 2 PINTS**

> 6 medium sized ears very fresh corn, white or yellow, husked and washed
>
> 2 cups water or Corn Stock (page 99)
>
> 1 teaspoon salt

Bring a large pot of water to a boil. Add the corn and blanch for 4 minutes. Over a large bowl, cut the kernels off the cob, then scrape the cobs to milk the corn juice.

Have ready 2 clean pint jars and bands, and new lids that have been simmered in hot water to soften the rubberized flange.

In a medium saucepan, bring the 2 cups water or stock to a boil over medium-high heat. Add the corn and corn milk. Bring back up to a boil, then turn off the heat. Pack the corn and milk into the jar leaving 1 inch of headroom. Remove any air bubbles with a butter knife. Add ½ teaspoon of salt per jar (the salt is not necessary for proper canning—only for flavor). Wipe the rims, place on the lids, and screw on the bands fingertip tight.

Process the jars in a pressure canner at 10/11 psi for 1 hour 25 minutes. (See "How to Pressure Can," page 379). There is no USDA data for processing quart jars. Be sure to make altitude adjustments when preserving (see page 389).

There may be some browning of the corn. This is due to staining by harmless metal ions present in the corn tissue, like iron. It's okay. But if it really bothers you, you can add 1 teaspoon of ascorbic acid to the boiling water or stock and stir to dissolve.

Pickled Corn Relish

I am in love with this simple relish, a perky accompaniment to broiled or fried fish. This recipe is a pared-down version of one in So Easy to Preserve. *I use cherry peppers, which are in season in the late summer and overlap for a few weeks with corn.* **Save the corncobs and the corn cooking water for making Corn Stock (page 99).** MAKES 3 HALF-PINTS

- 3 large ears corn, husked
- 2 heaping tablespoons plus a pinch of sugar
- ¾ cup white wine vinegar (5% acidity)
- ½ cup minced cherry pepper
- ¼ cup minced white onion
- 2 teaspoons pickling salt

Cut the kernels off the corncobs.

Bring a small pot of water to a boil over high heat and add a pinch of sugar. Add the corn kernels and boil until tender, about 5 minutes. Drain and set aside.

In a medium saucepan, combine the vinegar, cherry pepper, onion, 2 tablespoons sugar, and salt and bring to a boil over medium heat. Add the corn and heat through.

Have ready 3 clean half-pint jars and bands, and new lids that have been simmered in hot water to soften the rubberized flange. Spoon the relish into the jars, leaving ½ inch of headroom. Wipe the rims, place on the lids, and screw on the bands fingertip tight.

Process the jars in a water bath (see page 375) for 15 minutes. Be sure to make altitude adjustments when preserving (see page 389).

Mac and Cheese with Creamed Corn

This is a new take on the potluck classic. It's also a wonderful side dish for a barbecue. I use many garnishes with this dish, like chopped fresh chives, sautéed mushrooms, or a few drops of inexpensive truffle oil. SERVES 4

- 2 tablespoons olive oil
- 1 cup minced onion
- ½ cup minced celery
- 1 cup shredded Gruyère cheese (grated on the large holes of a box grater)
- 1 cup shredded jack or cheddar cheese (ditto)
- 1 cup grated Parmesan cheese
- 1 cup heavy cream
- 5 tablespoons unsalted butter, plus more for the baking dish
- 2 tablespoons white wine
- Salt and freshly ground black pepper
- ½ pound elbows or other small-cut pasta
- 1 pint Canned Creamed Corn (opposite)
- ¼ cup breadcrumbs (for homemade, page 362)
- ⅓ cup chopped scallions (optional)

Preheat the oven to 350°F. Butter an 11 × 6 × 2-inch baking dish. (I use an oval gratin dish.)

In a medium saucepan, heat the oil over medium heat. Add the onion and celery and cook until the onion is translucent, about 5 minutes. Scrape the onion and celery into the baking dish.

In the same saucepan, combine the cheeses, cream, butter, and white wine. Cook over low heat, stirring often, to melt the cheese. Season with salt and pepper to taste.

Bring a large pot of salted water to a boil and add the pasta. Cook until al dente and drain. Toss the pasta in the cheese sauce.

Add the corn. Pour into the baking dish and incorporate the celery and onions. Sprinkle with the breadcrumbs and scallions (if using).

Bake for 25 minutes, or until the breadcrumbs turn golden brown. Allow the casserole to rest for about 5 minutes before serving.

Broiled Seafood Skewers with Corn Relish

Nicely mixing hot and cold, soft and crispy, tart and mild, this is a great summer dish. You can substitute the squid and scallops in this recipe with peeled shrimp or hunks of monkfish (silver skin removed). I sometimes make these seafood skewers and serve them just with Pea Pesto (page 233). **SERVES 4**

- 1 pound squid, cleaned, with body cut into 2-inch-wide rings and the long tentacles trimmed
- 8 large scallops, hinge muscles removed (see photo)
- ½ cup olive oil
- 2 cups breadcrumbs (for homemade, page 362)
- 4 tablespoons chopped flat-leaf parsley
- Salt and freshly ground black pepper
- 1 cup Pickled Corn Relish (page 97)

Preheat the broiler. (Or prepare an outdoor grill to cook the seafood. Just be careful not to overcook.)

In a bowl, combine the squid, scallops, and ¼ cup of the oil. Toss together. Add the breadcrumbs, 2 tablespoons of the parsley, and salt and pepper to taste. Toss.

Skewer the breaded seafood on long metal or wood skewers (if you use wood skewers, wet them first so they don't burn). Do not pack the seafood too tightly or they won't cook where

HINGE MUSCLES ARE DISTINCT FROM THE REST OF THE SCALLOP

the pieces of fish touch. As you work, place the skewers over a baking dish (I usually use a small baking dish so the ends of the skewers can rest on the edges of the dish).

Broil until golden brown on all sides, about 10 minutes total. Sometimes the skewers are hard to turn; it helps to use tongs.

Serve the skewers with the corn relish.

VARIATION: You can also serve the seafood with fresh corn salad. In a large serving bowl, combine 2 cups of boiled corn kernels, ½ cup minced red bell pepper, and ½ cup white onion, olive oil, vinegar, minced parsley, and salt and pepper all to taste. Toss well. Serve the skewers on top of the salad.

Shrimp and Corn Casserole

I learned about this dish from Betty Fussell's I Hear America Cooking, *a wonderful collection of American recipes. This recipe has Southern roots, and it tastes like it: sweet, creamy, and rich. You can also make this recipe with 4 cups of fresh boiled corn kernels.* **If you can get head-on shrimp, save the heads and shells for Shrimp Shell Sauce (page 317). In any case, save the shells.** SERVES 4 TO 6

> 3 tablespoons unsalted butter
> 1 pound shrimp, peeled and deveined
> 1 cup minced onion
> 2 pints Canned Creamed Corn (page 96)
> 4 large eggs, separated
> ⅓ cup heavy cream
> Big pinch of cayenne pepper
> Salt and freshly ground black pepper

Preheat the oven to 300°F. Using 1 tablespoon of the butter, grease an 11 × 6 × 2-inch baking dish. (I use an oval gratin dish.)

Bring a large pot of water to a boil over high heat and drop in the shrimp. Boil until the flesh is pink and opaque, about 3 minutes. Drain and cut into bite-size pieces.

In a large saucepan, melt the remaining 2 tablespoons butter over medium heat. Add the onions and cook until they are translucent, about 5 minutes. Add the corn for about 5 minutes to warm.

In a large bowl, whisk together the egg yolks and cream. Add the corn mixture and combine well. Add the shrimp, cayenne, and salt and pepper and combine well.

In another large bowl, with a whisk or electric mixer, beat the egg whites until they form soft peaks. Fold the whites into the corn and shrimp mixture.

Pour the mixture into the buttered baking dish and bake for 25 minutes, or until the dish is bubbling and the top is just golden. Remove from the oven and let rest a few minutes before serving.

Corn Stock

You can add half an onion, a few peppercorns, or a few sprigs of fresh thyme to the stock for even more flavor. MAKES 1 QUART

> 6 corncobs, kernels removed
> 2 bay leaves
> Salt and freshly ground black pepper

Place the cobs in a large soup pot with enough water to cover, about 2 quarts. Add the bay leaves and bring to a boil over high heat. Reduce to medium-low heat and simmer, uncovered, until the stock is reduced by about half, about 40 minutes. Season with salt and pepper to taste.

Strain the stock. Transfer the stock to a quart jar and refrigerate or freeze (see the technique for making stocks, page 390).

For shelf-stable stock, pressure can it. (The canning time for corn stock is based on a vegetable stock recipe in the *Ball Complete Book of Home Preserving*.) Have ready 1 clean quart jar or 2 pint jars and bands, and new lids that have been simmered in hot water to soften the rubberized flange. Pour the stock into the jar(s) leaving 1 inch of headroom. Wipe the rims, place on the lids, and screw on the bands fingertip tight.

Process the corn stock in a pressure canner at 10/11 psi for 35 minutes. (See "How to Pressure Can," page 379.) Be sure to make altitude adjustments when preserving (see page 389).

Zucchini Soup with Corn Stock

The addition of corn stock to this otherwise basic recipe results in a particularly sweet dish. I make this in the summer when I have only a few cups of corn stock, made from the ears we ate for dinner the night before. This soup is delightful warm, but just as good cold. In which case, don't bother reheating the soup after you have pureed it. Just swirl in the crème fraîche, seasoning, and herbs, and chill. You can also freeze the soup without the crème fraîche. I like to garnish this soup with crunchy fried tortilla strips. **SERVES 4**

- 2 tablespoons olive oil
- 2 cups chopped zucchini
- 1 cup chopped onion
- 2 cups Corn Stock (page 99)
- ½ cup crème fraîche (for homemade, page 362) or sour cream
- Salt and freshly ground black pepper
- 2 tablespoons chopped fresh tarragon or cilantro
- 1 cup neutral oil, such as safflower, for frying
- 4 corn tortillas, cut into matchsticks

In a medium soup pot, heat the olive oil over medium heat. Add the zucchini and onion and cook until the vegetables are soft, 7 to 10 minutes.

CORN STOCK

In a food processor or blender, puree the zucchini and onions with the corn stock. Work in batches to avoid leaks and splatters.

Pour the soup back into the pot you cooked the zucchini in and bring to a boil over medium-high heat. Reduce the heat to low and add the crème fraîche. Simmer until the soup is warm, a few minutes. Season with salt and pepper to taste and add the tarragon.

In a small nonstick skillet, heat the oil for frying over high heat. Add the tortilla strips a few at a time and fry until golden, a matter of seconds. Drain on paper towels.

Serve the soup garnished with the tortilla strips.

CRANBERRIES

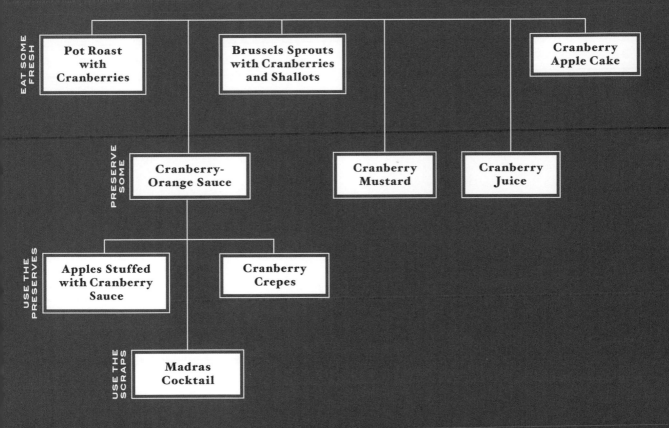

EAT SOME FRESH

Pot Roast with Cranberries

Brussels Sprouts with Cranberries and Shallots

Cranberry Apple Cake

PRESERVE SOME

Cranberry-Orange Sauce

Cranberry Mustard

Cranberry Juice

USE THE PRESERVES

Apples Stuffed with Cranberry Sauce

Cranberry Crepes

USE THE SCRAPS

Madras Cocktail

Pot Roast with Cranberries

This recipe is adapted from The Book of New New England Cookery. *It is warm, slightly sweet, tart, and rich. I used a classic Italian technique for braising the beef, which is both simple and elegant. It is excellent with mashed potatoes flavored with skordalia (for homemade, page 368).* SERVES 4

- 2 tablespoons olive oil
- One 2-pound chuck pot roast
- 1 cup fresh cranberries (frozen are okay, too)
- ½ cup water
- ¼ cup sugar
- ½ cup white wine
- 2 tablespoons horseradish (for homemade, page 364)
- One 3-inch cinnamon stick
- 1 fat garlic clove stuck with 6 whole cloves
- 2 cups chicken, beef, or mushroom stock (pages 89, 47, 190), or a combination
- 2 tablespoons chopped flat-leaf parsley, for garnish

In a large Dutch oven, heat the oil over medium-high heat. Add the beef and brown all over, about 10 minutes.

Meanwhile, in a small saucepan, combine the cranberries, water, and sugar and bring to a boil over medium-high heat. Cook until the cranberries are exploded looking, about 7 minutes.

Add the white wine to the beef and cook until the wine loses its winey smell, about 5 minutes. Add the horseradish, cinnamon stick, garlic, and cranberry mixture. Cook for a few minutes to heat through, and then add the stock. Reduce the heat to low, cover, and cook until the meat is very tender, about 2 hours 30 minutes.

Remove the meat gently (it wants to fall apart) and set aside. Strain the broth, discard the solids, and return the broth to the pot. Return the meat to the broth.

Serve in shallow bowls garnished with parsley.

Brussels Sprouts with Cranberries and Shallots

This is a beautiful, colorful dish that I love to serve at holiday dinners. When you blacken Brussels sprouts they become quite sweet, so the tart cranberries balance the dish well. **Save the bacon fat to pour into bean soups and stews.** SERVES 4 AS A SIDE DISH

- 4 slices bacon
- 1 pound Brussels sprouts
- 3 tablespoons olive oil
- Salt and freshly ground black pepper
- 1 cup fresh cranberries
- ½ cup sliced shallots
- 2 teaspoons minced garlic (optional)
- Extra virgin olive oil, for garnish

Preheat the broiler.

In a large nonstick skillet, cook the bacon over medium-high heat until the fat is rendered and the bacon is crisp. Drain on brown paper bags or paper towels. When cool enough to handle, crumble or chop the bacon into little bits.

Trim the scabby cut end of the Brussels sprouts and pull off any yellowed leaves. If the Brussels sprouts are large, halve them pole to pole (not along the equator or they'll fall apart).

Bring a large pot of water to a boil over high heat and add the Brussels sprouts. Boil until just tender, about 5 minutes. Drain and place on a baking sheet. Drizzle with 2 tablespoons of the olive oil and sprinkle with salt to taste. Broil for 8 or 9 minutes, until they are blackened on one side. Add the cranberries, flip the Brussels sprouts over, and continue broiling for another minute or two, just until the cranberries crack open. Remove from the broiler and set aside.

In a small skillet, heat the remaining 1 tablespoon olive oil over medium-high heat. Add the shallots and garlic (if using) and cook until the shallots are translucent, about 5 minutes.

To assemble the dish, *gently* combine the Brussels sprouts and cranberries. If you are too rough with the mixture the cranberries will bleed all over the Brussels sprouts: not very appetizing. Add a little salt to taste.

Garnish with the shallots and bacon bits. Drizzle with a little extra virgin olive oil and a few grinds of black pepper.

Cranberry Apple Cake

This cake has a very tender crumb, sweetness from the apples, and tartness from the cranberries and is light and moist. Sometimes I ice it with cream cheese icing: cream cheese, butter, and confectioners' sugar blended together, which is super tasty and rich. It also makes wonderful muffins (see Variation, page 104).

MAKES A 12-CUP TUBE CAKE

- 1 tablespoon unsalted butter, for the pan
- 2 large eggs
- 1 cup neutral oil, such as safflower
- 2 cups sugar
- 1 teaspoon vanilla extract (for homemade, page 361)
- 2 cups all-purpose flour
- 1 teaspoon baking soda

CRANBERRY APPLE CAKE (AS MUFFINS)

- 1 teaspoon ground cinnamon
- ½ teaspoon salt
- ¼ teaspoon grated nutmeg
- 3 cups shredded baking apples, such as Jonathans
- 1¼ cups fresh or thawed frozen cranberries, coarsely ground or finely chopped

Preheat the oven to 350°F. Butter a 12-cup capacity tube pan.

In a large bowl, beat together the eggs and oil. Add the sugar and vanilla and continue beating until the batter is thick, like cake icing, about 2 minutes.

Sift together the flour, baking soda, cinnamon, salt, and nutmeg. Add to the egg mixture. The batter will be quite thick. Stir in the apples and cranberries.

WILD CRANBERRIES COLLECTED ON LONG ISLAND, NEW YORK

Pour the batter in the pan. Tap the pan and shake it to evenly distribute the batter. Bake for 40 minutes, or until a cake tester inserted in the cake comes out clean (you'll smell the cake, too). Allow the cake to cool for a few minutes, then turn out the cake onto a rack. Serve at room temperature.

VARIATION

Cranberry Apple Muffins: Position the racks in the bottom and top thirds of the oven and preheat to 350°F. Line two 12-cup muffin tins with paper liners. Make the batter as directed and fill the muffin cups three-fourths full. Bake for 20 minutes, switching racks and rotating the pans front to back halfway through, until a cake tester inserted into a muffin comes out clean.

Cranberry-Orange Sauce

Cranberry sauce made from cranberries that haven't been pushed through a food mill will have some tough skins. Some people, like my husband, don't mind this. But the rough texture isn't nice in every application or for every taste. For a more refined sauce, you really must pass the cranberries through a food mill before canning. **The sauce throws off about 1 extra cup of juice. Save it to make a Madras Cocktail (page 108). MAKES 2 HALF-PINTS**

1 cup sugar, or more if you prefer a sweet rather than tart sauce

1 cup water

2 heaping cups fresh or frozen cranberries

1 cup orange juice

In a medium saucepan, dissolve the sugar in the water over medium-high heat. Boil for 2 minutes and then add the cranberries. Reduce the heat to medium-low, cover, and gently boil until the cranberries pop, about 5 minutes (it sounds like popcorn). Watch carefully—the berries easily foam up and boil over. Once the berries have exploded, uncover, and gently boil for another 20 minutes to reduce the syrup. The sauce is loose but easily mounds on a spoon. Stir in the orange juice. For a more refined sauce, press the cranberries and juice through a food mill.

Have ready 2 clean half-pint jars and bands, and new lids that have been simmered in hot water to soften the rubberized flange. Spoon the cranberries and juice into the jars leaving ½ inch of headroom. Wipe the rims, place on the lids, and screw on the bands fingertip tight.

Process the jars in a water bath (see page 375) for 15 minutes. Be sure to make altitude adjustments when preserving (see page 389).

Cranberry Mustard

This mustard is divine on turkey sandwiches and Chicken Croquettes (page 88), and an excellent condiment for pot roast or pastrami (page 61). You can alter the mustard powder, sugar, and mustard seed ratios, or add ground allspice, or really any spices you like. The Worcestershire sauce, however, is necessary. It just makes this mustard sing. This
recipe is from the Ball Complete Book of Home Preserving, *with some minor quantity and flavor adaptations.* MAKES 1 HALF-PINT

⅓ cup white wine or red wine vinegar (5% acidity)

2 tablespoons yellow mustard seeds

1½ cups fresh cranberries

1½ teaspoons Worcestershire sauce (for homemade, page 369)

3 tablespoons light brown sugar

¼ teaspoon mustard powder

Pinch of salt

In a small saucepan, bring the vinegar to a boil and add the mustard seeds. Remove from heat and allow the seeds to rest for about 15 minutes until they become saturated.

In a food processor, combine the cranberries and Worcestershire sauce and pulse to a thick paste. If necessary, add a few tablespoons of water to help the blades swirl.

In a medium saucepan, combine the mustard seeds, cranberry mixture, brown sugar, mustard powder, and salt. Bring to a boil and boil gently over medium-low heat until the mustard is thick, about 15 minutes.

Have ready 1 clean half-pint jar and band, and a new lid that has been simmered in hot water to soften the rubberized flange. Spoon the mustard into the jar leaving ¼ inch of headroom. Wipe the rim, place on the lid, and screw on the band fingertip tight.

Process the jars in a water bath (see page 375) for 10 minutes. You can double this recipe and process 1 pint for the same amount of time. Be sure to make altitude adjustments when preserving (see page 389).

Cranberry Juice

I love to have this juice on hand. Mixed with soda water, it makes a great nonalcoholic cocktail; straight, it's fabulous for your liver. Homemade cranberry juice is significantly better than that murky health food store cranberry juice or that awful Kool-Aid-y commercial stuff. This is pure heaven. I add sugar, but you don't have to, or you can add less or more. You can increase the recipe easily: every additional cup of cranberries and 1½ cups water will produce another cup of juice. You can process quarts of this juice for the same amount of time as pints. MAKES 3 PINTS

> 4 heaping cups fresh cranberries
>
> 6 cups water
>
> ½ cup sugar

In a large pot, combine the cranberries and water. Bring to a boil over medium heat and boil until the cranberries pop, about 5 minutes.

Arrange a jelly bag or a sieve lined with two layers of cheesecloth over a deep pot. Wet the bag or cheesecloth so it doesn't absorb any of the juice. Ladle the cranberries and water into the jelly bag and let the juice drip through into the pot, about 1 hour. Squeeze the bag to get all the juice.

Add the sugar to the juice. Bring to a boil over medium-low heat, allowing the sugar to gently dissolve. Don't let the juice and sugar come to a rapid boil or you could get a loose jelly!

Have ready 3 clean pint jars and bands, and new lids that have been simmered in hot water to soften the rubberized flange. Pour the cranberry juice into the jars leaving ½ inch of headroom. Wipe the rims, place on the lids, and screw on the bands fingertip tight.

Process the jars in a water bath (see page 375) for 15 minutes. Be sure to make altitude adjustments when preserving (see page 389). You might notice some sediment in the jars. It's okay.

Apples Stuffed with Cranberry Sauce

I love love love this recipe. It is so simple and the flavors are very bold and American. It is much better than straight cranberry sauce at Thanksgiving. You can make this dish with any cranberry sauce. SERVES 4

> 4 baking apples, such as Jonathan
>
> 4 heaping tablespoons Cranberry-Orange Sauce (page 104)
>
> 1 cup apple cider

Preheat the oven to 350°F.

Slice the stem end off the apples and using a corer or serrated spoon, scoop out the seeds, making a cavity large enough to hold 2 tablespoons in each apple. Trim the bottom of the apple so that it stands solidly. Stuff each apple with a heaping tablespoon of cranberry sauce.

Place the apples in an 8-inch square baking dish—or whatever they will fit in snugly; a cast-iron skillet will do, too. Pour the cider into the pan and place in the oven. Bake for 45 minutes, or until the apples are tender but not exploded looking. (Overcooking baked apples is one of my many kitchen afflictions. I even have a recipe that utilizes overcooked baked apples, page 9.)

Serve hot or at room temperature.

APPLES
STUFFED WITH
CRANBERRY
SAUCE

Cranberry Crepes

I like to serve these for breakfast or brunch. They are not sweet, more like blintzes, but less heavy. I don't bother keeping the crepes warm in the oven as I make them. I find that layering the cooked crepes with sheets of wax paper keeps them warm enough for me.

SERVES 4

¾ cup all-purpose flour

3 tablespoons granulated sugar

1 teaspoon baking powder

2 large eggs

⅔ cup whole milk

⅓ cup water

1 teaspoon grated orange zest, plus more for garnish

½ cup Cranberry-Orange Sauce (page 104)

½ cup cream cheese, at room temperature (4 ounces)

3 tablespoons cold unsalted butter

Confectioners' sugar, for garnish (optional)

In a large bowl, combine the flour, granulated sugar, and baking powder. In a separate bowl, whisk together the eggs, milk, water, and orange zest. Add the wet ingredients to the dry and whisk together. Refrigerate for about 30 minutes.

If you didn't do this when preparing the Cranberry-Orange Sauce, then push the cranberry sauce through a food mill to separate out the skins and combine it in a small bowl with the cream cheese.

See "Preparing Crepes" (page 395).

Spread the cranberry cream cheese onto the crepes and roll them up. Serve with a dusting of confectioners' sugar if you'd like. A little extra orange zest on top is nice, too.

MADRAS COCKTAIL

Madras Cocktail

I generally have this cocktail after I make Cranberry-Orange Sauce. But the cranberry juice refrigerates well and will hold for a few days.

MAKES TWO 6-OUNCE COCKTAILS

1 cup cranberry-orange juice (from Cranberry-Orange Sauce, page 104)

4 ounces vodka

Strain the cranberry-orange juice through a fine-mesh sieve. Combine with the vodka and serve in rocks glasses filled with ice.

CUCUMBERS

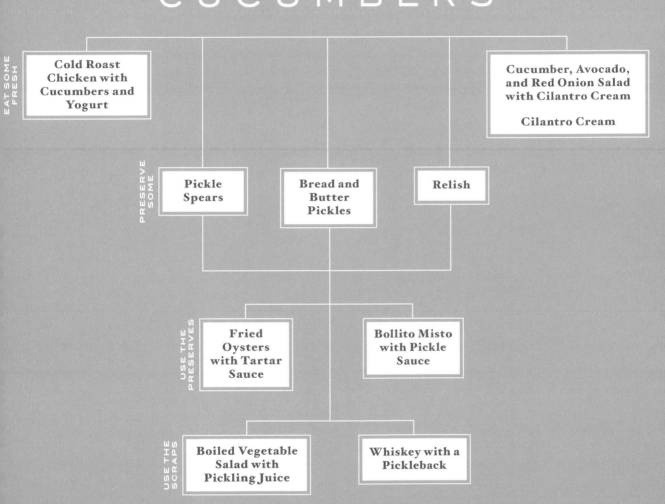

EAT SOME FRESH

Cold Roast Chicken with Cucumbers and Yogurt

Cucumber, Avocado, and Red Onion Salad with Cilantro Cream

Cilantro Cream

PRESERVE SOME

Pickle Spears

Bread and Butter Pickles

Relish

USE THE PRESERVES

Fried Oysters with Tartar Sauce

Bollito Misto with Pickle Sauce

USE THE SCRAPS

Boiled Vegetable Salad with Pickling Juice

Whiskey with a Pickleback

Cold Roast Chicken with Cucumbers and Yogurt

I make this dish in the summer, when a cold chicken dish is the most welcome. I like to serve it with pita bread, as the yogurt/cucumber combination is typical of eastern Mediterranean cuisine, but be sure to use young cucumbers: Big giant ones have lots of seeds (see Note). **The bones from a whole roasted chicken make a good stock, so save the carcass for Chicken Stock (page 89).** SERVES 4

>One 4-pound chicken
>
>½ lemon
>
>2 sprigs of fresh rosemary
>
>Handful of fresh oregano leaves or
>   1 tablespoon dried
>
>Salt and freshly ground black pepper
>
>Olive oil
>
>¼ cup white wine
>
>2 small cucumbers, peeled and cut into tiny
>   cubes
>
>1 cup plain yogurt (for homemade, page 370)
>
>2 tablespoons minced garlic (or skordalia,
>   for homemade, page 368)

Preheat the oven to 400°F.

Wash the chicken and dry it. Stuff the cavity of the chicken with the lemon, rosemary, and fresh oregano. If you use dried oregano, sprinkle it over the top of the bird. Truss the chicken (see page 83).

Place on a rack in a roasting pan. Sprinkle the bird with salt and pepper, drizzle with oil, and pour the wine in the pan. Roast for 1 hour, then cover and roast until the juices run clear and the internal temperature at the thigh is 165°F, another 20 minutes or so.

Remove the chicken and let it come to room temperature, then wrap it in foil and refrigerate for up to 24 hours. (You can also serve the chicken at room temperature.)

Twenty minutes before serving the chicken, make the cucumber sauce. In a bowl, combine the cucumber, yogurt, garlic, and salt to taste and let rest, covered for 20 minutes, to allow the flavors to meld. Keep in mind that the longer you let the cucumber sauce rest, the more water the cucumbers will release (a result of having added salt), which is delicious, but it will loosen the yogurt sauce.

Cut the roast chicken into serving pieces and slice the breast. Serve with the cucumber yogurt sauce.

Note: For easy seeding, carefully scrape the tip of a spoon along the center of the cucumber, carving out the seeds as you go.

Cucumber, Avocado, and Red Onion Salad with Cilantro Cream

The cilantro cream is wonderful with the salad; however, if you dump the cream on top and toss, you will end up with a very tasty but a very green looking salad. Like, bright green. So I prefer to drizzle the cream on, and not toss it in. You can also deconstruct the sauce, and simply add to the salad a handful of toasted pine nuts, a handful of chopped fresh cilantro, and a dollop of sour cream. The cilantro cream is also fabulous with Pork Tacos (page 261). SERVES 4

>2 large cucumbers, peeled, seeded, and sliced
>
>2 Hass avocados, peeled and sliced
>
>1 cup thinly sliced red onion
>
>3 tablespoons olive oil
>
>Juice from ½ lemon

Salt and freshly ground black pepper
Cilantro Cream (recipe follows)

Combine the cucumbers, avocados, and red onion in a serving bowl. Add the oil, lemon juice, and salt and pepper to taste and toss gently.

Drizzle the cilantro cream over the salad but do not toss, and serve.

CILANTRO CREAM

MAKES ABOUT ½ CUP

1 cup loosely packed cilantro

3 tablespoons chicken stock (for homemade, page 09) or water

2 tablespoons pine nuts

2 tablespoons sour cream or crème fraîche (for homemade, page 362)

Salt and freshly ground black pepper

In a blender or mini food processor, combine the cilantro, chicken stock, pine nuts, and sour cream and process to a very smooth puree. Season to taste.

Cucumber Pickles

Long (over 4-inch) cucumbers are used for eating, and the shorter, stubby ones are used for pickling, as they are convenient to pack into jars. Dill pickles are cucumber pickles cured with dill. Gherkins are cucumber cultivars grown for pickling. Cornichons are miniature gherkins. You don't have to peel a cucumber unless it has been waxed, and unfortunately many of the cucumbers in the grocery store are: You can tell because they are shiny and feel super-smooth, like plastic. Luckily, picklers are never waxed.

Cucumber pickles are safe, easy, and cheap to make, and I think everyone should give it a try, but don't be disappointed if your first batch is not perfect. If you produce shriveled-looking pickles, that's probably because you overprocessed (too much time in the hot water bath), or you used a too-intense vinegar and salt brine. Shriveled pickles don't look great but they are okay to eat. Hollow pickles happen when you use pickles that are too mature. They too are still safe to eat. But very soft, slippery pickles should be thrown away. They've spoiled because bacteria were able to flourish in the jar, usually the result of a poor seal or a brine with too little acid to kill the bacteria. Slippery, soft cucumbers are not to be confused with pickles that are just not crunchy, a perennial problem for picklers. The trick to crisp pickles is to start with crisp cucumbers and remove the blossom ends, which are a source of microbes that can cause spoilage.

CUCUMBER PICKLES

Pickle Spears

These are also known as picnic cucumbers and they are marvelous. You can dilly them by adding a dill flower to each jar. **The leftover brine, either from putting up the pickles or what is left after the pickles have been eaten, has numerous uses. See Iceberg Wedges with Ranch Pickle Juice Dressing (page 358) and Boiled Vegetable Salad with Pickling Juice (page 116), for example.**

MAKES 2 PINTS

> 1 pound pickling cucumbers
>
> 5 cups water
>
> 2½ tablespoons pickling salt
>
> 4 garlic cloves, peeled
>
> 2 small dried hot peppers
>
> ¾ cup distilled white vinegar (5% acidity)
>
> 1 tablespoon sugar

Cut the blossom ends off the cucumbers and slice lengthwise into spears. Cut them into lengths short enough to fit into a pint jar, but no higher than the screw marks on the jar. In a large bowl, combine the 4 cups of water and 1½ tablespoons of the salt. Add the spears and let them soak for 12 hours.

Have ready 2 clean pint jars and bands, and new lids that have been simmered in hot water to soften the rubberized flange. Drain and pack the spears into the jars. Tuck 2 garlic cloves and 1 hot pepper into each jar.

In a small saucepan, combine the vinegar, sugar, and remaining 1 cup water and 1 tablespoon salt. Bring to a boil over medium heat. As soon as it begins to boil, take it off the heat and pour over the spears, leaving ½ inch of headroom. Wipe the rims, place on the lids, and screw on the bands fingertip tight.

Process the jars in a water bath (see page 375) for 10 minutes for pints, 15 minutes for 1 quart jar. Be sure to make altitude adjustments when preserving (see page 389).

Bread and Butter Pickles

I make these to use on all types of sandwiches, like egg salad and Cuban sandwiches (page 356). **Be sure to save the leftover brine (see page 116).**

MAKES 3 PINTS

> 4 cups sliced pickling cucumbers, with blossom ends removed
>
> 1 cup sliced white onions
>
> 3 garlic cloves, smashed and peeled
>
> 1 tablespoon pickling salt
>
> A couple of trays of ice cubes
>
> 1 cup distilled white vinegar (5% acidity)
>
> 1⅓ cups sugar
>
> 1 teaspoon mustard seeds (brown, yellow, or a combination)
>
> ½ teaspoon turmeric

In a large bowl, combine the cucumbers, onions, garlic, and salt. Toss well and cover with ice cubes. Let rest for 3 hours. Drain.

In a large pot, combine the vinegar, sugar, mustard seeds, and turmeric and bring to a boil over medium heat. Add the cucumbers and simmer in the vinegar solution for 5 minutes.

Have ready 3 clean pint jars and bands, and new lids that have been simmered in hot water to soften the rubberized flange. Pack the cucumbers into the jars and cover with the vinegar solution leaving ½ inch of headroom. Be sure the garlic and spices are well distributed among the jars. Wipe the rims, place on the lids, and screw on the bands fingertip tight.

Process the jars in a water bath (see page 375) for 10 minutes. Be sure to make altitude adjustments when preserving (see page 389). Allow the pickles to rest 1 month or so to develop flavor.

Relish

I prefer relish to other pickled cucumber products because it works in so many other recipes, like homemade Tartar Sauce (right) and the piquant sauce for Bollito Misto (page 114), an Italian boiled dinner. Plus it is just really easy to put up, and doesn't call for a ton of cucumbers. Relish is wonderful with bell peppers as well. You can substitute ½ cup of the cucumbers with minced red bell peppers if you'd like.

MAKES 3 HALF-PINTS

> 1½ cups distilled or white wine vinegar (5% acidity)
>
> 3 tablespoons sugar
>
> 2 garlic cloves, minced
>
> 3¾ teaspoons pickling salt
>
> ¾ teaspoon dill seed
>
> 3½ cups finely chopped pickling cucumbers
>
> ½ cup finely chopped onion

In a small pot, combine the vinegar, sugar, garlic, salt, and dill seed. Bring to a boil over medium heat, add the cucumbers and onion, and stir to combine—it's okay if the vegetables are not covered with the vinegar solution. Cover, reduce the heat, and simmer for 10 minutes.

Have ready 3 clean half-pint jars and bands, and new lids that have been simmered in hot water to soften the rubberized flange. Pack the relish into the jars, and cover with the vinegar solution leaving ½ inch of headroom. Wipe the rims, place on the lids, and screw on the bands fingertip tight.

Process the jars in a water bath (see page 375) for 15 minutes. Be sure to make altitude adjustments when preserving (see page 389). The relish may look a bit washed out color-wise, but it's okay.

Tartar Sauce

Sometimes I prepare fried fish just so that I can have the tartar sauce. It's great with a whole flounder fillet, or fish sticks, calamari, or spearing (sometimes called whitebait, they're little silver minnows fried whole). **MAKES 1 CUP**

> 1 cup mayonnaise (for homemade, page 365)
>
> 3 tablespoons pickle relish, minced bread and butter pickles, or minced pickle spears (for homemade, above and opposite)
>
> 1 tablespoon minced fresh dill, parsley, or cilantro

In a small bowl, combine the mayonnaise, pickle, and herbs. Chill. To hold in the fridge for up to 4 days, place a piece of plastic wrap over the bowl, patted down on top of the tartar sauce, so it doesn't develop a skin.

Bollito Misto

One spring morning I went to Arthur Avenue, an Italian neighborhood in the Bronx, with my friend Alex Neil. Alex had just lost her mother and I thought it might be nice for us to hang out with my dad, who goes there every Friday to shop. Dad was eighty-five at the time, tough and sturdy as a work boot, and still cooking. His first book, *Italian Family Cooking* (1971), is the best Italian cookbook I know. If you find one on eBay, you'll probably be bidding against me.

Alex is an actress and once my dad got a load of her—she's like a delicate Jessica Lange— he became superfriendly and enthusiastic about showing her the neighborhood. He walked us to the 17,500-square-foot indoor marketplace at the epicenter of Arthur Avenue where we bought baby artichokes, broccoli rabe, herbs, and leeks. For every item Dad had a suggestion: poach the artichokes in chicken stock, bake the rabe in a hot oven with dried black olives, sauté the leeks as a base for *brodetto*, a fish stew.

There are a few sumptuous meat stores on Arthur Avenue, but Dad is loyal to Biancardi's, which carries everything the carnivore could desire: rabbit, goat, baby lamb, capon, duck, pig's feet, rack of lamb, veal, and all the offal available every day. When we entered Biancardi's, Sal said "Hi, Eddie," and they promptly began talking about a rabbit Dad got from d'Artagnan that was so big it fed seven people. "Seven damn people," Dad said. "Seven people?" Sal asked. "Yeah," replied Dad, "seven damn people." "Seven?" asked Sal, smiling so affectionately at my dad that my heart swelled. Alex and I walked the long display case, making our choices: osso buco, at a third of the cost in Manhattan, a fat capon breast stuffed with dried cranberries, and a long floppy flank steak, all of which Sal vacuum-packed so we could freeze them when we got home.

While my father took the bags to our car, Alex hugged me—"Thank you so much, this is so great"—and then Dad came back and told us that everyone was talking about the bollito misto (mixed boil) at Tra Di Noi, an excellent restaurant on 187th Street and would we like to have an early lunch? After consulting our phones idiotically for a few minutes, we decided life was too short not to have lunch with him that afternoon.

The bollito misto was beautiful: perfectly boiled pieces of beef tongue, short rib, chicken thigh, a potato, celery, and carrot. Warm in its silky broth, made sweet by the gelatin in the meats, it was an essay in graceful, uncomplicated cooking by chef/owner Marco Coletta. And yet what really blew me away—what always ends up blowing me away—was the simplest dish of all: the relish sauce that was served with the boiled meat. It was like a chimichurri, but sweeter, because of the addition of minced pickle, and so damn good that today I make bollito misto just so I can eat the sauce. But I also make it because it reminds me never to put off an opportunity to have lunch with people I love.

Fried Oysters
with Tartar Sauce

With a nice ripe tomato salad there isn't a more summery dinner. I usually use my own breadcrumbs, but for this dish I like a very crispy crust. Japanese panko breadcrumbs, widely available in grocery stores, do that best. You can use bottled oysters in this dish. Just drain them well (and use the stock in your next fish soup). You can also make a Po Boy sandwich by filling a soft white baguette with the fried oysters, tartar sauce, and shredded iceberg lettuce. SERVES 4

- 1 scant cup all-purpose flour (see Note)
- 2 large eggs, beaten
- 2 cups panko breadcrumbs, finely ground in the food processor
- 24 plump oysters, drained and patted dry
- Neutral oil, such as safflower, for frying
- Salt
- 1 lemon, cut into wedges
- 1 cup tartar sauce (for homemade, page 113)

Have ready 3 shallow bowls. Place the flour in one, the eggs in another, and the panko in a third. Dredge the oysters in the flour, dunk in the egg, and cover with the panko.

Meanwhile, in a large nonstick skillet, heat ½ inch of oil. Add the oysters and fry them until golden, a minute or two, then turn them over and fry for a few minutes more. Drain on brown paper bags or paper towels. Season with salt to taste.

Serve the oysters with the lemon wedges and tartar sauce.

Note: The best flour for frying is Wondra. It produces a very light, crispy crust. Indeed, sometimes I forgo the panko and simply dunk the oysters in milk, then in Wondra, and fry.

Bollito Misto
with Pickle Sauce

You can add Brussels sprouts, parsnips, or leeks to the bollito misto if you'd like, or substitute tongue, cotechino sausage, or bone-in beef shank for any of the meats. Think of this recipe more as a method. You may want to make the sauce first as it is best after resting a few hours, and you can vary the ingredients to your taste, adding capers, scallions, tarragon, and basil . . . whatever you have around. You can use just extra virgin olive oil as a dressing for bollito misto, too. Colman's mustard is good, as are pestos of all sorts. This recipe is adapted from Pleasures of the Good Earth *by Edward Giobbi.* SERVES 6

PICKLE SAUCE
- 2 tablespoons chopped flat-leaf parsley
- 1 tablespoon minced garlic
- 1 tablespoon relish (for homemade, page 113)
- 1 tablespoon minced red bell pepper
- Squirt of lemon juice
- Salt and freshly ground black pepper
- ¼ cup olive oil

BOLLITO MISTO
- 6 beef short ribs
- 12 cups water
- 1 medium onion, cut in quarters
- 2 ribs celery, cut into thirds
- 1 large bay leaf
- 6 chicken thighs, bone in, skin off
- 1 kielbasa sausage about 8 inches long
- 6 small potatoes, peeled
- 3 medium carrots, halved
- Salt and freshly ground black pepper

For the pickle sauce: Mince the parsley, garlic, relish, and red bell pepper together. If you use a food processor, be sure you pulse so that the sauce doesn't become creamy. Place in a bowl and add the lemon juice, and salt and black pepper to taste. Stir in the olive oil. Let marinate for a couple of hours.

For the bollito misto: In a large soup pot, combine the beef, water, onion, celery, and bay leaf. Cover, bring to a boil, and boil gently for 1 hour, skimming the scum as it rises. Add the chicken and cook 30 minutes. Add the kielbasa, potatoes, carrots, and salt and pepper to taste and cook 30 minutes.

Remove the meat and cut the kielbasa into slices. Remove the carrots and potatoes with a slotted spoon. Place the meat and vegetables on a platter. Strain the broth and defat it. Drizzle a bit of the broth over the meat to keep it moist. Serve the bollito misto with the relish sauce.

The broth is delicious. You can serve it as a first course: boil bird's nest pasta in the broth and serve with grated Parmesan and black pepper.

HOW TO USE PICKLE BRINE

I used to throw out pickle brine left in the jar, but now I save it for all sorts of uses—really, anywhere I use vinegar (except in canning). Below are two uses.

Boiled Vegetable Salad with Pickling Juice

Bring a large pot of water to a boil over high heat. Add small peeled potatoes and carrots cut into bite-size pieces and boil about 10 minutes, then add cauliflower cut into bite-size pieces and Brussels sprouts and continue boiling for another 10 minutes or so, until all the vegetables are tender. Drain and toss in a bowl with pickle juice, minced fresh dill, and black pepper. Drizzle with extra virgin olive oil. It's okay if there are some pickling spices in there, but remove hunks of garlic or hot pepper, or any big seeds that might not be easy to digest. Allow the vegetables to marinate for 20 minutes or so, until the flavors meld. You can put this dish in the refrigerator without the dill and it will just get better, but eat within 24 hours or so; add the dill before serving.

Whiskey with a Pickleback

The pickleback, a whisky chaser, has emerged as a byproduct of the hipster mixologist/fermenting phenomenon. It's certainly a great way to enjoy that wonderful leftover pickle juice from your jars (though not the brine from bread and butter pickles, because it's too sweet). Just serve a shot of good whiskey with a small glass of pickle juice on the side.

CURRANTS

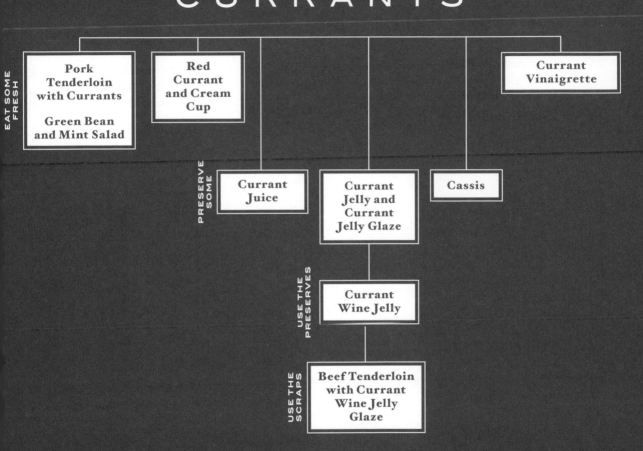

EAT SOME FRESH

Pork Tenderloin with Currants

Green Bean and Mint Salad

Red Currant and Cream Cup

Currant Vinaigrette

PRESERVE SOME

Currant Juice

Currant Jelly and Currant Jelly Glaze

Cassis

USE THE PRESERVES

Currant Wine Jelly

USE THE SCRAPS

Beef Tenderloin with Currant Wine Jelly Glaze

PORK TENDERLOIN
WITH CURRANTS

Pork Tenderloin with Currants

Currants add a lovely tart flavor to this sweet roasted pork. Plus it looks gorgeous. Plus it takes only 20 minutes to make. I love it with a Green Bean and Mint Salad (recipe follows). **SERVES 4**

- 1½ pounds pork tenderloin
- 2 tablespoons olive oil
- Salt and freshly ground black pepper
- 3 tablespoons minced garlic
- 2 tablespoons fresh thyme leaves
- 2 tablespoons balsamic vinegar
- ½ cup dry white or rosé wine
- ½ cup sliced shallots
- ¾ cup red currants
- ½ cup beef stock (for homemade, page 47)

Preheat the oven to 500°F.

Rub the tenderloin with the oil. Season the meat with salt and pepper and sprinkle garlic and thyme all over it. Place in a small baking pan and pour the vinegar over the meat. Add the wine and shallots to the pan.

Bake for 10 minutes, then add the currants. Bake for 10 minutes longer, or until the internal temperature of the roast is 145°F (lower than you may be used to, but this is the most updated USDA data). If the wine cooks off in less than 20 minutes, add the beef stock to the pan as soon as it looks dry. Remove from the heat and cover with foil. Allow the roast to rest about 5 minutes before carving.

GREEN BEAN AND MINT SALAD

This salad shows off the flavor of green beans better than any I know. And it gets better if it sits for a while—I usually make it about an hour before serving. **SERVES 4**

- 1 pound green beans, snapped into 2-inch pieces
- ½ cup chopped fresh mint
- 2 tablespoons extra virgin olive oil
- 1 tablespoon minced garlic
- 1 tablespoon fresh lemon juice
- Salt and freshly ground black pepper

Bring a large pot of water to a boil over high heat. Add the beans and boil them until they are bright green and tender, but still snappy, about 5 minutes. Drain the beans and run them under cold water to stop the cooking.

Toss the beans in a big serving bowl with ¼ cup of the mint, the oil, garlic, lemon juice, and salt and pepper to taste. Just before serving, toss in the last ¼ cup mint (to be sure to have some perky-looking herbs on the plate).

Red Currant and Cream Cup

This recipe is from The Home Book of German Cookery *(1979), with some changes in the quantities. It is basically a mousse. It is very simple, very tasty, very pretty, and can be prepared ahead of time.* **SERVES 4**

- 1 pound red currants
- ½ cup sugar
- 2 tablespoons cold water
- 2½ teaspoons unflavored powdered gelatin (1 envelope)
- 2 cups heavy cream

Set aside about ¼ cup of currants for the garnish. Pass the remaining currants through a food mill to remove the seeds and stems.

In a medium pot, combine the pulp and sugar and heat over medium heat to dissolve the sugar.

Meanwhile, place the water in a small bowl and sprinkle the gelatin on top. Stir to combine, and let rest for a few minutes to allow the gelatin to bloom (swell and soften).

Add the gelatin to the hot currant mixture and stir well, until the gelatin is thoroughly dissolved. Set aside and let come to room temperature.

In a large bowl, with an electric mixer, whip the cream until it forms soft peaks. Stir the currant mixture into the whipped cream until well combined. Spoon the red currant cream into 4 glasses and refrigerate for a few hours and up to 24. Serve garnished with the fresh currants.

Currant Juice

Few things are more healthful than a fresh cup of this vitamin C–rich juice in the morning, or, mixed with soda water and ice, a glass in the afternoon. For a less virtuous option, combine the juice with Guinness, hard cider, or lager beer. Unfortunately you can't make anything from the currant mash left over from straining off the juice, as you can with raspberries. The seeds are prohibitively bitter. The timing for canning this juice comes from the Ball Complete Book of Home Preserving. **MAKES ABOUT 3 CUPS**

> 2 pounds currants, black, red, white, or a combination
>
> 4 cups water
>
> Sugar (optional)

In a large heavy-bottomed pot, combine the currants and water and bring to a boil over medium-low heat. Gently boil for about 10 minutes. Remove the juice from the heat and let cool.

Arrange your jelly bag or a sieve lined with two layers of cheesecloth over a deep pot. Wet the bag or cheesecloth so it doesn't absorb any of the juice. Ladle the currant mash and water into the jelly bag and let the juice drip through into the pot. (You aren't supposed to squeeze the jelly bag because it can make the juice cloudy, but I do a little pressing anyway, to speed the process up, and have never had a problem.)

The juice is quite tart. You can reheat this juice with sugar to taste over medium heat, just long enough to dissolve the sugar. See page 393 for instructions on refrigerating and freezing juice.

To can, have ready 3 half-pints jars and bands, with new lids that have been simmered in hot water to soften the rubberized flange. Pour the juice into the jars leaving ¼ inch of headroom. Wipe the rims, place on the lids, and screw on the bands fingertip tight.

Process in a water bath for 15 minutes (see page 375). Be sure to make altitude adjustments when preserving (see page 389).

Currant Jelly

Currant jelly is excellent on toast but also perfect as a glaze on fruit tarts, lending a delicate layer of flavor and an appealing gloss. Sometimes I have about ⅓ cup of leftover jelly: too small an amount to can, but just enough to make Currant Wine Jelly (page 122). The timing for processing this jelly comes from the Ball Complete Book of Home Preserving. **MAKES 3 HALF-PINTS**

> 3 cups Currant Juice (left)
>
> 3 cups sugar

CURRANT JUICE

CURRANT JELLY

In a 6- to 8-quart heavy-bottomed pot, combine the currant juice and sugar. Bring to a boil over medium-low heat, allowing the sugar to dissolve. Increase the heat and boil the juice hard until a candy thermometer reaches 220°F at sea level, or 8°F over boiling temperature wherever you are. (To calculate the boiling temperature at your altitude, see page 389.) Watch the bubbles: When they take on color, the jelly is usually ready, about 20 minutes. You can also test the jelly by letting a spoonful cool in the fridge for a couple of minutes. If the jelly drips off the spoon in dribbles, it's not ready. If it shears off the spoon in a single drop, it is.

Have ready 3 clean half-pint jars and bands, and new lids that have been simmered in hot water to soften the rubberized flange. (See "How to Sterilize," page 389.) Pour the jelly into the jars leaving ¼ inch of headroom. Wipe the

rims, place on the lids, and screw on the bands fingertip tight.

Process the jars in a water bath (see page 375) for 10 minutes. Be sure to make altitude adjustments when preserving (see page 389).

CURRANT JELLY GLAZE

To use in sweet applications, melt 2 tablespoons of currant jelly in a small saucepan over low heat, less than a minute. Brush the melted jelly over open-faced fruit pastries, like tarts and galettes, after the pastry has come out of the oven. You can also dip whole strawberries in the hot jelly, then chill.

To use in savory applications, like on baked ham, roast lamb, pork roast, ribs, or poultry, heat ¼ cup currant jelly in a small saucepan over low heat until melted, less than a minute. Brush the melted jelly on the meat during the latter half of the cooking. You can also drizzle heated currant jelly over beef or lamb stew. It lends a delicate sweet tartness that adds an additional layer of flavor.

Currant Vinaigrette

This is a lovely vinaigrette made from a small amount of fresh currant juice rather than vinegar. It is especially good over butter lettuce or Boston lettuce. I hold the juice in the fridge and then make the vinaigrette fresh as I need it. **MAKES ½ CUP/ ENOUGH TO DRESS 8 SERVINGS OF SALAD**

2 tablespoons Currant Juice (page 120)

2 teaspoons mustard (for homemade, page 366)

Salt and freshly ground black pepper

6 tablespoons neutral oil, such as safflower

In a small bowl, whisk together the currant juice, mustard, and salt and pepper to taste. Add the oil in a slow drizzle, whisking all the while, until the vinaigrette thickens slightly.

Cassis

The first time I made cassis I have to say, I experienced a flush of DIY pride. I doused every glass of prosecco I served for an entire summer with the stuff. Cassis can also be added to white wine to make a Kir (named for a French mayor who popularized the drink), or to champagne, to make a Kir Royale. **MAKES ABOUT 1 PINT**

½ pound black currants, though red will do

1½ cups dry white or red wine

Sugar, as needed

Place the currants in a bowl and crush them slightly. Cover with the wine. Cover the bowl with plastic wrap and let it sit for 48 hours

Strain the currant mixture through a fine-mesh sieve into a bowl. Measure how much juice you have. Pour into a small saucepan. Add half that amount in sugar: So if you have 2 cups of juice, add 1 cup sugar.

Bring the juice and sugar mixture to a boil, then turn off the heat and let cool.

Pour into a sterilized 16-ounce bottle and cap—I just use an old vinegar bottle with a screw-on cap. (See "How to Sterilize," page 389.) The cassis will hold forever in the refrigerator, and months in the liquor cabinet.

Currant Wine Jelly

It is rare that every time you make a jelly recipe the volume will turn out exactly right. When I have that extra ⅓ cup or so that is just too small to can, I make this jelly with Pomona's Universal pectin. **MAKES 1 HALF-PINT**

⅓ to ½ cup leftover Currant Jelly (page 120)

¾ teaspoon calcium water (comes in the Pomona's package)

1 teaspoon powdered pectin

½ cup dry or sweet white, red, or rosé wine

Pour the jelly into a small saucepan and place over medium heat. Bring the jelly to a boil, take off heat, and add the calcium water and pectin, mixing well. Add the wine, return to the heat, and boil for 2 to 3 minutes.

Have ready 1 clean half-pint jar and band, and a new lid that has been simmered in hot water to soften the rubberized flange. Pour the jelly into the jar leaving ¼ inch of headroom. Wipe the rim, place on the lid, and screw on the band fingertip tight.

Process the jars in a water bath (see page 375) for 10 minutes. (It can be processed at the same time as Currant Jelly.) Be sure to make altitude adjustments when preserving (see page 389).

Beef Tenderloin with Currant Wine Jelly Glaze

This is a deceptively simple recipe for such a fancy dish. It's perfect for a Valentine's Day supper. The recipe doubles well, though watch the garlic. I like to serve this dish with Ginger Carrot Soufflé (page 70).

SERVES 2

2 beef tenderloin filets (about 6 ounces each)

Salt

½ cup beef stock (for homemade, page 47)

1 tablespoon minced garlic

1 tablespoon chopped fresh thyme leaves

10 black peppercorns, crushed

1 bay leaf

2 tablespoons Currant Wine Jelly (opposite)

½ cup dry white or red wine (optional)

Heat a cast-iron skillet over high heat until very hot. Season the beef and place in the skillet. Sear until well browned, about 2 minutes per side. Add the beef stock, garlic, thyme, peppercorns, and bay leaf and continue cooking over high heat for a minute or two, flipping the steaks over once or twice for medium rare. Spoon 1 tablespoon jelly over each filet, then remove the meat from the pan and allow it to rest for 5 minutes before serving.

You can make a little sauce with the pan drippings if you wish: Just add ½ cup wine to the skillet and bring to a boil. Reduce by half, strain the sauce through a small fine-mesh sieve, and pour half of the sauce onto the bottom of each plate. Place the filet on top.

BEEF TENDERLOIN WITH CURRANT WINE JELLY GLAZE

D U C K

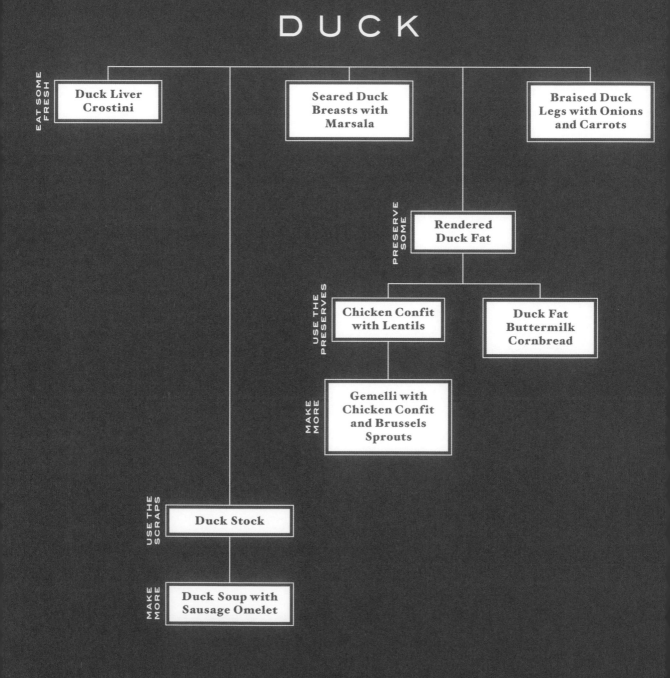

EAT SOME FRESH

Duck Liver Crostini

Seared Duck Breasts with Marsala

Braised Duck Legs with Onions and Carrots

PRESERVE SOME

Rendered Duck Fat

USE THE PRESERVES

Chicken Confit with Lentils

Duck Fat Buttermilk Cornbread

MAKE MORE

Gemelli with Chicken Confit and Brussels Sprouts

USE THE SCRAPS

Duck Stock

MAKE MORE

Duck Soup with Sausage Omelet

Duck Liver Crostini

Duck liver pâté spread on small pieces of toasted baguette makes a marvelous hors d'oeuvre. You can make this dish with chicken livers, too. **SERVES 2 AS AN APPETIZER**

- 1 large duck liver (around 60 grams)
- 1 tablespoon rendered duck fat (for homemade, page 126)
- 1 tablespoon unsalted butter
- 1 tablespoon minced shallots
- Salt and freshly ground black pepper
- 2 tablespoons brandy
- 1 teaspoon fresh lemon juice
- Hot sauce (for homemade, page 365)
- 1 teaspoon minced fresh thyme leaves
- 4 slices bread, toasted

Coarsely chop the liver.

In a small skillet, heat the duck fat and butter over high heat. Add the shallots and cook until translucent, a few minutes. Add the liver and salt and pepper to taste and cook until browned all over, about 5 minutes.

Using a mini food processor or a mortar and pestle, mash the livers with the brandy, lemon juice, and a few drops of hot sauce until smooth. Stir in the thyme and pack the pâté into a ramekin. Chill until it sets.

Serve smeared on the toasted bread.

Seared Duck Breasts with Marsala

This is a very basic, yet totally delicious way to prepare duck breast. You can add any herbs or spices you like to the marinade. You can also deglaze the pan with Red Wine Reduction Sauce (page 366) or Currant Jelly (page 120) instead of the Marsala. **Save the rendered duck fat and use it to sauté vegetables.** **SERVES 4**

- 2 boneless Pekin duck breasts
- 2 tablespoons olive oil
- 2 garlic cloves, smashed and peeled
- 6 sprigs of fresh thyme
- 1 bay leaf
- One 2-inch strip of lemon zest
- Salt and freshly ground black pepper
- 6 tablespoons dry Marsala or brandy
- 2 cups duck or chicken stock (for homemade, pages 131 or 89)
- 4 tablespoons (½ stick) unsalted butter
- 1 tablespoon fresh thyme leaves

Score the fat of the duck breasts in a crosshatch pattern with the tip of a sharp knife. Place the breasts in a bowl or plastic food storage bag with the oil, garlic, 2 sprigs of thyme, bay leaf, lemon zest, and salt and pepper to taste. Marinate unrefrigerated until the breasts come to room temperature. Remove the breasts from the marinade.

Place the breasts in a cold skillet fat-side down. Place the pan over low heat and very slowly cook the breasts, pouring off the fat as it renders off the duck. Cook until the duck is medium-rare, about 20 minutes. Press on the breasts with your finger. They should be quite firm to the touch. Increase the heat to high in order to crisp the skin. Cook for a few minutes, and then flip the breasts over to sear the other side, a few minutes more. Transfer the breasts to a cutting board, cover with foil to keep warm, and let rest for about 10 minutes. Pour off the rendered fat.

Add the Marsala to the pan and cook over medium heat, stirring to scrape the browned bits on the bottom of the pan. Add the stock, bring to a boil, and reduce by half. Swirl in the butter and thyme. Check the seasoning.

Slice the breasts. Pour the sauce over the meat and garnish with the remaining thyme sprigs.

Braised Duck Legs with Onions and Carrots

This is real home cooking, simple and hearty. I also cook duck legs in my homemade Sauerkraut with Caraway Seeds (page 60). Just add the sauerkraut in place of the carrots and onions. **When you brown the duck legs they will throw off a few tablespoons of fat. Use it to sauté vegetables. It is delicious, much better than butter.** SERVES 4

- 4 duck legs (drumsticks and thighs)
- 4 carrots, coarsely chopped
- 2 medium onions, coarsely chopped
- 2 to 3 cups duck stock (for homemade, page 131), chicken stock (for homemade, page 89), or a combination
- 4 garlic cloves, chopped
- ¼ cup chopped flat-leaf parsley
- Salt and freshly ground black pepper
- 12 tiny yellow potatoes, such as Yukon Gold or German Butterball (about ¾ pound)
- Bread, for serving

Preheat the oven to 350°F.

Heat a large Dutch oven over medium-high heat. Add the duck legs, reduce the heat to medium-low, and cook until they are browned all over, about 15 minutes. Remove the legs and transfer to a plate. Pour the fat out of the pan.

Return the Dutch oven to the heat. Add the carrots and onions and cook until the carrots are tender, about 10 minutes. Return the legs to the pot, add 2 cups of the stock, the garlic, parsley, and salt and pepper to taste. Cover, place in the oven, and bake for 30 minutes. Add the potatoes. If the pot looks dry, add another ½ cup to 1 cup of stock. Cover and bake 15 minutes longer, until the potatoes are tender.

Serve in bowls with big pieces of bread.

Rendered Duck Fat

Duck fat is rich but light, easy to digest, and just one of the best cooking fats. Use it to preserve meats, sauté vegetables, or in savory baking such as Duck Fat Buttermilk Cornbread (page 128). MAKES ABOUT 1 PINT

Cut off the fat and skin from a 5- to 6-pound duck (but leave some of the fat and skin on the legs, thighs, and breasts for cooking). Chop it and place in a small heavy pot over low heat. Cook the skin and fat until the fat is rendered and is clear, about 1 hour 45 minutes. Let cool to room temperature. Have ready a sieve lined with cheesecloth placed over a bowl. Strain the fat through the cheesecloth.

Have ready 1 sterilized pint jar, band, and lid. (See "How to Sterilize," page 389.) You do not need to use a new lid because you will not process this jar. Pour the fat into the jar. Wipe the rim, place on the lid, and screw on the band. The fat holds in the refrigerator for 3 months (at least).

Chicken Confit with Lentils

When there is chicken confit in the fridge, I know I have a delectable meal moments away. Confit is a preservation method where the fat acts as a barrier between the meat and spoilers. The brining stage for the poultry in a confit helps prevent the growth of microorganisms, and the cooking stage kills or disrupts spoilers, too. The key to successful confit preservation is keeping the meat totally covered in duck fat and then heating it thoroughly before serving (to an internal temperature of 165°F). The chicken thighs will keep in the refrigerator covered with duck fat for up to 2 weeks. The confit can also be prepared with duck legs. You can serve the chicken thighs whole on a bed of lentils, as here, or pull the meat off the bone and chop it for salads or in pasta dishes (like Gemelli with Chicken Confit, page 128).

SERVES 4

CHICKEN THIGHS IN DUCK FAT,
READY FOR THE OVEN

8 chicken thighs, bone-in, skin-on

Salt

2 sprigs of fresh thyme, or more, if desired

2 large garlic cloves, smashed and peeled

2 bay leaves

24 black peppercorns

4 cups rendered duck fat (for homemade, opposite)

8 small shallots or garlic cloves, peeled (optional)

1 cup brown lentils

Extra virgin olive oil

8 large scallions, minced

In a large bowl or sturdy plastic food storage bag, combine the chicken thighs, 2 tablespoons salt, thyme, smashed garlic, bay leaves, and peppercorns. Shake well to distribute the seasoning and refrigerate for 12 hours (overnight is best as there will be 4 hours of oven cooking coming up).

Preheat the oven to 250°F.

Remove the chicken thighs from the marinade and rinse off all the salt and herbs. Let the chicken rest for about 30 minutes in the refrigerator, wrapped in plastic, to allow the salt to distribute evenly throughout the chicken.

In a heavy-bottomed medium Dutch oven, melt the duck fat over medium heat. Tuck the thighs into the fat to cover. (You can add thyme sprigs and the shallots or garlic cloves at this point to add more flavor.) Place in the oven and bake for 3 to 4 hours, or until the chicken is tender. You can store the cooked chicken in the refrigerator at this point. Let the pot with the chicken return to room temperature, then refrigerate.

In a small saucepan, combine the lentils with water to cover. Bring to a boil over high heat, then reduce the heat to low, cover, and simmer until the lentils are tender, about 15 minutes. Dress the lentils with salt and a drizzle of olive oil. Toss in the scallions.

Wipe the fat off the chicken thighs (this doesn't need to be a thorough job). Heat a skillet over medium-high heat. Sear the thighs in the skillet, about 4 minutes on one side, 3 on the other (a bit longer if the chicken was very cold). Pour the lentils onto a platter and set the chicken thighs on top. Serve warm or at room temperature.

Duck Fat Buttermilk Cornbread

The duck fat makes this cornbread very, very rich. I love to serve it with a skillet of Feral Greens (page 231), Corn and Bean Soup (page 93), or chili. This cornbread recipe is from the 1964 edition of Joy of Cooking, *just with duck fat instead of bacon fat.*
SERVES 8

> 8 tablespoons rendered duck fat (for homemade, page 126), melted
>
> 2 cups all-purpose flour
>
> 1½ cups cornmeal
>
> 2 tablespoons sugar
>
> 1 tablespoon baking powder
>
> 1½ teaspoons salt
>
> 1 teaspoon baking soda
>
> 4 large eggs
>
> 2 cups buttermilk

Preheat the oven to 425°F.

Place 2 tablespoons duck fat in a 12-inch cast-iron skillet and place the skillet in the oven to heat while you prepare the batter.

In a large bowl, whisk together the flour, cornmeal, sugar, baking powder, salt, and baking soda. In another bowl, beat the eggs, then whisk in the buttermilk. Add the remaining 6 tablespoons melted duck fat. Add the wet ingredients to the dry ingredients and stir to combine.

Remove the skillet from the oven and swirl the fat around to coat the insides of the pan. Pour in the batter. Return the skillet to the oven. Be careful! This is when I always forget to put on an oven mitt. Bake for 25 to 30 minutes, or until the cornbread is golden.

Gemelli with Chicken Confit and Brussels Sprouts

I make blackened Brussels sprouts and use them throughout the week. They are fabulous as a room-temperature side dish served with a piece of grilled fish, or thrown into pasta dishes without tomatoes, like this one or Spaghettini in Trout Stock with Capers and Breadcrumbs (page 345). **SERVES 4**

> 12 large or 24 small Brussels sprouts
>
> 2 tablespoons olive oil, plus more as needed
>
> Salt and freshly ground black pepper
>
> 1 heaping teaspoon chopped garlic
>
> 1 small whole dried hot pepper
>
> 4 confit chicken thighs (page 127)
>
> ¾ pound gemelli or other short-cut pasta
>
> 4 tablespoons grated Parmesan cheese
>
> 2 tablespoons chopped flat-leaf parsley

Preheat the oven to 450°F.

DUCK FAT
BUTTERMILK
CORNBREAD

Duck

One summer day I helped my friend Marilee Gilman slaughter and process about 24 fat ducks. Marilee and her husband, Charlie, have a beautiful farm in Hotchkiss, Colorado, where they have grown or raised just about everything, from pigs to cutter bees. I love visiting the farm, so when Marilee told me she had this huge chore to do, I volunteered. I thought it would be fun.

Charlie did the killing and ran the birds through the picking machine. Then Marilee and I cleaned them: those tricky gallbladders! Look! A baby zucchini in the gullet! We set aside the gizzards, which were so tough to clean I have to say I kind of abandoned that job, and the livers, then more picking off all the little broken bits of feathers with our fingertips and fingernails and pliers and paring knives. My back hurt, my feet were sore. Marilee and I didn't even talk; we were so focused on getting the damn job done. Washing, chilling, and then the butchering. Off went the thighs and legs, zip went a little paring knife around the wishbone and easy off went the breast. I cut the fat off the carcass and put it in a separate container and then chucked the carcass in a bag. One after another, whap! Like a robot: thighs, wishbone, and breasts, fat, into the carcass bag. Whap! I started to float out of my body—I was still butchering and yet I could imagine cutting my thumb off. But I didn't and lived to help Marilee brown and then boil up the carcasses for stock, render the fat, then confit ten or so legs, freeze the breasts, confit the gizzards, and make up a batch of chicken liver pâté with Cognac.

It was the most exhausting afternoon I'd spent in years, but oh, the high of productivity!

Remove any yellowing leaves on the Brussels sprouts. Cut off the scabby bit of stem, but do not cut too much off or the sprouts will fall apart when you cook them. Bring a medium pot of water to a boil over high heat and add the Brussels sprouts. When the water comes back to a boil, drain. When the sprouts are cool enough to handle, halve the large ones pole to pole (not along the equator or the sprouts will fall apart).

Place the sprouts on a baking sheet and drizzle with the oil and sprinkle with salt. Bake until fork-tender and the outer leaves are blackened,

about 10 minutes. Transfer the sprouts to a bowl and add the garlic and hot pepper, and a little more oil. (You can make the sprouts up to 5 days ahead and refrigerate.)

Remove the confit chicken thighs from the fat. Scrape off most of the fat. You can either roast in the 450°F oven that you cooked the Brussels sprouts in, for about 10 minutes, until crispy, or sear in a hot dry skillet.

Allow the meat to cool enough to handle. Do not discard the rendered fat. Tear the meat off the bone and place in a serving bowl. Drizzle a tablespoon of the fat over it.

Bring a large pot of salted water to a boil and add the pasta. Cook until al dente, drain, and dump on top of the chicken confit. Add the Brussels sprouts and black pepper to taste. Toss. Garnish with the Parmesan cheese and parsley.

While this dish is great hot, it's good just warm as well, making it ideal for company. However, don't let it get too cool or the fat will congeal.

Duck Stock

Duck stock can be frozen or pressure canned. The processing time is based on canning duck meat. There is no data for duck stock yet, though it will likely be a 20-minute process, like other meat stocks. Among dozens of other uses, you can cook pasta in duck stock (try it in place of chicken stock in Spaghettini Cooked in Chicken Stock with Broccolini, page 91).

MAKES ABOUT 5 PINTS

> **Wings and carcass of one 5- to 6-pound duck, chopped in big pieces**
>
> **1 large onion, quartered**
>
> **2 carrots, quartered**
>
> **10 cups water**
>
> **½ cup coarsely chopped flat-leaf parsley**
>
> **2 sprigs of fresh thyme**
>
> **1 bay leaf**
>
> **½ teaspoon black peppercorns**

Preheat the oven to 500°F.

Place the duck wings and carcass, onion, and carrots in a roasting pan and roast for about 45 minutes, flipping them periodically, until the bones are browned.

Dump the bones into a stockpot. Add 2 cups of the water to the roasting pan and stir to loosen the browned bits. Pour the pan juices into the stockpot. Add the remaining 8 cups water, the parsley, thyme, bay leaf, and peppercorns. Bring the stock to a boil over medium-high heat, then reduce the heat to a simmer, cover, and cook for at least 2 hours, but longer—up to 8 hours—is better. The stock should just barely bubble. For the first hour or so, skim the top to remove precipitates like blood that will cloud your stock. The stock will also cloud if you let it come to a hard boil, because the boiling breaks down those precipitates into tiny bits and makes the stock murky.

Strain and defat the stock. (To defat, either chill the strained stock and then lift off the layer of fat, or use a gravy separator.) You should have about 5 pints.

ROAST THE DUCK BONES FIRST

Transfer the stock to 5 pint jars and refrigerate or freeze (see the technique for making stocks, page 390).

For shelf-stable stock, pressure can it. Have ready 5 clean pint jars and bands, and new lids that have been simmered in hot water to soften the rubberized flange. Pour the stock into the jars leaving 1¼ inches of headroom. Wipe the rims, place on the lids, and screw on the bands fingertip tight.

Process the jars in a pressure canner at 10/11 psi for 1 hour 5 minutes for pints, or you can process 2 quarts for 1 hour 15 minutes. (See "How to Pressure Can," page 379.) Be sure to make altitude adjustments when preserving (see page 389).

Duck Soup with Sausage Omelet

Putting an omelet in a soup may seem odd, but it's common in many culinary traditions. In Mexico, cheese omelets go in green chile soups, and the Italians add parsley and Parmesan omelets to their chicken stock. (I do it with cabbage stock, too.) This one is a light spin on a hearty soup from Gascony. It is robust and delicate at the same time. SERVES 4

4 tablespoons olive oil

½ cup chopped pancetta or bacon (about ¼ pound)

1 tablespoon minced garlic

1 medium onion, finely chopped

1 medium carrot, finely chopped

2 ribs celery, finely chopped

3 pints duck stock (for homemade, page 131)

Salt and freshly ground black pepper

4 large eggs

½ pound Italian sweet pork sausage (bulk or links with casings removed)

½ cup chopped flat-leaf parsley

In a large soup pot, heat 2 tablespoons of the oil over medium heat. Add the pancetta and cook until the fat begins to render, about 3 minutes. Add the onion, carrot, and celery and cook until they are tender, 6 to 8 minutes. Add the stock, bring to a boil, and reduce the heat to low. Simmer the soup for 15 minutes. Add salt to taste.

Meanwhile, in a medium bowl, beat the eggs and then combine them with the sausage meat and parsley. Add salt and pepper to taste. In a medium nonstick skillet, heat the remaining 2 tablespoons oil over medium heat. Add the egg mixture and cook until the edges of the omelet look dry and, when you lift the edge of the omelet with your spatula, you can see it is browning, about 6 minutes. Slide the omelet onto a plate. Invert the skillet over the omelet, and flip both plate and skillet so that the omelet falls back into the skillet, cooked side up. Continue cooking the omelet for another 3 or 4 minutes to brown the underside.

With a sharp knife cut the omelet into quarters and slide it into the soup. Continue simmering the soup for a few more minutes to make sure the omelet absorbs the stock, and then serve.

FENNEL

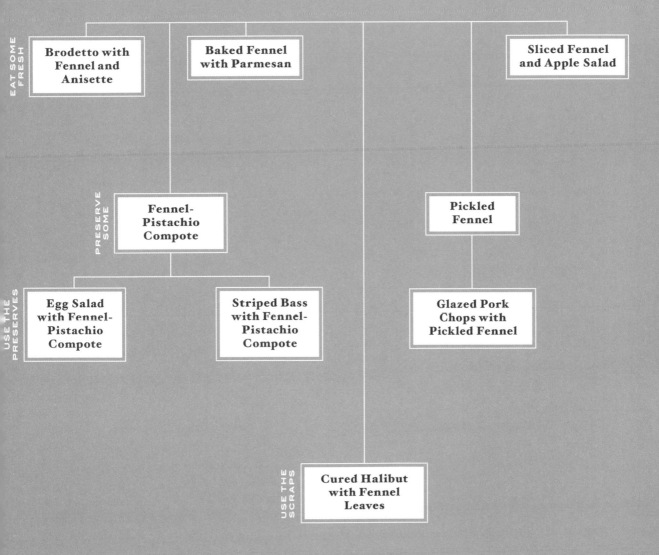

EAT SOME FRESH

Brodetto with Fennel and Anisette

Baked Fennel with Parmesan

Sliced Fennel and Apple Salad

PRESERVE SOME

Fennel-Pistachio Compote

Pickled Fennel

USE THE PRESERVES

Egg Salad with Fennel-Pistachio Compote

Striped Bass with Fennel-Pistachio Compote

Glazed Pork Chops with Pickled Fennel

USE THE SCRAPS

Cured Halibut with Fennel Leaves

Brodetto with Fennel and Anisette

Brodetto is a fish stew from the Adriatic coast of Italy, and best served over a big piece of bruschetta (toasted Italian bread). You can substitute any fish in this dish. The trick is variation—try to cook at least three different species. But be careful with delicate fish, like flounder or sand dabs, as they will sometimes fall apart. If you use squid, cut it into rings and cook separately in a small skillet in a few tablespoons of olive oil until fork-tender, 5 to 10 minutes, and add it to the stew just before serving. You can add or substitute a variety of vegetables, too, like peas, chopped asparagus, boiled fava beans, or sweet or pickled peppers. Tender vegetables (such as peas, favas, or pickled peppers) should go in at the same time as the fish. Hardier vegetables (such as raw peppers or asparagus) should go in at the same time as the fennel. The dish is also nice with small slices of boiled, peeled potatoes added at the end.

Save the fennel leaves for Cured Halibut with Fennel Leaves (page 140) or Fish Stock (page 311). Save the shrimp shells for Shrimp Shell Sauce (page 317). SERVES 4

- 4 tablespoons olive oil
- 1 medium onion, sliced
- 2 garlic cloves, thinly sliced
- 1 small fennel bulb, cored and thinly sliced
- ¼ cup white wine vinegar
- 4 large shrimp, peeled and deveined
- 4 large scallops, hinge muscle removed (see photo, page 98)
- ½ pound fish steaks such as sea bass, swordfish, or halibut, cut into 2-inch cubes
- Salt and freshly ground black pepper
- 4 tablespoons anisette
- Extra virgin olive oil, for serving
- 2 tablespoons chopped flat-leaf parsley, for garnish

In a large skillet, heat the 4 tablespoons oil over medium heat. Add the onion and garlic and cook until the onions turn translucent, about 5 minutes.

Add the fennel and vinegar and cook until the fennel is fork-tender, about 10 minutes. Add the shrimp, scallops, and fish chunks. You may need to add a bit of water if the pan seems dry. Add salt to taste. Cover and cook the seafood in the vegetables until the flesh is opaque, about 10 minutes. Keep in mind that if you substitute different fishes, some take longer to cook than others. If you use tiny bay scallops, for example, put them in after the bass. If you use monkfish, which is quite dense, put it in before any others. Add the anisette, cover, and simmer for 5 minutes to meld the flavors.

Give the brodetto a nice big drizzle of extra virgin olive oil and a few grinds of black pepper. Serve promptly garnished with parsley.

Note: The anisette really bumps up the flavor of the fennel in this dish. If you are going to Italy anytime soon, I highly recommend you buy a bottle of dry anisette. It is excellent to use with fish, and you can't get it here.

Baked Fennel with Parmesan

*This side dish is excellent with roasted poultry or as part of a vegetable platter. **Save the fennel leaves for Cured Halibut with Fennel Leaves (page 140) or to add to Fish Stock (page 311). If there is any liquid in the bottom of the baking pan after the fennel is cooked, save it to add flavor to fish stock.*** SERVES 4

FRESH FENNEL

BAKED FENNEL WITH PARMESAN

2 tablespoons olive oil

2 small fennel bulbs, cored and thickly sliced
lengthwise

1 large onion, thinly sliced (optional)

1 cup chicken stock (for homemade, page 89)

Salt and freshly ground black pepper

½ cup grated Parmesan cheese

Preheat the oven to 450°F.

Rub the bottom and sides of a medium
roasting pan with the oil. Add the fennel,
onion, if using, stock, and seasoning. Cover
with foil and bake for about 25 minutes, or
until the fennel is fork-tender. If there is liquid
in the bottom of the pan, pour it off. You can
serve the fennel garnished with Parmesan
cheese or, if you'd like, sprinkle the fennel with
Parmesan cheese and pop it under the broiler
for 3 to 4 minutes, until the cheese melts and
begins to turn golden.

VARIATION: To make a one-pot entrée,
brown pieces of chicken in the oven for about
20 minutes or so, pour off the chicken fat, and
then add the fennel, onion, stock, and salt and
pepper (omit the Parmesan) and bake for an
additional 25 minutes, until the fennel is done.

Sliced Fennel and Apple Salad

*This salad, delicate and tart, is a great palate cleanser
after a meal of roasted meats. You can add very thinly
sliced red onions or julienned radishes. Or instead of
slicing the ingredients, shred them to make a slaw.*
**Save the fennel leaves for Cured Halibut with
Fennel Leaves (page 140) or to add to Fish Stock
(page 311). A tablespoon of the leaves is a nice
garnish for this dish as well.** SERVES 4

1 medium fennel bulb, cored and sliced paper thin on a mandoline or with a very sharp knife (about 2 cups)

2 large Granny Smith apples, cored, quartered, and sliced paper thin (about 2 cups)

4 tablespoons extra virgin olive oil

Lemon juice to taste

Salt and freshly ground black pepper

In a serving bowl, gently combine the fennel, apple, oil, lemon juice, and salt to taste. Garnish with black pepper.

Fennel-Pistachio Compote

*I like to keep the ingredients chunky in this recipe and serve it as a salad. But when I want to use it more as a sauce, I grind it up. The compote can't be frozen or canned, so I preserve it in oil, which is only a prophylactic to keep new spoilers out of the jar. Eventually, the compote will ferment. So make it, refrigerate it, and try to use it within 10 days. I serve the fennel-pistachio compote with slices of mortadella, in egg salad, as a dressing for broiled fish, in grilled seafood salads, and even in a pasta dish with orecchiette. **Save the fennel leaves for Cured Halibut with Fennel Leaves (page 140) or to add to Fish Stock (page 311).** MAKES 1 PINT*

½ pound fennel (about ½ large bulb), cored

½ cup raw pistachios

½ cup olive oil, plus more to cover

2 tablespoons fresh lemon juice

1 teaspoon minced garlic

½ teaspoon salt

Freshly ground black pepper

Thinly slice the fennel, then chop into ½-inch pieces. Pulse-chop the pistachios in a mini food processor or chop with a knife. You don't want pistachio powder, just crushed nuts.

In a bowl, combine the fennel, pistachios, oil, and lemon juice to taste, garlic, salt, and pepper to taste.

Have ready 1 sterilized pint jar, band, and lid. (See "How to Sterilize," page 389.) You do not need to use a new lid because you will not process this jar.

Pack the compote into the jar leaving about 1 inch of headroom. Cover the compote with olive oil, leaving about ½ inch headroom. The compote holds in the refrigerator for up to 10 days. See "Preserving in Oil" (page 387).

Pickled Fennel

*I use fennel and vinegar in a couple of different recipes, like Brodetto with Fennel and Anisette (page 134) or as a vegetable bed for baked whole fish. Having pickled fennel on hand expedites these dishes. The USDA doesn't have any data for preserving pickled fennel, so I've used the processing times for pickled carrots. **Save the fennel leaves for Cured Halibut with Fennel Leaves (page 140) or to add to Fish Stock (page 311).** MAKES 1 PINT*

¾ pound fennel (1 medium bulb), cored

2 cups white wine vinegar or distilled white vinegar (5% acidity)

⅔ cup sugar

⅓ cup water

1 teaspoon pickling salt

¼ teaspoon celery seeds (optional)

¼ teaspoon caraway seeds (optional)

¼ teaspoon yellow or brown mustard seeds (optional)

1 sprig of fresh thyme (optional)

Cut the fennel into ¼-inch-thick slices—but not thinner or your finished pickle will be too wet.

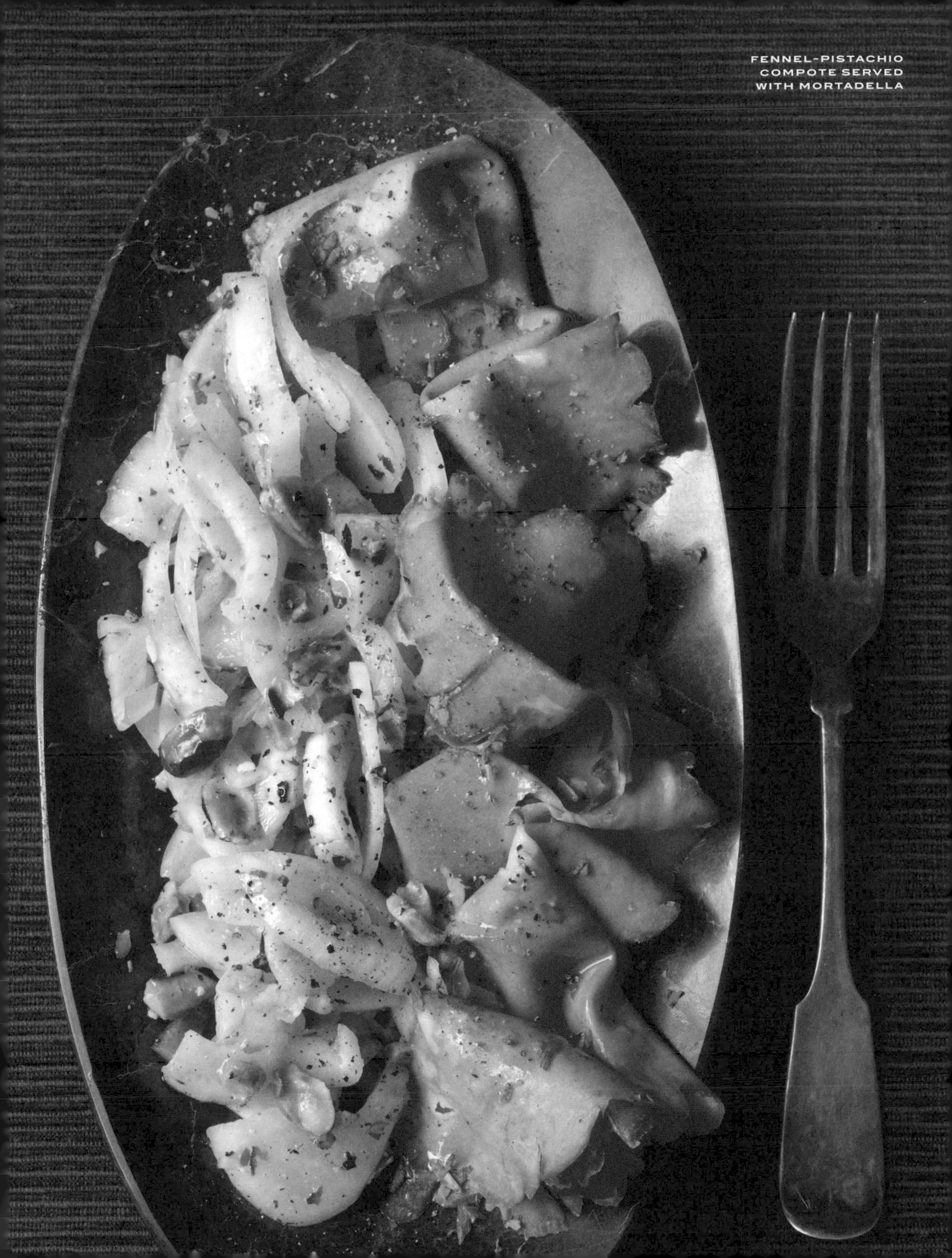

FENNEL-PISTACHIO COMPOTE SERVED WITH MORTADELLA

In a medium saucepan, combine the vinegar, sugar, water, and salt and bring to a boil over high heat. Reduce the heat to low and add the fennel. Cook until the fennel is partially cooked, about 5 minutes.

Have ready 1 clean pint jar and band, and a new lid that has been simmered in hot water to soften the rubberized flange. Place the seeds (if using) in the bottom of the pint jar. Pack the fennel into the jar leaving 1 inch of headroom. Tuck in the sprig of thyme (if using). Cover the fennel with the hot vinegar and fill the jar leaving ½ inch of headroom. Release any air bubbles by inserting the blade of a knife into the jar. Wipe the rim, place on the lid, and screw on the band fingertip tight.

Process the jars in a water bath (see page 375) for 15 minutes. Be sure to make altitude adjustments when preserving (see page 389).

Egg Salad with Fennel-Pistachio Compote

This dish perfectly exemplifies why putting a few products by is so worthwhile: The recipe takes 15 minutes to make and is absolutely delicious.
SERVES 4

> 8 large eggs
>
> 8 heaping tablespoons Fennel-Pistachio Compote (page 136), at room temperature
>
> 2 tablespoons minced red onion
>
> Salt and freshly ground black pepper
>
> 2 tablespoons chopped flat-leaf parsley

Place the eggs in a deep pot and cover with water. Cover and bring the water to a boil over medium heat. Turn off the heat and let the eggs

EGG SALAD WITH FENNEL-PISTACHIO COMPOTE

rest in the hot water for 12 minutes. Remove the eggs and let them come down to room temp. Peel and slice the eggs. Gently toss the eggs with the compote and the onion. Season with salt and pepper and garnish with parsley.

Striped Bass with Fennel-Pistachio Compote

This recipe works well with any non-oily fish, like halibut or flounder, as well as striped bass. You can also serve the compote with grilled fish. **SERVES 4**

> 2 tablespoons unsalted butter
>
> Salt and freshly ground black pepper
>
> 1½ pounds striped bass fillet (skin on or not—both are okay)
>
> ⅔ cup dry white wine
>
> 1 pint Fennel-Pistachio Compote (page 136), at room temperature

Preheat the oven to 400°F.

Butter a rimmed baking sheet big enough to hold the fillets. Sprinkle with salt. Place the fish fillet on the buttered sheet (skin side down if the skin is on). Pour the wine over the fish and lightly salt it. Place in the hot oven.

Cook the bass for about 15 minutes, or until the flesh flakes easily when prodded with a fork. A striped bass fillet is thick—around 2 inches—so it will cook longer than a thinner fillet, and a fillet with the skin on will cook a bit longer than one without. But the whole cooking process is relatively short, so in general you should just keep an eye on the fish so that it doesn't overcook.

Remove from the oven. Cut the fish into serving portions and top with the compote and pepper.

Glazed Pork Chops with Pickled Fennel

Both fennel and oranges are in season during the winter, and ingredients that are in season at the same time often marry well. **SERVES 4**

> 4 bone-in pork chops, about 1 inch thick (about 8 ounces each)
>
> Salt and freshly ground black pepper
>
> 1 tablespoon olive oil
>
> 1 to 1¼ cups fresh orange juice
>
> 2 tablespoons light brown sugar
>
> 1 pint Pickled Fennel (page 136)
>
> 2 tablespoons chopped flat-leaf parsley

Season the pork chops on both sides with salt and pepper.

In a skillet large enough to hold the pork chops in a single layer, heat the oil over medium-high heat. Add the pork chops and brown them on both sides, about 5 minutes.

Meanwhile, in a small bowl, combine 1 cup orange juice and the brown sugar, stirring to dissolve the sugar.

When the chops are browned, transfer them to a plate and cover with foil to keep warm.

Add the orange juice mixture to the skillet. When the cold juice hits the hot skillet it will boil fiercely, but just for a minute. You may need to turn your heat down a bit. Stir the juice, scraping the skillet with a wooden spoon to loosen the browned bits. Boil the orange juice at a medium to gentle boil for about 1 minute.

Return the chops and any juices that have accumulated on the plate. Flip the chops over to be sure they are thoroughly coated with juice. Spoon some of the hot juice over the chops. Keep the chops wet, and cook for about 10 minutes. The juice will thicken and may darken a bit: This is good. If the sauce becomes scant in the pan, add about ¼ cup more orange juice.

Use tongs or a fork to scoop the pickled fennel into the pan; you want some of the vinegar from the jar added to the skillet but not all. (Drained fennel will be too dry, and dumping all the contents in the skillet may make the dish too tart.) You can add more vinegar from the jar later if you want. Cook the chops until the fennel is hot and the meat is pinkish white or medium-well (an internal temperature of 145°F), about 5 minutes. Let rest for a few minutes, then serve sprinkled with parsley.

RUB IN THE CURE, ADD THE FLAVORING, WRAP, AND REFRIGERATE

Cured Halibut with Fennel Leaves

The preparation of this recipe is similar to gravlax (sugar/salt-cured salmon with dill). It produces flesh that is almost translucent and quite soft. You can prepare a sturdier version by curing the halibut longer, but I find it undermines the delicate flavor. It is wonderful as a first course, or served with thin pieces of black bread and a squirt of lemon juice as an hors d'oeuvre. **SERVES 4**

⅔ cup sugar

⅓ cup salt

1 pound skin-on halibut fillet

2 teaspoons ground fennel seeds

4 cups fennel leaves

Combine the sugar and salt. Lay a large piece of plastic wrap on your work surface and the fish on top. Massage the salt and sugar mixture into the fish. It's okay if not all the sugar and salt are absorbed. Sprinkle the fillet with the ground fennel seeds and then blanket the fish with the fennel leaves.

Wrap the fish tightly in the plastic wrap. Place the fish in a pan and place another pan on top that fits inside the lower pan. (I usually use two sizes of baking pans.) Weight down the upper pan with some canned goods—it doesn't have to be super heavy—a couple of full quart jars is good.

Place in the refrigerator and chill for 24 hours. Remove the fish and unwrap it. Discard the fennel and wipe off the sugar/salt liquid. Allow the fish to rest wrapped in a clean towel in the refrigerator for about 1 hour. (It's okay if it rests longer, but after a couple of hours you should wrap it in plastic.) Remove from the refrigerator and slice pieces of the fish as thinly as you can on an angle to the cutting board, as you would cured salmon.

The fish holds in the refrigerator for about 4 days.

F I G S

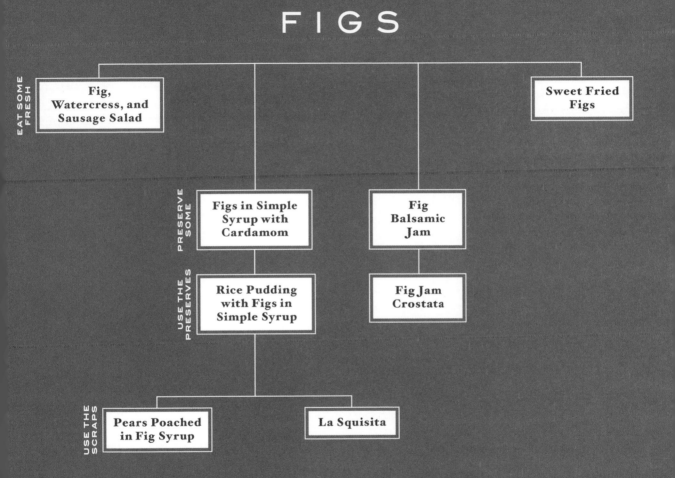

EAT SOME FRESH

Fig, Watercress, and Sausage Salad

Sweet Fried Figs

PRESERVE SOME

Figs in Simple Syrup with Cardamom

Fig Balsamic Jam

USE THE PRESERVES

Rice Pudding with Figs in Simple Syrup

Fig Jam Crostata

USE THE SCRAPS

Pears Poached in Fig Syrup

La Squisita

Fig, Watercress, and Sausage Salad

This is a terrific fall entrée salad. I prefer to use the skinny fresh pork sausage called luganica, but any pork sausage will do. Sometimes I substitute walnut oil for the olive oil in this recipe, which makes it even richer and enhances the walnut flavor. SERVES 4

- 1 pound fresh sausage links
- 2 big bunches watercress, tough stems removed (about 5 cups loosely packed)
- ¼ cup olive oil
- 2 tablespoons white wine vinegar
- Salt and freshly ground black pepper
- 16 fresh figs, such as Black Mission or Kadota (about 2 pounds), halved
- ½ cup walnuts (optional)
- ⅓ cup shaved Parmesan cheese (optional)

Prick the sausages all over and brown in a large dry skillet over medium heat for about 10 minutes. Add ½ cup water, cover, and steam for 5 minutes until the sausages are cooked through. Remove the cover and let the water boil off, allowing the sausages to take on a bit more color. Transfer the sausages to a cutting board and when cool enough to handle, cut into bite-size pieces.

Wash the watercress and coarsely chop.

In the bottom of a large salad bowl, combine the oil, vinegar, and salt and pepper to taste. Toss in the watercress, and then gently toss in the sausage, figs, and walnuts (if using). Garnish with the shaved Parmesan cheese, if you'd like.

Sweet Fried Figs

This is a very sexy dish—crunchy on the outside, warm and soft on the inside—that is super easy to make. But here's the rub: The more sugar you add to the batter, the more difficult it is for the batter to adhere to the figs. So you have to accept that the batter on these is not very sweet. I compensate by dusting the fried figs with confectioners' sugar. The batter adheres better to the Black Mission fig than it does to the Kadota. SERVES 4

- 1 cup all-purpose flour
- 1 cup light beer
- 6 tablespoons granulated sugar
- 1 teaspoon baking powder
- Pinch of salt
- Neutral oil, such as safflower, for frying
- 12 fresh Black Mission figs, stems on
- Confectioners' sugar, for dusting

In a large bowl, mix together the flour, beer, granulated sugar, baking powder, and salt. It is okay if there are a few lumps. Refrigerate for at least 30 minutes and up to 2 hours.

Pour 1½ to 2 inches of oil in a nonstick skillet. Heat over medium-high heat until very hot. Test it by throwing a dash of flour into the oil. If the flour pops, the oil is ready for frying.

Grab a fig by its stem and coat in the batter. Gently place the figs upright in the hot oil. Don't put too many figs in at once or it will bring down the temperature of the oil, and they mustn't touch or they will stick together. The batter on the figs will puff up some as they fry to a golden brown, in just a minute. Gently remove with tongs and drain on paper towels or brown paper bags.

Dust with confectioners' sugar.

SWEET
FRIED FIGS

Figs in Simple Syrup with Cardamom

These are really delicious preserves that throw off a pink fig-and-cardamom-infused syrup that I use in a few other applications such as Pears Poached in Fig Syrup (page 146) and a cocktail called La Squisita (page 146). **I also use the leftover syrup in my chamomile tea at night, in lieu of sugar or honey. The syrup holds for weeks in the fridge.** *Citric acid is widely available where canning supplies are sold.*
MAKES 2 PINTS

> 20 fresh Black Mission or Kadota figs, stems on
>
> 3 cups water
>
> 10 tablespoons sugar
>
> ½ teaspoon citric acid
>
> 12 green cardamom pods, cracked

In a large saucepan, combine the water and sugar and bring to a gentle boil over medium heat to dissolve the sugar. Add the figs and cook for 5 minutes.

Have ready 2 clean pint jars and bands, and new lids that have been simmered in hot water to soften the rubberized flange. Remove the figs from the syrup and pack them gently into the jars. Each jar should hold about 10 figs. Add ¼ teaspoon of citric acid and 6 cardamom pods to each jar. Ladle the syrup over the figs leaving ½ inch of headroom. Wipe the rims, place on the lids, and screw on the bands fingertip tight.

Process the jars in a water bath (see page 375) for 45 minutes for pints. Process 1 quart for 50 minutes with ½ teaspoon of citric acid in the jar. Be sure to make altitude adjustments when preserving (see page 389).

Fig Balsamic Jam

The idea for this jam came from a standard fig preparation: roasted figs drizzled with balsamic vinegar. There are many excellent uses for this savory jam, besides the simple joy of smearing it on a hunk of whole wheat toast. It's great slathered on roasted or braised duck, game birds, and pork about 15 minutes before cooking is completed, and fabulous as a filling for a Fig Newton–like tart (Fig Jam Crostata, opposite). **MAKES 2 PINTS**

> 2 pounds fresh figs, Black Mission or Kadota, stemmed
>
> 2 cups sugar
>
> ½ cup water
>
> ¼ cup plus 2 tablespoons balsamic vinegar

In a large heavy-bottomed pot, combine the whole figs, sugar, water, and ¼ cup of the vinegar over medium heat. Bring the mixture to a boil, mashing the figs. Once the figs are mashed and the sugar dissolved, reduce the heat to medium-low. Cook, uncovered, until the water has evaporated and the jam is thick and glossy, about 20 minutes.

Have ready 2 sterilized pint jars or 4 half-pint jars, bands, and new lids that have been simmered in hot water to soften the rubberized flange. (See "How to Sterilize," page 389.) Pour the fig mixture into the jars and add 1 tablespoon of balsamic vinegar to each pint (1½ teaspoons in each half-pint), leaving ¼ inch of headroom. Wipe the rims, place on the lids, and screw on the bands fingertip tight.

Process the jars in a water bath (see page 375) for 5 minutes for both half-pints or pints. Be sure to make altitude adjustments when preserving (see page 389).

Fig Jam Crostata

Extremely easy to make, this winter dessert tastes like a fancy Fig Newton. Serve with sweetened whipped cream or homemade crème fraîche (page 362). You can also make this crostata with Grape Must Concentrate (page 163). **SERVES 8**

PASTRY

1½ cups all-purpose flour

½ cup confectioners' sugar

6 tablespoons cold unsalted butter, cut into little pieces

2 large egg yolks, beaten

1 teaspoon vanilla extract (for homemade, page 361)

FILLING

½ cup walnuts

1 tablespoon sugar

1 pint Fig Balsamic Jam (opposite)

For the pastry: In a food processor, combine the flour, confectioners' sugar, butter, egg yolks, and vanilla and process until the dough comes together, a minute or so. Add a tablespoon of water if the dough fails to come together. (To make the pastry by hand, see page 395.) Press the crumbles together to form a ball of dough.

Wrap the dough in plastic wrap or wax paper and refrigerate until chilled, about 30 minutes.

Preheat the oven to 350°F.

Roll out the pastry into a round about 10 inches in diameter and ¼ inch thick and line a 10-inch tart pan with a removable bottom. Roll a rolling pin along the top edge of the tart pan to press away any extra dough.

For the filling: In a food processor, combine the walnuts and sugar and pulse to chop coarsely, or chop by hand. You can also use a mortar and pestle.

Spread the fig jam in the tart shell and sprinkle the walnut mixture on top.

Bake for 30 minutes, or until the crust is golden. Let the crostata cool. This will help the jam set.

Rice Pudding with Figs in Simple Syrup

I prefer my rice pudding (and risotto) soft and loose. But no matter how perfect it is when you finish cooking it, if you wait to serve it, rice pudding will thicken up and lose its luxuriousness. So this is one dish that must be served promptly. **SERVES 4**

2 cups whole milk

1 vanilla bean

1 pint Figs in Simple Syrup with Cardamom (opposite), drained, syrup reserved

2 tablespoons unsalted butter

½ cup carnaroli, vialone nano, or Arborio rice

In a medium saucepan, combine the milk and vanilla bean and warm over low heat. Do not let boil. Let the vanilla bean steep until soft, about 20 minutes.

Meanwhile, remove the stems from the figs and grind the figs in a food processor or blender to a puree. Or you can mash the figs by hand.

Remove the vanilla bean from the milk and slit it open lengthwise. With the edge of your knife, scrape the vanilla seeds out of the bean and add to the milk.

In a medium heavy-bottomed pot, melt the butter over medium heat. Add the rice and stir to coat. Strain the fig syrup and pour ½ cup into the rice. The rice will sizzle and boil. This is good. As soon as it settles down—less than a minute—add ½ cup of warm milk. Reduce the heat and stir the rice. Let the rice absorb the milk. As the rice absorbs the milk, keep adding more milk, ½ cup at a time. The rice will absorb the milk slowly at first, then as it expands it will absorb more quickly. You don't need to stir the rice constantly, but you do need to stir frequently, as stirring releases the starch in the rice that causes it to thicken.

When the rice is al dente, add the fig puree and stir it in. If the risotto is too tight, meaning it does not undulate in the bowl, add a bit of fig syrup to loosen. Serve promptly.

Pears Poached in Fig Syrup

The leftover fig syrup from canning figs is a beautiful pale lavender color. It makes a delightful poaching liquid for pears and lends a lovely aromatic fig flavor. You can substitute any leftover fruit syrup in this recipe, like peach, apricot, ginger, or cherry, but you may want to modify the amount of additional sugar. Some fruit syrups are sweeter than others. **SERVES 4**

2 slightly underripe Bosc pears

¾ cup fig syrup (from Figs in Simple Syrup with Cardamom, page 144)

¼ cup white wine

½ cup sugar

A few green cardamom pods

2 amaretti cookies, crumbled

Peel and halve the pears pole to pole. Core the pears but leave the stems on. Place the pears cored side up in a shallow pan with a fitted cover.

In a small saucepan, combine the fig syrup, wine, sugar, and cardamom pods, and heat over medium heat until the sugar dissolves.

Add the sugar syrup to the pears. Cover and poach over medium-low heat until the pears are tender, 10 to 15 minutes, turning the pears over about halfway through the cooking time. Remove the pears and set aside. Increase the heat to medium and reduce the liquid to a thick syrup, a few minutes. If you reduce too much, the syrup will get gluey, so be careful. Discard the cardamom pods.

Serve the pears garnished with the syrup and crumbled amaretti cookies.

La Squisita

My late Aunt Ada from Le Marche in Italy made a version of this drink in the evenings. When I asked her once what it was called, she said it is called "Squisita," or exquisite. Hot, boozy, comforting, it works better than Ambien. **SERVES 2**

6 tablespoons fig syrup (from Figs in Simple Syrup with Cardamom, page 144)

2 tablespoons bourbon

2 tablespoons sambuca, anisette, or pastis

In a small saucepan, heat the fig syrup over low heat. Remove from the heat and add the booze. Taste the drink—if it is too sweet for your taste, add some hot water. Divide between 2 heat-resistant glasses. Good night.

GINGER

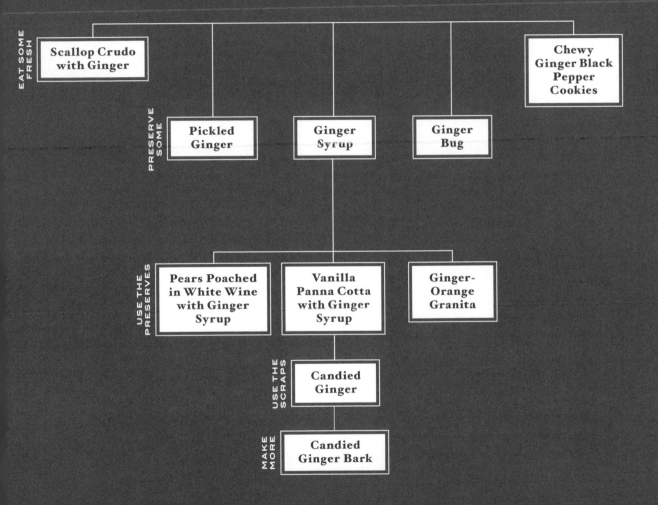

EAT SOME FRESH

Scallop Crudo with Ginger

Chewy Ginger Black Pepper Cookies

PRESERVE SOME

Pickled Ginger

Ginger Syrup

Ginger Bug

USE THE PRESERVES

Pears Poached in White Wine with Ginger Syrup

Vanilla Panna Cotta with Ginger Syrup

Ginger-Orange Granita

USE THE SCRAPS

Candied Ginger

MAKE MORE

Candied Ginger Bark

Scallop Crudo with Ginger

To thinly slice scallops in disks, place them in the freezer until very firm (but not frozen solid) first. You can also pound the scallop slices with a mallet to make them thinner, but be careful: The meat is delicate. Spring ginger is best in this dish. SERVES 4

- 2 tablespoons finely chopped fresh ginger
- 1 garlic clove, minced
- ½ teaspoon salt
- ¼ cup extra virgin olive oil
- 1 tablespoon fresh lemon juice
- 1 pound scallops, hinge muscle removed (see photo, page 98), thinly sliced into disks
- Freshly ground black pepper
- 2 tablespoons minced flat-leaf parsley, for garnish

Pile the chopped ginger, garlic, and salt on a cutting board. Using the side of a kitchen knife, mash these ingredients together very well. Transfer to a small bowl and stir in the oil and lemon juice. Add more salt or lemon juice to taste or olive oil if the mixture seems too lemony. (Alternatively, combine the ginger, garlic, salt, oil, and lemon juice in a food processor or blender and pulse to a puree.)

Place the scallop slices in a shallow bowl and add the ginger mixture. Make sure all parts of the slices are coated. Let rest for 15 minutes at room temperature before serving. You can also let the scallops rest in the fridge for a couple of hours. You don't have to serve the scallops at room temperature, but I think the flavors are more intense if you do.

Serve garnished with black pepper and parsley.

VARIATION: I have made this dish with swordfish, hake (a member of the cod family), and halibut and they are all good. You must use very fresh fish, of course, and as with all finfish that you plan to eat without cooking through, it's a good idea to freeze it for 15 hours prior to eating. This kills any parasitic worms that might be present, and also makes slicing easier. Gently pound the slices between two pieces of wax paper or plastic wrap to thin them out even more, but be careful: It is easy to pulverize the fish.

Chewy Ginger Black Pepper Cookies

This is a standard recipe for ginger cookies with a few adaptations that my family likes: fresh ginger and extra heat from black pepper. MAKES 48 COOKIES

- 2¼ to 2¾ cups all-purpose flour
- 1 teaspoon baking soda
- ½ teaspoon ground cinnamon
- ¼ teaspoon ground cloves
- ¼ teaspoon freshly ground black pepper
- ¼ teaspoon salt
- 2 heaping tablespoons grated fresh ginger or 2 teaspoons ground ginger
- 12 tablespoons (1½ sticks) unsalted butter, at room temperature
- 1 cup granulated sugar
- 1 large egg
- ¼ cup sorghum or molasses
- 2 cups raw sugar (such as demerara or turbinado)

Position two oven racks in the center of the oven and the upper third of the oven and preheat to 350°F.

In a large bowl, combine 2¼ cups of the flour, the baking soda, cinnamon, cloves, pepper, and salt. If using ground ginger, add it, too.

CHEWY GINGER BLACK PEPPER COOKIES

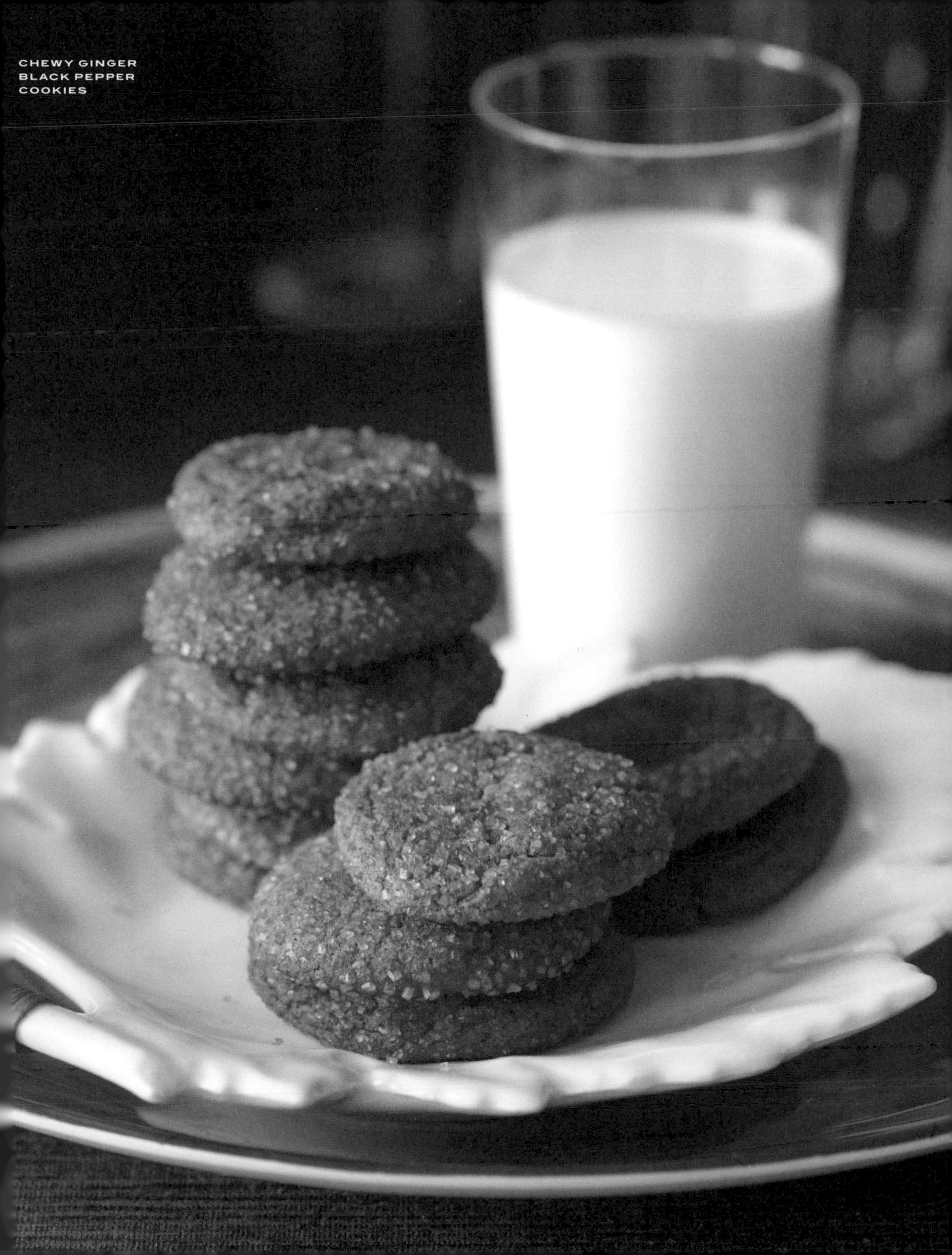

In another large bowl, with an electric mixer, beat the butter and granulated sugar until light. Adding them one at a time, and beating well after each addition, beat in the egg, sorghum, and fresh ginger (and any ginger juice). Add the flour mixture and beat to combine. If you can roll a bit of dough into a ball with your palms without the dough sticking, great. If not, add up to ½ cup more flour. The juicier the fresh ginger, the more flour you will need.

Place the raw sugar in a bowl. Roll the dough by heaping teaspoons into balls and then roll in the sugar. Place on baking sheets 1 to 2 inches apart. You can make these cookies larger if you'd like. I usually get about 15 cookies on a baking sheet. Do two sheets of cookies at a time.

Bake for 8 to 10 minutes, switching the upper and lower trays halfway through cooking, until the cookies flatten out and you can smell them. It is good to take them out even if they seem a bit soft on top; as long as they are dry, they are done. Let the cookies rest on the baking sheet for a few minutes, then transfer to a rack to cool.

Store in an airtight container for up to 4 days.

Pickled Ginger

I don't use pickled ginger often, just as a substitute for fresh ginger in some of my dishes, so I make only a small amount. It holds in the fridge for up to 6 months before losing its flavor and kick, and depending on the age of the ginger when harvested, will blush pink. Baby ginger is ideal for making pickled ginger. MAKES 1 CUP

- **1 cup loosely packed, thinly sliced, peeled baby ginger (available at farmers' markets in the fall or online)**
- **2 teaspoons salt**
- **¼ cup sugar**
- **¼ cup rice vinegar**

In a small bowl, combine the ginger and salt and cover with ice cubes. Refrigerate for 1 hour. This crisps up the ginger.

In a small saucepan, combine the sugar and vinegar and bring to a boil. Drain the ginger and add it to the vinegar solution. Bring to a boil, and then take off the heat.

Have ready 1 sterilized half-pint jar, band, and lid. (See "How to Sterilize," page 389.) You do not need to use a new lid because you will not process this jar. Pack the ginger in the jar and cover with the vinegar solution. Wipe the rim, place on the lid, and screw on the band. Refrigerate for up to 6 months.

Ginger Syrup

While some people think ginger syrup can be processed like a berry syrup, I refrigerate it for two reasons: Ginger has a pH of 5.6 to 5.9, above the safe limit for water bath processing without added acid, and I worry that pressure canning will decimate the flavor. So I refrigerate the syrup; it holds quite well for about a month. I add a chile pepper and some lemon zest to amp up the flavor, but that's just a matter of taste. I use the syrup on desserts like Vanilla Panna Cotta with Ginger Syrup (page 154) and Poached Pears in White Wine with Ginger Syrup (page 153). And you can use it to make a quick ginger ale: Combine 2 teaspoons per ½ cup soda water and stir, and then pour over ice. It is totally fresh, easy, and delicious. **When you strain the cooked ginger from the sugar syrup, save the ginger for Candied Ginger (page 154).** MAKES 1½ CUPS

Spring Ginger

After a winter of tough ginger roots in the
markets (and shrunken knobs with molding scars
in the crisper drawer of my fridge), it is with more
than a little excitement that I, and many other
ginger-lovers, welcome the spring ginger that
appears in Chinatown market stands in April
and May.

Spring ginger is young ginger: the immature
rhizomes (subterranean stems) of *Zingiber
officinale*. While we call it spring ginger, it is
actually a fall crop imported from countries
south of the equator that have the opposite
growing season. Indeed, most ginger sold in the
US is imported from China, India, Indonesia, Brazil, and Thailand.

Spring ginger has the same handlike shape as mature ginger, but it is plump and moist,
with a pink blush. In contrast to the thick-skinned, fibrous, and spicy mature ginger you are
used to seeing, spring ginger is juicy, tender, and the skin is so thin you don't have to peel it.
Just wash it and trim the cut surfaces.

There is a bit of a semantics kerfuffle in the marketplace. The names spring ginger, pink
ginger, baby ginger, and young ginger refer to the same plant at different stages of maturity
(ginger has an 11-month growing season). But the nomenclature is hardly codified, and what
name is used often depends on the user. Baby ginger, from the earliest harvest at 5 months,
is creamy white with vibrantly colored pink shoots, like a breakfast radish. It is traditionally
used to make *gari*, the pink ginger pickle served in Japanese cuisine. Because of its tender,
undeveloped fibers—it's the veal of ginger—baby ginger is ideal for candying. It is grown by
a handful of farmers in the US and is available in the fall in some farmers' markets. What is
commonly called spring or young ginger is adolescent ginger: It's 6 months (or more) mature
and ideal for cooking.

Fully mature ginger is found in markets year-round. Its pungency comes from nonvolatile
compounds called gingerols, which are concentrated in the skin. Mature ginger is great
for making ginger syrup because it is so spicy, and Ginger Bug (page 152) because the good
bacteria that ferments the sugar in the bug lives in the skin. The spiciness of ginger is relative
to its maturity: where there's more hide, there's more heat.

- **½ pound fresh ginger, peeled and sliced into thin disks**
- **2 cups water**
- **1½ cups sugar**
- **2 or 3 strips (2 inches long) lemon zest**
- **1 small dried hot pepper**

In a heavy-bottomed pot, combine the ginger, water, sugar, lemon zest, and hot pepper and bring to a boil over medium-high heat. Reduce the heat to low and simmer for 30 minutes. Then remove the pepper if you want to (I do). Continue cooking until the syrup is reduced by half, about 30 minutes. Watch the syrup and make sure you don't overcook it. If reduced too much, the syrup will crystallize when cool and you will find yourself scraping away at the candy in the bottom of your jar to get a spoonful of the stuff (although it still dissolves in soda and tastes great).

Let cool enough to handle. Strain. Have ready 3 sterilized half-pint jars, bands, and lids. (See "How to Sterilize," page 389.) You do not need to use new lids because you will not process these jars. (You can also use a 12-ounce bottle.) Pour the ginger syrup into the jars or bottle; wipe the rims, place on the lids, and screw on the bands. Refrigerate.

Ginger Bug

This is a marvelous fermented concoction that mixes well with a variety of syrups and juices to create carbonated drinks with added ginger flavor. It takes some tending and up to 10 days to really carbonate well, but the tending is very minor . . . easier than feeding the cat. **MAKES 1 QUART**

- **1 quart water, rested overnight in an open container at room temperature to dechlorinate (the chlorine will escape the water in the form of gas). You can boil the water for 20 minutes uncovered and cool it instead, though you will need to start with 50% more water.**
- **1 tablespoon plus 10 teaspoons minced unpeeled fresh ginger**
- **1 tablespoon plus 10 teaspoons raw sugar, such as demerara or turbinado**

Place the water in a gallon jar, leaving about 2 inches of headroom at the top. Add 1 table-spoon each of the ginger and sugar, place a lid on the jar, screw on the band fingertip tight, and give it a good shake. Leave the jar out on your counter.

For the next 10 days, every day add 1 teaspoon ginger and 1 teaspoon sugar. (If you miss a day or two it is no big deal.) This feeds the fermentation, increasing the amount of carbonation. When you give the jar a shake you will see the bubbles along the top of the liquid, and if you open it, it may really bubble up . . . and out!

Strain and pour into bottles, cap or cork, and refrigerate. The ginger bug will hold for about 1 month.

GINGER BUG

POACHED PEARS IN WHITE WINE
WITH GINGER SYRUP

Poached Pears in White Wine with Ginger Syrup

You can use any pear variety with this elegant recipe, even little Seckels, though I usually choose Bosc. Select pears that are not yet table ripe: very ripe pears may disintegrate during poaching. **SERVES 4**

- 4 pears, peeled, halved lengthwise, and cored (I use a melon baller to core the pears neatly)
- ⅓ cup orange juice
- ⅓ cup sugar
- ¼ cup sweet or dry white wine
- One 3-inch cinnamon stick
- 1 bay leaf
- 1 small slice peeled fresh ginger, the size of a nickel
- 1 strip (2 inches long) lemon zest
- 6 whole cloves
- ½ cup Ginger Syrup (page 150)
- A few pieces of candied ginger (optional; page 154), minced
- Crushed amaretti cookies, for garnish (optional)

Place the pears in a shallow pot with a fitted cover. Add the juice, sugar, wine, cinnamon, bay leaf, fresh ginger, lemon zest, and cloves. Cover and poach over medium-low heat until the pears are tender, about 10 minutes. Remove the pears and set aside. Reduce the liquid and spices for a few minutes to thicken. Strain the liquid and add to the pears. (You can hold the pears in their syrup for a few days in the fridge, though they do get a little soggy after 24 hours.)

Serve the pears with warmed, room temp, or cooled ginger syrup. Garnish with candied ginger bits, if desired. Crushed amaretti cookies are nice, too.

Vanilla Panna Cotta with Ginger Syrup

This is a heavenly dessert that is perfect for company because it can be made up to 8 hours ahead. (After which the panna cotta may get tough. That's because the longer gelatin rests, especially in a cool environment, the more rubbery it gets.) The recipe is adapted from a basic vanilla panna cotta by David Lebovitz, whose blog The Sweet Life in Paris *is one of my favorites.* **SERVES 4**

> **Neutral oil, such as safflower, for the ramekins**
>
> **2 cups heavy cream**
>
> **½ cup sugar**
>
> **1 heaping teaspoon ground ginger**
>
> **2½ teaspoons unflavored powdered gelatin (1 envelope)**
>
> **3 tablespoons water**
>
> **½ cup Ginger Syrup (page 150)**
>
> **Freshly ground black pepper, for garnish**

Lightly oil four ½-cup ramekins.

In a saucepan, combine the cream, sugar, and ground ginger and heat over medium-low heat, whisking to dissolve the sugar. Remove from the heat.

Sprinkle the gelatin over the water in a large bowl to bloom (swell and soften). Pour the warm cream and sugar mixture over it (straining it through a fine-mesh sieve if the ground ginger did not dissolve thoroughly in the cream). Whisk until the gelatin is dissolved.

Pour the mixture into the ramekins. Refrigerate for 4 to 6 hours.

To serve, run a sharp knife around the edge of the panna cotta and tap the ramekin upside down onto a dessert plate. Use the tip of your knife to loosen the panna cotta.

Garnish with warmed, room temperature, or chilled ginger syrup and a few grinds of fresh black pepper.

Ginger-Orange Granita

Delicate and light, this is a perfect dessert for a late-night meal. **MAKES 2 CUPS**

> **2 cups orange juice, or a mixture of orange and tangerine juice**
>
> **½ cup Ginger Syrup (page 150)**

Combine the juice and ginger syrup and prepare according to the technique for making granita on page 393.

Candied Ginger

I make this wonderful candy with the disks of ginger left over from making Ginger Syrup, but you can make it with fresh ginger if you'd like. To use fresh ginger, boil peeled disks for 30 minutes until tender, then drain and add the sugar as described below. The ginger is preserved by dehydration. **MAKES ¼ POUND**

> **¼ pound ginger left over from making Ginger Syrup (page 150)**
>
> **1 cup sugar**

In a bowl, combine the ginger pieces and sugar. Toss well. Pour the sugar and ginger pieces onto a baking sheet. You may need to press some sugar into pieces of ginger that seem juicy, usually the thicker ginger disks. Allow the ginger to dry out. I leave it on the kitchen counter overnight, uncovered. When ready, the ginger should feel dry and rubbery.

Store in a clean jar with a screw-on top. Holds indefinitely.

Candied Ginger Bark

You can use milk chocolate or semisweet chocolate in this recipe, though I prefer semisweet. And actually, you can totally forget about the ginger and just substitute with minced candied grapefruit or orange peel, dried cherries, apricots, raisins, dried coconut, or chopped nuts, even a sprinkle of smoked coarse sea salt. **MAKES ½ POUND**

  8 ounces high-quality semisweet chocolate,
  like Ghirardelli or Valrhona, coarsely chopped

  ½ cup or more minced Candied Ginger
  (opposite)

Have ready a baking sheet lined with wax paper or parchment paper. In a double boiler or bowl set over a pot of hot water, melt the chocolate over medium heat. Spread the melted chocolate evenly on the lined baking sheet. It should be about the thickness of very thick paint, or about as thick as lemon peel. Sprinkle with the minced candied ginger. Be sure you distribute the ginger evenly, and press down bits that don't adhere to the chocolate.

Refrigerate for a few hours, until the bark is very hard. Break up the bark into manageable pieces.

To store, place the bark in a plastic container or a candy box. The bark will hold in the refrigerator for a few weeks. If it gets a white bloom on it, don't worry. This happens when the temperature of the chocolate fluctuates (did you leave it out overnight after a dinner party?). It doesn't mean your chocolate has gone bad, it just means the cocoa butter has separated a bit.

CANDIED GINGER

GRAPES

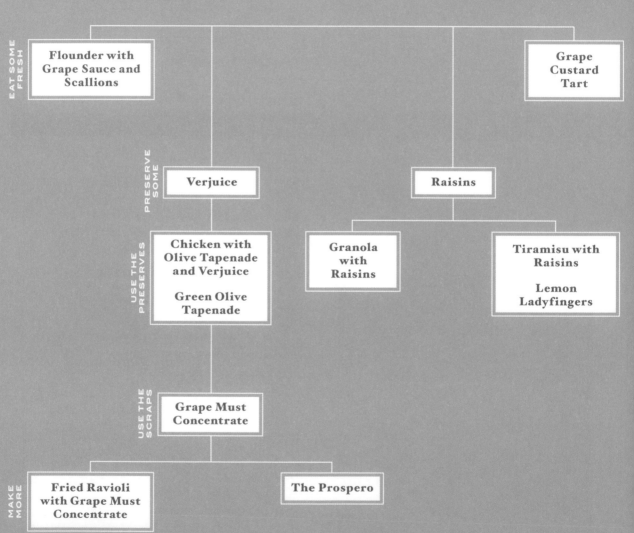

EAT SOME FRESH

Flounder with Grape Sauce and Scallions

Grape Custard Tart

PRESERVE SOME

Verjuice

Raisins

USE THE PRESERVES

Chicken with Olive Tapenade and Verjuice

Green Olive Tapenade

Granola with Raisins

Tiramisu with Raisins

Lemon Ladyfingers

USE THE SCRAPS

Grape Must Concentrate

MAKE MORE

Fried Ravioli with Grape Must Concentrate

The Prospero

Flounder with Grape Sauce and Scallions

This dish, with a delicate wine and butter sauce and a handful of sweet seedless grapes, is perfect for late summer when seedless grapes like Niagaras and wine grapes are available in farmers' markets. As the season progresses, the grapes develop seeds, which won't work here. Don't use grocery store green grapes, which are too tart. You can substitute a range of fish in this recipe, from grouper and halibut to tilapia, sole, or skate. **SERVES 4**

- 1½ pounds flounder or other white fish fillet, cut into 4 serving pieces
- About 3 cups fish stock (for homemade, page 311) or water
- Salt and freshly ground black pepper
- 1 cup white wine
- 4 tablespoons (½ stick) unsalted butter
- 1½ cups sweet seedless grapes (about a handful per serving)

FLOUDER WITH GRAPE SAUCE AND SCALLIONS

- 1 cup chopped scallions
- 2 tablespoons fresh lemon juice

Place the fish in a large skillet and add enough stock to come halfway up the fish. Bring to a very gentle boil over medium-low heat and poach the fish until the fish flakes easily when prodded with a fork, about 5 minutes.

Gently remove the fish to a serving platter, season with salt, and wrap in foil to keep it warm.

Add the wine to the poaching stock and increase the heat to medium. Bring to a boil and cook until the sauce has reduced by half, about 10 minutes. Whisk in the butter, 1 tablespoon at a time. Add the grapes, scallions, and lemon juice. Cook until the skins of the grapes burst, about 5 minutes. Season with salt to taste.

Serve the fish with the sauce poured over it and garnished with pepper.

Grape Custard Tart

This tart originated in Alsace. It is sophisticated, with a delicate taste, and stupid easy. You need sweet seedless grapes for this recipe. Taste the grapes before you make this tart. If the grapes are sour, the tart will not be as good. You can also use 2 cups of golden raisins. **SERVES 8**

PASTRY

- 1½ cups all-purpose flour
- ½ cup confectioners' sugar
- 6 tablespoons cold unsalted butter, cut up
- 2 large egg yolks, beaten
- 1 teaspoon vanilla extract (for homemade, page 361)

FILLING

4 cups sweet seedless grapes

½ cup granulated sugar

½ cup sour cream or crème fraîche (for homemade, page 362)

4 large eggs

For the pastry: In a food processor, combine the flour, confectioners' sugar, butter, egg yolks, and vanilla and process until the dough comes together, a minute or so. (To make the pastry by hand, see page 395.) Press the crumbles together to form a ball of dough.

Wrap the dough in plastic wrap or wax paper and refrigerate until chilled, about 30 minutes.

Preheat the oven to 350°F.

Roll out the pastry into a round about 10 inches in diameter and ¼ inch thick and line a 10-inch tart pan with a removable bottom. Roll a rolling pin along the top edge of the tart pan to press away any extra dough.

For the filling: Pour the grapes onto the pastry. Bake about 10 minutes, until the crust is beginning to color and the grape skins split open.

Meanwhile, in a medium bowl, combine the sugar, sour cream, and eggs and mix well.

Remove the tart from the oven. Pour the egg mixture over the grapes and return the tart to the oven. Bake for about 30 minutes, or until the custard has just set. It will look puffed up. This is okay. Do not overcook.

Remove the tart from the oven and let cool to room temperature. The tart will deflate. This is okay, too. I like to serve this tart plain.

Verjuice

*This is one of my favorite pantry staples. It is made from semiripe wine grapes or sweet table grapes like Niagara. Verjuice is similar to vinegar but has a fruity flavor, wonderful for deglazing poultry and fish. If you can verjuice it will be still (not fermented). If you refrigerate it with a cap on, it will ferment and may spew all over when you open the bottle, so if you want to keep it in the fridge, make sure the cap allows for some air to escape the bottle. You can also pasteurize the verjuice by holding it at 175°F for 20 minutes and then bottling it in a sterilized bottle. It will hold in the refrigerator for months this way. **Save the skins to make a Prospero cocktail (page 164).** MAKES 1 PINT*

1 quart semiripe seedless green or red grapes

VERJUICE

Pass the grapes through a food mill, then through a sieve. Bottle the juice. You can refrigerate it or can it.

To can, have ready 1 sterilized pint jar and band, and a new lid that has been simmered in hot water to soften the rubberized flange. Pour the juice into the jar leaving ¼ inch of headroom. Wipe the rim, place on the lid, and screw on the band fingertip tight.

Process the jar in a water bath (see page 375) for 5 minutes. Be sure to make altitude adjustments when preserving (see page 389).

Chicken with Olive Tapenade and Verjuice

You can substitute the tapenade with 1 cup of pitted, smashed green olives in this super savory dish. This is wonderful served with a bowl of rice. **Save the back, wing tips, and neck to make about a pint of Chicken Stock (page 89).** SERVES 4

>   4 tablespoons olive oil
>   Salt and freshly ground black pepper
>   One 4-pound chicken, cut into serving pieces
>   ½ cup Verjuice (page 158)
>   ½ cup Green Olive Tapenade (recipe follows)
>   2 tablespoons chopped flat-leaf parsley, for garnish

In a large nonstick or seasoned cast-iron skillet, heat 3 tablespoons of oil over medium heat. Salt the chicken and add to the oil. Cook for about 25 minutes, turning frequently, to brown the chicken all over.

Add the verjuice to the pan, reduce the heat to medium-low, and boil for 10 minutes, moving the chicken pieces about as you scrape up the browned bits on the bottom of the pan. Add the tapenade, cover, and cook for 10 minutes to meld the flavors.

Garnish the chicken with black pepper and parsley.

GREEN OLIVE TAPENADE

I use tapenade in many dishes: I use it to make last-minute crostini, add dollops of it to spaghettini al'olio, smear it on fish fillets and then cook them in parchment, sprinkle it on pizza, or slip it under the skin of a roaster chicken. See "How to Preserve in Oil" (page 387) for information on preserving the tapenade. MAKES 1 CUP

>   1 cup green olives, pitted (see Note)
>   ¼ cup pine nuts
>   2 tablespoons water
>   1 to 2 tablespoons olive oil
>   1 garlic clove, peeled (or more to taste)
>   1 tablespoon fresh thyme leaves
>   1 tablespoon capers
>   2 tablespoons golden raisins (optional but very good; for homemade, opposite)

In a food processor, combine the olives, pine nuts, water, 1 tablespoon olive oil, garlic, thyme, and capers and pulse to blend to a coarse paste. If the tapenade is a little dry add another tablespoon of oil. Add the raisins (if using) and pulse once or twice to blend.

Note: To quickly remove olive pits, smash the olive with the flat side of a cook's knife. This cracks the flesh and exposes the pit.

RAISINS

If you are so lucky as to get a load of grapes at a great price, why not make raisins? Homemade raisins are more tender and flavorful than commercial ones. Just don't use grapes with seeds.

Place the grapes in a pot of boiling water for 30 seconds. Drain. Place the grapes in the trays of a food dehydrator so they are not touching. Set your dryer to 135°F. The grapes should dry for about 12 hours, until they are leathery. See "How to Dry" (page 385) for information on oven-drying and "conditioning" the dried grapes.

Tiramisu with Raisins

This is best if it rests overnight, so it's perfect for company. You can buy ladyfingers, but homemade ones don't disintegrate when soaked the way commercial ones do. I have also made this recipe with 1 cup of fresh red currants heated up in 2 tablespoons of sugar instead of the raisins. **SERVES 4**

- ⅓ cup brewed espresso, at room temperature
- ⅓ cup dark rum
- ⅓ cup brandy
- 2 large very fresh organic eggs, separated
- ¼ teaspoon salt
- 6 tablespoons sugar
- ¾ cup mascarpone cheese, at room temperature
- 4 heaping tablespoons raisins (for homemade, above)
- 16 Lemon Ladyfingers (page 162)
- 4 teaspoons grated semisweet chocolate

In a wide bowl, combine the espresso, rum, and brandy.

In a bowl, with an electric mixer or whisk, beat the egg whites with the salt until they form soft peaks, slowly adding 3 tablespoons of the sugar as you go, about 1 minute.

TIRAMISU WITH RAISINS

In a separate bowl, beat the egg yolks with the remaining 3 tablespoons sugar until the eggs are light, a few minutes. Fold in the mascarpone. Fold a few spoonfuls of the whites into the yolks to lighten them, and then fold in the rest of the whites.

Place the raisins in a steamer and steam for about 1 minute, until they are hot and plump.

Soak the ladyfingers in the espresso mixture until they are thoroughly soft.

Have ready 4 half-pint jars. To each jar add, in this order, 4 ladyfingers lining the edge of the jar, 2 to 3 tablespoons of mascarpone cream, 1 tablespoon raisins, and 2 to 3 tablespoons of mascarpone cream, and top with 1 teaspoon chocolate. Screw on the lids. Refrigerate for at least 4 hours, but overnight is best. Serve chilled.

LEMON LADYFINGERS

MAKES ABOUT 24 COOKIES

> 2 large eggs, separated
> 5 tablespoons granulated sugar
> Pinch of salt
> 1 heaping teaspoon grated lemon zest
> ¼ cup cornstarch
> ¼ cup all-purpose flour
> Confectioners' sugar, for dusting

Position a rack in the center of the oven and preheat to 350°F. Line a baking sheet with parchment paper or a silicone baking mat.

In a bowl, with an electric mixer or whisk, beat the egg whites until they form soft peaks, slowly adding the granulated sugar as you go, about 1 minute. Add the salt and whisk to combine. Whisk in the yolks and mix to combine. Add the lemon zest and whisk to combine.

Sift the cornstarch and flour into the egg mixture and, using a spatula, fold to combine.

Fill a pastry bag fitted with a ½-inch plain tip with the batter. Squeeze out sticks about 2 inches long on the prepared baking sheet. Sprinkle the ladyfingers with a heavy dusting of confectioners' sugar.

Bake the ladyfingers for 15 minutes, or until they are just golden. Cool for a few minutes on the pan before transferring to a rack to cool completely. Store in an airtight container for about 1 week.

Granola with Raisins

Not only is it very easy to make homemade granola, it is fresher and therefore more delicious than anything you can buy. You can add maple syrup with the wet ingredients, chopped nuts of all sorts, or dried fruits like cherries, cranberries, or chopped apricots in any combination, to make the granola your own. Honestly? I use whatever I have on hand, but here's a foundational recipe. **MAKES 2½ CUPS**

> 2 tablespoons honey
> 1 tablespoon olive oil
> 1 teaspoon vanilla extract (for homemade, page 361)
> 2 cups rolled oats
> 1 tablespoon brown sugar
> ¼ cup slivered almonds
> ¼ cup raisins (for homemade, page 161)
> Pinch of salt

Preheat the oven to 300°F.

In a large bowl, stir together the honey, oil, and vanilla. Add the oats, brown sugar, almonds, raisins, and salt and mix well.

LEMON LADYFINGERS

Spread the granola out onto a baking sheet. Bake for 25 minutes, shaking the pan periodically, until golden brown.

Let cool, and then store in an airtight jar. Stays fresh for a few weeks.

Grape Must Concentrate

I make this concentrate with the skins and seeds left over from making grape jelly and Verjuice (page 158). You can also make this seedy crushed grapes; don't add water and boil for half the time before straining. The concentrate is thick with particulate matter, almost grainy, and very, very rich. I use both red and white grapes, but I don't add sugar, though you can do so safely. Use this concentrate in place of the fig jam in Fig Jam Crostata (page 145). The timing for processing this concentrate is based on USDA data for processing grape jam. **MAKES 1 HALF-PINT**

> 1½ pounds grape skins, seeds, stems (about 3 cups)

Place the grape mash in a very large, heavy-bottomed pot or Dutch oven. Add enough water to barely cover the mash. Bring to a low boil and cook over medium-low heat for about 1 hour, until the mash has broken down and released its remaining juices into the water.

Arrange a jelly bag or a sieve lined with two layers of cheesecloth over a deep pot. Wet the bag or cheesecloth so it doesn't absorb any of the juice. Ladle the must and liquid into the jelly bag and let the juice drip through into the pot. Go ahead and press the jelly bag: This is not a clear jelly. You should have about 2 cups of juice.

Return the juice to the pan and cook over medium-low heat until it has reduced by half and is like molasses, 30 to 40 minutes.

Have ready 1 sterilized half-pint jar and band, and a new lid that has been simmered in hot water to soften the rubberized flange. Pour the concentrate into the sterilized jar leaving ¼ inch of headroom. Wipe the rim, place on the lid, and screw on the band fingertip tight.

Process the jar in a water bath (see page 375) for 5 minutes. Be sure to make altitude adjustments when preserving (see page 389).

Fried Ravioli with Grape Must Concentrate

This is a traditional Italian Christmas dessert composed of wine grape concentrate, walnuts, and chocolate. You can also use Fig Balsamic Jam (page 144) or Baked Cherry Jam with Orange Zest (page 76) in this recipe. **MAKES 12 TO 16 RAVIOLI**

> PASTA
> 1½ cups all-purpose flour
> A pinch of salt
> 2 large eggs
> Olive oil
>
> FILLING
> ½ cup Grape Must Concentrate (left)
> ⅓ cup chopped walnuts
> ⅓ cup grated semisweet chocolate (use the large holes of a box grater)
>
> Natural oil, such as safflower, for frying
> Confectioners' sugar, for garnish

For the pasta: Combine the flour and salt on a board. Make a mound with a well. Crack the eggs into the well. Using a fork, gradually combine the flour with the eggs. When half of the flour is incorporated, switch to using your hands. Combine the flour and eggs thoroughly, then knead for about 15 minutes, until the pasta is smooth and pliable. Rub a few drops of olive oil all over the dough, cover it in plastic wrap, and leave it at room temperature for about 1 hour.

For the filling: In a small bowl, combine the concentrate, walnuts, and chocolate.

Cut the pasta in half. Press each half through the rolls of a pasta machine, in ever decreasing widths, until the pasta has passed through the narrowest width. (If you roll out by hand, just keep at it: You want the pasta to be as thin as you can get it, about 1/16 inch.) Lay the pasta out on a floured board. Place teaspoon-size dollops of the filling mixture on one sheet of pasta spaced about 3 inches apart. Place the second sheet of pasta on top. Cut the ravioli out (I use a 3-inch round cutter). Have ready a small cup of water. Wet the tines of a fork and press firmly all along the edges of the ravioli to seal.

Pour about ¾ inch of vegetable oil into a medium nonstick skillet. Heat the oil over medium-high heat until it is very hot. (You can test the oil by tossing a pinch of flour in. If it boils up furiously, the oil is ready.) Do not let the oil smoke or your ravioli could burn.

Carefully place the ravioli, a few at a time, in the hot oil and cook for about 10 seconds on each side, until they are golden brown and puffy. Remove with a slotted spoon and drain on paper towels.

Allow the ravioli to cool for a few minutes, then dust with confectioners' sugar and serve. Watch out! The filling is hot.

The Prospero

I call this cocktail the Prospero because my dad buys his wine grapes every fall from Prospero Grapes in Pleasantville, New York. After we press the grapes, there is plenty of flavor in the must—the leftover mash of skins and seeds. If your grape-pressing project is large, then you may have enough must to make Grape Must Concentrate (page 163); if you have made the Verjuice recipe (page 158), then you will have enough leftover must to make a delicious cocktail. **MAKES 4 COCKTAILS**

1 cup grape must
¼ cup sugar
½ cup bourbon

Mash the must and sugar together with a mortar and pestle. Place the sugar/must mixture into a jar and add the bourbon. Shake hard. Pass through a fine-mesh sieve. Pour over ice.

GRAPE MUST

LEMONS

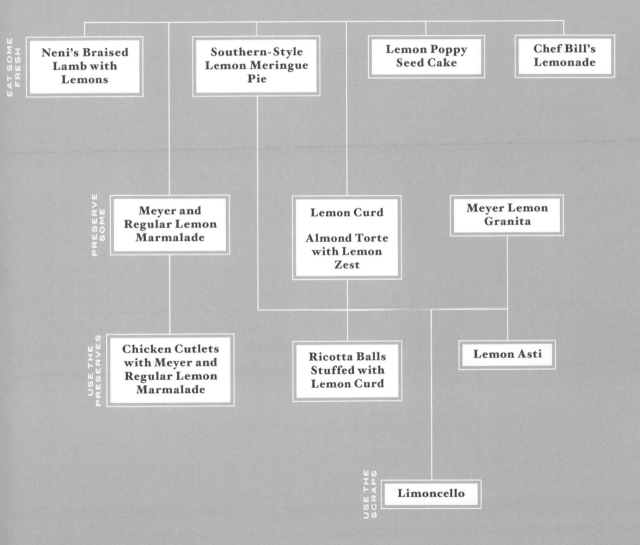

EAT SOME FRESH

Neni's Braised Lamb with Lemons

Southern-Style Lemon Meringue Pie

Lemon Poppy Seed Cake

Chef Bill's Lemonade

PRESERVE SOME

Meyer and Regular Lemon Marmalade

Lemon Curd

Almond Torte with Lemon Zest

Meyer Lemon Granita

USE THE PRESERVES

Chicken Cutlets with Meyer and Regular Lemon Marmalade

Ricotta Balls Stuffed with Lemon Curd

Lemon Asti

USE THE SCRAPS

Limoncello

> When you think a dish needs more salt, think again. It may just need acid. A squirt of lemon juice will brighten up the dish.

Neni's Braised Lamb with Lemons

Neni Panourgia and I were class moms together and knowing her was the best thing about the experience. Many times we had "meetings" over marvelous dinners, and this recipe is typical of her Greek kitchen. Her husband, Stathis, calls it "lamb marmalade." Indeed it is: The sauce is thick and lemony, and the meat is impossibly tender. Serve with rice, if you'd like. **When you peel the lemons for this recipe, save the zest for making Almond Torte with Lemon Zest (page 172), Limoncello (page 175), or Lemon Extract (page 361).** SERVES 4 TO 6

2 tablespoons olive oil

2 pounds boneless lamb leg, cut into 8 large pieces

2 cups sliced onions

1 tablespoon sliced garlic

Salt and freshly ground black pepper

2 cups water

2 lemons, zest, pith, and seeds removed, and chopped

In a large Dutch oven or heavy-bottomed pan, heat the oil over medium heat. Add the lamb, cover, and cook until the lamb loses its color, about 5 minutes. Add the onions, garlic, and pepper to taste. Cover, reduce the heat to medium-low, and continue cooking for a few minutes, then add ½ cup water. Reduce the heat to low, cover, and cook until the liquid is cooked out, about 30 minutes. Add another ½ cup water, cover, and cook 30 minutes more. If the liquid cooks out quicker, then add another ½ cup water. At this point the sauce will be like butterscotch, the meat tender. Add the lemons and another ½ cup water if there is no liquid left (but the less water the better!) and salt to taste. Cover and cook for an additional 20 minutes until the lemon is totally broken down and incorporated into the sauce.

Southern-Style Lemon Meringue Pie

Lemon meringue pie is the ultimate lemon dessert. It was my favorite as a child, and I remember the intense pleasure of its light sweetness. It was the first recipe I learned to make (it was from the 15th edition of The Memphis Cookbook, *1972) when I was still a schoolgirl in pigtails. I used to sell my pies to my mother's friends for their dinner parties, as I recall, for $5 a pie. You can make a chocolate meringue pie by substituting the lemon juice and zest with ½ cup melted semisweet chocolate. Add an additional tablespoon of water if you do.* SERVES 6 TO 8

CRUST

1½ cups all-purpose flour

½ cup confectioners' sugar

6 tablespoons cold unsalted butter, cut up

2 large egg yolks

1 teaspoon vanilla extract (for homemade, page 361)

CUSTARD FILLING

5 large eggs

¾ cup plus 1 tablespoon granulated sugar

¼ cup water

¼ cup fresh lemon juice

1 tablespoon grated lemon zest

4 tablespoons (½ stick) unsalted butter, cut into tablespoons

For the crust: In a food processor, combine the flour, confectioners' sugar, butter, egg yolks,

NENI'S
BRAISED LAMB
WITH LEMONS

and vanilla and process until the dough comes together, a minute or so. Add a tablespoon of cold water if the dough fails to come together. (To make the pastry by hand, see page 395.) Press the crumbles together to form a ball of dough.

Form into a disk and wrap in plastic wrap or wax paper and refrigerate until chilled, about 30 minutes.

Preheat the oven to 350°F.

Roll out the pastry about 10 inches in diameter and ⅛ inch thick and place in a 9-inch pie plate. Flute the edge of the dough with your thumb and forefinger, or press the edges down with a fork. Prick the crust with the tines of a fork and bake for 10 to 15 minutes, or until the crust is golden.

Reduce the oven temperature to 300°F.

For the filling: Separate 3 of the eggs and place the whites in a bowl in the fridge. In a medium bowl, whisk together the egg yolks and remaining 2 whole eggs. Adding them one at a time, and whisking well to combine after each addition, whisk in ¾ cup of the granulated sugar, water, lemon juice, and zest. Transfer the egg mixture to a double boiler and bring the water to a low boil over medium heat. (I often use a round-bottomed bowl or copper pot over a pot of hot water in lieu of a double boiler as the custard cooks more evenly.) Whisk the egg mixture until it is frothy, and then stir in the butter, 1 tablespoon at a time. Cook, whisking constantly or at least very often, until the custard thickens, 8 to 10 minutes. It should be the consistency of yogurt and very smooth. Don't overcook or the custard will be cakey. Take the custard off the heat.

In a bowl, with an electric mixer or whisk, beat the whites until they thicken, then beat in the remaining 1 tablespoon granulated sugar. Continue beating until the meringue forms soft peaks.

Pour the custard into the crust and cover the custard with the meringue. Bake for 15 minutes, or until the tips of the meringue are golden.

Allow the pie to come to room temperature before serving. The custard needs a little time to set.

Lemon Poppy Seed Cake

This recipe is an adaptation of one of my favorites from Maida Heatter, America's grande dame of desserts. I've amped up the lemon flavor and added poppy seeds, as well as cake flour, which makes the crumb especially tender. This recipe doubles nicely; it's handy to have around the holidays. You can also prepare this recipe as cupcakes, but shorten the cooking time by about 5 minutes. In this recipe I top the cake with an icing that is smooth and loose enough to drizzle down the sides of the cake, but sometimes I make it with a lemon glaze composed of 1 part lemon juice and 2 parts sugar. SERVES 8

CAKE

8 tablespoons (1 stick) plus 2 tablespoons unsalted butter, at room temperature

¼ cup breadcrumbs (for homemade, page 362), ground fine

1 cup all-purpose flour

½ cup plus 1 tablespoon cake flour

1 teaspoon baking powder

½ teaspoon salt

1 cup granulated sugar

2 large eggs

½ cup whole milk

Grated zest of 1 large lemon (about
2 tablespoons)

2 teaspoons lemon extract (for homemade,
page 361)

2 heaping tablespoons poppy seeds

ICING

½ cup confectioners' sugar

2 tablespoons fresh lemon juice

For the cake: Preheat the oven to 350°F. Butter a 9-inch tube pan with the 2 tablespoons of butter. Dust with the breadcrumbs. Tap out any breadcrumbs that don't stick to the butter.

In a medium bowl, sift the all-purpose flour, cake flour, baking powder, and salt. In a separate medium bowl, with an electric mixer, beat the remaining 8 tablespoons butter and the granulated sugar until creamy. Add the eggs, one at a time, beating well after each addition until the mixture is pale yellow and fluffy. Adding one at a time in this order, and beating well after each addition, add half the flour mixture, ¼ cup of the milk, the remaining flour, and remaining ¼ cup milk. Beat in the lemon zest, lemon extract, and poppy seeds.

Pour the batter into the tube pan and bake for 25 minutes, or until a cake tester inserted into the cake comes out clean. Do not overcook. You will smell it when it is done.

Turn the cake out of the pan onto a rack, setting it right side up.

For the icing: In a small bowl, stir together the confectioners' sugar and 1 tablespoon of the lemon juice. Add the remaining 1 tablespoon lemon juice in tiny increments until the icing is loose enough to drizzle over the sides of the cake.

Set the rack with the cake on it over a piece of newspaper (for easier cleanup). Using a spoon, pour the icing over the top of the cake and let it drizzle down the sides. The icing will harden as the cake cools.

To get the most juice from your lemons, press and roll the lemon on a hard surface with the palm of your hand before squeezing.

Chef Bill's Lemonade

Bill Moss was my teacher at the French Culinary Institute (now called The International Culinary Center) in New York City. He was a wonderful instructor who made up a batch of this ambrosia for every session. Bill was prone to puns. He wrote them on the kitchen blackboard announcing the day's subject: "Who let the dogs out? Oeuf! Oeuf! Oeuf! Oeuf!" **MAKES 1 GALLON**

2 large lemons, scrubbed (see Note, page 175)

2 large limes, scrubbed

2 oranges, scrubbed

2 cups superfine sugar (see Note)

Ice

Cold water

Halve the lemons, limes, and oranges. Using a wooden reamer or a spoon, squeeze the juice and pulp into a 4-quart jug. Put all of the rinds into the jug as well. Add the sugar, then fill the jug to the top with ice. Add enough cold water to come to the top, stirring constantly to dissolve the sugar. (Putting a long-handled spoon or ladle into the jug before you add the ice will make the mixing process easier because it will already be down there and you don't have to force it through the cubes.) Some of the ice will melt down as you stir. Allow the lemonade to sit for at least 30 minutes before serving so the flavors develop completely.

Note: If you don't have superfine sugar, you can make your own by grinding granulated sugar in a food processor.

Meyer and Regular Lemon Marmalade

You can use any combination of lemons in this recipe: all Meyer, a mix, or all lemon; they're all good. **When you juice the lemons for this recipe, save the zest for making Almond Torte with Lemon Zest (page 172), Limoncello (page 175), or Lemon Extract (page 361).** MAKES 2 HALF-PINTS

- 1 pound Meyer lemons, scrubbed (see Note, page 175)
- 1 cup sugar
- ½ cup fresh regular lemon juice (3 to 4 lemons)
- 1 teaspoon unsalted butter (optional)

Take the peel off the Meyer lemons in as big pieces as you can. Cut most of the white pith off the inside of the peels by scraping away with a paring knife. If lots of pith is stuck to the fruit, you must pick it off. It's okay if you don't get all the pith off the fruit and the peel.

Cut the lemon peels into little matchsticks. You need about ½ cup.

Remove the seeds from the fruit by cutting the fruit in half along the equator and popping out the seeds with the tip of a paring knife. Grind the fruit in a food processor or blender to a chunky pulp. You should have about 1 cup of pulp. But measure what you have (there can be some variations depending on the lemons) and adjust the sugar accordingly: You will need

1 cup of sugar for every 1 cup of pulp. Pour the pulp into a medium bowl.

In a small saucepan, combine the matchsticks with water to cover (½ to ¾ cup). Cook over medium heat until the rinds are tender, about 25 minutes. Cool, then add the rinds and water to the pulp and let it rest for 2 to 4 hours, covered, at room temperature, or overnight, covered, in the fridge.

In a large, wide, heavy-bottomed pot, combine the pulp mixture, sugar, and lemon juice. The marmalade will thicken more quickly in a wide pot than a deep one. To avoid a messy foam-up, be sure the pot is deep enough to only fill halfway. You can also add a teaspoon of butter: it helps control the foam. Boil over medium-high heat for 20 to 30 minutes, removing the foam as it builds up, and stirring the marmalade down, until a candy thermometer reaches 220°F at sea level, or 8°F over boiling temperature wherever you are. (To calculate the boiling temperature at your altitude, see page 389.) Or you can test the jell by letting a spoonful cool in the fridge for a couple of minutes. If the marmalade wrinkles when you push it with your finger, it is ready to can. This is a loose marmalade, but if it comes out stiff, don't worry. Just warm it up before using it in the recipes.

Have ready 2 sterilized half-pint jars and bands, and new lids that have been simmered in hot water to soften the rubberized flange. Pour the marmalade into the jars leaving ¼ inch of headroom. Wipe the rims, place on the lids, and screw on the bands fingertip tight.

Process the jars in a water bath (see page 375) for 5 minutes. Be sure to make altitude adjustments when preserving (see page 389).

Lemon Curd

This recipe, developed by the University of Georgia Extension, originally called for bottled lemon juice. But fresh lemon juice is just as acidic and has more flavor. You will need 5 large lemons to make this curd. Just don't use Meyer lemons, which aren't acidic enough (unless you aren't planning to can it). You can use this curd to make a quick Southern-Style Lemon Meringue Pie (page 166)—just substitute the custard with 4 cups of curd. I hate recipes that call for a ton of egg yolks and then leave you stuck with all those whites, so check out Almond Torte with Lemon Zest (page 172). It will use up most of those whites.

MAKES 3 TO 4 HALF-PINT JARS

2½ cups sugar

½ cup grated lemon zest

7 large egg yolks

4 large eggs

1 cup fresh lemon juice

1½ sticks (6 ounces) cold unsalted butter, cut into small pieces

LEMON CURD

In a food processor, grind the sugar for about 1 minute until it is superfine. Combine the sugar and lemon zest in a small bowl and set aside for 30 minutes.

In the top of a double boiler (not over heat), whisk together the egg yolks and whole eggs. Slowly whisk in the sugar-zest mixture, blending until well mixed and smooth. Whisk in the lemon juice and then add the butter pieces to the mixture.

Bring the water in the double boiler to a gentle boil over medium-low heat. Place the upper compartment of the double boiler or a round-bottomed bowl over the boiling water, keeping it at a low boil. Cook, stirring gently but constantly with a spoon to prevent the mixture from sticking, until the mixture

reaches 170°F. Use a thermometer to monitor the temperature.

Remove the upper compartment of the double boiler from the heat and continue to stir the curd gently until it thickens, about 5 minutes. Strain the curd through a fine-mesh sieve into a glass or stainless steel bowl and discard the zest.

Have ready 4 clean half-pint jars and bands, and new lids that have been simmered in hot water to soften the rubberized flange. (You may only need 3 jars.) Pour the hot strained curd into the jars leaving ½ inch of headroom. Release any air bubbles by inserting a butter knife into the jar. Wipe the rims, place on the lids, and screw on the bands fingertip tight.

Process the jars in a water bath (see page 375) for 15 minutes. Be sure to make altitude adjustments when preserving (see page

ALWAYS SCRUB LEMONS BEFORE ZESTING AND FREEZE EXTRA ZEST!

389). The curd is shelf stable for 4 months. Browning or separation may occur. The curd should be discarded if this occurs.

You can also freeze the curd. Pour the strained curd into freezer-safe containers and chill in the refrigerator. When cool, place in the freezer. The curd will hold for 1 year. Thaw in the refrigerator.

Almond Torte with Lemon Zest

This is an adaptation of a French recipe from International Home Cooking *from the United Nations International School, where my daughter was a student. I've added almond and lemon flavors, and poppy seeds. I love it because it uses up extra egg whites. The recipe is best served fresh from the oven, as over time the cake will collapse on itself.* **SERVES 8**

- 8 tablespoons (1 stick) unsalted butter, melted, plus 1 tablespoon cold butter
- 6 large egg whites
- 1 cup granulated sugar
- 1 cup finely ground almonds
- ½ cup all-purpose flour
- 2 teaspoons almond extract
- 1½ teaspoons grated lemon zest
- 1 tablespoon poppy seeds (optional)
- Confectioners' sugar or whipped cream, for garnish

Preheat the oven to 375°F. Use the 1 tablespoon cold butter to grease a 10-inch cake pan.

In a large bowl, with an electric mixer or whisk, beat the egg whites until they are light but not stiff, then beat in the granulated sugar. Stir in the ground almonds, flour, melted butter, almond extract, lemon zest, and poppy seeds (if using) and mix well.

Pour the batter into the pan and bake for 35 minutes, or until a cake tester inserted into the center of the cake comes out clean.

Place the cake on a rack until the pan is cool enough to handle, then flip over onto a serving plate.

Serve promptly, garnished with confectioners' sugar or whipped cream.

Meyer Lemon Granita

I use this lemon granita as the base for a totally decadent dessert to serve after a fish dinner: Lemon Asti (page 174). When I'm squeezing lemons for a recipe but not zesting them, I will save the squeezed lemon shells: Cleaned up, they make a lovely service cup for the granita. The lemon shells freeze well, but freeze them on a baking sheet first, then put them in a plastic food storage bag. That way you can pull out the number of cups you need, rather than defrosting the whole lot. You can also substitute the Meyer lemon juice with a combination of regular lemon juice with some orange juice, to your taste, to get a similar result.
MAKES 3 CUPS

> 2 cups water
>
> 1 cup sugar
>
> ½ cup Meyer lemon juice (about 4 lemons)

In a small saucepan, combine the water and sugar and heat over medium heat, stirring until the sugar dissolves. Take the syrup off the heat and let come down to room temperature. Stir in the lemon juice. You are basically making lemonade: If it is good to drink, it will make a good granita.

Prepare according to the technique for making granitas on page 393.

Chicken Cutlets with Meyer and Regular Lemon Marmalade

You can make this dish with any citrus marmalade, as long as it isn't super sweet. Also, a very dense marmalade may need a little extra stock to ensure the sauce is saucy. Kids love it. **SERVES 4**

> 4 tablespoons (½ stick) unsalted butter
>
> All-purpose flour, for dredging
>
> Salt and freshly ground black pepper
>
> 4 chicken cutlets, about 6 ounces each
>
> ¾ cup chicken stock (for homemade, page 89)
>
> ¼ cup Meyer and Regular Lemon Marmalade (page 170)
>
> 2 tablespoons chopped flat-leaf parsley

In a large well-seasoned cast-iron or nonstick skillet, heat the butter over medium heat. (If you use a nonstick skillet, the browned bits that lend flavor to the sauce will be scant.) In a shallow bowl, combine the flour with salt and pepper to taste. Dredge the cutlets in the flour and add them to the pan. Cook until golden brown on both sides, about 12 minutes total. Remove the chicken and wrap in foil to keep warm.

Pour the stock into the skillet and stir with a wooden spoon to scrape up the browned bits. Let the stock come to a boil and cook for a few minutes, then swirl in the marmalade.

Return the cutlets to the pan and spoon the sauce over them. If the marmalade seems sticky, add a bit more stock (or water if you've no stock left). Check the seasoning and serve sprinkled with parsley.

Ricotta Balls Stuffed with Lemon Curd

Your dinner companions are not going to believe it when you serve this dish: fritters filled with warm lemon curd? And it really isn't complicated to make.

SERVES 4

> ½ pound (about 1 heaping cup) ricotta cheese (for homemade, page 367)
>
> ½ cup all-purpose flour
>
> 2 medium eggs, beaten
>
> 2 tablespoons brandy
>
> 1 tablespoon granulated sugar
>
> 2 teaspoons baking powder
>
> 1 teaspoon grated lemon zest
>
> Pinch of salt
>
> Neutral oil, such as safflower, for frying
>
> 1 half-pint Lemon Curd (page 171)
>
> Confectioners' sugar, for garnish

In a medium bowl, combine the ricotta, flour, eggs, brandy, granulated sugar, baking powder, lemon zest, and pinch of salt. Mix them well, cover the bowl, and refrigerate the batter for 1 hour.

Pour 1 inch of oil into a large well-seasoned cast-iron or nonstick skillet and heat until very hot over medium-high heat. Test to make sure the oil is hot by dropping a bit of the batter in the oil. If the oil boils violently, turn it down a bit. You want the oil to be very hot, but not so hot that the exterior of the ricotta ball browns immediately.

Drop rounded tablespoons of the batter into the hot oil and fry, a few at a time, until golden, about 4 minutes. Ricotta balls brown quickly, but that doesn't mean they are done inside. Just let them cook 1 minute after they have turned golden brown and they will be dry and fluffy inside. (If the ricotta balls turn dark brown it is okay—they won't taste burnt.) Drain the ricotta balls on paper towels or brown paper bags, flipping them over once to be sure they drain all over.

Spoon the lemon curd into a pastry bag fitted with a ¼-inch (or smaller) plain tip. Carefully insert the pastry tip into a ricotta ball and squeeze in about 1 teaspoon of lemon curd. The ricotta ball will swell slightly in your hand and feel heavy. Don't overstuff. It may take a couple of tries for you to get the feel for this, but once you do you will be able to whip through the rest of the balls.

Garnish with confectioners' sugar and serve promptly.

Lemon Asti

Asti (which used to be called Asti Spumante) is a sweet sparkling Italian wine from the Piedmont region. Typically served with dessert, it's also opened on special occasions for giving toasts. You can add a shot of vodka with the lemon granita, which is intoxicating in every sense. My friend Jim Sullivan calls the combination "ambrosia." I like to serve this dessert after a fish dinner. **SERVES 6**

> ½ bottle Asti, chilled
>
> 1½ cups lemon granita (for homemade, page 173)

Open the Asti a few minutes before using to let the bubbles settle down. For each serving, scoop ¼ cup lemon granita into a champagne glass and top with Asti.

Limoncello

Limoncello is easy to make, and a wonderful treat to have on hand. But to do it right, you have to give it time. I hide my jar in order to forget about it while it ages. Even after bottling, the limoncello will continue to mellow. That last glass is the best. **Save the lemons for Neni's Braised Lamb with Lemons (page 166).**
MAKES 1½ PINTS

- 4 lemons, scrubbed (see Note)
- 1 pint vodka
- 1 cup water
- ¾ cup sugar

Zest the lemons with a vegetable peeler. Be sure not to include any pith. You need ⅓ cup.

Combine the vodka and lemon zest in a pint jar. Screw on the lid and shake it up. Set aside for about 1 month, shaking it periodically. This is where the flavor comes from: It is like a giant batch of lemon extract.

Transfer the lemon vodka to a quart jar.

In a small saucepan, heat the water over medium heat and add the sugar. When the sugar dissolves, take the pan off the heat. Let cool and then add to the lemon vodka. Give it a few shakes, and put the limoncello away for another month.

LIMONCELLO

Filter the limoncello, first through cheesecloth, then through a coffee filter. Bottle and store. It holds forever, though I keep mine in the fridge because I like to serve it cold. If you see a ring of crud on the inside of the bottle, it is because the filtration was not adequate. But it's okay.

Note: Commercial lemons are, unfortunately, waxed. The wax itself is not harmful, but it can trap pesticides or fungicides on the peel. Scrub the lemons with soap and hot water. The lemons will no longer look shiny. This is good.

LOBSTER

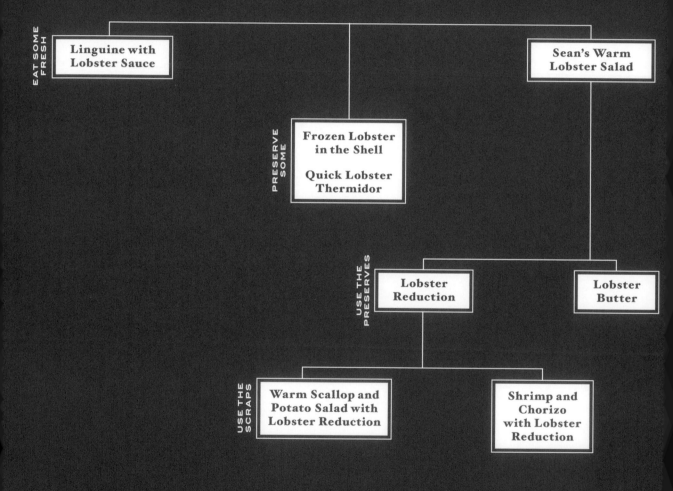

EAT SOME FRESH

Linguine with Lobster Sauce

Sean's Warm Lobster Salad

PRESERVE SOME

Frozen Lobster in the Shell

Quick Lobster Thermidor

USE THE PRESERVES

Lobster Reduction

Lobster Butter

USE THE SCRAPS

Warm Scallop and Potato Salad with Lobster Reduction

Shrimp and Chorizo with Lobster Reduction

Lobster Preparation

You must either cook your lobsters live or kill them immediately before cooking. Once a lobster dies, decomposition sets in quickly. A hard-shell lobster will hold in your refrigerator (wrapped in a damp paper bag) for a day or two, but it's best to cook your lobsters promptly.

To kill a lobster before cooking, turn the lobster on its back (if you chill it in the freezer first it will become quite passive—something worth doing if you boil lobsters live as they won't flip about as much) and insert the tip of your knife between the first pair of legs below the claws and cut straight down. This will cut the lobster's head between its eyes and kill it quickly.

If you're not cooking the lobster whole, chop off the head and claws. Remove a long antenna and fold it in half. Ready? Insert the antenna into the lobster's anus at the bottom of the abdomen (where it meets the tail). Pull out the antenna. The colon track will come with it. It's the same as deveining a shrimp, only without cutting into the meat. Halve the head lengthwise, and halve the tail lengthwise or cut into sections at the segments in the carapace.

Once cooked, note that the white stuff is cooked blood. (It is blue in the raw.) The green stuff, or tomalley, is the hepatopancreas, a kind of combination liver and pancreas. The red stuff, or coral, which is black when raw, is immature roe. All are edible and to some diners, choice.

Linguine with Lobster Sauce

When I was young we ate this dish all summer long and sometimes on Christmas Eve, as part of La Vigilia, the Feast of the Seven Fishes. It has a very light tomato sauce that doesn't overwhelm the flavor of the meat. You can also make this dish with 8 cleaned blue crabs. SERVES 4

¼ cup olive oil

1 cup minced green bell peppers

¼ cup chopped flat-leaf parsley

1 tablespoon minced garlic

2 live lobsters (about 1¼ pounds each), cut into big pieces (see "Lobster Preparation," left)

2 cups crushed tomatoes (for homemade, page 328)

¼ cup chopped fresh basil

¼ cup chopped fresh mint

Salt and hot pepper flakes

¾ pound linguine

In a very large skillet, heat the oil over medium heat. Add the bell peppers, parsley, and garlic. Cook a few minutes, then add the lobsters (including the heads) and cook for about 5 minutes. Add the tomato puree, basil, mint, and salt and pepper flakes to taste. Cover and cook, turning the lobster occasionally, until the sauce smells aromatic and the lobster shells turn red, about 30 minutes.

Remove the skillet from the heat and take the lobster pieces out of the sauce. Remove the meat from the lobster shells. This is slightly messy, but the smaller you cut the lobsters in the first place, the easier the job. Discard the heads: They've thrown off flavor and that is enough. Chop the meat into bite-size pieces and return to the sauce.

Bring a large pot of salted water to a boil and add the linguine. Cook until al dente and drain.

Add the linguine to the sauce. Place the skillet back over medium heat and toss the pasta, sauce, and lobster meat. Check the seasoning and serve promptly.

Sean's Warm Lobster Salad

I made this dish for New Year's Eve a few years back and one of my guests, Sean Sullivan, who writes the blog Spectacularly Delicious, *loved it and insisted I put it in this book, which is why I named the dish after him. You can make all of the parts of this salad ahead of time. There is about ⅔ cup of lobster meat per pound of lobster in the shell.* **Save the lobster heads and shells for Lobster Reduction (page 180) or Lobster Butter (page 180).** SERVES 4

> 4 live lobsters (about 1¼ pounds each)
>
> 1 celery root about the size of a grapefruit
>
> ½ cup mayonnaise (for homemade, page 365)
>
> 12 small yellow potatoes, such as Yukon Gold or German Butterball
>
> Salt and freshly ground black pepper
>
> 1 tablespoon chopped fresh tarragon or mint

Chill the lobsters in the freezer to passify them. Bring a large pot of heavily salted water to a boil. Drop in the lobsters. (You can also kill the lobsters before dropping them into the boiling water; see "Lobster Preparation," page 177.) Boil the lobsters for 6 to 7 minutes. Remove and set aside. When the lobsters are cool enough to handle, remove the tails and claws, crack them and remove the meat. Chop the meat in bite-size pieces (though it is nice to leave a few large pieces, like the claw meat, intact for garnish).

Peel the celery root and cut it into thin slices, then julienne the slices (about 1½ cups). Rinse and toss with the mayonnaise. (At this point you can chill the celery root for up to 24 hours.)

Bring a large pot of salted water to a boil. Add the potatoes and boil until they are tender, about 20 minutes. Peel off the skins if you'd like and cut the potatoes in half.

Rewarm the lobster by dunking it in a pot of boiling water and draining.

In a serving bowl, gently combine the celery root, lobster, and potatoes. Add salt and pepper to taste and garnish with tarragon and lobster claws, if you left a few whole.

FROZEN LOBSTER IN THE SHELL

On occasion I have an extra lobster, left over when someone had to cancel for dinner, or when the lobsters were relatively cheap. It's good to know you can freeze lobsters, and that they freeze well. The meat is perfectly sweet, and the lobster holds for about 9 months.

Kill the lobster and devein (see "Lobster Preparation," page 177). Fill a large pot with 2 quarts of water and ½ cup salt. (This is a 2% salt brine.) Bring the water to a boil over a high heat and blanch the lobster for 1 minute. (You can freeze raw lobster, but it is not as good because the meat can develop off-flavors.) Drain.

Chill the lobster in the refrigerator for 30 minutes, then dry the lobster and place it in a freezer plastic food storage bag (or better, if you have a vacuum sealer, vacuum-pack the lobster) and freeze. You can freeze lobster whole, or freeze just the tails, or remove the meat and freeze only the meat, in which case add enough milk (whole or fat-free) to the bag to lightly coat the lobster meat. This helps the meat retain its moisture.

Thaw frozen lobster in the refrigerator. Boil in a 2% salt brine for 12 to 15 minutes before serving. Thawed lobster meat (out of the shell) can also be steamed for 10 minutes before serving.

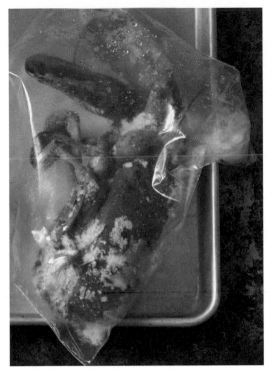

FROZEN LOBSTER

Quick Lobster Thermidor

This is a good recipe for frozen lobsters because if the meat gets a little tough, it doesn't matter. You are chopping it up anyway. This dish, which is basically a flavored béchamel mixed with lobster meat and cheese, is indulgent and delicious. Keep in mind it can take up to 24 hours to thaw a lobster in the refrigerator. SERVES 4

Salt and freshly ground black pepper

2 frozen lobsters (2 pounds each), thawed in the refrigerator, or large tails

3 tablespoons unsalted butter

¼ cup minced shallots

3 tablespoons all-purpose flour

1 cup whole milk

Dash of grated nutmeg

2 tablespoons chopped fresh tarragon

1 tablespoon mustard (for homemade, page 366)

6 tablespoons grated Parmesan cheese

2 tablespoons chopped flat-leaf parsley, for garnish

Preheat the oven to 400°F.

Fill a large pot with 2 quarts of water and ½ cup salt. Bring to a boil over high heat and add the lobster. Boil for 12 to 15 minutes to cook through, then drain.

When cool enough to handle, remove the heads and save to make Lobster Butter or Lobster Reduction (both on page 180). Remove the meat from the claws. With a pair of poultry shears, cut each tail through the shell and the flesh in half lengthwise. Carefully remove the meat and save the lobster tail shells intact. Coarsely chop the tail and claw meat and set aside.

In a medium saucepan, melt the butter over medium-high heat. Add the shallots and cook until soft, about 30 seconds. Add the flour and whisk to combine. Cook the flour for a minute, until the edges are sizzling, then reduce the heat to medium and add the milk slowly, whisking all the while. The sauce will thicken in a minute or two. Whisk in the nutmeg and salt and pepper to taste. Take the sauce off the heat and add the tarragon and mustard and stir to combine. Add the lobster meat and 2 tablespoons of the Parmesan.

Scoop the lobster mixture into the tail shells and place on a baking sheet. Sprinkle with the remaining cheese and place in the oven. Bake until the stuffing is golden, about 10 minutes. Sprinkle with parsley and serve promptly.

Lobster Butter

Use this lobster butter to flavor pasta with fish sauces (like Linguine Fini in Mussel Broth, page 207), or to dress a piece of roasted or broiled fish. **MAKES ½ CUP**

- 1 cooked lobster head
- 8 tablespoons (1 stick) unsalted butter

Place the lobster head in a heavy pot over medium heat. Using a wooden spoon or a handle-less rolling pin, break the head up in as small pieces as you can. I use poultry shears to help the process along. Do not add water. Add the butter and let it melt as you continue to break up the lobster pieces, about 5 minutes.

Reduce the heat to low. Cook the butter and the shells very gently for another 5 minutes. The butter will turn orange. This is very good.

Strain the butter and shells through a sieve. Then pack the remaining lobster bits and the butter clinging to them in damp cheesecloth and press out the remaining butter/juices. You should have 6 to 7 tablespoons of orange melted butter.

Pour the lobster butter into a mold or ½-cup jar. Holds in the refrigerator for about 1 month or it can be frozen.

Lobster Reduction

This stuff is so glamorous, it's like having caviar in the house. And to think it's made from just shells. I use it to flavor fish dishes, like Shrimp and Chorizo (page 182) and Warm Scallop and Potato Salad (page 182). You can make this recipe with shrimp or crayfish too, or a combination. The first step is to make a lobster stock, which can also be used to make bisque or cook pasta (see "Preparing Pasta in Stocks,"

page 392) or can be frozen. I don't add salt to this reduction because the lobster shells are naturally salty. **MAKES 2 HALF-PINTS**

- 5 lobster carcasses (heads and shells), about 3 pounds
- 2 quarts fish stock (for homemade, page 311), chicken stock (for homemade, page 89), or water
- 2 cups chopped fennel stalks and leaves (optional)
- 1 bunch scallions, white parts only
- 2 carrots, cut in big pieces
- 2 ribs celery, cut in big pieces
- 1 onion, cut in big pieces
- 3 garlic cloves
- 10 or so sprigs of fresh thyme
- 2 bay leaves

Combine all of the ingredients in a large soup pot. Cover and bring to a gentle boil over medium to medium-low heat. Cook for 2 hours, every once in a while taking off the top and stirring the ingredients around, and breaking up the carcasses with a big spoon. The smell is good, but quite intense.

Cool and strain. Discard the shells. You should have about 5 to 6 cups of brown stock.

Put the lobster stock in a pot and bring to a gentle boil over medium to medium-low heat. Boil, partially covered, until the stock reduces by half or more, about 1 hour. Strain the stock and then a second time, using ever finer sieves. The finer the strain, the more elegant the sauce.

Transfer the stock to 2 half-pint jars and refrigerate or freeze (see the technique for making stocks, page 390). If you see any sediment in the jar, don't worry. It's just fine bits of lobster and vegetable that got through your sieve.

SHRIMP AND
CHORIZO WITH
LOBSTER
REDUCTION

Shrimp and Chorizo with Lobster Reduction

If you have all the ingredients assembled you can toss together this dish in a matter of minutes. The dried chorizo is rather chewy, which I like, or you can use smoked or fresh chorizo, but you have to cook fresh chorizo separately, slice, and then use in the recipe below. Sometimes I stir a cup or two of cooked rice into the sauté, or add a few slices of feta cheese and a handful of dill, or substitute clams for the shrimp. **Save the shrimp shells for Shrimp Shell Sauce (page 317).** SERVES 4

- 1 tablespoon olive oil
- 1 tablespoon minced garlic
- 1¼ pounds small shrimp, peeled and deveined
- ½ pound dried chorizo sausage (two 9-inch links—they're skinny), sliced
- 6 tablespoons Lobster Reduction (page 180)
- 3 tablespoons chopped cilantro

In a large skillet, heat the oil over medium heat. Add the garlic. As soon as the garlic takes on color, about 1 minute, add the shrimp, chorizo, and lobster reduction. Cook until the shrimp turn pink, about 5 minutes. If the lobster reduction gets thick, add a little water to loosen it. In the last minute of cooking, toss in the cilantro.

Warm Scallop and Potato Salad with Lobster Reduction

This very impressive, delicious dish looks like something you'd get in a restaurant. I served it as a first course on a winter evening recently. First we ate raw foraged Long Island oysters dressed with crushed cranberry, then this scallop recipe, then Cod with Sweet Potatoes (page 307). Then baba au rhum with vanilla ice cream for dessert. It was one of my all-time favorite dinners. SERVES 4

- 2 tablespoons olive oil
- 6 tablespoons Lobster Reduction (page 180)
- 12 large scallops, hinge muscle removed (see photo, page 98)
- 2 cups arugula
- 1 tablespoon lemon juice
- ⅓ cup mayonnaise (for homemade, page 365)
- 2 teaspoons minced garlic
- 4 small pieces (about 2 inches square) bruschetta (toasted Italian bread)
- 8 small white creamer or fingerling potatoes, boiled, peeled, and halved
- Salt and freshly ground black pepper

In a medium skillet, combine the oil and lobster reduction (you need the olive oil because otherwise the lobster reduction will reduce very quickly into a super thick syrup that can easily burn). Place the pan over medium heat. As soon as the lobster reduction has started to boil, add the scallops and cook about 2 minutes on each side. The scallops are done when they begin to crack. Spoon the reduction sauce over the scallops as they cook. Remove from the heat.

In a bowl, toss the arugula with the lemon juice. In a small bowl, combine the mayonnaise and garlic.

Assemble each plate. (You can do this as a platter, of course, but it will look like a mess after the first person has served herself.) Place ½ cup of arugula in the center of the plate. Place a piece of bruschetta on top. Place 4 potato halves around the salad. Place 3 scallops on top of the bruschetta. Drizzle with lobster reduction and garnish with 1 tablespoon of the garlic mayonnaise.

CULTIVATED MUSHROOMS

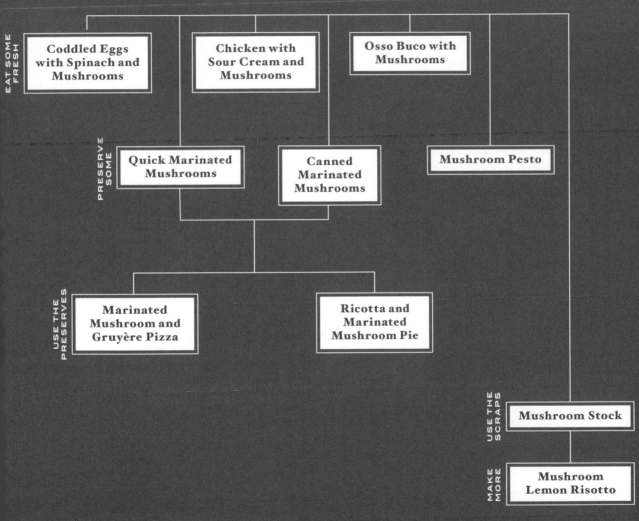

EAT SOME FRESH

Coddled Eggs with Spinach and Mushrooms

Chicken with Sour Cream and Mushrooms

Osso Buco with Mushrooms

PRESERVE SOME

Quick Marinated Mushrooms

Canned Marinated Mushrooms

Mushroom Pesto

USE THE PRESERVES

Marinated Mushroom and Gruyère Pizza

Ricotta and Marinated Mushroom Pie

USE THE SCRAPS

Mushroom Stock

MAKE MORE

Mushroom Lemon Risotto

Mushroom Preparation

Don't wash any mushrooms until you are ready to cook or preserve them. But do wash all mushrooms prior to cooking. Likewise, if you buy dried wild mushrooms you should rehydrate them to check for dirt before throwing them into your dishes. You can eat all parts of a mushroom, though some have tough stems, particularly shiitake. If a stem feels woody or tough, remove and save it for the stockpot.

Mushroom Cooking Basics

When you cook mushrooms be careful not to fill the skillet. Because they release so much water (up to 70 percent in some species), mushrooms crowded into a pan will end up steaming rather than sautéing. You can pour off the mushroom liquid as you cook (but save it: it's like mushroom stock). Cook mushrooms until their juices evaporate, or even until they are dry and caramelized.

Coddled Eggs with Spinach and Mushrooms

This is a recipe I learned from a Jacques Pépin show a few years ago. I was, at the time, something of a mushroom snob, turning up my nose at white button mushrooms. But there is never good reason for snobbery. Indeed, since I've made this great brunch or late-dinner dish, and seen such a venerable chef loving the champignon, I have changed my tune. You can use more mushrooms and less spinach in this recipe if you'd like. I often prepare this dish just with mushrooms, in which case, I use 1 to 1½ pounds. You can also replace the spinach with Canned Caramelized Onions (page 210). **SERVES 4**

2 tablespoons unsalted butter or rendered duck fat (for homemade, page 126)

½ pound white button mushrooms, sliced

1 tablespoon olive oil

1 pound spinach, stemmed and torn

4 eggs

4 tablespoons heavy cream

Salt and freshly ground black pepper

Preheat the oven to 350°F. Use 1 tablespoon of the butter to grease four 1½-cup ramekins.

In a large nonstick skillet, heat the remaining 1 tablespoon butter over medium heat. Add the mushrooms and cook until golden, about 10 minutes. Pour the cooked mushrooms into a bowl and keep warm.

Heat the olive oil in the same skillet over medium heat. Add the spinach, cover, and let wilt—less than 5 minutes. Remove the spinach from the heat.

Divide the spinach and mushrooms among the ramekins. Crack an egg into each ramekin. Add 1 tablespoon cream to each ramekin, and season to taste. Place the ramekins in a baking pan. Fill the baking pan with enough hot water to come halfway up the sides of the ramekins. Bake for 8 to 10 minutes, or until the whites of the eggs are set.

Chicken with Sour Cream and Mushrooms

This sweet dish is wonderful with any mushroom, but especially champignon. Sometimes I add a little sweet paprika after the sour cream has been introduced. You can also substitute plain yogurt (for homemade, page 370) for the sour cream. **SERVES 4**

1½ pounds boneless, skinless chicken thighs (see Note)

Salt and freshly ground black pepper

2 tablespoons unsalted butter

1 pound white button mushrooms, sliced

1 medium onion, finely chopped

1 tablespoon minced garlic

¼ cup dry white wine

1 tablespoon all-purpose flour

1 cup chicken stock (for homemade, page 89)

¼ cup sour cream

Squeeze of lemon juice

Chopped flat-leaf parsley, for garnish

Season the chicken with salt and pepper. In a large nonstick skillet, heat the butter over medium heat. Add the chicken and brown, about 5 minutes on each side. Remove the chicken and set aside.

Add the mushrooms and onion to the pan and cook until the mushrooms are tender and the onions are translucent, about 10 minutes. Add the garlic and wine. Cook until the wine evaporates, 3 to 5 minutes. Add the flour and stir to coat the mushrooms. Add the stock and let come to a boil, stirring to thicken the sauce. Return the chicken and any accumulated juices to the pan. Cover and cook over medium-low heat until the chicken is cooked through, about 15 minutes. You may need a bit more stock to keep everything very moist.

Push the chicken to the side of the pan and stir the sour cream into the sauce. Stir in the lemon juice. Recombine the chicken with the sauce, adjust the seasoning, and serve garnished with parsley.

Note: If you use chicken breasts, which take longer to cook, cut each breast into 4 pieces.

Osso Buco with Mushrooms

This is my father's osso buco recipe. Like all of his cooking, it is simple, honest, and savory. The leftover bones, meat, and vegetable remnants soaked in gelatin and fat make an awesome base for a lentil, chickpea, or bean soup. Just add the beans and water and cook until the beans are tender, and throw in any leftover mushrooms and the gremolata, too. You can substitute beef shanks, though they take a bit longer to cook. Use any mushroom in this recipe, but I like oyster mushrooms and portobellos best. **SERVES 4**

All-purpose flour, for dredging

4 pieces veal shank (1½ to 2 inches thick, about 8 ounces each)

2 tablespoons olive oil

2 garlic cloves, peeled

½ large onion, chopped

1 large carrot, chopped

2 tablespoons chopped fresh basil or 2 teaspoons dried

Salt and freshly ground black pepper

1 cup white wine

2 cups crushed tomatoes (for homemade, page 328)

2 tablespoons unsalted butter

½ pound mushrooms, sliced (about 2 cups)

GREMOLATA

2 tablespoons minced flat-leaf parsley

1 tablespoon minced garlic

1 tablespoon minced fresh sage or 1 teaspoon dried

1 teaspoon grated lemon zest

Preheat the oven to 400°F.

Place about ½ cup of flour on a plate and dredge the veal. In a Dutch oven with a fitted lid, heat the oil over medium-high heat. Add the veal shanks and brown about 5 minutes on one side, then add the garlic cloves. Flip the

OSSO BUCO WITH MUSHROOMS

Quick Marinated Mushrooms

These mushrooms will marinate in the fridge and hold for 10 days. I use them on crostini, mixed with grilled scallops to make an antipasto salad, on Marinated Mushroom and Gruyère Pizza (page 189, and in Ricotta and Marinated Mushroom Pie (page 190). You can sauté the mushrooms in 100 percent coconut oil if you'd like. It lends a subtle sweetness. You can also roast the mushrooms instead of sautéing them (see variation below). **MAKES ABOUT 3 PINTS**

> 1½ pounds mixed mushrooms, composed of 4 different kinds, like white button, shiitake, oyster, and maitake mushrooms
>
> 4 tablespoons plus 1¾ cups olive oil
>
> 4 sprigs of fresh thyme
>
> One 4-inch sprig of fresh rosemary
>
> 1 bay leaf
>
> 1 small dried hot pepper
>
> ½ teaspoon grated lemon zest
>
> 1 tablespoon minced garlic (or more if you'd like)
>
> ¼ cup fresh lemon juice
>
> Salt and freshly ground black pepper

shanks and brown for about 5 minutes on the other side. Add the onion, carrot, basil, and salt and pepper to taste. Continue browning the shanks, cooking until the onions are soft, about 5 minutes more. Add the wine, reduce the heat to low, and cook until the wine evaporates, about 10 minutes. Add the tomatoes and butter. Cover and simmer the osso buco for a few minutes to meld the flavors, and then place the pot in the oven. Bake for 30 minutes.

Remove the pot and add the mushrooms. Reduce the heat to 350°F and return the pot to the oven. Bake for another 30 minutes, or until the shanks are meltingly tender.

Meanwhile, for the gremolata: Combine all the ingredients in a small bowl.

Remove the shanks and serve with the vegetable sauce. Garnish with the gremolata.

Clean and slice the mushrooms, but do not mix them together. Different mushrooms cook at different rates, so it is best to cook them one species at a time.

In a large nonstick skillet, heat 1 tablespoon of the oil. Add one species of mushroom, and cook until they are golden and fork-tender. Some will release quite a bit of liquid, and you should cook those until their liquid has mostly evaporated. All mushrooms will cook within 10 minutes. Pour the cooked mushrooms into a large nonreactive bowl, and continue cooking the remaining species of mushrooms, using 1 tablespoon oil per batch.

QUICK
MARINATED
MUSHROOMS

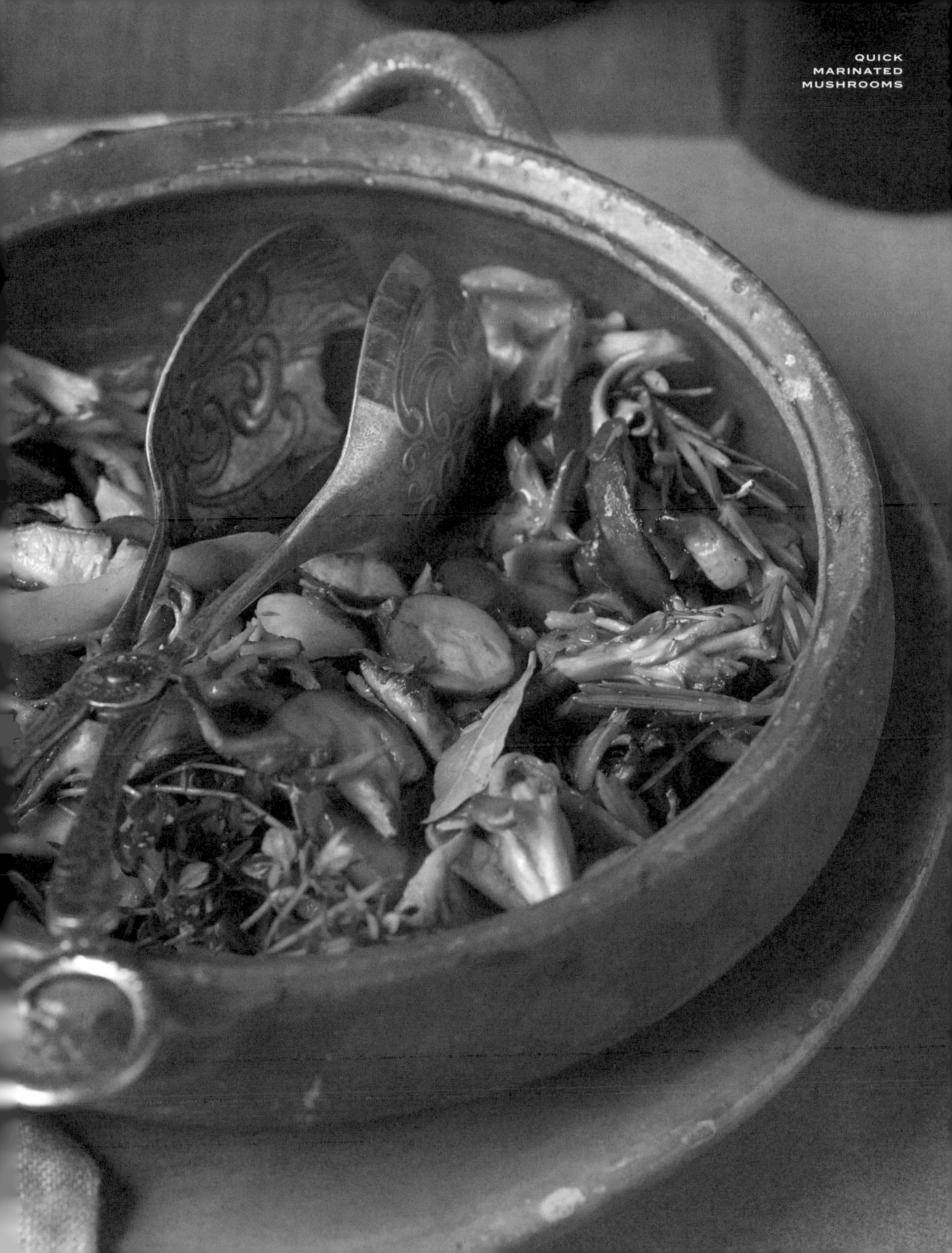

Once all the mushrooms are cooked and in the large bowl, add the thyme, rosemary, bay leaf, hot pepper, lemon zest, garlic, remaining 1¾ cups olive oil, the lemon juice, and salt and pepper to taste.

Have ready 3 sterilized pint jars, bands, and lids. (See "How to Sterilize," page 389.) You do not need to use new lids because you will not process these jars. Spoon the mushrooms into the jars. Wipe the rims, place on the lids, and screw on the bands. (See "How to Preserve in Oil," page 387.)

Fish out the bay leaf and hot pepper before serving.

VARIATION

Roasted Marinated Mushrooms: Roasted mushrooms lend a caramel-y, nutty flavor to the recipe. Preheat the oven to 400°F. Chop the mushrooms to a uniform size (I like bigger rather than smaller pieces) and place on a baking sheet. Sprinkle with 2 tablespoons olive oil and salt. Bake until the mushrooms are tender. They will be golden and slightly crispy on the edges, about 10 minutes. Marinate as directed in the main recipe.

Canned Marinated Mushrooms

I have simplified the USDA's standard recipe for marinated mushrooms to highlight a few key Italian tastes: oregano, garlic, hot pepper, and bay. The simpler the flavor of the canned food, the more I can do with it once the can is opened. I have made this recipe with wild mushrooms like chopped porcini, which will never be tested by the USDA but I think is safe. **MAKES 2 OR 3 HALF-PINT JARS**

1 pound white button mushrooms

2 tablespoons fresh lemon juice

¾ cup white distilled vinegar (5% acidity)

½ cup olive oil

1 teaspoon pickling salt

1 teaspoon dried oregano

2 or 3 garlic cloves, sliced

2 or 3 small dried hot peppers

2 or 3 small bay leaves

In a medium pot, combine the mushrooms and lemon juice. Add water to cover (2 or so cups should do it). Bring to a boil over high heat, then reduce the heat and simmer for 5 minutes. Drain.

In a small saucepan, combine the vinegar, oil, salt, and oregano. Bring to a boil over medium heat.

Have ready 2 or 3 clean half-pint jars and bands, and new lids that have been simmered in hot water to soften the rubberized flange. In each jar place 1 sliced garlic clove, 1 hot pepper, and 1 bay leaf. Add the hot mushrooms and cover with the oil and vinegar mixture leaving ½ inch of headroom. Wipe the rims, place on the lids, and screw on the bands fingertip tight.

Process the mushrooms in a water bath (see page 375) for 20 minutes. Be sure to make altitude adjustments when preserving (see page 389).

Mushroom Pesto

You can use this product in all the places you would use finely chopped sautéed mushrooms (duxelles): in Beef Wellington, on top of crostini, stuffed in chicken legs, or in a Stuffed Boned Chicken (page 85). **MAKES 1 CUP**

¼ pound mushrooms, such as maitake, oysters, and white button (all one kind or a combination)

3 tablespoons olive oil

¼ cup pine nuts

1 large garlic clove

1 teaspoon chopped fresh thyme

Salt and freshly ground black pepper

Mushroom Stock (page 190), chicken stock (for homemade, page 89), or water (optional)

Preheat the oven to 400°F.

Chop the mushrooms to a uniform size, in largish pieces about 2 inches long. Spread the mushrooms on a baking sheet and sprinkle with 1 tablespoon of the oil. Roast for 10 minutes, or until just golden brown.

Transfer the roasted mushrooms to a food processor and add the remaining 2 tablespoons oil, pine nuts, garlic, thyme, and salt and pepper to taste. Pulse to finely chop. If you want a very smooth pesto, add stock or water to thin it out.

Have ready 1 sterilized half-pint jar, band, and lid. (See "How to Sterilize," page 389.) You do not need to use a new lid because you will not process this jar. Pack the pesto in the jar. Freeze (see "How to Freeze Foods," page 382) or preserve in oil (see "How to Preserve in Oil," page 387).

Marinated Mushroom and Gruyère Pizza

This savory pizza is great with cocktails. Make sure you drain the mushrooms so the pizza isn't oily. If I am using mushrooms from the bottom of the jar, I even blot them on a paper towel. **MAKES ONE 18 × 13-INCH PIZZA**

DOUGH

¾ cup room temperature water

2¼ teaspoons (1 envelope) active dry yeast

3 tablespoons olive oil, plus more as needed

Pinch of salt

2½ cups all-purpose flour

Semolina flour, for flouring the board

TOPPING

1 cup grated Gruyère cheese

1 cup Quick or Canned Marinated Mushrooms (page 186 or opposite), drained and chopped

2 tablespoons chopped flat-leaf parsley

For the dough: In a bowl, combine the water, yeast, oil, and salt. Add the all-purpose flour and knead a few times until the dough comes together. It will be rather sticky. It's okay. Remove the dough from the bowl and set aside. Rub the bowl with a little oil. Return the dough to the bowl. Cover with a damp towel and leave in a very warm spot and let rise until the dough has doubled in size, about 2 hours. Push the dough down, deflating it, then let it rise in the bowl again for 20 minutes.

Preheat the oven to its very hottest temperature. Mine is 500°F.

Roll out the pizza dough on a semolina-floured board about ½ inch or less thick. Place on a large baking sheet or, if you have one, a pizza stone that has been preheated in the oven for 15 minutes. Place the pizza in the oven and bake for 5 minutes, until the dough looks chalky.

For the topping: Sprinkle the Gruyère, mushrooms, and parsley over the dough. Brush a little oil along the crusty edge of the pizza.

Return the pizza to the oven and bake about 5 minutes more, until the edges of the pizza are browned and the cheese is melted.

Ricotta and Marinated Mushroom Pie

This savory pie is wonderful at buffets and potlucks because it travels well and cuts cleanly. I make this recipe with Marinated Baby Artichokes with Hot Pepper (page 28) as well. **MAKES ONE 9-INCH PIE**

DOUGH

2 cups all-purpose flour

½ teaspoon salt

2 large eggs

8 tablespoons (1 stick) cold unsalted butter, cut into small pieces, plus 1 tablespoon for the pie plate

½ teaspoon active dry yeast

1 teaspoon room temperature water

FILLING

2 pounds ricotta cheese (for homemade, page 367) or two 15-ounce containers (about 4 cups)

¼ pound boiled ham, cubed (about 1 cup)

1 cup Quick or Canned Marinated Mushrooms (page 186 or 188), drained

2 egg whites

3 tablespoons chopped flat-leaf parsley

½ teaspoon grated nutmeg

Salt and freshly ground black pepper

Place the flour, salt, eggs, and the 8 tablespoons of butter in a food processor. Combine the yeast and water in a small cup and allow the yeast to bloom, a few minutes. Add to the flour mixture. Process the dough for about 45 seconds, until it forms a ball or many small balls. (To make the pastry by hand, see page 395.)

Divide the dough into two disks, one a little larger than the other. Wrap them in wax paper and let rest in the refrigerator for 30 minutes.

Preheat the oven to 350°F. Grease a deep 9-inch pie plate with the 1 tablespoon of butter.

For the filling: In a large bowl, combine the ricotta, ham, mushrooms, egg whites, parsley, nutmeg, and salt and pepper to taste.

On a lightly floured surface, roll out the larger dough disk to about 10 inches in diameter and about ⅛ inch thick. Fit the dough into the pie plate and allow a little dough to overhang the edge.

Scrape the ricotta and mushroom mixture into the pie shell.

On a lightly floured surface, roll out the remaining dough to about 9 inches in diameter and ⅛ inch thick. Place this crust on top of the pie. Crimp the edges to seal, trim, and cut a few slashes in the top crust. Brush the top of the crust with a little water or beaten egg and bake for 1 hour, or until the crust is golden brown.

Serve hot or at room temperature.

Mushroom Stock

Even if you only have a cup or two of mushrooms stems, it's worth making stock. This recipe can be easily halved or doubled, and more or less of any of the ingredients will work fine. No matter how small an amount of mushroom stock you have, use it the next time you cook meat in a soup, stew, or braise: The meaty flavor of mushrooms enhances the flavor of meat dishes. **MAKES 1 PINT**

2 cups mushroom stems, cleaned

¼ onion

1 celery rib

1 garlic clove

2 sprigs of fresh thyme

2 sprigs of flat-leaf parsley

4 black peppercorns

1 small bay leaf

In a small soup pot, combine the mushroom stems, onion, celery, garlic, thyme, parsley, peppercorns, and bay leaf. Cover with about 2 inches of water, cover the pot, and bring to a boil over medium heat. Reduce the heat to medium-low and cook until the liquid is light brown and you can smell the mushroomy fragrance, about 30 minutes. (When you're making small amounts of stock, watch to be sure you don't lose it all to evaporation.) Strain the stock.

Transfer the stock to a pint jar and refrigerate or freeze (see the technique for making stocks, page 390).

For shelf-stable stock, pressure can it. Have ready 1 clean pint jar and band, and a new lid that has been simmered in hot water to soften the rubberized flange. Pour the hot stock in the jar leaving 1 inch of headroom. Wipe the rim, place on the lid, and screw on the band fingertip tight. Process the jar in a pressure canner at 10/11 psi for 45 minutes (pints and half-pints only). (See "How to Pressure Can," page 379.) Be sure to make altitude adjustments when preserving (see page 389).

Mushroom Lemon Risotto

This is a lemony risotto that goes well with seafood. Try serving fried soft-shelled crabs or grilled shrimp on top. If you don't have enough mushroom stock, you can use a combination of mushroom and chicken stock. **SERVES 4**

  3 tablespoons olive oil
  1 cup minced onion
  1 cup carnaroli, vialone nano, or Arborio rice
  ½ cup white wine

  4 cups mushroom stock (for homemade, opposite), room temperature
  Salt and freshly ground black pepper
  1 tablespoon unsalted butter
  1 tablespoon minced garlic
  2 tablespoons grated lemon zest
  3 tablespoons fresh lemon juice
  ½ cup grated Parmesan cheese
  2 tablespoons minced flat-leaf parsley

In a 4-quart heavy-bottomed pot, heat the oil over medium heat. Add the onion and cook until the onion becomes translucent, about 5 minutes. Add the rice and stir until the rice is covered with oil and loses its opaque quality, about 2 minutes. Add the wine. It will boil rapidly. It's okay. Cook until the wine is absorbed, about 30 seconds. Stir in 1 cup of mushroom stock and cook until the rice absorbs almost all the stock, about 5 minutes. The rice may stick, so stir often, though you don't have to stir it constantly. Continue adding mushroom stock by the cup, stirring until each is absorbed, until you have used a total of 3 cups of stock. Add salt to taste.

Stir in the butter and garlic. Stir in pepper to taste, then add the remaining 1 cup stock, the lemon zest, and lemon juice. Cook the rice until it has absorbed all of the stock, stirring all the while. The rice will absorb the stock quickly as it gets closer to being done. Test the rice for doneness by sampling a grain. It should be yielding but firm to the bite, and the texture of the overall dish should be as soft as porridge.

Check the seasoning. Serve promptly, garnished with Parmesan and parsley.

WILD
MUSHROOMS

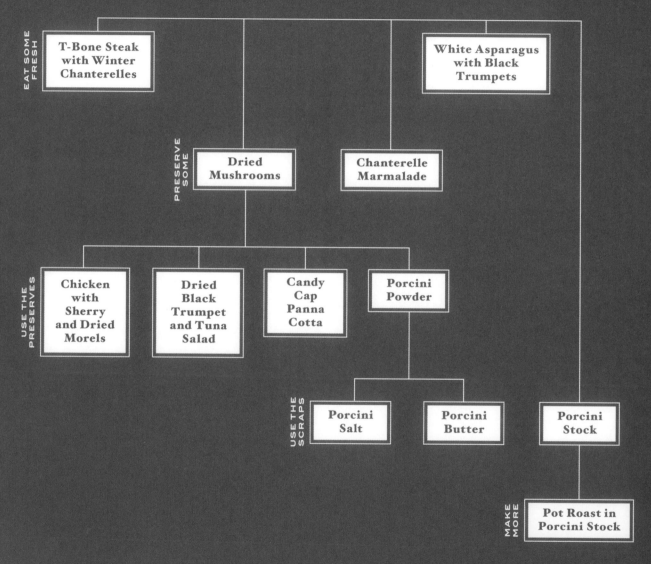

EAT SOME FRESH

T-Bone Steak with Winter Chanterelles

White Asparagus with Black Trumpets

PRESERVE SOME

Dried Mushrooms

Chanterelle Marmalade

USE THE PRESERVES

Chicken with Sherry and Dried Morels

Dried Black Trumpet and Tuna Salad

Candy Cap Panna Cotta

Porcini Powder

USE THE SCRAPS

Porcini Salt

Porcini Butter

Porcini Stock

MAKE MORE

Pot Roast in Porcini Stock

T-Bone Steak with Winter Chanterelles

On a mushroom hunt with Sonoma-based preserver and gleaner Elissa Rubin-Mahon, we found a load of Craterellus tubaeformis, *known as the yellow foot or winter chanterelle. Some people wrongly disparage this mushroom, which is delicately peaty and perfect, says Elissa, cooked with Scotch. You can substitute any tender wild mushroom but switch the Scotch for brandy if you do.* SERVES 4

- 2 T-bone steaks (about 1 pound each)
- 2 tablespoons olive oil
- Salt and freshly ground black pepper
- 5 tablespoons Scotch whiskey
- ½ cup chicken stock (for homemade, page 89)
- 2 pounds winter chanterelle mushrooms
- 4 tablespoons (½ stick) unsalted butter, cut into pieces
- 2 tablespoons chopped fresh thyme, for garnish

Rub the steaks with the oil and season with salt and pepper to taste. Heat a well-seasoned cast-iron skillet over medium-high heat. Add the steaks and pan-fry them until medium-rare (145°F), about 10 minutes on the first side, and 5 on the second. For rare, cook it to 130°F (or use the thumb test, page 42). Remove the steaks, cover with foil, and keep warm.

Wipe the fat out of the skillet. While holding the pan off the heat, add the Scotch and chicken stock to the skillet. It will bubble up. Return to the heat and loosen the browned bits with a spatula. Reduce by about one-fourth. Add the chanterelles. Cook until the mushrooms are soft, about 10 minutes. Swirl in the butter and add salt and pepper to taste.

Slice the steak against the grain and garnish with the mushrooms. Sprinkle with the thyme.

White Asparagus with Black Trumpets

I first had this dish at D'Artagnan, a much beloved but now defunct Gascon restaurant in Midtown Manhattan. White asparagus have a mild flavor that showcases the mushrooms. Clean black trumpets carefully. Because they are black it is easy to miss bits of forest debris. You can substitute other mushrooms, such as morels, in this elegant recipe. SERVES 4

- 1 pound white asparagus
- 1 bay leaf
- 4 tablespoons (½ stick) unsalted butter
- 2 tablespoons sliced shallots
- 1½ cups black trumpet mushrooms
- ¼ cup white wine
- Salt and freshly ground black pepper
- 2 tablespoons minced flat-leaf parsley (optional)

Lay the asparagus in a shallow pot or pan and add enough water to come halfway up the sides of the asparagus. Add the bay leaf and bring to a low boil over medium heat. Cover and poach the asparagus until they are fork-tender, about 5 minutes. Remove from the water, wrap in foil, and keep warm.

In a small nonstick skillet, heat 2 tablespoons of the butter over medium heat. Add the shallots and cook until they are translucent, a few minutes. Add the black trumpets and cook until they are fork-tender, about 5 minutes. Add the wine and continue cooking to reduce the liquid by half, a few minutes more. Cut up the remaining 2 tablespoons of butter and swirl it in just until melted.

To serve, pour the mushrooms on top of the poached asparagus. Season with salt and pepper to taste. Garnish with parsley, if you'd like.

MORELS

BLACK
TRUMPETS

CANDY
CAPS

DRIED MUSHROOMS

To prepare mushrooms for drying, wash them and allow them to drain thoroughly. Cut large mushrooms (over 2½ inches long) into lengthwise slices; cut large morels in half. Do not refrigerate mushrooms after they have been washed.

To dry in a dehydrator: Place the mushrooms cut side up in the trays of a food dehydrator. Do not pack them tightly. Set your dryer to 135°F. Mushrooms dry at different rates, but they all must dry until they are brittle. Morels and sliced porcini dry in about 8 hours, depending on their size. The more tender mushrooms like candy caps (of which there are several species, but *Lactarius fragilis*, a maple-flavored mushroom, is my favorite) and black trumpets are brittle in about 6 hours.

To dry in an oven: Morels are treated differently (see below), but for other mushrooms, slice large specimens and dry them on a wire rack in your oven as described in "How to Dry" (page 385). It should take the same amount of time to dry in the oven as it does in a dehydrator.

To dry morels in an oven: Thread morel mushrooms through the stem with a needle threaded with about 6 inches of dental floss. Tie the morels to a rack in your oven so they hang caps down and are well separated; adjust your oven racks to accommodate two layers of hanging morels, if you have that many. Remove any unused racks. Morels should take about 8 hours to dry in the oven.

Condition dried mushrooms as described in "How to Dry" (page 385).

To rehydrate dried mushrooms: Place them in a bowl of cool water, with a ratio of about 1 part mushroom to 3 parts water. To keep the mushrooms submerged, fill a food storage bag with water, seal it, and place it on top of the mushrooms. After 10 to 20 minutes, they will be soft and have returned to their fresh shape, ready to cook. Taste the water. If it has good flavor, strain it and use when cooking the mushrooms. (Always cook morels. Never eat them raw as they contain a substance that can cause stomach upset, but that is neutralized when heated.)

Chanterelle Marmalade

I first tasted this scrumptious marmalade at a potluck held by the New York Mycological Society. The recipe is adapted from one by a mushroom enthusiast, Long Litt Woon, who lives in Norway. I like to serve this marmalade on a cheese plate and in a cheese sandwich. **MAKES 1 PINT**

> ½ pound chanterelle mushrooms
>
> 1¼ cups water
>
> ½ cup sugar
>
> ½ cup white wine vinegar
>
> ¼ cup minced onion
>
> 6 prunes, pitted and chopped
>
> 3 garlic cloves, minced
>
> 1 teaspoon minced fresh ginger
>
> 3 green cardamom pods
>
> One 2-inch cinnamon stick
>
> 1 bay leaf
>
> ¼ teaspoon mustard seeds
>
> Salt and freshly ground black pepper

Chop the mushrooms into bite-size pieces. Heat a dry skillet over medium-high heat and add the mushrooms. Cook the mushrooms until they release their liquid, and the liquid evaporates, about 10 minutes.

In a small saucepan, combine the mushrooms, water (see Note), sugar, vinegar, onion, prunes, garlic, ginger, cardamom, cinnamon, bay leaf, mustard seeds, and salt and pepper to taste. Cook the marmalade, uncovered, over medium-low heat until the liquid reduces and is syrupy, about 20 minutes. It will be amber colored and very delicious.

Have ready 1 sterilized pint jar, band, and lid. (See "How to Sterilize," page 389.) You do not need to use a new lid because you will not process this jar. Pour the marmalade into the jar. Place on the lid and screw on the band. The marmalade holds in the refrigerator for about 3 months. Remove the cardamom pods, cinnamon stick, and bay leaf before serving.

Note: Chanterelles freeze well. Blanch them in boiling water for 2 minutes, drain, and freeze, or sauté them in butter or oil until they release their liquid, then freeze them in their liquid. If using frozen chanterelles in this recipe, thaw and squeeze out the excess water and save it to use in the marmalade cooking step. But taste the water first: Sometimes chanterelle water can be bitter. If it's good to use, then replace some of the regular water with an equal amount of the mushroom water you squeezed out.

CHANTERELLE MARMALADE

Chicken with Sherry and Dried Morels

This is a poor man's version of the very elegant French regional dish poulet vin jaune, *chicken braised with a white wine from Château-Chalon. I use sherry instead, which has a similar flavor. You can make this dish with dried or fresh morels (see Variation).* SERVES 4

> At least 1 cup dried morels (see page 195), but more if you've got them
>
> 2 tablespoons unsalted butter
>
> 8 bone-in, skin-on chicken thighs (or other chicken parts)
>
> 2 cups dry sherry
>
> Salt and freshly ground black pepper
>
> ½ cup heavy cream
>
> 2 tablespoons chopped fresh tarragon, for garnish

Place the mushrooms in a bowl of cool water to cover. Soak until the mushrooms are softened, 10 to 20 minutes. Strain the soaking liquid and reserve.

In a Dutch oven with a fitted lid, heat the butter over medium heat. Add the chicken and lightly brown all over, about 20 minutes. Add the sherry, the rehydrated morels, no more than 1 cup of the soaking liquid (save the rest for another use), and salt and pepper to taste. Bring to a boil. Then reduce the heat to low, cover, and gently boil until the chicken is very tender, about 40 minutes.

Transfer the chicken to a platter, wrap in foil, and keep warm. You will probably have about 2 cups of sauce (sherry and drippings combined). Stir in the cream, increase the heat to medium, and cook, uncovered, to reduce the sauce by about one-third. Check the seasoning and return the chicken to the pot. Cook for 5 minutes to heat through.

Serve garnished with the tarragon.

VARIATION
Chicken with Sherry and Fresh Morels:
Brown the chicken as directed. Add the sherry and salt and pepper to taste. Bring to a boil, then reduce to a gentle boil and cook for 20 minutes. Add ½ pound fresh morels, left whole if 2 inches long or smaller, otherwise cut in half lengthwise. Re-cover and continue cooking until the chicken is very tender, about 20 minutes longer. Proceed with the rest of the recipe as written.

Dried Black Trumpet and Tuna Salad

My friend Elissa made sandwiches with this salad for our mushroom hunt one year. The salad can be made ahead of time and holds in the refrigerator for a few days. Bring to room temperature before serving. You can substitute other tender wild mushrooms for the trumpets and you can add sliced hard-boiled eggs, chopped flat-leaf parsley, and/or a drizzle of extra virgin olive oil as a garnish. It's also great mixed with sliced boiled potatoes. **SERVES 2**

- 8 ounces dried black trumpet mushrooms (see page 195)
- ¼ cup olive oil
- 2 tablespoons white wine vinegar
- 1 tablespoon chopped fresh thyme
- 1 teaspoon minced garlic
- 2 half-pints tuna packed in olive oil (for homemade, page 301), drained
- 1 heaping tablespoon minced red onion
- Shaved Parmesan cheese
- Salt and freshly ground black pepper

Soak the trumpets in cool water until they are soft, about 10 minutes. Swish them in the water to remove any grit and drain.

Bring a medium pot of water to a gentle boil over medium heat and add the mushrooms. Gently boil until the mushrooms are fork-tender, about 10 minutes. Drain and place the mushrooms in a bowl. Add the olive oil, vinegar, thyme, and garlic. Mix gently and let rest for about 30 minutes. (You can do this ahead of time. Just cover with plastic wrap and refrigerate. The mushrooms will hold for about 5 days.)

Add the tuna to the mushrooms and gently toss. Add the onions and toss. Add shaved Parmesan and salt and pepper to taste.

Serve at room temperature.

Candy Cap Panna Cotta

If the rest of the world were to discover candy cap mushrooms, there wouldn't be any more for us. When you pick candy caps, your skin smells like maple syrup. When you eat them, your sweat smells like maple syrup. When you make love, well, yes. Some people bake with candy caps. I like to push a couple of dried candy caps into baked apples, or throw them in with poaching pears, which is divine.

You can buy candy caps from online mushroom purveyors like Far West Fungi. However, there are a cluster of species collectively called candy caps, and some are sweeter than others. If you find that the mushrooms are bitter, just add more sugar and cook them longer. Besides panna cotta, you can use candy cap sauce on cheesecake, baked apples, bread pudding, vanilla ice cream, and ricotta cream. Use the cooked mushrooms as a substitute for raisins in Tiramisu with Raisins (page 161). **SERVES 4**

PANNA COTTA

2 cups heavy cream

½ cup sugar

Neutral oil, such as safflower, for the ramekins

3 tablespoons cold water

1 envelope (¼ ounce) unflavored powdered gelatin

CANDY CAP SAUCE

4 heaping tablespoons dried candy cap mushrooms (see page 195)

1½ cups water

About ½ cup sugar

For the panna cotta: In a saucepan, combine the cream and sugar and heat over medium-low heat, stirring to dissolve the sugar. Remove from the heat.

Lightly oil four ½-cup ramekins.

Pour the water into a medium bowl and sprinkle in the gelatin. The gelatin will soften in a minute. Pour the warm cream and sugar mixture over it. Stir until the gelatin is dissolved.

Divide the cream mixture among the ramekins. Refrigerate for 4 to 6 hours (but not longer than 12 hours or it may get tough).

Meanwhile, for the candy cap sauce: Soak the candy caps in the water for about 10 minutes, until the mushrooms are soft. Remove the mushrooms and strain the liquid through a fine-mesh sieve to remove any forest grit. Pour the candy cap soaking liquid and the mushrooms into a small heavy-bottomed pot. Add ½ cup sugar. Bring the syrup to a low boil over medium-low heat and simmer until the mushrooms are very tender, about 20 minutes. The mushrooms will become sweeter over time. Give the syrup a taste and see if you need more sugar. Reduce the syrup to about ¾ cup.

The sauce holds in the refrigerator for a few days, but it can get pretty gummy—you'll need to add water to reheat. I like to serve it at room temperature.

To serve, remove the panna cotta by running a sharp knife around the edge of each ramekin and unmold by tapping onto a serving dish. Add a couple of tablespoons of candy cap syrup with a few mushrooms on top of each.

PORCINI POWDER

To make porcini powder, simply grind dried porcini in a spice grinder. You will notice a lot of porcini dust when you open the top of the grinder. Don't worry about it. It's mostly dried spores. One and a half cups of loosely packed dried porcini mushrooms will grind up to about ½ cup of powder. You can keep excess powder in a clean jar for about a year. I use porcini powder lots of ways: to make Porcini Salt (below), Porcini Butter (opposite), in pasta al'olio and risotto, but one of my favorites is as a rub on meat. Beef rubbed with the porcini powder, seared, and cooked as a pot roast is fabulous.

Porcini Salt

I like to use a coarse sea salt, but kosher salt works too. I use porcini salt as a finisher, sprinkled on beef, eggs, and pasta with mushrooms. It also makes a great gift. MAKES ABOUT ¼ CUP

4 tablespoons very coarse salt (or slightly less if you are using a finer grain of salt)

2 tablespoons Porcini Powder (above)

In a spice grinder, combine the salt and porcini powder. Grind until well combined. Place in a small airtight container and store in the pantry for up to a year.

CROSTINI WITH PORCINI BUTTER AND SUMMER TRUFFLES

Porcini Butter

My friend Daniel Winkler, a mycologist with whom I traveled in Tibet in search of the elusive caterpillar mushroom, showed me this recipe. It's one of those products that falls under my "should be illegal it's so good" heading. Use the butter to spread on steaks or a piece of fish or to melt on top of an omelet, as a dressing for a simple spaghetti with garlic and oil, or smeared on toast. **MAKES ½ POUND**

> ½ pound (2 sticks) high-quality lightly salted or unsalted butter (I use lightly salted creamery butter from the farmers' market)
>
> 3 tablespoons Porcini Powder (opposite)
>
> Salt (optional)

Let the butter come to room temperature. In a small bowl, stir the butter and porcini powder until well combined. If you used unsalted butter, add salt to taste. Spoon the butter into a glass tub with a plastic top and refrigerate

until firm. You can freeze the butter for up to 8 months, after which its flavor will decline, or hold in the refrigerator for a couple of weeks.

Porcini Stock

In contrast to mushroom stock made with the stems and odd bits of mixed mushrooms, porcini stock is made with the pores (which have the same function as gills on other mushrooms) on the underside of the cap. As the mushroom matures, the pores become spongy and can turn green. For years I threw the pores away. But during a visit to our cabin in Colorado (where we collect porcini in abundance), the renowned mushroom hunter David Campbell told me the pores make an excellent stock. You can use this stock to make Mushroom Lemon Risotto (page 191), as a soup base, in a Pot Roast in Porcini Stock (page 200), or in a Bollito Misto (page 115). **MAKES 2 QUARTS**

> 1 quart porcini pores, removed from the underside of the cap (they pull off easily), and any stem or cap bits
>
> 1 large onion, cut into quarters
>
> Bunch of fresh thyme
>
> 1 teaspoon black peppercorns
>
> 1 bay leaf
>
> About 3 quarts water
>
> Salt

In a large soup pot, combine the mushroom pores, onion, thyme, peppercorns, and bay leaf. Add water to cover, cover the pot, and bring to a boil over medium heat. Reduce the heat to medium-low and boil gently for about 45 minutes. The stock will be greenish brown and slightly gooey, like aloe. It's okay. Uncover and boil for another 15 minutes or so, to reduce by about one-third. Strain the stock.

Transfer the stock to quart jars and refrigerate or freeze (see the technique for making stocks, page 390).

For shelf-stable stock, pressure can it, but in pint jars only. Follow the instructions for Mushroom Stock (page 190). Be sure to make altitude adjustments when preserving (see page 389).

Pot Roast in Porcini Stock

I love pot roasts for the garnishes. Serve this one with horseradish (for homemade, page 364) mixed with unsweetened whipped cream; skordalia (for homemade, page 368); or a quick sauté of olive oil, minced garlic, a handful of chopped mushrooms, the grated zest from half a lemon, and salt and pepper to taste. Leftover pot roast and its juices and vegetables make a wonderful base for lentil or bean soup. Just add dried lentils or rehydrated beans and water and boil until the beans are tender. **SERVES 6**

3 tablespoons unsalted butter

2 pounds chuck or rump roast

Salt and freshly ground black pepper

4 tablespoons Porcini Powder (page 198; optional)

1 cup coarsely chopped onions

3 large garlic cloves, peeled

½ cup dry white wine

1 quart Porcini Stock (page 199), plus more if needed

About 10 sprigs of fresh thyme

1 bay leaf

1 cup cut carrots (2-inch-long pieces)

1 cup cut celery (2-inch-long pieces)

2 tablespoons chopped flat-leaf parsley

In a large Dutch oven, heat the butter over medium-high heat. Season the meat with salt and pepper to taste, and if you have any porcini powder, rub it on the meat. Brown the meat all over in the butter, about 10 minutes. Add the onions and garlic and cook until the onions are translucent, about 5 minutes. Add the wine and boil it hard for a few minutes until it mostly evaporates. Add the stock, thyme, and bay leaf. Cover and cook over medium-low heat until the meat is tender, about 1 hour 30 minutes. Check after 1 hour to be sure the pot roast isn't getting dry. If it is, add more porcini stock, or if you don't have it, then chicken, beef, or vegetable stock, or water.

Add the carrots and celery. Continue cooking until they are tender, about 15 minutes.

Serve the pot roast in thick slices or hunks with the boiled carrots and celery, ladled with the juices and garnished with parsley.

PORCINI

MUSSELS

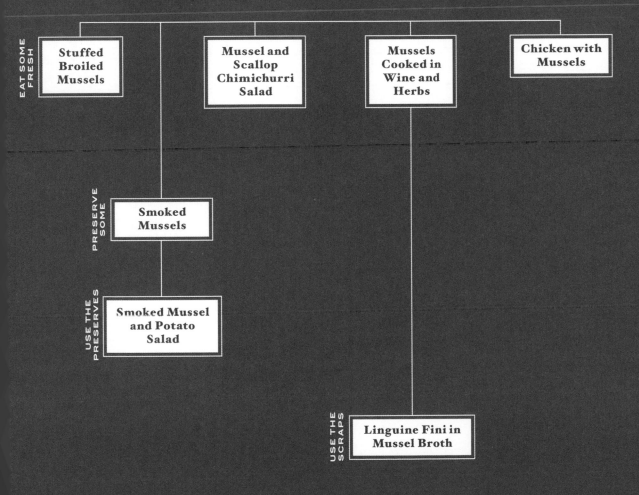

EAT SOME FRESH

Stuffed Broiled Mussels

Mussel and Scallop Chimichurri Salad

Mussels Cooked in Wine and Herbs

Chicken with Mussels

PRESERVE SOME

Smoked Mussels

USE THE PRESERVES

Smoked Mussel and Potato Salad

USE THE SCRAPS

Linguine Fini in Mussel Broth

STUFFED
BROILED
MUSSELS

Mussel Preparation

When buying mussels look at the harvest or "use by" date. Mussels quickly deteriorate after they have died, so look for specimens with tightly closed shells. Often, mussels will open their shells even though they are still alive. But when you tap on their shells they will close again. It is important to inspect every mussel while cleaning them. I like to cut or yank off the beard but you don't have to. Just be sure the mussels are tightly closed and the shell unbroken. A good test to determine whether a closed mussel is alive or not is to twist the mussel between your fingers. If the mussel is dead the upper and lower shell will slide back and forth. Mussels should smell fresh as the ocean.

Refrigerate mussels in a bowl covered with a damp towel. Don't store them in an airtight container, plastic bag, or water. You can keep them in the fridge for a day or two, but drain the small amount of liquid that they release each day.

Stuffed Broiled Mussels

*The first time I made this dish was on a hot plate and in a toaster oven. My sister and I threw a party when we lived in a raw TriBeCa loft that didn't have a proper kitchen. We made hundreds of these stuffed mussels that we bought in Chinatown for $.99 a pound. You can stuff clams and oysters the same way. **After boiling the mussels, strain the broth and save it for Linguine Fini (page 207).***

SERVES 4 AS AN APPETIZER

4 pounds mussels, scrubbed

2 cups white wine

2 cups water

1 small onion, peeled

Bunch of flat-leaf parsley stems

1 bay leaf

½ cup breadcrumbs (for homemade, page 362)

1 tablespoon minced flat-leaf parsley

1 teaspoon minced garlic

2 tablespoons olive oil

Salt and freshly ground black pepper

Juice of ½ lemon

Place the mussels, wine, water, onion, parsley stems, and bay leaf in a large pot. Cover and bring to a boil over medium heat. Steam the mussels until they open, about 8 minutes. Discard any mussels that do not open.

Preheat the broiler.

Open the mussels and loosen the meat, leaving it in the lower shell. Discard the upper shells. Place the mussels on a large baking sheet.

In a medium bowl, combine the breadcrumbs, minced parsley, garlic, olive oil, and salt and pepper to taste. Sprinkle the breadcrumb mixture over the mussel meat. Drizzle the lemon juice over the mussels.

Place the mussels under the broiler and broil for a minute, until the breadcrumbs brown. Don't walk away! They burn easily.

Mussel and Scallop Chimichurri Salad

*This cold fish salad is perfect in the summer. You can add chopped avocado and sliced boiled potatoes. I've even served it over a bowl of Marilee's Coleslaw (page 58). **After cooking the scallops in the mussel broth, strain the broth. You should have about 1 pint. Pour the broth into a jar and refrigerate for Linguine Fini (page 207).*** **SERVES 4 AS AN APPETIZER**

MUSSEL AND SCALLOP CHIMICHURRI SALAD

3 pounds mussels, scrubbed

1 cup white wine

½ cup coarsely chopped onion

¼ cup chopped fresh dill

1 orange, quartered

1 small dried hot pepper

8 large scallops, hinge muscle removed (see photo, page 98)

CHIMICHURRI SAUCE

1 cup coarsely chopped flat-leaf parsley

¼ cup white wine vinegar

½ cup olive oil

1 tablespoon coarsely chopped garlic

Salt and freshly ground black pepper

Place the mussels in a soup pot with the wine, onion, and dill. Squeeze the juice from the quartered oranges into the pot and add the orange rinds. Add the chile pepper, cover, and bring to a boil over high heat. Steam the mussels until they open, about 8 minutes.

Discard any mussels that did not open. Remove the pot from the heat and allow the mussels to cool enough to handle. Remove the meat from the shells, place in a bowl, and set aside. Discard the shells.

Bring the liquid in the pot back to a gentle boil over medium heat and add the scallops. Poach the scallops until they become opaque and crack, about 8 minutes. Remove them with a slotted spoon and cut them into quarters. Put them in the bowl with the mussels.

For the chimichurri sauce: In a food processor or blender, combine the parsley, vinegar, olive oil, garlic, and salt and pepper to taste. Pulse to grind to a very loose sauce. I like flakes of parsley big enough to see, though you can grind the chimichurri very fine if you'd like. You should have about ½ cup.

Toss the chimichurri with the mussels and scallops. You can serve right away, or refrigerate overnight. Let the salad warm up a bit at room temperature before serving, however.

Mussels Cooked in Wine and Herbs

Steamed mussels make a great light supper or first course. The recipe is very adaptable. You can add more or less onion, green pepper, herbs, or garlic. Just don't overcook them. Once the mussels are open, they are ready. Be sure to save the leftover broth. (I even save it when I go to restaurants and order this dish. Even when someone else orders this dish actually, which I guess is kind of tacky, but not if you know what great stuff it is.) I like to serve these mussels with bread to sop up the juices. SERVES 4

- 5 pounds mussels, scrubbed
- 3 cups white wine
- 2 cups water
- 1 cup finely chopped fennel (it's okay to use the tops)
- ½ cup finely chopped green bell pepper
- ½ cup finely chopped onion
- ½ cup finely chopped celery
- ⅓ cup finely chopped cilantro
- 3 sprigs of fresh oregano
- 2 garlic cloves, finely chopped
- 1 small hot dried pepper
- ½ lemon
- 1 bay leaf
- Salt and freshly ground black pepper

Place the mussels, wine, water, fennel, bell pepper, onion, celery, cilantro, oregano, garlic, hot pepper, lemon, bay, and salt and pepper to taste in a big pot. Cover and bring to a boil over medium heat. Boil until the mussels open,

about 8 minutes. Discard any mussels that did not open. You can serve the mussels in a bowl at this point, or strain the broth and serve it with the mussels, either in or out of the shell.

Chicken with Mussels

This is Italian surf and turf. It is a dish my dad often made in the summer with mussels we harvested ourselves, and is wonderful served family style. **Save the chicken neck, back, and wing tips for Chicken Stock (page 89).** SERVES 4

- One 3-pound chicken, cut into serving pieces
- Salt and freshly ground black pepper
- 2 tablespoons olive oil
- 2 garlic cloves, smashed and peeled
- 1 cup white wine
- 2 tablespoons chopped fresh basil
- 2 tablespoons chopped fresh mint
- 1 teaspoon dried oregano
- 2 cups crushed tomatoes (for homemade, page 328)
- 1 cup minced green bell pepper
- 3 pounds mussels, scrubbed
- 2 tablespoons chopped flat-leaf parsley

Season the chicken with salt and pepper. In a large skillet, heat the olive oil over medium heat. Add the chicken and garlic. Cook until the chicken is browned on one side, 5 to 10 minutes. Turn the chicken over and add the wine, basil, mint, and oregano. Cook for 5 minutes more. Add the tomatoes and bell pepper. Cover and cook until the sauce is thick and the chicken is cooked through, about 20 minutes.

Add the mussels, cover, and cook until the mussels open, 5 to 10 minutes. Discard any mussels that did not open.

Remove most of the mussels from the shell, and return to the stew. I like to leave about one-fourth of the mussels still in the shell so people know what they are eating. Check the seasoning. Garnish with parsley and serve promptly.

Smoked Mussels

Smoking mussels consists of four stages: cooking, brining, smoking, and then packing in oil. They can also be pressure canned. My best results are with large wild mussels or the big green New Zealand mussels. Prince Edward Island mussels, the kind you normally see in grocery stores, are too small for smoking—you only end up getting about ¼ pint per pound. I love smoked mussels dipped in mayonnaise (page 365). **Strain the broth from cooking the mussels and save for another use.** MAKES 2 HALF-PINTS

> 2 pounds New Zealand green-lipped mussels (about 24)
>
> 3 cups water
>
> ½ cup white wine
>
> 1 small onion, quartered
>
> 1 bay leaf
>
> 1 small hot dried pepper
>
> 2 tablespoons pickling salt
>
> 1 tablespoon alder chips
>
> About 1 cup olive oil

Place the mussels, 1 cup of the water, the wine, onion, bay leaf, and hot pepper in a big pot. Cover and bring to a boil over medium-high heat. Cook until the mussels open, about 8 minutes, then remove from the heat. Discard any mussels that did not open. As soon as the mussels are cool enough to handle, remove the meat from the shells.

In a large bowl, combine the remaining 2 cups water and the salt and add the mussels. Soak for about 5 minutes. They will plump up. Drain and dry with a towel.

Prepare your stovetop smoker (see "How to Smoke Indoors," page 384) with the wood chips. Lay the mussels on the rack, close the smoker, and place over medium-high to high heat. Smoke the mussels for 10 minutes, and then take off the heat. Remove the mussels from the smoker. (For how to make your own smoker, see page 384.)

Have ready 2 sterilized half-pint jars, bands, and lids, or 1 pint jar, band, and lid. (See "How to Sterilize," page 389.) You do not need to use new lids because you will not process these jars. Pack the mussels in the jars and cover with olive oil. Wipe the rims, place on the lids, and screw on the bands. (See "Preserving in Oil," page 387.)

Holds in the refrigerator for up to 10 days.

Smoked Mussel and Potato Salad

This warm salad is perfect for a late dinner entrée. In small portions it makes for a good first course, too. **Save the mussel-flavored oil to use in place of olive oil next time you make a fish dish. It will add additional flavor.** SERVES 4

> 16 small white potatoes
>
> 1 pint Smoked Mussels (left), at room temperature
>
> Salt and freshly ground black pepper
>
> 2 tablespoons chopped flat-leaf parsley

Bring a large pot of water to a boil, then add the potatoes. Boil until fork-tender, about 10 minutes. Drain and peel, then cut into bite-size pieces. (Or you can roast them in a 375°F oven for about 25 minutes.)

Reserving the oil, drain the mussels. Toss the mussels with the potatoes in a serving dish. Add enough of the drained oil to glisten the potatoes. Season with salt and pepper to taste, but check first because you may not need any salt. Toss with the parsley and serve.

Linguine Fini in Mussel Broth

This intensely flavorful pasta calls for cooking the linguine in mussel broth. The pasta is not drained as it absorbs the broth and throws off starch, which thickens any remaining broth into a sauce. It is refined enough for company yet couldn't be simpler if you have the broth on hand. I usually make this dish a day or two after I've prepared a recipe with mussels. The strained broth freezes well (see techniques for stocks, page 390). The broth works perfectly in this recipe once thawed. SERVES 2

> 4 cups mussel broth (from preparing Mussels Cooked in Wine and Herbs, page 205)
>
> ½ pound linguine fini or spaghettini
>
> Salt and freshly ground black pepper
>
> 3 tablespoons olive oil
>
> 1 tablespoon minced garlic
>
> 1 tablespoon chopped anchovies (see Note)
>
> ½ cup mixed chopped tender herbs such as cilantro, tarragon, dill, basil, and parsley
>
> 1 cup mussel meats (optional)

In a pasta pot, bring the mussel broth to a boil over medium heat. Add the pasta and a big pinch of salt. See page 392 for instructions on how to cook pasta in stock.

Meanwhile, in a small saucepan, heat the olive oil over medium-low heat. Add the garlic and anchovies and cook until the garlic sizzles, but do not let it brown. Add the herbs and cook for a few more minutes.

Toss the oil and herb mixture into the pot with the pasta and combine well. Check the seasoning. Serve promptly, garnished with mussel meats if you'd like.

Note: I prefer whole anchovies cured in salt, available in Italian markets. Soak them for 10 minutes to remove the salt, then rinse and fillet them.

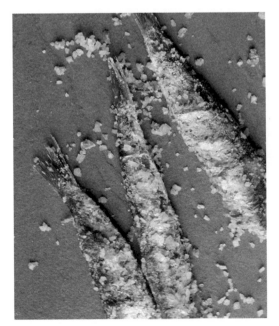

ANCHOVIES IN SALT

ONIONS

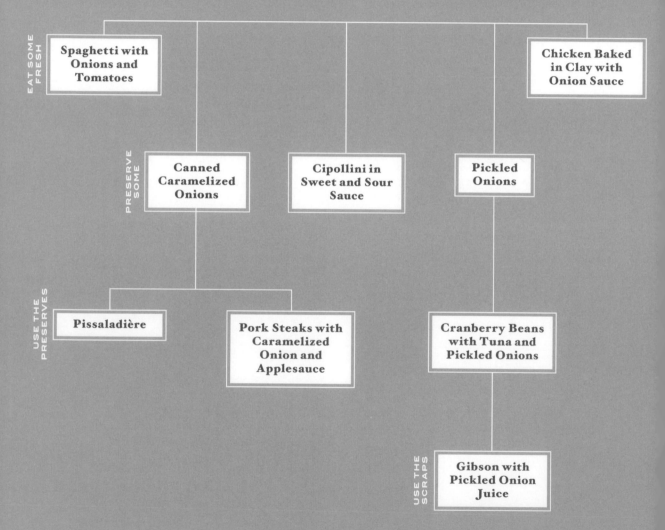

EAT SOME FRESH

Spaghetti with Onions and Tomatoes

Chicken Baked in Clay with Onion Sauce

PRESERVE SOME

Canned Caramelized Onions

Cipollini in Sweet and Sour Sauce

Pickled Onions

USE THE PRESERVES

Pissaladière

Pork Steaks with Caramelized Onion and Applesauce

Cranberry Beans with Tuna and Pickled Onions

USE THE SCRAPS

Gibson with Pickled Onion Juice

Spaghetti with Onions and Tomatoes

I have loved this sweet, filling family recipe my whole life. When I was a student on a tight budget, it was a lifesaver. **SERVES 4**

- 3 tablespoons olive oil
- 3 large onions, sliced (about 3 heaping cups)
- 1 pound spaghetti
- 1 cup crushed tomatoes (for homemade, page 328)
- 1 cup whole milk
- Salt and freshly ground black pepper
- 3 tablespoons grated Parmesan cheese
- 2 tablespoons chopped flat-leaf parsley

In a large heavy-bottomed pot, heat the oil over medium heat. Add the onions and cook until translucent, about 10 minutes. Do not brown the onions.

Meanwhile, bring a large pot of salted water to a boil and add the pasta. Cook for 6 minutes, about half the time it takes for pasta to cook to the point of al dente. Drain.

Add the tomato puree and milk to the onions. Cover and boil gently over low heat for about 5 minutes. (Don't worry if it looks curdled; the starch in the pasta will bind the milk and tomatoes to make a silky sauce.) Stir in the drained spaghetti and finish cooking the spaghetti in the sauce. If the sauce is too tight, add a bit more milk to loosen it up. Season with salt and pepper to taste.

Serve garnished with Parmesan and parsley. A few extra grinds of black pepper is nice, too.

SPAGHETTI WITH ONIONS AND TOMATOES

Chicken Baked in Clay with Onion Sauce

The ancient method of cooking in clay results in exceedingly tender foods. It's what a Romertopf, a clay roaster, does. In this recipe a whole chicken is wrapped in clay. After it comes out of the oven, the clay can be painted with bright-colored poster paints before it is brought to the table. You can take the time to paint the clay because the meat stays hot inside its clay oven for up to an hour. I made this dish with my kids when they were young, and they loved every aspect of its preparation, from forming a lifelike chicken in clay, to painting the wings, and finally, to the delightful moment when their most elemental, violent selves broke through and they smashed the clay to bits, revealing, like a piñata, the treat within. The quick onion sauce is key: It adds a wonderful sweetness to this tender dish. The recipe originally appeared in 1971 in Italian Family Cooking, *my dad's first cookbook.* **SERVES 4 TO 6**

One 4-pound chicken

1 garlic clove, cut into slivers

1 tablespoon fresh rosemary leaves
or 1 teaspoon dried

Salt and freshly ground black pepper

1 tablespoon olive oil or unsalted butter

1 tablespoon chopped fresh thyme
or 1 teaspoon dried

5 pounds sculptor's clay (use earth clay, not
Plasticine)

2 tablespoons unsalted butter

1 large onion, sliced

1 cup dry Marsala wine

Preheat the oven to 350°F.

Slip the garlic under the skin of the chicken. Place the rosemary and salt and pepper to taste in the cavity. Rub oil or butter over the bird and sprinkle with the thyme and salt and pepper to taste.

Wrap the chicken in foil, leaving no open seams. Set aside about 2 handfuls of clay. Cover a work surface with a large garbage bag and roll out the clay to about ¾ inch think. Wrap the clay around the foiled chicken, making sure none of the foil peeks through. With the 2 handfuls of clay, form a chicken head and tail. Use a teaspoon, fork, and/or butter knife to create the impression of feathers along the neck and sides of the bird. Reserve a couple of tablespoons of clay in case you need it to seal any cracks as the chicken bakes (see next step).

Place the chicken in a shallow baking pan and bake for 1 hour to dry out the clay so it will be less likely to crack. Then turn up heat to 450°F and continue baking for 45 minutes. Check the clay from time to time to see if it has cracks and steam is escaping. If it does, stuff the crack with more clay.

Remove the chicken and allow the clay to cool for about 15 minutes. Paint the clay with water-based poster paints if you'd like.

Meanwhile, in a large skillet, heat the butter over medium heat. Add the onion and cook until soft, about 5 minutes. Add the wine and cook until the liquid is reduced by half, another 5 minutes.

Crack the clay chicken open. Open the foil over a platter to retain the juices. The smell is delightful. Add the juices to the wine and onion mixture. Simmer the sauce over low heat while you carve the chicken. Lay the chicken on the platter and serve with the sauce poured over it.

Canned Caramelized Onions

Caramelized onions are perfect served with cheese or or eggs, or to make French onion soup or the French pizza, Pissaladière (page 212). Any kind of onion— white, yellow, or red—will work for this recipe, but I usually use Spanish onions. Two pounds of fresh onions generally make 3 caramelized cups. The pounds of pressure and timing for caramelized onions are based on the USDA recommendation for canning whole boiled onions. MAKES 3 HALF-PINTS

¼ cup olive oil

2 pounds onions, thinly sliced

Salt (optional)

Heat the oil in the largest skillet you have or divide the oil and heat in two 9-inch skillets over medium-low heat. Add the onions in a single layer (if you pile them they will steam and not caramelize well). Start the onions over medium-low heat (if they pick up a little brown color, that's good), but after about 5 minutes, reduce the heat to low and cook the onions for 45 minutes until caramelized, stirring occasionally. You can add salt to taste if you'd like, or salt the onions when you use them in a recipe.

Have ready 3 clean half-pint jars and bands, and new lids that have been simmered in hot water to soften the rubberized flange. Pack the onions into the jars leaving 1 inch of headroom. Wipe the rims, place on the lids, and screw on the bands fingertip tight.

Process the jars in a pressure canner at 10/11 psi for 40 minutes. (See "How to Pressure Can," page 379.) Be sure to make altitude adjustments when preserving (see page 389).

Cipollini in Sweet and Sour Sauce

The classic Italian preparation is to braise cipollini in a vinegar tomato sauce. This recipe combines the same ingredients but allows the pressure canner to do the cooking. The result is an excellent quick side dish for grilled steak—just dump them out of the jar and into a pan and heat. The timing is based on USDA data for pressure canning whole boiled onions.
MAKES 3 PINTS

> 2 cups crushed tomatoes (for homemade, page 328)
> ¾ cup white wine vinegar (5% acidity)
> 4 tablespoons sugar
> 1 teaspoon pickling salt (optional)
> 2 pounds cipollini onions, peeled (about 25 the size of a silver dollar)

In a large pot, combine the tomato puree, vinegar, sugar, and salt (if using). Bring to a boil and add the onions. Boil gently for 5 minutes.

Have ready 3 clean pint jars and bands, and new lids that have been simmered in hot water to soften the rubberized flange. Pack the jars with the onions and cover with the tomato sauce leaving 1 inch of headroom. Wipe the rims, place on the lids, and screw on the bands fingertip tight.

Process the jars in a pressure canner at 10/11 psi for 40 minutes. (See "How to Pressure Can," page 379.) Be sure to make altitude adjustments when preserving (see page 389).

Pickled Onions

I make these with cipollini onions mainly because they are so pretty, and I get inspired to do it when they are in during the winter months. But you can pickle pearl onions, too, or chopped white onions. I save the leftover onion-flavored vinegar for Gibsons (page 213), my favorite cocktail. You can add spices like celery seed and mustard seed and it won't change the safety of the recipe. **MAKES 2 HALF-PINTS**

> 1½ cups distilled white or white wine vinegar (5% acidity)
> ½ cup sugar
> ¼ cup water
> ½ teaspoon pickling salt
> 2 cups tiny cipollini onions, peeled

In a medium pot, combine the vinegar, sugar, water, and salt and heat over medium heat. As soon as the sugar has dissolved, add the onions. Boil for 5 minutes.

Have ready 2 clean half-pint jars and bands, and new lids that have been simmered in hot water to soften the rubberized flange. Pack the onions into the jars and cover with the vinegar solution leaving ½ inch of headroom. Wipe the rims, place on the lids, and screw on the bands fingertip tight.

Process the jars in a water bath (see page 375) for 10 minutes. Be sure to make altitude adjustments when preserving (see page 389).

Pissaladière

Pissaladière is a specialty of Nice—a kind of flaky pizza-like tart with onions, niçoise olives, and anchovies. It's a fast and easy dish to make if you have the caramelized onions on hand. **SERVES 4 AS AN APPETIZER**

- 1 sheet (10 × 15 inches) frozen puff pastry, thawed in the refrigerator
- 1 half-pint Canned Caramelized Onions (page 210)
- 12 niçoise olives, pitted and sliced
- 2 whole anchovies or 4 anchovy fillets (see Note, page 207), chopped
- Salt and freshly ground black pepper

Preheat the oven to 450°F. Place a baking sheet in the oven to heat up.

Lay the puff pastry sheet on a silicone baking mat or piece of parchment paper and roll up the sides of the pastry to create a raised edge. Spread the caramelized onions over the pastry, then dot with olives and anchovies. Season with salt and pepper to taste.

Place the pissaladière on the hot baking sheet and bake for 10 to 15 minutes. You'll smell it and the pastry will be golden brown and puffy. Almost immediately after removing from the oven it will deflate, so serve promptly.

CIPOLLINI ONIONS

Pork Steaks with Caramelized Onion and Applesauce

This is a quick and satisfying dinner, my style of fast food because I often have both the applesauce and the caramelized onions on hand. You can also use fresh peeled and sliced apples. Put them in at the same time as the wine. **SERVES 4**

- 3 tablespoons unsalted butter
- 1½ pounds boneless center-cut pork chops, thin sliced
- Salt and freshly ground black pepper
- 1 cup dry white wine
- 1 cup applesauce (for homemade, page 10)
- ½ pint Canned Caramelized Onions (page 210)
- 2 tablespoons fresh thyme leaves

In a large skillet, heat the butter over medium heat. Season the pork chops and add them to the skillet. Cook until golden brown on both sides, about 5 minutes. Add the wine, cover, and cook until the wine is reduced and the internal temperature of the pork is 145°F, about 10 minutes. Uncover, add the applesauce and onions and cook until they are hot, about 5 minutes. Garnish with the thyme and serve.

Cranberry Beans with Tuna and Pickled Onions

Fresh cranberry beans, also known as borlotti beans, are usually sold in their long red freckled shells during the winter. I like to serve this dish with bruschetta. **SERVES 4 AS AN APPETIZER**

- 1½ pounds fresh cranberry beans in the pod, shelled (about 1¾ cups)
- 1¾ cups chicken stock (for homemade, page 89)
- 1 teaspoon salt
- 2 half-pints tuna packed in olive oil (for homemade, page 301), drained
- ½ cup Pickled Onions (page 211), thickly sliced or halved if small
- Juice from ½ lemon
- Freshly ground black pepper
- 2 tablespoons minced flat-leaf parsley

In a medium pot, combine the beans, chicken stock, and salt. Boil, uncovered, over medium heat until the beans are tender but al dente, about 25 minutes. The red speckles on the beans will fade and the beans will turn pinky beige.

Drain off any remaining stock and transfer the beans to a serving bowl. Add the tuna and onions to the beans and gently toss. Add the lemon juice and pepper to taste and combine gently. Garnish with minced parsley.

Serve at room temperature.

Gibson with Pickled Onion Juice

The Gibson is my drink and, like all martini drinkers, I am all about the garnish. After extensive experimenting, I realized that it was the tart sweetness in home-pickled onions that made the drink sing. Tiny pearl onions are a fine fit for a martini glass, but a bummer to peel and pickle, and when I thought about it, I never eat the onion anyway. So now I make Gibsons with the pickling juice from my home-pickled onions and it is perfect, and I supply it to numerous stressed-out girlfriends, particularly Diane, around the time she is doing her potato pancake party (see page 13). **SERVES 1**

- 1½ ounces gin or vodka
- ¼ teaspoon dry vermouth
- ¼ teaspoon (or more) juice from Pickled Onions (page 211)

Pour the liquor, vermouth, and pickle juice into a cocktail shaker with ice cubes. Shake very vigorously. Strain into a martini glass.

ORANGES

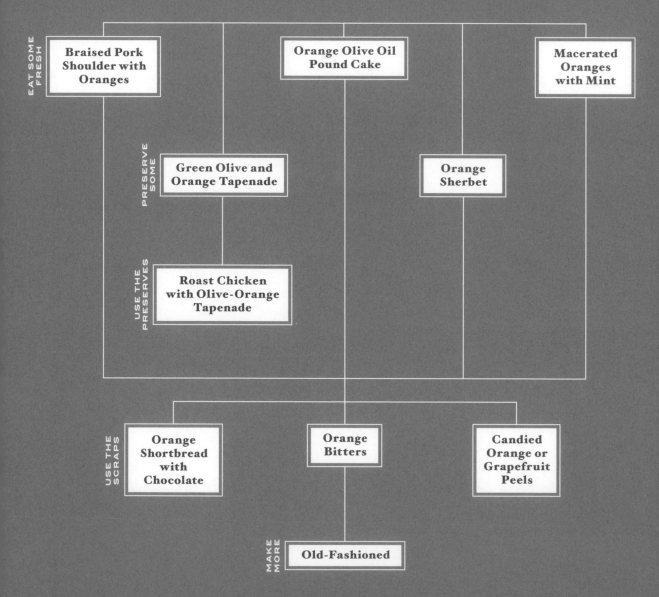

EAT SOME FRESH

Braised Pork Shoulder with Oranges

Orange Olive Oil Pound Cake

Macerated Oranges with Mint

PRESERVE SOME

Green Olive and Orange Tapenade

Orange Sherbet

USE THE PRESERVES

Roast Chicken with Olive-Orange Tapenade

USE THE SCRAPS

Orange Shortbread with Chocolate

Orange Bitters

Candied Orange or Grapefruit Peels

MAKE MORE

Old-Fashioned

Braised Pork Shoulder with Oranges

This combination of pork and orange is sweet and unctuous. The leftovers (if there are any) are wonderful next to a scrambled egg. The pork is marinated 12 hours, but a couple of hours is okay. **Before you juice the oranges, grate the zest and save it for Pound Cake (right) or Orange Shortbread (page 219), or remove the zest in strips and save for Orange Bitters (page 221). Zest holds for about 4 days in the fridge, or can be frozen or dried (see page 221).** SERVES 4 TO 6

- 3 pounds bone-in pork shoulder
- 1 tablespoon paprika (sweet or a combination of sweet and hot)
- 1 tablespoon ancho chile powder
- 2 oranges, juiced
- 1 lemon, juiced
- 2 limes, juiced
- ½ cup white wine
- 3 tablespoons olive oil
- 3 garlic cloves, smashed and peeled
- 3 sprigs of flat-leaf parsley
- One 3-inch sprig of rosemary
- 1 teaspoon salt
- ½ teaspoon freshly ground black pepper

Rub one side of the pork with the paprika and the other side with the ancho. Place in a large zipseal plastic food storage bag or large bowl.

In a small bowl, combine the citrus juices, wine, olive oil, garlic, parsley, rosemary, salt, and pepper. Pour the marinade into the bag or bowl and distribute around the meat. Refrigerate 12 hours (overnight is good), turning the meat over once or twice.

Preheat the oven to 400°F. Allow the meat to come to room temperature.

Place the meat and marinade in a roasting pan (a 9 × 9 × 2-inch pan fits well—the meat should be snug in the pan). Cover with foil and bake for 2½ to 3 hours, until the meat is falling off the bone. It will be swimming in fat.

Remove the garlic, rosemary, and parsley. Spoon the fat off the drippings (or use a gravy separator). Serve the drippings poured over the meat.

Orange Olive Oil Pound Cake

My criteria when it comes to recipes are these: Is it tasty enough that I will crave it over and over? Is it easy? And does it look pretty? This recipe hits those marks. It is moistest, richest, most flavorful pound cake I have ever made. MAKES ONE 9-INCH LOAF

- 1 tablespoon unsalted butter, for the pan
- 2 cups all-purpose flour
- 1 tablespoon baking powder
- Pinch of salt
- 3 large eggs
- 1¼ cups sugar
- 1 cup olive oil
- ½ cup whole milk
- 2 tablespoons brandy
- 2 tablespoons orange liqueur, such as Cointreau
- 1 tablespoon grated lemon zest
- 1 tablespoon grated orange zest
- ½ cup fresh orange juice

Preheat the oven to 325°F. Butter a 9 × 5-inch loaf pan.

In a medium bowl, whisk together the flour, baking powder, and salt. In a large bowl, whisk together the eggs and 1 cup of the sugar. Whisk in the olive oil, milk, brandy, liqueur, lemon zest, orange zest, and ¼ cup of the orange juice. Add the dry ingredients and whisk to combine. The batter is wet. It's okay.

Pour the batter into the loaf pan and bake for 1 hour 5 minutes to 1 hour 10 minutes, until a cake tester inserted in the cake comes out clean. You will smell the cake when it is done. Remove the cake from the oven and let cool enough to handle, then flip over onto a rack to cool thoroughly.

Meanwhile, in a small bowl, combine the remaining ¼ cup sugar and ¼ cup orange juice.

Turn the cake right side up. Using a pastry brush, brush the glaze all over the cake. Allow the glaze to harden some before serving.

Macerated Oranges with Mint

I like to serve these orange slices laid out on a platter: They are beautifully shiny. You can also make this dish with navel orange or tangerine segments. See the variation, below, for a savory version of this dish.
SERVES 4

Oranges

My grandparents used to winter in West Palm Beach, at a development called The Lost Tree Club. In the 1970s it was popular with Southern businessmen and it had a genteel conventional air. The crowd was old-world gracious, with head-patting grandpas in charge of regional banks and trim white-haired ladies in Elizabeth Arden lipstick who threw cocktail parties before driving one block to take their guests to dinner at the clubhouse (my grandmother Elinor, from Memphis, loved the "Boo-fay" with its display of cold shellfish on ice, punctuated with halved lemons). My sister and I used to visit during our Christmas break from school in snowy Vermont, and we couldn't wait to bake ourselves crisp on the beach.

The small house, which faced the sea, was cool and turquoise and pink. There was always a supply of bottled Cokes in the fridge, next to a tray of cold stuffed eggs. My grandparents seemed happiest if we were not asking them too many questions, and so, in our bikinis and puka shell necklaces, we slowly invited our middle-aged wrinkles. The Lost Tree Club is where I smoked my first cigarette (a Vantage) and drank my first cocktail (a Grasshopper). And it is where I first tasted fresh-squeezed Honeybell juice.

Honeybells, also known as Minneola tangelos, are not really oranges. They are a hybrid of a tangerine (which is a hybrid of an orange) and a grapefruit. Nonetheless, it is the "orange" that I love, and eat, most. Indeed, it was one of the great delights of my adulthood to realize I could order Honeybells and have them sent to dreary, wintry New York. To me, they simply represent the bliss of teenagerism: those first forays into adult party behavior, the utter inability to imagine middle age, much less death, and the great joy of guilt-free idleness.

MACERATED ORANGES

GREEN OLIVE AND ORANGE TAPENADE

4 oranges

¼ cup sugar

¼ cup fresh lemon juice

¼ cup rum

16 whole cloves

2 tablespoons slivered mint

Remove the peel and pick the pith off the oranges and slice the flesh into rounds. Remove the seeds.

In a large bowl, combine the sugar, lemon juice, rum, and cloves. Be sure to count how many cloves you add because you will need to remove them before serving. Mix well. Add the oranges and toss gently. Leave at room temperature to macerate for a couple of hours, or place the oranges in the fridge and let macerate overnight.

Before serving, remove the cloves and garnish with the mint.

VARIATION: To prepare savory macerated oranges, toss the orange slices in olive oil, lemon juice, and salt and pepper. Let macerate. You can also add sliced raw fennel to the oranges. Serve as a salad garnished with pitted dried black olives.

Green Olive and Orange Tapenade

This tapenade is great spread on crostini as an hors d'oeuvre, smeared on broiled or grilled fish, or tucked under the skin of a roast chicken (page 110). I also combine it with home-canned tuna to make a savory pasta sauce. For variety, add 2 tablespoons blanched almonds, a clove of garlic, 1 teaspoon of capers, and orange zest (see photo on page 217). **MAKES 1 HALF-PINT**

1 cup meaty green olives, smashed and pitted
　　　　(I use Cerignola)

　　½ cup fresh orange juice

　　1 tablespoon sugar

In a food processor, combine the olives, orange juice, and sugar and pulse to blend. I leave it a bit coarse. You can also grind the tapenade with a mortar and pestle.

Have ready 1 sterilized half-pint jar, band, and lid. (See "How to Sterilize," page 389.) You do not need to use a new lid because you will not process this jar. Spoon the tapenade into the jar. You can preserve the tapenade in oil (see "How to Preserve in Oil," page 387). Holds in the refrigerator for up to 10 days.

Orange Sherbet

In the South, folks use orange soda for sherbet, but I prefer this recipe, which is clean and fresh, but still rich from the milk. Serve in orange shells that have been sliced flat on the bottom. **MAKES 1 PINT**

　　1 teaspoon grated orange zest

　　1 cup fresh orange juice

　　½ cup whole milk

　　¼ cup superfine sugar

In a medium bowl, combine the orange zest, orange juice, milk, and sugar and stir to dissolve the sugar. Chill in the refrigerator.

Transfer the chilled mixture to an ice cream maker and freeze according to the manufacturer's directions (or make by hand; see page 394).

ORANGE SHERBET

Roast Chicken with Olive-Orange Tapenade

If you want to have a sauce to go with this chicken, then add a few tablespoons of the tapenade to the roasting juices shortly before the chicken is done. ***Save the carcass for Chicken Stock (page 89).*** **SERVES 4**

　　One 4-pound chicken (see Note)

　　¼ cup Green Olive and Orange Tapenade
　　　　(page 217)

　　1 tablespoon olive oil

　　1 orange, halved

　　4 garlic cloves, smashed and peeled

　　Two 3-inch sprigs of fresh rosemary

　　Salt and freshly ground black pepper

　　½ cup white wine

　　½ cup chicken stock (for homemade, page 89),
　　　　vegetable stock, or water

Preheat the oven to 425°F.

Loosen the skin over the breast of the chicken. (You can do this by easing your fingers under the skin and loosening the membrane that holds it down. Eventually you will get your whole hand under the skin, a weirdly satisfying feeling.) Press the tapenade under the skin, covering the breast meat. Rub the outside of the bird with the olive oil. Squeeze the orange juice over the bird. Place the squeezed orange inside the cavity. Insert the garlic and rosemary into the cavity as well. Season the bird with salt and pepper and truss it with kitchen twine (see "How to Truss a Chicken," page 83).

Place the chicken on a rack over a roasting pan. Add the wine to the pan and roast for about 15 minutes, until the bird is golden brown all over.

Reduce the oven temperature to 350°F and continue roasting about 40 minutes longer, or until the juices of the chicken run clear.

Remove the chicken from the rack and let it rest on a platter for about 5 minutes before carving.

Meanwhile, defat the pan drippings if you wish (the chicken fat is greasy but totally delicious). Place the pan with the drippings on top of the stove. Add the stock and cook over medium-high heat, scraping up the browned bits in the pan. Serve the pan drippings with the chicken.

Note: When making stock with the carcass (see page 89), throw the orange, garlic, and rosemary into the pot as well.

Orange Shortbread with Chocolate

I can only keep these in the house for a nanosecond, I think because they appeal to tastes both young and old. You can dress these up by dipping the ends of the cookies in melted chocolate (as here) or make them savory by grinding up ½ cup salty mixed nuts and pressing them on top of the shortbread before baking.

MAKES 12 BARS

- 1 cup all-purpose flour
- 8 tablespoons (1 stick) unsalted butter, at room temperature
- ¼ cup plus 1 tablespoon sugar
- 1 tablespoon grated orange zest
- ¼ teaspoon salt
- 1 cup semisweet chocolate chips

Preheat the oven to 375°F.

In a food processor, pulse to combine the flour, butter, ¼ cup of the sugar, the orange zest, and salt (or combine by hand) until crumbly. Place the dough in an 8 × 8-inch baking pan and pat it down evenly to fill the pan. Prick the dough all over with a fork and sprinkle the remaining 1 tablespoon sugar over it. Score the dough into 12 even bars.

Bake until golden, about 15 minutes. Let the shortbread cool in the pan.

Meanwhile, in a double boiler or bowl set over a pan of hot water, melt the chocolate.

Cut the cool shortbread bars through and dip the ends in the chocolate. Or drizzle the chocolate over the shortbread while in the pan and let harden, then cut the bars. Store in a cookie tin for a couple of days.

ORANGE
SHORTBREAD
WITH CHOCOLATE

Orange Bitters

During one election season my husband and I checked out of the inane televised coverage and found relief in the 1963 epic comedy, It's a Mad, Mad, Mad, Mad World. *In one of our favorite scenes (and there are many), the actor Jim Backus plays an inebriated pilot who abandons the controls to make an Old-Fashioned "just like Granddaddy used to make." We made ours with homemade orange bitters, and the drink got us through the election. The bitters take weeks to make, though very little effort, and is a pretty fabulous holiday gift.* **MAKES 1 PINT**

> Dried zest from 2 large oranges (see Note)
> 6 coriander seeds
> 6 allspice berries
> 6 whole cloves
> 3 green cardamom pods, cracked
> 1 star anise pod
> 1 pint vodka
> 1 cup water
> 3 tablespoons sugar

In a quart jar, combine the orange zest, coriander, allspice, cloves, cardamom, and star anise. Pour in the vodka. Place on the lid, screw on the band, and give the jar a good shake. Let the bitters rest on your counter for about 2 weeks, shaking every day or so.

Reserving the zest and spices, strain the vodka back into the jar. In a small saucepan, combine the reserved zest and spices with the water. Bring to a boil over high heat, then reduce the heat to low, cover, and simmer for about 10 minutes. Turn off the heat and let cool.

Add the water and zest and spices to the jar with the vodka. Let this rest for another week, although it is okay if it rests longer.

Strain out the solids and discard. Return the liquid to the jar. Add the sugar and stir to dissolve. Let the bitters rest another week, then strain through a coffee filter and pour into a clean bottle. The bitters hold forever.

Note: To dry the orange zest, peel off the zest in strips with a vegetable peeler. Preheat the oven to the lowest setting. Spread the zest on a baking sheet and bake for 40 minutes.

Old-Fashioned

MAKES 1 COCKTAIL

> 1½ ounces bourbon
> 2½ teaspoons orange bitters (for homemade, left)

Pour the bourbon and bitters into a rocks glass, stir to combine, and add ice.

Candied Orange or Grapefruit Peels

As a rule, I remove citrus zest before juicing, either by grating or peeling to produce strip zest. Always scrub fruit before zesting (see Note, page 175). This candying technique is from Jacques Pépin.

Julienne about 1 cup zest. Place in a small pot and cover with water. Heat over high heat until the water comes to a boil. Then drain the zest and run it under cold water. In a small saucepan add the zest, 1 cup of water, and ½ cup of sugar. Bring to a boil over medium heat and cook, uncovered, about 5 minutes, until the syrup is thick. Pour another ½ cup of sugar in a cookie tray. Add the zest and coat with the sugar. Allow to dry for an hour or so. Place in a container and refrigerate. Holds for months.

PEACHES

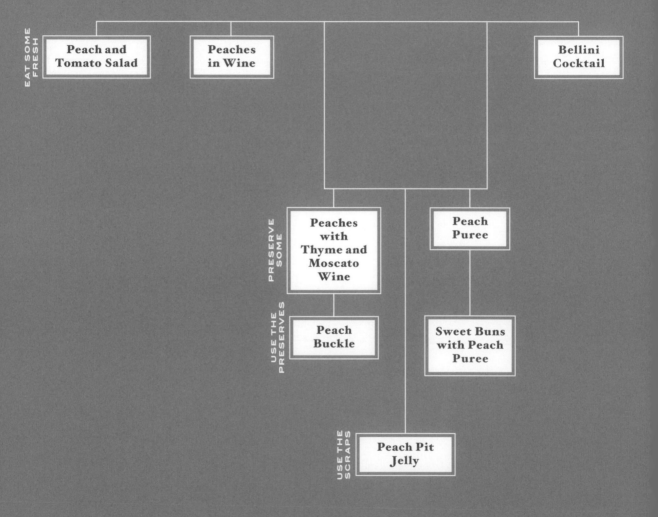

EAT SOME FRESH

Peach and Tomato Salad

Peaches in Wine

Bellini Cocktail

PRESERVE SOME

Peaches with Thyme and Moscato Wine

Peach Puree

USE THE PRESERVES

Peach Buckle

Sweet Buns with Peach Puree

USE THE SCRAPS

Peach Pit Jelly

Of the hundreds of varieties, peaches pretty much fall into two categories: yellow-fleshed peaches are generally clingstone, which means the flesh hugs the pit, and white-fleshed varieties are generally freestone, meaning the pit separates easily from the flesh. The clingstones are super juicy and best for canning, and freestones are less, well, sticky and easier to eat without having to change your T-shirt afterward. I pretty much always use clingstone peaches in my recipes, though they are more of a hassle to handle.

Peach and Tomato Salad

There is nothing better at the height of summer than this room-temperature salad. Use slicing tomatoes and peaches that have not been refrigerated for the best flavor. **SERVES 4**

PEACH AND TOMATO SALAD

4 cups tomato wedges

3 cups peach wedges

1 cup sliced onion (sweet or red are best)

3 to 4 tablespoons extra virgin olive oil

1 to 2 tablespoons white wine vinegar, champagne vinegar, or fruit vinegar

Salt and freshly ground black pepper

2 tablespoons chopped cilantro, for garnish

In a serving bowl, gently combine the tomatoes, peaches, onion, olive oil, vinegar, and salt and pepper to taste. You may want to adjust the olive oil and vinegar ratio to your taste. Garnish with the cilantro.

Bellini Cocktail

This cocktail was originally served at Harry's Bar in Venice. It's named for the painter, Giovanni Bellini, who used a beautiful peachy color in his paintings. You can make it with prosecco, Asti, champagne, or cava. **SERVES 4**

1 large peach

1 bottle cold prosecco or other sparkling wine

Bring a small pot of water to a boil. Add the peach, count off 30 seconds, and then remove. The peel should slide off. Halve and pit the peach.

Place the peach flesh into a food processor or blender and puree.

Place a tablespoon or two of puree in the bottom of each champagne flute. Top with the prosecco.

Peaches with Thyme and Moscato Wine

This recipe is a great way to use leftover sweet wine from a dinner party. I like to serve these preserves with whipped cream or crème fraîche (for homemade, page 362), or use them to make a skillet tart. Substitute them for apricots in the Apricot-Raisin Skillet Tart (page 20); it works just as well with peaches. **Save the peach peels and pits for Peach Pit Jelly (page 227). Save the syrup used to poach the peaches to add to lemonade or iced tea as a peachy sweetener.** *You can substitute peeled Bosc or Bartlett pears or plums (just prick plum skins) for the peaches in this recipe.* **MAKES 3 PINTS**

1½ tablespoons ascorbic acid

2 pounds peaches

1 cup sugar

1 cup water

¾ cup Moscato or other sweet wine

6 sprigs of fresh thyme

3 strips (2 inches long) lemon zest

To retain the peaches' color, combine the ascorbic acid with 4 cups water. Stir to dissolve.

Bring a large pot of water to a boil. Add the peaches, count off 30 seconds, and then remove. The peels should slide off. Halve and pit the peaches. Slice the peaches (or cut them into chunks if you prefer) and drop them into the ascorbic acid dip. Let rest for about 5 minutes. Drain.

Meanwhile, in a large saucepan, combine the sugar and the water and bring to a boil over medium heat.

Add the drained peaches to the hot syrup and bring to a boil again. Take the peaches off the heat.

PEACHES IN WINE

Have ready 3 clean pint jars and bands, and new lids that have been simmered in hot water to soften the rubberized flange. Fish the peaches out of the syrup and place them in the jars. Add ¼ cup Moscato, 2 thyme sprigs, and a piece of lemon zest to each jar. If the Moscato doesn't cover the peaches, add some of the syrup from the saucepan, but leave ½ inch of headroom. Remove any air bubbles by inserting a butter knife into the jar. Wipe the rims, place on the lids, and screw on the bands fingertip tight.

Process the jars in a water bath (see page 375) for 20 minutes. Be sure to make altitude adjustments when preserving (see page 389). There may be some discoloring of the fruit at the top of the jar over time. It's okay.

PEACHES IN WINE, THE ULTIMATE ITALIAN DESSERT

This dessert is a revelation for first-timers. It is so fresh, so elegant, so elemental: it embodies the Italian food perspective. Use only very fresh peaches that have not been refrigerated for the best flavor, and whatever wine you were drinking at lunch or dinner.

Place one freestone peach per person in a large bowl of cool water, and supply enough fruit knives. Diners slice their peach with its peel directly into their wine glasses. Cover with additional wine, and allow the peaches to macerate for a few minutes. Use your forks to capture pieces of wine-soaked peach.

Peach Puree

This is a great product to have on hand, to pour into batters, to make soufflés, and add to sauces ... the only problem with it is that peach puree oxidizes to a beige color and ascorbic acid doesn't seem to help. Nonetheless, the flavor is great. You can substitute the cardamom pods with 1 teaspoon ground ginger or cinnamon and/or ¼ teaspoon grated nutmeg if you'd like. **Save the peach peels and pits for Peach Pit Jelly (page 227).** MAKES 3 HALF-PINTS

- 2 pounds peaches
- 1 cup sugar
- 1 tablespoon fresh lemon juice
- 1 tablespoon green cardamom pods (optional)

Bring a large pot of water to a boil. Add the peaches, count off 30 seconds, and then remove. The peels should slide off. Halve and pit the peaches.

Transfer the peach flesh to a food processor and puree. Pour the puree into a large saucepan and bring to a high simmer over medium heat. Add the sugar, lemon juice, and cardamom (if using).

Continue simmering until the sugar dissolves, about 10 minutes. Discard the cardamom pods.

Have ready 3 clean half-pint jars and bands, and new lids that have been simmered in hot water to soften the rubberized flange. Pour the puree into the jars leaving ½ inch of headroom. Wipe the rims, place on the lids, and screw on the bands fingertip tight.

Process the jars in a water bath (see page 375) for 15 minutes. Be sure to make altitude adjustments when preserving (see page 389).

Peach Buckle

Using peaches canned in sweet wine makes this cake fast and sophisticated. You can use fresh peaches in this recipe, too, or other fruit, fresh or canned. (Save the syrup drained from the peaches to sweeten tea and lemonade.) In a spring 2013 issue of People *magazine, I found a lovely recipe for a strawberry tart from television star Gail Simmons. The batter for this buckle is hers and it's very good!* SERVES 6

- 8 tablespoons (1 stick) plus 1 tablespoon unsalted butter, at room temperature
- 1 cup all-purpose flour
- 1 teaspoon baking powder
- Pinch of salt
- ½ cup plus 3 tablespoons sugar
- 2 large eggs
- 1 teaspoon vanilla extract (for homemade, page 361)
- ½ pint Peaches with Thyme and Moscato Wine (opposite), drained, or 1 cup sliced fresh peaches
- 2 tablespoons coarsely ground hazelnuts

Preheat the oven to 350°F. Butter an 8-inch springform pan with 1 tablespoon butter.

PEACH BUCKLE

In a medium bowl, whisk together the flour, baking powder, and salt. In a separate bowl, with an electric mixer, cream the stick of butter and ½ cup of the sugar. Add the eggs, one at a time, beating well after each addition. Beat in the vanilla. Add the flour mixture and mix well.

Pour the batter into the springform pan. Insert 6 or so pieces of peach into the batter in a concentric pattern. The peaches do not have to be covered, as the batter will rise around them as it bakes. Do not put more peaches in the batter or the cake will be too moist.

In a small bowl, combine the ground hazelnuts and 1 tablespoon of the sugar. Sprinkle the hazelnut mixture over the top of the batter. Sprinkle the remaining 2 tablespoons sugar over the hazelnut mixture.

Bake the buckle for about 25 minutes, or until the top is golden brown and a cake tester

inserted into the buckle comes out clean. Remove from the oven and let cool, then remove the springform.

Sweet Buns with Peach Puree

There is nothing quite so satisfying as a fresh-from-the-oven sweet bun. You can use any fruit puree in this recipe, such as Apricot-Orange Puree (page 19) or Strawberry Puree (page 322). **MAKES 12 BUNS**

> 3¾ cups all-purpose flour
>
> 2¼ teaspoons (1 envelope) active dry yeast
>
> ⅓ cup granulated sugar
>
> Pinch of salt
>
> 1 cup plus 2 to 3 tablespoons whole milk
>
> 7 tablespoons unsalted butter, at room temperature
>
> 1 large egg
>
> ¼ cup water
>
> ½ pint Peach Puree (page 225)
>
> ½ cup chopped pecans
>
> ¼ cup packed light brown sugar
>
> ⅓ cup confectioners' sugar

In a stand mixer with the whisk attachment, combine 2¼ cups of the flour, the yeast, granulated sugar, and salt. (Or in a large bowl, mix everything by hand.)

In a small saucepan, heat 1 cup of the milk over medium heat until it starts to bubble around the edges. Take the milk off the heat and add 5 tablespoons of the butter. Whisk to melt the butter.

In a small bowl, whisk together the egg and water.

With the machine running, slowly add the milk mixture to the flour. Add the egg and continue mixing until the ingredients are well blended.

Switch to the dough hook attachment. Add ½ cup flour and blend. Add another ½ cup flour. If the dough is still sticky, add up to ½ cup more. Remove the dough from the bowl and knead on a flat surface a few times, then place it in a big bowl covered with a damp cloth and let rise in a warm place for 2 hours.

Preheat the oven to 375°F. Use the remaining 2 tablespoons butter to grease 12 cups of a muffin tin.

In a small bowl, combine the peach puree, pecans, and brown sugar.

Roll out the dough on a floured board about 12 inches square and ½ inch thick. Smear on the peach-pecan mixture and loosely roll up the dough as you would a jelly roll. With a sharp knife, cut the roll of dough crosswise into 12 disks, and place each disk in a muffin cup. Allow the buns to rise again for 30 minutes.

Bake for 20 minutes, or until golden brown.

Meanwhile, in a small bowl, whisk together the confectioners' sugar and enough milk (2 to 3 tablespoons) to make a drizzling icing.

While the buns are still hot, drizzle the icing on top and let it run down the sides. Serve immediately.

Peach Pit Jelly

This recipe, which works with pear peels, too, comes from Ginger Saylor, and it is a winner. Peach pit jelly has a kind of furry quality, very homey and bed and breakfasty. This jelly calls for powdered pectin; I prefer Pomona's. The processing time comes from the Ball Complete Book of Home Preserving.

MAKES 2 HALF-PINTS

4 cups peach peelings and pits

About 6 cups water

1 tablespoon fresh lemon juice

2 teaspoons calcium water (included in the Pomona's package)

2 cups sugar

2½ teaspoons powdered pectin

Place the peach peelings and pits in a large pot and cover with the water. Bring to a low boil over medium-low heat, cover, and cook for 30 minutes.

Remove from the heat and pour the peelings and water into a bowl. Place in the fridge overnight or up to 3 days. (This step intensifies the flavor, but it is okay to skip it.)

Arrange a jelly bag or a sieve lined with two layers of cheesecloth over a deep pot. Wet the bag or cheesecloth so it doesn't absorb any of the juice. Ladle the peelings and water into the jelly bag and allow the juice to drip into the pot.

In a large saucepan, combine the peach juice, lemon juice, and calcium water. Bring to a boil over medium heat.

In a bowl, combine the sugar and pectin very well. Add to the boiling juice. Allow the mixture to return to a boil, and cook, stirring, until the sugar has dissolved.

Have ready 2 clean half-pint jars and bands, and new lids that have been simmered in hot water to soften the rubberized flange. Pour the jelly into the jars leaving ½ inch of headroom. Wipe the rims, place on the lids, and screw on the bands fingertip tight.

Process the jars in a water bath (see page 375) for 10 minutes. Be sure to make altitude adjustments when preserving (see page 389).

PEAS

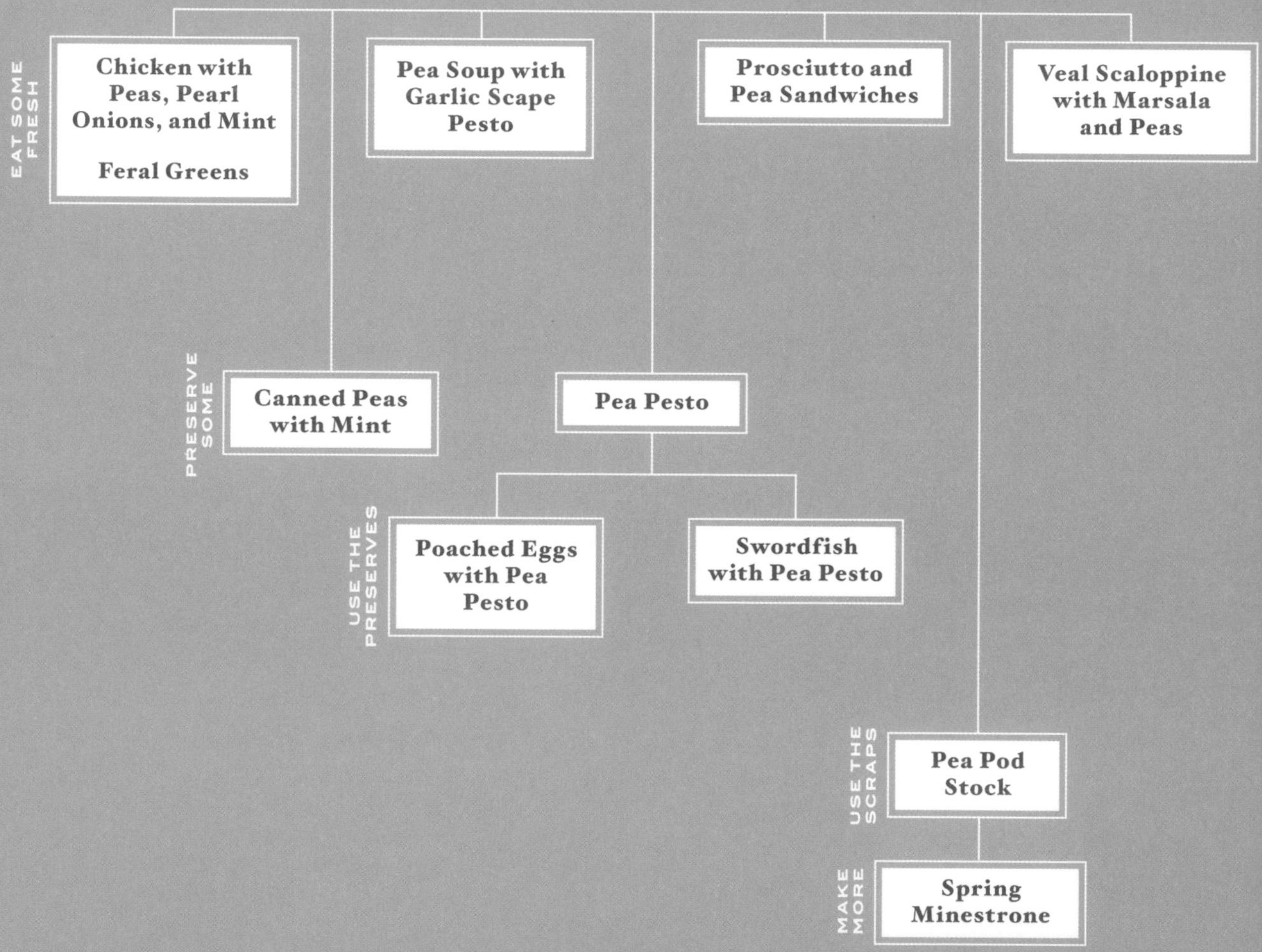

EAT SOME FRESH

Chicken with Peas, Pearl Onions, and Mint

Feral Greens

Pea Soup with Garlic Scape Pesto

Prosciutto and Pea Sandwiches

Veal Scaloppine with Marsala and Peas

PRESERVE SOME

Canned Peas with Mint

Pea Pesto

USE THE PRESERVES

Poached Eggs with Pea Pesto

Swordfish with Pea Pesto

USE THE SCRAPS

Pea Pod Stock

MAKE MORE

Spring Minestrone

Pea Soup with Garlic Scape Pesto

The garlic scape pesto, which yields 2 cups—more than you need for this recipe—can be used in lots of ways, and holds well in the fridge for up to 10 days. Try adding a tablespoon to a Linguine Fini in Mussel Broth (page 207) or as a sauce for grilled fish or steak. If you want to make it just for this recipe, then reduce the quantities by three-quarters (you only need ½ cup). I sometimes skip the pesto and serve crème fraîche (for homemade, page 362) with this soup. **Save the pea pods for Pea Pod Stock (page 236).**
MAKES ABOUT 1 QUART

GARLIC SCAPE PESTO

1 pound garlic scapes, coarsely chopped

¾ cup blanched sliced almonds or pine nuts

¼ cup olive oil

¼ cup chicken stock (for homemade, page 89)

1 tablespoon fresh lemon juice (optional)

Salt and freshly ground black pepper

PEA SOUP

2 cups shelled fresh peas (about 2 pounds in the pod)

3 cups chicken stock (for homemade, page 89)

¼ cup white wine

Juice of ½ lemon

Salt and freshly ground black pepper

GARLIC SCAPE PESTO

For the pesto: In a food processor, puree the scapes and almonds to a fairly smooth paste. Add the olive oil and chicken stock. You may have to adjust the liquid: add more if the pesto is very thick. Add lemon juice if you'd like, and season with salt and pepper to taste.

For the soup: In a medium pot, combine the peas, chicken stock, and wine. Bring to a boil over medium-high heat and cook gently until the peas are soft, about 10 minutes. Pass the peas and stock through a food mill. Return the pea puree to the pot and add the lemon juice and season with salt and pepper to taste.

Pour the warm soup in bowls and garnish each bowl with 2 tablespoons of the pesto. Stir in the pesto as you eat the soup.

Chicken with Peas, Pearl Onions, and Mint

This is a typical rustic Italian dish: one pot, a vegetable, and a protein. Simple and seasonal—and perfect served with what I call Feral Greens (recipe follows), the spring shoots of the previous summer's broccoli rabe, turnip, and kale crops. **Save the chicken neck, back, and wing tips for making Chicken Stock (page 89). Save the pea pods for Pea Pod Stock (page 236). SERVES 4**

CHICKEN WITH PEAS,
PEARL ONIONS, AND MINT

2 tablespoons olive oil

One 4-pound chicken, cut into serving pieces

Salt and freshly ground black pepper

One 3-inch sprig of fresh rosemary

1½ cups pearl onions

½ cup white wine

1 tablespoon chopped fresh thyme or
   1 teaspoon dried

1½ cups shelled fresh peas (about 1½ pounds
   in the pod)

Pinch of sugar

4 tablespoons (½ stick) unsalted butter, cut up

2 tablespoons chopped fresh mint

Preheat the oven to 400°F.

In a large ovenproof skillet with a fitted cover, heat the oil over medium-high heat. Add the chicken and brown it for about 5 minutes, then add the salt and pepper and rosemary. Continue cooking until the chicken browns, turning often, about 15 minutes. Add the onions and cook them until they turn translucent, about 5 minutes. Pour off the chicken fat if lots has accumulated (but leave a few tablespoons in for flavor). Add the wine and thyme. Cover and simmer for 5 minutes, then uncover and cook until the wine has mostly evaporated.

Meanwhile, place the peas in a small saucepan and cover with water. Add the sugar and bring to a gentle boil over medium heat.

Drain the peas and add to the chicken, along with the butter and mint. Cover and place in the oven. Bake for 10 minutes until the peas are tender and the chicken reaches an inner temperature of 165°F.

Check the seasoning and serve.

FERAL GREENS

A farmer is going to harvest as much of his vegetables as he can and then plant a new crop in the spring. But those that don't get harvested may go to seed. A feral green is the spindly, wild looking vegetable that comes up from those seeds. There isn't much of a market for them, but that's because most consumers don't know how absolutely fantastic they are. Feral greens are slightly bitter, excruciatingly tender, and loaded with vitamins and minerals. Even when they are in flower, they are delicious. Serve them as a side or as part of an entrée. I like to poach eggs on top of the vegetables while they are still in the skillet. SERVES 4 TO 6

4 pounds feral greens, such as broccoli rabe,
   turnip greens, and kale

¼ oup olive oil

3 tablespoons minced garlic

1 small dried hot pepper, chopped

Salt

Trim the tough ends off the greens. Bring a large pot of water to a boil over high heat. Add the greens to the boiling water; once the water comes up to a boil again, drain the greens.

In a large cast-iron skillet, heat the oil over medium heat. Add the garlic and hot pepper. Cook until the garlic becomes aromatic, a couple of minutes. Do not burn the garlic. Add the greens and toss in the oil and garlic. If the pan seems dry, add a little water. Cover and cook over medium heat until tender, about 10 minutes. I like to cut up the greens with kitchen scissors. Add salt to taste.

Prosciutto and Pea Sandwiches

*This is a specialty of a famous sandwich stop in Forte dei Marmi, an Italian resort that has been popular with artists and socialites for decades. **Save the pea pods for Pea Pod Stock (page 236).*** MAKES 4 SANDWICHES

- 1 cup shelled fresh peas (from 1 pound peas in the pod)
- 2 tablespoons unsalted butter, at room temperature
- 2 tablespoons grated Parmesan cheese
- 4 pieces focaccia, split, or 8 thin slices Italian bread
- 4 slices prosciutto crudo

Place the peas in a small pot and just cover with water. Bring to a low boil over medium heat and cook until the peas are tender, about 10 minutes. Drain the peas and mash them with a fork. You can mash them to a puree, but I like to leave them semiwhole.

In a small bowl, combine the butter and Parmesan cheese.

Spread the Parmesan butter inside each piece of bread. With a fork, press the peas on top. Add the prosciutto and lay on the top piece of bread.

Veal Scaloppine with Marsala and Peas

*This is a lovely spring dish that takes advantage of seasonal ingredients: veal, peas, and mint. **Save the pea pods for Pea Pod Stock (page 236).*** SERVES 4

- 1½ cups shelled fresh peas (about 1½ pounds in the pod)
- 1¼ pounds veal scaloppine

PROSCIUTTO AND PEA SANDWICHES

- ½ cup all-purpose flour
- Salt and freshly ground black pepper
- 6 tablespoons unsalted butter
- 1 cup dry Marsala wine
- 1 cup minced onion (1 medium)
- 2 tablespoons minced fresh mint, for garnish

In a medium saucepan, combine the peas and just enough water to cover them and bring to a boil over medium heat. Cook until they are tender, about 10 minutes. Drain and set aside.

Dredge the veal in the flour and season it with salt and pepper to taste. In a large nonstick skillet, heat 4 tablespoons of the butter over medium-high heat. Add the veal and cook, turning, until it is golden, a few minutes on each side. Add the Marsala and cook until the sauce thickens, a few more minutes.

Meanwhile, in a small saucepan, heat the remaining 2 tablespoons butter over medium heat and add the onions. Cook until translucent, about 5 minutes.

Add the sautéed onions and the peas to the skillet with the veal. Cook for 5 minutes more to meld the flavors. Check the seasoning and serve promptly, garnished with the mint.

Canned Peas with Mint

When I can peas I like to add some of the ingredients that I use when I cook fresh peas, like mint and white wine. You can substitute lemon juice for white wine (use 1 scant tablespoon per pint) or thyme for the mint. The flavor of garlic tends to wash out when you pressure can it, so I don't use it and just add fresh garlic when I warm up the peas to serve them. Use the peas as a quick winter side dish, warmed with butter and minced garlic. **Save the pea pods for Pea Pod Stock (page 236).** MAKES 2 PINTS

- 4 cups shelled fresh peas (about 4 pounds in the pod)
- 6 tablespoons white wine
- 2 teaspoons salt
- 4 to 6 fresh mint leaves

Have ready 2 clean pint jars and bands, and new lids that have been simmered in hot water to soften the rubberized flange. Pour the peas into the jars. Add 3 tablespoons white wine, 1 teaspoon salt, and 2 to 3 mint leaves to each jar. Cover the peas with boiling water leaving 1 inch of headroom. Wipe the rims, place on the lids, and screw on the bands fingertip tight.

Process the jars in a pressure canner at 10/11 psi for 40 minutes; you can also process 4 half-pints or 1 quart jar for the same amount of time. (See "How to Pressure Can," page 379.) Be sure to make altitude adjustments when preserving (see page 389). The peas settle nicely into the jar, and should look quite plump, though the color will be washed out.

Pea Pesto

Pea pesto is a condiment, a sauce, a flavor enhancer. I spread it on grilled skirt steak marinated in horseradish (for homemade, page 364) and on lamb chops. I sauce spaghettini with pea pesto (just boil the pasta in chicken stock and toss in the pea pesto and garnish with toasted breadcrumbs) and I dress cold roast chicken with pea pesto and homemade yogurt (for homemade, page 370). I broil or grill seafood skewers and serve them on a pillow of pea pesto; I sauté scallops or swordfish in the pan with pea pesto (Swordfish with Pea Pesto, page 235); and serve poached eggs on an English muffin spread with pea pesto (Poached Eggs with Pea Pesto, page 234). For extra zing, you can add a tablespoon of horseradish to every cup of peas. MAKES 3 CUPS

- 2 cups chicken stock (for homemade, page 89)
- 4 cups shelled fresh peas (about 4 pounds in the pod)
- 1 to 2 tablespoons chopped garlic
- 1 to 2 tablespoons fresh lemon juice
- Salt and freshly ground black pepper

In a large saucepan, bring the chicken stock to a boil over medium heat. Add the peas, reduce the heat, and boil the peas gently until tender, about 10 minutes for large peas (smaller ones cook more quickly). Drain and reserve the stock.

Place the peas in a food processor with 1 cup of the reserved stock, 1 tablespoon garlic, 1 tablespoon lemon juice, and salt and pepper to taste. Process to a smooth puree. At this point taste the cream and adapt it to your taste. If you'd like more lemon juice, add it. Missing

VARIATION: PEA PESTO WITH PIGNOLI AND
HORSERADISH

PEA PESTO

that garlic heat? Add it. Not creamy (which can happen if the peas are not cooked quite enough or if they are starchy)? Add more stock.

Place the puree in one-cup containers or half-pint freezer jars leaving 1 inch of headroom and freeze. See "How to Freeze Foods," page 382.

Poached Eggs with Pea Pesto

For a breakfast, I like to serve these eggs on an English muffin. For a dinner, I go for a slice of bruschetta (toasted Italian bread) rubbed with a little olive oil. Bruschetta is less sweet and more hearty than a muffin. **MAKES 1 SERVING**

    4 tablespoons Pea Pesto (page 233)

    2 to 4 tablespoons chicken stock (for
       homemade, page 89)

    1 English muffin, split, or 2 slices bruschetta

    Unsalted butter or olive oil

    1 teaspoon distilled white vinegar

    2 large eggs

    1 teaspoon fresh thyme leaves

    Salt and freshly ground black pepper

In a small saucepan, combine the pea cream and 2 tablespoons of chicken stock and heat over low heat. The cream should be soft and loose, like yogurt, so add more stock 1 tablespoon at a time as you need it.

Toast the English muffin and spread with a little butter, or toast the Italian bread and drizzle a bit of oil on it.

Bring a medium pot of water to a high simmer over medium-low heat. Add the vinegar. Swirl the water with a spoon to create a gentle whirlpool. Crack one egg into a ramekin or

POACHED EGGS WITH PEA PESTO

Swordfish with Pea Pesto

This is a fast, unusual dish that is good with halibut, Chilean sea bass, or other white-fleshed fish; you just need fillets that can be cut into 2-inch chunks. This dish is wonderful served on top of large pieces of bruschetta. **SERVES 4**

- 4 tablespoons olive oil
- 1 large white onion, sliced
- 2 tablespoons minced garlic
- Hot pepper flakes
- ½ cup white wine vinegar
- 3 tablespoons chopped flat-leaf parsley
- 1 cup Pea Pesto (page 233)
- ½ cup chicken stock (for homemade, page 89)
- Salt and freshly ground black pepper
- 1½ pounds swordfish, cut into 2-inch chunks
- 2 tablespoons finely chopped fresh mint, for garnish (optional)

other small bowl and then slide the egg into the center of the whirlpool. The vinegar and the whirlpool effect help keep the whites from dispersing in the water. Cook for a few minutes, until the whites are cooked through but the yolk is still soft.

In the meantime, spread 1 tablespoon of pea pesto on each piece of bread.

Gently remove the egg with a slotted spoon and place on the bread. Repeat for the second egg.

Gently spoon the remaining pea pesto on top of the eggs.

Garnish with the thyme leaves and season with salt and pepper to taste. (I love to use a gourmet salt on this dish.)

In a medium skillet, heat 2 tablespoons of the oil over medium heat. Add the onion, garlic, and pepper flakes to taste. Cook the onion until it is translucent, about 5 minutes. Add the vinegar and parsley. Reduce the heat to medium-low and cook until the vinegar evaporates, a few minutes. Add the pea pesto and the stock. Stir to combine. Bring the sauce to a boil and then remove from the heat. Season with salt and pepper to taste.

In a large well-seasoned cast-iron skillet, heat the remaining 2 tablespoons olive oil over medium heat. Season the fish with salt and pepper. Add to the pan and sauté until golden on all sides, about 5 minutes.

Add the pea pesto sauce and combine gently. Garnish with fresh mint, if you'd like.

PEA POD STOCK

I've boiled the stems, the pods, and the tough outer leaves of just about every vegetable I cook to see what's worth saving to make stock. In some cases, once is enough. But in other cases, like pea pods, vegetable scraps can delicately flavor water. I hold the stock in the fridge in a quart jar, and the next time I need water—for boiling pasta, or adding to soup or stew—I use it. This stock brings a sweet undertone. You can add an onion to the stock if you'd like, or herbs. A small batch, like a pint, is perfect to keep around and will last for 3 or 4 days in the refrigerator. And if you have a lot, make Spring Minestrone (below)!

To make 1 quart of pea pod stock, remove the stems and wash the pods from 2 pounds of peas. Place the pods in a soup pot and cover with about 5 cups of water. Bring to a boil over medium heat, and boil for about 30 minutes. There might be some oil-like patches on top of the water. It's okay. Strain. The stock will be very pale green and smell gently but distinctly of peas. To freeze, see "How to Freeze Foods," page 382.

Spring Minestrone

A lot of vegetables go into this dish and others could go in as well, like fresh peas. You can forfeit the pesto and just garnish this room-temperature soup with olive oil and chopped parsley, if you'd like, or make the pesto with mint instead of basil, which goes very well with the pea flavors. You can even replace the pesto in this recipe with Pea Pesto (page 233).

SERVES 4

SOUP

6 cups **Pea Pod Stock** (above)

2 cups chopped cabbage

1 cup chopped onion

1 cup chopped zucchini

1 cup diced red potato

1 cup snapped green beans

Salt and freshly ground black pepper

PESTO

1 cup fresh basil leaves

¼ cup grated Parmesan cheese

5 tablespoons extra virgin olive oil

3 tablespoons pine nuts

1 tablespoon chopped garlic

Salt

1 cup tubettini pasta (see Note)

¼ cup grated Parmesan cheese

For the soup: In a medium soup pot, combine the pea pod stock, cabbage, and onion. Cover, bring to a boil over medium heat, and boil gently 30 minutes. Add the zucchini, potato, and green beans. Cover and cook another 30 minutes until the potatoes are tender. Stir in salt and pepper to taste. Remove from the heat and let cool, uncovered.

Meanwhile, for the pesto: In a food processor, combine the basil, Parmesan, olive oil, pine nuts, garlic, and salt to taste. Puree and set aside.

Once the soup is cool stir in the pesto.

Bring a small pot of salted water to a boil over high heat and add the tubettini. Cook until al dente. Drain.

To serve, add a portion of pasta to the bottom of each bowl and ladle the minestrone over it. Garnish with the Parmesan.

Note: Cook pasta for soup as needed. If you add pasta to the soup pot, then your leftover soup will be plagued by soft gummy pasta.

PEPPERS:
SWEET, CHERRY, AND HOT

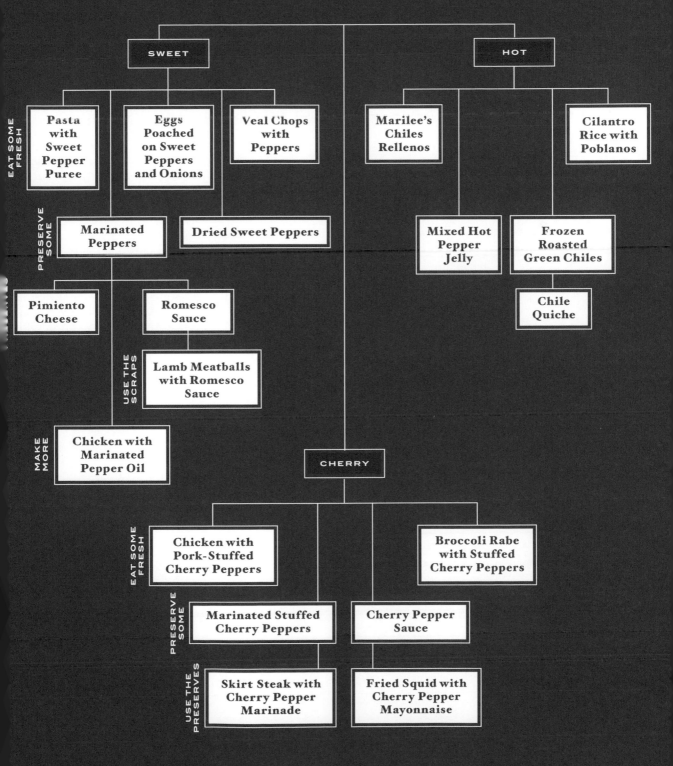

SWEET

EAT SOME FRESH

- Pasta with Sweet Pepper Puree
- Eggs Poached on Sweet Peppers and Onions
- Veal Chops with Peppers

PRESERVE SOME

- Marinated Peppers
- Dried Sweet Peppers

- Pimiento Cheese
- Romesco Sauce

USE THE SCRAPS

- Lamb Meatballs with Romesco Sauce

MAKE MORE

- Chicken with Marinated Pepper Oil

HOT

- Marilee's Chiles Rellenos
- Cilantro Rice with Poblanos

- Mixed Hot Pepper Jelly
- Frozen Roasted Green Chiles

- Chile Quiche

CHERRY

EAT SOME FRESH

- Chicken with Pork-Stuffed Cherry Peppers
- Broccoli Rabe with Stuffed Cherry Peppers

PRESERVE SOME

- Marinated Stuffed Cherry Peppers
- Cherry Pepper Sauce

USE THE PRESERVES

- Skirt Steak with Cherry Pepper Marinade
- Fried Squid with Cherry Pepper Mayonnaise

Handling Hot Peppers

To clean raw cherry and hot peppers, use rubber gloves. Halve the pepper (with cherries, at the equator) and scrape out the seeds and ribs—which are the hottest parts—with a spoon. I use a serrated grapefruit spoon and it works great.

Roasting and Peeling Peppers

Some recipes call for the peppers to be charred and the skin to be removed. You can do this under the broiler or on top of a gas burner directly on the heat. Cooking on the burner, where you place a couple of peppers on each burner and turn them with tongs until they are blistered all over, is more work, but easier to control. Under the broiler is more convenient and faster, but the peppers easily overcook. I use the broiler with the door open so I can watch them more closely.

Heat the broiler to hot. Place the peppers on a baking sheet and place under the broiler about 6 inches from the heat. Turn the peppers as they blister. It takes about 5 minutes for a tray of peppers to roast. As soon as you can handle the peppers, remove the skin. Usually, the skin will slip off in a few big peels. If some skin sticks, it's okay. Remove the seedpod, and rinse out the seeds.

Pasta with Sweet Pepper Puree

When I was a kid my dad came up with a version of this recipe and he was delighted that no one could figure out the source of the beautiful ruddy pink sauce. Kids love the sweetness of this dish. Indeed, I have loved it for forty years. You can use the pepper sauce in other recipes as you would marinara.

SERVES 4

3 tablespoons olive oil

2 pounds sweet red peppers (8 to 10 peppers), cored and sliced

1½ cups sliced onions

2 tablespoons chopped fresh basil

Salt and freshly ground black pepper

¾ cup chicken stock (for homemade, page 89)

1 pound short-cut pasta, like penne or farfalle

2 tablespoons chopped flat-leaf parsley, for garnish

¼ cup grated Parmesan cheese, for garnish

In a large skillet, heat the oil over medium heat. Add the peppers and onions, and cook until the onions become translucent, about 5 minutes. Add the basil and salt and pepper to taste and cook until the peppers are soft, about 15 minutes longer. If the peppers cook too fast—if they begin to brown—then reduce the heat. The peppers need to cook gently, without browning, until they are absolutely limp and soft.

Transfer the pepper mixture to a food processor or blender and add the stock. (Do this in batches if you are using a blender.) Puree until very smooth. For a more refined sauce, pass the sauce through a sieve or food mill.

Bring a large pot of salted water to a boil over high heat and add the pasta. Cook until al dente and drain. Toss the pasta and pepper sauce together. Garnish with the parsley and Parmesan and serve promptly.

EGGS POACHED ON SWEET PEPPERS AND ONIONS

½ cup grated Parmesan cheese, for garnish

2 tablespoons chopped flat-leaf parsley, for garnish

In a large skillet with a fitted lid, heat the olive oil over medium heat. Add the peppers and onions and cook until the peppers are almost soft, about 8 minutes. Add the tomatoes and basil and cook until all the vegetables are soft, about 10 minutes. Add salt to taste.

With the back of a spoon, create 8 indentations in the vegetables. Carefully crack the eggs in the indentations. Don't let the eggs touch the bare bottom of the pan or the sides or they will burn or stick. Reduce the heat to medium-low, cover the pan, and simmer until the whites of the eggs are set, 6 to 8 minutes. Season with salt and pepper and sprinkle with the Parmesan and parsley. Serve promptly.

Eggs Poached on Sweet Peppers and Onions

This is the perfect summer dinner: light, fresh, nutritious, and easy. It is simply cooked vegetables with eggs poached on top. You can use any vegetable combination you like (zucchini, onion, and boiled potatoes, for example) but if you don't use tomatoes you will need to compensate for the lack of moisture by adding about ½ to ¾ cup chicken stock, vegetable stock, or water to the vegetable sauté. **SERVES 4**

¼ cup olive oil

2 sweet red peppers, sliced

2 medium onions, sliced

2 large tomatoes, peeled, seeded, and coarsely chopped (see Note, page 240)

2 tablespoons chopped fresh basil or 1 teaspoon dried

Salt and freshly ground black pepper

8 large eggs

Veal Chops with Peppers

I don't cook veal chops often (they are quite extravagant), but when I do, it's usually in the summertime, when I can make this dish with sweet red peppers and vine-ripe tomatoes. **SERVES 4**

6 tablespoons olive oil

2 cups sliced sweet red peppers (about 3 peppers)

4 loin veal chops, about 1 inch thick

Salt and freshly ground black pepper

1 cup sliced onion

½ cup white wine

1 cup peeled, seeded, and coarsely chopped tomato (see Note, page 240)

Preheat the oven to 400°F.

In a large skillet, heat 3 tablespoons of the oil over medium-high heat. Add the peppers and cook until they are soft, about 10 minutes. It's okay if they scorch a bit.

Season the veal with salt and pepper. In a large ovenproof pot, heat the remaining 3 tablespoons of oil over medium-high heat. Add the veal and sear until browned all over, about 5 minutes. Add the onions and wine and cook until the wine has evaporated, 3 to 5 minutes. Add the tomato and cook for 5 to 8 minutes to reduce and thicken the sauce. Add the peppers and place in the oven.

Bake for 10 to 15 minutes, or until the meat is cooked to medium-well (the very palest pink) and the sauce is thick.

Note: To peel and seed a tomato, bring a pot of water to a boil and drop in the tomato. Remove it after 30 seconds and peel off the skin. Halve the tomato at the equator, and push out the seeds with your thumb. You don't have to remove every seed.

Chicken with Pork-Stuffed Cherry Peppers

A flavor bomb, this dish highlights the fragrant hot cherry pepper. I make it for company because the dish is unusual, very seasonal, and warms up well, so I can enjoy the cocktail hour, too. If you find seeded pickled cherry peppers in the deli section of your supermarket, you can skip the first step in the recipe. SERVES 4

- 12 cherry peppers, stemmed, seeded, and rinsed
- 1 cup water
- 1 cup white wine vinegar
- 2 tablespoons olive oil
- 4 bone-in, skin-on chicken legs (separated into thighs and drumsticks) or 8 chicken thighs

- Salt and freshly ground black pepper
- ⅓ cup white wine
- One 3-inch sprig of fresh rosemary
- 1¼ cups sliced onion (1 large)
- 1 tablespoon minced garlic
- 1 large (6 inch) Italian sweet sausage
- ½ cup chicken stock (for homemade, page 89)
- 2 tablespoons chopped flat-leaf parsley, for garnish (optional)

In a medium pot, combine the cherry peppers, water, and vinegar. Bring to a boil over medium-high heat and cook until the peppers lighten in color, from red to bright orange, and are pliable, about 5 minutes. Drain and set aside.

In a large skillet, heat the oil over medium heat. Season the chicken with salt and pepper to taste. Add to the skillet and cook until browned all over, about 20 minutes, turning once or twice. Add the white wine and rosemary and cook until the wine has mostly evaporated, about 5 minutes. Add the onion and garlic and cook until the onion is soft, about 5 minutes.

Remove the casing on the sausage. Roll the sausage meat into little balls about the size of marbles and stuff them into the cavities of the cherry peppers. Add the stuffed peppers and the stock to the skillet with the chicken. Cover and cook over medium-low heat for 15 minutes for the flavors to meld and the pork to cook. It will be pale in color. Uncover and cook until the sauce reduces by about half, 10 to 15 minutes longer.

Serve garnished with parsley, if you'd like.

CHICKEN WITH
PORK-STUFFED
CHERRY PEPPERS

Broccoli Rabe with Stuffed Cherry Peppers

This is a variation of Chicken with Pork-Stuffed Cherry Peppers (page 240) that I absolutely adore. Adding the peppers to broccoli rabe makes a hearty dish, and if you add cooked spaghettini or orecchiette once the rabe comes out of the oven, the dish becomes even more satisfying. When buying rabe, look for perky, dark green bunches with lots of flowerettes and fresh stem ends. SERVES 4

> 12 cherry peppers, stemmed, seeded, and rinsed
>
> 1 cup water
>
> 1 cup white wine vinegar
>
> 1 large (6 inch) Italian sweet sausage
>
> 2 bunches broccoli rabe (about 2 pounds)
>
> 6 tablespoons olive oil
>
> 2 tablespoons minced garlic
>
> Salt and freshly ground black pepper
>
> ¾ pound spaghettini or orecchiette pasta (optional)
>
> ⅓ cup grated Parmesan cheese

Preheat the oven to 400°F.

In a medium pot, combine the cherry peppers, water, and vinegar. Bring to a boil over medium-high heat and cook until the peppers lighten in color, from red to bright orange, and are pliable, about 5 minutes. Drain. Remove the casing from the sausage. Roll the sausage meat into little balls about the size of marbles and stuff them into the cavities of the cherry peppers.

Wash the rabe and cut off the tough stem ends. Bring a large pot of water to a boil and drop in the rabe. As soon as the water comes back to a boil, remove the rabe. (Keep the boiling water if you're making the pasta.) Place the rabe in a medium-large roasting pan. Add the olive oil,

garlic, and salt and pepper to taste, and bake for about 10 minutes, or until the rabe begins to look dried out. Add the cherry peppers, tucking them into the vegetable, and cook for another 10 minutes, or until the meat in the cherry peppers is cooked through (it will be pale in color).

If you're adding pasta, bring the rabe cooking water back to a boil. Add the pasta and cook until al dente. Drain. Remove the rabe from the oven. Remove the peppers and add the pasta to the rabe. Mix the pasta and rabe well. You may need to sprinkle a bit of olive oil on top of everything if the vegetable seems a bit dry. Return the peppers to the pan.

Adjust the seasoning and garnish with the Parmesan.

Marilee's Chiles Rellenos

My friend Marilee Gilman of Four Directions Farm in Colorado makes the best chiles rellenos I've ever had: lightly battered and fried poblano peppers stuffed with cheese and served on a puddle of tomato sauce. I usually make this for a first course, but you can double the pepper recipe to serve as an entrée (you won't need to double the tomato puree). I like to serve the peppers with a variety of condiments, like quartered limes, sour cream, chopped avocado, and/ or black beans dressed with lime juice and cilantro. SERVES 4

> 4 poblano peppers (see Note)
>
> ½ cup grated mozzarella cheese
>
> ½ cup grated Gruyère cheese
>
> 2 eggs, separated
>
> Salt and freshly ground black pepper
>
> 1 tablespoon olive oil
>
> ¼ cup chopped onion

2 cups fresh peeled and seeded tomato puree (for homemade, page 328)

Neutral oil, such as safflower, for frying

Char and peel the poblanos (see "Roasting and Peeling Peppers," page 238). Cut a small slit in each pepper and slip in scissors to cut loose the seedpod leaving the stem end still attached to the rest of the pepper.

Combine the cheeses in a small bowl. Loosely pack about ¼ cup of cheese into each pepper. Close the peppers with a toothpick.

In a small bowl, beat the egg yolks. In a large bowl, with an electric mixer or whisk, beat the egg whites with a pinch of salt until they are stiff.

In a small saucepan, heat the olive oil over medium heat. Add the onion and cook until the onions are translucent, about 5 minutes. Add the tomato puree and cook at a low boil for about 15 minutes to reduce the puree a bit. You will smell cooked tomatoes. Season to taste. Set aside and cover to keep warm.

Pour ½ inch of vegetable oil into a medium nonstick skillet. Heat over medium-high heat. The oil is hot enough when a pinch of flour flicked into the oil boils rapidly.

Dip the stuffed peppers into the egg yolks, then the egg whites, and place in the hot oil. Fry until golden brown, less than a minute, then carefully turn over with tongs. Fry for another 30 seconds or so, then drain on paper towels or brown paper bags. Season with salt.

To serve, pour a puddle of the tomato sauce in the bottom of a plate. Place the fried pepper on top.

Note: Smell the poblanos in the store. If they smell hot, they will be. And sometimes they won't smell hot, but will be anyway. That's why I always buy a few extra: Because while a slightly hot poblano is divine, a too-hot pepper is frustratingly hard to eat.

Cilantro Rice with Poblanos

This is a dish I learned from Diane Kennedy's The Cuisines of Mexico. *The recipe calls for parsley, but I prefer cilantro, and I started adding nuts and raisins one year and have used them ever since. You can omit them, if you'd like.* **SERVES 4**

1 medium onion, chopped (about 1 cup)

⅓ cup water

½ cup chopped cilantro

1 garlic clove, chopped

Salt

4 small poblano peppers

2 tablespoons olive oil

1 cup long-grained white rice

2 cups whole milk (or whey left over from making ricotta, page 367)

¼ cup slivered almonds

¼ cup golden raisins (for homemade, page 161)

4 strips (1 × 4 inches) Monterey jack or Cheddar cheese

In a blender, combine the onion, water, cilantro, and garlic and process until they are liquefied. Add salt to taste.

Char and peel the peppers (see "Roasting and Peeling Peppers," page 238). Cut a small slit in each pepper and slip in scissors to cut loose the seedpod leaving the stem end still attached to the rest of the pepper.

In a Dutch oven with a fitted top, heat the oil over medium heat. Roll the oil around so that it coats the inside of the dish. Add the rice and cook it until it begins to color, about 3 minutes. Be sure to stir often, to keep the rice from sticking. Add the cilantro puree to the rice and stir it well. It will bubble up ferociously, and then settle down. Cook the rice and cilantro water over medium-low heat, covered, until the rice has absorbed all the liquid and is beginning to look dried out, about 15 minutes.

Stir in the milk, cover the Dutch oven, and cook the rice for 10 minutes over medium-low heat. Stir in salt to taste, then the almonds and raisins, re-cover, and continue cooking until the rice is very tender and soft (it should be rather loose, like risotto), about 5 minutes longer.

Insert 1 strip of cheese into each pepper.

When the rice is cooked, dig 4 small trenches in the rice and insert a stuffed poblano in each trench. Cover and let the heat from the rice melt the cheese in the peppers, a few minutes. Serve promptly.

Marinated Peppers

Marinated chopped peppers are an incentive to make great food fast. Just the fact that I can spoon the peppers out of a jar and not even have to cut them up has led to spontaneous and delicious dishes. For example, I like to toss these peppers with boiled shrimp, garnished with parsley, or I make a quick dip/spread by mashing the peppers with feta cheese or softened goat cheese and dill or cilantro.

MAKES 3 PINTS

- 2 pounds sweet red peppers (8 to 10 peppers)
- 2 cups white wine vinegar (5% acidity)
- 1 cup fresh lemon juice (5 large lemons; save the zest for recipes in "Lemons," page 165)
- 1 cup olive oil
- 2 tablespoons minced garlic
- 2 tablespoons dried oregano
- 1½ teaspoons pickling salt

Char and peel the peppers (see "Roasting and Peeling Peppers," page 238). Allow the peppers to come down to room temperature. Halve the peppers and remove the seedpod and stems. Chop the peppers.

In a medium saucepan, combine the vinegar, lemon juice, olive oil, garlic, oregano, and salt and bring to a boil over medium heat. Add the peppers and toss them in the marinade.

Have ready 3 clean pint jars (or a combination of half-pints and pints) and bands, and new lids that have been simmered in hot water to soften the rubberized flange. Spoon the peppers into the jars and cover with the marinade, making sure the garlic and oregano are distributed evenly throughout the jars. Leave ½ inch of headroom. Wipe the rims, place on the lids, and screw on the bands fingertip tight.

Process the jars in a water bath (see "How to Water Bath Can" page 375) for 15 minutes. Be sure to make altitude adjustments when preserving (see page 389). If the jars seem a little greasy, it is okay. Just wipe them down with a bit of vinegar. The peppers may float at first but don't worry; they will settle down.

Dried Sweet Peppers

Dried peppers lend a lovely sweetness to soups, stews, and sauces. They also make a fabulous pesto, which I've used on bruschetta, tossed with spaghetti and seared scallops, and served with grilled steak (page 247). **ABOUT ¼ POUND DRIED PEPPERS**

5 pounds sweet red peppers

Wash the peppers, halve them, and remove the seeds and stems. If the peppers are very large, cut them in quarters lengthwise. Bring a large pot of water to a boil over high heat and blanch the peppers for about 4 minutes. Drain.

Place the peppers cut side up in the trays of a food dehydrator (or see page 385 for instructions on oven-drying). Do not pack them tightly. Set your dryer to 135°F. The peppers should take 8 to 12 hours. See "How to Dry" (page 385) for information on "conditioning" the dried peppers. Keep the peppers in jars in the pantry or in the fridge, or covered in olive oil in the fridge (see "How to Preserve in Oil," page 387).

To rehydrate, soak the peppers in cool water for about 10 minutes or drop them directly into soups, stews, and sauces.

Marinated Stuffed Cherry Peppers

Every fall I put up a few jars of cherry peppers stuffed with a breadcrumb mixture and covered in oil, to serve with egg dishes throughout the year. The USDA recommendations say you can hold foods under oil in the fridge for 10 days, but that won't do here, as the peppers need to age for 2 weeks refrigerated before eating. I go ahead and refrigerate anyway; if no spoilers get in the jar, they hold for months. The main problem you might encounter is fermentation of the breadcrumbs. You can tell right away if they have fermented when you taste them— it won't hurt you to give it a nibble. They will taste too strong and vinegary, and have an acetone-like smell. You don't have to worry about spoilers like the bacteria that causes botulism, because this is a refrigerated product. You can add fresh or dried herbs, nuts, raisins, or any spices without a second thought, but I avoid cheese and meat as they more quickly succumb to spoilers.

If, after you finish eating the peppers, you have the pepper-flavored marinade liquid left over— don't throw it away! It is a fabulous instant marinade for skirt steak (page 252). **MAKES 3 HALF-PINTS**

2 cups distilled white vinegar (5% acidity)

1 cup water

16 cherry peppers, stemmed and seeded

1¾ cups breadcrumbs (for homemade, page 362)

1 to 2 tablespoons olive oil, plus oil for the jars

1½ tablespoons minced garlic

1½ tablespoons minced flat-leaf parsley

Salt and freshly ground black pepper

In a medium pot, bring the vinegar and water to a boil. Drop in the peppers and boil gently for about 5 minutes. Don't let the peppers get too soft. They should be pliable but firm. If you can squeeze the peppers gently with your tongs without any cracking or squashing, they are perfect. Drain the peppers and reserve the vinegar.

In a bowl, combine the breadcrumbs, 1 to 2 tablespoons of olive oil (the breadcrumbs need to be damp—not wet), the garlic, parsley, and salt and pepper to taste.

MARINATED STUFFED CHERRY PEPPERS

Note: As the peppers age, some of the breadcrumbs may come loose and float in the vinegar solution or darken over time. It's okay. Just pack your peppers tighter next year. The oil may become thick and white or beady at refrigerator temperatures—that's okay, too.

Cherry Pepper Sauce

I use cherry pepper sauce as a topping for bruschetta or in pasta dishes, smeared on top of broiled fish, or mixed with eggs. I learned to make this from the ladies in the Mount Carmel food shop on Arthur Avenue in the Bronx. Note the sauce takes 5 days to make. **MAKES 1 HALF-PINT**

> 1 pound cherry peppers (about 20), stemmed, seeded, and coarsely chopped
>
> 2 cups white wine vinegar
>
> ¼ cup olive oil
>
> Salt

Place the cherry peppers in a bowl and cover with the vinegar. Cover the bowl with plastic wrap and refrigerate 5 days.

Drain the peppers and pat them dry. (You can save the spicy vinegar if you like to use in salad dressings.) Place the peppers in a food processor and pulse to grind. Add the olive oil in a drizzle, pulsing as you go. You may need a bit more oil: The peppers should be about the consistency of pickle relish. Add salt to taste.

Have ready 1 sterilized half-pint jar, band, and lid. (See "How to Sterilize," page 389.) You do not need to use a new lid because you will not process this jar. Pour the sauce into the jar. It holds for at least 10 days in the refrigerator.

When the peppers are cool enough to handle, stuff with the breadcrumb mixture. I use a teaspoon to fill the pepper, then with my thumb, pack in the breadcrumbs. The more packed the breadcrumbs, the better. But be careful not to tear the peppers.

Have ready 3 sterilized half-pint jars, bands, and lids. (See "How to Sterilize," page 389.) You do not need to use new lids because you will not process these jars. Pack the peppers into the jars with the breadcrumbs facing the glass. This holds the breadcrumbs in place.

Carefully pour the vinegar into the jars to come about two-thirds the way up the jar. Top with olive oil—enough so the peppers are covered in oil. Place on the lids and screw on the bands. (See "How to Preserve in Oil," page 387.) Age the peppers in the refrigerator (see Note) for about 2 weeks before eating.

FROZEN ROASTED GREEN CHILES

There are two camps regarding freezing roasted chiles: those who think it is better to freeze with the roasted skins on and seedpods intact, and those who clean them thoroughly before freezing. As to peeling, if you have a gas oven, which allows you to char the chile skin quickly at a high heat, then it is okay to freeze with the skins on. They will come off well when you thaw them. However, with the lower heat of an electric oven, the chile skin takes longer to char, which will cook the flesh some, making the chile susceptible to tearing during the peeling process. In this case it is better to peel before freezing. Roast the chiles as instructed in "Roasting and Peeling Peppers" (page 238) and then peel them. When it comes to the seedpods, I leave them in to give the chiles a little volume instead of being flat strips, which are rather delicate. But if you prefer an already cleaned chile ready to go, remove the seedpods by cutting a small hole in the chile and slipping in small scissors to cut loose the seedpod leaving the stem end still attached to the rest of the pepper. You can also remove the seedpod and stem end of the pepper altogether. Pack into freezer bags. Six pounds of fresh green chiles will yield three 4-ounce bags of frozen. Thaw the chiles in the refrigerator or in a bowl of cool water. Peeled chiles need not be totally thawed in order to cook them—just soft enough to chop.

Mixed Hot Pepper Jelly

This jelly can be hot, depending on the mix of chiles. At the farmers' market I go to in New York City there is a pepper farm that sells pint baskets of mixed peppers: cherry, Fresno, habanero, and jalapeño. I just stem and seed them all (wear rubber gloves and don't touch your nostrils, eyes, or lips) and mince them in the food processor. I serve this jelly with cheese, on cream cheese sandwiches, tucked into scones (page 281), and as a meat condiment. Try it with Bollito Misto (page 115) or instead of the cucumber and yogurt sauce for Cold Roast Chicken (page 110). I use Pomona's Universal pectin. The processing time is based on a pepper jelly recipe in the Ball Complete Book of Home Canning. **MAKES 3 HALF-PINTS**

> 1 cup stemmed, seeded, finely chopped mixed chile peppers
>
> 1 cup distilled white vinegar (5% acidity)
>
> 1½ teaspoons calcium water (comes in the Pomona's package)
>
> 2½ cups sugar
>
> 2 teaspoons powdered pectin

In a medium pot, combine the chiles and vinegar. Bring to a boil over medium heat, add the calcium water, then reduce the heat and simmer for 5 minutes.

Combine the sugar and pectin in a bowl. Be sure the pectin is well combined. Pour the sugar into the pot with the chiles. Increase the heat, bring to a boil, and boil gently until the sugar has dissolved.

Have ready 3 clean half-pint jars and bands, and new lids that have been simmered in hot water to soften the rubberized flange. Pour the jelly into the jars leaving ¼ inch of headroom. Wipe the rims, place on the lids, and screw on the bands fingertip tight.

Process the jars in a water bath (see "How to Water Bath Can," page 375) for 10 minutes. Be sure to make altitude adjustments when preserving (see page 389).

DRIED SWEET PEPPER PESTO

Puree 12 rehydrated dried peppers (see page 245), ¼ cup blanched almonds, ¼ cup olive oil, 1 garlic clove, 1 tablespoon chopped flat-leaf parsley, and salt and pepper to taste in a food processor. If you'd like, you can preserve the pesto in oil for about 10 days (see "How to Preserve in Oil," page 387).

Pimiento Cheese

I've eaten pimiento cheese with my relatives in the South where it has never gone out of fashion, but it wasn't until I started putting up my own marinated peppers that I really got into making it myself. Homemade mayonnaise is key. Serve with crostini, crackers, and celery sticks, or spread on bread to make pimiento sandwiches. **When you drain the marinated peppers, either reserve the marinade for Chicken with Marinated Pepper Oil (page 251), or pour it back in the jar with the rest of the peppers.** MAKES ABOUT 1¾ CUPS

- ½ cup mayonnaise (for homemade, page 365)
- ½ cup grated sharp cheddar cheese
- ½ cup soft goat cheese or cream cheese (or a combination), at room temperature
- ⅓ cup chopped marinated peppers (for homemade, page 244), drained
- Salt and cayenne pepper

In a medium bowl, with an electric mixer, beat together the mayonnaise, cheddar, and goat cheese (or cream cheese) until it is as smooth as possible. Add the drained peppers and salt and cayenne to taste. Pour into a bowl and chill in the fridge.

Romesco Sauce

Romesco sauce is a lively Catalonian pesto full of roasted garlic flavor. Serve it with grilled shrimp, over cold sliced boiled beets, and with lamb meatballs (opposite). The romesco sauce freezes perfectly. You can also cover the sauce with oil and hold it in the refrigerator for about 10 days. **When you drain the marinated peppers, save any oil you don't use for Chicken with Marinated Pepper Oil (page 251).** MAKES ABOUT 1 CUP

- 1 garlic bulb, peels on (see Note)
- 2 small dried chipotle chiles
- 4 dried tomatoes (for homemade, page 331)
- 1 cup chopped marinated peppers (for homemade, page 244), drained, oil reserved
- ⅓ cup toasted pine nuts
- Salt

Preheat the oven to 400°F.

Place the garlic bulb on a baking sheet in the middle of the oven and roast for 15 minutes until very tender.

In a small bowl, soak the dried chiles in ½ cup water until soft, about 10 minutes, then drain. In a separate bowl, soak the dried tomatoes in ½ cup water until soft, about 10 minutes, but do not drain.

In a food processor, or with a mortar and pestle, combine 2 cloves roasted garlic, chiles, tomatoes, tomato soaking water, marinated peppers, pine nuts, and salt to taste and puree. If needed, to keep the sauce soft and loose, add the oil reserved from draining the peppers 1 tablespoon at a time.

To make the sauce very smooth, press through a fine-mesh sieve. If you are going to serve immediately or freeze, add water to loosen to the consistency of yogurt. Do not add water if you are going to preserve in oil.

To freeze, pour the sauce into a freezer container leaving ½ inch of headroom. To preserve in oil, see "How to Preserve in Oil," page 387.

Note: Even though I only need 2 garlic cloves for this recipe, I roast a whole bulb to combine with butter and smear onto grilled meat.

Lamb Meatballs with Romesco Sauce

Now, Forager, *a film about mushroom hunting, has a scene where a character makes lamb meatballs with romesco sauce. It's the kind of food scene I love: sensuous, but unsentimental. The combination of lamb and romesco is typical of the Basque kitchen.*

SERVES 4

- 1 pound ground lamb
- ¼ cup minced onion
- ¼ cup breadcrumbs (for homemade, page 362)
- 3 tablespoons water
- 1 large egg, beaten
- 2 tablespoons chopped flat-leaf parsley
- ½ teaspoon ground cumin
- Salt and freshly ground black pepper
- ¼ cup white wine
- ½ pint Romesco Sauce (opposite), at room temperature

Preheat the broiler. Lightly oil a baking sheet.

In a large bowl, combine the lamb, onion, breadcrumbs, water (which helps keep the meatballs tender), egg, parsley, cumin, and salt and pepper to taste. I use my hands. Make 24 meatballs the size of golf balls, and then flatten them slightly.

Place the meatballs on the baking sheet and broil for about 7 minutes, or until golden brown. Flip the meatballs over. If there is a lot of fat, pour it off. Sprinkle the wine over the meatballs and continue cooking for another 5 minutes until the meatballs are cooked through.

Serve the meatballs with the romesco sauce.

MAKING LAMB MEATBALLS

Fried Squid with Cherry Pepper Mayonnaise

When my son was young, he was so infatuated with squid that we didn't eat it for years. But this dish changed his mind. **SERVES 4**

- 2 cups milk
- 1½ pounds cleaned squid, body cut into rings and tentacles trimmed
- ¼ cup Cherry Pepper Sauce (page 246)
- ½ cup mayonnaise (for homemade, page 365)
- Vegetable oil, for frying
- 1 cup Wondra flour (see Note)

Pour the milk into a large bowl and add the squid.

Drain the cherry pepper sauce (and return the drained oil back to the jar). In a small bowl, stir together the mayo and cherry pepper sauce.

CHILE QUICHE

Pour about 1 inch of vegetable oil into a medium nonstick skillet and heat over medium-high heat. The oil must be very hot. You can test it by throwing a dash of flour into the oil. If the flour pops, the oil is ready for frying.

Pour the flour into a paper bag or bowl. Drain the squid and toss in the flour. Shake the squid to remove excess flour and gently place in the hot oil. Fry in batches, until golden brown, a few minutes. Drain on paper towels or brown paper bags.

Serve the squid in a basket with a dipping bowl of cherry pepper mayo.

Note: You can use all-purpose flour for frying, but Wondra produces a much lighter fried food.

Chile Quiche

The trick to a high, light quiche is lots of milk and cream. For this dish I use frozen roasted chiles. For a nice variation, substitute 1 cup soft goat cheese for ½ cup of the milk and ½ cup of the cream. **SERVES 4**

PASTRY

- 1½ cups all-purpose flour, plus more for the rolling out
- 6 tablespoons cold unsalted butter, cut into little pieces
- 2 large eggs
- ¼ teaspoon salt

FILLING

- 4 large eggs
- 1½ cups whole milk
- 1½ cups heavy cream
- Salt and freshly ground black pepper
- ⅓ cup grated Parmesan cheese
- 1 heaping cup thawed and chopped Frozen Roasted Green Chiles (page 247)

Position a rack in the upper third of the oven and preheat to 350°F.

For the pastry: In a food processor, combine the flour, butter, eggs, and salt and process until the dough comes together, a minute or so. (To make the pastry by hand, see page 395.) Press the dough together to form a disk. Wrap the dough in plastic wrap or wax paper and refrigerate until chilled, about 30 minutes.

Meanwhile, for the filling: In a large bowl, whisk together the eggs, milk, cream, and salt and pepper to taste until totally smooth. Stir in the Parmesan.

Roll out the dough on a floured surface about 10 inches in diameter and ⅛ inch thick. Roll the dough up onto the rolling pin and transfer to a standard 8-inch cake pan. Pat the dough into the sides of the pan. Trim the pastry to the edge of the pan.

Spread the chiles in the bottom of the pie shell. Pour in the custard. Bake the quiche for about 50 minutes, or until the custard is just set and puffy. You will smell it when it is ready. Do not overcook the quiche or it will be tough. Remove and let rest for a few minutes before cutting.

Chicken with Marinated Pepper Oil

By the time you have finished the Marinated Peppers (page 244), you will probably have about ¼ cup of marinade per pint jar left over. That's all you need to flavor a chicken dinner for two. You can use boneless chicken thighs if you like: they will cook a bit quicker. **SERVES 2**

- 1 tablespoon olive oil
- 1 pound skinless chicken thighs on the bone
- Salt and freshly ground black pepper
- ½ cup white wine
- ¼ cup pepper marinade (left over from Marinated Peppers, page 244)
- 1 tablespoon finely chopped flat-leaf parsley, for garnish

In a large skillet, heat the oil over medium heat. Season the chicken with salt and pepper and add it to the skillet. Brown the chicken all over, about 15 minutes. Add the wine and cook for 15 minutes more until the thighs are cooked through. Add the marinade and cook for about 5 minutes, flipping the chicken thighs to coat them in the marinade.

Serve garnished with the parsley.

Skirt Steak with Cherry Pepper Marinade

The leftover marinade in your jar of Marinated Stuffed Cherry Peppers (page 245) is delicious stuff, and flavors skirt steak very well. SERVES 4

- 1½ pounds skirt steak
- 4 tablespoons cherry pepper marinade (left over from Marinated Stuffed Cherry Peppers, page 245)
- A few sprigs of fresh thyme
- Salt
- 1 lemon, halved
- 4 cups baby arugula, washed
- ¼ cup vinaigrette (for homemade, page 368)

Remove the silvery membrane that sheathes the meat. Cut the steak into 4 pieces. Place the meat in a plastic food storage bag or bowl and add the cherry pepper marinade, thyme,

and salt. Squeeze the lemon juice into the bag, then toss the halves in too. You can refrigerate the meat for 2 to 24 hours, but the meat should be room temperature when you are ready to cook it.

Heat your outside grill or grill pan to very hot. Remove the steaks from the marinade but don't wipe the marinade off. Lay the steaks on the grill and sear each side for about 30 seconds once, and then repeat. Ideally, you'll create a nice crosshatched sear, but my steaks usually don't look so tidy. Check the seasoning.

Allow the steak to rest for 5 minutes before slicing against the grain.

Meanwhile, combine the arugula and vinaigrette.

Serve the arugula salad on top of the steak (or under, if you'd like).

SKIRT STEAK IN CHERRY PEPPER MARINADE

PLUMS

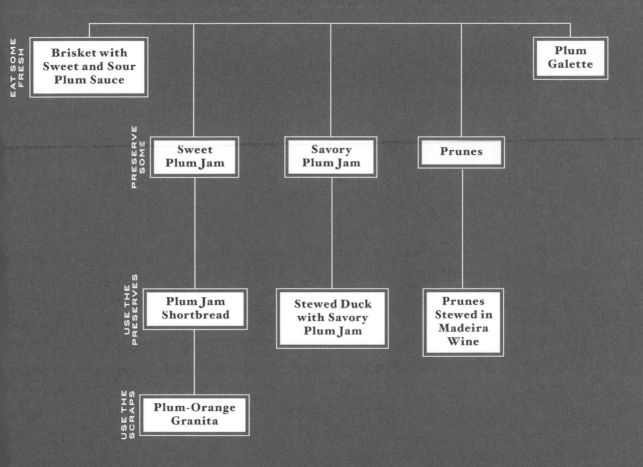

EAT SOME FRESH

Brisket with Sweet and Sour Plum Sauce

Plum Galette

PRESERVE SOME

Sweet Plum Jam

Savory Plum Jam

Prunes

USE THE PRESERVES

Plum Jam Shortbread

Stewed Duck with Savory Plum Jam

Prunes Stewed in Madeira Wine

USE THE SCRAPS

Plum-Orange Granita

Brisket with Sweet and Sour Plum Sauce

You can use fresh plums in this dish or substitute plum jam (see Note). This brisket is wonderful with a puree of root vegetables, like carrots, turnips, or potatoes. The recipe works with most any plum, from big juicy Victorias to Italian prune plums. **SERVES 4 (HEARTILY)**

- 1 pound plums, pitted and coarsely chopped
- ½ cup sugar
- ½ cup chopped onion
- ½ cup water
- ¼ cup wine vinegar (red or white, doesn't matter)
- 2 garlic cloves, chopped
- 2 teaspoons salt
- 1 teaspoon freshly ground black pepper
- 1 teaspoon mustard powder
- 1 teaspoon fresh thyme leaves
- ½ teaspoon rubbed sage
- 2 pounds brisket, extra fat and silver skin removed, cut into a few large pieces
- 2 tablespoons bacon or duck fat (for homemade, page 126), or vegetable oil
- 2 cups beef stock (for homemade, page 47)

Preheat the oven to 350°F.

In a medium pot, combine the plums, sugar, onion, water, vinegar, and garlic. Bring to a boil over medium-high heat and boil for about 20 minutes. For a smooth sauce, allow the plum mixture to cool, then puree in a food processor. Or leave chunky style.

Meanwhile, in a spice grinder or with a mortar and pestle, grind the salt, pepper, mustard powder, thyme, and sage together. Rub this mixture all over the brisket.

FRESH PLUMS

In a large Dutch oven, melt the bacon or duck fat over medium heat. Add the beef and brown all over, about 5 minutes. Add the plum sauce and beef stock, cover, and place in the oven. Bake for 2 hours, or until the brisket has completely broken down. Adjust the seasoning.

Note: You can substitute 1 cup Sweet Plum Jam (page 256) for the fresh plums and sugar. Add it to the pot with the onion, water, vinegar, and garlic.

Plum Galette

I love all types of fruit galettes, but my favorites are plum and rhubarb (see page 289): They are both sweet and tart. There is little that is as gloriously simple and delicious as a ripe plum galette and a cup of coffee. Serve the galette with whipped cream or ice cream, if you'd like. **SERVES 6 TO 8**

PASTRY

1½ cups all-purpose flour

8 tablespoons (1 stick) cold unsalted butter, cut into little bits

1 tablespoon sugar

Pinch of salt

⅓ cup cold water

FILLING

1 pound plums

1 tablespoon fresh lemon juice

½ cup plus 4 tablespoons granulated sugar

4 tablespoons all-purpose flour

½ cup blanched peeled almonds

3 tablespoons unsalted butter, cut into little bits

Egg wash: 1 egg yolk beaten with 1 tablespoon water

For the pastry: In a food processor, combine the flour, sugar, butter, and salt and process until blended, a minute or so. Add the water and process until little balls form. (To make the pastry by hand, see page 395.) Press the dough together to form a disk. Wrap the dough in plastic wrap or wax paper and refrigerate until chilled, about 30 minutes.

Preheat the oven to 350°F.

For the filling: Pit the unpeeled plums and thinly slice. Toss with the lemon juice and place them in a colander set over a bowl. Some plum juice will be released. This is good.

In a small bowl, combine ½ cup of the granulated sugar and 2 tablespoons of the flour. In a food processor, combine the almonds and 2 tablespoons of granulated sugar and 2 tablespoons of flour. Pulse to finely chop the nuts.

On a silicone baking mat or piece of parchment paper, roll out the pastry into a large round

about 12 inches in diameter. It's okay if it isn't perfectly round but don't make it too thin: This pastry needs to be a bit on the robust side. Transfer the pastry on its baking mat to a baking sheet. Spread the nut mixture in the center of the pastry, leaving a 3-inch border all around.

In a bowl, toss the plums with the sugar and flour mixture, then arrange them over the nut mixture in concentric circles. Distribute the butter bits on top of the fruit. Gently fold the border of dough over the plums. The center of the galette should be open.

Brush the egg wash over the dough. Sprinkle the remaining 2 tablespoons granulated sugar on top of the dough—the egg wash will help it adhere.

Bake for 25 to 30 minutes, or until the crust is golden brown. Remove and let come to room temperature. If some juice breaks through the crust it is okay. When the galette cools, the juice will thicken.

PRUNES

The best prune plums are the small, dark, oval Italian prune plums. They are dense and not so juicy. About 2 pounds of prune plums will make ½ pound of prunes. Blanch the prune plums for 1 minute in boiling water to crack the skins. Or you can slit the skin with a knife.

Place the plums in the trays of a food dehydrator (or see page 385 for instructions on oven-drying). Do not pack them tightly. Set your dryer to 135°F. Dry the plums for 12 hours. Press the pits out the blossom ends of the fruit, then return to the dryer and continue to dry until leathery, 4 to 6 hours longer. See "How to Dry" (page 385) for information on "conditioning" the prunes.

Rehydrate the prunes in an equal amount of cold water (boiling water will make them slimy), or, do as they do in Gascony and rehydrate in

Armagnac. Prunes stewed in booze (like port wine, fortified wine, and red wine) are great with just whipped cream, but are also wonderful chopped and used in meat and duck stews.

Sweet Plum Jam

I use this jam in savory recipes, as a topping for shortbread (page 258), or just spread on a bagel. **There is always some jam left after canning, either sticking to the sides of the pan, or maybe a little extra jam that didn't fit in the jars. Save it to make Plum-Orange Granita (page 259).** MAKES 3 HALF-PINTS

> 1½ pounds plums, halved and pitted
>
> 1 cup water
>
> 1½ cups sugar
>
> 1 tablespoon lemon juice

In a large, wide heavy-bottomed pot, combine the plums and water and bring to a boil over medium-high heat. Mash the plums as they soften. (I use a potato masher.) Once the plums are thoroughly softened, add the sugar and lemon juice. Turn the heat up to high to dissolve the sugar. Be careful the jam doesn't scorch. Use a candy thermometer to determine the temperature: The jam will jell at 220°F at sea level, or 8°F over boiling temperature wherever you are. (To calculate the boiling temperature at your altitude, see page 389.) It should take about 15 minutes. If the temperature doesn't get up high enough, cook it a little longer with the cover off so the ratio of juice to sugar diminishes. The jam is ready when it mounds on a spoon.

Have ready 3 sterilized half-pint jars and bands, and new lids that have been simmered in hot water to soften the rubberized flange. Pour the jam into the jars leaving ¼ inch of headroom. Wipe the rims, place on the lids, and screw on the bands fingertip tight.

Process the jars in a water bath (see page 375) for 5 minutes Be sure to make altitude adjustments when preserving (see page 389).

Savory Plum Jam

I make this savory jam to use in duck, goose, or pheasant stews. The processing time for this jam is based on the USDA timing for plum and tomato jam. MAKES 3 HALF-PINTS

> 1½ pounds plums, halved and pitted, skins on
>
> 1 cup water
>
> ½ cup sugar
>
> 1 cup minced dried tomatoes (for homemade, page 331)
>
> Three 3-inch sprigs of fresh rosemary

In a large heavy-bottomed pot, combine the plums, water, and sugar and bring to a low boil over medium heat. Boil gently until the plums are very soft and beginning to thicken, about 15 minutes. Add the dried tomatoes and rosemary. Turn off the heat and allow the sauce to rest for about 10 minutes.

Have ready 3 sterilized half-pint jars and bands, and new lids that have been simmered in hot water to soften the rubberized flange. Pour the jam into the jars leaving ¼ inch of headroom. Tuck a sprig of rosemary into each jar. Remove any air bubbles by sliding a butter knife into the jar. Wipe the rims, place on the lids, and screw on the bands fingertip tight.

Process the jars in a water bath (see "How to Water Bath Can" page 375) for 5 minutes for half-pints. Be sure to make altitude

STEWED DUCK
WITH SAVORY
PLUM JAM

adjustments when preserving (see page 389). There may be some discoloring of the fruit at the top of the jar, but it's okay.

Stewed Duck with Savory Plum Jam

This stew is so easy if you have Savory Plum Jam on hand, but you can still make the dish using whatever preserved plums you can scrounge up—just add fresh rosemary and dried tomatoes. You can substitute game birds like pheasant for the duck in this recipe. Sometimes I add a few dashes of Asian-Style Hot Oil (page 360) to the burritos. SERVES 4

> 2 pounds duck, cut in parts
>
> 2 cups red wine
>
> 2 cups chicken stock (for homemade, page 89)
>
> 1 cup Savory Plum Jam (page 256)
>
> ¼ cup soy sauce
>
> 2-inch piece fresh ginger, peeled
>
> 8 large flour tortillas
>
> 2 tablespoons chopped cilantro, for garnish

Preheat the broiler. Place the duck parts on a rimmed baking sheet. Broil for about 10 minutes to brown, flipping over once. Transfer the duck to a large pot along with any juices in the pan. Add the wine, chicken stock, plum jam, soy sauce, and ginger. Bring to a boil over medium-high heat, then reduce the heat to medium, cover, and cook at a gentle boil for 1½ hours, until the duck is tender. Allow the duck to cool in the stock.

Strain and defat the stock (I use a gravy separator) and reserve. Remove the meat from the bones (discard the bones) and chop the meat into small pieces. Set aside. Return the strained stock to the pot and boil over medium heat until the stock is reduced by half, about 15 minutes. Add the chopped meat back to the gravy. Heat the meat through.

Serve the meat rolled up in warm flour tortillas, sprinkled with cilantro, and drizzled with the sauce.

Plum Jam Shortbread

This shortbread with any combination of jam and nuts—like apricot and almonds, peach and pecans, and raspberry and hazelnuts—is a winner. You can also add lemon, vanilla, or other flavor extract to the dough. Shortbread gets tough when refrigerated for more than 48 hours, and because of the plums you do need to refrigerate these squares. So I try not to make more than I plan to eat in a day. SERVES 4 TO 6

> 1 cup all-purpose flour
>
> 8 tablespoons (1 stick) unsalted butter, at room temperature
>
> ¼ teaspoon salt
>
> ½ cup plus 2 tablespoons sugar
>
> 1 cup Sweet Plum Jam (page 256)
>
> 3 tablespoons chopped walnuts

Preheat the oven to 300°F.

In a food processor, pulse to combine the flour, butter, salt, and ½ cup of the sugar until crumbly. (Or combine by hand.) Dump the dough into an 8 × 8-inch baking pan. Pat the dough evenly to fill the pan. Prick the dough all over with a fork. Pour the jam on top.

In a food processor, or with a mortar and pestle, grind the walnuts with the remaining 2 tablespoons sugar. Sprinkle the walnut mixture over the plum jam.

PRUNES STEWED IN MADEIRA WINE

Bake for 35 minutes, or until the edges of the shortbread are golden and the jam is bubbling. Remove the shortbread and let cool in the pan. When the shortbread is cool, cut it into quarters and remove from the pan. Then cut the quarters into bars with a sharp knife.

Serve or wrap the squares in plastic wrap and refrigerate. They keep for 2 days.

Prunes Stewed in Madeira Wine

I love serving this dessert after a rich, meaty dinner. It is excellent with a dollop of whipped cream or crème fraîche (for homemade, page 362). Note the prunes need to rehydrate for 24 hours. **SERVES 4**

1 pound pitted prunes (for homemade, page 255)

2 cups Madeira wine

6 tablespoons raisins (for homemade, page 161)

Two 2-inch strips lemon zest

Two 3-inch cinnamon sticks

2 tablespoons sugar

Place the prunes in a bowl and cover with the wine. Cover and let rest at room temperature for 24 hours.

Pour the prunes and wine into a small saucepan. Add the raisins, lemon zest, cinnamon, and sugar. Heat over medium heat until most of the wine has evaporated, 10 to 15 minutes. Remove the cinnamon and lemon zest. Serve at room temperature, warm, or cool.

Plum-Orange Granita

I make this granita when I can plum jam. The canning pot always has leftover jam sticking to the sides, and you'll end up with maybe ¼ cup of jam in the bottom of the pot that doesn't fit into a jar. Don't wash that pot! Deglaze with orange juice and make granita. This is a great technique that you can do with most fruit canning remnants. **MAKES 1¼ CUPS**

1 cup orange juice

¼ cup Sweet Plum Jam (page 256)

Pour the orange juice into the pot with the leftover plum jam, and scrape the bottom and sides to combine the plums with the juice. If the plum remnants are rather sticky, then do this over low heat. Once the orange juice and plums are thoroughly combined, pour the liquid into a metal container and chill in the refrigerator. Prepare according to the technique for making granita on page 393.

PORK

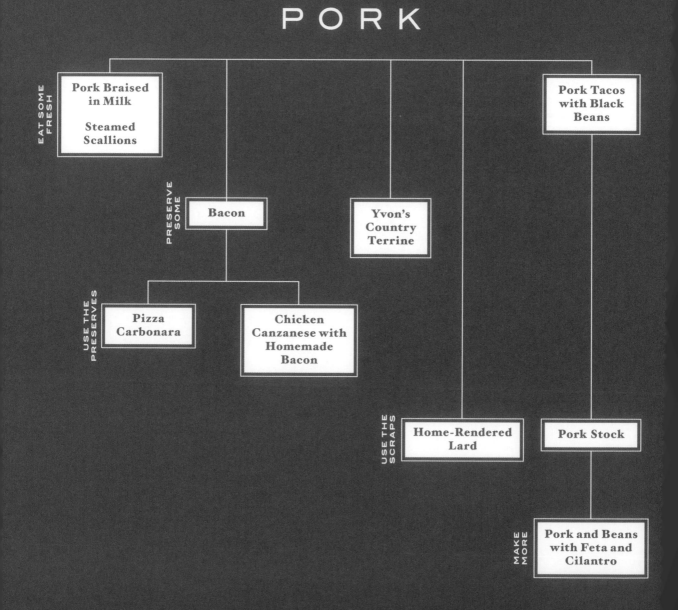

EAT SOME FRESH

Pork Braised
in Milk

Steamed
Scallions

Pork Tacos
with Black
Beans

PRESERVE SOME

Bacon

Yvon's
Country
Terrine

USE THE PRESERVES

Pizza
Carbonara

Chicken
Canzanese with
Homemade
Bacon

USE THE SCRAPS

Home-Rendered
Lard

Pork Stock

MAKE MORE

Pork and Beans
with Feta and
Cilantro

Pork Braised in Milk

I often make this dish after making Ricotta Cheese (page 367) to use up the whey. It creates a silky sauce. You can flavor this pork with garlic and sage instead of rosemary and shallots. The pork is wonderful served on mashed potatoes with Steamed Scallions (recipe follows). **SERVES 4**

- 1½ pounds pork tenderloin
- Salt and freshly ground black pepper
- 2 tablespoons unsalted butter
- 2 tablespoons minced shallots or 1 tablespoon minced garlic
- Three 3-inch sprigs of fresh rosemary
- 1 bay leaf
- 2 cups whole milk or whey left over from making Ricotta Cheese (page 367)

Season the tenderloin with salt and pepper. In a medium Dutch oven or other heavy-bottomed pot, heat the butter over medium heat. (It's okay to cut the tenderloin in half to fit your pot.) Add the pork and sear all over, about 15 minutes. Add the shallots, rosemary, and bay leaf. Add the milk (or whey) and let come to a boil. Then reduce the heat to a gentle boil, partially cover, and braise the pork until it is well done, about 1 hour 40 minutes. Check the milk periodically, and using a skimmer, remove the curdles. The sauce below the curdles is light and silky. (You will have very few curdles if you use whey.)

Remove the meat and wrap in foil to keep warm. Bring the sauce back to a boil over medium heat and reduce by one-third, about 15 minutes, scraping up any browned bits from the bottom that might be left over from searing. Remove the rosemary sprigs and bay leaf. Adjust the seasoning. Slice the pork and serve with the milk sauce.

STEAMED SCALLIONS

This recipe is an Italianized version of one from a favorite cookbook, The Cuisine of Normandy *by Princess Marie-Blanche de Broglie.* **The dark-green scallion tops are chewy when steamed, so trim them off and save to use raw on a dish like Roast Beet Salad with Feta, Scallions, and Cilantro (page 50) or to make scallion pesto (see Tuna with Scallion Pesto, page 305).** **SERVES 4**

- 28 large scallions
- 2 tablespoons unsalted butter
- Salt and freshly ground black pepper
- 2 tablespoons lemon juice
- ¼ cup grated Parmesan cheese

Trim the scallions to include 3 inches of the dark-green tops. Place the scallions in a vegetable steamer and steam until tender, about 2 minutes.

In a large skillet, heat the butter over medium heat. Add the scallions, tossing them in the butter for about a minute. Add salt and pepper to taste. Transfer to a serving platter. Dress the scallions with the lemon juice and garnish with the cheese. Serve warm.

Pork Tacos with Black Beans

When I have a crowd of 25 or more I make this recipe, which I got from my friend Neni Panourgia. I serve it with black turtle beans (though sometimes we just go to our neighborhood Cuban joint and buy a few orders), Pickled Onions (page 211), and Cilantro Cream (page 111). **Save the pork bone and leftover tough bits to make Pork Stock (page 268).** **SERVES 6 TO 8**

PORK TACOS WITH
BLACK BEANS

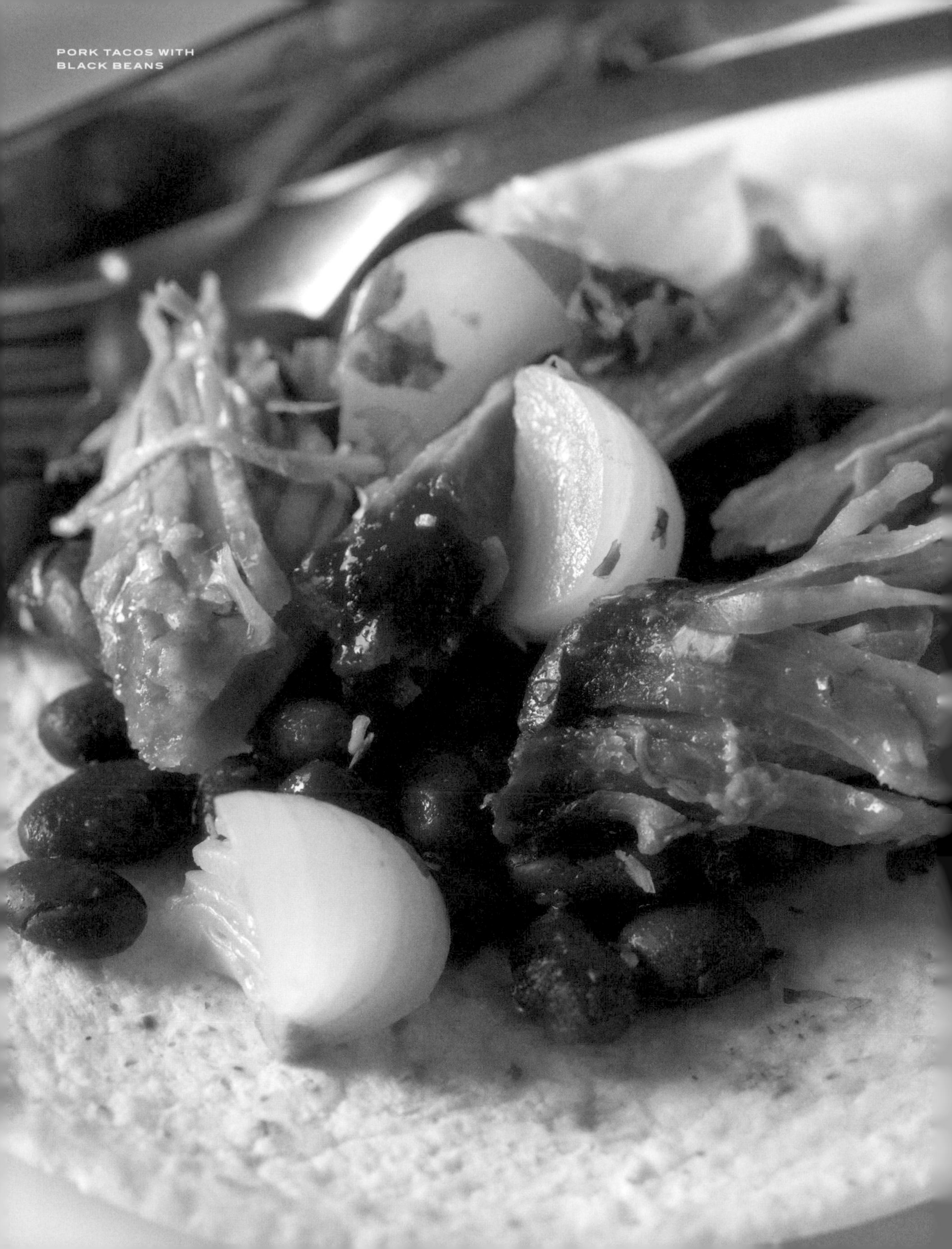

1 tablespoon salt

1 teaspoon freshly ground black pepper

3 pounds bone-in pork shoulder

2 tablespoons chopped garlic

3 tablespoons mustard (Dijon or homemade, page 366)

½ cup fresh lemon juice

BEANS

1 cup dried black beans, soaked overnight and drained

3 cups chicken stock (for homemade, page 89) or beef stock (for homemade, page 47)

Salt

8 flour tortillas, warmed

½ pint Pickled Onions (page 211; optional)

Cilantro Cream (page 111)

Preheat the oven to 400°F.

For the pork: In a small bowl, combine the salt and pepper. Score the fat of the pork in a diamond pattern and rub the salt and pepper all over the shoulder, and push the garlic into the slits. Then cover the whole roast with mustard (I pat the mustard on with my hands).

Place the pork fat side down in an oiled roasting pan and roast for 15 minutes. Then turn the roast over, fat side up, and roast for another 15 minutes. Pour the lemon juice over the shoulder. Reduce the oven temperature to 325°F and roast the pork, uncovered, for 2½ to 3 hours, basting periodically. You can tell when the roast is done because the tip of the bone will be exposed and the meat will fall away from the bone. The fat should be well browned and mostly rendered.

Meanwhile, for the beans: In a medium pot, combine the beans, stock, and salt to taste. Bring to a boil over high heat, and then reduce the heat to medium-low. Cover and gently boil the beans until they are fork-tender, about 50 minutes.

Remove the pork shoulder from the oven, pour off the drippings, and save (see Note).

Pull the pork off the bone (you can't really cut it off in any tidy way). Fork about ¼ cup of meat into each warmed flour tortilla. Add 1 or 2 tablespoons black beans and a few pickled onions (if using) and a drizzle of cilantro cream.

Note: The drippings will be 50 percent fat. To use, strain and defat it and combine the drippings in a saucepan with an equal amount of beef stock and some chopped fresh thyme. Cook to reduce the sauce by about 25 percent. You will have a lovely sauce to use with this or another dish, like Pork and Beans with Feta and Cilantro (page 269).

Bacon

This delicious recipe calls for roasting the meat in a low oven after a 1-week curing period. The bacon must be refrigerated and keeps for about 2 weeks. Curing and roasting kills spoilers, and refrigeration retards the growth of any spoilers that might remain. However, the bacon has to be very dry before wrapping and refrigerating. I learned the salt and sugar ratios, and basic technique, from Charcuterie, *written by Michael Ruhlman and Brian Polcyn. You can adjust the spices without affecting the safety of the recipe, but don't change the quantity of salt.*

MAKES 2½ POUNDS

2½ pounds slab pork belly, rind on

3 tablespoons pickling salt

1½ tablespoons light brown sugar

1 tablespoon black peppercorns

1 tablespoon coriander seeds

1 tablespoon juniper berries

1 large garlic clove, minced

Rinse and dry the meat. Place it on a large piece of wax paper.

With a mortar and pestle or spice grinder, grind the salt, brown sugar, peppercorns, coriander seeds, juniper berries, and garlic to the consistency of kosher salt (some of the seasoning ingredients will become powdery, which is okay).

Rub the seasonings all over the meat. Put the meat in a plastic food storage bag (along with any leftover seasoning) and place in a baking pan. Place another smaller baking pan on top and weight it with a brick or canned goods. Refrigerate for 1 week, turning the meat daily. (Don't forget to replace the weights.) Over the course of the week, brine will develop in the bag. It won't be sopping wet, but you will see puddles of water in the bag. This is good.

After 1 week, remove the pork belly, rinse it, and dry it very well. Place the meat in a baking dish and cover with plastic wrap or foil. Refrigerate for 24 hours. This allows the salt to equalize throughout the cells of the meat.

Preheat the oven to 200°F. Place the meat in a clean baking dish and bake uncovered for 2 to 2½ hours, until the internal temperature of the meat reaches 150°F. The bacon will brown all over and smell spicy and strong. Do not overcook the bacon or the meat will become tough and the fat will render. Best to check the internal temperature of the bacon with a meat thermometer after about 1½ hours.

Remove the meat when it is cool enough to handle and cut off the rind (see Note). To store, dry the meat very well, wrap in wax paper, and place in a plastic food storage bag in the refrigerator. It will hold for about 2 weeks.

Or freeze the bacon. I chop half the bacon into cubes and freeze 1-cup bags to use in salads and in Chicken Canzanese (page 266).

Note: Save the rind. Cut it into chunks and freeze. Rind bits add excellent flavor to soups.

Yvon's Country Terrine

My friend Yvon Gross, a Frenchman and proprietor of the Leroux Creek Vineyards, taught me this easy terrine. You can make it in just about any mold, covered with foil with a few holes poked in it to vent the steam produced by the cooking meat. You can use pork liver instead of calf's liver if you prefer, and you can increase the amount of liver by up to 6 ounces in this recipe—both adaptations are more typically French. MAKES ONE 9-INCH LOAF

2 pounds boneless pork shoulder with lots of fat on it (if the shoulder is 50 percent fat, that's ideal)

10 ounces calf's liver

½ cup brandy

1 large egg

5 teaspoons finely chopped flat-leaf parsley

1 tablespoon finely chopped garlic

2 teaspoons finely chopped fresh thyme

2 teaspoons finely chopped fresh rosemary

2 teaspoons finely chopped fresh basil (optional)

2 teaspoons salt

1 teaspoon freshly ground black pepper

Position an oven rack in the lower third of the oven and preheat to 375°F.

Coarsely chop the pork shoulder with fat. Separately, coarsely chop the liver. A very sharp knife helps.

Working in batches, grind the pork shoulder with fat in a food processor or meat grinder. If using a food processor, do this in small batches, as the blade will have to work hard at first to grind up the meat. The texture should be like sausage meat. It will be heavy and thick. It is okay for there to be little clumps of fat, but it should not be stringy. Place the ground pork with fat in a large bowl.

Place the liver in a food processor or meat grinder and pulse to grind. It will liquefy some but should be mostly chunky. That liquefied liver will create the smooth interstices in the terrine.

Add the liver to the pork along with the remaining ingredients and mix well by hand. (The herbs will get mucky if you put them in the food processor.) When the ingredients are combined they will smell aromatic and tasty. You can do a taste control at this point: Make a small patty of the mixture and fry as you would a slider and taste for seasoning. Add more garlic or salt or herbs if you'd like.

Pour the mixture into a 9 × 5-inch loaf pan. You don't have to grease it—there is enough fat in the terrine. With a spatula, smooth the mixture into every corner of the pan, popping any air bubbles and condensing the mixture. Smooth the top and cover with a lid that has holes or foil punctured with a small hole about the size of the end of a chopstick. Place the terrine in a large baking pan and add enough hot water to come halfway up the sides of the loaf pan. Place in the oven and bake for 1½ hours, or until the internal temperature (slip a thermometer into the vent hole) reaches 165°F.

Turn off the oven and let the terrine rest for 15 minutes. Remove the terrine from the oven and tip the pan to drain off the excess fat.

Allow the terrine to cool completely before gently flipping it over onto a cutting board. Wrap the terrine in foil to freeze, or refrigerate for up to 5 days. Serve in slices with homemade Pickle Spears (page 112).

Pizza Carbonara

The trick to making this pizza is precooking the eggs. If you were to cook the eggs on top of the pizza, you'd end up either with undercooked eggs or overcooked crust. It is best to prebake the crust, as the toppings are precooked and only need to be heated. My friend John Zito makes this pizza with quail eggs. SERVES 4

CRUST

¾ cup room temperature water

2¼ teaspoons (1 envelope) active dry yeast

3 tablespoons olive oil, plus more for the bowl

Pinch of salt

2½ cups all-purpose flour

Semolina flour, for dusting

TOPPING

2 tablespoons olive oil

2 cups chopped bacon (for homemade, page 263)

3 cups sliced onions

2 teaspoons minced garlic

1 cup grated Parmesan cheese

2 tablespoons chopped flat-leaf parsley

8 small eggs

Freshly ground black pepper

For the dough: In a bowl, combine the water, yeast, oil, and salt. Add the all-purpose flour and knead a few times until the dough comes together. It will be rather sticky. It's okay. Remove the dough from the bowl and set aside. Rub the bowl with a little oil. Return the dough to the bowl. Cover with a damp towel and leave in a very warm spot and let rise until the dough has doubled in size, about 2 hours. Push the dough down, deflating it, then let it rise in the bowl again for 20 minutes.

Preheat the oven to its very hottest temperature. Mine is 500°F.

Roll out the pizza dough on a semolina-floured board to the size and shape of a large baking sheet and place on a baking sheet. Place the dough in the oven and bake for about 5 minutes, until it looks chalky.

For the topping: In a large pot, heat 1 tablespoon of the oil over high heat and add the bacon. Cook the bacon until it renders its fat, about 5 minutes, then add the onions and garlic. Cook until the onion is translucent, about 5 minutes. Pour off the excess fat.

To assemble the pizza, top the crust with the bacon and onion mixture (I use tongs to place the mixture on the crust), and sprinkle with the Parmesan and parsley. Brush the edges of the crust with the remaining tablespoon of olive oil. Return the pizza to the oven and bake until the cheese melts and the crust becomes golden, about 5 minutes.

Meanwhile, heat a large nonstick skillet over medium-high heat and crack the eggs into it. Fry the eggs sunny-side up until the whites are opaque.

To serve, place the eggs evenly on the pizza and, with a spatula, crack the yolks. Garnish with black pepper. Cut into 8 serving pieces and serve promptly.

Chicken Canzanese with Homemade Bacon

Chicken Canzanese is a dish from Abruzzi in Italy that my father used to make for Sunday lunch when I was a child, and I make different versions of it for my family all the time because it is an easy, one-pot recipe that needs little attention. The dish is wonderful with sliced morel mushrooms added at the end. SERVES 4

8 chicken thighs, bone in, skin on

½ cup finely diced bacon (for homemade, page 263)

2 tablespoons chopped fresh sage

1 heaping tablespoon finely chopped garlic

10 black peppercorns

4 whole cloves

2 bay leaves

Two 2-inch sprigs of fresh rosemary

1 small dried hot pepper

1 cup dry white wine

Salt

3 tablespoons chopped flat-leaf parsley

Place the chicken thighs in a single layer skin side down in a large sauté pan with a fitted lid. Sprinkle the diced bacon, sage, garlic, peppercorns, cloves, bay leaves, rosemary, hot pepper, and wine over the chicken. Cover and cook over medium heat for 30 to 35 minutes until the skin of the chicken is rendered and brown and easily pulls away from the bottom of the pan. Remove the cover and cook for an additional 5 minutes to allow the wine and steam to evaporate. Check the seasoning. The chicken will be ivory colored and moist, the sauce golden and aromatic.

To serve, place the chicken thighs on a serving platter and pour the drippings and bits of cooked herbs and garlic all over. Don't forget to fish out the whole cloves and remove most of the peppercorns. Garnish with parsley.

The Pig Roast

Every other summer my husband gets a hankering to throw a whole pig roast at our cabin in Colorado. We invite everyone we know, and it's wonderful and rowdy and a tremendous pain in the ass. First, I have to give up my controlling tendencies, and let a passel of middle-aged men and their gray ponytails run rampant in the kitchen. Then there's the problem of getting a pig that's not too humongous. We buy our pigs from local organic farmers in Delta County. Sometimes our timing is good and we get a nice 50- to 75-pounder, but sometimes the only available pig is 200 plus pounds. One year we got such a monster that two of the three men who flopped it on the picnic table to stuff it developed hernias.

Usually we fill the pig with fennel bulbs and garlic, rosemary and oregano from the garden, and plenty of salt and pepper—though one year there was a bounty of *Boletus* mushrooms growing in the West Elk Mountains and we stuffed the pig with porcini stems and an armful of thyme. We wrap the pig in miles of cheesecloth until it looks like a big fat pink mummy. It is quite a process, with bees buzzing everywhere and frequent "conferences," where the guys lubricate themselves with shots of tequila. Once the men have filled a pit in the backyard with wood from our scraggly apple trees and set the fire, we wait. And eat, and drink. For 6 hours the fire is stoked until finally it is allowed to die out and the pig is put into a chicken wire basket and heaved on top of the hot stones. By this time I am usually in bed, but I can hear the men grunting as they bury the pig and pat the dirt hard with the backs of their shovels.

The next day is a flurry of activity as we prepare buttermilk cornbread, barbecue sauce, tarragon pesto, a huge pot of beans, and avocado and cucumber salad. Our guests bring desserts, and by late afternoon the sideboard is laden with cherry pies and peach cobblers. We open bottle after bottle of wine from the local vineyards and I put out every plate, every knife and fork, and every glass that I have. The moment of truth comes when we remove the pig from the pit. Is it done? We never know for sure. There have been years when we've had to do a quick butcher job and finish the Jurassic-size hunks of meat in the oven. But always by the time the kids are parking the farm trucks in the front pasture, the cabin has filled with the delectable smell of sweet flesh and pungent herbs riding in on the canyon's eternal minerally breeze.

Home-Rendered Lard

The types of fat typically used to make rendered lard are leaf lard (which is from around the kidneys), belly fat, and back fat (the layer of fat beneath the skin). Leaf lard is the whitest and purest fat, and the most versatile when it comes to cooking because of its mild taste. Have the butcher grind it up for you. To grind it yourself, place the lard in the freezer for 30 minutes or so to make it less sticky, then chop into at least ½-inch cubes. You can render fat on top of the stove, but I prefer to do it in the oven, where the fat is less likely to scorch. Lard is a wonderful substitution for butter in pastry and an excellent fat for frying.
MAKES 1 PINT

1½ pounds chopped pig fat (about 4 cups)

Preheat the oven to 225°F.

Spread the fat in a large roasting pan and put the pan in the oven. You want to heat the fat enough to liquefy, but not enough to burn it, so every 10 minutes or so, check the fat. Stir the fat to move the pieces around. Cracklings will form. These are browned bits of connective tissue that cannot be rendered. Remove them with a slotted spoon as they brown. (Drained, the cracklings will be rather soft, but if you heat them in a hot oven to crisp them up, they can be used as a garnish on other foods, like soups, beans, and gratins.)

It takes about 1 hour 30 minutes for the lard to render, sometimes longer. Let the lard render slowly. It makes for a better product. Once the fat is totally melted, ladle the clear fat into a metal sieve over a metal bowl to separate out any remaining cracklings.

Have ready a sterilized pint jar, band, and lid. (See "How to Sterilize," page 389.) You do

HOME-RENDERED LARD

not need a new lid because you will not be processing this jar. Line a sieve with a layer of cheesecloth and pour the fat through the cheesecloth and into the pint jar.

Wipe the rim, place on the lid, and screw on the band. The lard will hold in the fridge for 3 months. It will get quite hard, so remove the amount you want to use and let it warm up a bit before using.

Pork Stock

This is a very rich stock, wonderful for cooking beans, or as a base for a bean soup. I always make it from the bone left over from a pork shoulder recipe, like Pork Tacos (page 261) or Braised Pork Shoulder with Oranges (page 215). **MAKES ABOUT 6 CUPS**

1 pork bone

½ large onion

3 medium carrots, cut in large pieces

1 cup coarsely chopped flat-leaf parsley

½ lemon

2 bay leaves

1 teaspoon black peppercorns

8 cups water

Salt

Place the pork bone, onion, carrots, parsley, lemon, bay leaves, and peppercorns in a large soup pot. Cover with the water. Bring to a boil over high heat, then reduce the heat to low. Gently boil the stock, partially covered, for 2½ hours.

Add salt to taste. Strain the stock and discard the bones. Defat the stock with a gravy separator, or chill the stock, then remove the cooled layer of fat with a fork.

Transfer the stock to pint jars and refrigerate or freeze (see the technique for making stocks, page 390).

For shelf-stable stock, pressure can it. Have ready 3 clean pint jars and bands, and new lids that have been simmered in hot water to soften the rubberized flange. Pour the pork stock into the jars leaving 1 inch of headroom. Wipe the rims, place on the lids, and screw on the bands fingertip tight.

Process the jars in a pressure canner at 10/11 psi for 20 minutes for pints, 25 minutes for 1 quart (see "How to Pressure Can," page 379). Be sure to make altitude adjustments when preserving (see page 389).

Pork and Beans with Feta and Cilantro

I make this dish as a side, as an entrée, for lunch, for dinner, with eggs for brunch. It is all-purpose, and very tasty. It's also forgiving and adaptable. I make it even if I have no leftover pork—the stock flavors the beans very well. Try different kinds of beans, and garnishes, like chopped avocado, tomatoes, or pickled peppers. For this recipe, I soak dried cannellini beans in salted water overnight. SERVES 4

1½ cups dried cannellini beans, soaked overnight with a big pinch of salt and drained

4 cups Pork Stock (opposite)

1 tablespoon fresh lemon juice

1 tablespoon minced garlic

Salt and freshly ground black pepper

2 cups chopped leftover cooked pork

½ cup chopped onions (white or red)

½ cup crumbled feta cheese

½ cup finely chopped cilantro

Hot sauce (for homemade, page 365), for serving

In a large pot, combine the soaked beans and pork stock. Bring to a boil over medium-high heat, then reduce the heat to medium low, cover, and boil gently for 20 minutes. Add the lemon juice, garlic, and salt and pepper to taste. Continue to boil gently, covered, for 10 minutes more, then add the pork and cook uncovered until the beans have absorbed the stock and are tender, about 20 minutes. Add more stock or water if needed to keep the beans moist.

Pour the beans and pork into a serving dish. Check the seasoning. Garnish with the onions, feta, and cilantro. Serve with hot pepper sauce.

RADISHES WITH GREENS

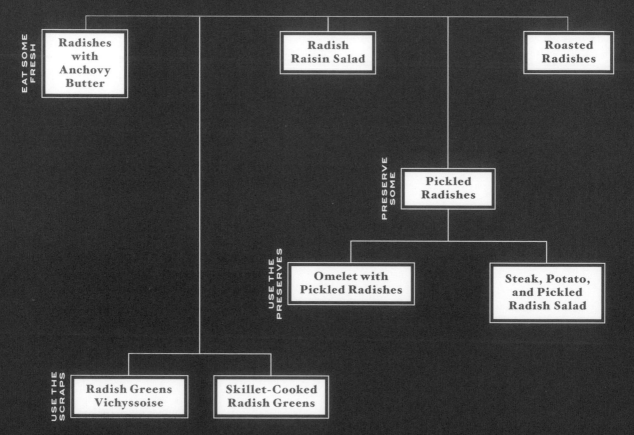

EAT SOME FRESH

Radishes with Anchovy Butter

Radish Raisin Salad

Roasted Radishes

PRESERVE SOME

Pickled Radishes

USE THE PRESERVES

Omelet with Pickled Radishes

Steak, Potato, and Pickled Radish Salad

USE THE SCRAPS

Radish Greens Vichyssoise

Skillet-Cooked Radish Greens

Radishes with Anchovy Butter

Radishes are the perfect hors d'oeuvre: They whet the appetite and keep your breath fresh. Choose small firm radishes about 1 inch in diameter. French breakfast radishes are perfect for this kind of noshing. **Save the radish greens for Skillet-Cooked Radish Greens (page 275) or Radish Greens Vichyssoise (page 275).** MAKES ½ CUP BUTTER, ENOUGH FOR 8 SERVINGS

> 2 bunches radishes, such as French breakfast, greens removed (about 20 small)
>
> 8 tablespoons (1 stick) unsalted butter, at room temperature
>
> 1 whole anchovy (see Note) or 2 anchovy fillets, minced
>
> 1 tablespoon minced fresh chives (optional)
>
> Salt and freshly ground black pepper

If the radishes are large, cut them into bite-size pieces.

In a bowl, combine the butter, anchovies, chives (if using), and salt and pepper to taste until smooth. Pack this mixture into a mold (I usually use a ramekin). Sealed in a container, the butter will hold in the fridge for a month.

To eat family-style, dip the radishes into the butter. You can also chill the butter and cut it into individual pieces, then allow to soften at room temperature to serve.

Note: I prefer whole anchovies cured in salt, available at Italian markets. Soak them for 10 minutes to remove the salt, then rinse and fillet them. You don't have to get all the bones, just the spine.

RADISHES WITH ANCHOVY BUTTER

Radish Raisin Salad

This is an easy, unusual side dish or first course. You can add shaved Parmesan cheese if you'd like. **Save the radish greens for Skillet-Cooked Radish Greens (page 275) or Radish Greens Vichyssoise (page 275).** SERVES 4

> 4 cups sliced or grated radishes
>
> 1 cup golden raisins (for homemade, page 161)
>
> ¼ cup extra virgin olive oil
>
> Salt and freshly ground black pepper, to taste

Combine all of the ingredients in a serving bowl and serve at room temperature.

Roasted Radishes

*This recipe couldn't be simpler. The flavor is earthy and delicate at the same time. **Save the radish greens for Skillet-Cooked Radish Greens (page 275) or Radish Greens Vichyssoise (page 275)**.* SERVES 4

> 2 bunches radishes (about 20 small), greens removed
>
> 2 tablespoons minced shallots
>
> 2 tablespoons olive oil
>
> Salt and freshly ground black pepper

Preheat the oven to 400°F.

Bring a large pot of salted water to a boil and drop in the radishes. Cook until almost fork-tender and pale, about 5 minutes, depending on the size of the radishes. Drain and retain the water.

Spread the radishes in a medium roasting pan. If they are not uniform in size, cut the larger ones in half or whatever is needed to match the smallest radish. Drizzle oil over the shallots, and season with salt and pepper to taste. Add a couple of tablespoons of the radish cooking water and place in the oven. Roast for 15 minutes, until the radishes are just golden, shaking the pan once during baking to turn them over.

Pickled Radishes

I love the beautiful warm pink color of these pickles. The taste is sweetly hot, and using a mandoline to slice the radishes ensures a delicate pickle. Unfortunately, there is no USDA-approved recipe for canning pickled radishes, but since they are pretty much available year-round, I just put up a new half-pint when I run out. They hold for a few months in the refrigerator. MAKES 1 HALF-PINT

> ½ cup white wine or champagne vinegar
>
> ½ cup sugar
>
> ½ teaspoon salt
>
> 6 radishes, very thinly sliced (1 heaping cup)
>
> 1 large shallot, cut into eighths

In a small saucepan, combine the vinegar, sugar, and salt and heat over medium-low heat, stirring until the sugar dissolves. Add the radishes and shallots. Heat until the vinegar just begins to boil, then remove from the heat.

Have ready 1 sterilized half-pint jar, band, and lid. (See "How to Sterilize," page 389.) You do not need to use a new lid because you will not process this jar. Pack the radishes and shallots into the jar and refrigerate. Allow the radishes to cure 1 week before serving. Save the extra pickling liquid to use in salad dressing.

Omelet with Pickled Radishes

It is one of those quirks of recipe development that something so totally simple can be so divine, but the crisp, sweet, tart radishes on top of a simple omelet is as fine as anything I've eaten. SERVES 4

> 8 eggs
>
> ½ cup heavy cream
>
> Salt and freshly ground black pepper
>
> 4 tablespoons (½ stick) unsalted butter
>
> 1 half-pint Pickled Radishes (left)

In a bowl, beat together the eggs and cream and season with salt and pepper to taste.

In each of two small nonstick skillets (I like to make two omelets at a time, though you can make one big omelet as well), heat 1 tablespoon of the butter over medium heat. Add one-fourth of the egg mixture and let cook for a few minutes. Slightly scramble the eggs, making sure the bottom of the pan is still covered with egg. This makes the omelet a bit fluffier. Allow the omelets to cook without disturbing for a few minutes more. When the bottom is golden brown, fold one third of the omelet into the middle, then the other third of the omelet over, as if folding a napkin. Flip the whole omelet over so the seams can cook. Repeat to make 2 more omelets.

Garnish with the radishes and serve promptly.

Steak, Potato, and Pickled Radish Salad

I make simple seared steak and potato salad throughout the summer and everyone in my family loves it. But adding pickled radishes really takes it to another level, both in terms of the snappy flavor they add, and the lovely pink color. **SERVES 4**

- 8 medium potatoes (I like Yukon Gold)
- ¼ cup extra virgin olive oil
- 4 teaspoons coarsely ground black pepper
- 1½ pounds thick-cut (1 inch or more) sirloin steak, trimmed (see Note)
- 1 half-pint Pickled Radishes (opposite), drained, ¼ cup pickling liquid retained
- Salt
- 2 tablespoons minced flat-leaf parsley

Bring a large pot of salted water to a boil over medium-high heat. Add the potatoes and boil them until they are just tender, about 25 minutes. Drain the potatoes and run them under cold water to stop the cooking. Peel and slice the potatoes, place them in a salad bowl, and drizzle with 2 tablespoons of oil.

Pat the pepper onto the steak. Place a large cast-iron skillet over high heat and heat it until it is very hot. Reduce the heat to medium-high, add the steak, and sear for 4 minutes on one side. Turn the steak over. Salt the seared side and sear it for another 4 minutes. Turn the steak back over, salt it, and sear it for another 3 minutes. Turn the steak one final time and sear for another 3 minutes. This is an Italian technique: It gives you a great sear without any burn. Take the steak off the heat and let it come down to room temperature.

Slice the steak into very thin strips about 3 inches long and add to the potatoes. Add the radishes, pickling liquid, remaining 2 tablespoons of olive oil, and salt to taste, and gently toss to combine. Garnish with the parsley.

Note: If your steak is thinner than 1 inch, it will only take a few minutes per side to sear.

STEAK, POTATO, AND PICKLED RADISH SALAD

SKILLET-COOKED
RADISH GREENS

Skillet-Cooked Radish Greens

The first time I cooked radish greens I was surprised at how sweet and tender they were. I'd been throwing them away for years, before my friend Daphne, a farmer in Paonia, Colorado, told me the Greeks made horta *with them. (Horta is a bit like the Italian* verdura trovata, *a mélange of sautéed "found" or wild vegetables; see also Feral Greens, page 231.) Sometimes the radish greens will be lacy with insect holes. Farmers will plant radish rows between more valuable crops to draw insects. I eat them anyway. To make this into an entrée, poach eggs on top (see Eggs Poached on Sweet Peppers and Onions, page 239). You can also make a pasta dish: Cook ¾ pound* orecchiette *until al dente, drain, and toss with the greens. Garnish with grated Parmesan cheese.* **I save the water I used to cook the radish greens in the fridge for soup.** **SERVES 4 AS A SIDE DISH**

- ½ pound radish greens (weight of 2 typical bunches)
- 2 tablespoons olive oil, plus more for serving
- 1 tablespoon minced garlic
- Salt
- Hot pepper flakes or 1 small hot pepper

Bring a large pot of salted water to a boil. Add the radish greens and cook until the water returns to a boil. Reserving the cooking water, drain the greens and chop into bite-size pieces.

In a medium skillet, heat the oil over medium heat. Add the garlic and cook for a few minutes, until you can smell it. Do not brown. Add the radish greens and cook until they are tender, about 10 minutes. Add a little of the cooking water if the greens are dry. Add salt and pepper flakes to taste. Serve with a drizzle of olive oil.

Radish Greens Vichyssoise

I love this soup both warm and chilled. Sometimes I add garnishes of bacon bits or croutons or minced dill, but really, the soup's charm is its simplicity. Just remember it consists of 2 of everything and everything cooks for 3. **SERVES 4**

- 2 tablespoons unsalted butter
- 2 cups thinly sliced leek whites (2 fat leeks; save the green parts for Chicken Stock, page 89)
- 2 cups chopped small white potatoes (about ½ pound)
- 2 cups chopped radish greens (about ½ pound)
- 2 cups chicken stock (for homemade, page 89)
- 2 cups heavy cream
- 2 tablespoons fresh lemon juice (or more to taste)
- Salt and freshly ground black pepper
- 2 tablespoons julienned radishes or minced chives, for garnish (optional)

In a large heavy-bottomed pot, heat the butter over medium-high heat. Add each vegetable, one at a time, allowing it to cook for 3 minutes before adding the next one to the pot. Add the chicken stock and bring to a boil, then reduce the heat to medium-low, cover, and gently boil the soup until the potatoes are very tender, about 30 minutes.

Puree the soup with an immersion blender (or in a standard blender or food processor in batches; but let the soup cool first so that it is easier to handle).

Return the puree to the pot and stir in the cream. Cook at a simmer for a few minutes, until the soup is hot. Add the lemon juice and salt and pepper to taste.

Serve the soup hot or chilled. Garnish with radishes or chives, if you'd like.

RASPBERRIES

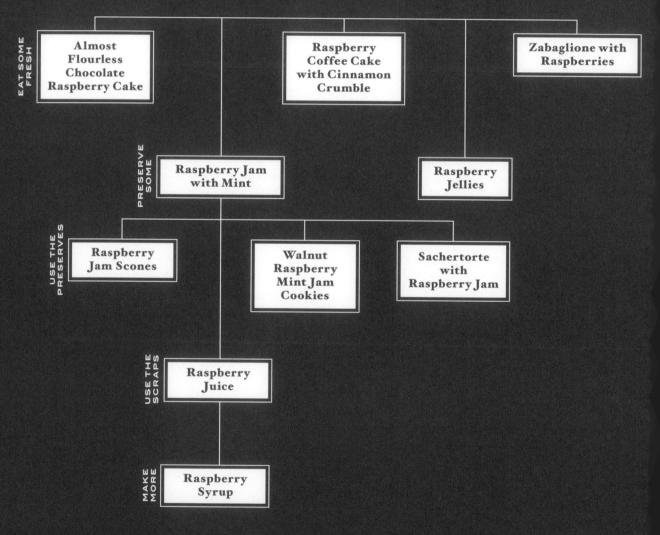

EAT SOME FRESH

Almost Flourless Chocolate Raspberry Cake

Raspberry Coffee Cake with Cinnamon Crumble

Zabaglione with Raspberries

PRESERVE SOME

Raspberry Jam with Mint

Raspberry Jellies

USE THE PRESERVES

Raspberry Jam Scones

Walnut Raspberry Mint Jam Cookies

Sachertorte with Raspberry Jam

USE THE SCRAPS

Raspberry Juice

MAKE MORE

Raspberry Syrup

Almost Flourless Chocolate Raspberry Cake

This dense, rich cake accentuates the great combination of raspberries and chocolate. It is adapted from Maida Heatter's Sour Cherry Chocolate Torte. I use raspberries and walnuts instead of cherries and almonds. **MAKES ONE 8-INCH CAKE**

- 12 tablespoons (1½ sticks) unsalted butter, at room temperature, plus 1 tablespoon for the pan
- 4 graham cracker squares
- 6 ounces semisweet chocolate, coarsely chopped
- ¾ cup granulated sugar
- 3 large eggs
- 1 teaspoon vanilla extract (for homemade, page 361)
- ⅔ cup sifted all-purpose flour
- ⅓ cup ground walnuts
- Pinch of salt
- 1 cup raspberries
- Confectioners' sugar or whipped cream, for serving (optional)

Preheat the oven to 350°F. Use 1 tablespoon butter to butter an 8-inch springform pan. Grind the graham crackers in a food processor or with a mortar and pestle. Dust the buttered pan with the graham crumbs. Tap out the excess.

In a double boiler or bowl set over a pan of hot water, melt the chocolate over medium-low heat.

In a large bowl, with an electric mixer, cream the butter and granulated sugar. Add the eggs one at a time, beating well after each addition. Mix in the chocolate and vanilla. Add the flour, walnuts, and salt and combine well.

Pour half the batter into the pan. Place the raspberries in a layer on top of the batter. Pour the remaining batter on top.

Bake for 45 to 50 minutes, until a cake tester inserted in the cake comes out clean. You will know the cake is done when you can smell it. Don't let it bake much after you get that first whiff.

Allow the cake to cool on a rack, and then remove the springform sides. Garnish with confectioners' sugar or serve with whipped cream, if you'd like.

Raspberry Coffee Cake with Cinnamon Crumble

This recipe is adapted from an old, tattered Woman's Exchange of Memphis cookbook. The cake is moist and sweet and best eaten right away, as the crumb toughens after a day or so. You can use Peach Puree (page 225) or Apricot-Orange Puree (page 19) in this recipe instead of the raspberries. Just swirl the puree over the batter. **SERVES 8**

CAKE
- 1 tablespoon unsalted butter, melted, plus softened butter for the pan
- 1 large egg
- ¾ cup granulated sugar
- 1 cup sour cream
- 1 teaspoon vanilla extract (for homemade, page 361)
- 1½ cups all-purpose flour
- 2 teaspoons baking powder
- ¼ teaspoon baking soda
- ¾ teaspoon salt

TOPPING
- ½ cup packed light brown sugar
- 2 tablespoons all-purpose flour
- 2 tablespoons unsalted butter, at room temperature
- ½ teaspoon ground cinnamon
- 1 cup raspberries

For the cake: Preheat the oven to 375°F. Butter an 8 × 8-inch baking pan.

In a bowl, with an electric mixer, beat the egg until it is frothy. Add the granulated sugar and melted butter and continue beating until the mixture is light and fluffy. Add the sour cream and vanilla and blend well. Sift the flour, the baking powder, baking soda, and salt together. Add the flour mixture to the sour cream mixture and blend them well.

For the topping: In a small bowl, combine the brown sugar, flour, butter, and cinnamon and mash it up with your fingers. It should be crumbly. If it is very wet and greasy, add a teaspoon of flour at a time until you can drop it off your fingers.

Pour the batter into the pan. Sprinkle the raspberries on top of the batter and sprinkle the topping over the raspberries.

Bake for 25 to 30 minutes, or until a cake tester inserted into the cake comes out clean. Do not overcook: This should be a moist cake.

Zabaglione with Raspberries

The best possible pan for cooking zabaglione is an unlined, round-bottomed copper pot set over a pot of boiling water, though any metal bowl will do. You can also use a double boiler, but unless the double boiler insert has a rounded bottom, the zab doesn't cook as evenly. This dish is traditionally served in a coupe glass—that cup-shaped champagne glass that Napoleon supposedly modeled on Josephine's bosom. If you don't have one, use any wide-mouthed, shallow glass. **SERVES 4**

4 egg yolks

¼ cup sugar

½ cup sweet Marsala wine

16 raspberries

Bring a saucepan of water to a rolling boil over medium heat.

In a metal bowl (that will sit over the top of, but not all the way in, the saucepan), whisk together the egg yolks, sugar, and Marsala. Place the bowl over the boiling water and reduce the heat to medium-low. With a whisk, beat the zabaglione constantly for about 3 minutes. During that time the egg mixture will go from egg yellow to foamy beige to a frothy, putty-colored stuff the consistency of soft meringue. Remove from the heat. If you notice any caking in the corners of the pan, it is overcooking. Take the zabaglione off the heat immediately.

Pour the zabaglione into the glasses and garnish with raspberries. They will drop to the bottom of the zab. This is good. Serve promptly.

Raspberry Jam with Mint

If you don't mind the seeds in raspberries, or the raspberries you are using are not very seedy to start with, then skip the food mill stage of this delicious recipe. I have made this jam with what I thought were raspberries without too many seeds, only to discover they actually had lots. So while the jam was still hot I pressed it through a sieve. I lost half the volume, but the result was wonderful. Steeping mint in the jam lends a delicate flavor. The longer you steep the mint, the stronger the flavor. ***After putting the raspberries though the food mill, save the raspberry mash to make Raspberry Juice (page 283).*** **MAKES 2 HALF-PINTS**

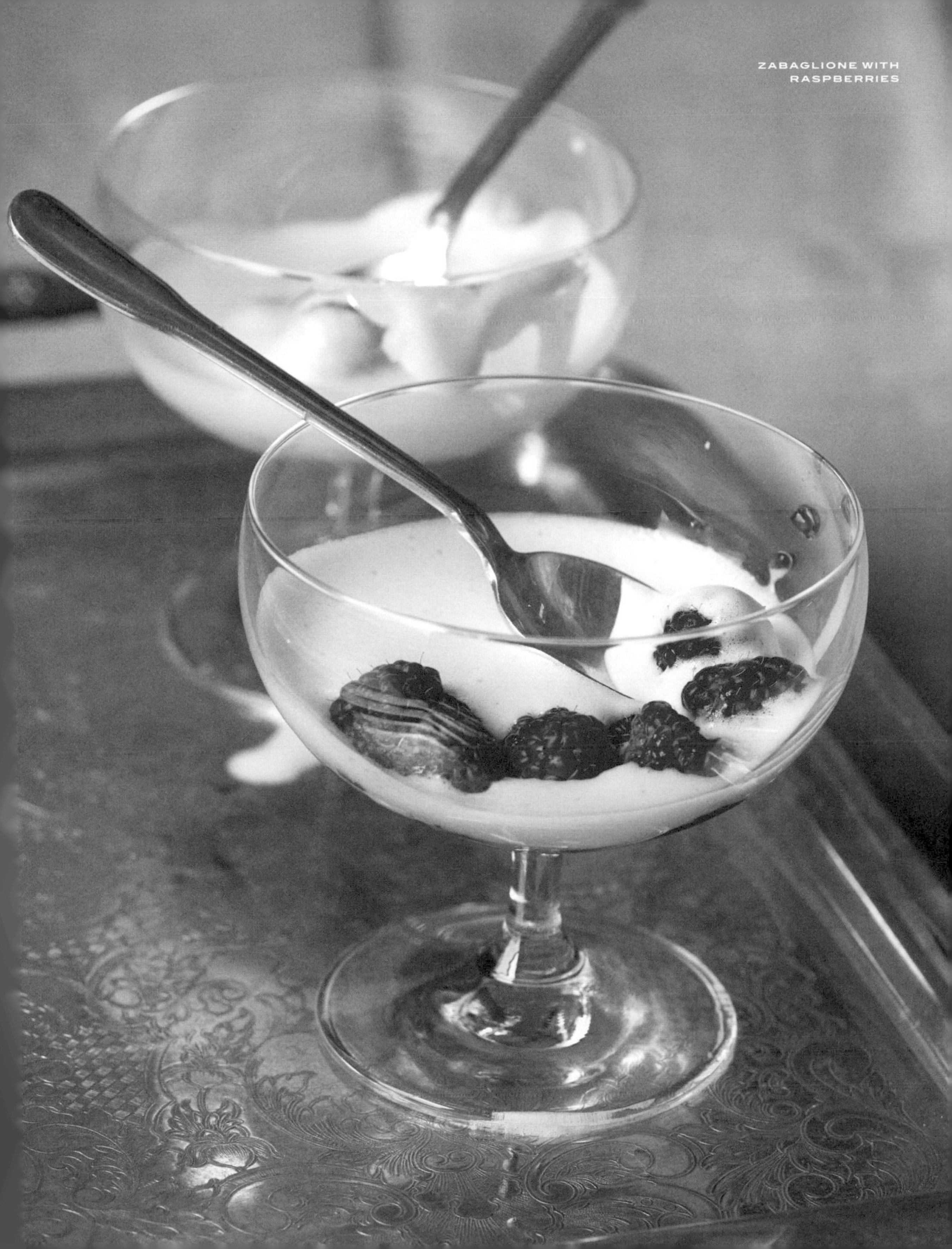
ZABAGLIONE WITH RASPBERRIES

5 cups raspberries

½ cup water

3 cups sugar

2 tablespoons lemon juice

2 leafy sprigs of mint

Place the raspberries in a large heavy-bottomed pot with the water and heat over medium heat for a few minutes. Pass the raspberries and water through a food mill to remove the seeds. You should have about 2 cups of puree.

Return the raspberry puree to the heavy-bottomed pot and add the sugar and lemon juice. Bring to a rapid boil over high heat and cook the jam until it is very thick, about 30 minutes, stirring frequently so the jam doesn't scorch. In the last few minutes of cooking, add the mint sprigs. Check the temperature with a candy thermometer. It will jell at 220°F at sea level, or 8°F over boiling temperature wherever you are. (To calculate the boiling temperature at your altitude, see page 389.) Or you can place a tablespoon of the jam in the fridge to chill. If it falls off the spoon in a clump, it's ready.

Have ready 2 sterilized half-pint jars and bands, and new lids that have been simmered in hot water to soften the rubberized flange. (See "How to Sterilize," page 389.) Remove the mint sprigs. Pour the jam into the jars leaving ¼ inch of headroom. Wipe the rims, place on the lids, and screw on the bands fingertip tight.

Process the jars in a water bath (see page 375) for 5 minutes for both half-pints or 1 pint. Be sure to make altitude adjustments when preserving (see page 389). There may be some discoloring of the fruit at the top of the jar over time. It's okay.

RASPBERRY SAUCE

You can take the raspberry puree from the first step of making raspberry jam and use it to make a fresh raspberry sauce instead. Just add sugar and lemon juice to taste and heat to dissolve the sugar. You can then water bath can it just as you would for the jam, using the same timing. The sauce is terrific in all kinds of desserts: drizzled into pound cake batter, poured over ice cream, or puddled under poached pears.

Raspberry Jellies

Homemade jellies are easy to make, and the taste explodes with raspberry flavor. They hold well in the fridge for about 10 days, but don't sugar them until you are ready to serve, as the sugar tends to liquefy. **After draining the raspberries in the jelly bag, save the raspberry mash to make Raspberry Juice (page 283). MAKES ABOUT 20 JELLIES THE SIZE OF DICE**

2 cups raspberries

2½ cups water

½ cup unflavored powdered gelatin (8 envelopes)

¾ cup sugar, plus more for coating

½ cup corn syrup

Place the raspberries and 2 cups of the water in a small saucepan and heat over medium heat until the raspberries are very soft, about 5 minutes.

Arrange a jelly bag or a sieve lined with two layers of cheesecloth over a deep pot. Wet the bag or cheesecloth so it doesn't absorb any of the juice. Ladle the raspberries and their water into the jelly bag and let the juice drip through into the pot. You aren't supposed to squeeze the jelly bag because it can make the jelly cloudy, but I do a little pressing anyway,

RASPBERRY JELLIES

Raspberry Jam Scones

These scones are versatile. You can use other jams or add raisins, dried cherries or cranberries, or grated cheddar cheese to the dough. To freeze, place the scones on a baking sheet, freeze, and then pack into freezer bags. **MAKES 14 SCONES**

> 2 cups all-purpose flour, plus more for kneading
>
> ⅓ cup sugar
>
> 2 teaspoons baking powder
>
> Scant ½ teaspoon salt
>
> 6 tablespoons cold unsalted butter, cut into tiny pieces
>
> ½ cup heavy cream
>
> 2 large eggs
>
> Grated zest of 1 lemon
>
> 1 teaspoon lemon extract (for homemade, page 361)
>
> ¼ cup Raspberry Jam with Mint (page 278)

to speed the process up, and have never had a problem. Measure the juice. You should have about 1¼ cups.

Place the gelatin in ½ cup of water. Allow it to soften for a few minutes.

Meanwhile, in a medium pot, combine the raspberry juice, sugar, and corn syrup and bring to a boil over medium heat. Add the softened gelatin and whisk to dissolve.

Pour the raspberry mixture into a wet pan—I use a 9-inch loaf pan—and refrigerate for about 2 hours. Flip the jelly onto a smooth surface and remove the pan. Cut the jelly into cubes the size of playing dice. Store in a plastic or glass container lined with paper towels for up to 10 days.

Before serving, roll the jellies in sugar.

Preheat the oven to 400°F. Line a baking sheet with parchment paper or a silicone baking mat.

Sift together the flour, sugar, baking powder, and salt into a large bowl. Add the butter and with your fingers, mash the butter into the flour. I rub the flour and butter between my hands to mix well until there are no clumps of butter remaining.

In a small bowl, whisk together the cream, 1 of the eggs, the lemon zest, and extract. Add the cream mixture to the dough and stir to combine.

Pour the dough onto a floured board and knead a few times. The dough will be soft, but will hold together. Roll out to about a 1-inch thickness and with a round cookie cutter cut into 12 biscuit-size rounds. With your rolling pin, roll out the scones into ovals about ½ inch thick. Place 1 teaspoon of jam at one end of the

RASPBERRY JAM SCONES

oval, and then fold the other end over. Reroll the leftover dough and make two more scones.

Place the scones on the baking sheet. Whisk together the remaining egg and 2 tablespoons water. Brush the egg wash over the scones.

Bake for 20 minutes, or until the scones are golden brown and the jam is bubbling and beginning to dribble out.

Note: I prefer to make small scones, as large ones are just too bready for me.

Sachertorte with Raspberry Jam

I collect region-specific cookbooks, and this recipe is derived from one of my favorites, The Art of Viennese Pastry *(1969). I always thought sachertorte was too complicated to make at home*

until I learned how from the author Marcia Colman Morton. SERVES 6

> 8 tablespoons (1 stick) unsalted butter, plus 1 tablespoon for buttering the pan, at room temperature
>
> 6 ounces semisweet chocolate morsels
>
> ¾ cup granulated sugar
>
> 6 eggs, separated
>
> 1 teaspoon vanilla extract (for homemade, page 361)
>
> ¾ cup sifted all-purpose flour
>
> ½ cup blanched almonds, ground
>
> Pinch of salt
>
> 1 half-pint Raspberry Jam with Mint (page 278)
>
> Confectioners' sugar or whipped cream for garnish (see Note)

Preheat the oven to 350°F. Butter an 8-inch springform pan.

Bring a medium saucepan of water to a boil over high heat. Turn off the heat. Place a large metal or glass bowl over the water. Pour the chocolate morsels into the bowl and allow to melt, stirring occasionally until smooth. Remove the bowl from the water and allow the chocolate to come to room temperature.

With an electric mixer or by hand, cream the butter and ½ cup of the granulated sugar in a large bowl. Add the egg yolks one at a time, beating after adding each one. Add the chocolate and vanilla and stir to combine.

With an electric mixer, in a large bowl beat the egg whites until thickened, then add the remaining ¼ cup granulated sugar in a slow stream, beating all the while, until the egg whites are stiff.

Combine the flour, almonds, and salt in a small bowl.

Fold the egg whites and the flour mixture alternately into the chocolate. Pour the batter into the baking pan and bake for 60 minutes, until a cake tester inserted into the cake comes out clean. Remove the cake and allow it to rest in the pan overnight.

Slice the cake in half at the waist. Spread the jam on the lower half of the cake, and replace the upper half on top. Garnish with confectioners' sugar or whipped cream.

Note: Sachertorte traditionally calls for a chocolate glaze icing, but I find it too intense.

Walnut Raspberry Mint Jam Cookies

Thumbprint cookies are a great way to finish off a jar of jam. Raspberry goes well with walnut, but try mixing fig and walnut, apricot and almond, cherry and hazelnut. **MAKES 24 COOKIES**

- ⅓ cup sugar
- ⅓ cup walnuts
- 1¼ cups all-purpose flour
- 8 tablespoons (1 stick) unsalted butter, at room temperature
- 1 teaspoon vanilla extract (for homemade, page 361
- Pinch of salt
- ¼ cup Raspberry Jam with Mint (page 278)

In a food processor, combine the sugar and walnuts and finely grind. (It is okay to do a rougher grind: It creates a more textured cookie.) Add the flour, butter, vanilla, and salt and pulse to form a dough. (You can also make the dough by hand. Grind the sugar and walnuts with a mortar and pestle, then combine it with the flour, butter, salt, and vanilla in a bowl.)

Roll the dough into a log, wrap in plastic wrap or wax paper, and refrigerate for at least 30 minutes and up to a couple of hours.

Preheat the oven to 300°F.

Cut the cookie log crosswise into disks about ½ inch thick. Place the disks on an ungreased baking sheet. Stick your thumb in the center of each cookie to make an indentation. Spoon about ½ teaspoon raspberry jam into the indentation.

Bake for 10 minutes, until the cookies are golden and the jam is bubbling. Let cool on the pan long enough for the jam to set.

Raspberry Juice

I can't bear to throw out the seedy raspberry mash left over from straining raspberries when I make jam, so I run the mash through the jelly bag a second time. The result is a lovely medium-weight juice, great to drink straight, or to use as a soda syrup (see Raspberry Syrup, page 284). You do not have to make syrup to make a raspberry soda, however. You can make raspberry soda by combining 1 part raspberry juice to 2 parts soda water, and adding simple syrup (sugar dissolved in water) to taste. Likewise, you can combine 1 part raspberry juice to 2 parts lemonade or iced tea, and add simple syrup to taste. The juice holds in the refrigerator for a few days or you can process it in a water bath. The timing for this recipe comes from the Ball Complete Book of Home Preserving. **MAKES 2 CUPS**

- ½ cup raspberry mash (left over from making Raspberry Jam with Mint, page 278)
- 2 cups water

In a medium pot, combine the raspberry mash and water and bring to a boil over medium heat. Reduce the heat to medium-low and cook for about 5 minutes. Remove the mash from the heat and let cool.

Arrange a jelly bag or a sieve lined with two layers of cheesecloth over a deep pot. Wet the bag or cheesecloth so it doesn't absorb any of the juice. Ladle the raspberry mash and water into the jelly bag and let the juice drip through into the pot. You aren't supposed to squeeze the jelly bag because it can make the juice cloudy, but I do a little pressing anyway, to speed the process up, and have never had a problem. Measure the juice. You should have about 2 cups.

You can refrigerate the juice (it holds well for days) or you can water bath can it for longer storage.

Have ready 1 clean pint jar and band, and a new lid that has been simmered in hot water to soften the rubberized flange. Pour the juice into the jar leaving ¼ inch of headroom. Wipe the rim, place on the lid, and screw on the band fingertip tight.

Process the jars in a water bath (see page 375) for 15 minutes. Be sure to make altitude adjustments when preserving (see page 389).

Raspberry Syrup

Raspberry juice is the base for this raspberry syrup, a great flavor enhancer for lemonade (page 169), soda (just add soda water), and iced tea. **MAKES 1 HALF-PINT**

    2 cups Raspberry Juice (page 283)

    ½ cup sugar

RASPBERRY SODA

Place the raspberry juice in a medium pot and boil over high heat until the juice is reduced by one-third, about 10 minutes. Add the sugar and continue boiling over low heat until reduced to 1 cup, about 10 minutes longer. Once you add sugar, the juice wants to foam up, so keep the heat low and your eye on it.

Refrigerate for a few weeks or water bath can for longer storage.

Have ready 1 clean half-pint jar and band, and a new lid that has been simmered in hot water to soften the rubberized flange. Pour the syrup into the jar leaving ½ inch of headroom. Wipe the rim, place on the lid, and screw on the band fingertip tight.

Process the jar in a water bath (see page 375) for 10 minutes. Be sure to make altitude adjustments when preserving (see page 389).

RHUBARB

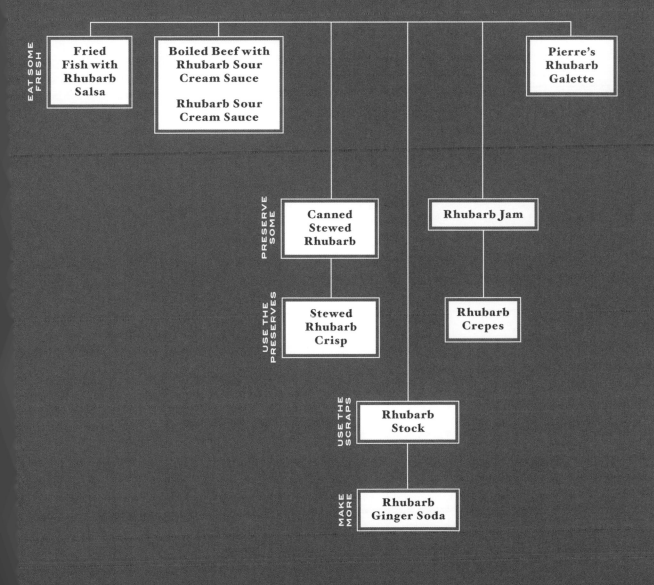

EAT SOME FRESH

Fried Fish with Rhubarb Salsa

Boiled Beef with Rhubarb Sour Cream Sauce

Rhubarb Sour Cream Sauce

Pierre's Rhubarb Galette

PRESERVE SOME

Canned Stewed Rhubarb

Rhubarb Jam

USE THE PRESERVES

Stewed Rhubarb Crisp

Rhubarb Crepes

USE THE SCRAPS

Rhubarb Stock

MAKE MORE

Rhubarb Ginger Soda

Fried Fish
with Rhubarb Salsa

Rhubarb salsa perks up fried fish. I prefer sole or flounder fillet, but tilapia and sand dabs are good too. You can also fry the fish chunk-style, as is typical with grouper or cod. You don't need to peel rhubarb unless it is old and becomes tough. **But don't discard old peels: They can be boiled to make Rhubarb Stock (page 292).** SERVES 4

SALSA

1 cup minced green or red rhubarb

3 tablespoons olive oil

2 tablespoons minced red bell peppers or chopped marinated peppers, drained (for homemade, page 244)

1 tablespoon minced scallions

1 tablespoon minced shallot

1 small jalapeño pepper, seeded and minced

1 tablespoon minced cilantro

Juice of ½ lemon

Salt and freshly ground black pepper

FISH

¾ cup all-purpose flour

3 eggs

2 cups fine breadcrumbs (for homemade, page 362) or panko

Neutral oil, such as safflower, for frying

4 sole or flounder fillets (¼ to ⅓ pound each)

Salt

A Rhubarb Digression

I learned about rhubarb from George Lang, who owned Café des Artistes in New York City, and who also owned a famous restaurant in Budapest called Gundel. In 1998 I went there to report on Gundel's chicken paprika for *Saveur* magazine. I was a little embarrassed to have traveled so far to write about one dish, and so I asked the maître d' to keep it simple: I only needed to taste the chicken and do an interview with the chef. But when I arrived for dinner I was led to the wine cellar, where a table for one was set with a flight of about a dozen wineglasses. A translator, waiter, sommelier, and the chef, a man with a humongous moustache wearing a toque and a number of medals pinned to his coat, stood around the table. With great pride and many dramatic flourishes of the "Voilà!" variety, they served me full portions of almost everything on the menu—and remember, Hungarian food, at least in the 1990s, was seriously robust—paired with marvelous regional wines. I manfully ate dish after dish, until I came to the main event, a half chicken glistening with gorgeous oily paprika sauce. I was so full I could do no more than take a nibble, lick a bit of the sauce off a spoon, and nod in delight. The next morning, sick with a food hangover, I was mortified to think I had failed by spoiling my appetite prior to eating the dish—the only dish—I was there to cover. But it turned out okay, because while I was novice enough to eat everything put in front of me, I was wise enough to recognize that the story was not really the chicken, but rather the exuberance and excitement of a country whose doors, and food, had only recently been reopened to the world.

For the salsa: Have ready a bowl of ice water. Bring a small pot of water to a boil over medium-high heat. Add the rhubarb and blanch for 30 seconds. Drain and drop the rhubarb into the bowl of ice water. Drain well.

In a bowl, combine the rhubarb, olive oil, bell peppers, scallions, shallot, jalapeño, cilantro, lemon juice, and salt and black pepper to taste.

For the fish: Have ready 3 shallow bowls. Place the flour in one, beat the eggs in another, and place the breadcrumbs in a third. Pour ¼ inch of oil into a medium nonstick skillet and heat over medium-low heat until it pops when you flick a bit of flour into it.

Dredge the fillets in the flour, dunk in the egg, then coat with the breadcrumbs. Fry until golden brown, a few minutes, then flip over and fry the other side, a minute or two more. Remove and drain on paper towels. Salt to taste.

Serve the fillets topped with the salsa.

Boiled Beef with Rhubarb Sour Cream Sauce

This is a tangy, delicious dish, adapted from George Lang's Cuisine of Hungary. **SERVES 4**

   2 tablespoons unsalted butter
   Salt
   1¾ pounds top round
   ¼ cup white wine
   ½ lemon
   A few sprigs of fresh thyme
   A few sprigs of flat-leaf parsley
   1 bay leaf
   10 black peppercorns
   1 small onion, peeled
   2 carrots, cut in half
   2 cups chicken stock (for homemade, page 89)
   Rhubarb Sour Cream Sauce (recipe follows)
   Chopped flat-leaf parsley, for garnish

In a Dutch oven, heat the butter over medium-high heat. Salt the beef (you might have to cut it into a few big pieces) and add it to the butter. Brown on all sides, about 5 minutes. Add the wine, lemon, thyme, parsley sprigs, bay leaf, and peppercorns. Cover and boil the wine for a few minutes. Remove the cover and add the onion, carrots, and chicken stock. Cover, reduce the heat to medium-low, and cook until the beef is very tender, about 1 hour 15 minutes. Remove the beef and strain the sauce.

Serve the beef in slices or hunks on top of a puddle of the sauce. Serve with a dollop of rhubarb sour cream sauce. Garnish with parsley.

BOILED BEEF WITH RHUBARB SOUR CREAM SAUCE

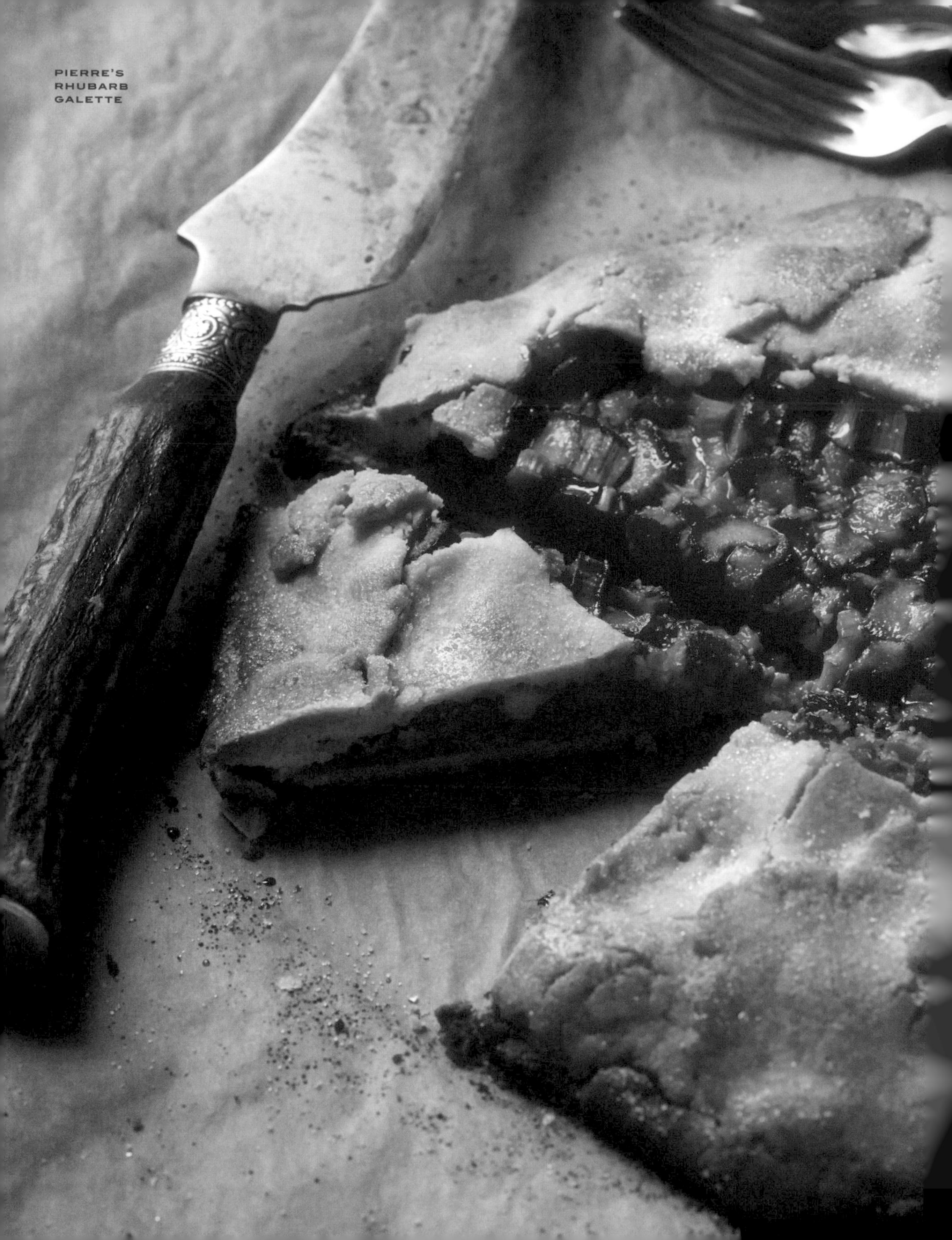

PIERRE'S RHUBARB GALETTE

RHUBARB SOUR CREAM SAUCE

This versatile sauce is great with stewed and roasted meats. **Save the rhubarb blanching water to make Rhubarb Stock (page 292).** MAKES ABOUT 1 CUP

⅓ cup finely chopped green or red rhubarb

¼ cup sour cream

½ teaspoon sugar

½ teaspoon salt

In a small pot of boiling water, blanch the rhubarb for a minute or two. Drain well. Combine the rhubarb with the sour cream, sugar, and salt.

Pierre's Rhubarb Galette

The spring after Pierre Franey died (he wrote the popular 60-Minute Gourmet column with Craig Claiborne for the New York Times*), a bunch of his friends got together and made a lunch in his honor. Jacques Pépin made this galette. To me, it looks like a great broken heart.* SERVES 6 TO 8

PASTRY

1½ cups all-purpose flour

8 tablespoons cold unsalted butter, cut up

1 tablespoon sugar

Pinch of salt

⅓ cup cold water

FILLING

⅔ cup blanched almonds

½ cup plus 2 tablespoons granulated sugar

1 tablespoon all-purpose flour

1 pound red rhubarb, chopped

2 tablespoons unsalted butter, cut into small bits

TOPPING

¼ cup Currant Jelly (page 120; optional)

1 tablespoon granulated sugar

For the pastry: In a food processor, combine the flour, sugar, butter, and salt and process until blended, a minute or so. Add the water and process until little balls form. (To make the pastry by hand, see page 395.) Press the dough together into a disk. Wrap the dough in plastic wrap or wax paper and refrigerate until chilled, about 30 minutes.

Meanwhile, for the filling: Grind the almonds with 2 tablespoons of granulated sugar and the flour. You can do this in a food processor or with a mortar and pestle.

Preheat the oven to 375°F.

On a silicone baking mat or piece of parchment paper, roll out the pastry into a large round about 12 inches in diameter. It's okay if it isn't perfectly round but don't make it too thin: This pastry needs to be a bit on the robust side. Transfer the pastry on its baking mat to a baking sheet. Spread the almond mixture in the center of the pastry, leaving a 3-inch border all around.

Place the rhubarb on top of the almond mixture and sprinkle the remaining ½ cup granulated sugar on top. Dot the top of the fruit with the butter. Gently fold the border of dough over the fruit, leaving the center open.

Bake for 1 hour, or until the pastry is golden brown and the fruit is bubbling.

Let the galette cool slightly.

For the topping: In a small saucepan, heat the jelly over medium-low heat. Brush the hot jelly over the top of the whole galette. Sprinkle the granulated sugar over the crust and let come to room temperature before serving.

Canned Stewed Rhubarb

This is the simplest preserve, just rhubarb cooked with sugar. It is loose and perfect for dessert, served plain or with whipped cream and garnished with blanched, toasted almonds. I've used the stewed rhubarb to make ice cream sundaes (with whipped cream and toasted almonds) and mixed it with gelatin. See the recipe for Tomato Aspic (page 333) and replace the marinara sauce with 2 cups of stewed rhubarb. It makes a groovy Mad Men-*type dessert. Red rhubarb maintains its color well, though processing does fade the color some. Green rhubarb, which tastes the same as red rhubarb, cooks to a pinkish brown color. To help maintain the color, you can add chopped strawberries.* **Save the steaming liquid for Rhubarb Stock (page 292) or drink it warm mixed with honey.** MAKES 2 HALF-PINTS

CANNED STEWED RHUBARB

2½ cups chopped red rhubarb (about ¾ pound)
¼ cup chopped strawberries (optional)
½ cup sugar (or more to taste)

In a steamer, steam the rhubarb over 2 cups of boiling water until soft, 3 to 4 minutes.

In a large pot, combine the rhubarb, strawberries (if using), and sugar. Bring to a boil over medium heat and then take off the heat.

Have ready 2 clean half-pint jars and bands, and new lids that have been simmered in hot water to soften the rubberized flange. Pour the stewed fruit into the jars leaving ½ inch of headroom. Wipe the rims, place on the lids, and screw on the bands fingertip tight.

Process the jars in a water bath (see page 375) for 15 minutes. (If you make a bigger batch of stewed rhubarb, you can put it up in pints or quarts; the processing time will be the same.) Be sure to make altitude adjustments when preserving (see page 389). There may be some discoloring of the fruit at the top of the jar over time. It's okay.

Rhubarb Jam

This is a lovely, soft jam to which you can add up to ¼ cup chopped strawberries. If you want to double the recipe cook the rhubarb in batches of no more than 4 cups so it thickens quickly without scorching the fruit. MAKES 2 HALF-PINTS

4 cups chopped rhubarb (about 1 pound)
1½ cups sugar
4 tablespoons chopped strawberries (optional)
2 tablespoons grated lemon zest
2 tablespoons fresh lemon juice

Place the rhubarb in a wide pot and add the sugar, strawberries (if using), lemon zest, and lemon juice. Bring to a boil over medium heat. Stir often, and watch carefully to be sure the fruit doesn't scorch. Cook until the juice evaporates and the jam thickens, about 30 minutes. When you push the jam around in the pot with your spoon, you should see the bottom of the pan. Chill a spoonful of jam for a few minutes. If it does not spread when you wiggle the spoon, the jam is ready.

Have ready 2 sterilized half-pint jars and bands with new lids that have been simmered in hot water to soften the rubberized flange. Pour the jam into the jars leaving ¼ inch of headroom. Wipe the rims, place on the lids, and screw on the bands fingertip tight.

Process the jars in a water bath (see page 375) for 5 minutes for half-pints or 1 pint. Be sure to make altitude adjustments when preserving (see page 389). There may be some discoloring of the fruit at the top of the jar over time. It's okay.

VARIATION

Rhubarb-Ginger Jam: Add 2 tablespoons minced fresh ginger along with the sugar.

Stewed Rhubarb Crisp

Rhubarb is a classic crisp and pie filling, as its nickname, the pieplant, attests. You will need to double the Canned Stewed Rhubarb recipe in order to make this crisp for 4. SERVES 4

   ¼ cup blanched almonds
   4 cups Canned Stewed Rhubarb (opposite)
   ½ cup all-purpose flour
   ¼ cup packed light brown sugar

   3 tablespoons unsalted butter, at room
      temperature
   Pinch of salt
   ¼ cup yogurt (for homemade, page 370; optional)

Preheat the oven to 400°F.

Heat a small skillet over high heat and add the almonds. Cook, shaking frequently, until they are toasted. You will smell them when they are done. Remove the almonds and coarsely grind in a food processor or with a mortar and pestle.

Fill four 1-cup ramekins with the stewed rhubarb. It will reduce a bit in volume when you bake it, so fill the ramekins to the top. Or use a 4-cup baking dish.

In a small bowl, combine the flour, brown sugar, almonds, butter, and salt. With your fingers, press the butter through the dry ingredients until the butter is well distributed. The crumble should be, well, crumbly, but also feel just slightly moist.

Divide the crumble evenly among each ramekin, and place the ramekins on a baking sheet. Bake for 10 to 15 minutes, or until the crumble is crisp. The ramekins are hot, and there may be some bubbling of rhubarb juice over the edges, so I serve each on a little plate. Serve with a dollop of yogurt, if you'd like. The crisp is great hot, but very good at room temperature, too.

Rhubarb Crepes

These sweet crepes, using batter adapted from an old copy of The Joy of Cooking, *are great for either breakfast or dessert. A sprinkle of toasted almonds is lovely on top. I usually serve 2 crepes per person.*
SERVES 4

¾ cup all-purpose flour

¼ cup granulated sugar

1 teaspoon baking powder

¼ teaspoon salt

2 large eggs, beaten

⅔ cup whole milk

⅓ cup water

½ pint Rhubarb Jam (page 290)

2 to 3 tablespoons cold unsalted butter

Confectioners' sugar, for garnish

In a large bowl, whisk together the flour, granulated sugar, baking powder, and salt. In a separate bowl, whisk together the eggs, milk, and water. Add the wet ingredients to the dry and whisk briefly. Ignore the lumps. Refrigerate for about 30 minutes.

Heat the jam in a small saucepan. Add a little water if it seems sticky. You want the jam to be thick but soft.

To cook the crepes, see "Preparing Crepes," page 395. To assemble the crepes, spread about 1 tablespoon of jam on each crepe. Roll the crepe up like a blintz. Continue with the remaining crepes. Garnish with confectioners' sugar.

RHUBARB STOCK

During the month or so that I am cooking with rhubarb, I keep an ongoing quart jar of water in the fridge that I reuse to blanch or boil the rhubarb. Over time the water gets heavier and more flavorful, until by the end of the season I have a stock that I can use to make Rhubarb Ginger Soda (right).

To make rhubarb stock, cover chopped rhubarb bits and ends (no leaves!!!) or the peelings with 2 inches of water and boil about 15 minutes over medium heat. Strain and retain the water in a jar in the fridge. If the water is boiled (including for a rhubarb cooking project) every third day, no spoilers will have a chance to grow.

Rhubarb Ginger Soda

I use swing-cap bottles for this soda and store them in my fridge. It never lasts long. You can also make this soda by adding seltzer water and simple syrup to the rhubarb stock, but you must drink it right away. The seltzer water will not keep its fizz for long. MAKES THREE 17-OUNCE BOTTLES

3 tablespoons sugar

6 tablespoons water

4 cups Rhubarb Stock (left)

2 cups Ginger Bug (page 152)

In a small saucepan, heat the sugar and water over medium heat until the sugar dissolves, a minute or so. Allow the syrup to cool.

Combine the rhubarb stock and ginger bug. Add the simple syrup a tablespoon at a time until you reach your desired sweetness. Funnel into 3 bottles, cap the bottles, and refrigerate.

RHUBARB GINGER SODA

SALTWATER FISH
SALMON

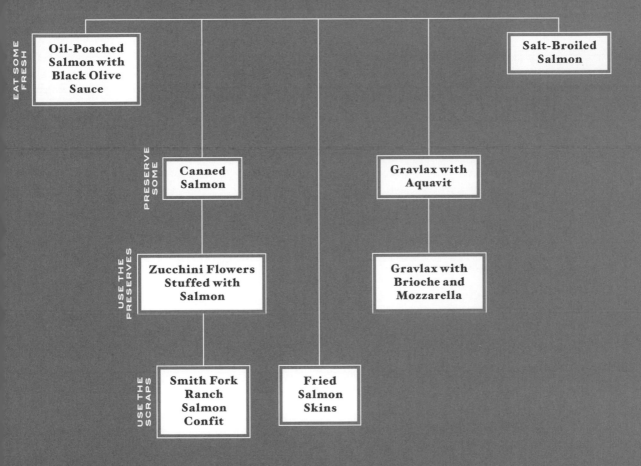

EAT SOME FRESH

Oil-Poached Salmon with Black Olive Sauce

Salt-Broiled Salmon

PRESERVE SOME

Canned Salmon

Gravlax with Aquavit

USE THE PRESERVES

Zucchini Flowers Stuffed with Salmon

Gravlax with Brioche and Mozzarella

USE THE SCRAPS

Smith Fork Ranch Salmon Confit

Fried Salmon Skins

Oil-Poached Salmon with Black Olive Sauce

The trick to oil-poached salmon is keeping the oil temperature low. Use a deep-frying thermometer to regulate the temperature of the poaching oil and your salmon will be perfectly tender. The black olive sauce is a little shocking to look at (it's black), but totally delicious. **Save the skins for frying (see page 299).**

SERVES 4

> SAUCE
>
> **1 cup dried black olives, pitted**
>
> **4 garlic cloves, peeled**
>
> **1 cup chicken stock (for homemade, page 89)**
>
> **Salt**
>
> POACHED SALMON
>
> **1½ pounds skinless salmon fillet, cut into 4 pieces**
>
> **2 cups light olive oil or other vegetable oil (it doesn't have to be good stuff)**
>
> **Freshly ground black pepper**
>
> **2 tablespoons minced flat-leaf parsley**

For the sauce: Place the olives, garlic, and chicken stock in a food processor or blender and puree. Add salt to taste. Pass the sauce through a sieve to ensure it is very smooth. This makes about 1 cup of sauce.

For the poached salmon: Check the salmon for any pin bones by running your fingers along the flesh. Remove any bones you encounter with tweezers. In a medium pot, slowly bring the oil to 150°F over medium-low heat. Add the salmon and gently poach at this temperature for 20 minutes. Drain the salmon and pat dry.

Lay a puddle of olive sauce on the plate and place a piece of salmon on top. Garnish with a few grinds of black pepper and the parsley.

Salt-Broiled Salmon

I learned this dish from a great cookbook called The Essentials of Japanese Cooking *by Tokiko Suzuki, a well-known Japanese food authority. It is a method I think all cooks should have in their pocket.*

SERVES 4

> **1½ pounds salmon fillet, skin on (1 to 1½ inches thick), cut into 8 pieces**
>
> **2 teaspoons salt**

Preheat the broiler. Set the rack 6 inches below the broiler.

Check the salmon for any pin bones by running your fingers along the flesh. Remove any bones you encounter with tweezers. Sprinkle the salt all over the salmon and let it rest for 5 minutes while the broiler heats. You will notice the fish will sweat a bit. This is good.

Place the fish skin side down on a rack set over a rimmed baking sheet. Broil 5 minutes, then cover the fish with foil and broil another 5 to 8 minutes longer.

Serve promptly.

Canned Salmon

Home-canned salmon is tender and moist, and not at all fishy. You can preserve salmon scaled, with the skin on, but I find it easy to remove the skin. Just slip a long sharp knife between the skin and flesh and press down on the knife with one hand while wiggling the skin away with the other. Remove pin bones with tweezers. You can double, triple, or quadruple this recipe: It's basically ½ pound salmon per half-pint. With the exception of tuna (page 301) all fish, including salmon, are canned without liquid. The salmon extrudes quite a bit of water during processing, as well as rich fat. If you topped off your jars with oil or water, your seals would fail. You can also lightly smoke salmon before canning it: The method is the same as putting up the raw fish, but USDA data requires canned smoked salmon to be processed for 10 minutes longer in a 16- to 22-quart canner.

If you have any leftover, oddball bits of salmon, save them to make Smith Fork Ranch Salmon Confit (page 298). Save the skins for Fried Salmon Skins (page 299). **MAKES 4 HALF-PINTS**

> 2 pounds salmon fillet, skinned, pin bones removed
>
> 2 teaspoons pickling salt

Have ready 4 clean half-pint jars and bands, and new lids that have been simmered in hot water to soften the rubberized flange.

Cut the salmon into 2-inch chunks and press them into the jars leaving 1 inch of headroom. Do not add any liquid. Place ½ teaspoon salt in

each jar. Wipe the rims, place on the lids, and screw on the bands fingertip tight.

Process the jars in a pressure canner at 10/11 psi for 1 hour 40 minutes for 4 half-pints or 2 pints. Note most pressure canner manufacturers recommend fish be processed in a 21-quart or larger canner. (See "How to Pressure Can," page 379.) Be sure to make altitude adjustments when preserving (see page 389).

Canned salmon can be eaten right away. If little crystals form in the inside of your jars, don't worry: this is just magnesium ammonium phosphate, a naturally occurring mineral in fish's bodies that crystallizes under certain conditions. They are not dangerous. You may also see creamy white matter in the jars. This is fat, and fat is good!

Gravlax with Aquavit

Gravlax is a terrific hors d'oeuvre served with rye crisps, emulsified mustard, and lemon wedges. I douse my gravlax with aquavit, the Scandinavian liquor, and the result is a super creamy fish. Gravlax is cured in salt (salt wreaks havoc on spoilers) and is refrigerated (which retards spoilers). It lasts in the refrigerator for 10 days. (See "How to Cure," page 383.) **MAKES TWO 1-POUND FILLETS**

> 2½ pounds salmon, cut into two fillets with the skin on, preferably from the same fish, so that the fillets fit together neatly (choose fillets from the center of the fish; they're meatier)
>
> ⅔ cup sugar
>
> ⅓ cup kosher salt
>
> 1 bunch fresh dill
>
> ¼ cup aquavit

CANNED SALMON

If you use wild salmon, place it in the freezer for 7 days at -10°F or 15 hours at -31°F before preparing gravlax, or buy frozen wild salmon. Freezing kills any parasites that may be present in the fish. Farm-raised salmon is unlikely to carry parasites. (I prefer organic Scottish farm-raised. It's fatty and makes a luscious gravlax.)

Be sure the salmon you buy stays chilled up until the moment you cure it: about 38°F is ideal. Rinse the fillets and then gently run your fingers along the flesh, feeling for any bones. Remove with needle-nosed pliers or tweezers. Be careful to avoid bruising the salmon.

Combine the sugar and salt in a bowl.

Lay the salmon fillets on your counter, skin side down. Sprinkle half of the sugar/salt mixture onto each fillet. Gently rub as much of the mixture into the flesh of the two fillets as you can, without bruising the meat (you won't be able to rub it all in—it's okay). Lay one salted fillet down on a large piece of plastic wrap, skin side down. Completely cover it with half of the fresh dill. (You may leave the stems on.) Sprinkle the aquavit over the dill, and then add the remaining fresh dill. Place the other salted fillet directly on top, flesh side down, like a sandwich. Some of the sugar/salt mixture will fall off. It's okay. Pile any extra sugar/salt mixture along the ends of the fillets. Wrap the plastic wrap securely around the fish, and then wrap more plastic so that it is snug. Place the fish in a large zipseal plastic food storage bag, press out the air, and fold the bag around the fish tightly. The salt pulls the water out of the tissue of the fish and dissolves in these juices to create a brine. It is important that the juices produced by salting the fish not escape, as gravlax must baste in its brine to cure.

Set the fish in a pan. Place a smaller pan on top of the fish and weight with a few bricks or canned goods. (You can also load a heavy bag of rice or beans on top.) Refrigerate. It will need to cure for at least 48 and up to 60 hours. (You will get the most tender gravlax by curing for 48 to 52 hours.) Turn the fish over every 12 hours.

After curing, remove the plastic wrap from around the fish. The fillets will have reduced in thickness, sometimes by almost half. Scrape off the dill and wipe the fish clean. If there is a white film on the fish, don't worry: It is impurities that have been drawn from the flesh by the salt. Just wipe it off with a clean kitchen towel. The fish can be eaten at this point. However, you can add additional flavorings, which are very good (see Note).

Wrap the fish in wax paper. It will hold in the refrigerator for 10 days.

To slice gravlax, lay the fillet on a cutting board, skin side down. With a long flexible knife, slice paper-thin pieces on an angle to the cutting board. Start slicing the fish at the top of the fillet, about one-third down the length of the fish, sliding the blade toward the skin as you go. If you cut pieces straight up and down, you will find yourself sawing through the tough skin. You can preslice the fish and keep it in the refrigerator in wax paper, but the slices will dry out much faster than if you slice to order.

Note: After the gravlax has cured, you can add more flavorings, though you don't have to. Coat the fish with finely chopped dill. Or rub each fillet with 1 tablespoon aquavit, then pat on a freshly ground mix of ½ teaspoon white pepper, 1 teaspoon black pepper, 2 teaspoons dill seed, 2 teaspoons fennel seed, and 2 teaspoons caraway seed.

Zucchini Flowers Stuffed with Salmon

This dish works best with young, stiff flowers (for information about zucchini flowers, see page 352). You can also stuff these flowers with Smoked Trout Pâté (page 344) or the tuna and ricotta mixture from the stuffed tomatoes (page 305). **SERVES 8 AS AN APPETIZER**

- **16 zucchini flowers**
- **1 cup all-purpose flour**
- **1 cup lager beer**
- **1 teaspoon baking powder**
- **Salt**
- **½ pint canned salmon (for homemade, page 294), drained**
- **⅓ cup sour cream**
- **Dash of Worcestershire sauce (for homemade, page 369)**
- **Dash of hot sauce (for homemade, page 365)**
- **Neutral oil, such as safflower, for frying**
- **Lemon wedges or mayonnaise (for homemade, page 365), for serving**

Check the insides of the zucchini flowers for insects and shake them out. Brush the dirt off the flowers, but do not wash them or your flowers won't be crisp when you fry them.

In a bowl, combine the flour, beer, baking powder, and a pinch of salt and refrigerate for about 1 hour.

In a small bowl, combine the salmon, sour cream, Worcestershire sauce, and hot sauce and mash them together until the mixture becomes smooth (or you can use your food processor, but avoid over processing or the filling will be too wet). Either use a plastic pastry bag or a plastic bag with a small hole cut out at one corner. Spoon a couple of tablespoons of the salmon into the wide end of the bag and press the salmon down toward the tip by twisting the top. With one hand, gently open the petals of a zucchini flower. With the other hand, pipe the salmon in. You will need at least 1 tablespoon of the salmon mixture per flower. Repeat this process with the remaining flowers.

Pour ¾ inch of oil into a large nonstick or well-seasoned cast-iron skillet. Heat the oil over high heat. The oil must be very hot. You can test it by throwing a dash of flour into the oil. If the flour pops, the oil is ready for frying.

Dunk the flowers in the batter and place them gently in the hot oil. Don't put too many flowers in at once or it will bring down the temperature of the oil, and they mustn't touch sides or they will stick together. Do not flip the flowers over until you can see the lower edges have turned golden brown, about 2 minutes. (If you are using an iron skillet and the flowers stick, let them cook 30 seconds more.) Turn the flowers over with tongs and fry for an additional minute, then remove them and drain on paper towels or brown paper bags. Sprinkle the fried flowers with salt.

Do not add more battered flowers to the oil until you are sure the oil has come up in temperature again.

Serve with lemon wedges or mayonnaise.

Gravlax with Brioche and Mozzarella

Gravlax turns a lovely pink in this swanky dish. It is a bit messy to serve, so for a more refined presentation, you can make it in individual ramekins. Note that the simple brioche recipe calls for letting the dough rest overnight in the refrigerator. **SERVES 6**

BRIOCHE

¼ cup whole milk, at room temperature

1 tablespoon sugar

1⅛ teaspoons active dry yeast (a heaping teaspoon will do)

2 cups all-purpose flour, sifted

8 tablespoons (1 stick) unsalted butter, at room temperature

4 large eggs

½ teaspoon salt

FILLING

4 tablespoons olive oil

1 pound mozzarella, sliced ¼ inch thick

½ pound sliced gravlax (for homemade, page 295)

Egg wash: 1 egg white whisked with 1 tablespoon water

For the brioche: In a small bowl, combine the milk and ½ tablespoon of the sugar. Add the yeast and dissolve. Add ½ cup of the flour and mix well. Cover and let rise in a warm place until fluffy, about 30 minutes.

In a stand mixer, with the dough hook attachment, combine the remaining 1½ cups flour with the remaining ½ tablespoon sugar. Beat in the butter, 2 of the eggs, and the salt. Add the flour and yeast mixture and beat again. Add the remaining 2 eggs, one at a time, beating thoroughly. (You can also do this with a hand mixer or by hand.) Cover and let rise until fluffy, 3 to 4 hours. Beat the dough again and refrigerate overnight.

Preheat the oven to 400°F.

For the filling: Place 2 tablespoons of the olive oil in a 9-inch deep dish pie plate. Add a layer of sliced mozzarella, then a layer of gravlax and so on, until the pie plate is filled.

Remove the dough from the refrigerator, turn it out of the bowl and punch it into a rough disk 10 inches in diameter. Place the dough on top of the filled pie plate. Allow some dough to fall over the lip. With a knife, cut an X into the top of the dough for steam to escape. Using a pastry brush, brush the egg wash over the dough.

Bake for 20 to 25 minutes, or until the brioche is browned. Using a sharp knife, cut off any dough that has fallen over the edge of the plate. Let rest about 10 minutes before serving.

Smith Fork Ranch Salmon Confit

This is an excellent hors d'oeuvre with a sparkling wine. Serve at room temperature with toast tips or rye crisps. Seth Bateman, the gifted chef at Smith Fork Ranch in Crawford, Colorado, also serves the confit as a first course, with shaved cucumber tossed in a bit of vinaigrette and garnished with capers. **MAKES 1 CUP**

½ pound salmon fillets, skin and pin bones removed, finely chopped (see Note)

1 tablespoon sugar

2 tablespoons salt

8 tablespoons (1 stick) unsalted butter

1 tablespoon minced fresh dill

In a zipseal plastic food storage bag, combine the salmon, sugar, and salt and refrigerate for 1 hour 30 minutes.

Meanwhile, in a small saucepan, melt the butter over low heat. When the butter is liquefied, skim off any solids that have floated to the top and pour off the clear, clarified butter into a small bowl, leaving the white gunk at the bottom of the pot. These are the milk solids from the butter. Discard (sadly, it is not useful stuff as it burns quickly).

Remove the salmon from the bag, place in a sieve, and rinse off the salt and sugar. Add the salmon to the bowl with the butter and toss to combine. Add the dill and pack into a small jar—a half-pint will usually do, but a pretty serving jar is nice, too. The confit can hold in the refrigerator for a week.

Note: I usually make this with the leftover bits of salmon from canning (page 294).

Fried Salmon Skins

Fried salmon skins are like bacon from the sea. I crumble them to garnish other fish dishes, or just eat them hot off the draining paper. (The oil creates a rather intense smell, so if you are having company, you may want to put off the frying until after they've gone home.) Three quarters of a pound of salmon fillet, an ample serving for two, will yield about six 1-inch-wide pieces of skin. **ABOUT ½ CUP SKINS**

    6 strips (1 inch wide) of salmon skin (you will
        get more skin per pound if you select fillets
        from the tail end of the fish)
    2 tablespoons salt
    ½ cup neutral oil, such as safflower, for frying

FRIED SALMON SKIN

Check the skins for scales. If you feel any, then place the skin on a flat surface. While holding the skin down with one hand, scrape the scales in the opposite direction from how they lie with the blunt side of a knife. Trim off any excess flesh that may be stuck to the skin. Place the salmon skin in a small bowl with the salt and let it rest for 10 minutes. Remove the skin, rinse, and dry well.

In a small nonstick skillet, heat the oil over high heat. Add the skins. They will curl up as soon as they hit the oil. Flip them over with your tongs and promptly pat them flat in the oil. If they are very thin, the skins will fry in 3 to 4 minutes. Watch carefully. It takes a second for the skins to go from golden brown and crispy to burnt.

Drain on paper towels or brown paper bags.

SALTWATER FISH
TUNA

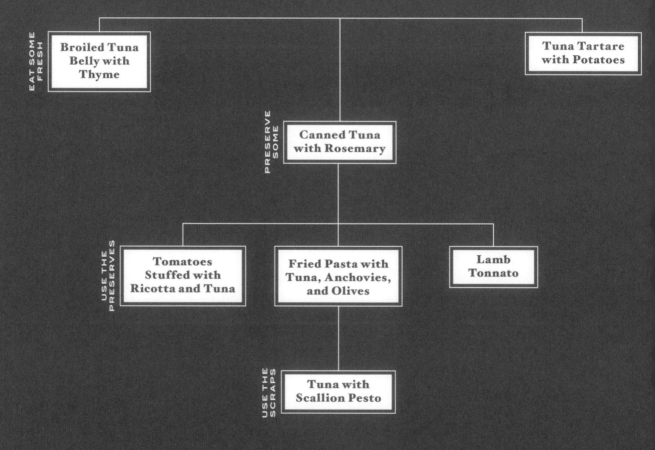

EAT SOME FRESH

Broiled Tuna Belly with Thyme

Tuna Tartare with Potatoes

PRESERVE SOME

Canned Tuna with Rosemary

USE THE PRESERVES

Tomatoes Stuffed with Ricotta and Tuna

Fried Pasta with Tuna, Anchovies, and Olives

Lamb Tonnato

USE THE SCRAPS

Tuna with Scallion Pesto

Broiled Tuna Belly with Thyme

For years tuna belly was inexpensive, but now that people have figured out this fatty cut is really luscious, it's gotten a bit pricey. A quick broil with herbs and a garnish of good extra virgin olive oil is just about perfection. I like to serve this dish with boiled, peeled potatoes rolled in a hot pan with minced parsley and butter. SERVES 4

    2 to 3 tablespoons extra virgin olive oil

    1½ pounds tuna belly, usually sold in one piece about ¾ inch thick

    Salt and freshly ground black pepper

    10 sprigs of fresh thyme

Preheat the broiler.

Rub about 1 tablespoon oil onto a small baking sheet. Add the tuna belly. Season with salt and pepper, lay the thyme on top, and sprinkle with 1 to 2 tablespoons oil.

Place 6 inches under the broiler and broil for 5 to 10 minutes, until the flesh is opaque. Do not turn over.

Tuna Tartare with Potatoes

A couple of times a year we get a big hunk of pristinely fresh tuna from our friend Joey Jacinto, who catches it off the coast of Long Island. We almost always have it raw, in a room-temperature salad like this one. Sometimes I add a few dashes of Asian-Style Hot Oil (page 360) to the tartare. SERVES 4

    2 pounds tuna, chopped

    4 medium potatoes, boiled, peeled, and sliced into rounds

    ⅓ cup minced white onion

    ¼ cup extra virgin olive oil

    2 tablespoons fresh lemon juice (or to taste)

    Salt and freshly ground black pepper

    2 tablespoons minced flat-leaf parsley

Gently combine the tuna, boiled potatoes, onion, olive oil, lemon juice, and salt and pepper to taste in a serving bowl. Garnish with the parsley.

Canned Tuna with Rosemary

Preparing tuna for canning is simple. Check the tuna for any blood vessels—they will look like red strings—and cut them out with a sharp knife. Don't worry if some parts of the meat are dark red; the color comes from blood in the meat or natural variations in the meat. Dark meat may turn purple after canning, but it's okay to eat. I put up tuna in light olive oil, but you can put it up in water, too. **Save the bits and ends of tuna that don't fit into the jars to make Tuna with Scallion Pesto (page 305).** MAKES 12 HALF-PINTS

    7 pounds very fresh tuna, with skin, bones, and any stringy blood vessels removed

    6 teaspoons pickling salt

    12 teaspoons fresh rosemary leaves

    Italian olive oil (not extra virgin)

Have ready 12 clean half-pint jars and bands, and new lids that have been simmered in hot water to soften the rubberized flange.

Cut the tuna into 2- to 3-inch chunks and pack them into the jars. Ideally, the chunks of tuna meat should be as large as you can manage to pack in the jars. Fill the gaps between the large chunks with small bits of tuna. To the top of each jar add ½ teaspoon salt and 1 teaspoon rosemary. Pour in enough olive oil to cover the fish, leaving 1 inch of headroom at the top of the jar. Using a butter knife, press aside the tuna so the oil can fill any air pockets between the chunks of tuna.

Wipe the rims, place on the lids, and screw on the bands fingertip tight. (If you put a dab of white vinegar on the cloth you use to wipe the rims, the oil will clean off more easily.)

Process the jars in a pressure canner at 10/11 psi for 1 hour 40 minutes. (See "How to Pressure Can," page 379.) Be sure to make altitude adjustments when canning (see page 389). Tuna should age 3 to 6 months to mellow the flavor.

If little crystals form in the inside of your jars, don't worry. This is magnesium ammonium phosphate, a naturally occurring mineral in fish's bodies. They are not dangerous. You may also see bits of creamy white matter in the jars. This is fat, and fat is good!

Fried Pasta with Tuna, Anchovies, and Olives

This is an on-demand dish. It works best in a small nonstick skillet with each serving prepared individually, but for quicker service you can use two large nonstick skillets with half the ingredients in each. Cut the finished fried pasta in half to serve. Fedelini pasta will give you the best crust. A thicker strand of pasta, like spaghetti, won't, and angel hair gets tangled. This is a good recipe for using excess cooked pasta. SERVES 4

2 tablespoons olive oil, plus more for frying

¾ cup pitted dried black olives

3 tablespoons chopped anchovy fillets (see Note)

4 tablespoons chopped flat-leaf parsley

2 tablespoons minced garlic

Pinch of hot pepper flakes

Salt

¾ pound fedelini pasta

2 half-pints Canned Tuna with Rosemary (page 301), drained

¼ cup grated pecorino cheese

In a small saucepan, heat 2 tablespoons of oil over medium heat. Add the olives, anchovies, 2 tablespoons of the parsley, garlic, and pepper flakes and cook until the flavors meld and the garlic is soft, about 4 minutes. Pour the olive mixture into a large bowl.

Bring a large pot of salted water to a boil and add the pasta. Cook until al dente, then drain and add to the olive mixture. Add the tuna, the remaining 2 tablespoons parsley, and pecorino, and combine well. The pasta should be a bit dryer than you would normally serve it.

Heat a bit of oil in a 7-inch nonstick skillet and add one-fourth of the pasta. Flatten the pasta with a spatula and cook for about 5 minutes until the pasta becomes brown and crusty on the bottom. Slide the pasta onto a plate. Put another plate on top and flip over, then slide the pasta back into the skillet to brown the pasta on the second side—it will take a few minutes less on the second side. Keep warm while you repeat for the remaining servings.

Note: I prefer whole anchovies cured in salt, available in Italian markets. Soak them for 10 minutes to remove the salt, then rinse and fillet them. You don't have to get all the bones, just the spine.

Lamb Tonnato

The Italian classic vitello tonnato *calls for veal, but I think it is wonderful with lamb. The tuna sauce is also good on pasta, garnished with lots of chopped parsley.* **SERVES 4**

- 2 pounds lamb roast or boned leg
- Salt and freshly ground black pepper
- 2 tablespoons olive oil
- ½ cup chicken stock (for homemade, page 89)

TUNA SAUCE
- ½ pint Canned Tuna with Rosemary (page 301), drained
- 1 tablespoon fresh lemon juice
- 1 small garlic clove, minced
- 1 tablespoon olive oil
- Salt and freshly ground black pepper
- ⅓ cup chicken stock (for homemade, page 89)

- ½ lemon, thinly sliced into rounds
- 1 tablespoon capers

Preheat the oven to 350°F.

Season the roast with salt and pepper. In a large skillet, heat the oil over high heat. Add the roast and brown it all over, about 10 minutes. Remove it and place in a roasting pan with a rack. Add the stock to the skillet and scrape with a wooden spoon to release the browned bits. Pour the stock over the roast. Transfer to the oven and roast for 35 minutes for medium-rare. Remove and let it rest at least 10 minutes, then chill in the refrigerator.

LAMB TONNATO

TUNA WITH
SCALLION
PESTO

Meanwhile, for the tuna sauce: In a food processor, combine the tuna, lemon juice, garlic, oil, and salt and pepper to taste and puree, slowly pouring in the stock. Pour the sauce into a bowl and chill in the refrigerator.

When you are ready to serve, slice the lamb as thinly as you can. Serve the lamb with the tuna sauce, and garnish with the lemon slices and capers.

Tomatoes Stuffed with Ricotta and Tuna

This is a terrific first course in the summer. I like to serve these tomatoes with a piece of bruschetta rubbed with a raw or roasted garlic clove. You can also stuff zucchini flowers with this mixture (page 297). **Save the scooped-out tomato flesh to add to your next recipe calling for tomato.** SERVES 4

  2 large tomatoes (about ½ pound), at room temperature

  ½ cup ricotta cheese (for homemade, page 367)

  1 half-pint Canned Tuna with Rosemary (page 301), drained

  Salt and freshly ground black pepper

  2 tablespoons minced flat-leaf parsley

  1 lemon, cut into wedges

Cut the tomatoes in half at the equator. Scoop out the insides leaving a tomato shell about ½ inch thick.

Combine the ricotta, tuna, and salt and pepper to taste in a small bowl. Spoon the tuna mixture into the tomatoes. Garnish with the parsley and serve with the lemon wedges, or give each tomato a squirt of lemon juice before serving.

Tuna with Scallion Pesto

You can serve the cool, spicy scallion pesto with other fish, either raw or cooked. Or serve it by itself as an antipasto with bruschetta; or spooned into vegetable soups—use it to replace the pestos in Pea Soup (page 229) or Spring Minestrone (page 236)—and on pasta dishes like Linguine Fini in Mussel Broth (page 207). This recipe makes about ¾ cup delicious scallion pesto. SERVES 4

  ½ cup coarsely chopped scallion greens (about ½ bunch; save the whites for steaming, page 261)

  3 tablespoons pine nuts

  1 garlic clove, minced (optional)

  3 tablespoons extra virgin olive oil

  2 teaspoons fresh lemon juice

  Salt

  1 pound tuna (see Note), chopped

In a food processor or blender, combine the scallion greens, pine nuts, garlic (if you want the extra heat), olive oil, lemon juice, and salt to taste and process to a thick sauce. (I like to leave it a bit on the coarse side, but a smooth puree is nice too.)

Toss the scallion pesto and tuna together in a serving bowl.

Note: I make this with the pieces of tuna that didn't make it into the jars for Canned Tuna with Rosemary (page 301). Often that's less than a pound.

SALTWATER FISH
WHITE-FLESHED FISH

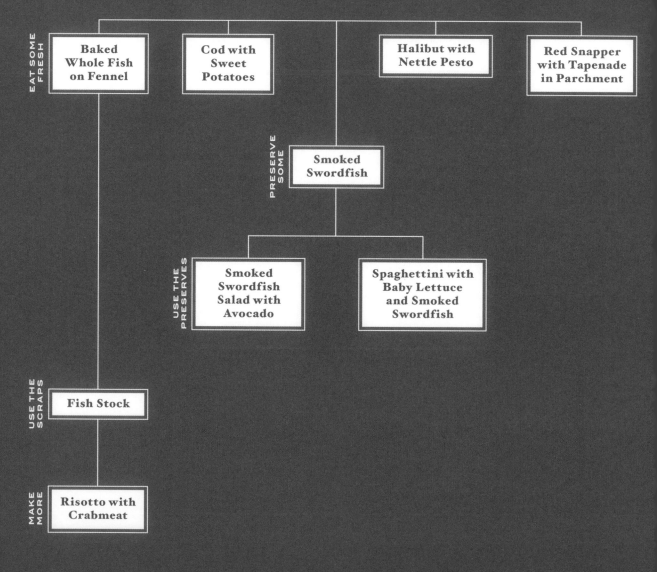

EAT SOME FRESH

Baked Whole Fish on Fennel

Cod with Sweet Potatoes

Halibut with Nettle Pesto

Red Snapper with Tapenade in Parchment

PRESERVE SOME

Smoked Swordfish

USE THE PRESERVES

Smoked Swordfish Salad with Avocado

Spaghettini with Baby Lettuce and Smoked Swordfish

USE THE SCRAPS

Fish Stock

MAKE MORE

Risotto with Crabmeat

Baked Whole Fish on Fennel

It's good to cook a whole fish, because then you have the head and bones for fish stock (page 311), but you can also make this recipe with chunks of fish. Just cook the fennel until almost done, around 20 minutes, tuck the chunks of fish into the fennel, and return to the oven. It will cook in about 15 minutes. Garnish with black pepper, extra virgin olive oil, and a bit of Parmesan cheese on the vegetable. **SERVES 4**

    3 cups sliced fennel (about 1 large bulb)

    2 cups sliced onions (about 2 medium)

    1 tablespoon sliced garlic

    ¼ cup olive oil, plus some for drizzling over
        the fish

    One 3-pound or two 1½-pound whole dressed
        fish, such as snapper or sea bass

    1 small bunch of flat-leaf parsley

    Salt and freshly ground black pepper

    ½ lemon

    Extra virgin olive oil, for garnish

Preheat the oven to 375°F.

In a medium bowl, toss together the fennel, onions, garlic, and ¼ cup of olive oil. Place the vegetables in the bottom of a roasting tray with a fitted rack. Oil the rack. Stuff the fish cavity with the parsley, drizzle the fish with olive oil, and season with salt and pepper to taste. Place the rack over the vegetables and place the fish on the rack. Bake for about 30 minutes, 20 minutes for the smaller fish, more or less depending on the thickness of the fish. Cook until the flesh pulls away easily with a fork and the internal temperature is 145°F.

To serve, remove the fish and place on a cutting board. Remove the parsley. Fillet the fish: Cut off the head, the tail, and the dorsal fins. (This will be easy as the meat is cooked

BAKED WHOLE FISH ON FENNEL

and the bones are soft.) Slice along the midline of one side of the fish, cutting the fillet in half. Gently pull off the two fillets. Lift the spine off the bottom fillet and leave it whole.

Toss the vegetables together in a serving plate and place the fillets on top. Squeeze the lemon juice over the fish, and garnish with a drizzle of extra virgin olive oil, and a few grinds of black pepper.

Cod with Sweet Potatoes

The sweet potatoes and tomato sauce can be prepared ahead of time, and the fish cooks quickly, so this is a great dish for company. You can also use bass or halibut fillets, but avoid really delicate fillets, like sole, as they tend to fall apart in the sauce. **SERVES 4**

1 pound small sweet potatoes (about 4)

2 tablespoons olive oil

2 medium onions, finely chopped

4 garlic cloves, finely chopped

1 cup chopped tomatoes, fresh or canned (for homemade, page 328)

Salt and freshly ground black pepper

1½ pounds codfish fillet, cut into 2-inch chunks

2 tablespoons extra virgin olive oil

2 tablespoons chopped flat-leaf parsley

Preheat the oven to 450°F. Bake the sweet potatoes for about 45 minutes, or until they are fork-tender. When they are cool, peel them and cut into thick slices. Leave the oven on.

In a medium skillet with a fitted ovenproof lid, heat the olive oil over medium heat. Add the onions and garlic and cook until the onions become translucent, about 5 minutes. Add the tomatoes. Cover the skillet and simmer the vegetables over medium-low heat for 10 minutes, or until the tomatoes break up. Add salt and pepper to taste. Add the sweet potato slices.

Place the fish pieces in the sauce so that the pieces do not overlap. Add salt to taste and cover the skillet. Place the skillet in the oven and bake for about 10 minutes, or until the fish is white and flaky. Adjust the seasoning.

Sprinkle the fish and sweet potatoes with the extra virgin olive oil and parsley and serve promptly.

Halibut with Nettle Pesto

Nettles taste a bit like spinach, but more wild. They sting, so handle with gloves. If you gather them wild and you do get stung, look for a nearby jewelweed (they often grow together). Rub some jewelweed juice on the sting and it will go away. Once nettles are blanched, or even soaked in cold water, their sting (actually, a collection of chemicals delivered by needlelike hairs on the leaves and stem) is neutralized. The nettle pesto can be frozen (see "How to Freeze Foods," page 382). SERVES 4

⅓ pound nettles (about 2 cups chopped)

2 tablespoons olive oil

¼ cup pine nuts

⅔ cup chicken stock (for homemade, page 89), warmed

1 teaspoon grated lemon zest

Salt and freshly ground black pepper

1¼ pounds skin-on halibut or other rich, white-fleshed fish

1 lemon, quartered

Preheat the oven to 500°F.

Bring a medium pot of water to a boil over high heat and drop in the nettles. Once the water returns to a boil, drain the nettles. The water will turn black. Discard.

In a small skillet, heat 1 tablespoon of the oil over medium heat and add the nettles. Cook until they are very soft, about 5 minutes. Transfer the nettles to a food processor and add the pine nuts, chicken stock, lemon zest, and salt to taste and pulse to grind. I like my pesto rather coarse, but you can puree it to a smooth blend if you'd prefer. Either way, the pesto should be rather loose, like porridge.

Salt the fish to taste. Drizzle 1 tablespoon of oil in a baking sheet and place the fish on top. Roast the fish for about 10 minutes, or until the flesh flakes apart when gently prodded with a fork. (Alternatively, you can pan-cook the fish. Use a lightly oiled nonstick skillet and

HALIBUT WITH NETTLE PESTO

cook the fish flesh side down until just golden, about 5 minutes, then flip the fish over and cook an additional 5 minutes, until the skin is crispy.)

Serve the fish on top of a puddle of the nettle pesto, garnished with a few grinds of black pepper, and a lemon quarter.

Red Snapper with Tapenade in Parchment

Cooking in parchment means there are no pots to wash up. You can substitute the tapenade with a pesto (any kind, really), and the leeks and mushrooms with other vegetables. Just note that the cooking time is short, so some vegetables, like bell peppers, would need to be precooked. **SERVES 4**

2 tablespoons olive oil

2 leeks, whites only, washed and julienned

4 teaspoons minced garlic

¼ cup chicken stock (for homemade, page 89)

3½ ounces enoki mushrooms or other white mushroom such as sliced white button or julienned royal trumpets

4 red snapper fillets (about 6 ounces each)

Salt and freshly ground black pepper

Generous ¼ cup Green Olive Tapenade (page 160)

2 tablespoons fresh lemon juice

4 sprigs of fresh thyme

¼ cup white wine

Place an oven rack in the center of the oven. Preheat the oven to 350°F.

In a medium skillet, heat the olive oil over medium heat. Add the leeks and garlic and cook until the garlic is fragrant, a few minutes. Add the chicken stock, cover, and gently poach the leeks until they are soft, about 5 minutes.

Cut 4 pieces of parchment about 12 inches square. Fold the parchment in half, and then open it again. For each serving, place one-fourth of the leeks on the lower half of a parchment square (not in the middle). Place one-fourth of the enoki mushrooms on top of the leeks. Lay a fish fillet on top of each portion. Season with salt and pepper and smear a heaping tablespoon of tapenade on top. Add 1 teaspoon lemon juice and a sprig of thyme to each. Drizzle 1 tablespoon of white wine over each portion.

Fold the free half of the paper over the food and crimp the edges of the paper. You do this by folding the edges of the paper in pleats.

Place 2 parchment packets on each of 2 baking sheets and place in the oven. Bake for

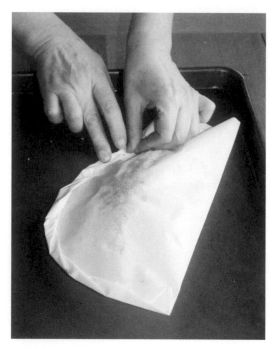

PLEATING PARCHMENT PACKETS

swordfish in the brine and let it rest in the refrigerator for about 1 hour. This is important because to safely store smoked fish in the refrigerator, you need to introduce adequate salt into the flesh. Salt is what preserves smoked fish.

Drain, rinse, and return the swordfish to a bowl with clean cold water. Allow the fish to soak about 30 minutes. Drain and pat dry. Smoke does not deposit well on wet fish.

Prepare your stovetop smoker (see "How to Smoke Indoors," page 384) with the wood chips. Lay the swordfish on the rack, close the smoker, and place over medium-high to high heat. Smoke the swordfish for 35 minutes, and then take off the heat. Remove the swordfish from the smoker and let come to room temperature. (For how to do this in your oven, see page 384.)

Wrap in paper towels or wax paper so moisture does not settle on the surface. Place in a plastic container. Holds in the refrigerator for 10 days.

12 minutes. The paper will look crispy. It's okay. I like to serve the fish in its parchment pouch. When the diner opens it up, a lovely aroma emerges and the fish is moist and flavorful.

Smoked Swordfish

Swordfish is particularly well suited for smoking, as the flesh is sweet and fatty. You can also play around with seasonings: Try dusting the steaks with sweet paprika before smoking. MAKES 2½ POUNDS

- **1 cup pickling salt**
- **7 cups cold water**
- **3 pounds fresh swordfish steaks, whole or in chunks, skinned, washed, and patted dry**
- **1½ tablespoons alder chips**

In a large bowl, combine the salt and water. Stir the salt to dissolve in the water. Place the

Smoked Swordfish Salad with Avocado

This is a rich main-dish salad. I serve it with pieces of bruschetta. You can substitute 2 cups of cooked, room-temperature cannellini beans for the potatoes. SERVES 4

- **¾ pound Smoked Swordfish (left), sliced**
- **1½ cups artichoke hearts, canned or thawed frozen, or marinated artichokes (for homemade, page 28), drained (see Note)**
- **1 avocado, sliced**
- **3 tablespoons minced fresh chives**
- **¼ cup extra virgin olive oil**

Juice from ½ lemon

Salt and freshly ground black pepper

4 medium Yukon Gold potatoes, boiled, peeled, and sliced crosswise

2 tablespoons minced flat-leaf parsley

In a large bowl, combine the swordfish, artichoke hearts, avocado, chives, 3 tablespoons of the olive oil, lemon juice, and salt and pepper to taste. Toss gently.

Lay the potatoes on a serving platter and dress them with the parsley, remaining 1 tablespoon olive oil, and salt and pepper to taste. Spoon the swordfish salad on top and serve.

Note: Marinated artichokes are more flavorful than frozen or canned in water, so if you use them, add the olive oil and lemon juice in tablespoon increments to avoid overdressing.

Spaghettini with Baby Lettuce and Smoked Swordfish

In this simple yet snazzy dish, the heat from the pasta wilts the lettuce, so be sure you use very tender greens. You can also make this pasta without the fish and just garnish with grated Parmesan cheese. **SERVES 4**

¾ pound spaghettini

2 teaspoons mustard, Dijon or homemade (page 366)

1 tablespoon fresh lemon juice

6 tablespoons vegetable oil

½ pound baby lettuces, washed

Salt and freshly ground black pepper

½ pound Smoked Swordfish (opposite), sliced

Bring a large pot of salted water to a boil over high heat and add the spaghettini. Cook until al dente and drain.

Meanwhile, in a small bowl, whisk together the mustard and lemon juice. Slowly add the oil, whisking all the while, until the oil is emulsified.

Toss the hot pasta and vinaigrette together in a serving bowl. Add the lettuces and toss, distributing them throughout. Season with salt and pepper to taste. Lay the sliced swordfish over the pasta and serve.

Fish Stock

This fish stock can be made with the head and bones of a cooked or uncooked white fish. If you have only 1 pound of bones you should still make the stock. Just reduce the quantities of the other ingredients by two-thirds. Fennel, leeks, and tomatoes go very well in fish stock, so add them with the onions if you have them on hand. Lazy? Skip the sautéing step and just throw all of the raw ingredients into the pot and bring to a boil. The stock will still be good and far more flavorful than anything bought at the store. The pressure-canning timing is from a fish chowder base recipe in Stocking Up, *a reliable preserving guide.*

MAKES ABOUT 7 CUPS

3 tablespoons olive oil

1 medium onion, coarsely chopped

1 celery rib, chopped

2 garlic cloves, chopped

2½ to 3 pounds white-fleshed-fish heads (gills removed) and bones

8 cups water

½ cup chopped flat-leaf parsley, stems included

½ lemon

½ teaspoon black peppercorns

3 bay leaves

Salt

In a medium pot, heat the oil over medium heat. Add the onion, celery, and garlic and cook until the onions become translucent, about 5 minutes. Add the fish heads and bones, water, parsley, lemon, peppercorns, bay leaves, and salt to taste. Cover and bring to a boil over high heat. Then reduce the heat to low, uncover, and boil gently for 1 hour. Strain the stock. Discard the bones and vegetables.

Transfer the stock to jars and refrigerate or freeze (see the technique for making stocks, page 390).

For shelf-stable stock, pressure can it. Have ready 3 clean pint jars and bands, and new lids that have been simmered in hot water to soften the rubberized flange. Fill the jars with hot stock leaving 1 inch of headroom. Wipe the rims, place on the lids, and screw on the bands fingertip tight. Process the jars in a pressure canner at 10/11 psi for 1 hour. (See "How to Pressure Can," page 379.) Be sure to make altitude adjustments when preserving (see page 389).

Risotto with Crabmeat

This risotto is light but satisfying. You can substitute shrimp for the crab, or leave off the seafood garnish altogether. The fish stock is key to its delicate flavor. For more flavor, garnish with a dollop of Scallion Pesto (page 305). **SERVES 4**

RISOTTO
2 tablespoons olive oil

½ cup finely chopped onion (about ½ medium)

2 tablespoons finely chopped garlic (about 4 cloves)

1 cup carnaroli, vialone nano, or Arborio rice

½ cup dry white wine

3 tablespoons finely chopped flat-leaf parsley

About 4 cups warm fish stock (for homemade, page 311)

¼ cup grated Parmesan cheese

Salt and freshly ground black pepper

CRABMEAT GARNISH
1 tablespoon olive oil

1 tablespoon finely chopped garlic

8 ounces lump crabmeat

1 tablespoon chopped flat-leaf parsley

¼ cup dry Marsala wine or sherry

Salt and freshly ground black pepper

For the risotto: In a deep saucepan, heat the olive oil over medium heat. Add the onion and garlic and cook until the onions become translucent, about 5 minutes. Add the rice, wine, and parsley. Bring the wine to a boil and cook, uncovered, until the rice absorbs the wine, about 5 minutes. Then add enough fish stock to cover the rice (about 1 cup). Stir frequently until the rice absorbs the stock. Continue adding stock (about a cup at a time) and stirring as the rice cooks. The rice will cook slowly at first, but then more quickly. When the rice is tender, 25 to 30 minutes, add the Parmesan and salt and pepper to taste. The texture of the risotto should be like porridge.

For the crabmeat garnish: In a small skillet, heat the olive oil over medium heat. Add the garlic and when it begins to take on color, a couple of minutes, add the crabmeat, parsley, Marsala, and salt and pepper to taste. Cover and simmer for about 5 minutes, until the wine evaporates.

Serve each portion of risotto with a helping of crabmeat on top.

SHRIMP

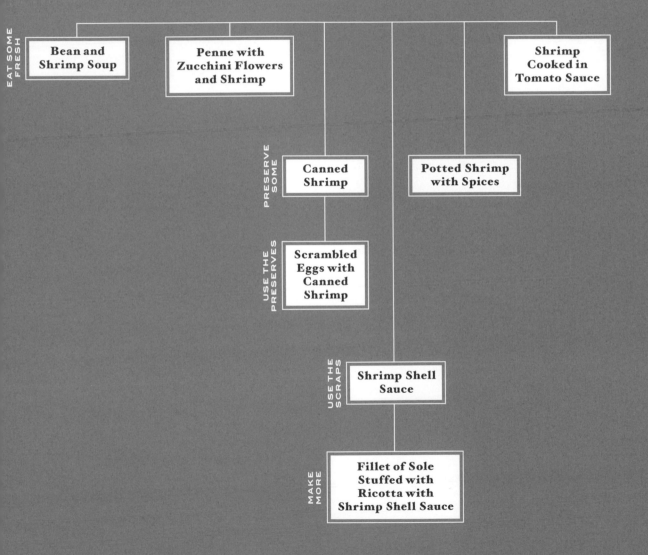

EAT SOME FRESH

Bean and Shrimp Soup

Penne with Zucchini Flowers and Shrimp

Shrimp Cooked in Tomato Sauce

PRESERVE SOME

Canned Shrimp

Potted Shrimp with Spices

USE THE PRESERVES

Scrambled Eggs with Canned Shrimp

USE THE SCRAPS

Shrimp Shell Sauce

MAKE MORE

Fillet of Sole Stuffed with Ricotta with Shrimp Shell Sauce

Buy shell-on shrimp because the shell protects the meat from handling and environmental factors, like melting ice. And when possible, buy shrimp with the head on. Not only is it a sign of freshness, but also those heads are packed with flavor.

Bean and Shrimp Soup

*This is one of my family's favorite winter soups. With a salad and a loaf of Italian bread, it is perfect on a cold night. Sometimes I add a sliced kielbasa sausage or chorizo with the shrimp. In the winter I use fresh cranberry beans. Otherwise, I soak any number of different beans, like cannellini or Great Northern beans, overnight in salted water to rehydrate them before using in the recipe. About 1 heaping cup of dried cannellini beans produces about 3 cups of rehydrated beans. **Save the shrimp shells for Shrimp Shell Sauce (page 317).** SERVES 4*

2 tablespoons olive oil

¼ cup chopped pancetta or 4 slices bacon, chopped

2 cups chopped onions (about 2 medium)

2 tablespoons chopped garlic (3 or 4 cloves)

2 cups crushed tomatoes (for homemade, page 328)

3 cups beans, fresh or rehydrated dried

2 tablespoons chopped flat-leaf parsley

2 tablespoons chopped fresh basil (optional)

3 inches Parmesan cheese rind (optional)

Salt and freshly ground black pepper

12 large shrimp, peeled and deveined

In a large soup pot, heat the oil over medium-high heat. Add the pancetta and cook until the fat is rendered, about 5 minutes. Add the onions and garlic and cook until the onions become translucent, about 5 minutes. Add the tomatoes and cook until the tomatoes break

up, another 5 minutes or so. Add the beans, parsley, basil (if using), cheese rind (if using), and salt and pepper to taste. Add water to cover (6 to 8 cups), bring to a boil, then reduce the heat and cook the soup at a gentle boil for 1 hour 45 minutes, stirring often.

When the beans are tender, remove the cheese rind and add the shrimp. Cook until the shrimp are pink and opaque, about 5 minutes. Check the seasoning and serve either hot or at room temperature. Sometimes I garnish with a little Parmesan cheese, a sprinkle of chopped parsley, or a drizzle of olive oil.

Penne with Zucchini Flowers and Shrimp

*If you don't have zucchini flowers, you can use grated zucchini, but reduce the quantity to 1½ cups. **Save the shrimp shells for Shrimp Shell Sauce (page 317).** SERVES 4*

5 tablespoons extra virgin olive oil

1 medium onion, coarsely chopped

10 large zucchini flowers, chopped (about 2 cups)

1 tablespoon unsalted butter

1 tablespoon fresh basil chiffonade (see Note)

Salt and freshly ground black pepper

1 to 1½ cups chicken stock (for homemade, page 89)

¼ teaspoon saffron threads

¾ pound penne or other small-cut pasta, such as farfalle

2 garlic cloves, finely chopped

¾ pound shrimp, peeled and deveined

2 tablespoons finely chopped flat-leaf parsley

In a medium skillet, heat 3 tablespoons of the olive oil over medium heat. Add the onions and cook until they become translucent, about 5 minutes. Add the zucchini flowers, butter, basil, and salt and pepper to taste. Cover and simmer until the flowers are soft, about 10 minutes.

Meanwhile, in a small saucepan, heat 1 cup of the chicken stock over medium heat. Add the saffron, cover, and simmer until the saffron threads dissolve, about 5 minutes.

Add the stock to the zucchini flower mixture, cover, and simmer until the stock is aromatic, another 10 minutes.

Transfer the sauce to a food processor and puree until it is the consistency of light cream. If it is too thick, warm up ½ cup chicken stock in a small saucepan over medium heat and add to the sauce a few tablespoons at a time.

Bring a large pot of salted water to a boil and add the pasta. Cook until al dente and drain.

Meanwhile, in a medium skillet, heat the remaining 2 tablespoons olive oil over medium heat. Add the garlic, shrimp, and salt and pepper to taste, and cook until the shrimp turn pink, about 4 minutes.

Toss the zucchini flower sauce and the pasta in a large serving bowl. Garnish with the shrimp and parsley.

Note: To chiffonade basil, lay the leaves on top of each other. Roll them up like a cigar, and thinly slice crosswise. When you unfurl the leaves you will have a tangle of thin slices.

Shrimp Cooked in Tomato Sauce

I often serve this as a first course with bruschetta, but didn't start putting cheese on top until I'd had a similar dish at my friend Neni's house: shrimp in tomato sauce with feta and dill. To serve as an entrée (which you may want to do after tasting it), just double the ingredients. **Save the shrimp shells for Shrimp Shell Sauce (page 317).** SERVES 4 AS A FIRST COURSE

> 2 tablespoons olive oil
>
> 2 tablespoons minced garlic
>
> ½ teaspoon hot pepper flakes (or more to taste)
>
> 2 cups crushed tomatoes (for homemade, page 328)
>
> Salt
>
> 16 medium shrimp, peeled and deveined
>
> ½ cup crumbled ricotta salata (see Note) or feta cheese
>
> 2 tablespoons chopped flat-leaf parsley (if you use ricotta) or fresh dill (if you use feta)

In a medium saucepan, heat the oil over medium heat. Add the garlic and pepper flakes and cook until the garlic begins to sizzle, a minute or so. Add the tomatoes and salt to taste and cook until the tomatoes break up and are gently boiling, about 10 minutes. You will smell them.

Add the shrimp and cook them until they are pink, about 5 minutes.

Serve the shrimp in a ladle of sauce, garnished with cheese and parsley or dill.

Note: I use my homemade ricotta (page 367), because it's dry enough to crumble.

Canned Shrimp

I've tried canning tiny Maine shrimp, which I love, but pressure canning is simply too tough on such a delicate critter. Medium to large shrimp are better for canning. **MAKES 2 PINTS**

> 1 tablespoon plus ¾ teaspoon pickling salt
> ¼ cup distilled white vinegar (5% acidity)
> 8 cups water
> 1 pound shell-on medium to large shrimp

In a large pot, combine 1 tablespoon of the salt, the vinegar, and 4 cups of water and bring to a boil over high heat. Add the shrimp (shells on) and boil in the brine for for 8 to 10 minutes. Drain the shrimp (discard the brine). Rinse the shrimp and remove the shells.

In a medium pot, combine the remaining ¾ teaspoon salt and 4 cups water and bring to a boil.

Have ready 2 clean pint jars and bands, and new lids that have been simmered in hot water to soften the rubberized flange. Pack the shrimp into the jars leaving a little more than 1 inch of headroom. Cover the shrimp with the hot brine leaving 1 inch of headroom. Wipe the rims, place on the lids, and screw on the bands fingertip tight.

Process the jars in a pressure canner at 10/11 psi for 45 minutes for either pints or 4 half-pints. (See "How to Pressure Can," page 379.) Be sure to make altitude adjustments when preserving (see page 389).

Potted Shrimp with Spices

Potted shrimp is a kind of spicy shrimp confit. It is wonderful as an hors d'oeuvre right out of the jar, served with toast tips. I've made this with tiny Maine shrimp (divine) and medium shrimp. Traditionally, potted shrimp calls for mace, but you can flavor the shrimp any way you like. **Save the shrimp shells for Shrimp Shell Sauce (opposite).** **MAKES 1 HALF-PINT**

> 8 tablespoons (1 stick) unsalted butter
> 2 large garlic cloves
> Pinch of grated nutmeg
> Pinch of paprika
> ½ pound medium shrimp, peeled and deveined, cut into bite-size pieces
> Salt
> 1 tablespoon fresh lemon juice

In a small saucepan, melt the butter over low heat. Pour the melted butter through

POTTED SHRIMP WITH SPICES

cheesecloth to remove the milk solids from the butter. Wipe out any milk solids from the saucepan, return the clarified butter to the pan, and add the garlic, nutmeg, and paprika. Simmer for 5 minutes. Skim off the foam. Remove the garlic and add the shrimp. Poach very gently for 10 minutes. Season with salt and the lemon juice and stir.

Have ready a sterilized half-pint jar, band, and lid. (See "How to Sterilize," page 389.) You don't need a new lid because the jar won't be processed. Pack the shrimp into the jar and cover with the butter. Refrigerate. It will be ready to eat in 24 hours, and will hold in the refrigerator for up to 10 days.

Scrambled Eggs with Canned Shrimp

You can make this dish with fresh shrimp of course, and garnish with parsley, cilantro, tarragon, dill, or chives. **SERVES 4**

8 eggs

2 tablespoons unsalted butter

1 tablespoon minced garlic

1 pint Canned Shrimp (opposite), drained and sliced in half end to end

2 to 3 tablespoons crème fraîche (for homemade, page 362) or sour cream, to taste

2 tablespoons grated Parmesan cheese

Salt and hot pepper flakes

Break the eggs into a small bowl and whisk. In a large nonstick skillet, melt the butter over medium heat. Add the garlic and cook for 1 minute, just to soften a bit. Add the shrimp and cook until they just begin to color, about 2 minutes, then add the eggs. Reduce the heat

to low. Slowly scramble the eggs to your taste, but I like them soft, about 5 minutes. Just before they are done, add the crème fraîche, Parmesan, and salt and pepper flakes to taste.

Shrimp Shell Sauce

This exquisite sauce is perfect on top of Risotto with Crabmeat (page 312), or on Fillet of Sole Stuffed with Ricotta (page 318). **MAKES 1 PINT**

1 tablespoon unsalted butter

¼ cup minced onion

2 teaspoons minced garlic (about 2 garlic cloves)

Heads and shells from 1 pound shrimp

¼ cup white wine

2½ cups crushed tomatoes (for homemade, page 328)

Salt and freshly ground black pepper

In a medium saucepan, heat the butter over medium heat. Add the onion and garlic and cook until the onion is translucent, about 5 minutes. Add the heads and shells and the wine and cook until the wine almost evaporates, about 5 minutes. Add the tomatoes and salt and pepper to taste, cover, and cook over medium-low heat for 45 minutes.

Transfer the sauce and shells to a food processor and puree. Press the puree through a fine-mesh sieve into a bowl. Wrap the remaining solids in a piece of cheesecloth and squeeze the juice into the sauce. The sauce can be refrigerated or frozen.

To refrigerate, have ready a sterilized pint jar, band, and lid. (See "How to Sterilize," page 389.) You don't need a new lid because the jar won't be processed. Pour the hot sauce in the

SOFTEN THE SHELLS IN WINE BEFORE ADDING TOMATOES

jar, cap, and refrigerate. Use it within 3 days, or bring the sauce to a boil every third day. You will lose some volume doing this.

To freeze, simply pack into a freezer-safe jar or food-grade plastic container. Be sure to leave about 1 inch of headroom, as the sauce will expand when frozen.

Fillet of Sole Stuffed with Ricotta with Shrimp Shell Sauce

This is the final dish my family eats as part of La Vigilia, The Feast of the Seven Fishes, served on Christmas Eve. You can add lump crabmeat to the ricotta stuffing if you'd like, or sautéed shrimp to the sauce. **SERVES 4**

1 cup ricotta cheese (for homemade, page 367)
4 tablespoons finely chopped flat-leaf parsley
Pinch of grated nutmeg
Salt and freshly ground black pepper
4 sole fillets (about 4 ounces each)
¼ cup dry white wine
1 cup Shrimp Shell Sauce (page 317)

Preheat the oven to 450°F.

In a bowl, combine the ricotta, 2 tablespoons of the parsley, the nutmeg, and salt and pepper to taste. Lay the fillets out and place 1 to 2 tablespoons of the stuffing in the center of each fillet. Roll the fillet and gently place, seam side down, in an 8 × 8-inch baking dish. Add the white wine to the pan. Bake for 15 minutes, or until the fish is opaque.

Add the shrimp sauce and cook for about 5 minutes more, until the sauce is hot. Serve the fish garnished with the remaining 2 tablespoons parsley.

STRATEGY BERRIES

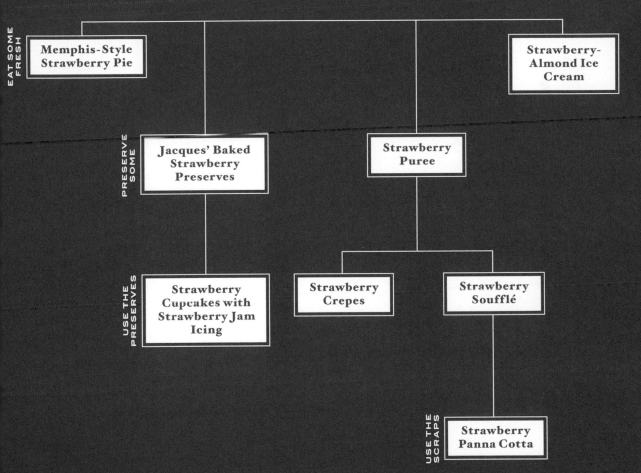

STRAWBERRIES

EAT SOME FRESH
- Memphis-Style Strawberry Pie
- Strawberry-Almond Ice Cream

PRESERVE SOME
- Jacques' Baked Strawberry Preserves
- Strawberry Puree

USE THE PRESERVES
- Strawberry Cupcakes with Strawberry Jam Icing
- Strawberry Crepes
- Strawberry Soufflé

USE THE SCRAPS
- Strawberry Panna Cotta

Memphis-Style Strawberry Pie

This is the way they make strawberry pie in Memphis, Tennessee, and I think it is heavenly. But don't make it out of season. Only fresh local strawberries will pack the flavor punch you need for this recipe. You can also make the pie with a graham cracker crust (see Note). **MAKES ONE 10-INCH PIE**

1½ cups all-purpose flour

½ cup confectioners' sugar

6 tablespoons cold unsalted butter

3 large egg yolks

½ teaspoon vanilla extract (for homemade, page 361)

¾ pound strawberries, hulled

1 can (14 ounces) sweetened condensed milk

¼ cup fresh lemon juice

In a food processor, combine the flour, confectioners' sugar, butter, 2 of the egg yolks (beaten together), and vanilla and process until the dough comes together, a minute or so. Add a tablespoon of cold water if the dough fails to come together. (To make the pastry by hand, see page 395.) Press the dough into a disk. Wrap the dough in plastic wrap or wax paper and refrigerate until chilled, about 30 minutes.

Preheat the oven to 350°F.

Roll out the dough 10 inches in diameter and ⅛ inch thick and line a 10-inch pie plate. Trim dough to fit the edge of the pie plate and press down the edge with the tines of a fork. You can use pie weights to keep the crust bottom smooth. I don't bother, though on occasion there is some bubbling of the crust. In which case, pop it with a fork. Bake the crust for about

MEMPHIS-STYLE STRAWBERRY PIE

15 minutes, or until golden brown. Remove and let cool slightly, but leave the oven on.

In a blender or food processor, combine the strawberries, remaining 1 egg yolk, the condensed milk, and lemon juice and blend.

Pour the strawberry mixture into the pie crust and bake for 15 minutes, or until the pie has just set. Cool to room temperature. Chill for a few hours before serving.

Note: For a graham cracker crust, combine 6 tablespoons melted butter with 12 crushed graham cracker squares and ¼ cup granulated sugar. Press into a 10-inch pie plate. Bake for 15 minutes at 375°F. Let cool, then fill with strawberry filling and bake according to the recipe.

Strawberry-Almond Ice Cream

Almonds are a lovely addition to classic strawberry ice cream, a must-do recipe in the early summer when the berries come in. Remember, strawberries do not continue to ripen after harvesting, so choose fruit that has been picked fully ripened. If you see white flesh near the stem, that is an indication the strawberry was picked too soon. **MAKES 1½ PINTS**

- 1 cup heavy cream
- 1 cup whole milk
- 2 large eggs, beaten
- ½ cup sugar
- 1 teaspoon vanilla extract (for homemade, page 361)
- 1 heaping cup coarsely chopped strawberries
- 4 heaping tablespoons slivered almonds

In a heavy-bottomed pot, combine the cream and milk. Heat over medium-high heat until the milk is very hot but not boiling, a few minutes. Set aside.

In a bowl, combine the eggs and sugar and whisk until they are well blended. Add a few tablespoons of the hot milk to temper the eggs (too much hot milk all at once will create egg curdles), then transfer the warmed egg mixture back to the pot with the milk in it. Return to a low heat and cook, stirring all the while, until the mixture thickens, about 5 minutes. You can tell the mixture has thickened enough if the custard coats the back of a spoon. Add the vanilla. Pour the custard into a stainless steel bowl or other cold-conductive container and chill in the refrigerator until very cold.

Transfer the chilled mixture to an ice cream maker. Add the strawberries and almonds and freeze according to the manufacturer's directions. (To make the ice cream by hand, see page 394.) It's okay if the ice cream is not totally dense like commercial ice cream. In fact, it is done when it looks like gelato: heavy and soft.

Transfer to a freezer-safe container and freeze. It will harden up like commercial ice cream. Holds for about 3 months.

Jacques' Baked Strawberry Preserves

This Jacques Pépin technique thickens the strawberries and juice by dehydrating the fruit through slow cooking. It creates a preserve with chunks of fruit that are soft and thick enough to spread with little sugar and no added pectin. The technique works with other fruits that are not excessively juicy, like apricots, sweet cherries, and rhubarb. **There are often quite a few tablespoons of juice left in the** *pan that you don't pack into the jar. Save this to make Strawberry Panna Cotta (page 325) or strawberry soda (syrup plus soda water).* MAKES 1 HALF-PINT

> **2 heaping cups cut-up strawberries, cut so they are about the same size**
>
> **½ cup sugar**

Preheat the oven to 200°F.

Place the strawberries on a rimmed baking sheet and sprinkle the sugar on top. Place in the oven and bake for 1 hour 30 minutes. Every once in a while flip the berries over, or stir them around with a spatula. When the berries are very soft, remove from the pan.

Have ready 1 sterilized half-pint jar and band, and a new lid that has been simmered in hot water to soften the rubberized flange. (See "How to Sterilize," page 389.) Pack the fruit into the jar leaving ¼ inch of headroom. Wipe the rim, place on the lid, and screw on the band fingertip tight.

Process the jar in a water bath (see page 375) for 5 minutes. Be sure to make altitude adjustments when preserving (see page 389). Some berries may float in the jar. It's okay. As soon as the jar is sealed, flip it over and the juice and berries will recombine.

Strawberry Puree

I prefer to use small, flavorful farmers' market strawberries for jams, but for a puree it's okay to use the big commercial strawberries, though organic always tastes better. I love to have this puree on hand because I can quickly flavor desserts, like crepes, soufflés, and panna cotta. MAKES 2 HALF-PINTS

> **4 cups strawberries, hulled**
>
> **½ cup water**
>
> **½ cup sugar**
>
> **1 teaspoon fresh lemon juice**

In a heavy-bottomed pot, combine the strawberries and water and mash. Cook over medium-low heat for a few minutes, bringing the strawberries to a gentle boil. Take off the heat and let cool enough to handle, then press the strawberry mash with a spoon through a sieve or food mill. You are going for a thick but smooth and seed-free puree.

Pour the puree back into the pot and heat over medium-low heat. Add the sugar and stir to dissolve, a few minutes. Stir in the lemon juice and remove from the heat.

Allow the puree to cool enough to handle and, if necessary, pass the puree through a finer sieve to remove any remaining seeds.

Have ready 2 sterilized half-pint jars and bands, and new lids that have been simmered in hot water to soften the rubberized flange. (See "How to Sterilize," page 389.) Fill the jars with the puree leaving ¼ inch of headroom. Wipe the rims, place on the lids, and screw on the bands fingertip tight.

Process the jars in a water bath (see page 375) for 5 minutes. Be sure to make altitude adjustments when preserving (see page 389). The juice and pulp may separate. You can flip over the jars after they have sealed, and you can always mix the juice and pulp together once you open the jar. There may be some discoloring of the fruit at the top of the jar over time. It's okay.

Strawberry Cupcakes
with Strawberry Jam Icing

These are pretty cupcakes, with a tender crumb and delicious flavor. You can double the recipe to make a cake: Bake in 2 greased 8-inch round cake pans. The cakes cook for about 5 minutes longer. You can use other jams for the icing. **MAKES 12**

CUPCAKES

2 cups cake flour

2 teaspoons baking powder

½ teaspoon salt

8 tablespoons (1 stick) unsalted butter, at room temperature

1 cup granulated sugar

1 egg

1 teaspoon vanilla extract (for homemade, page 361)

¾ cup whole milk

12 small strawberries (optional)

ICING

4 tablespoons (½ stick) butter, at room temperature

1 tablespoon heavy cream

2 tablespoons strawberry preserves (for homemade, below)

1 teaspoon vanilla extract (for homemade, page 361)

1½ to 2 cups confectioners' sugar

Preheat the oven to 350°F. Line 12 cups of a muffin tin with paper liners or grease them well.

For the cupcakes: Sift the cake flour with the baking powder and salt into a medium bowl. In a separate bowl, cream together the butter and granulated sugar. Add the egg and vanilla and mix well. Add half the milk and mix well. Resift half the flour mixture into the bowl and mix well. Add the remaining milk and mix well. Resift, add the remaining flour, and mix well.

Place a strawberry (if using) into each muffin cup, then add about ¼ cup of batter on top of each strawberry.

Bake for about 25 minutes, or until a cake tester inserted into a cupcake comes out

About Strawberry Jam

Most canners start with strawberry jam. Because of strawberries' high acidity, they are safe to water bath can, but it can be difficult to get a nice set. There are a few techniques to try.

• Combine the strawberries and sugar and add pectin, or combine the strawberries with a pectin-rich fruit (with the peel on), like apples or lemons. If adding pectin, follow the manufacturer's instructions (I prefer Pomona's Universal pectin—you can use less sugar). If adding pectin-rich fruit, boil until the strawberries mound on a spoon.

• Bake the strawberries (see Jacques' Baked Strawberry Preserves, page 321).

• Make a confiture by macerating the strawberries with lemon juice and sugar and simmering until the juice is released. Then separate the juice from the fruit and cook to 220°F at sea level, or 8°F over boiling temperature wherever you are. (To calculate the boiling temperature at your altitude, see page 389.) Recombine with the fruit.

• Cook down a ratio of 1½ cups fruit to 1 cup of sugar, plus 2 tablespoons of lemon juice, until the volume is reduced by half. This is what I do when I have an extra pint of strawberries.

clean. The tops will be golden brown and look smooth. Cool in the muffin tin on a rack.

Meanwhile, for the icing: In a metal bowl, with an electric mixer, cream the butter and beat in the cream until smooth. Beat in the jam and vanilla until smooth. Beat in 1½ cups of the confectioners' sugar. If the frosting is thick and spreadable, do not add more sugar. But if you went a little heavy on the jam, you may need another ½ cup of confectioners' sugar to compensate for the extra moisture. Place the bowl of icing over a pot of boiling water and cook for about 5 minutes, stirring vigorously as it heats up. The icing will become glossy and smooth, and the raw taste of the sugar will disappear. Remove the icing from the heat and let cool down. Beat again when it is cool. It will be thick enough to spread again. If it is too thick, add another teaspoon of cream. Avoid adding additional confectioners' sugar after you have heated the icing or you will taste that raw sugar again.

Remove the cooled cupcakes from the muffin tin and ice the cupcakes.

Strawberry Crepes

I love these crepes drizzled with a little extra puree on top. The batter holds well in the fridge overnight, making for a quick breakfast. The crepes are quite good served at room temperature, too. **MAKES 8 CREPES**

> ¾ cup all-purpose flour
>
> 3 tablespoons granulated sugar
>
> 1 teaspoon baking powder
>
> Pinch of salt
>
> 2 large eggs, beaten
>
> ½ cup Strawberry Puree (page 322)
>
> ⅓ cup whole milk

> ¼ cup water
>
> 2 tablespoons unsalted butter
>
> Confectioners' sugar, for garnish

In a large bowl, whisk together the flour, granulated sugar, baking powder, and salt. In a separate bowl, whisk together the eggs, strawberry puree, milk, and water. Add the liquid ingredients to the dry ingredients and whisk quickly, just to combine. Ignore the lumps. Refrigerate the batter for about 1 hour.

To cook the crepes, see "Preparing Crepes," page 395.

Garnish with confectioners' sugar and a drizzle of additional strawberry puree, if you'd like.

Strawberry Soufflé

This soufflé is delicate and a bit tangy—not as intense as I usually like my foods, but I can easily inhale two servings because it is so light and sweet. If you live at altitude, you will need to make this with a béchamel base (see High-Altitude Soufflé, page 79). **SERVES 6**

> 2 tablespoons unsalted butter, for the ramekins
>
> ⅓ cup granulated sugar, plus more for dusting
>
> 3 eggs, separated
>
> 6 tablespoons Strawberry Puree (page 322)
>
> Pinch of salt
>
> ¼ teaspoon cream of tartar
>
> Confectioners' sugar, for garnish

Position a rack in the middle of the oven and preheat to 350°F. Butter six 1-cup ramekins and dust with granulated sugar.

In a bowl, with an electric mixer, beat the yolks and ⅓ cup granulated sugar until the egg is light and falls from the beater in ribbons. Beat in the strawberry puree, combine, and set aside.

STRAWBERRY SOUFFLÉ

Using clean beaters, beat the egg whites with the salt and cream of tartar until stiff and glossy.

Add a large spoonful of the egg whites to the egg yolk mixture to lighten it. Then fold in the remaining egg whites carefully. Fill the ramekins, place on a baking sheet, and bake for 20 minutes.

Serve promptly with a dusting of confectioners' sugar.

Strawberry Panna Cotta

I make this dish with the strawberry syrup left over from Jacques' Baked Strawberry Preserves (page 321). You can also make it with Strawberry Puree (page 322) or Apricot-Orange Puree (page 19). Panna cotta can be made a day in advance, but not more or it will become tough. This panna cotta is more creamy than slick. **SERVES 4**

- 1 teaspoon neutral oil, such as safflower
- 3½ teaspoons unflavored powdered gelatin (about 1½ envelopes)

- 3 tablespoons cool water
- 2 cups half-and-half
- ¼ cup sugar
- 1 scant teaspoon vanilla extract (for homemade, page 361)
- 1 cup strawberry syrup

Grease four 1-cup ramekins with the oil.

Sprinkle the gelatin over the water in a small bowl and let soften.

In a small saucepan, combine the half-and-half, sugar, and vanilla and cook over medium-low heat until almost boiling, a few minutes. Remove from the heat and whisk in the strawberry syrup. Then whisk in the gelatin, making sure it is totally dissolved. Allow the mixture to cool to room temperature. Once cool, stir, and pour the cream into the ramekins and refrigerate for 2 to 4 hours, until set.

To serve, slip a sharp thin knife around the edge of the panna cotta, turn the ramekin upside down, and tap firmly onto a plate.

STRAWBERRY PANNA COTTA

TOMATOES

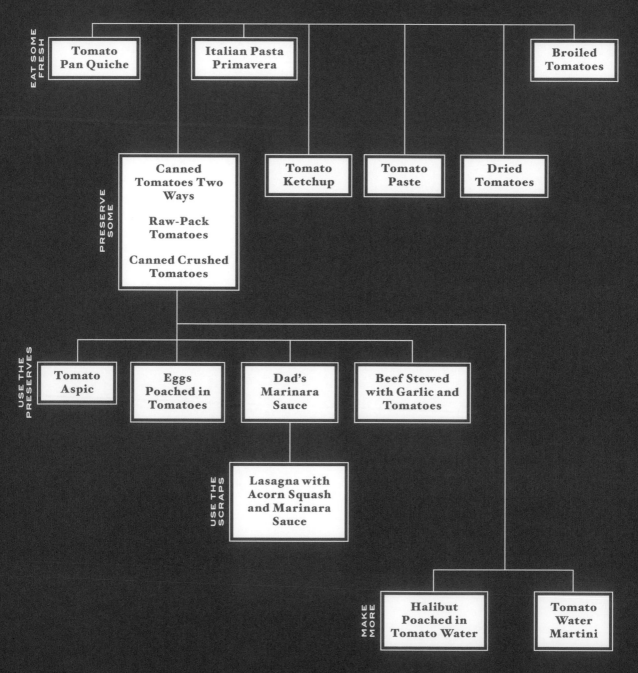

EAT SOME FRESH

Tomato Pan Quiche

Italian Pasta Primavera

Broiled Tomatoes

PRESERVE SOME

Canned Tomatoes Two Ways

Raw-Pack Tomatoes

Canned Crushed Tomatoes

Tomato Ketchup

Tomato Paste

Dried Tomatoes

USE THE PRESERVES

Tomato Aspic

Eggs Poached in Tomatoes

Dad's Marinara Sauce

Beef Stewed with Garlic and Tomatoes

USE THE SCRAPS

Lasagna with Acorn Squash and Marinara Sauce

MAKE MORE

Halibut Poached in Tomato Water

Tomato Water Martini

Tomato Pan Quiche

This is a perfect way to highlight the big taste of fresh summer tomatoes. This pan quiche is rustic but light, served directly from the skillet. Serve with a green salad. **SERVES** 4

- 1 to 2 tablespoons olive oil, for the pan
- 8 eggs
- 2 cups heavy cream
- Salt and freshly ground black pepper
- 2 tablespoons minced garlic
- 2 cups chopped fresh tomatoes, drained if very wet
- ½ cup chopped mozzarella or grated Parmesan cheese
- ¼ cup chopped flat-leaf parsley or basil, or a combination

Preheat the oven to 375°F. Oil a well-seasoned 9-inch cast-iron skillet or an ovenproof nonstick skillet.

In a large bowl, whisk together the eggs, cream, and salt and pepper to taste. Pour the egg mixture into the skillet. Add the garlic, tomatoes, cheese, and herbs. Place the skillet in the oven and bake for 40 to 45 minutes, or until the eggs are golden brown and puffy. Remove from the oven and let cool enough to serve. The eggs will deflate some. It's okay.

Italian Pasta Primavera

This is the traditional Italian recipe for pasta primavera. In contrast to recipes with chopped vegetables or cream, in Italy, "spring pasta" utilizes the first tomatoes of the season and not much else. Plum tomatoes work best in this recipe because they are meaty and not too juicy. **SERVES** 4

- 3 cups chopped fresh plum tomatoes
- 3 tablespoons chopped fresh basil
- 1 tablespoon chopped garlic
- 4 tablespoons extra virgin olive oil
- Salt and freshly ground black pepper
- 1 pound spaghetti or spaghettini
- ¼ cup grated Parmesan cheese
- 2 tablespoons chopped flat-leaf parsley

Finely chop the tomatoes, basil, and garlic together and combine in a serving bowl with 3 tablespoons of oil, and salt and pepper to taste. (Alternatively, put the ingredients in a food processor and pulse to blend.)

Bring a large pot of salted water to a boil over high heat and add the pasta. Cook until al dente, drain, and toss it in a serving bowl with the raw sauce. Garnish each portion with a drizzle of extra virgin olive oil, the Parmesan, and parsley.

Broiled Tomatoes

Serve these hot or room temperature as a side dish. For variation, you can also put a small sprig of rosemary in each tomato, or sprinkle with breadcrumbs before broiling. **SERVES** 4

- 2 large fresh tomatoes, halved at the equator
- 4 small garlic cloves, slivered
- 4 teaspoons chopped fresh oregano or 2 teaspoons dried
- Salt and freshly ground black pepper
- ¼ cup olive oil

Preheat the broiler (you can make these in a toaster oven, too).

Place the tomatoes in a small baking pan cut side up. Stick each tomato with a few slivers of garlic. (This is preferable to sprinkling garlic on top; when the garlic is buried in tomato flesh it's protected from burning.) Sprinkle the tomatoes with the oregano, salt and pepper to taste, and the olive oil.

Place under the broiler and broil until the herbs are almost browned, 5 to 10 minutes, depending on how close to the heat the tomatoes are.

CANNED TOMATOES TWO WAYS

RAW-PACK TOMATOES

MAKES 4 PINTS

> 5 pounds tomatoes
> Boiling water (optional)
> 2 fresh basil leaves per jar (optional)
> ½ teaspoon pickling salt per jar (optional)
> ¼ teaspoon citric acid per jar

Have ready 4 very clean pint jars and bands, and new lids that have been simmered in hot water to soften the rubberized flange. You don't need to sterilize the jars, as you will be processing them for more than 10 minutes.

Halve the tomatoes and pack them into the jars. I usually get 1½ large tomatoes in a pint jar. Press down to release the juices. If the tomatoes aren't juicy, add enough boiling water to fill the jar, leaving ½ inch of headroom. With a butter knife, free any air bubbles caught in the jar.

Slip 2 basil leaves into each jar, if you'd like. Add ½ teaspoon salt (if using) and ¼ teaspoon citric acid to each jar. Wipe the rims, place on the lids, and screw on the bands fingertip tight.

USE A COLANDER TO CATCH JUICES

Process the jars in a water bath (see page 375) for 40 minutes for pints or 45 minutes for 2 quarts. Be sure to make altitude adjustments when preserving (page 389).

CANNED CRUSHED TOMATOES

MAKES 4 PINTS

> 5 pounds tomatoes
> ½ teaspoon pickling salt per jar (optional)
> ¼ teaspoon citric acid per jar

Bring a large pot of water to a boil over high heat. Add as many tomatoes as will comfortably fit in your pot and blanch for 10 seconds. The skins will look light and shiny. The water doesn't need to come back to a boil before you blanch the remaining tomatoes.

Working over a colander set over a bowl to catch juices, slit the tomato skin with a paring

About Canning Tomatoes

I can tomatoes two ways: the grade A way, which is to peel, seed, crush, and heat the tomatoes before processing, and the grade B way, which is to shove raw halved tomatoes into the jar and process. The latter is called raw-packing, and perfect if you are short on time. The downside is when it comes time to cook the tomatoes in a recipe you'll want to remove those skins and seeds by pushing the tomatoes through a food mill. Tomato skins tend to curl in the sauce, and the seeds will add bitterness to your dishes.

I estimate a little over a pound of tomatoes per pint jar, but if you have more or less tomato product than jars designated in the recipe, then process half-pints (they process for the same amount of time as pints and can be done in the same water bath batch). Don't process jars that are not full (leaving ½ inch headroom) or your seals may fail.

Tomatoes usually have a pH of 4.5 or 4.6, which is right on the borderline for foods you can safely process in a water bath. Different circumstances, like harvesting practices, and different cultivars can vary the acidity of tomatoes just enough to tip them into the iffy category, so you should acidify them by adding ¼ teaspoon citric acid or 2 tablespoons lemon juice per pint. Or alternatively, can them in a pressure canner instead of a water bath. (Citric acid is available wherever canning supplies are sold, or online.)

When peeling, seeding, and crushing tomatoes (which I do by squeezing the tomato flesh in my fist), do it over a colander set over a bowl. You will get lots of beautiful light tomato water. You can also remove the skin and seeds by running the tomatoes through an Italian tomato press or a large food mill.

Sometimes with canned crushed tomatoes, I find the pulp has separated from the juice. This is caused by an enzyme in the tomato that activates when the tomato is exposed to air, either by peeling, cutting, or crushing. The enzyme breaks down pectin, and the solids and liquids separate. The sooner those peeled, cut, or crushed tomatoes hit the heat the better, as heat stops the enzymatic action. Still, it happens. I just flip over the jars after they have sealed and let them cool upside down. This usually remixes the pulp and liquids, but if it doesn't, don't worry. The pulp and juice will remix when you are cooking. Sometimes some of the puree will be pressed out of the jars during processing, or even dribble out a bit after you remove the boiling jars from the water. As long as your seals are tight by the time the jars are completely cool, it's okay.

You probably won't encounter much separation with raw-pack tomatoes. But there will be some mighty compression of the fruit, especially when processing at high altitude. The tomatoes may look washed out and fill only three-fourths of the jar, but they are fine.

I add salt for flavor, but you don't have to. You could put in dried oregano if you'd like. Since the herb is dehydrated, there is no fear of spoilers hitching a ride into your jar.

Do not add onion and garlic to crushed tomatoes because the addition of low-acid vegetables could alter the overall acidity in your jar. I recommend you put up tomatoes plain, then add them to your onions and carrots or whatever and make your sauce fresh.

knife and peel it off. The skins will come off easily. Cut the tomato in half pole to pole and remove the stem. Push the seeds and seed jell out with your thumb. Crush the tomato over a pot with your hands (a few chunks are okay) or you can grind the peeled and seeded tomatoes in a food processor. All the juice accumulated in the bowl can be added to the canning jars or saved for other uses (see Tomato Water, page 336).

Transfer the crushed tomatoes to a large saucepan and bring to a gentle boil over medium-low heat. Boil gently for 5 minutes. The tomatoes may get a bit foamy on top. It's okay.

Have ready 4 clean pint jars and bands, and new lids that have been simmered in hot water to soften the rubberized flange. Place ½ teaspoon salt (if using) and ¼ teaspoon citric acid in each jar. Ladle in the hot tomatoes leaving ½ inch of headroom. With a butter knife, free any air bubbles caught in the jar. Wipe the rims, place on the lids, and screw on the bands fingertip tight.

Process the jars in a water bath (see page 375) for 35 minutes for pints or 45 minutes for 2 quarts. Be sure to make altitude adjustments when preserving (see page 389).

Tomato Ketchup

Homemade ketchup has three basic elements: onion, tomato, and a combination of vinegar and spices. You can alter the quantities or types of spices, but the onion/tomato/vinegar ratio must remain the same. This recipe is adapted from one tested by the Michigan State University Extension. **MAKES 2 HALF-PINTS**

¼ teaspoon hot pepper flakes

¼ teaspoon whole cloves

1-inch piece of cinnamon stick, crushed

¼ teaspoon ground allspice

1 teaspoon celery seed

6 tablespoons white distilled vinegar (5% acidity)

5 cups Canned Crushed Tomatoes (page 328) or fresh or Raw-Pack Tomatoes (page 328) that have been pushed through a food mill to remove skin and seeds

6 tablespoons chopped onion

2 tablespoons sugar

½ teaspoon pickling salt

In a spice bag or a square of cheesecloth, combine the pepper flakes, whole cloves, cinnamon, allspice, and celery seed. Pour the vinegar into a small saucepan and add the spice bag. Bring the vinegar to a boil over medium-high heat, then cover and remove from the heat.

Pour the tomatoes and onion into a large heavy-bottomed pot. Bring to a boil over medium heat. Reduce the heat to medium-low and gently boil uncovered for 20 minutes, stirring frequently to be sure the tomatoes don't scorch. At this point, for a smooth product, run the tomato mixture through a food mill or blend with a regular blender or an immersion blender.

Remove the spice bag from the vinegar and pour the vinegar into the tomato mixture. Add the sugar and salt. Combine well and continue to boil gently for 45 minutes, until the tomato mixture is thick enough to spoon but runny enough to pour—you will have about 2 cups.

Have ready 2 clean half-pint jars and bands, and new lids that have been simmered in hot water to soften the rubberized flange. Pour the ketchup into the jars leaving ⅛ inch of headroom. Use a butter knife to loosen any air bubbles in the jar. Wipe the rims, place on the lids, and screw on the bands fingertip tight.

Process the jars in a water bath (see page 375) for 15 minutes for both half-pints or 1 pint. Be sure to make altitude adjustments when preserving (see page 389).

Tomato Paste

In Le Marche, where my father's family is from, tomato paste is used sparingly in winter recipes, to "stain" a pasta dish, or to add richness and flavor to a meat sauce or stew. Beyond salt, this paste is unseasoned. However, you can add dried oregano, black pepper, bay leaf, and/or garlic cloves to the tomato paste if you'd like; just remember to remove the garlic cloves before processing. The processing time may seem long relative to the size of the jar, but that is due to the density of the paste. Plum tomatoes are best here because they are less juicy than slicers. I used the Ball Complete Book of Home Preserving *for processing times.* MAKES 1 CUP/4 QUARTER PINTS

> **8 cups Canned Crushed Tomatoes (page 328) or fresh or Raw-Pack Tomatoes (page 328) that have been pushed through a food mill to remove skin and seeds**
>
> **⅛ teaspoon citric acid per jar**
>
> **¼ teaspoon pickling salt per jar (optional)**

Pour the tomato puree into a large heavy-bottomed pot. Bring to a boil over medium heat, then reduce the heat to low and simmer until the tomatoes round in a spoon and there is no liquid left (the puree should come down to 1 cup paste), 3 to 3½ hours. Stir often, making sure the tomatoes at the bottom of the

pot do not scorch. As the tomatoes reduce, you will need to reduce the temperature more and more. If you reduce the pot size as you go, you will decrease the chance of scorching the paste.

Have ready 4 clean quarter-pint jars (see Note) and bands, and new lids that have been simmered in hot water to soften the rubberized flange. Place ⅛ teaspoon citric acid and ¼ teaspoon salt (if using) in each jar.

Spoon the tomato paste into the jars, leaving ½ inch of headroom. Tap the jars against your countertop to pack the paste. Check for air bubbles and slide the blade of a butter knife into the jar to release them. Wipe the rims, place on the lids, and screw on the bands fingertip tight.

Process the jars in a water bath (see page 375) for 45 minutes. Be sure to make altitude adjustments when preserving (see page 389).

Note: You can use 2 half-pint jars, but since you will probably only use a tablespoon or two of paste for any given recipe, you may find the smaller jars are more useful. If you want to process half-pints, add ¼ teaspoon citric acid and ½ teaspoon salt to each jar. They process for the same amount of time as the quarter-pints.

Dried Tomatoes

Dried tomatoes add a subtle but deep flavor to stews and soups. You can also grind dried tomatoes into a pesto (with olive oil, garlic, pine nuts, and salt) or submerge dried tomatoes in oil, but you must keep them in the fridge, where they will hold for 10 days (often longer). There is no USDA data for home pressure canning or water bath canning dried tomatoes in oil. MAKES ½ POUND

14 pounds San Marzano or plum tomatoes

½ teaspoon citric acid

2 quarts water

To prepare the tomatoes, wash, core, and cut pole to pole in slices about ½ inch thick. Remove the seeds and seed jell. In a bowl, combine the citric acid and water. Soak the tomato slices in the water for 10 minutes. Remove and drain.

Place the tomato slices in the trays of a food dehydrator (or see page 385 for instructions on oven-drying). Do not pack them tightly. Set your dryer to 135°F. The tomatoes should take 8 to 12 hours, until they are crisp. See "How to Dry" (page 385) for information on "conditioning" the dried tomatoes. Keep the dried tomatoes in jars in the pantry or in the refrigerator. Or cover them in olive oil and store in the refrigerator for up to 10 days.

Eggs Poached in Tomatoes

The trick to this delightful recipe is to take the eggs off the heat as soon as the whites are set because this dish is really splendid when the yolks are soft and runny. Serve with hunks of toasted Italian bread rubbed with a raw garlic clove and sprinkled with olive oil and salt. When I want to serve this to company and make it a little fancier, I make it in individual ramekins. I ladle the sauce into the ramekins, crack one or two eggs into each, and cover with foil. I cook the ramekins in a water bath (a large shallow pan with boiling water to come halfway up the sides of the ramekins) and cook over low heat until the whites are set. SERVES 2

2 tablespoons olive oil

½ cup chopped onion

2 garlic cloves, minced

2 cups Canned Crushed Tomatoes (page 328) or Raw-Pack Tomatoes (page 328) that have been pushed through a food mill to remove skin and seeds

1 tablespoon unsalted butter

Salt and freshly ground black pepper

4 large eggs

2 tablespoons minced flat-leaf parsley

In a medium saucepan, heat the oil over medium heat. Add the onion and garlic and cook until the onion is translucent, about 5 minutes. Add the tomato puree and cook, boiling gently, until the sauce is reduced by about one-third, about 15 minutes. Add the butter and salt to taste.

Gently crack the eggs into the sauce, reduce the heat a bit so the sauce stays at a hot simmer, and cover. It should only take 4 or 5 minutes for the whites to cook. Add a bit of salt to the eggs and black pepper to taste. Garnish with parsley and serve.

Dad's Marinara Sauce

This is the best marinara sauce: It has a soft consistency, is naturally sweet, and foolproof. Plus it only takes about 30 minutes to make. The sauce freezes well (see "How to Freeze Foods," page 382).
MAKES 4 CUPS

¼ cup olive oil

2 medium onions, chopped

2 medium carrots, chopped

2 large garlic cloves, chopped

4 cups Canned Crushed Tomatoes (page 328) or Raw-Pack Tomatoes (page 328) that have been pushed through a food mill to remove skin and seeds

1 tablespoon chopped fresh basil

1 teaspoon dried oregano

Salt and freshly ground black pepper

4 tablespoons (½ stick) unsalted butter

In a large saucepan, heat the oil over medium heat. Add the onions, carrots, and garlic. Cook until the vegetables are soft, about 10 minutes. Add the tomato puree and cook for 15 minutes, or until the sauce is bubbling. Do not overboil or the sauce will get too thick. Turn down the heat if you have to.

Push the sauce through a food mill or puree the vegetables in a blender or with an immersion blender.

Return the sauce to the heat, add the basil and oregano, and season with salt and pepper to taste. Cook until the herbs become fragrant, another 15 minutes. Add the butter, stir until it is melted, and serve.

Tomato Aspic

I make tomato aspic with marinara sauce but you can also make it with gazpacho or just fresh tomato puree flavored like a Bloody Mary (minus the booze). It is a great summer dish. Use 1¼ teaspoons powdered gelatin per cup of tomato product. I make ½-cup ramekins of this aspic, garnish it with homemade mayonnaise (page 365), and serve it with bruschetta or with boiled shrimp placed in the bottom of each ramekin or on the side. You can double the recipe and make the aspic in a ring mold, too. **SERVES 4**

1 teaspoon olive oil

2½ teaspoons unflavored powdered gelatin (1 envelope)

2 tablespoons cool water

2 tablespoons hot tap water

2 cups Dad's Marinara Sauce (opposite)

Grease four ½-cup ramekins with the oil.

Sprinkle the gelatin over the cool water in a small bowl and let soften, and then add the hot water to dissolve, stirring constantly. The gelatin has to be thoroughly dissolved before you add the sauce.

Pour the marinara into the bowl with the gelatin and whisk together well. Pour the mixture into the ramekins and refrigerate until firm, 3 to 4 hours.

To loosen the aspic, place the bottom of the ramekins in a skillet of hot water for a few seconds, minding it so that it doesn't melt. Return the aspic to the fridge for a few minutes to reset the edges, then flip over onto a plate, tap the bottom of the ramekin, and the aspic will slip out.

Lasagna with Acorn Squash and Marinara Sauce

Since lasagna is time-consuming, I usually make two and freeze one. Use this recipe to make a meat lasagna by layering Bolognese sauce and besciamella (page 42). You can use sliced grilled zucchini or eggplant instead of the squash, or forfeit the vegetable altogether. **MAKES ONE 9 × 9 × 2-INCH LASAGNA, 6 SERVINGS**

1 acorn squash (about 3 pounds)

3 large eggs

8 tablespoons grated Parmesan cheese

Salt and freshly ground black pepper

1 pound ricotta cheese (for homemade, page 367)

2 tablespoons finely chopped flat-leaf parsley

¼ teaspoon grated nutmeg

8 cups Dad's Marinara Sauce (opposite), warmed

6 sheets (9 × 9-inch) no-boil lasagna (12 no-boil lasagna noodles)

Preheat the oven to 500°F.

Halve the squash lengthwise and remove the seeds. Place on a baking sheet cut side down and bake until soft, about 40 minutes. Leave the oven on but reduce the temperature to 400°F.

Peel the squash and pass the flesh through a ricer. (Alternatively, blend the squash in the food processor for a minute to get it started, but do not blend until smooth or the squash will be too wet. Then finish off the mashing by hand with a fork or potato masher.) Place the squash in a bowl and add 1 of the eggs, 2 tablespoons of the Parmesan, and salt and pepper to taste.

In another bowl, combine the ricotta, remaining 2 eggs, 3 tablespoons of the Parmesan, the parsley, nutmeg, and salt and pepper to taste.

Pour about 1 cup of marinara sauce in the bottom of the 9 × 9 × 2-inch baking pan. Make layers in this order: 1 sheet of pasta, ⅓ cup squash, about 1 cup sauce; then 1 sheet pasta, about ⅓ cup ricotta, 1 cup sauce. Continue with this sequence until you have reached the top of the pan, about 6 layers. Don't press down on the lasagna sheets. Finish with the remaining sauce and then sprinkle 3 tablespoons of Parmesan on top the lasagna.

Cover with foil and bake for about 40 minutes, until the lasagna is bubbling. Allow the lasagna to rest about 5 minutes before cutting.

Beef Stewed with Garlic and Tomatoes

In this very rich and succulent stew, the acid in the tomatoes breaks down the beef, lending tremendous flavor. I love this dish because you assemble it, disappear for a couple of hours, and poof! It's done.

SERVES 6

> 3 pounds beef, such as London broil or tri-tip, fat mostly removed
>
> Salt and freshly ground black pepper
>
> 4 tablespoons olive oil
>
> 4 cups Canned Crushed Tomatoes (page 328) or Raw-Pack Tomatoes (page 328) that have been pushed through a food mill to remove skin and seeds
>
> 2 bulbs garlic, cloves separated and peeled
>
> 2 teaspoons dried oregano
>
> ⅓ cup minced flat-leaf parsley, plus 2 tablespoons for garnish
>
> 2 tablespoons unsalted butter
>
> Italian bread, for serving

Preheat the oven to 300°F.

Season the beef with salt and pepper. Cut the meat into a few large pieces. In a large Dutch oven, heat the oil over high heat. Add the meat and cook, turning often, until the meat is browned all over, about 10 minutes.

Add the tomato puree, garlic, oregano, and parsley. Cover the pot and place in the oven. Bake for 3 hours and then check the meat. It's done when it can be torn easily with the tines of a fork. The sauce will have cooked way down. Depending on the cut, the meat can take up to another hour to completely surrender.

Check the seasoning, swirl the butter into the tomato sauce, and serve the meat on a platter garnished with chopped parsley and a loaf of Italian bread.

HALIBUT
POACHED IN
TOMATO WATER

TOMATO WATER

Whenever you peel, cut, and seed tomatoes, do so over a colander placed over a bowl to catch the flavorful juice. A pound of tomatoes, especially juicy ones, will yield about ½ cup of tomato water. This is great stuff to add to your canned tomatoes, but also to use for cooking thin pasta (page 392), as a poaching liquid for fish, like halibut (below), or to make cocktails, like Bloody Marys.

After collecting the juice in a bowl, transfer to a sterilized quart jar. Note that the water will likely separate. There will be a fine red pulp and yellowish water. You can use just the yellowish water—it has great flavor—or shake the jar up and your dishes will have little flecks of the red tomato throughout.

Halibut Poached in Tomato Water

This is a perfect luncheon dish, wonderful hot, but also great served at room temperature with a dollop of homemade mayonnaise (page 365). **SERVES 4**

> Salt and freshly ground black pepper
> 1¼ pounds halibut fillets, about 2 inches thick
> 1 quart Tomato Water (above), lightly salted
> ¼ cup fresh basil chiffonade (to chiffonade, see Note, page 315)

Lightly salt the fish. Place the fish in a medium sauté pan with a fitted top. Add the tomato water: it should come halfway up the fish. Bring the tomato water to a gentle boil over medium heat. Cover and gently poach the fish, until it flakes easily, 9 to 12 minutes. Cut the fish into 4 portions.

Remove the fish and set aside. Increase the heat to high and cook to reduce the tomato water by about half. Pour the tomato water into the bottom of 4 shallow bowls, place a fish fillet on top, and add some freshly ground black pepper. Garnish with the basil.

Tomato Water Martini

Midway between my cabin in Colorado and the airport in Denver is Kelly Liken restaurant. I love to stop there for a good dinner and a tomato martini. Kelly macerates chopped fresh tomatoes, jalapeño peppers, garlic, and salt for at least 30 minutes, and then presses their combined juices through cheesecloth and adds the juice to a vodka martini. This recipe is an adaptation using tomato water left over from canning. **MAKES 2 COCKTAILS**

> 5 ounces Tomato Water (left)
> ¼ teaspoon minced jalapeño pepper
> 1 small garlic clove, minced
> Pinch of salt
> 5 ounces vodka
> 1½ ounces dry vermouth

Combine the tomato water, jalapeño, garlic, and salt and let steep for 30 minutes. Strain.

In a cocktail shaker, combine the tomato water, vodka, and vermouth and fill with ice. Shake vigorously and strain into chilled martini glasses.

TOMATO WATER MARTINI

TROUT

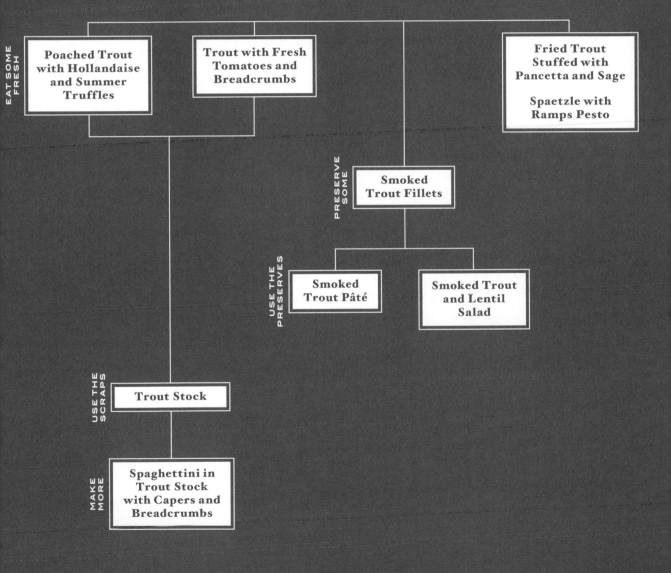

EAT SOME FRESH

Poached Trout with Hollandaise and Summer Truffles

Trout with Fresh Tomatoes and Breadcrumbs

Fried Trout Stuffed with Pancetta and Sage

Spaetzle with Ramps Pesto

PRESERVE SOME

Smoked Trout Fillets

USE THE PRESERVES

Smoked Trout Pâté

Smoked Trout and Lentil Salad

USE THE SCRAPS

Trout Stock

MAKE MORE

Spaghettini in Trout Stock with Capers and Breadcrumbs

Poached Trout with Hollandaise and Summer Truffles

This is a special-occasion dish, but you can dress it down with 1 pound of sautéed white button mushrooms or chanterelles in place of the truffles. I use canned summer truffle peelings from D'Artagnan in this recipe. They are woodsy and nutty tasting. **Save the trout heads and bones to make Trout Stock (page 344).** SERVES 4

4 to 6 large lettuce leaves (depending on whether you are cooking 1 fish or 2)

One 4-pound or two 2-pound whole cleaned trout, head(s) on

1 large bunch mint, dill, tarragon, parsley, or a combination, with the stems on

Salt and freshly ground black pepper

2 cups dry white wine

2 cups water

HOLLANDAISE

1½ tablespoons fresh lemon juice

3 large egg yolks

¼ cup boiling water

8 tablespoons (1 stick) unsalted butter, melted

Salt

½ cup summer truffle peelings (*Tuber aestivum*) or thin sliced burgundy truffles (*Tuber uncinatum*)

Freshly ground black pepper

Preheat the oven to 350°F.

Bring a large pot of water to a boil. Add the lettuce leaves and blanch to soften, about 30 seconds. Remove and drain.

Stuff the fish with the herbs, using the hard stems to secure them inside. Season the fish with salt and pepper to taste.

POACHED FILLETS, READY FOR SAUCE

Pour the wine and water into a 9 × 13-inch baking pan. Place the pan over medium heat on top of the stove. Bring the wine and water almost to a boil, a few minutes. (You preheat the liquid in order to speed up the cooking in the oven, and so avoid overcooking the fish.) Turn off the heat and place the fish in the pan. The liquid should come about one-third up the fish's side. Depending on how round the trout is, you may need less or more liquid; adjust the liquid. Cover the fish with the lettuce leaves (parchment paper or foil will also do).

Place the fish in the oven and bake, until the skin pulls away from the flesh easily, about 30 minutes for the 4 pound trout, 20 minutes for the 2 pounders.

Remove the fish from the pan and as soon as you can handle it, remove the skin and take the fillets off the bone. Place on a platter.

For the hollandaise: In a small saucepan, warm the lemon juice over low heat—do not boil. Fill the bottom chamber of a double boiler with water and bring to a boil over medium heat. Reduce the heat to low and add the egg yolks to the upper chamber and whisk. Add 1 tablespoon of the boiling water (I retrieve it from the double boiler) to the yolks and whisk to combine. Do this until you have added a total of 4 tablespoons boiling water to the egg yolks. Then whisk vigorously until the eggs thicken to about the consistency of a zabaglione or egg custard sauce. Whisk in the warm lemon juice to combine. Remove the eggs from the heat and slowly add the melted butter, whisking all the while, until the sauce is thick and shiny, just a minute or two. Add salt to taste.

Pour the hollandaise sauce over the fish. Add the truffle peelings and garnish with pepper to taste. Serve promptly because the hollandaise will congeal if left to cool.

Trout with Fresh Tomatoes and Breadcrumbs

This recipe has typical Italian flavors: wine, herbs, garlic, and olive oil. **Save the trout heads and bones for Trout Stock (page 344).** SERVES 4

- 2 tablespoons olive oil
- 2 whole butterflied trout (2 pounds each)
- ½ cup minced fresh herbs, such as parsley, thyme, or chives
- 2 tablespoons chopped garlic
- 2 tablespoons fresh lemon juice
- Salt and freshly ground black pepper
- 1 cup white wine
- 1½ cups breadcrumbs (for homemade, page 362)
- 2 cups chopped fresh tomatoes
- Extra virgin olive oil

Preheat the broiler.

Rub the olive oil in the bottom of a large baking pan or skillet. Place the trout in the pan. Sprinkle the herbs and garlic over the trout. Sprinkle with lemon juice, and salt and pepper to taste. Add the wine to the pan and place about 6 inches under the broiler. Broil for 5 minutes, then sprinkle the breadcrumbs on top of the fish and continue broiling 2 to 5 more minutes, until the breadcrumbs are browned and the flesh is opaque.

Garnish the trout with the chopped tomatoes and a drizzle of extra virgin olive oil. Check the seasoning, and serve promptly.

FRIED TROUT
STUFFED
WITH
PANCETTA
AND SAGE

VARIATION: You can add the tomatoes to the fish before broiling. It will take a minute or two longer for the fish to cook.

Fried Trout Stuffed with Pancetta and Sage

This is my favorite way to fry "brookies," or little trout. You can do the same with small whiting, too, but don't try this with a large trout: The skin tends to get too brown before the flesh is cooked through inside. **Save the heads and bones for stock. They won't make much, but who cares? A pint of Trout Stock (page 344) is a blessing.** *I serve this dish with Spaetzle with Ramps Pesto (recipe follows).*

SERVES 4

> 4 small cleaned trout (½ pound each), heads removed
>
> Salt and freshly ground black pepper
>
> 12 very thin slices pancetta
>
> 8 large fresh sage leaves
>
> Flour, for dredging (I prefer Wondra)
>
> Neutral oil, such as safflower, for frying
>
> 1 lemon, cut into quarters

Pat the trout dry. Salt and pepper the trout inside. Roll up 3 slices of pancetta and insert into the trout cavity. Insert 2 big sage leaves into each cavity, too.

Tie the fish with kitchen twine as you would a roast: Cut a piece of twine about 8 inches long for each fish. Tie a small loop at one end of the twine. Wrap the twine once around the body of a trout near its head (or where its head was). Pass the end of the twine through the loop and pull it tight. Pull the twine along the spine and hold it in place a few inches down the fish with one hand. Wrap the twine around the fish's body with the other hand, and tie it off at the top (or

continue wrapping, depending on the size of the fish). Repeat with the remaining trout.

Dredge the fish in flour, and salt and pepper the exterior of the fish. Pour ½ inch of oil into a large nonstick skillet and heat until very hot. Add a dash of flour to the hot oil. If it pops, then the oil is hot enough. Add the fish. Fry for a few minutes on each side until golden brown. Tip the skillet to make sure hot oil gets into the cavity and fries the inside of the fish as well.

Drain the fish on paper towels or brown paper bags. Cut off the twine and serve the fish with lemon quarters.

SPAETZLE WITH RAMPS PESTO

SERVES 4

Ramps are wild onions with a garlicky flavor that come in season in early spring. Some people make raw ramps pesto, but I think it is too grassy and intense. If you cook the ramps you'll get the pungent flavor without the sharpness. To make spaetzle, all you need is a colander, though a spaetzle maker is ideal. You can also forgo the ramps and simply toss the cooked spaetzle with butter, salt, and pepper.

> RAMPS PESTO
>
> 2 tablespoons olive oil
>
> 1 heaping cup chopped ramps, bulbs and leaves
>
> ½ cup pine nuts
>
> 3 tablespoons chicken stock (for homemade, page 89)
>
> ½ teaspoon fresh lemon juice
>
> Salt
>
> SPAETZLE
>
> 2 cups all-purpose flour
>
> 3 large eggs, beaten
>
> ⅔ cup whole milk
>
> Salt

SPAETZLE

With a spatula, press the batter through the holes in the colander. This will produce little squiggles of pasta, which will float to the top of the water when they are done. Scoop them out with a slotted spoon and place in a bowl. (A spaetzle maker will regulate the size of the noodles. It's awesome.)

Toss the spaetzle in the pesto and check the seasoning.

Smoked Trout Fillets

Home-smoked trout is more tender than commercially smoked fish, and easy too. This process brines and smokes a trout fillet in 30 minutes. The brining stage helps undermine microbial growth in your finished product. **MAKES 1½ POUNDS**

> 1½ pounds trout fillets
>
> ½ cup pickling salt
>
> 2 cups water
>
> Flavorings (optional): pinch of cayenne pepper, 1 teaspoon paprika, ½ teaspoon garlic or onion powder, or a combination
>
> 1 tablespoon light brown sugar
>
> Freshly ground black pepper
>
> 1 tablespoon alder chips

For the ramps pesto: In a small skillet, heat 1 tablespoon of the olive oil over medium heat. Add the ramps and cook until wilted, a few minutes.

Transfer the cooked ramps to a food processor and add the pine nuts, chicken stock, lemon juice, salt to taste, and remaining 1 tablespoon olive oil. Pulse to grind to the consistency of a pesto. This pesto can be frozen. (See "How to Freeze Foods," page 382.)

For the spaetzle: In a bowl, whisk together the flour and eggs, then slowly add the milk, whisking all the while. Add salt to taste.

Bring a large pot of salted water to a boil over high heat. Pour the batter into a colander (not a sieve) and hold it over the boiling water.

Remove any small bones from the trout with tweezers.

Make the brine: In a large bowl, dissolve the salt in the water. If you'd like, add the optional flavorings. Place the fish in the brine and let rest for 15 minutes, then rinse it and dry it very well. Pat on the brown sugar and season with the black pepper.

Prepare your stovetop smoker (see "How to Smoke Indoors," page 384) with the wood chips. Lay the trout fillets on the rack, close the smoker, and place over a medium-high to high heat. Smoke the trout for 15 minutes. Don't oversmoke the fillets or they will be dry or even burn. Remove from the heat and let the fish rest in the smoker while it comes down in temperature. I usually take it out after about 40 minutes. (For how to do this in your oven, see page 384.)

Wrap in paper towels and parchment or wax paper so moisture does not settle on the surface. Place in a plastic container or wrap in foil. Holds in the refrigerator for 10 days.

SMOKED TROUT FILLETS

Smoked Trout and Lentil Salad

This salad is excellent as part of an antipasto or as a lunch or dinner salad. You add all sorts of toppings. I use red onion here, but you can use a cup of chopped scallions, shallots, or sautéed garlic scapes; minced radish; a tablespoon of horseradish (for homemade, page 364) or skordalia (for homemade, page 368); herbs of all sorts; or a handful of arugula or watercress. Sometimes I substitute boiled potatoes for the lentils, in which case, I use mustard vinaigrette (for homemade, page 368), but you could make any potato salad in your repertoire, and just garnish with the smoked trout. Boom. **SERVES 4**

> ¾ cup brown lentils
>
> 3 cups water
>
> ½ cup minced red onion
>
> 4 tablespoons extra virgin olive oil
>
> 3 to 4 tablespoons fresh lemon juice or white wine vinegar
>
> Salt and freshly ground black pepper
>
> 1 heaping cup smoked trout (for homemade, opposite)
>
> 2 tablespoons minced flat-leaf parsley

In a medium saucepan, combine the lentils and water and bring to a boil over high heat. Reduce the heat to medium-low and gently boil the lentils until al dente, about 10 minutes. Do not boil lentils rapidly or half will be cooked right and the other half will be mucky and their skins will separate. Drain the lentils and pour them into a serving bowl.

Add the red onion and toss gently. Add the olive oil, lemon juice, and salt and pepper to taste, and toss gently. Add the smoked trout and combine carefully so that the trout doesn't break up too much. Garnish with the parsley.

Smoked Trout Pâté

This is one of my go-to hors d'oeuvres. It is wonderful spread on black bread, sliced boiled potatoes, sliced cucumbers, or as a replacement for the salmon filling in fried zucchini flowers (page 297). **MAKES ABOUT 1 CUP**

- 1 cup shredded smoked trout (for homemade, page 342)
- ¼ cup sour cream or crème fraîche (for homemade, page 362)
- 2 tablespoons minced shallots
- 1 teaspoon horseradish (for homemade, page 364) or more to taste
- 1 teaspoon fresh lemon juice
- Salt and freshly ground black pepper

In a small bowl, mash together the trout, sour cream, shallots, horseradish, lemon juice, and salt and pepper to taste to make a paste. If you are not going to eat it right away, cover the pâté with plastic wrap and refrigerate so it doesn't dry out.

Trout Stock

This is an aromatic stock that you can refrigerate or freeze. There is no USDA data for canning freshwater fish stock, but there is data for processing trout, so that's the timing used in this recipe. I use this stock to cook spaghettini, as a base for fish soup, in place of the water in Mussels Cooked in Wine and Herbs (page 205), and as a liquid when cooking other fish dishes. **MAKES 3 PINTS**

- Heads, bones, tails, and skin from about 2 pounds trout
- 3 cups chopped fennel stalks and leaves or leeks (optional)
- 3 celery ribs, cut into big pieces
- ½ large onion (with the peel, if you like)

TROUT STOCK

A few sprigs of flat-leaf parsley

1 bay leaf

8 cups water

In a large soup pot, combine the trout bones and trimmings, fennel (if using), celery, onion, parsley, bay leaf, and water and bring to a boil over medium-high heat. Reduce the heat to low, cover, and boil gently until the stock is aromatic, 1 to 2 hours. If you used fennel tops, the stock will be pale green. Strain the stock.

Transfer the stock to pint jars and refrigerate or freeze (see the technique for making stocks, page 390).

For shelf-stable stock, pressure can it. Have ready 3 clean pint jars and bands, and new lids that have been simmered in hot water to soften the rubberized flange. Pour the hot stock into the jars leaving 1 inch of headroom.

Process the jars in a pressure canner at 10/11 psi for 1 hour 40 minutes. (See "How to Pressure Can," page 379.) Be sure to make altitude adjustments when preserving (see page 389).

Spaghettini in Trout Stock with Capers and Breadcrumbs

This recipe is extremely simple—perfect for a last-minute supper—yet elegant enough to serve at a dinner party. Using homemade trout stock and homemade breadcrumbs make the difference here, so really try to avoid the store-bought stuff. Sometimes I garnish this dish with chopped anchovies, smoked mussels, or tuna (preferably home-canned, but Italian tuna packed in oil and drained is very good).

SERVES 4

¾ pound spaghettini

6 cups Trout Stock (opposite)

1½ cups breadcrumbs (for homemade, page 362)

3 tablespoons capers (see Note)

2 tablespoons minced garlic

3 tablespoons minced flat-leaf parsley

Salt and freshly ground black pepper

Extra virgin olive oil

¼ cup grated Parmesan cheese

Cook the pasta in the stock according to the technique on page 392. When the pasta has absorbed the stock, take it off the heat.

In the meantime, toast the breadcrumbs: heat a large skillet over high heat. Spread the breadcrumbs in the skillet and toast, flipping occasionally, until the breadcrumbs are brown, a minute or two.

Toss the breadcrumbs, capers, garlic, parsley, and salt and pepper to taste into the pot with the cooked pasta. Transfer to a serving platter, add a good drench of extra virgin olive oil, and garnish with the Parmesan. (This pasta dish is not overly wet with sauce. Its flavor derives from cooking the pasta in the fish stock.)

Note: I prefer salt-packed capers. To use them in this recipe, soak them in water for 10 minutes to reduce the saltiness. Drain and blot them dry on paper towels.

WATERMELONS

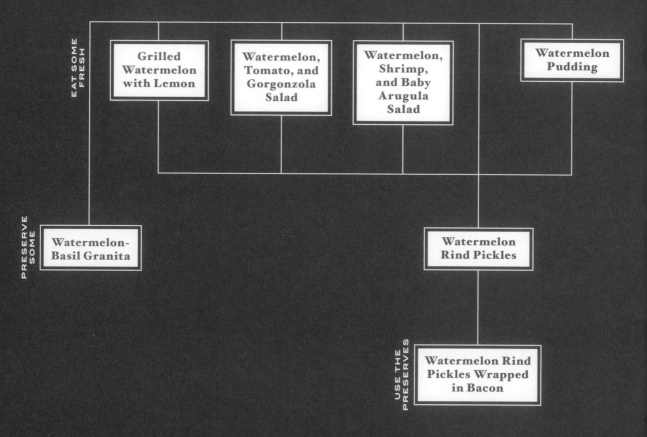

EAT SOME FRESH

Grilled Watermelon with Lemon

Watermelon, Tomato, and Gorgonzola Salad

Watermelon, Shrimp, and Baby Arugula Salad

Watermelon Pudding

PRESERVE SOME

Watermelon-Basil Granita

Watermelon Rind Pickles

USE THE PRESERVES

Watermelon Rind Pickles Wrapped in Bacon

Grilled Watermelon with Lemon

I remember running around on the lawn in a frenzy of watermelon-induced madness, just letting my face get totally saturated with watermelon juice and spitting seeds at the gods. Now, I eat watermelon with a knife and fork and salt, which is also very nice. Grilled watermelon is delicious served with grilled meats and fish. My friend Susan Murrmann dunks her watermelon in teriyaki sauce before grilling, which is surprisingly tasty. But I like it simple or, at most, with crumbled feta on top. **Save the rind to make Watermelon Rind Pickles (page 350).** SERVES 4

    Salt and freshly ground black pepper
    4 slices (2 inches thick) watermelon, rind
        removed
    Olive oil, for drizzling
    4 lemon wedges

Preheat a grill to medium-high.

Salt the watermelon and let it rest on a rack for about 10 minutes. Rinse off the salt and pat dry.

Drizzle olive oil all over the watermelon. Grill for a few minutes on each side, and garnish with black pepper. Serve with lemon wedges.

Watermelon, Shrimp, and Baby Arugula Salad

I use a melon baller to scoop out the watermelon—it makes a perfect bite size. **Save the rind to make Watermelon Rind Pickles (page 350). Save the watermelon juice for Watermelon-Basil Granita (page 349) or just drink it on its own. Save the shrimp shells for Shrimp Shell Sauce (page 317).** SERVES 4

    1 pound shell-on shrimp
    Juice of ½ lemon
    ¼ cup mayonnaise (page 365)
    2 cups watermelon cubes
    3 cups baby arugula
    Salt and freshly ground black pepper

Bring a large pot of salted water to a boil. Add the shrimp. Remove them when the shrimp turn pink, about the time the water starts to boil again. Drain and remove the shells. Cut the shrimp into bite-size pieces. Place the shrimp in a large bowl, toss with the lemon juice, and chill.

Toss the chilled shrimp with the mayonnaise. Gently toss in the watermelon and arugula. Add salt and pepper to taste.

Watermelon, Tomato, and Gorgonzola Salad

The combination of watermelon and tomato, which was on every restaurant menu a decade ago, is particularly good. You can substitute feta for the Gorgonzola if you'd like, but keep in mind that some fetas are quite salty. Cut the watermelon over a bowl to capture the watermelon juice. Drink it on its own or save for Watermelon-Basil Granita (page 349). **Save the rind to make Watermelon Rind Pickles (page 350).** SERVES 4

    1⅓ cups 1-inch chunks of tomato
    1⅓ cups seeded 1-inch chunks of watermelon
        (about 1⅓ pounds watermelon on the rind)
    ½ cup crumbled Gorgonzola cheese
    ¼ cup extra virgin olive oil
    Juice of ½ lemon
    Salt and freshly ground black pepper
    2 tablespoons chopped fresh basil

WATERMELON,
TOMATO, AND
GORGONZOLA
SALAD

In a large serving bowl, gently toss together the tomatoes, watermelon, Gorgonzola, olive oil, lemon juice, and salt to taste. Garnish with pepper and the basil.

Watermelon Pudding

This is a version of a Sicilian dish called gelo di mellone. *It's a typical summer dessert in Palermo. Cut the watermelon over a bowl to capture the watermelon juice.* **Drink it on its own or save for Watermelon-Basil Granita (right). Save the rind to make Watermelon Rind Pickles (page 350).** SERVES 4

- 2 cups seeded watermelon chunks (from about 2 pounds watermelon on the rind)
- ⅓ cup cornstarch
- ½ cup sugar
- 1 tablespoon fresh lemon juice
- Whipped cream, for serving (optional)

Puree the watermelon chunks in a blender or food processor, then push through a fine-mesh sieve into a bowl.

In a medium saucepan, whisk together the cornstarch and sugar. Whisk in the watermelon juice until the cornstarch is thoroughly combined with the juice. Place over high heat and bring to a full boil, whisking all the while, and add the lemon juice. The pudding will thicken within a minute, even suddenly. Take it off the heat.

Pour the pudding into a serving bowl or 4 serving glasses (I like to serve this in cuvée champagne glasses), cover with plastic wrap, and refrigerate until the pudding is set, a few hours. Serve with sweetened whipped cream, if you'd like.

Watermelon-Basil Granita

This is the most refreshing granita and holds all summer in the freezer. The basil syrup is great stuff to have on hand to flavor fruit salads or use in cocktails, so you might want to double the recipe. It will hold in the refrigerator for a month or so. Cut the watermelon over a bowl to capture the watermelon juice. **Drink it on its own. Save the rind to make Watermelon Rind Pickles (page 350).** MAKES 1 QUART

- 1 cup water
- 1 cup loosely packed fresh basil leaves
- ¾ cup sugar
- 3 cups seeded, chopped watermelon (from about 3 pounds watermelon on the rind)
- 2 tablespoons fresh lemon juice
- ½ teaspoon salt

In a small saucepan, bring the water to a boil over medium-high heat. Put the basil in a sieve and set it in the boiling water for 30 seconds. Remove the basil and set it aside. Add the sugar to the boiling water and cook the mixture until reduced by half, about 10 minutes. Set the syrup aside to cool. Transfer the cooled syrup to a blender. (If the syrup is too stiff, just warm it up over medium heat and add a few tablespoons of water.) Add the blanched basil and puree it until it is smooth. Strain the mixture through a fine-mesh sieve and refrigerate it until you are ready to use it.

Place the watermelon in a blender or food processor and puree. Add the lemon juice, salt, and basil syrup. Combine well.

Transfer the mixture to a cold-conductive pan and prepare according to the technique for granitas on page 393.

Watermelon Rind Pickles

I thought watermelon pickles were a Southern thing, but Imogene Wolcott published a recipe for them in The New England Yankee Cookbook *in 1939, so I guess it's a watermelon thing. I like to serve them with Bollito Misto (page 115) and wrapped in bacon (right).* **MAKES 3 HALF-PINTS**

> 5½ cups water
>
> 2 tablespoons pickling salt
>
> 2 cups watermelon rind, white part only, cut into 1-inch pieces
>
> 1½ cups distilled white vinegar (5% acidity)
>
> 1½ cups sugar
>
> 1 lemon, sliced

Pour 4 cups of the water into a big bowl and add the salt. Stir to dissolve the salt. Add the watermelon rind and let rest overnight in the fridge.

The next day, in a medium saucepan, combine 1½ cups water, the vinegar, and sugar and bring to a boil over medium heat to dissolve the sugar. Reduce the heat and simmer 5 minutes. Drain the rinds. Return the rinds to the bowl, add the lemon slices, and cover with the hot vinegar solution. Let rest while you prepare the jars.

Have ready 3 clean half-pint jars and bands, and new lids that have been simmered in hot water to soften the rubberized flange. Pack the rinds and lemon slices into the jars and cover with the vinegar solution leaving ½ inch of headroom. Be sure the lemon slices are well distributed among the jars. Wipe the rims, place on the lids, and screw on the bands fingertip tight.

Process the jars in a water bath (see page 375) for 10 minutes. Be sure to make altitude adjustments when preserving (see page 389).

Watermelon Rind Pickles Wrapped in Bacon

These very American hors d'oeuvres are the perfect balance of sweet and salty, kind of suburban and totally delicious. I can imagine them served at a party in a John Updike novel. **SERVES 4**

> 5 slices bacon (for homemade, page 263)
>
> 15 pieces watermelon rind pickle

Preheat the oven to 400°F. Line a baking sheet with parchment paper or use a nonstick baking sheet.

Cut the bacon crosswise into thirds. Wrap each piece of watermelon pickle in a piece of bacon and secure with a toothpick. Place the pickles on the baking sheet and bake for about 15 minutes, or until the bacon is crispy.

WATERMELON RIND PICKLES WRAPPED IN BACON, READY FOR THE OVEN

ZUCCHINI

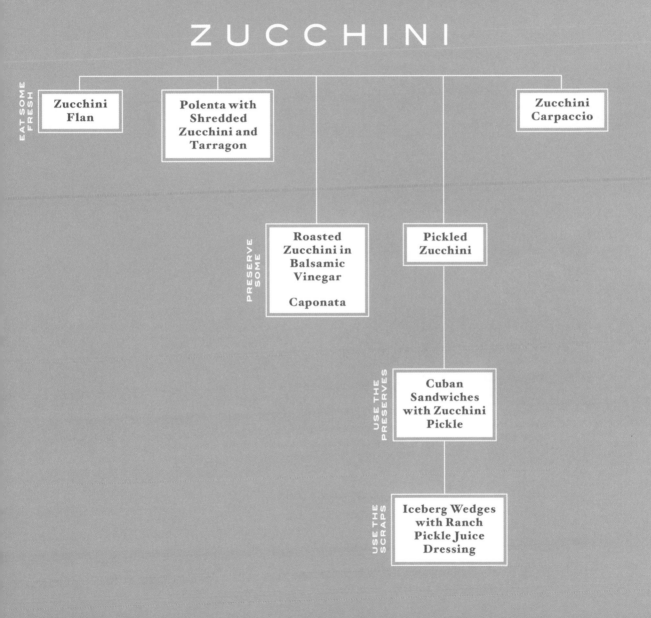

EAT SOME FRESH

Zucchini Flan

Polenta with Shredded Zucchini and Tarragon

Zucchini Carpaccio

PRESERVE SOME

Roasted Zucchini in Balsamic Vinegar

Caponata

Pickled Zucchini

USE THE PRESERVES

Cuban Sandwiches with Zucchini Pickle

USE THE SCRAPS

Iceberg Wedges with Ranch Pickle Juice Dressing

Zucchini Flowers

When choosing zucchini flowers for frying, select male flowers that are young and not flopped open: it is easier to fry a stiff-petaled flower, although you can fry open flowers, too. In the picture below, the female flower is on top, the male below. The males grow straight up on thin green stems. The females grow from the end of a baby zucchini. Females are collected with the baby zucchini attached. You only need one male per plant to keep the females happy (nature is consistent after all). The rest you can pick off and eat. Check the inside for bees and other bugs and shake them out. Don't wash zucchini flowers, because they may disintegrate. If you have reason to believe they have been recently sprayed with pesticides, let some time pass, maybe a rainfall, then pick.

Zucchini Flan

This flan is baked in individual ramekins. You can either serve them in the ramekins, or for a fancier presentation, you can line the ramekins with very thin slices of zucchini before pouring in the zucchini mixture. See the Variation, below. **Save the water from squeezing the zucchini. It is flavorful and excellent used in place of plain water in vegetable dishes. (It holds in the refrigerator for a few days.)** SERVES 6 AS A FIRST COURSE

4 cups unpeeled grated zucchini (1¼ pounds)

2 tablespoons olive oil

1½ cups minced onion

2 tablespoons chopped fresh tarragon

4 tablespoons (½ stick) unsalted butter

¼ cup all-purpose flour

1 cup whole milk

Salt and freshly ground black pepper

½ cup grated Parmesan cheese

2 large eggs, beaten

Preheat the oven to 375°F.

Place the grated zucchini in a couple of sheets of dampened cheesecloth and squeeze out the water over a bowl (I do this in 2-cup batches).

In a medium skillet, heat the oil over medium heat. Add the onion and cook until translucent, about 5 minutes. Add the zucchini and cook until it is very soft, about 10 minutes. Add the tarragon and continue cooking until all the zucchini water has cooked out and the bottom of the skillet is dry. Let the zucchini come to room temperature.

Use 1 tablespoon of the butter to grease six 1-cup ramekins.

In a small saucepan, melt the remaining 3 tablespoons butter over medium heat. Add the flour and stir well. When the flour begins to sizzle after a minute or so, whisk in the milk in a steady stream, whisking all the while. Add salt and pepper to taste. Continue to whisk as the béchamel thickens, about 3 minutes. The sauce should be about the thickness of heavy cream, maybe a bit thicker. Take off the heat and let come to room temperature.

Combine the zucchini mixture and the sauce. Stir in the Parmesan and eggs. Divide the mixture among the buttered ramekins.

Place the ramekins in a pan and fill the pan with hot water, enough to come halfway up the sides of the ramekins. Place in the oven and bake for 45 minutes, or until the flans are just golden and puffed-up looking.

VARIATION: To line the flans with zucchini, use a mandoline to slice very thin planks from a zucchini about 8 inches long and 2 inches in diameter. You will need 2 planks per ramekin. Butter the ramekins and line with the zucchini, cutting to fit the perimeter and depth of the ramekin. Add the zucchini and egg mixture and bake as described above. Once cooked, turn the flan out on a plate.

Polenta with Shredded Zucchini and Tarragon

I've been making pasta with this shredded zucchini and tarragon combo for years, but lately I've put it on pizza (just spread the vegetables and mozzarella over the dough and cook as you would regular pizza) and then my brother—who loves the recipe—tried it on polenta, which is even better. **SERVES 4**

- ¼ cup olive oil
- 2 medium onions, finely chopped
- 4 garlic cloves, minced (2 tablespoons)
- 2 medium zucchini, grated on the large holes of a box grater
- 2 tablespoons finely chopped fresh tarragon
- Salt and freshly ground black pepper

POLENTA
- 4 cups water
- 1 teaspoon salt
- 1 cup fine or coarse yellow cornmeal

- ½ cup grated Parmesan cheese

In a large skillet, heat the olive oil over medium heat. Add the onions and garlic and cook until the onions become translucent, about 5 minutes. Add the zucchini and cook the vegetables until the zucchini releases its water and the water cooks out, about 10 minutes. Add the tarragon and salt and pepper to taste.

For the polenta: In a medium saucepan, bring the 4 cups water and salt to a boil over high heat. Add the cornmeal in a thin stream, whisking all the while. Reduce the heat to low and cook, covered, for 5 minutes, or until the water is absorbed and the cornmeal has lost its raw taste.

Preheat the broiler.

Spread the polenta into a 12 × 8-inch baking pan. Let the polenta sit for 5 to 10 minutes to firm up. Spread the zucchini mixture over the top and sprinkle with the Parmesan. Place 6 inches under the broiler and broil for about 5 minutes, or until the cheese is melted.

Zucchini Carpaccio

You need firm, very fresh zucchini for this dish, which makes a lovely salad or side. **SERVES 4**

- 2 zucchini (6 to 8 inches long), stem end removed
- Extra virgin olive oil
- Lemon juice to taste
- Salt and freshly ground black pepper
- 1 small red onion, thinly sliced (see Note)
- 1 cup crumbled feta cheese (I prefer French— it's less salty)
- 2 tablespoons minced flat-leaf parsley

ZUCCHINI CARPACCIO

Shave the zucchini lengthwise on a mandoline or cut as thin as you can. You can press down hard with a vegetable peeler to get the ribbons as well. Place on a platter and add olive oil, lemon juice, and salt to taste. Toss carefully. Let the zucchini marinate for about 15 minutes but no more than 20 minutes or the dish will become soggy.

Break the onion up into rings and sprinkle over the zucchini. Sprinkle with the feta, parsley, and pepper and serve.

Note: If you used a mandoline for the zucchini, you can slice the red onion on it too, but do not slice paper thin or the onion will have a hairy mouthfeel.

Roasted Zucchini in Balsamic Vinegar

The Italians use balsamic vinegar mostly as a garnish on roasted vegetables. I make an investment in the good stuff and use it in just a few dishes, like this recipe. You can add chopped parsley between the layers of zucchini, if you'd like, and/or minced garlic. The vinegar helps preserve the zucchini, but it must be refrigerated. I often serve this as part of a room temperature vegetable platter including Caponata (opposite) and a Watermelon, Tomato, and Gorgonzola Salad (page 347). The zucchini is also wonderful in a caprese salad. **SERVES 4**

¼ cup olive oil

3 large zucchini (about 12 inches long), cut into slabs 4 to 6 inches long and ½ inch thick

Salt

About ⅓ cup balsamic vinegar

Preheat the oven to 500°F.

Rub the oil onto 2 baking sheets, preferably nonstick. Place the zucchini slices on the sheets. Do not overlap. Turn the zucchini over so that oil lightly coats both sides. Sprinkle with salt to taste. Roast for about 10 minutes, or until they begin to brown. Turn the slices over and roast for an additional 5 minutes, or until golden brown. (Alternatively, do this on the grill. Brush the zucchini with the olive oil and grill on both sides, about 10 minutes altogether.)

Place the slices in a nonreactive bowl one layer at a time, drizzling balsamic vinegar and salt between the layers. Cover and refrigerate. Holds in the refrigerator for about 10 days. Serve at room temperature.

CAPONATA

Serve this as a salad, or, for a fancier presentation, pack the caponata in ramekins and tap over a plate to release. You can add more or less capers and pine nuts in this recipe, if you like. You can also toss the caponata with 1 diced avocado, or 1 drained half-pint tuna, or 1 cup diced pear (I like Anjou best).

SERVES 4

2 tablespoons olive oil

¾ pound eggplant, peeled and finely diced

1 medium onion, finely diced

1 celery rib, finely diced

1 small tomato, coarsely chopped

2 tablespoons white wine vinegar

2 teaspoons sugar

2 tablespoons capers (see Note)

1 tablespoon pine nuts

Salt and freshly ground black pepper

2 tablespoons chopped flat-leaf parsley

In a large skillet, heat the olive oil over medium heat. Add the eggplant and cook over medium-high heat, stirring often until lightly browned, about 15 minutes.

With a slotted spoon, transfer the eggplant to a medium bowl. Add the onions to one side of the skillet and the celery to the other side. Reduce the heat, cover, and cook, stirring occasionally. When the celery is tender, in about 10 minutes, add the tomato. Mix the vegetable together, cover, and continue to cook for 10 minutes longer. Add the eggplant.

In a small saucepan, heat the vinegar and sugar together. As soon as the mixture boils, add the capers, pine nuts, and salt and pepper to taste. Simmer for 1 minute, then add to the eggplant mixture. Cook over low heat for 5 minutes. Adjust the seasoning.

Transfer to a serving bowl and garnish with the parsley.

Note: I prefer salt-packed capers. To use them in this recipe, soak them in water for 10 minutes to reduce the saltiness. Drain and blot on paper towels.

GRILLED ZUCCHINI

Pickled Zucchini

*You can use these pickles just as you would bread and butter pickles. Adding or changing the spices (mustard seed and turmeric are good) won't affect the safety of the recipe. **I always save the extra pickling liquid for Boiled Vegetable Salad with Pickling Juice (page 116) or for Ranch Pickle Juice Dressing (page 358).** The processing time for this recipe comes from the* Ball Complete Book of Home Preserving. **MAKES 2 HALF-PINTS**

½ pound zucchini, washed and sliced into thin rounds

½ cup thinly sliced onion

2 garlic cloves, peeled

½ tablespoon pickling salt

Ice cubes

½ cup white wine vinegar (5% acidity)

¼ cup sugar

¼ teaspoon caraway seeds

¼ teaspoon coriander seeds

¼ teaspoon celery seeds

In a large bowl, combine the zucchini, onion, garlic, and salt. Cover with ice cubes and let rest on the counter for 2 hours. (The ice cubes will melt. It's okay.)

In a medium pot, combine the vinegar, sugar, caraway seeds, coriander seeds, and celery seeds. Bring to a boil over medium heat. Drain the vegetables and add them to the vinegar mixture. Using tongs, make sure all the vegetables are well saturated in the pickling liquid. Bring back to a boil, and then remove from heat.

Have ready 2 clean half-pint jars and bands, and new lids that have been simmered in hot water to soften the rubberized flange. Place the zucchini mixture in the jars and cover with the pickling liquid leaving ½ inch of headroom. Make sure the spices are well distributed. Use a butter knife to release any air bubbles in the jar. Wipe the rims, place on the lids, and screw on the bands fingertip tight.

Process the jars in a water bath (see page 375) for 10 minutes. Be sure to make altitude adjustments when preserving (see page 389).

Cuban Sandwiches with Zucchini Pickle

*This recipe is adapted from one my friend Richard Ampudia used to serve in his Cafe Habana. You only need about a pound of meat to make 4 sandwiches, so you will have leftovers. Try Pork and Beans with Feta and Cilantro (page 269). It's very good. **Save the extra pickling liquid for Boiled Vegetable Salad with Pickling Juice (page 116) or for Ranch Pickle Juice Dressing (page 358).*** **MAKES 4 SANDWICHES**

4 pounds boneless pork butt

6 garlic cloves, crushed

1 green bell pepper, cut in large pieces

1 medium white onion, cut in large pieces

1 cup white wine vinegar

½ cup fresh lime juice

¼ cup grapefruit juice

¼ cup orange juice

2 tablespoons dried oregano

1½ teaspoons achiote seasoning

1½ teaspoons adobo powder

Salt and freshly ground black pepper

½ cup mayonnaise (for homemade, page 365)

¼ cup canned chipotle peppers in adobo sauce

1 loaf seedless Italian bread

¼ pound thin sliced Swiss cheese

1 half-pint Pickled Zucchini (left), drained

ICEBERG WEDGES
WITH RANCH
PICKLE JUICE
DRESSING

Score the pork fat with a sharp knife. Rub the garlic all over the pork. In a Dutch oven large enough to hold the pork, combine the bell pepper, onion, vinegar, lime juice, grapefruit juice, orange juice, oregano, achiote, adobo, and salt and black pepper to taste. Marinate the pork in the refrigerator for 12 hours, making sure you turn the meat a few times.

Preheat the oven to 400°F.

Roast the pork in its marinade, covered, for 2½ hours, or until the meat is tender and falling off the bone. Remove the pan from the oven and let cool. Remove the pork (do not discard the liquid) and shred or slice the meat.

In a food processor, blender, or with a mortar and pestle, combine the mayonnaise and chipotle peppers until it is pink in color. It should taste quite spicy.

Split the bread horizontally and toast slightly. Smear the chipotle mayonnaise on the bread. Then layer on the Swiss cheese, pickled zucchini, the shredded or sliced pork, and a little bit of the cooking juice and close the sandwich.

Heat a large skillet over low to medium heat. Place the sandwich in the hot skillet (you may need to cut the sandwich in half to fit: it's okay) and set a smaller skillet on top and press down to sear. When the bread is crispy, remove from the skillet and cut into quarters.

Iceberg Wedges with Ranch Pickle Juice Dressing

I love an iceberg lettuce salad in the summer, especially with a nice ranch pickle juice dressing. You don't have to use only zucchini pickle juice in this recipe, but if you use other pickle juices, then add the juice 1 tablespoon at a time and taste as you go, as pickle brines vary in tartness. This recipe makes enough dressing for ½ cup per person because, to me, an iceberg wedge without enough dressing is rabbit food. **SERVES 4**

> 4 large garlic cloves, peeled
> 6 tablespoons mayonnaise (for homemade, page 365)
> 6 tablespoons sour cream
> 6 tablespoons buttermilk
> 2 tablespoons strained juice from Pickled Zucchini (page 356)
> 2 tablespoons minced fresh chives or dill
> Freshly ground black pepper
> 1 large head iceberg lettuce, cut in quarters

Make a garlic paste by mashing the garlic with a garlic press, a mortar and pestle, or by scraping the garlic on your counter with the flat side of the knife.

In a small bowl, mix together the mashed garlic, mayonnaise, and sour cream. Whisk in the buttermilk. Whisk in the pickle juice. Stir in the chives or dill and black pepper. You can store the dressing in a sterilized jar in the fridge for about 1 week. (See "How to Sterlize," page 389.)

Ladle ½ cup of dressing over each wedge.

CONDIMENTS, NECESSITIES, AND LUXURIES

Asian-Style Hot Oil

Vanilla Extract

Lemon Extract

Crème Fraîche

Cured Olives

Herb Butter

Herb Syrup

Horseradish

Hot Vinegar Sauce

Mayonnaise

Mustard

Red Wine Reduction Sauce

Ricotta Cheese

Skordalia

Mustard Vinaigrette

Worcestershire Sauce

Yogurt

I STARTED MAKING HOMEMADE CONDIMENTS shortly after I got in the habit of making homemade mayo once a week. That's because every time I used a homemade condiment instead of a commercial one in a recipe, the recipe tasted better.

So now I also make my own baking extracts, mustard, horseradish, breadcrumbs, vinaigrette, verjuice, hot sauce, cocktail onions, ketchup, tomato paste, Worcestershire sauce, ginger syrup, red wine reduction sauce, and more. Dairy products like homemade yogurt, crème fraîche, and ricotta are stupid-easy to make. I don't always have them all on hand, of course. I run out of stuff, or don't get around to making olives one year. But in general I make all these things year round, and not over a marathon weekend or some other such torture, but just when I am tooling around in the kitchen anyway. I'll set some mustard seeds out to soak, or grind up yesterday's leftover baguette in the food processor to make breadcrumbs. (Most condiments can be made quickly.) Vanilla pods get dunked in a vial of vodka. A quart of milk is made into ricotta in a few minutes. Leftover red wines get reduced to a reduction, a mound of minced garlic left over from cooking a big dinner party makes skordalia, which holds in the fridge for a week and doesn't lose its oomph. Leftover herbs get minced into compound butters. These little preparations offer flavors that often hold a recipe together. They make my food more delicious, and I benefit from all the other perks of doing it myself: value, quality, local sourcing, and beating the system. So even though it is very easy to just buy a jar of horseradish or mayo, at the end of the day, it's just not worth it.

A COLLECTION OF CONDIMENTS

Asian-Style Hot Oil

I make an Asian hot sauce to serve with Stewed Duck (page 258) and Tuna Tartare with Potatoes (page 301). I learned how to infuse oils of this kind from Mark Bittman, who is a master at making things easy. **MAKES ONE 8-OUNCE BOTTLE**

> 1 cup neutral oil, such as safflower
> 1 tablespoon hot pepper flakes
> 1 teaspoon Szechuan peppers
> One 2-inch cinnamon stick
> 1 teaspoon sesame seeds
> 2 whole star anise

In a small pot, combine the oil, pepper flakes, Szechuan pepper, cinnamon, sesame seeds, and star anise and heat over medium heat just to the point where there are bubbles sizzling along the perimeter of the pan. You will smell the spices. Cover, remove from the heat, and let steep until cool. It's okay to forget it for a day.

Strain and pour the oil into an 8-ounce bottle. You don't have to refrigerate this oil for safety reasons, but the flavor will stay strong for longer if you do so. It will hold for 6 months at least.

Baking Extracts

You can make an extract with any flavoring. Whether you are making a flavoring for baking or simply flavoring an alcohol for drinking is a matter of ratios: the ratio of the solid food to the solvent plus the amount of time they spend together. So lots of lemon zest soaking in a small amount of vodka over a long time will produce lemon extract for baking purposes, whereas if you increase the amount of vodka and soak it for less time, you will get a lemony vodka for making cocktails. When making extracts, however, the percentage of ethanol in the alcohol (its proof) matters: The higher the proof, the more bitter flavors you will extract.

I use 80-proof alcohol for making extracts because I usually have vodka on hand. In general, bacteria can't survive in alcohol that is 40 percent ethanol (80 proof), but molds can survive. To hedge my bets, I sterilize my jars before filling them. But it's pretty unlikely any mold will develop.

Commercial baking extracts are sweetened, and I sweeten mine slightly, but you don't have to.

Dark bottles protect extracts from light, which can degrade the flavor of the extract. Extracts become stronger over time, so keep that in mind when using extracts in recipes. For example, if I'm using a newly minted extract, I add a little extra to my batters. You can feed the extract over time. If you are getting low, make up another batch and add it to the jar right on top of the old extract.

Vanilla Extract

If you want to use tall, skinny decorative bottles, you can simply fill the bottles with the sugar and vodka solution, and insert the vanilla beans directly into the bottle and allow it to steep. **MAKES ½ CUP**

> ½ cup 80-proof vodka (40% ethanol)
>
> 1 teaspoon sugar (optional)
>
> 3 vanilla beans

In a small saucepan, combine the vodka and sugar and warm just enough to dissolve the sugar. (Skip this step if you go sugar-free.)

Have ready a sterilized half-pint jar with a sterilized lid and band. (See "How to Sterilize," page 389.) Pour the vodka into the jar. With a sharp knife, split the vanilla beans lengthwise and scrape the seeds with the edge of a paring knife into the vodka. Break up the vanilla pods into a few small pieces and add them to the jar. Give the bottle a few good shakes and store in a cool dark place. Every day or so give the bottle a shake. The extract should be ready in about 1 month.

You can strain the extract and store it in a decorative bottle, or you can leave the pods in: The extract will continue to age over time, just getting stronger and better.

Lemon Extract

Little particulate matter may come off the lemon; it's okay. You can substitute the lemon with orange to make orange extract. **MAKES ½ CUP**

> 1 lemon, scrubbed
>
> ½ cup 80-proof vodka (40% ethanol)
>
> 1 teaspoon sugar (optional)

With a vegetable peeler zest the lemon in strips.

In a small saucepan, combine the vodka and sugar and warm just enough to dissolve the sugar. (Skip this step if you go sugar-free.)

Have ready a sterilized half-pint jar with a sterilized lid and band. (See "How to Sterilize," page 389.) Pour the vodka into the jar. Add the lemon zest. Give the bottle a few good shakes and store in a cool dark place. Every day or so give the bottle a shake. The extract should be ready in about 1 month.

You can strain the extract and store it in a decorative bottle, or you can leave the zest in: The extract will continue to age over time, just getting stronger and better.

BREADCRUMBS

Grind up stale bread (1 or 2 days old) in a food processor to a small crumb. Include all different types of stale bread, whatever you have around. Bagels, too. Varied texture and colors make the breadcrumbs better. Pour into a freezer bag, press out the air, and freeze. Keep adding breadcrumbs to the bag. The breadcrumbs hold well for 3 months in the freezer. Don't add salt or spices. Better to add the seasoning when you use the crumbs.

To use, simply spoon out the amount of breadcrumbs you need. There may be some clumping, but don't worry. It is easy to break up the clumps with your fingers. Toast the crumbs, or use them plain, depending upon the recipe.

Crème Fraîche

I use this cream in place of whipped cream on desserts, and in place of sour cream in savory dishes and baking. It is very easy to make, much easier than finding commercial crème fraîche, and lighter.
MAKES 2 CUPS

> 2 cups heavy cream
> 3 tablespoons whole buttermilk

Have ready 1 sterilized quart jar, band, and lid. (See "How to Sterilize," page 389.)

Combine the cream and buttermilk in the quart jar, give it a good shake, and set it on your kitchen counter overnight. If your house is really cold, put the jar near the radiator.

The crème fraîche will thicken up in 12 to 24 hours, sometimes a little longer, and become mildly acidic.

The crème fraîche will keep in the fridge for 2 to 3 weeks.

Cured Olives

If you have access to fresh olives, it's worth learning how to cure them. I don't go the curing-with-lye route: Anything that requires goggles isn't for me. But lye is the quicker cure, and worth exploring if that is your bag. I use these olives to make Green Olive Tapenade (page 160). **MAKES 1 QUART**

> 25 fresh green olives (fewer if you use the giant Cerignola)
> ½ cup white wine vinegar (5% acidity)
> 3 tablespoons pickling salt
> Sliced lemons
> Garlic cloves
> Dried oregano

Cut a slit in each olive, in the flesh but not through to the pit. Place in a quart jar and cover with water. Fill a zipseal plastic food storage bag with water and put it on top to ensure all the olives stay submerged. Change the water daily until the olives lose their bitterness, at least 1 week and up to 3 weeks. They will turn army green. It's okay. It's also okay if you miss a day here and there. I keep them near the sink as a reminder to change the water.

When the olives have lost their bitterness, drain and pack into a clean quart jar. In a bowl, combine the vinegar, salt, and 4 cups water, mixing to dissolve the salt. Add lemon slices, garlic cloves, and oregano, to your taste. Cover the olives with the brine and cap. Refrigerate and let rest for a month. The olives will get darker and the taste will mellow.

Herb Butter

While herb butter is the least of preserving exotica, it is possibly one of the most useful to have on hand. I have experimented with a variety of herbs and they all work, except you must mince them small: Leafy bits of herbs oxidize easily when you cook with the butter. The butter can stay frozen but after 6 months it will lose some of its oomph. You can also flavor butter with Parmesan cheese, minced olives, paprika, or chiles. **MAKES THREE 2-OUNCE LOGS**

- 1½ sticks (6 ounces) unsalted butter, at room temperature
- 6 tablespoons minced flat-leaf parsley or other fresh herb
- 2 tablespoons minced garlic
- 1 tablespoon grated lemon zest
- Salt and freshly ground black pepper

FRESH THYME AND SAGE

In a small bowl, blend together the butter, herbs, garlic, lemon zest, and salt and pepper to taste with a rubber spatula. Alter the seasonings to your taste.

Dump the butter into the middle of a piece of wax paper about 12 inches long. Roll the butter up in the wax paper, massaging it into a tidy log about 3 inches long and 2 inches in diameter. Chill. Cut the roll in thirds, pack into freezer bags, and freeze.

To use, transfer the butter to the refrigerator until you are ready to use it in a recipe.

Herb Syrup

Of all the herb syrups, I prefer basil and mint syrups, though you can make this syrup with any fresh herb. Herb syrups are wonderful additions to teas, lemonade, cocktails, and to macerated, baked, and poached fruits. Herb syrup makes a simple panna cotta or slice of cheesecake really divine.

MAKES 1 CUP

> 1¼ cups water
>
> ¾ cup sugar
>
> 1 cup fresh herb leaves, washed
>
> Green food coloring (optional)

In a small saucepan, combine the water and sugar and bring to a boil over medium-low heat, stirring to dissolve the sugar. Add the herb leaves and cook until the syrup is reduced by half, about 10 minutes, maybe a bit longer. Pour the syrup into a blender to puree the herbs. Strain the syrup through a fine-mesh sieve. You can add a drop of green food coloring if you'd like (not too much, or it looks nuclear). When cool enough to handle, pour into a squeeze bottle and refrigerate. The syrup holds for about 1 month.

Horseradish

While available all year, horseradish root is best in spring. The full flavor of this product lasts about a month in the refrigerator, at which point its flavor begins to dissipate (though it is still good). Horseradish may brown slightly. It's okay. If you want it to retain its white color, add a pinch of ascorbic acid per half-pint. **MAKES 2 HALF-PINTS**

> 1 pound fresh, firm horseradish root, peeled and washed (about ¾ pound cleaned)
>
> 1¼ cups distilled white vinegar (see Note)

> 1½ teaspoons salt
>
> 1 tablespoon sugar (optional; sugar counteracts some of the bitterness of horseradish)

Cut the horseradish root into chunks and place in the food processor. Pulse to grind. I like it fine. It will be a bit dry, something like coconut. (If the fumes are really intense, set up a small fan to blow them away from you while you finish the recipe.) Add the vinegar, salt, and sugar (if using).

Have ready 2 sterilized half-pint jars, bands, and lids. (See "How to Sterilize," page 389.) Pack the horseradish in the jars and refrigerate. You can freeze as well, but the horseradish won't last any longer than refrigerated.

Note: You can use white wine, rice, or cider vinegar as well.

LOIN LAMB CHOPS WITH HORSERADISH PESTO

I have used this horseradish crust on other meats, like beef eye round, and it is terrific. Avoid the temptation to add more oil: The crust stays on the meat quite well. I often prepare these chops in the morning, let them marinate all day in the fridge, and when it is time to make dinner, pop them under the broiler.

SERVES 4

> ¼ cup horseradish (for homemade, left)
>
> 2 tablespoons fresh thyme leaves
>
> 3 garlic cloves
>
> 1 tablespoon extra virgin olive oil
>
> Salt and freshly ground black pepper
>
> 4 loin lamb chops (about 6 ounces each)
>
> Oil, for greasing the rack

In a food processor, combine the horseradish, thyme, garlic, olive oil, and salt and pepper to taste and grind to a coarse pesto-like consistency. Pat the horseradish pesto on both sides of the chops, seal in a plastic food storage bag, and refrigerate up to 12 hours or cook right away.

Preheat the broiler.

Oil the rack of a broiler pan and place the chops on the rack. Broil the lamb about 6 inches from the heat for 6 to 8 minutes, or until they are golden on top (monitor it carefully so they don't burn). Flip the chops over and broil on the other side, 4 to 5 minutes, until golden.

Serve promptly.

Hot Vinegar Sauce

This is the most elemental of hot sauces. You can play with the flavor by adding other types of peppers, and different vinegars, as well as onions, or shallots. Use rubber gloves when handling hot peppers!

MAKES 1 CUP

- 1 cup distilled white vinegar
- ¼ cup seeded and chopped jalapeño chiles (preferably red, 2 ounces)
- 1 garlic clove, smashed
- A big pinch of salt

In a small pot over medium-low heat, simmer the vinegar, chiles, garlic, and salt for 5 minutes.

Pour the sauce in a blender and puree until smooth.

Have ready a sterilized pint jar, band, and lid. (See "How to Sterilize," page 389.) Pour the sauce into the jar and, with the lid loosely closed, leave in a dark place for at least 1 week.

Pour the vinegar into a sterilized bottle with a spout and cap and refrigerate. Holds for up to 1 year. The vinegar will mellow some over time.

Mayonnaise

I use mayonnaise all the time. In egg and chicken salads and on sandwiches of all sorts, of course, but I also add horseradish and serve it with boiled shrimp or roast beef, mix it with crabmeat and black pepper to serve on endive leaves, fold some in with cream cheese and marinated peppers to make pimiento cheese, and combine it with buttermilk to make ranch dressing. I add herbs and serve it with fried zucchini flowers, or dollop it on poached fish. I mix mayonnaise with garlic to make aioli and throw it into fish stews, or serve it with boiled root vegetables. Once you've gotten used to homemade mayonnaise, there's no going back to supermarket stuff. Mayonnaise calls for raw egg yolks, so use very fresh organic eggs. I buy them at the farmers' market in season, and off-season in the organic grocery store.

MAKES 1 CUP

- 2 large fresh organic egg yolks
- 2 tablespoons mustard, Dijon or homemade (page 366)
- 1 tablespoon fresh lemon juice
- Salt and freshly ground black pepper
- 1 cup neutral oil, such as safflower oil

In a stainless steel bowl, whisk together the egg yolks, mustard, lemon juice, and salt and pepper to taste. Add the oil in a slow, thin drizzle, whisking all the while. It will start to emulsify immediately. If it does not, it is most likely because you poured the oil in too quickly. You can try to whisk the mayonnaise vigorously to emulsify it anyway.

Check the seasoning and overall flavor. If it is too acidic, add another couple of tablespoons of oil in a slow drizzle. If it is not acidic enough, add lemon juice. Whisk in a teaspoon of water if you are not planning to use all the mayonnaise right away to prevent separation.

Spoon the mayonnaise into a half-pint jar and refrigerate for up to 4 days.

Mustard

Mustard is miraculous. The volatile oil in the seed has antimicrobial properties, so, combined with vinegar and salt, you can refrigerate it indefinitely. It is even shelf stable without being canned, although it does tend to dry out.

Mustard is versatile: You can add spices like turmeric (that's what makes American-style mustards such a bright yellow), or honey to make honey mustard, or tarragon to make Bordeaux-style mustard. You can use yellow, brown, or black mustard seeds: Yellow is the mildest and black is the spiciest. You can play around with the flavors of vinegar—like rice, wine, or fruit-enhanced—and even the quantity of vinegar. I make a half-pint at a time, about what I'll use over the course of a couple of months, and as a result, I experiment on a regular basis. You should, too. **MAKES 1 HALF-PINT**

> ¼ cup mustard seeds
>
> 3 tablespoons vinegar
>
> 3 tablespoons water or white wine
>
> 2 tablespoons olive oil
>
> 2 tablespoons mustard powder
>
> 2 tablespoons honey
>
> ½ teaspoon salt

In a small bowl, cover the seeds with the vinegar and water. Soak overnight, or even longer, until the seeds have absorbed all the liquid and are soft enough to mash between your fingers.

Place the softened seeds in a food processor and add the oil, mustard powder, honey, and salt. (I add mustard powder to make the mustard smoother.) Pulse to puree, a few seconds, but do not overpuree or the mustard will become whipped and be hard to spread. Less grinding will produce a seedier mustard, which is very good. You can also grind the mustard with a mortar and pestle. It takes longer, but might give you better control.

Pack into a half-pint jar and refrigerate. Holds forever.

Red Wine Reduction Sauce

More often than I like to admit, I will open various bottles of wine that I end up not finishing because I found them tannic, or too whatever. These bottles use up precious real estate in the kitchen, and I always think to myself I'll just make a beef stew with red wine, but I hardly ever do. Nor will I serve a wine that I don't enjoy drinking. That's when it is time to make red wine reduction sauce. Red wine reduction doesn't freeze well, so I think it's best to make the reduction and just use it within a couple of weeks. It's great as a sauce on game and beef. You can add a tablespoon of minced shallots, onion, celery, or herbs, or a couple of peeled garlic cloves when you add the stock, if you'd like. They will add flavor. The food writer Josh Eisen showed me this recipe. **MAKES 1 PINT**

> 4 cups red wine (a combination of red and white is okay, too)
>
> 2 cups beef stock (for homemade, page 47) or chicken stock (for homemade, page 89)

Pour the wine into a saucepan. Bring to a low boil over medium heat and boil, uncovered, until the wine is reduced to 2 cups, 10 to 15 minutes. Add the stock and reduce by half again, another 10 to 15 minutes. Strain the reduction through cheesecloth to remove any residue.

Have ready 1 sterilized pint jar, band, and lid. (See "How to Sterilize," page 389.) Pour the sauce into the sterilized jar. Holds in the refrigerator for about 2 weeks.

Ricotta Cheese

I make a ricotta that is blissfully dry, which works well in my recipes for ravioli, lasagna, and as a garnish on salads and pasta dishes. (In fact, you can replace any feta cheese in any of the recipes in this book with this ricotta.) If you want a creamy ricotta, to serve dressed with a fruit syrup (or the candy cap mushroom sauce, page 197) or to spread on crostini or to make cannoli cream (see page 368), then you need to add some cream to the recipe: Replace 1 cup of the whole milk with heavy cream. Goat milk makes a creamier ricotta as well.

Ricotta-making produces a lot of whey, which you can use in lieu of milk in Pork Braised in Milk (page 261). **MAKES 1 CUP**

- **4 cups whole organic milk**
- **½ teaspoon salt**
- **2 tablespoons distilled white vinegar**

Have ready a colander lined with cheesecloth placed over a large bowl. Place the milk and salt in a large heavy-bottomed pot. Slowly bring the milk to 185°F. The milk will sizzle at the perimeter of the pot. Take the milk off the heat and stir in the vinegar. The curds will precipitate promptly. Allow them to form, a couple of minutes. Pour the milk and curds through the cheesecloth. Allow the curds to drain for an hour or so, then squeeze the curds in the cheesecloth and pack in a bowl. The ricotta holds for about 2 days in the refrigerator.

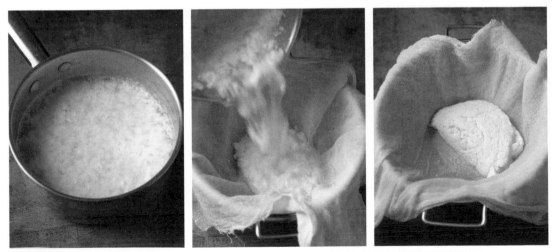

HEAT THE MILK TO 185°F. ADD THE VINEGAR AND ALLOW CURDLES TO FORM. POUR THROUGH A CHEESECLOTH AND DRAIN THE CURDS. SAVE THE WHEY TO POACH PORK (PAGE 261).

CANNOLI CREAM

To make cannoli cream, combine 2 cups ricotta (page 367) with 5 tablespoons sugar, ½ teaspoon vanilla extract (page 361), and ½ cup heavy cream beaten with 1 tablespoon sugar until it forms peaks. You can add minced citron, pistachios, or tiny chocolate chips if you'd like. Refrigerate for at least 1 hour before using. Holds in the refrigerator for about 2 days. Wonderful served with fresh fruit.

Skordalia

I use skordalia, an intense garlic paste used in Greek cooking, as a garnish or for flavoring recipes. I got this recipe from my friend Neni Panourgia, the best amateur cook of Greek cuisine I know. She explained to me that skordalia can be made with bread or potatoes, but if you make it with bread it can be refrigerated for about a month, whereas potato-based skordalia only lasts a week. **MAKES 1 HALF-PINT**

> 1 slice stale white sandwich bread (but not sourdough), crusts removed
>
> ⅓ cup water
>
> ¼ cup coarsely chopped garlic
>
> Salt
>
> 1 tablespoon white wine vinegar
>
> ¼ cup olive oil

Soak the bread in the water. Squeeze out the water and set the bread aside.

Mash the garlic and ½ teaspoon salt together to make a paste. (I just mash them directly on a cutting board, using the flat side of my chef's knife.)

In a mini food processor, combine the bread, garlic paste, and vinegar. With the machine on, slowly drizzle in the oil, or add the oil in small amounts and pulse between additions. Process until smooth, or as smooth as you like it. You can also make the skordalia with a mortar and pestle.

Check the seasoning.

Have ready 1 sterilized half-pint jar, band, and lid. (See "How to Sterilize," page 389.) Pack the skordalia into the jar and refrigerate. Holds for about 1 month.

Mustard Vinaigrette

A vinaigrette is simply about experience—the feel of the oil as it emulsifies—and once you've got it, it takes 2 minutes to make forever after. Vinaigrette can be stored for several days in the refrigerator, and while it will eventually separate, with the acid settling to the bottom and the oil floating to the top, you can almost always whisk it back together. You can alter the tastes of vinaigrette by playing around with the basic ingredients: Lemon juice or flavored vinegars; different types of oils; varieties in mustards; shallots, minced onions, minced pickled onions, and garlic; fresh herbs and dry spices. The basic recipe is really just a template. **MAKES ½ CUP**

> 1 large shallot, minced
>
> 2 teaspoons mustard, Dijon or homemade (page 366)
>
> 2 teaspoons fresh lemon juice
>
> Salt and freshly ground black pepper
>
> ½ cup neutral oil, such as safflower

Place the shallot in a small bowl. Add the mustard, lemon juice, and salt and pepper to taste. Whisk together. Then add the oil in a slow, thin drizzle while you whisk. It will start to emulsify immediately. If it does not, it is most likely because you poured the oil in too fast. You can try to whisk the vinaigrette vigorously to emulsify.

Check the seasoning and overall flavor. If it is too acidic for your taste, add another couple of tablespoons of oil in a slow drizzle. If it is not acidic enough, add lemon juice to your taste.

Spoon the vinaigrette into a half-pint jar and refrigerate for up to 4 days.

Worcestershire Sauce

I use Worcestershire sauce for a few recipes, like Chicken Croquettes (page 88) and Bloody Marys. I guess I thought Worcestershire sauce was immortal, because I never looked at the expiration date on my bottle of Lea and Perrins. I didn't even know there was an expiration date! There is, and mine had expired years earlier. Since obviously I don't use it often, I only need to make a cup at a time. Basically, the ingredients are simmered together, then aged, and then bottled. MAKES 1 CUP

- ½ teaspoon yellow mustard seeds
- ½ teaspoon salt
- ½ teaspoon black peppercorns
- ½ teaspoon whole cloves
- 4 green cardamom pods, cracked
- 1 cup distilled white vinegar
- ½ cup sliced shallots
- ¼ cup tamarind concentrate
- ¼ cup molasses
- 2 tablespoons soy sauce
- 2 garlic cloves, smashed and peeled
- One 2-inch cinnamon stick
- 2 anchovy fillets (see Note), chopped
- 1 small dried hot pepper
- A 1-inch piece fresh ginger, peeled and chopped
- ¼ cup sugar

With a mortar and pestle, or in a spice or coffee grinder, combine the mustard seeds, salt, peppercorns, cloves, and cardamom pods. Grind them together coarsely.

Pour the spices into a dry skillet over medium heat. When you will smell the spices (about a minute), remove from the heat and transfer to a medium pot. Add the vinegar, shallots, tamarind, molasses, soy sauce, garlic, cinnamon stick, anchovy, hot pepper, and ginger. Bring to a boil over medium heat, then reduce the heat to low and simmer for 10 minutes.

In a small skillet, cook the sugar over medium heat until it dissolves and turns an amber color, a few minutes. Remove from the heat and add to the vinegar mixture. Gently boil the sauce over low heat for 10 to 15 minutes. Different aromas will come up, then disappear: first the anchovies, then the vinegar, and then the tamarind. When you smell the tamarind, the sauce is ready. Pour the sauce into a pint jar and refrigerate for 2 to 3 weeks. It will thicken in the refrigerator and smell very rich and spicy. That's good.

Have ready a sterilized 8-ounce bottle with a cap. (See "How to Sterilize," page 389.) Strain the sauce to remove the solids and pour it into the bottle. Refrigerate for up to a year (at least).

Note: I prefer whole anchovies cured in salt, available in Italian markets. Soak them for 10 minutes to remove the salt, then rinse and fillet them. You don't have to get all the bones, just the spine.

Yogurt

Homemade yogurt is much lighter than commercial products. Yogurt is simply fermented milk. When certain bacteria are added to milk they produce lactic acid as a result of fermentation. Lactic acid makes the milk taste tart (by lowering the pH) and makes the milk proteins thicken. The lower pH dissuades the growth of pathogenic bacteria. When making yogurt the culture, or starter, needs to come from yogurt with active or live bacteria. **MAKES 4 HALF-PINTS**

> 4 cups whole milk
>
> 2 tablespoons plain organic yogurt with live bacteria

Heat the milk over low heat. When it is between 110° and 115°F, stir in the yogurt very well.

Have ready 4 sterilized half-pint jars, bands, and lids. (See "How to Sterilize," page 389.) Pour the inoculated milk into the jars.

There are a few ways to incubate the yogurt. I wrap the jars in towels and place them in a box in the kitchen, but you can pack them in any contained space, like a cooler or a covered roasting pan. Some people leave them overnight in their gas oven, turned off, as the pilot light generates enough heat.

Leave the jars for 6 to 8 hours, then check how they are doing. If the yogurt is thick, then it is done and you can refrigerate it. If not, leave them to incubate longer. I usually just leave them overnight, and by morning they are ready to eat.

The yogurt holds for up to 1 month in the refrigerator. Be sure to save a few tablespoons of your yogurt to start your next batch.

HOMEMADE YOGURT WITH POACHED EGGS

Talk about a last-minute meal, this traditional Greek dish, called tsilbiri, *is very silky, wonderfully comforting, and takes just minutes to prepare. (I wrote in my notes "OMG delicious! Worth the price of the book.") It's cool, warm, buttery, salty. I like to serve it with grilled Italian bread.* **SERVES 4**

> 2 cups plain whole-milk yogurt (for homemade, left)
>
> 1 teaspoon white vinegar
>
> 4 large eggs
>
> 4 tablespoons (½ stick) unsalted butter
>
> Salt and freshly ground black pepper

Spoon ½ cup yogurt into each of 4 small bowls.

Bring a medium pot of water to a high simmer over medium-low heat. Add the vinegar. Swirl the water with a spoon to create a gentle whirlpool. Crack one egg into a ramekin or other small bowl and then slide the egg into the center of the whirlpool. The vinegar and the whirlpool effect help keep the whites from dispersing in the water. Cook for a few minutes, until the whites are cooked through but the yolk is still soft. Gently remove the egg with a slotted spoon and place it on top of a bowl of yogurt. Continue with the remaining eggs.

Meanwhile, in a small skillet, heat the butter over medium heat. Cook until the butter turns amber brown (not dark brown) and smells nutty, a minute or so.

Pour brown butter over each egg and garnish with salt and pepper.

PRESERVING AND RECIPE TECHNIQUES

ABOUT PRESERVATION

Preserving is about prolonging the shelf life of foods by killing or neutralizing the agents that would otherwise cause them to spoil.

In home preservation we are after one of two scenarios: Either kill all spoilers, or retard the growth of spoilers (you can't get sick from a spoiler that is inert). That's done by heating, cooling, acidifying, or dehydrating foods to a point where spoilers can't survive or grow. Spoilers are naturally occurring enzymes, fungi, and bacteria that make your food inedible.

Enzymes cause decomposition. They are naturally occurring in all living things. Enzymes are most active between 85° and 120°F, which is why refrigeration slows decomposition. Enzymes are destroyed by heating food to 140°F and above.

Molds and yeasts are fungi. Molds are that white or blue fuzz that grows on leftovers in your fridge and yeasts are microscopic organisms that cause fermentation. Some molds and yeasts are introduced into foods, like blue cheese and bread. Others spoil or sour foods unappetizingly. Molds and yeasts cannot grow in freezing temperatures, although they can survive; and they start to bloom from 50° to 100°F. They can be destroyed at temperatures from 140°F and above.

Bacteria are the big bugaboo in canning. There are two classes of bacteria: relatively fragile germs like *Salmonellae* that can survive in frozen food and when exposed to temperatures above 45°F can activate. They can be killed at 140°F (well below boiling) if held at that temperature for a prescribed amount of time, and much quicker at higher temperatures. Other bacteria, like *Staphylococcus* and *Clostridium botulinum,* the bacteria that causes botulism, may be inactive at lower temperatures and in acidified solutions, but to kill them you need to expose them to a high temperature: 240°F for a sustained length of time, obtainable only with a pressure canner.

This book is composed of recipes using a variety of preserving techniques that inhibit the growth of spoilers in your food. That said, throw away preserved foods that look or smell nasty.

> If your preserved food looks and smells good, yet you are still worried about its safety, then before tasting, boil the food in an open pan for 10 minutes (plus 1 minute for each additional 1,000 feet above sea level). Canned corn is the exception. It should be boiled for 20 minutes at sea level, plus any altitude modification. This will sterilize your food by destroying any molds, yeasts, or bacteria, including any botulin toxin that may be present.

HOW TO PRESERVE

What you put in the jar is what you get out of the jar, so put up foods that are in season. Don't put up foods that are on their way out. Preserving is not a way to postpone eating something that has been aging in your refrigerator. Rather, preserving is a way of capturing a food's peak freshness for the future.

Water Bath Canning

Water bath canning is used to process high-acid foods like fruits and pickled vegetables for long-term storage. The food is packed into clean or sterilized glass jars with sealable lids and boiled in water for a prescribed amount of time. The heat generated by the water bath kills or arrests spoilers and establishes a sealed container where new spoilers cannot be introduced by pushing the air out of the tissues of the foods and jar, and creating a vacuum seal. These conditions, combined with the high acidity of the food within the jar, ensure that harmful microorganisms do not develop and the food is safe to store on the shelf. Because spoilers, including *Clostridium botulinum,* cannot develop in a high-acid environment, foods that have a pH of 4.6 or lower are safe to water bath can.

The processing times for water bath canning are calculated based on the density of the food in the jar (it takes longer for the heat to penetrate a very thick product), the acidity of the food in the jar (the higher the acidity, the shorter the processing time), and the size of the jar of food (it takes longer to heat up a quart than it does a pint), and the altitude at which you are processing. In this book the recipes call for water bath processing

two types of products: fruit products like jams and juices with a pH of 4.6 or less (or those bumped down to 4.6 or less by the addition of acid), and pickled products, like pickled zucchini, which are made with low-acid vegetables but achieve a safe level of acidity by the addition of vinegar and/or salt.

ABOUT JAMS AND JELLIES

Fruit preserves are made from whole or chopped fruit. Jams are made from mashed fruit, and jellies are made from juice. Making jams and jellies can be maddening, as the same recipe, used twice, can produce different results. That's because, in order to set, jellies and jams need a balance of sugar, acid, pectin (a naturally occurring substance that helps bind cells), and water. Different fruits have different levels of juiciness, acidity, and pectin, and those levels can be affected by a variety of factors, like weather conditions when the fruit was growing or the ripeness of the fruit when prepared. Some fruits must be acidified. Some need added pectin. And since pectin breaks down as fruit ripens, it's a good idea to use about 25 percent underripe fruits—which are more acidic, too—when making jams and jellies. Because evaporation of water is a factor in successful jamming, it takes less time to get a small pot of jam or jelly to set than a large one, so if you want to double a recipe, do so in small batches and use a wide, heavy-bottomed pan to increase the evaporative surface. To test whether your jelly or jam has set, place a spoonful in the fridge for a few minutes until chilled. If it falls off the spoon in clumps, it will set after canning. Given the right mix of pectin, sugar, and acid, jams and jellies will reach the jell stage 8°F above boiling. Water boils at 212°F at sea level, so the jell stage in New York City is 220°F. For every increase of 1,000 feet in altitude, the temperature of boiling water drops 1.8°F. So at my cabin in Colorado, which is just shy of 7,000 feet, water boils at 203.6°F. The jell stage, then, is reached when the thermometer reads 211.6°F.

I use Pomona's Universal Pectin, which doesn't tie me to a particular recipe or oblige me to add pectin-high fruits to my jam. It is a citrus-based pectin that allows you to use less sugar than other commercial pectins. It is widely available in stores and online, and I use it in a handful of recipes in this book.

ABOUT PICKLING

There are two approaches to pickling: with salt and with vinegar (though when you pickle with vinegar you usually add salt as well).

There are two methods of salt pickling: dry-salt and brined. The dry-salt method combines dry salt with vegetables in quantities above what you would add for seasoning purposes. Watery juices are pulled from the vegetables, and this liquid combines with the salt to create brine—a salty, watery solution. With the brine method, a vegetable is placed in a combination of salt and water. With both methods, the vegetables rest, covered in brine, for a prescribed amount of time. In some cases the vegetables are allowed to ferment in this submerged, airless state. Fermentation is the process by which natural bacteria in the foods convert the sugars into lactic acid. Lactic acid, which supplies that yummy sour taste, is a natural preservative: Microorganisms do not grow in lactic acid because of its high acidity. As a result, low-acid foods like cabbage can be safely water bath canned after it has fermented.

Pickling with vinegar is a much quicker process. It's what we usually do when making cucumber pickles. The vegetable does not ferment. Usually, the vegetable rests for a short time in a brine (in order to add crispness and flavor), is drained, often brought to a boil in a vinegar solution, packed into jars, covered in the remaining hot vinegar solution, and water bath canned for long-term preservation. The acetic acid in vinegar, which is colorless and flavorless, brings up the acidity of the vegetable to a point where no microorganisms can thrive. When the recipe calls for vinegar that is 5% acid that means the vinegar is 5% acetic acid. Acetic acid is what gives vinegar its sour, tart taste. You can use any vinegar you like in pickling as long as it is at least 5% acidity, though some vinegars work better than others. I use distilled white vinegar, cider vinegar, and white wine vinegar. Balsamic and red wine vinegar will darken your pickles.

If your water is good to drink, it is likely good to pickle with. However, hard water (mineral-rich water) and heavily chlorinated water can interfere with the formation of lactic acid. If this is the case, and you want to ferment vegetables, you have two options. Either use distilled water, or boil your tap water for 15 minutes then let it sit covered for 24 hours. You will detect a scum on top and sediment on the bottom. Skim off the scum, and pour the water into a container, leaving the sediment behind. (Filtered water is not as effective in reducing minerals and salts.)

I use pickling or canning salt. Pickling salt is pure granulated salt without anticaking agents that can cause the pickling liquid to turn cloudy. Avoid iodized table salts: they have additives that prevent it from dissolving completely. Kosher salt's large crystals do not dissolve quickly so if you use it be sure the crystals dissolve. You also need to increase the measurement of kosher salt and that increase varies depending on the brand. Sea salt can include minerals that may adversely affect your pickling. Ferment foods in a stoneware, glass, or a food-grade plastic crock; and brine in nonreactive bowls. When brining foods, especially those that brine for some time, you must be sure the food stays submerged. A simple way to accomplish this is to fill a heavy-duty plastic food storage bag with brine. It will be heavy enough to keep the vegetables below the liquid. And if you spring a leak, it's no problem, because only brine will drip into your crock.

HOW TO WATER BATH CAN

There are four steps to water bath canning: (1) Preparing the food and the jars, (2) packing the jars with the food and wiping the rims, (3) boiling the jars in water, and (4) allowing the jars to cool.

1. Ready the jars. (I prefer lid and band-style jars because they seal predictably, and wide-mouthed jars because they are easiest to pack.) Food and jars that will be processed in a water bath for 10 minutes or more at sea level (plus 1 to 2 minutes per 1,000 feet of altitude) do not need to be sterilized. Food and jars that are processed for less time must be sterilized first by boiling the jars and bands for 10 minutes at sea level (plus 1 minute per 1,000 feet altitude). You need new lids for every processing and you can purchase these separately. Prepare the lids for canning by simmering them in hot water to soften the rubberized flange. This only takes a minute or two.

2. Pack food into jars leaving the prescribed amount of headroom and release any air

I PREFER THREE-PIECE CANNING JARS—THEY'RE RELIABLE.

bubbles that are trapped in the jar with a utensil like a butter knife. Headroom allows for a small increase in the volume of the product or for the foods to bubble as they are canned. If you don't leave enough headroom, some of the food might be forced out of the jars with the air, which could compromise your seal. Too much headroom can cause a buildup of pressure inside the jar, leading to cracks in the glass, discoloration of foods, or seal failure. Wipe the rim of the jar: Sticky bits of food can inhibit the seal. Place the prepared lid on the jar. Screw on the bands "fingertip" tight, just tight enough to close with your fingertips, not cranked with your palm. This is because you want all the air in the jar to be able to escape during the water bath processing.

3. Place the jars in a deep pot with a rack so the water can circulate around the jars. Also, without a rack, the jars will rattle while they are boiling and may break—and the sound will drive you crazy. (I use a rack made by wiring together canning bands.) The pot must be deep enough to cover the jars with 2 inches of water and then still have an additional couple of inches so the boiling water doesn't erupt all over your stove. If I am putting up just one jar, I use my asparagus cooker. Cover the jars with hot water (140°F for uncooked foods, 180°F for cooked) and bring to a boil over high heat. Boil the jars for the prescribed amount of time. Processing times must be adjusted for altitude. (See "Altitude Adjustments," page 389.) Boiling water, whether it is boiling violently or mellowly, is still boiling at the same temperature, so you can reduce the heat as long as the water continues to boil. If at any time the water is no longer covering the jars, add additional *boiling* water. If the water stops boiling at any time, you need to bring the water back up to a boil and start your timing over from the beginning. Turn off the heat and let the jars rest in the water for about 5 minutes. Remove the jars and place them on a towel or rack.

4. Allow the jars to rest untouched for 12 to 24 hours. The cooling stage in water bath processing is important because the rubber flange on the lid will be soft coming out of the water bath and needs to stiffen to complete the seal. Don't tighten the bands. If you hear a popping sound, it's okay. It indicates your jars have sealed. Once cool, check the seals. Unscrew the band and lift the jar by the edges of the lid. If you can lift the jar, the seal is good. If the lid comes off, the seal has failed and you must refrigerate and eat the product, or reprocess the jars with new lids following the same procedure. Label the jars and store them in a cool dark place for up to a year (except where noted in the recipes). You do not need to store the jars with the bands on. Refrigerate after opening.

Pressure Canning

Even though pressure canning requires a bulky and expensive piece of equipment, it is the most liberating form of canning. It is very safe and easy to do once you understand the basic steps. If I make a large pot of beef or chicken stock, I automatically pressure can it in pints. It takes just 20 minutes.

In pressure canning, foods are processed in glass jars under pressurized heat. Steam builds up in the airtight cavity of the pressure canner, accomplishing the same thing as a water bath canner, but at a higher temperature (240°F). This technique kills all spoilers. Pressure canning is used when processing low-acid foods (pH 4.6 and higher), like poultry, meat, and fish, and vegetables without added acid.

The amount of time you pressure can does not change, whether you live in Florida or Colorado. However, altitude effects the amount of pressure you use. This is because the higher the altitude, the lower the atmospheric pressure. You compensate for this discrepancy by adding pressure in the canner. Altitude adjustments depend on the kind of pressure canner you have, and that information is described below.

PARTS OF A PRESSURE CANNER

A pressure canner lid has three to five parts, depending on the model:

- A gauge, which displays the amount of pressure.

- A steam vent, which, when open, allows steam to escape from the canner. When the steam vent is closed, either by capping it with a weight or flipping it to its closed position, steam can build up pressure in the canner. The steam vent will be forced open if too much pressure builds up in the canner.

- An overpressure plug that will automatically vent steam if the steam vent is clogged.

- A gasket (in some models), which is a rubber ring between the lid and pot that ensures an airtight seal.

- A safety lock (in some models), which prevents you from opening the lid before the canner is safely depressurized.

In the base or pot of the canner is a rack, sometimes two if you have a large canner. These racks are just steel disks with holes in them. They don't fit into the canner in any special way. You just drop one rack in the bottom of the canner, and for those who are into large batch canning, another rack that fits on top of the first layer of jars and upon which the next layer of jars is placed.

GET THE RIGHT CANNER FOR YOU

You must use a pressure canner, not a pressure cooker. A pressure cooker does not achieve enough pressure to safely can most foods. When you buy a pressure canner sometimes it will be described as a pressure canner/cooker. This is okay. You can cook in a canner. You just can't can in a cooker. Pressure canners come in a variety of sizes, based on their total liquid capacity. A 10-quart canner (the smallest USDA-recommended size), will process 4 quart-sized jars of food. Buy a pressure canner based on the circumstances of your kitchen and the stuff you want to can. Here's what to look for:

- If you have a gas stove, all pressure canner types will work.

- If you have an electric stove with burners, or a ceramic top stove, you must use a smooth-bottomed canner that doesn't overhang the burner by more than 2 inches, otherwise you won't generate enough heat to can safely. Canners with a rounded or ridged bottom won't pick up enough heat to do the job. Additionally, large canners can set off the built-in sensor in some ceramic top stoves that lowers the heat if the output is too high. This is a drag because if your pressure drops, you have to stop timing, bring it back up to pressure, and then start timing all over again.

- All pressure canner types can safely can meat, poultry, and vegetable products.

- If you want to process fish, check the pressure canner manufacturer's guidelines. Some state that fish cannot be safely processed in their smaller canners because they depressurize too quickly. The USDA data recommends smoked fish be processed in a 16-quart canner or larger, but does not state canner size in their other fish-canning recommendations.

- Modern pressure canners come in two styles of locking lid mechanisms: thumbnuts, which are tightened by hand, and slide closures, which slide into a locked position.

Both thumbnut and slide closures work equally well, although the slide closure may give the beginner more confidence, as there is no question of whether the lid is on tightly enough. Thumbnuts will not feel like they are locking down the lid: There's a narrow gap between the lid and body, but don't worry. It's okay.

- Inside the lid of some slide closure canners is a rubber gasket. Gaskets age, of course, and may need to be replaced periodically. You need to check it before each use to be sure it isn't cracked or torn.

- Pressure canner gauges come in two styles: the weighted gauge and the dial gauge (and some canners have both, which is my preference). A weighted gauge is a weight with three settings—5 pounds, 10 pounds, and 15 pounds—or three separate weights that fit over the steam vent on the lid. The 5-pound

setting is not used for pressure canning. It is used for pressure cooking. Five pounds psi (per square inch) is not enough pressure to preserve. Ten pounds of pressure is applied at sea level, and 15 pounds of pressure is used at altitudes above 1,000 feet. Weighted gauges are great because they don't need to be calibrated. The downside is some models rattle at intervals: Too much pressure and it rattles constantly, too little and it rattles infrequently. Other models maintain a jiggle. You just have to get used to using them.

- Dial gauges are just that: A little pointer indicates on a scale exactly how much pressure is in the canner. Dial gauges are nice because you know exactly what's going on in there. However, dial gauges should be tested every couple of years to be sure they remain accurate. You can bring the lid of your canner to the Extension Office associated with your state university and have it tested against a master gauge. It is not uncommon for a dial gauge to stray a pound or two up or down. Up is not a problem when it comes to safety, but you don't want to be canning at less pressure than is necessary. You can't recalibrate a dial gauge, so you compensate by bringing the pressure up or down (by applying more or less heat) equal to the psi you are off. If your gauge goes off by over 2 pounds, however, you should replace it. Food canned at altitudes up to 2,000 feet in dial gauge pressure canners must be processed at 11 psi. The 1-pound difference between the two gauge types reflects differences in the canners' construction. For dial gauge canners add ½ pound of pressure for every 1,000 feet over 2,000 feet altitude, but don't

change the processing time. Round up; so at an altitude of 3,500 feet, add 1 pound of pressure, for a total of 12 pounds.

HOW TO PRESSURE CAN

There are five steps to pressure canning. (1) Preparing the food and the jars, and packing the jars with the food and wiping the rims, (2) venting the canner, (3) processing at the right pressure for the prescribed amount of time, (4) venting the canner again, and (5) allowing the jars to cool.

1. You don't have to sterilize jars before pressure canning because the process will do that job for you. Just clean the jars well before getting started. Pack food into jars leaving 1 inch of headroom and release any air bubbles that are trapped in the jar with a butter knife. Wipe the rim of the jar: Sticky bits of food can inhibit the seal. You need new lids for every processing. Prepare the lids for canning by simmering them in hot water to soften the rubberized flange. This only takes a minute or two. Screw on the bands "fingertip" tight, just tight enough to close with your fingertips, not cranked with your palm. This is because you want the air in the jar to be able to escape during processing. Place the rack in the bottom of your pressure canner. Place 2–3 inches of hot water (140°F at sea level) in the bottom of your pressure canner. The water will create the steam when heated. If you want shiny jars, add ½ teaspoon of white distilled vinegar to the water. Place the jars on the rack. It is okay if the water comes up the sides of the jar. Avoid tipping the jars. Lock the top into position as per the instructions for

your pressure canner. Remove the pressure regulator from the steam vent. Heat the canner over high heat.

2. Steam will come out of the steam vent. Allow steam to be released from the vent in a continuous stream for 10 minutes. This is important because air trapped in the canner lowers the temperature and results in underprocessing. After 10 minutes, depending on the type of canner you have, either put the petcock in the off position or put the pressure regulator (the weighted gauge) over the steam vent.

3. Start watching your dial gauge, or listening to your weighted gauge. It will take up to 10 minutes for the canner to pressurize. If you are using a dial gauge, heat the canner until the appropriate pressure based on your altitude is reached. Start to reduce the heat a bit when the dial gauge reaches 2 pounds of pressure less than your target so the pressure still rises, but more slowly. You want to hit your pressure and maintain it. With a weighted gauge, the weight will begin to rock when it achieves the right pressure. In some models you'll hear a rattle, then a pause; a rattle, then a pause. In other models it spits and rattles constantly. But if it hardly ever rattles, with minutes between rattles, that means your pressure has dipped below what is needed to preserve safely.

Maintain the pressure canner at the right pressure for the amount of time prescribed in the recipe. Check periodically to ensure the pressure stays at the right psi. Usually, once you've got the heat right, the pressure will become stable. If you are a little over, it's okay. If the pressure dips, you have to stop timing, bring the canner back up to pressure by increasing the heat, and then start the timing over from the beginning. Remember, the timing for processing is particular to the size of the jar described in the recipe. You can process smaller jars for the same amount of time, but larger jars may need a different time.

4. When you've processed your jars for the prescribed amount of time, turn off the heat and allow the pressure to drop naturally. (If you use an electric stove, slide the canner off the burner since the burner continues to generate heat after it has been turned off.) Do not force the cooling, but don't just take the canner off the heat and go away for the weekend. You need to hang around a bit longer, until the safety lock releases, or the pressure regulator reads 0, indicating that the pressure has decreased and you can safely remove the lid. (Don't leave your jars in the canner to cool overnight; it is still hot in the canner even after the pressure is down, and the jars may overprocess. Your jars won't be unsafe, but the food may be mushy.) When the canner is depressurized, remove the vent weight or gauge (or open the petcock) away from you. Wait 10 minutes, then remove the lid, opening it away from you as there may still be some hot steam inside.

5. Place the jars on a towel or rack. Don't retighten the bands. As in the case of water bath canning, the cool down is part of the process. Some of the food in the jars may still be boiling. Allow the jars to rest untouched for 12 to 24 hours. Check the seals: Unscrew the band and lift the jar by

the edges of the lid. If you can lift the jar, the seal is good. Should any of your jars fail to seal, refrigerate and eat the product; or you can reprocess the jars with new lids, following the same procedure. Label the jars and store them in a cool dark place for up to a year, depending on the recipe. You do not need to store the jars with the bands on. Refrigerate after opening.

Freezing

This is the process in which semicooked or cooked food is solidified at temperatures between 0° and 32°F, which slows the metabolism of foods and the spoilers that may live on them. Some spoilers are destroyed and those that aren't are inert. With proper thawing and/or prompt cooking, spoilers on foods that have been frozen will never amount to anything. Freezing, which seems so simple, can actually be done well or poorly. Here's why.

In freezing, water in the cells of the food crystallizes and, as a result, expands. The slower the freezing process, the larger the ice crystals, which can cause the cell walls of the food to rupture: This is what makes thawed foods mushy, and is most evident in the case of starchy foods, like peas. (That's why when you see a product labeled "flash frozen," it's a good thing.)

For best results, freeze at 0°F. If your freezer is warmer, the foods won't hold as nicely for the full time. I use the blueberry test: If my bag of frozen blueberries is not rock solid, I know I'm not at 0°F. Overpacking the freezer can lower its temperature, so try not to freeze more than 3 pounds of food per cubic foot of freezer space. With every 10° increase in temperature above 0°F in your freezer, the foods will decrease in quality, in some cases significantly. If you have a warmer freezer, use the food sooner. Fluctuating freezer temperatures can cause some degradation of the quality of your frozen foods as well. If the foods slightly thaw and then refreeze, the tiny ice crystals in the cells grow larger and damage the cell walls even more. Temperature fluctuations can also cause the water in the food to migrate out of the tissues, and that leads to drier, tougher food (this is particularly a problem with frozen meat). Frozen foods remain safe indefinitely, but the quality is affected over time. See FoodSafety.gov for optimum storage times for particular foods.

Avoid freezing foods with high water content, like lettuce, because when the water in the tissue freezes and expands, it ruptures the cell walls. The more water in the vegetable, the more ice crystals, the more expansion, the more cell rupturing, and the soggier the thawed product.

Sometimes the flavor of spices, herbs, and seasonings is altered as a result of freezing. Spices like black pepper and garlic can become bitter when frozen. Salt can just dumb down

Freezer Burn

Freezer burn is a pale, rough spot on your food. It occurs when the food is exposed to air in the freezer, causing dehydration and oxidation. The food deteriorates and develops a stale taste and a dry, tough texture in the area of the burn. It won't hurt you, but it is unpalatable. You can cut freezer burn off the food it has affected. As long as the rest of the food is free of freezer burn, it will taste okay.

and lose its oomph. These flavoring agents are best added when cooking the frozen foods in a recipe.

HOW TO FREEZE FOODS

There are three steps to freezing foods properly: (1) Blanching or cooking the food (except in the case of proteins and fruits; some fruits are pretreated with an antidarkening agent); (2) packing the foods in the right kind and size of container; (3) chilling the food in the fridge and then placing in the freezer.

1. Most vegetables and mushrooms should be blanched, if not cooked, prior to freezing to inactivate the enzymes in them. If you freeze without a precooking stage, the enzymes will continue to age the product—albeit slowly—and undermine the flavor, texture, and color of the food. Blanching is not the optimum treatment for proteins and fruits. Proteins are frozen raw. Fruits are also frozen raw—either as is or in a light (20 percent sugar) or medium (30 percent sugar) syrup. A sugar syrup helps fruits retain their texture and color. Certain fruits, like apples, apricots, nectarines, and peaches, may lose their vibrant color during freezing. These can be dipped in a solution of ¼ teaspoon ascorbic acid (it's just vitamin C and widely available wherever you buy canning supplies) dissolved in 1 quart water.

2. Be sure to use freezer-safe plastic containers or bags (it will indicate that on the box), because freezer-safe containers and bags are moisture/vapor proof. This is important because if the food inside the container or bag is exposed to air, you'll get freezer burn. (And don't reuse freezer bags for freezing.)

For purees, I use plastic freezer containers or "can and freeze" canning jars (rather than "standard" canning jars, which can break). When freezing soft foods like stocks, purees, and sauces, leave about 1 inch of headroom in your freezer container to allow the food to expand during freezing. If you don't, and your container lids bulge open, your product may get freezer burn.

3. Chill the food before freezing. The more quickly a product freezes, the smaller the ice crystals, and your food will retain its texture better. For small pieces of food (such as fresh berries or blanched, chilled cut-up vegetables), arrange them on a baking sheet and freeze, then loosen them with a spatula, and pack into freezer bags or containers. This way the food won't freeze in a clump, and will be more manageable if you only want to defrost a portion.

THAWING FOODS SAFELY

The safest way to thaw frozen foods is in the refrigerator. You can also thaw in cold water. When you do, keep the food in its leakproof container or bag so that bacteria don't slip in via the soaking water and to ensure the food doesn't get waterlogged, which will undermine its texture. You can store the thawed food for a few days in the fridge until you are ready to use it. If you thaw in the microwave, however, you need to cook the food right away, as the food has been warmed enough for bacteria to grow. You can refreeze thawed foods that are either partially frozen or still cold, around 40°F. Refreezing, while safe, does undermine the quality of the product because the already traumatized cells of the foods are hit again with expanding ice crystals.

Curing

Curing is the art of preserving food with salt via a dry cure (combining the food with dry salt) or a brine (soaking the food in salted water). Salt urges water from cells, which dehydrates the flesh. Since spoilers need moisture to grow, salt-cured foods provide an inhospitable environment for microbes. Likewise, salt enters and dehydrates the microbes themselves, causing havoc with their ability to survive. The information on page 374 regarding pickling salt is true for salt used in curing.

A dry cure is composed of salt (and sometimes sugar to counteract the harshness of the salt) and spices or flavorings. It is rubbed onto foods, allowed to rest for a prescribed amount of time and then removed. A brine is composed of salt and water, and sometimes sugar and flavorings. Foods are soaked in the brine for a prescribed amount of time and then rinsed. The cured foods in this book last about 2 weeks in the refrigerator and the meat is brown. That's because I don't use curing salt, which is salt mixed with nitrate or a combination of nitrite and nitrates. (Among other attributes, nitrite keeps cured meat pink.)

Smoking (inundating a food with hot or cold smoke) is often performed in conjunction with curing.

HOW TO CURE

There are four steps to curing: (1) For dry-curing, rubbing the salt mixture on the food and chilling for a prescribed amount of time; for brining, soaking the food in a cold brine solution for a given amount of time; (2) washing off the salt mixture or the brine; (3) allowing the food to rest in the fridge—dry if salted, in plain water if brined—so that the salt may equalize throughout the flesh; (4) refrigerating the food; or smoking or cooking the product and then refrigerating it.

1. Pat on the dry-cure or place the food in the brine. Brine in nonreactive crocks and pans and wrap dry-cured foods in plastic wrap. Chill in the refrigerator (though this can be done in other cold environments, too). How long you refrigerate is based on the thickness of the product, as a successful cure is the complete penetration of the food by salt.

2. Wash the salt off the food thoroughly or rinse off the brine.

3. An important factor in curing is clearing, or allowing the salt to complete the task of equalizing throughout the food after the surface has been washed. Because the greatest concentration of salt is on the surface of the food, it needs to have the opportunity to complete its penetration into the meat: Salt will seek equilibrium throughout all the cells given the time to do so. To do this in dry-curing, wrap the washed meat in plastic wrap and let rest in the refrigerator for a prescribed amount of time so the salt can disperse evenly. In brining, soak the food in clean cold water in the refrigerator for a prescribed amount of time, which accomplishes the same thing. As in curing, the larger and thicker the food product, the longer it will take to clear. If you don't clear the food, it will be very salty.

4. Store the finished cured product in a plastic food storage bag in the refrigerator or freezer. Or cook the product and store in a plastic food storage bag in the refrigerator or freezer; or smoke the product (see "How to Smoke Indoors," page 384).

Smoking

Smoking, a common second part of the curing process, adds flavor, and kills microorganisms through heat. It is an excellent process for proteins. Small amounts of food can easily be smoked in or on your stove safely. Smoking will cook foods if there is ample heat and smoke. For indoor smoking, you can buy a smoker or rig one with a cast-iron skillet fitted with a 10-inch footed cake rack and a fitted lid. If you have a cast-iron Dutch oven with a fitted top, that's perfect. If necessary, you can make a rack by wiring canning bands together.

You need wood chips to smoke foods. They are widely available. I get Cameron brand wood chips online. Alder wood is great for fish; apple and cherry are good for poultry; hickory and oak for beef and pork. Pecan, maple, and mesquite are fun to play with, but be careful: Too much mesquite will make your food bitter. Don't use conifer chips or needles. They leave a nasty taste on the food.

HOW TO SMOKE INDOORS

There are three steps to smoking: (1) Drying the cured food to be smoked; (2) placing the food in the smoker; (3) drying, packing, and refrigerating the smoked food.

1. Pat dry the food. Smoke doesn't adhere well to wet surfaces.

2. Place the food in the smoker. If you use a commercial stovetop smoker like a Cameron, place wood chips on the floor of the smoker, then fit in the tray and the rack. The food is placed on the rack and the lid is almost completely closed. Place the smoker over the heat and as soon as wisps of smoke begin to appear, close the lid the rest of the way. Smoke for the amount of time in the recipe. To make a smoker, line a heavy skillet or pot with foil (for easy cleanup) and tear a hole about 2 inches in diameter in the center at the bottom. Place a rack in the pan and heat the pan over high heat until very hot, a few minutes, then add wood chips, as per the recipe, in the hole in the foil so the chips are resting on the bottom of the pan itself, not on foil. In a minute you will see wisps of smoke come off the chips. Place the food on the rack and cover the pan. I often lay down another piece of foil under the top of the skillet to ensure a tighter seal. (Nonetheless, my rigs always leak some as does my Cameron stovetop smoker. A little leaking is okay, but if too much smoke escapes there will not be enough heat to cook the food, so ensure the tightest seal possible.)

3. When your smoked foods are cool enough to handle, dry them very well before refrigerating or freezing. Because smoked food can sweat, the moisture released by the food will condense and settle on the surface of the food and create a moist spot where mold can grow. To prevent that, I wrap the smoked food in paper towels before placing it in the plastic food storage bag. Home-smoked foods last about 10 days in the fridge or can be frozen.

Drying

Drying is a great way to preserve lots of different foods, particularly certain fruits, herbs, and mushrooms. In fact, the flavor of some herbs, like oregano, and certain mushrooms, like candy caps and porcini, are intensified when dried. I mainly dry foods if I have a bounty, as it takes about 10 pounds of fresh food to produce 1 pound of dried food. Every fall I dry oregano and marjoram, wild mushrooms, a bagful of tomatoes, and another of sweet red peppers to use through the winter.

Drying is dehydrating a food of most of its moisture. When you remove the moisture from foods you remove one of the things spoilers need to survive: water. Eighty percent of the water must be removed from fruit in order to make it inhospitable to spoilers. For vegetables, you need to remove 90 percent of the water. The reason why you don't have to remove as much water from fruits as you do vegetables is because fruits are naturally high in acid, and it is the combination of dehydration and acidity that creates a safe product. Vegetables and mushrooms are low-acid foods, so they must be dryer than fruits in order to retard the growth of spoilers. The best way to tell if your food is dehydrated properly is by feel. Fruits should be from leathery and pliable to crisp. Vegetables and mushrooms must be crisp.

The sweet spot for drying foods is a temperature between 95° and 140°F. Lower than 95°F, and mold and other spoilers could grow on your food during the 4 to 24 hours it takes to dry food. Too high (above 140°F) and foods will cook on the outside, but the inside of the food will still be too moist. Air circulation is helpful, as it wicks moisture away from the food.

There are lots of drying methods, but success depends on air movement, humidity, and temperature. You can dry food outside, but you will need 3 sunny days without humidity to succeed, and you must protect

your food from dust and insects by wrapping the trays in cheesecloth or nylon or plastic screening (just not metal, which can throw weird flavors onto your food). The USDA does not recommend solar collectors or microwaves for drying, because they can easily cook your foods, leaving some moisture inside. You are best off drying at home in your oven, or with an electric dehydrator. I use a Nesco dehydrator.

HOW TO DRY

There are three steps to drying foods: (1) Prepping and/or pretreating the foods, (2) drying the foods for the prescribed amount of time, (3) conditioning the foods.

1. Prepare foods for drying by cutting them into uniform pieces. Slices dry more effectively than chunks. To make vegetable chips, slice with a mandoline.

   Most vegetables and some fruits should be blanched prior to drying. When you cut into a vegetable or fruit, it activates a naturally occurring enzyme that breaks down the pectin—it's the enzyme that causes decomposition. When you blanch the vegetable or fruit by dunking in boiling water, the heat deactivates the enzyme. Additionally, the residual heat from blanching will help the drying process begin more quickly. Some fruits, like cherries and blueberries, are blanched to crack the skins. This helps them dry more effectively. Pat the fruit or vegetables dry after blanching.

Some fruits benefit from a pretreatment with ascorbic acid (vitamin C) to hold the color. (Commercial operations use sulfur to retain the color and elasticity of dried fruit.) You can make a simple bath composed of 1 teaspoon ascorbic acid (or 3,000 milligrams of crushed vitamin C tablets) dissolved in 2 cups of water. Fruits

DRIED APRICOTS

are immersed for 3 to 5 minutes depending on the fruit. You can also immerse fruits in lemon or pineapple juice, but it will affect the flavor. Each recipe in this book describes the particular pretreatment for that food.

2. The juicier the food, the longer it will take to dry, but expect anywhere from 4 to 12 or more hours to complete the process. To dry in an electric dehydrator, you just fill the trays, set the temperature, and leave it to do its thing. Fruits, mushrooms, and vegetables dry at 135°F with an electric dehydrator. Place foods cut side up in drying trays to avoid sticking.

If you want to use your oven, the food can be laid directly on the racks, or a finer rack can be inserted, or you can string and hang the food in the oven. Set your oven to its lowest temperature (most ovens don't go below 200°F). An ordinary oven will hold 4 to 6 pounds of dried food, but a lighter load will dry faster than a heavier load. Be sure there are about 3 inches of vertical room between the racks and about 3 inches of room between the food and the inside walls of the oven. Leave the oven door slightly open, 4 to 6 inches for electric stoves and 1 to 2 inches for gas, for air circulation. If you have a convection feature on your oven it will help to turn it on. Check the oven temperature with an oven thermometer: You should maintain a consistent temperature of 140°F for best results. Dry the food for the amount of time recommended in the recipes.

3. Place the dried foods in a large jar and shake them up every day for a week to 10 days. This is called conditioning the food.

About Olive Oil

When preserving in oil, what oil you use matters. Mechanically extracted olive oils—usually the most expensive varieties—will stay fluid at lower temperatures than cheaper oils, which are made by heat or chemical extraction. So a high-quality olive oil is best when preserving foods in oil and then refrigerating. Olive oil will solidify at 42°F. It becomes buttery and white, or, in the case of oil with added vinegar, the oil will separate from the vinegar in little balls. This is okay. Oil rancidity is occasionally a problem (the shelf life of oil is about 15 months). Rancid oil has a nasty, stale taste. It's not poisonous, nor does it occur in conjunction with the development of botulin toxin or any other spoiler. It happens when the polyunsaturated fats in vegetable oil oxidize. Oxidation is a chemical reaction that causes the fats to decompose when exposed to air, sunlight, or heat, in turn producing obnoxious odors and flavors. Rancidification can also undermine the nutrients in oil by degrading some vitamins. Refrigeration slows down the march toward rancidity because it is a cool, dark environment but doesn't stop it because the oil is still exposed to air (what remains between the cork and the oil in the bottle).

It distributes the moisture—the 10 to 20 percent that remains—throughout the food.

To store dried food, place it in an airtight container in a cool, dark place, like your pantry. I recommend you put up dried foods in small packages or jars because if there is any spoilage, then at least only a small percentage will go bad. In warm, humid regions like Florida, it may be best to keep your dried foods in the refrigerator. Food stored at 52°F will last two to three times longer than dried foods stored at 70°F. In general, dried foods last about 1 year.

Preserving in Oil

This process is not a permanent preservation method, but rather, a way to extend the refrigerator life of certain foods. Foods are pre-cooked—which kills many spoilers—or prepared and covered in oil, and sometimes oil and vinegar or lemon juice, and refrigerated. As air cannot penetrate olive oil, it acts as a prophylactic between the foodstuff and the environment, putting off the growth of spoilers longer than simple refrigeration. You must refrigerate all foods preserved in oil to avoid the growth of spoilers, and foods preserved in oil and refrigerated should be used within 10 days. You can't water bath can foods preserved in oil. The downside of preserving in oil, besides the fact that it doesn't hold food for that long, is the food becomes saturated with oil, and so is useful only in recipes to which you would have added oil anyway.

HOW TO PRESERVE IN OIL

There are three steps to preserving in oil: (1) Preparing the food, (2) packing the food in sterilized jars and covering with oil, (3) refrigerating.

1. Prepare the food as described in the recipe.

2. Sterilize the jars by boiling for 10 minutes at sea level and pack in the food. Release any air bubbles as these can harbor spoilers. Cover the food with oil. In cases where there is a lot of space in the jar to be filled

with oil, you may need to revisit the jar to see if the food is still covered and add more oil.

3. Refrigerate for up to 10 days. If you have added vinegar or lemon juice to the jar it will hold longer, but there are no USDA recommendations as to how long. I find that a product like Marinated Stuffed Cherry Peppers (page 245), which are packed in a combination of oil and vinegar, will hold about 6 months in the fridge.

As you use the food preserved in oil, it is important to avoid introducing spoilers to the jar. If you're using just some of the food from the jar, spoon the oil off the top of the jar and measure out the amount of food you wish to use. Press the remaining ingredients back down into the jar, packing them as tightly as you can, and re-cover with the same or new oil. Do this quickly and return the jar to the fridge: Do not allow the jar to hang around at room temperature as spoilers may be introduced, or those present in the jar may activate.

Preserving with Alcohol

Preserving with booze is sometimes called "toxic inhibition" because alcohol is an inhospitable environment for microorganisms. It is a terrific way to put up fruit, and it's very easy: no water bath processing necessary. You just combine fresh fruit and sugar and cover with alcohol, bottle, and store on the shelf. The alcohol softens the fruit, usually in a matter of months.

Fruit preserves and jams can be topped off with a tablespoon of alcohol for flavoring. You can do this safely as spirits have a pH

PRESERVING IN OIL

of approximately 4.0 and wine of 3.0. These kinds of preserves are water-bath processed.

Fruits can be preserved by maceration with alcohol, and they don't necessarily have to be processed in a water bath, like Bachelor's jam. In this classic boozy fruit preserve, you layer berries, usually, and sugar, then drown them in 80-proof alcohol and let it soak for weeks in a cool, dark place. It will hold in your fridge or on the shelf for up to a year, although the fruit must stay submerged in the alcohol.

Moving toward the less fruity, more alcoholic products, extracts are simply heavily infused spirits. The flavoring rests in the booze for weeks, even months, creating a concentrated flavor, like Vanilla Extract (page 361) or Lemon Extract (page 361), or flavored spirits, like liqueurs (flavored with nuts or spices) and cordials (flavored with fruit). I make cordials with the leftover fruit-flavored syrup I get from canning fruit. Cherry Bounce (page 80) is simply cherry syrup, rum, brandy, and water. But you can use the same recipe to make apricot bounce, peach bounce, apple bounce, even Concord grape bounce. Limoncello (page 175) is simply vodka or another neutral spirit that has lemon peels steeped in it, then combined with simple syrup. To make liqueurs (albeit lightly flavored ones) add a flavoring, like a handful of dried chamomile, to a bottle of grappa, gin, sake, or light rum. Let the flavoring steep in the booze until the taste is where you like it, strain, and bottle. Try cinnamon sticks, whole cloves, whole nutmeg, dried mushrooms, a hunk of semisweet chocolate, dried mint, coffee beans, or dried hot pepper. Fresh herbs, like basil, will make a mucky infusion. Cordials and liqueurs can be stored in your liquor cabinet and last forever.

A Final Word on Canning

Except where noted, I use USDA data for the processing times of the canned goods in this book. In some cases I used data produced by state university extension labs, part of the National Institute of Food and Agriculture. Processing data is key to safe canning, so while substitutions of spices or herbs, and additions of dried flavorings like black pepper or cinnamon, are okay, do not change the processing times, and be aware that processing times (and psi in pressure canning) are calibrated for specific jar sizes and altitudes.

How to Sterilize

Cover jars or bottles, bands, and lids with water and boil vigorously for 10 minutes.

Altitude Adjustments

Be aware of altitude adjustments. All the recipes in this book are written for cooks at sea level.

To sterilize jars: For every 1,000 feet in altitude, boil an additional 1 minute (it takes 10 minutes at sea level).

For water bath canning: If the processing time at sea level is 20 minutes or less, add 1 minute of processing time for each 1,000 feet above sea level: add 2 minutes for every 1,000 feet if the processing time is more than 20 minutes. And round up: If you live at 3,500 feet, process for 4,000 feet altitude.

For pressure canning: You need to add pressure, not increase the time. For weighted gauge pressure canners, increase the pressure to 15 pounds if you live between 1,000 and 10,000 feet above sea level. For dial gauge pressure canners, add ½ pound pressure for every 1,000 feet above 2,000 feet altitude.

For blanching vegetables prior to freezing: Add 1 minute blanching time if you live above 5,000 feet.

Molds: When to Scrape and When to Scrap

There are zillions of mold spores in the atmosphere floating around, hoping to land on something they like to eat. Let's say a spore lands on a package of cream cheese you've left on the counter for a few minutes while you smeared your bagel. You close the package and put it in the fridge. A few days later, there's a blue bloom on it. What to do? Well, mold grows in all directions from the point of germination, so while the blue stuff on the surface is just the sporulated part of the fungus, the microscopic fungus is growing hemispherically as well. The softer the product, the easier the fungus can penetrate, so you can assume that in the case of cream cheese or yogurt, as wide as the mold spot is, the mold has grown as deep. In these cases you should throw away the moldy product. However, the mold on dense, hard cheeses like Parmesan can be scraped (depending on how far advanced it is) because it takes longer for the fungus to penetrate it. The hard/soft rule applies to most foods: Throw out soft cured meats with mold but hard cured meats may be scraped. Throw out cooked or soft raw foods with mold, including bread. In the case of some hard raw foods, like onions, you can usually cut off the spoiled part, including ample margins.

RECIPE TECHNIQUES

Many of the products I make from the waste stream of primary ingredients are variations on a few primary ideas: stocks, juices, syrups, zests. In the recipe section you will find recipes with specific information: ingredients, amounts, directions, and any special handling. But below you will find the techniques for making these products, as well as a few techniques that simply show up often in these pages.

Preparing Stocks

I use stocks not just to make soups and risotto, but also in place of water in other dishes in order to amp up the flavor of the recipes, from boiling pasta to thinning a sauce to braising meat. When I make large amounts of stock I can or freeze it; smaller amounts, even as little as a pint, go in the fridge to be used at the first opportunity. Below is the basic technique for making stocks. In some cases the recipes will stray from this technique.

Place the scraps (stems, tough leaves, bones) and the additional flavoring ingredients (see individual recipes) in a medium or large soup pot depending on how much stuff you have. If you are making stock from a handful of mushroom stems a small pot will do.

Cover the scraps and other ingredients with about 2 inches of water. (Or use two parts flavor to three parts water—a good ratio determined by cookbook author Michael Ruhlman.) Bring to a boil, reduce the heat to medium-low, cover, and gently boil the stock. Vegetables, mushrooms, and fish will deliver flavor to the water in about an hour. But poultry, pork, and beef bones need at least 2 hours. Skim off the scum that rises to the surface while the stock is boiling. I usually remove the cover during the last 15 minutes or so of cooking in order to reduce and concentrate the stock. Strain the liquid. In the case of meat or poultry stocks, defat the stock with a gravy separator, a cheap, fabulous tool that every serial stock maker will treasure, or chill the broth in a bowl in the refrigerator for a couple of hours. The fat will rise to the top and harden. Remove the fat. Measure the amount of stock you have.

To store stock in the refrigerator, have ready the appropriate-size jars. I like to use quart jars, mainly to save space. Sterilize the jars, bands, and lids. Pour the stock into the jars; wipe the rims, place on the lids, and screw on the bands. You can store the stock in the refrigerator indefinitely, as long as you sterilize the stock every fourth day. The stock will reduce in volume every time you do this. (See page 389 for how to sterilize.)

To store stock in the freezer, be sure to use freezer-safe jars or plastic containers. You don't have to sterilize the jars but they need to be very clean. Pour the stock into the jars (I prefer pints) leaving 2 inches of headroom. You can freeze all the stocks for up to a year though the quality degenerates over time.

To store stock in the pantry, it must be pressure canned to be shelf stable. The times for individual foods will be in the stock recipes. Please also note the size of jars in the recipes, as this is important to the times required. I like to can stock in pint jars. (And in the case of the fish stocks, you have to. Keep in mind the recommendations of your particular canner when processing fish products.) Often I will only need a cup or two of stock for a recipe, so pints are more efficient for me. Process the jars at 10/11 pounds of pressure (at sea level) for the amount of time prescribed in the individual recipes. Be sure to make any altitude adjustments (page 389).

You can process different kinds of stock (or any product for that matter) at the same time, as long as you process them all at the longest time required for any individual product. For example, if you want to process pints of beef stock, which takes 20 minutes, and pints of vegetable stock, which takes 30 minutes, in the same load, you would need to process the lot for 30 minutes.

While there is no USDA data for canning mushroom, fish (freshwater or saltwater), or duck stocks, there is data for sliced mushrooms, duck meat, trout meat, and fish soup. To process stocks using timing intended

COOKING PASTA IN STOCK

BAKED CHERRIES

CHERRY SYRUP

for meat is undoubtedly overkill, but until the USDA does the testing, the only 100-percent sure way to preserve these stocks is to use the data that exists.

Preparing Pasta in Stocks

Cooking pasta in stock is a fabulous way to get another meal out of a pot of bones and stems and peels. The pasta absorbs the flavors from the stock and leaches out starch, which thickens the stock to create a savory sauce. You can make the pasta saucy or soupy with more stock, or tight and dry with less stock. Both versions are delicious and versatile. It is best to use thin spaghetti (spaghettini) or thin linguine (linguine fini). They will absorb the stock more efficiently. Thicker pasta will work, but you will need more stock and the taste will be wheaty. Very thin pasta like

fedelini is good, but it absorbs fast, and tends to get knotted and overcooked. If I use stock to cook fedelini, I prefer to serve it as a soup.

You will need about 1 pint of stock for every ¼ pound of thin pasta. Bring the stock to a boil in your pasta pot over medium-high heat. Season the stock to taste. Add the pasta. It will be stiff and stick out of the stock. Be patient. Gently push down the pasta, and after about 5 minutes it will soften and collapse into the stock. Stir often, as the pasta tends to stick together. Cook the pasta in the stock until it is al dente. You will notice the starch from the pasta thickens the stock to create a sauce. Add a little more stock or water if the pasta gets sticky. Do not overcook the pasta. It is best to serve this pasta loose. Toss in the various flavorings and garnishes as specified in individual recipes.

Preparing Juices

Not to be confused with juiced fresh fruits—a primo product described below—you can also make "captured" juices while preparing foods for cooking or canning. To do this, I prep fruits over a colander set in a bowl. The peels and seeds from tomatoes, for example, are very juicy. So are the peels from ripe peaches, and pitting sour cherries produces a lot of juice. If you press the scraps against the holes of the colander you may well end up with a cup or two of juice. To refine the juice, line a sieve with wet cheesecloth. Place the sieve over a bowl and pour the juice through the cheesecloth. (You can also save the juice-flavored water left over after boiling or blanching fruits and vegetables, like rhubarb or beets.)

It is easy to make juice from fresh fruits. Wash and prepare the fruit, removing the stems and blossom ends of apples and pits of stone fruits, and cutting large fruits into smaller pieces. Place the fruit in a large shallow pot and barely cover with water. Bring the water to a gentle boil over medium-high heat and cook until the fruit looks exploded. Arrange a jelly bag or a sieve lined with two layers of cheesecloth over a deep pot. Wet the bag or cheesecloth so it doesn't absorb any of the juice. Ladle the fruit and its cooking water into the jelly bag and let the juice drip through into the pot. You aren't supposed to squeeze the jelly bag because it can make the juice cloudy, but I do a little pressing anyway, to speed the process up, and have never had a problem. Measure the juice. Very generally, 3 cups of fruit cooked in enough water to cover will produce 1 cup of juice. Less water will make a more intense juice.

To store juice in the refrigerator, have ready sterilized jars, bands, and lids (see page 389). Pour the juice into the jars. Wipe the rims, place on the lids, and screw on the bands. You can store the juice in the refrigerator for 2 or 3 days. To store juice in the freezer, be sure to use freezer-safe jars or plastic containers. You don't have to sterilize the jars, but they need to be very clean. Pour the juice into the jars leaving 2 inches of headroom. You can freeze any of the juices in this book for up to 1 year.

All juices can be water bath canned, though not all can well. Orange and lemon juices, for example, are better frozen. Prepare and process as per the individual recipes. Be sure to make altitude adjustments when preserving (see page 389).

Preparing Granitas

Juices and flavored waters are perfect for making granitas. To make a granita, flavor the juice with sugar and, if you'd like, lemon juice, to your taste. Heat the juice and sugar together to dissolve the sugar. If the juice is thick, you can make a light syrup (10 percent sugar, so ⅓ cup sugar for every 3¼ cups of water), or heavier syrup with a greater percentage of sugar if you like it sweeter. In general, the greater the sugar-to-juice ratio, the more like a slushy your granita will be (which is not necessarily a bad thing). You also need to be careful when spiking granitas with booze. I have found that a granita will still freeze if there are no more than 3 tablespoons of 70-proof alcohol (like flavored brandy) for every 2 cups of juice.

Pour the sweetened juice or flavored water into a metal pan. Place in the freezer and every 15 to 30 minutes, run the tines of a fork through the ice to break up the crystals. Over the course of about 3 hours, the crystals will get small and crumbly.

After that, if you want a refined granita, pour into a food processor and pulse to grind the crystals. Then return the granita to the pan and refreeze, running the tines of the fork through it every 15 minutes or so for another 30 minutes. You can also make granita in your ice cream maker. Just follow the manufacturer's instructions for making sorbet.

Once done, you can pack the granita into a freezer-safe container; it can hold in the freezer for up to 1 year.

Preparing Fruit Syrups

Fruit syrups are simply fruit juice combined with sugar and cooked down to a syrupy consistency. Fruit syrups can be prepared fresh, of course (see below), but I tend to use the syrups that are left behind from cooking and canning projects. It's mainly a matter of capturing the leftover syrup from the bottom of the preserving pot and, if the volume is sparse, adding water, juice, or even wine. The syrup is cooked a few minutes longer with the additional liquid.

Syrups are fabulous as a sauce: Any serving of panna cotta, rice pudding, cheesecake, poached fruit, or ice cream benefits from a drizzle of syrup. Syrups are also useful in making cocktails and flavoring hot and cold tea. Syrups also make wonderful homemade sodas. Add 1 part syrup to 2 parts sparkling water, and pour over ice to serve.

To make syrups fresh, start with this simple formula: 1 cup of juice to 1 cup sugar. I use more sugar (1¼ cups) with tart fruits. Pour the juice into a saucepan and add the sugar.

Bring to a boil over medium heat, stirring to be sure the sugar doesn't scorch, then reduce the heat to a simmer for a minute or so. The syrup will be viscous, but still runny. Expect some minor variability in preparing syrups, depending on the kind of fruit you use. For example, some high-pectin fruits will threaten to jell if you boil the syrup too long. This will give you a thicker end product. But when you are ready to use it, just heat it up to loosen it, or add water.

To store syrup in the refrigerator, sterilize the jars, bands, and lids (see "How to Sterilize," page 389). Pour the syrup into the jars. Wipe the rims, place on the lids, and screw on the bands. You can store the syrup in the refrigerator for months.

Syrups, because of their high sugar content, can be difficult to freeze. If the syrup is more than 50 percent sugar it won't get hard, but that doesn't affect the safety at all. To store syrup in the freezer, be sure to use freezer-safe jars or plastic containers. You don't have to sterilize the jars, but they need to be very clean. Pour the syrup into the jars leaving 2 inches of headroom. You can freeze syrups for up to a year.

You can water bath can all fruit syrups. Process the jars for the amount of time prescribed in the individual recipes. Be sure to make altitude adjustments when preserving (see page 389).

Preparing Ice Cream by Hand

Ice cream makers are convenient, and there are small hand-crank models that work very well. But if you don't have an ice cream maker, no worries: Pour the cold ice cream mixture into a metal pan and place in the freezer. After about

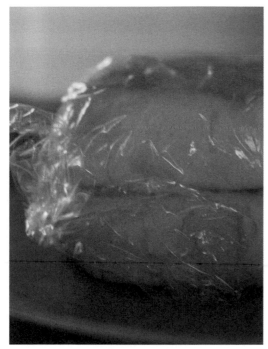

PASTRY

30 minutes, stir the mixture vigorously. You can use an electric hand mixer, or simply lots of elbow grease. There is a direct relationship between how refined the ice crystals of the ice cream are and the amount of stirring you do. Return to the freezer and check again in another 30 minutes and stir vigorously again. Keep doing this until the ice cream comes together and is firm. Spoon the ice cream into a plastic container and freeze. Ice cream holds for about 1 month in the freezer.

Preparing Pastry by Hand

I mainly use my food processor for pastry but, of course, pastry can be handmade, and honestly, it is more delicate if it is.

To make pastry by hand, measure the dry ingredients into a bowl. Use a pastry blender or 2 table knives to cut the fat into the dry ingredients, until the mixture is crumbly, like granola, or squeeze the butter and flour mixture between your fingers until it is well blended. If you want a superflaky pastry, grab a walnut-size piece of pastry and smear it with the palm of your hand against a stone or plastic surface (wood doesn't work as well). Continue with the rest of the dough. Press the dough into a disk, wrap in plastic wrap, and refrigerate for at least 30 minutes and up to 24 hours before rolling out.

Preparing Crepes

Follow the recipe for preparing the crepe batter.

Have ready 5 pieces of wax paper about 12 inches square. Heat a crepe pan or a small nonstick skillet over medium-high heat. Rub the lump of cold butter around the pan, leaving a thin coating of butter.

Ladle 2 tablespoons of batter into the pan and immediately tip the pan to spread the batter evenly over the bottom. Cook until air holes appear in the crepe, about 1 minute. Flip the crepe and cook 20 seconds more. Flip the crepe onto the wax paper. I usually place two 6-inch-diameter crepes on each sheet of wax paper, to save paper. (The first crepe is almost always funny looking. Don't worry. There is enough batter.) Repeat with the remaining batter and butter. The pan will get progressively hotter, so moderate the temperature by either lowering the heat or taking the pan off the flame for a minute. Otherwise, you will need to swirl the batter faster and faster as it will set as soon as it hits the hot metal.

ACKNOWLEDGMENTS

Making a book is an ecosystem of a sort, too. It is composed of many systems and individual acts that work in concert to create something vivid and alive. It's not just about me. Too bad, then, that the credit for such an ecosystem is hard to fit on one page, but I'm going to try

First, to those who helped make this book. Editors buy a lot of books, or have books other editors bought foisted upon them. When your editor really loves your project, it can be like a life jacket. My editor Doris Cooper's delight in this book was evident at all times and her skillful critiques and kind encouragement kept me from sinking into laziness and grumpiness. All writers should be so lucky. Thanks to Angela Miller, my trusted friend and adviser, and the brilliant Pam Krauss, whose judgment and character is precious to me. Many thanks to Ben Fink, who brought grace to every photograph and ease to every photo shoot. Copyeditor Kate Slate is, simply, a genius. Christine Tanigawa oversaw editorial production, a huge job with a book like this. Thanks to Rae Ann Spitzenberger: there were a lot of moving parts in this project, but she pulled it all together in a beautiful design. Jane Treuhaft, Marysarah Quinn, and Jim Massey oversaw everything one sees in this book, and Kate Tyler and Carly Gorga in the publicity and marketing departments shepherded this project into the world. To all of you, many thanks.

Second, to those who abetted the development of my ideas for this book. I first went public with the ecosystem paradigm in a lecture at the Denver Botanical Gardens in 2010, and then in various articles for *Food & Wine, Saveur, Martha Stewart Living,* and the *New York Times,* and in my now-defunct blog, *Well-Preserved,* which was hosted by the *Denver Post.* Thanks to all those colleagues for their enthusiasm, especially Tucker Shaw.

Third, to those upon whom the safety of this book depends. When writing preserving recipes there are rarely more than tiny changes in quantities and techniques that can be made safely, and we all are (hopefully) using USDA data. So, like most canners, I am greatly in the debt of the many food scientists in the extension system, in the industry, and at the National Center for Home Preservation, but especially Dr. Elizabeth L. Andress.

Fourth, to those who inspire. I am a child of the first wave of the American food revolution, and owe a huge debt of thanks to those chefs and authors who blazed the trail and influenced me, some I know, some I knew, some I have never met, but most of all my dad, Edward Giobbi.

Fifth, to those who support with love and advice. How many friends and relatives have helped with recipes, or eaten crappy ones, or just generally pretended to be excited when I talked about this book for the umpteenth time? When I typed out the list it was too long to fit in this space. That's when I realized I am very, very rich.

And finally, to Kevin, who, when I was answering preserving questions at a farmers' market, commented that he would be glad to handle any dishwashing questions. Enough said.

INDEX

A

Alcohol, preserving with, 388–89
Almond(s)
  Dried Cherry Chunkies, 80
  Garlic Scape Pesto, 229
  Pierre's Rhubarb Galette, 289
  Plum Galette, 254–55
  Sachertorte with Raspberry
    Jam, 282–83
  -Strawberry Ice Cream, 321
  Torte with Lemon Zest, 172–73
Anchovy(ies)
  Butter, 271
  Pissaladière, 212
  Tuna, and Olives, Fried Pasta
    with, 302
Apple(s), 7–15
  Applesauce, 10
  Baked, with Bread Pudding, 9
  Cranberry Cake, 103–4
  Cranberry Muffins, 104
  and Fennel, Sliced, Salad, 135–36
  Juice Granita, 15–16
  Lady, Basil Jelly, 10–11
  Peel Jelly Stock, 14–15
  Smoked Pork Butt, and Onion
    Sauté, 8
  Stewed, with Red Cabbage, 8
  Stuffed with Cranberry Sauce,
    106
Applesauce, 10
  Cake with Raisins and Walnuts,
    14
  and Caramelized Onion, Pork
    Steaks with, 212–13
Apricot(s), 16–23
  Baked, with Mascarpone
    Cream, 17
  Chocolate Truffles, 22–23
  Dried, 20
  -Orange Ice Cream, Beulah's, 21
  -Orange Puree, 19
  and Raisins, Canned, 19
  -Raisin Skillet Tart, 20–21
  Shrub, 23
  and Tarragon, Braised Chicken
    with, 17
Artichoke(s), 24–30
  Baby, Marinated, with Hot
    Pepper, 28–29
  Constantinople Style, 27–28
  Marinade and Potatoes,
    Sausages with, 30
  Marinated, and Parsley,
    Chicken with, 30

  Marinated, Shrimp with, 29–30
  and Mint, Braised Lamb with,
    27
  and Ricotta, Spaghetti with, 25
  Smoked Swordfish Salad with
    Avocado, 310–11
  trimming, 25
Arugula
  Baby, Watermelon, and Shrimp
    Salad, 347
  Skirt Steak with Cherry Pepper
    Marinade, 252
Asparagus, 31–40
  Dilly, 35–36
  Dilly, and Cauliflower Salad,
    36–37
  Frittata with Parmesan, 32–33
  Pesto, 35
  Pesto, Ravioli with, 38–39
  Risotto, 40
  Roasted, Soft-Shell Crabs with,
    32–33
  Shaved, Pea, and Pea Shoot
    Salad, 33–35
  Stock, 37
  trimming, 32
  White, with Black Trumpets,
    193
Avocado
  Cucumber, and Red Onion
    Salad with Cilantro Cream,
    110–11
  Smoked Swordfish Salad with,
    310–11

B

Bacon
  and Beets, Farfalle with, 50
  Fried Trout Stuffed with
    Pancetta and Sage, 341
  Homemade, 263–64
  Homemade, Chicken
    Canzanese with, 266–67
  Pizza Carbonara, 265–66
  Watermelon Rind Pickles
    Wrapped in, 350
Basil
  Lady Apple Jelly, 10–11
  Pesto, 236
  -Watermelon Granita, 349
Bean(s)
  Black, Pork Tacos with, 262–63
  and Corn Soup, 93–95
  Cranberry, with Tuna and
    Pickled Onions, 213

  Green, and Mint Salad, 119
  and Pork with Feta and
    Cilantro, 269
  and Shrimp Soup, 314
Beef, 41–48. See also Veal
  Boiled, with Rhubarb Sour
    Cream Sauce, 287
  Bollito Misto with Pickle Sauce,
    115–16
  Brisket with Sweet and Sour
    Plum Sauce, 254
  Bull Shot Cocktail, 48
  Canned, 44–45
  Canned, Pot Pie, 45–46
  Cannelloni, 46–47
  Cheeks, Braised, with Cloves,
    43–44
  estimating doneness, 42
  Filet Mignon with Gorgonzola
    Sauce, 43
  Flank Steak with Carrot Top
    Pesto, 71
  Pasta alla Bolognese with
    Besciamella, 42–43
  Pasta Genovese, 66
  Pastrami with Sauerkraut,
    61–62
  Pot Roast in Porcini Stock, 200
  Pot Roast with Cranberries, 102
  Skirt Steak with Cherry Pepper
    Marinade, 252
  Steak, Potato, and Pickled
    Radish Salad, 273
  Stewed with Garlic and
    Tomatoes, 334
  Stock, 47
  Stock with Poached Eggs and
    Meatballs, 47–48
  T-Bone Steak with Winter
    Chanterelles, 193
  Tenderloin with Currant Wine
    Jelly Glaze, 123–24
Beet(s), 49–55
  and Bacon, Farfalle with, 50
  buying, 50
  Canned, 52–54
  Canned, with Tuna, 54
  Granita, 55
  greens, removing, 50
  Greens Gratin, 55
  Jam, 52
  Pickled, 51–52
  Pickled, Stuffed Eggs with, 54
  Roast, Salad with Feta,
    Scallions, and Cilantro, 50–51

Berries, 6. *See also* Cranberry(ies); Raspberry(ies); Strawberry(ies)
Bourbon
Bull Shot Cocktail, 48
Eggnog, 9–10
La Squisita, 146
Old-Fashioned, 221
The Prospero, 164
Brandy
Cherry Bounce, 80
Tiramisu with Raisins, 161
Bread Pudding, Baked Apples with, 9
Breads
Duck Fat Buttermilk Cornbread, 128
Gravlax with Brioche and Mozzarella, 298
making crumbs with, 362
Raspberry Jam Scones, 281–82
Sweet Buns with Peach Puree, 226–27
Broccolini, Spaghettini Cooked in Chicken Stock with, 91
Broccoli Rabe with Stuffed Cherry Peppers, 242
Brussels Sprouts
and Chicken Confit, Gemelli with, 128–31
with Cranberries and Shallots, 102–3
Butter
Anchovy, 271
Herb, 363
Lobster, 180
Porcini, 199

C
Cabbage, 56–64
Leaves Stuffed with Veal, 57–58
Marilee's Coleslaw, 58
Pastrami with Sauerkraut, 61–62
Penne with, 58
Polenta with Sauerkraut and Sausage, 61
Red, Stewed Apples with, 8
Sauerkraut with Caraway Seeds, 60
Stock, 62–63
Stock, Scrippelle in, 63–64
Cakes
Almond Torte with Lemon Zest, 172–73
Applesauce, with Raisins and Walnuts, 14
baking as muffins, 5

Chocolate Raspberry, Almost Flourless, 277
Cranberry Apple, 103–4
Lemon Poppy Seed, 168–69
Orange Olive Oil Pound, 215–16
Peach Buckle, 225–26
Raspberry Coffee, with Cinnamon Crumble, 277–78
Sachertorte with Raspberry Jam, 282–83
Strawberry Cupcakes with Strawberry Jam Icing, 323–24
Candy
Apricot Chocolate Truffles, 22–23
Dried Cherry Chunkies, 80
Raspberry Jellies, 280–81
Carrot(s), 65–71
Artichokes Constantinople Style, 27–28
with Butter and Fennel Seeds, 68
Canned Ginger, 69
Jam, 69
and Onions, Braised Duck Legs with, 126
Pasta Genovese, 66
and Shallots, Veal Stew with, 67
Soufflé, Ginger, 70
Top Pesto, 70–71
Top Pesto, Flank Steak with, 71
Cassis, 122
Cauliflower and Dilly Asparagus Salad, 36–37
Cheese
Asparagus Frittata with Parmesan, 32–33
Baked Apricots with Mascarpone Cream, 17
Baked Fennel with Parmesan, 134–35
Beet Greens Gratin, 55
Cannoli Cream, 368
Cherry-Ricotta Strudel, 73–74
Corn and Potato Gratin, 93
Cuban Sandwiches with Zucchini Pickle, 356–58
Filet Mignon with Gorgonzola Sauce, 43
Fillet of Sole Stuffed with Ricotta with Shrimp Shell Sauce, 318
Gravlax with Brioche and Mozzarella, 298
Lasagna with Acorn Squash and Marinara Sauce, 333–34
Mac and, with Creamed Corn, 97–98

Marilee's Chiles Rellenos, 242–43
Marinated Mushroom and Gruyère Pizza, 189
Pimiento, 248
Pizza Carbonara, 265–66
Ravioli with Asparagus Pesto, 38–39
Ricotta, 367
Ricotta and Marinated Mushroom Pie, 190
Ricotta Balls Stuffed with Lemon Curd, 174
Roast Beet Salad with Feta, Scallions, and Cilantro, 50–51
Spaghetti with Artichokes and Ricotta, 25
Tiramisu with Raisins, 161
Tomatoes Stuffed with Ricotta and Tuna, 305
Watermelon, Tomato, and Gorgonzola Salad, 347–49
Zucchini Carpaccio, 353–54
Cherry(ies), 72–81
Bounce, 80
Chocolate Chip Ice Cream, 74–76
Dried, Chunkies, 80
grown in Colorado, 75
Jam, Baked, with Orange Zest, 76–77
pitting, 73
-Ricotta Strudel, 73–74
Soufflé, 79
Sour, Corn Cakes with, 73
swapping berries for, 6
Sweet, Ancho Pork with, 78
Sweet, Dried, 77
Sweet or Sour, Canned, 76
Chicken, 82–91
Baked in Clay with Onion Sauce, 209–10
Bollito Misto with Pickle Sauce, 115–16
Braised, with Apricots and Tarragon, 17
Canned, 86
Canzanese with Homemade Bacon, 266–67
Cold Roast, with Cucumbers and Yogurt, 110
Confit and Brussels Sprouts, Gemelli with, 128–31
Confit with Lentils, 127–28
Croquettes, 88–89
Cutlets with Meyer and Regular Lemon Marmalade, 173–74

Chicken (*continued*)
cutting into parts, 83
with Garlic and Rosemary, 84
Gizzard Confit, 86–87
Gnocchi in Broth, 88
Gnocchi with Sage Butter, 87
with Marinated Artichokes and
Parsley, 30
with Mussels, 205–6
with Olive Tapenade and
Verjuice, 160
with Peas, Pearl Onions, and
Mint, 229–31
with Pepper Marinade, 251–52
with Pork-Stuffed Cherry
Peppers, 240
and Potato Gnocchi with
Marinara Sauce, 87
Roast, with Olive-Orange
Tapenade, 218–19
with Sherry and Dried Morels,
196–97
with Sherry and Fresh Morels,
197
with Sour Cream and
Mushrooms, 184–85
Stock, 89
Stock, Spaghettini Cooked in,
with Broccolini, 91
Stuffed Boned, 85
trussing, 83
Zia Ada's Stracciatella, 91
Chocolate
Candied Ginger Bark, 155
Chip Cherry Ice Cream,
74–76
Dried Cherry Chunkies, 80
Fried Ravioli with Grape Must
Concentrate, 163–64
Orange Shortbread with, 219
Raspberry Cake, Almost
Flourless, 277
Sachertorte with Raspberry
Jam, 282–83
Truffles, Apricot, 22–23
Cilantro
Cream, 111
Rice with Poblanos, 243–44
Cod with Sweet Potatoes, 307–8
Coffee Cake, Raspberry, with
Cinnamon Crumble, 277–78
Coleslaw, Marilee's, 58
Confit
Chicken, and Brussels Sprouts,
Gemelli with, 128–31
Chicken, with Lentils, 127–28
Chicken Gizzard, 86–87

Salmon, Smith Fork Ranch,
298–99
Cookies and bars
Chewy Ginger Black Pepper,
148–50
Lemon Ladyfingers, 162
Orange Shortbread with
Chocolate, 219
Plum Jam Shortbread, 258–59
Walnut Raspberry Mint Jam,
283
Corn, 92–100
and Bean Soup, 93–95
Canned Creamed, 96
Creamed, Mac and Cheese with,
97–98
husks, drying, 93
Ice Cream, 95–96
Pickled, Relish, 97
and Potato Gratin, 93
Relish, Broiled Seafood Skewers
with, 98
and Shrimp Casserole, 99
Stock, 99–100
Stock, Zucchini Soup with, 100
Cornmeal
Corn Cakes with Sour Cherries,
73
Duck Fat Buttermilk
Cornbread, 128
Polenta with Sauerkraut and
Sausage, 61
Polenta with Shredded Zucchini
and Tarragon, 353
Crabs
Risotto with Crabmeat, 312
soft-shell, buying, 33
Soft-Shell, with Roasted
Asparagus, 32–33
Cranberry(ies), 101–8
Apple Cake, 103–4
Apple Muffins, 104
Crepes, 108
Juice, 106
Madras Cocktail, 108
Mustard, 105
-Orange Sauce, 104–5
Pot Roast with, 102
Sauce, Apples Stuffed with, 106
and Shallots, Brussels Sprouts
with, 102–3
Crème Fraîche, 362
Crepes
Cranberry, 108
preparing, 395
Rhubarb, 291–92
Strawberry, 324

Cucumber(s), 109–16
Avocado, and Red Onion Salad
with Cilantro Cream, 110–11
Bread and Butter Pickles, 112–13
pickles, preparing, 111
Pickle Spears, 112
Relish, 113
Tartar Sauce, 113
and Yogurt, Cold Roast
Chicken with, 110
Cupcakes, Strawberry, with
Strawberry Jam Icing, 323–24
Curd, Lemon, 171–72
Currant(s), 117–23
Cassis, 122
Jelly, 120–21
jelly glaze, uses for, 121
Juice, 120
Pork Tenderloin with, 119
Red, and Cream Cup, 119–20
Vinaigrette, 122
Wine Jelly, 122
Wine Jelly Glaze, Beef
Tenderloin with, 123–24

D
Desserts. *See also* Cakes; Cookies
and bars
Apple Juice Granita, 15–16
Apples Stuffed with Cranberry
Sauce, 106
Apricot-Raisin Skillet Tart,
20–21
Baked Apples with Bread
Pudding, 9
Baked Apricots with
Mascarpone Cream, 17
Beet Granita, 55
Beulah's Apricot-Orange Ice
Cream, 21
Candy Cap Panna Cotta, 197–98
Cannoli Cream, 368
Cherry Chocolate Chip Ice
Cream, 74–76
Cherry-Ricotta Strudel, 73–74
Cherry Soufflé, 79
Corn Ice Cream, 95–96
Cranberry Crepes, 108
Fig Jam Crostata, 145
Fried Ravioli with Grape Must
Concentrate, 163–64
Ginger-Orange Granita, 154
Grape Custard Tart, 157–58
Lemon Asti, 174–75
Memphis-Style Strawberry Pie,
320–21
Meyer Lemon Granita, 173

Orange Sherbet, 218
Peaches with Thyme and
    Moscato Wine, 224
Pears Poached in Fig Syrup, 146
Pierre's Rhubarb Galette, 289
Plum Galette, 254–55
Plum-Orange Granita, 259
Poached Pears in White Wine
    with Ginger Syrup, 153
Prunes Stewed in Madeira
    Wine, 259
Red Currant and Cream Cup,
    119–20
Rhubarb Crepes, 291–92
Rice Pudding with Figs in
    Simple Syrup, 145–46
Ricotta Balls Stuffed with
    Lemon Curd, 174
Southern-Style Lemon
    Meringue Pie, 166–68
Stewed Rhubarb Crisp, 291
Strawberry-Almond Ice Cream,
    321
Strawberry Crepes, 324
Strawberry Panna Cotta, 325
Strawberry Soufflé, 324–25
Sweet Fried Figs, 142
Tiramisu with Raisins, 161
Vanilla Panna Cotta with
    Ginger Syrup, 154
Watermelon-Basil Granita, 349
Watermelon Pudding, 349
Zabaglione with Raspberries,
    278
Dilly Asparagus, 35–36
Dilly Asparagus and Cauliflower
    Salad, 36–37
Dips and spreads. See also Jam;
    Jelly; Marmalade; Pesto;
    Preserves
    Anchovy Butter, 271
    Green Olive and Orange
        Tapenade, 217–18
    Green Olive Tapenade, 160
    Herb Butter, 363
    Lemon Curd, 171–72
    Lobster Butter, 180
    Mayonnaise, 365–66
    Mustard, 366
    Pimiento Cheese, 248
    Porcini Butter, 199
    Rhubarb Salsa, 286–87
    Smoked Trout Pâté, 344
Drinks. See also Juice
    Apricot Shrub, 23
    Bellini Cocktail, 223
    Bull Shot Cocktail, 48

Cassis, 122
Chef Bill's Lemonade, 169–70
Cherry Bounce, 80
Eggnog, 9–10
Gibson with Pickled Onion
    Juice, 213
La Squisita, 146
Limoncello, 175
Madras Cocktail, 108
Old-Fashioned, 221
The Prospero, 164
Rhubarb Ginger Soda, 292
Tomato Water Martini, 336
Whiskey with a Pickleback, 116
Duck, 124–32
    Breasts, Seared, with Marsala,
        125–26
    Fat, Rendered, 126
    Fat Buttermilk Cornbread, 128
    Legs, Braised, with Onions and
        Carrots, 126
    Liver Crostini, 125
    processing, description of, 130
    Soup with Sausage Omelet, 132
    Stewed, with Savory Plum Jam,
        258
    Stock, 131–32

E
Eggnog, 9–10
Eggplant
    Caponata, 355
Egg(s)
    Asparagus Frittata with
        Parmesan, 32–33
    Coddled, with Spinach and
        Mushrooms, 184
    Duck Soup with Sausage
        Omelet, 132
    Eggnog, 9–10
    Omelet with Pickled Radishes,
        272–73
    Pizza Carbonara, 265–66
    Poached, and Meatballs, Beef
        Stock with, 47–48
    Poached, Homemade Yogurt
        with, 370
    Poached, with Pea Pesto, 234–35
    Poached in Tomatoes, 332
    Poached on Sweet Peppers and
        Onions, 239
    Salad with Fennel-Pistachio
        Compote, 138
    Scrambled, with Canned
        Shrimp, 317
    Scrippelle in Cabbage Stock,
        63–64

Stuffed, with Pickled Beets, 54
Zia Ada's Stracciatella, 91
Extracts
    Lemon, 361–62
    preparing, 361
    Vanilla, 361

F
Fennel, 133–40
    and Anisette, Brodetto with,
        134
    and Apple, Sliced, Salad, 135–36
    Baked, with Parmesan, 134–35
    Baked Whole Fish on, 307
    Leaves, Cured Halibut with,
        140
    Pickled, 136–38
    Pickled, Glazed Pork Chops
        with, 139
    -Pistachio Compote, 136
    -Pistachio Compote, Egg Salad
        with, 138
    -Pistachio Compote, Striped
        Bass with, 138–39
    Seeds and Butter, Carrots with,
        68
Fig(s), 141–46
    Balsamic Jam, 144
    Jam Crostata, 145
    La Squisita, 146
    in Simple Syrup, Rice Pudding
        with, 145–46
    in Simple Syrup with
        Cardamom, 144
    Sweet Fried, 142
    Syrup, Pears Poached in, 146
    Watercress, and Sausage Salad,
        142
Fish. See also Anchovy(ies);
    Salmon; Trout; Tuna
    Baked Whole, on Fennel, 307
    Brodetto with Fennel and
        Anisette, 134
    Cod with Sweet Potatoes,
        307–8
    Cured Halibut with Fennel
        Leaves, 140
    Fillet of Sole Stuffed with
        Ricotta with Shrimp Shell
        Sauce, 318
    Flounder with Grape Sauce and
        Scallions, 157
    Fried, with Rhubarb Salsa,
        286–87
    Halibut Poached in Tomato
        Water, 336
    Halibut with Nettle Pesto, 308–9

Fish (*continued*)
  Red Snapper with Tapenade in
    Parchment, 309–10
  saltwater white-fleshed, 306–12
  Smoked Swordfish, 310
  Smoked Swordfish Salad with
    Avocado, 310–11
  Spaghettini with Baby Lettuce
    and Smoked Swordfish, 311
  Stock, 311–12
  Striped Bass with Fennel-
    Pistachio Compote, 138–39
  substituting types of, in
    recipes, 6
  Swordfish with Pea Pesto, 235
Flounder with Grape Sauce and
  Scallions, 157
Frittata, Asparagus, with
  Parmesan, 32–33
Fruits. *See also specific fruits*
  citrus, note about, 6
  swapping types of, in recipes, 6

G
Galettes
  Plum, 254–55
  Rhubarb, Pierre's, 289
Garlic
  Gremolata, 185–86
  and Rosemary, Chicken with,
    84
  Skordalia, 368
  and Tomatoes, Beef Stewed
    with, 334
Garlic Scape Pesto, 229
Ginger, 147–55
  Black Pepper Cookies, Chewy,
    148–50
  Bug, 152
  Candied, 154
  Candied, Bark, 155
  Carrots, Canned, 69
  Carrot Soufflé, 70
  mature, about, 151
  -Orange Granita, 154
  Pickled, 150
  -Rhubarb Jam, 291
  Rhubarb Soda, 292
  Scallop Crudo with, 148
  spring, about, 151
  Syrup, 150–52
  Syrup, Poached Pears in White
    Wine with, 153
  Syrup, Vanilla Panna Cotta
    with, 154
Gizzard, Chicken, Confit, 86–87
Glaze, currant jelly, uses for, 121

Gnocchi
  in Broth, 88
  Chicken and Potato, with
    Marinara Sauce, 87
  with Sage Butter, 87
Grains. *See also* Cornmeal; Rice
  Granola with Raisins, 162–63
Granita
  Apple Juice, 15–16
  Beet, 55
  Ginger-Orange, 154
  Meyer Lemon, 173
  Plum-Orange, 259
  preparing, 393–94
  Watermelon-Basil, 349
Granola with Raisins, 162–63
Grapefruit
  or Orange Peels, Candied, 221
  substituting other citrus for, 6
Grape(s), 156–64. *See also*
    Raisin(s)
  Custard Tart, 157–58
  Must Concentrate, 163
  Must Concentrate, Fried Ravioli
    with, 163–64
  The Prospero, 164
  Sauce and Scallions, Flounder
    with, 157
  Verjuice, 158–60
Gravlax
  with Aquavit, 295–96
  with Brioche and Mozzarella,
    298
Green Bean and Mint Salad, 119
Greens
  beet, cutting off, 50
  Beet, Gratin, 55
  Carrot Top Pesto, 70–71
  Feral, 231
  Flank Steak with Carrot Top
    Pesto, 71
  Radish, Skillet-Cooked, 275
  Radish, Vichyssoise, 275
  swapping types of, in recipes, 6
  Utica, 67–68

H
Halibut
  Cured, with Fennel Leaves,
    140
  with Nettle Pesto, 308–9
  Poached in Tomato Water, 336
Ham
  Prosciutto and Pea Sandwiches,
    232
  Ricotta and Marinated
    Mushroom Pie, 190

Herb(s). *See also specific herbs*
  Butter, 363
  swapping types of, in recipes, 6
  Syrup, 364
  and Wine, Mussels Cooked in,
    205
Horseradish, 364
Horseradish Pesto, 364–65

I
Iceberg Wedges with Ranch
  Pickle Juice Dressing, 358
Ice Cream
  Apricot-Orange, Beulah's, 21
  Cherry Chocolate Chip, 74–76
  Corn, 95–96
  preparing by hand, 394–95
  Strawberry-Almond, 321
Icing, Strawberry Jam, 323–24

J
Jam
  about, 373–74
  Beet, 52
  Carrot, 69
  Cherry, Baked, with Orange
    Zest, 76–77
  Fig Balsamic, 144
  fruit, swapping types of, in
    recipes, 6
  Plum, Savory, 256–58
  Plum, Sweet, 256
  Raspberry, with Mint, 278–80
  Rhubarb, 290–91
  Rhubarb-Ginger, 291
  strawberry, tips for preparing,
    323
Jellies, Raspberry, 280–81
Jelly
  about, 373–74
  Currant, 120–21
  currant, glaze, uses for, 121
  Currant Wine, 122
  Lady Apple Basil, 10–11
  Mixed Hot Pepper, 247
  Peach Pit, 227
Jelly Stock, Apple Peel, 14–15
Juice
  Cranberry, 106
  Currant, 120
  fruit, swapping types of, in
    recipes, 6
  preparing, 393
  Raspberry, 283–84

K
Ketchup, Tomato, 330–31

L

Ladyfingers, Lemon, 162
Lamb
    Braised, with Artichokes and
        Mint, 27
    Braised, with Lemons, Neni's,
        166
    Chops, Loin, with Horseradish
        Pesto, 364–65
    Meatballs with Romesco Sauce,
        249
    Tonnato, 303–5
Lard, Home-Rendered, 268
Lemon(s), 165–75
    Asti, 174–75
    Braised Lamb with, Neni's, 166
    brightening up dishes with, 166
    Chef Bill's Lemonade, 169–70
    Curd, 171–72
    Curd, Ricotta Balls Stuffed
        with, 174
    Extract, 361–62
    Gremolata, 185–86
    juicing, 169
    Ladyfingers, 162
    Limoncello, 175
    Meringue Pie, Southern-Style,
        166–68
    Meyer, Granita, 173
    Meyer and Regular, Marmalade,
        170
    Meyer and Regular, Marmalade,
        Chicken Cutlets with, 173–74
    Mushroom Risotto, 191
    Poppy Seed Cake, 168–69
    substituting other citrus for, 6
    Zest, Almond Torte with,
        172–73
Lentil(s)
    Chicken Confit with, 127–28
    and Smoked Trout Salad, 343
Lettuce
    Baby, and Smoked Swordfish,
        Spaghettini with, 311
    Iceberg Wedges with Ranch
        Pickle Juice Dressing, 358
Liver
    Duck, Crostini, 125
    Yvon's Country Terrine,
        264–65
Lobster, 176–82
    Butter, 180
    freezing, 178
    preparing, 177
    Reduction, 180
    Reduction, Shrimp and Chorizo
        with, 182

Reduction, Warm Scallop and
    Potato Salad with, 182
Sauce, Linguine with, 177
thawing, 178
Thermidor, Quick, 179
Warm, Salad, Sean's, 178

M

Marmalade
    Chanterelle, 195–96
    Meyer and Regular Lemon, 170
Mayonnaise, 365–66
Meat. See Beef; Lamb; Pork; Veal
Meatballs
    Lamb, with Romesco Sauce, 249
    and Poached Eggs, Beef Stock
        with, 47–48
Mint
    Canned Peas with, 233
    and Green Bean Salad, 119
Muffins
    baking as cakes, 5–6
    Cranberry Apple, 104
Mushroom(s), 183–200
    Candy Cap Panna Cotta, 197–98
    Chanterelle Marmalade, 195–96
    Chicken with Sherry and Dried
        Morels, 196–97
    Chicken with Sherry and Fresh
        Morels, 197
    cultivated, 183–91
    cultivated, cooking basics, 184
    cultivated, preparing, 184
    Dried Black Trumpet and Tuna
        Salad, 197
    Lemon Risotto, 191
    Marinated, and Gruyère Pizza,
        189
    Marinated, and Ricotta Pie, 190
    Marinated, Canned, 188
    Marinated, Quick, 186–88
    Osso Buco with, 185–86
    Pesto, 188–89
    Porcini Butter, 199
    porcini powder, preparing, 198
    Porcini Salt, 198–99
    Porcini Stock, 199–200
    Pot Roast in Porcini Stock, 200
    Red Snapper with Tapenade in
        Parchment, 309–10
    Roasted Marinated, 188
    and Sour Cream, Chicken with,
        184–85
    and Spinach, Coddled Eggs
        with, 184
    Stock, 190–91
    Stuffed Boned Chicken, 85

swapping types of, in recipes, 6
T-Bone Steak with Winter
    Chanterelles, 193
White Asparagus with Black
    Trumpets, 193
wild, 192–200
wild, drying, methods for, 195
wild dried, rehydrating, 195
Mussel(s), 201–7
    Broth, Linguine Fini in, 207
    buying and storing, 203
    Chicken with, 205–6
    Cooked in Wine and Herbs, 205
    and Scallop Chimichurri Salad,
        203–5
    Smoked, 206
    Smoked, and Potato Salad,
        206–7
    Stuffed Broiled, 203
Mustard, 366
    Cranberry, 105
    Vinaigrette, 368–69

N

Nettle Pesto, 308–9
Nuts. See also Almond(s); Pine
    Nuts; Walnut(s)
    Fennel-Pistachio Compote, 136

O

Oats
    Granola with Raisins, 162–63
Oil, 387–88
Oil, Hot, Asian-Style, 360–61
Olive(s)
    Black, Sauce, 294
    Cured, 362–63
    Green, and Orange Tapenade,
        217–18
    Green, Tapenade, 160
    -Orange Tapenade, Roast
        Chicken with, 218–19
    Pissaladière, 212
    Tapenade and Verjuice, Chicken
        with, 160
    Tuna, and Anchovies, Fried
        Pasta with, 302
Omelets
    with Pickled Radishes, 272–73
    Sausage, Duck Soup with, 132
    Scrippelle in Cabbage Stock,
        63–64
Onion(s), 208–13
    Apples, and Smoked Pork Butt
        Sauté, 8
    Caramelized, and Applesauce,
        Pork Steaks with, 212–13

Onion(s) (*continued*)
  Caramelized, Canned, 210–11
  and Carrots, Braised Duck Legs
    with, 126
  Cipollini in Sweet and Sour
    Sauce, 211
  Pearl, Peas, and Mint, Chicken
    with, 229–31
  Pickled, 211–12
  Pickled, and Tuna, Cranberry
    Beans with, 213
  Pickled, Juice, Gibson with, 213
  Pissaladière, 212
  Sauce, Chicken Baked in Clay
    with, 209–10
  and Sweet Peppers, Eggs
    Poached on, 239
  and Tomatoes, Spaghetti with, 209
Orange(s), 214–21
  -Apricot Puree, 19
  Bitters, 221
  Braised Pork Shoulder with, 215
  Chef Bill's Lemonade, 169–70
  -Cranberry Sauce, 104–5
  -Ginger Granita, 154
  and Green Olive Tapenade,
    217–18
  Honeybells, about, 216
  Macerated, with Mint, 216–17
  Old-Fashioned, 221
  Olive Oil Pound Cake, 215–16
  -Olive Tapenade, Roast Chicken
    with, 218–19
  or Grapefruit Peels, Candied, 221
  -Plum Granita, 259
  Sherbet, 218
  Shortbread with Chocolate, 219
  substituting other citrus for, 6
  Zest, Baked Cherry Jam with,
    76–77
Oysters, Fried, with Tartar Sauce,
  115

P
Pancakes
  Corn Cakes with Sour Cherries,
    73
  Potato, with Applesauce, 13
Pancetta and Sage, Fried Trout
  Stuffed with, 341
Panna Cotta
  Candy Cap, 197–98
  Strawberry, 325
  Vanilla, with Ginger Syrup, 154
Parsley
  Chimichurri Sauce, 204–5
  Gremolata, 185–86

Pasta
  alla Bolognese with Besciamella,
    42–43
  Beef Cannelloni, 46–47
  Broccoli Rabe with Stuffed
    Cherry Peppers, 242
  Chicken and Potato Gnocchi
    with Marinara Sauce, 87
  cooking in stock, 392
  Farfalle with Beets and Bacon, 50
  Fried, with Tuna, Anchovies,
    and Olives, 302
  Fried Ravioli with Grape Must
    Concentrate, 163–64
  Gemelli with Chicken Confit
    and Brussels Sprouts, 128–31
  Genovese, 66
  Gnocchi in Broth, 88
  Gnocchi with Sage Butter, 87
  Lasagna with Acorn Squash and
    Marinara Sauce, 333–34
  Linguine Fini in Mussel Broth,
    207
  Linguine with Lobster Sauce, 177
  Mac and Cheese with Creamed
    Corn, 97–98
  Penne with Cabbage, 58
  Penne with Zucchini Flowers
    and Shrimp, 314–15
  Primavera, Italian, 327
  Ravioli with Asparagus Pesto,
    38–39
  Spaetzle with Ramps Pesto,
    341–42
  Spaghettini Cooked in Chicken
    Stock with Broccolini, 91
  Spaghettini in Trout Stock with
    Capers and Breadcrumbs, 345
  Spaghettini with Baby Lettuce
    and Smoked Swordfish, 311
  Spaghetti with Artichokes and
    Ricotta, 25
  Spaghetti with Onions and
    Tomatoes, 209
  swapping types of, in recipes, 6
  with Sweet Pepper Puree, 238
Pastrami with Sauerkraut, 61–62
Pastry, preparing by hand, 395
Peach(es), 222–27
  Bellini Cocktail, 223
  Buckle, 225–26
  Pit Jelly, 227
  Puree, 225
  Puree, Sweet Buns with, 226–27
  with Thyme and Moscato Wine,
    224
  and Tomato Salad, 223

Pears
  Poached, in White Wine with
    Ginger Syrup, 153
  Poached in Fig Syrup, 146
Pea(s), 228–36
  and Marsala, Veal Scaloppine
    with, 232–33
  with Mint, Canned, 233
  Pearl Onions, and Mint,
    Chicken with, 229–31
  Pesto, 233–34
  Pesto, Poached Eggs with,
    234–35
  Pesto, Swordfish with, 235
  pod stock, preparing, 236
  and Prosciutto Sandwiches, 232
  Shaved Asparagus, and Pea
    Shoot Salad, 33–35
  Soup with Garlic Scape Pesto,
    229
  Spring Minestrone, 236
Pepper(s), 237–52
  Ancho Sauce, 78
  Cherry, Marinade, Skirt Steak
    with, 252
  Cherry, Marinated Stuffed,
    245–46
  Cherry, Mayonnaise, Fried
    Squid with, 249–51
  Cherry, Pork-Stuffed, Chicken
    with, 240
  Cherry, Sauce, 246
  Cherry, Stuffed, Broccoli Rabe
    with, 242
  Chile Quiche, 251
  Cilantro Rice with Poblanos,
    243–44
  freezing roasted chiles, 247
  hot, handling, 238
  Hot, Mixed, Jelly, 247
  Hot Vinegar Sauce, 365
  Marilee's Chiles Rellenos, 242–43
  Marinade, Chicken with, 251–52
  Marinated, 244
  Pimiento Cheese, 248
  roasting and peeling, 238
  Romesco Sauce, 248
  Sweet, and Onions, Eggs
    Poached on, 239
  Sweet, Dried, 245
  Sweet, Puree, Pasta with, 238
  sweet dried, making pesto with,
    247
  Veal Chops with, 239–40
Pesto, 236
  Asparagus, 35
  Carrot Top, 70–71

dried sweet pepper, preparing, 247
Garlic Scape, 229
Horseradish, 364–65
Mushroom, 188–89
Nettle, 308–9
Pea, 233–34
Ramps, 341–42
Scallion, 305
swapping types of, in recipes, 6
Pickle brine, serving ideas, 116
Pickled Beets, 51–52
Pickled Corn Relish, 97
Pickled Fennel, 136–38
Pickled Ginger, 150
Pickled Onions, 211–12
Pickled Radishes, 272
Pickled Zucchini, 356
Pickles
    best cucumbers for, 111
    Bread and Butter, 112–13
    Dilly Asparagus, 35–36
    Pickle Spears, 112
    pickling methods, 374–75
    preparing, 111
    Watermelon Rind, 350
Pickle Sauce, 115–16
Pies
    Lemon Meringue, Southern-Style, 166–68
    Ricotta and Marinated Mushroom, 190
    Strawberry, Memphis-Style, 320–21
Pig roasts, 267
Pimiento Cheese, 248
Pine Nuts
    Nettle Pesto, 308–9
    Ramps Pesto, 341–42
    Romesco Sauce, 248
    Scallion Pesto, 305
Pissaladière, 212
Pistachio-Fennel Compote, 136
Pizza
    Carbonara, 265–66
    Marinated Mushroom and Gruyère, 189
Plum(s), 253–59
    dried prunes, rehydrating, 256
    Galette, 254–55
    Jam, Savory, 256–58
    Jam, Savory, Stewed Duck with, 258
    Jam, Sweet, 256
    Jam Shortbread, 258–59
    -Orange Granita, 259
    prune, how to dry, 255

Prunes Stewed in Madeira Wine, 259
Sauce, Sweet and Sour, Brisket with, 254
Polenta
    with Sauerkraut and Sausage, 61
    with Shredded Zucchini and Tarragon, 353
Poppy Seed(s)
    Almond Torte with Lemon Zest, 172–73
    Cake, Lemon, 168–69
Pork, 260–69. See also Bacon; Ham; Sausage(s)
    Ancho, with Sweet Cherries, 78
    and Beans with Feta and Cilantro, 269
    Beef Stock with Poached Eggs and Meatballs, 47–48
    Braised in Milk, 261
    Butt, Smoked, Apples, and Onion Sauté, 8
    Chops, Glazed, with Pickled Fennel, 139
    Cuban Sandwiches with Zucchini Pickle, 356–58
    Home-Rendered Lard, 268
    and pig roasts, 267
    Shoulder, Braised, with Oranges, 215
    Steaks with Caramelized Onion and Applesauce, 212–13
    Stock, 268–69
    Tacos with Black Beans, 262–63
    Tenderloin with Currants, 119
    Yvon's Country Terrine, 264–65
Potato(es)
    and Artichoke Marinade, Sausages with, 30
    Artichokes Constantinople Style, 27–28
    Bollito Misto with Pickle Sauce, 115–16
    Braised Duck Legs with Onions and Carrots, 126
    and Chicken Gnocchi with Marinara Sauce, 87
    and Corn Gratin, 93
    Gnocchi in Broth, 88
    Gnocchi with Sage Butter, 87
    Pancakes with Applesauce, 13
    Radish Greens Vichyssoise, 275
    and Scallop Salad, Warm, with Lobster Reduction, 182
    Sean's Warm Lobster Salad, 178
    and Smoked Mussel Salad, 206–7

Smoked Swordfish Salad with Avocado, 310–11
Steak, and Pickled Radish Salad, 273
Sweet, Cod with, 307–8
Tuna Tartare with, 301
Veal Tail Stew with, 44
Pot Pie, Canned Beef, 45–46
Poultry. See Chicken; Duck
Preserves. See also Jam; Jelly
    about, 373–74
    Strawberry, Jacques' Baked, 321–22
    swapping types of, in recipes, 6
Preserving
    altitude adjustments, 389
    curing, 383–84
    drying, 385–87
    freezing, 381–82
    goals of, 392
    pickling, 374–75
    preserving in oil, 387–88
    preserving with alcohol, 388–89
    pressure canning, 376–81, 389
    processing times, 389
    smoking, 384
    water bath canning, 373–76, 389
Prosciutto and Pea Sandwiches, 232
Pudding
    Bread, Baked Apples with, 9
    Rice, with Figs in Simple Syrup, 145–46
    Watermelon, 349

Q
Quiche
    Chile, 251
    Tomato Pan, 327

R
Radicchio di Treviso, Broiled, 84
Radish(es), 270–75
    with Anchovy Butter, 271
    Greens, Skillet-Cooked, 275
    Greens Vichyssoise, 275
    Pickled, 272
    Pickled, Omelet with, 272–73
    Pickled, Steak, and Potato Salad, 273
    Raisin Salad, 271
    Roasted, 272
Raisin(s)
    and Apricots, Canned, 19
    -Apricot Skillet Tart, 20–21
    drying grapes for, 161
    Granola with, 162–63

Radish Salad, 271
Tiramisu with, 161
and Walnuts, Applesauce Cake
with, 14
Ramps Pesto, 341–42
Raspberry(ies), 276–84
Chocolate Cake, Almost
Flourless, 277
Coffee Cake with Cinnamon
Crumble, 277–78
Jam, Sachertorte with, 282–83
Jam Scones, 281–82
Jam with Mint, 278–80
Jellies, 280–81
Juice, 283–84
Mint Jam Walnut Cookies,
283
sauce, preparing, 280
Syrup, 284
Zabaglione with, 278
Recipes
substituting ingredients in,
5–6
techniques, 390–95
tools for, 5
Red Snapper with Tapenade in
Parchment, 309–10
Relish, 113
Relish, Pickled Corn, 97
Rhubarb, 285–92
Crepes, 291–92
Galette, Pierre's, 289
-Ginger Jam, 291
Ginger Soda, 292
Jam, 290–91
Salsa, Fried Fish with, 286–87
Sour Cream Sauce, 289
Sour Cream Sauce, Boiled Beef
with, 287
Stewed, Crisp, 291
Stewed Canned, 290
stock, preparing, 292
Rice. See also Risotto
Cilantro, with Poblanos,
243–44
Pudding with Figs in Simple
Syrup, 145–46
Risotto
Asparagus, 40
with Crabmeat, 312
Mushroom Lemon, 191
Rosemary
Canned Tuna with, 301–2
and Garlic, Chicken with, 84
Rum
Cherry Bounce, 80
Tiramisu with Raisins, 161

S

Sage
Butter, Gnocchi with, 87
Gremolata, 185–86
and Pancetta, Fried Trout
Stuffed with, 341
Salads
Boiled Vegetable, with Pickling
Juice, 116
Caponata, 355
Cucumber, Avocado, and Red
Onion, with Cilantro Cream,
110–11
Dilly Asparagus and
Cauliflower, 36–37
Dried Black Trumpet and Tuna,
197
Egg, with Fennel-Pistachio
Compote, 138
Fig, Watercress, and Sausage
Salad, 142
Green Bean and Mint, 119
Iceberg Wedges with Ranch
Pickle Juice Dressing, 358
Marilee's Coleslaw, 58
Mussel and Scallop
Chimichurri, 203–5
Peach and Tomato, 223
Radish Raisin, 271
Roast Beet, with Feta, Scallions,
and Cilantro, 50–51
Shaved Asparagus, Pea, and Pea
Shoot, 33–35
Sliced Fennel and Apple,
135–36
Smoked Mussel and Potato,
206–7
Smoked Swordfish, with
Avocado, 310–11
Smoked Trout and Lentil, 343
Steak, Potato, and Pickled
Radish, 273
Tuna Tartare with Potatoes,
301
Warm Lobster, Sean's, 178
Warm Scallop and Potato, with
Lobster Reduction, 182
Watermelon, Shrimp, and Baby
Arugula, 347
Watermelon, Tomato, and
Gorgonzola, 347–49
Zucchini Carpaccio, 353–54
Salmon, 293–99
Canned, 294–95
Confit, Smith Fork Ranch,
298–99
Gravlax with Aquavit, 295–96

Gravlax with Brioche and
Mozzarella, 298
Oil-Poached, with Black Olive
Sauce, 294
Salt-Broiled, 294
Skins, Fried, 299
Zucchini Flowers Stuffed with,
297
Salsa, Rhubarb, 286–87
Salt, Porcini, 198–99
Sandwiches
Cuban, with Zucchini Pickle,
356–58
Pastrami with Sauerkraut,
61–62
Prosciutto and Pea, 232
Sauces. See also Pesto
Ancho, 78
Apricot-Orange Puree, 19
Black Olive, 294
Cherry Pepper, 246
Chimichurri, 204–5
Cilantro Cream, 111
Cranberry-Orange, 104–5
Hollandaise, 338–39
Marinara, Dad's, 332–33
Pickle, 115–16
raspberry, preparing, 280
Red Wine Reduction, 366–67
Rhubarb Sour Cream, 289
Romesco, 248
Shrimp Shell, 317–18
Skordalia, 368
Tartar, 113
Tomato Ketchup, 330–31
Tuna, 303–5
Vinegar, Hot, 365
Worcestershire, 369
Sauerkraut
with Caraway Seeds, 60
Pastrami with, 61–62
and Sausage, Polenta with, 61
Sausage(s)
Bollito Misto with Pickle Sauce,
115–16
Broccoli Rabe with Stuffed
Cherry Peppers, 242
Chicken with Pork-Stuffed
Cherry Peppers, 240
Fig, and Watercress Salad, 142
Omelet, Duck Soup with, 132
with Potatoes and Artichoke
Marinade, 30
and Sauerkraut, Polenta with,
61
Shrimp and Chorizo with
Lobster Reduction, 182

Scallion(s)
  Pesto, 305
  Steamed, 261
Scallop(s)
  Brodetto with Fennel and
    Anisette, 134
  Broiled Seafood Skewers with
    Corn Relish, 98
  Crudo with Ginger, 148
  and Mussel Chimichurri Salad,
    203–5
  and Potato Salad, Warm, with
    Lobster Reduction, 182
Scones, Raspberry Jam, 281–82
Seafood. See Fish; Shellfish
Shellfish. See also Crabs; Lobster;
    Mussel(s); Scallop(s); Shrimp
  Broiled Seafood Skewers with
    Corn Relish, 98
  Fried Oysters with Tartar Sauce,
    115
  Fried Squid with Cherry Pepper
    Mayonnaise, 249–51
  swapping types of, in recipes, 6
Sherbet, Orange, 218
Sherry
  and Dried Morels, Chicken
    with, 196–97
  and Fresh Morels, Chicken
    with, 197
Shortbread
  Orange, with Chocolate, 219
  Plum Jam, 258–59
Shrimp, 313–18
  and Bean Soup, 314
  Brodetto with Fennel and
    Anisette, 134
  Canned, 316
  Canned, Scrambled Eggs with,
    317
  and Chorizo with Lobster
    Reduction, 182
  Cooked in Tomato Sauce, 315
  and Corn Casserole, 99
  with Marinated Artichokes,
    29–30
  Potted, with Spices, 316–17
  shell-on, buying, 314
  Shell Sauce, 317–18
  Shell Sauce, Fillet of Sole
    Stuffed with Ricotta with, 318
  Watermelon, and Baby Arugula
    Salad, 347
  and Zucchini Flowers, Penne
    with, 314–15
Sole, Fillet of, Stuffed with Ricotta
    with Shrimp Shell Sauce, 318

Soufflés
  Cherry, 79
  Ginger Carrot, 70
  Strawberry, 324–25
Soups. See also Stews; Stock
  Bean and Shrimp, 314
  Beef Stock with Poached Eggs
    and Meatballs, 47–48
  Corn and Bean, 93–95
  Duck, with Sausage Omelet, 132
  Gnocchi in Broth, 88
  Pea, with Garlic Scape Pesto,
    229
  Radish Greens Vichyssoise, 275
  Scrippelle in Cabbage Stock,
    63–64
  Spring Minestrone, 236
  Zia Ada's Stracciatella, 91
  Zucchini, with Corn Stock, 100
Sour cream, substitutes for, 6
Spaetzle with Ramps Pesto,
    341–42
Spinach and Mushrooms, Coddled
    Eggs with, 184
Squash. See also Zucchini
  Acorn, and Marinara Sauce,
    Lasagna with, 333–34
Squid
  Broiled Seafood Skewers with
    Corn Relish, 98
  Fried, with Cherry Pepper
    Mayonnaise, 249–51
Stews
  Brodetto with Fennel and
    Anisette, 134
  Chicken with Mussels, 205–6
  Veal, with Carrots and Shallots,
    67
  Veal Tail, with Potatoes, 44
Stock
  Asparagus, 37
  Beef, 47
  Cabbage, 62–63
  Chicken, 89
  cooking pasta in, 392
  Corn, 99–100
  Duck, 131–32
  Fish, 311–12
  Lobster Reduction, 180
  Mushroom, 190–91
  pea pod, preparing, 236
  Porcini, 199–200
  Pork, 268–69
  preparing, 390–92
  rhubarb, preparing, 292
  swapping types of, in recipes, 6
  Trout, 344–45

Strawberry(ies), 319–25
  -Almond Ice Cream, 321
  Crepes, 324
  Cupcakes with Strawberry Jam
    Icing, 323–24
  jam, tips for preparing, 323
  Jam Icing, 323–24
  Panna Cotta, 325
  Pie, Memphis-Style, 320–21
  Preserves, Jacques' Baked,
    321 22
  Puree, 322
  Soufflé, 324–25
Striped Bass with Fennel-Pistachio
    Compote, 138–39
Strudel, Cherry-Ricotta, 73–74
Sweet Potatoes, Cod with, 307–8
Swordfish
  with Pea Pesto, 235
  Smoked, 310
  Smoked, and Baby Lettuce,
    Spaghettini with, 311
  Smoked, Salad with Avocado,
    310–11
Syrups
  fruit, swapping types of, in
    recipes, 6
  Ginger, 150–52
  Herb, 364
  preparing, 394
  Raspberry, 284

T
Tacos, Pork, with Black Beans,
    262–63
Tapenade
  Green Olive, 160
  Green Olive and Orange,
    217–18
  Red Snapper with, in
    Parchment, 309–10
Tarts
  Apricot-Raisin Skillet, 20–21
  Fig Jam Crostata, 145
  Grape Custard, 157–58
  Pierre's Rhubarb Galette, 289
  Pissaladière, 212
  Plum Galette, 254–55
Tiramisu with Raisins, 161
Tomato(es), 326–36
  Aspic, 333
  Broiled, 327–28
  canned, two ways, 328–30
  Canned Crushed, 328 30
  canning process, 329
  Cipollini in Sweet and Sour
    Sauce, 211

Tomato(es) (*continued*)
  Dad's Marinara Sauce, 332–33
  Dried, 331–32
  Eggs Poached in, 332
  Fresh, and Breadcrumbs, Trout
    with, 339–41
  and Garlic, Beef Stewed with,
    334
  Italian Pasta Primavera, 327
  Ketchup, 330–31
  Lasagna with Acorn Squash and
    Marinara Sauce, 333–34
  Marilee's Chiles Rellenos,
    242–43
  and Onions, Spaghetti with,
    209
  Pan Quiche, 327
  Paste, 331
  and Peach Salad, 223
  Raw-Pack, 328
  Romesco Sauce, 248
  Sauce, Shrimp Cooked in, 315
  Shrimp Shell Sauce, 317–18
  Stuffed with Ricotta and Tuna,
    305
  water, about, 336
  Water, Halibut Poached in, 336
  Water Martini, 336
  Watermelon, and Gorgonzola
    Salad, 347–49
Trout, 337–45
  Fillets, Smoked, 342–43
  with Fresh Tomatoes and
    Breadcrumbs, 339–41
  Fried, Stuffed with Pancetta
    and Sage, 341
  Poached, with Hollandaise and
    Summer Truffles, 338–39
  Smoked, and Lentil Salad, 343
  Smoked, Pâté, 344
  Stock, 344–45
  Stock, Spaghettini in, with
    Capers and Breadcrumbs, 345
Truffles, Apricot Chocolate, 22–23
Truffles, Summer, and
    Hollandaise, Poached Trout
    with, 338–39
Tuna, 300–305
  Anchovies, and Olives, Fried
    Pasta with, 302
  Belly, Broiled, with Thyme, 301
  Canned Beets with, 54
  and Dried Black Trumpet
    Salad, 197
  and Pickled Onions, Cranberry
    Beans with, 213

  and Ricotta, Tomatoes Stuffed
    with, 305
  with Rosemary, Canned, 301–2
  Sauce, 303–5
  with Scallion Pesto, 305
  Tartare with Potatoes, 301

V
Vanilla Extract, 361
Vanilla Panna Cotta with Ginger
    Syrup, 154
Veal
  Beef Stock with Poached Eggs
    and Meatballs, 47–48
  Cabbage Leaves Stuffed with,
    57–58
  Chops with Peppers, 239–40
  Osso Buco with Mushrooms,
    185–86
  Scaloppine with Marsala and
    Peas, 232–33
  Stew with Carrots and Shallots,
    67
  Tail Stew with Potatoes, 44
Vegetable(s). *See also specific*
    vegetables
  Boiled, Salad with Pickling
    Juice, 116
  Spring Minestrone, 236
Verjuice, 158–60
Verjuice and Olive Tapenade,
    Chicken with, 160
Vinaigrettes
  Currant, 122
  Mustard, 368–69
Vinegar Sauce, Hot, 365
Vodka
  Bull Shot Cocktail, 48
  Gibson with Pickled Onion
    Juice, 213
  Lemon Extract, 361–62
  Limoncello, 175
  Madras Cocktail, 108
  Orange Bitters, 221
  Tomato Water Martini, 336
  Vanilla Extract, 361

W
Walnut(s)
  Almost Flourless Chocolate
    Raspberry Cake, 277
  Fig Jam Crostata, 145
  Fried Ravioli with Grape Must
    Concentrate, 163–64
  and Raisins, Applesauce Cake
    with, 14

  Raspberry Mint Jam Cookies,
    283
Watercress, Fig, and Sausage
    Salad, 142
Watermelon, 346–50
  -Basil Granita, 349
  Grilled, with Lemon, 347
  Pudding, 349
  Rind Pickles, 350
  Rind Pickles Wrapped in
    Bacon, 350
  Shrimp, and Baby Arugula
    Salad, 347
  Tomato, and Gorgonzola Salad,
    347–49
Whiskey with a Pickleback, 116
Wine
  Bellini Cocktail, 223
  Cassis, 122
  Currant Jelly, 122
  Lemon Asti, 174–75
  Madeira, Prunes Stewed in, 259
  Moscato, and Thyme, Peaches
    with, 224
  Red, Reduction Sauce, 366–67

Y
Yogurt
  and Cucumbers, Cold Roast
    Chicken with, 110
  Homemade, 370
  Homemade, with Poached
    Eggs, 370
  substitutes for, 6

Z
Zabaglione with Raspberries,
    278
Zucchini, 351–58
  Carpaccio, 353–54
  Flan, 352–53
  flowers, for frying, 352
  Flowers and Shrimp, Penne
    with, 314–15
  Flowers Stuffed with Salmon,
    297
  Iceberg Wedges with Ranch
    Pickle Juice Dressing, 358
  Pickle, Cuban Sandwiches with,
    356–58
  Pickled, 356
  Roasted, in Balsamic Vinegar,
    354–55
  Shredded, and Tarragon,
    Polenta with, 353
  Soup with Corn Stock, 100